THE
American Woman's
COOK BOOK

Edited and Revised by
Ruth Berolzheimer
Director, Culinary Arts Institute

From THE DELINEATOR COOK BOOK
Edited by The Delineator Institute
and
Martha Van Rensselaer and Flora Rose, *Directors,*
College of Home Economics, Cornell University

NATIONAL BINDING

Published by
CONSOLIDATED BOOK PUBLISHERS, CHICAGO
1947

A

Table of Contents

List of Illustrations

~~~~~~~~

iv

LIST OF ILLUSTRATIONS

v

LIST OF ILLUSTRATIONS

AT YOUR SERVICE

Unless otherwise specified, all recipes are based on service for six persons. When cooking for more, multiply the ingredients in direct proportion. When fewer are to be served, divide by two or three as necessary. A full discussion of the problems of small quantity preparations is found in the chapter entitled "Cooking for Two."

THE *Color* PLATES

The full-color illustrations in The American Woman's Cook Book reproduce with striking fidelity the tempting texture of nicely browned chicken, the appetizing hue of roast beef done to a turn, and the verdant crispness of leafy salads. They show precisely how attractive a properly prepared dish should appear when served.

The development of printing reproduction in full color of difficult food subjects is a fascinating story. The color pages in The American Woman's Cook Book required not only the skillful preparation of the dishes to be photographed, but also an advanced photographic technique which makes possible the brilliant colors and superb craftsmanship of modern photoengraving. The beautiful pages which have been included in this volume effectively vitalize the recipes and add inspiration to the occupation of cooking.

The Carnation Company, producer of Irradiated Carnation Milk, was among the first to present pictorially in full, natural color many of the appealing dishes which grace our dinner tables. In admiration of their supreme achievement, we extend our grateful thanks for permission to reproduce their color plates in The American Woman's Cook Book. These pages have been generally acclaimed as the outstanding examples of modern full-color printing in the field of food illustration.

The editor wishes to acknowledge the generous and wholehearted cooperation of those who put at our disposal the beautiful photographs and color plates which appear in this book.

American Can Company
Appalachian Apple Service, Inc.
Armour and Company
The Best Foods, Inc.
Booth Fisheries Corporation
California Fruit Growers Exchange
Campbell Soup Company
Canned Salmon Industry
Chicago Flexible Shaft Company
Corn Products Refining Company
Corning Glass Works
Cranberry Canners, Inc.
Fostoria Glass Company
Fruit Dispatch Company
Gaper Catering Company
General Electric Company
General Foods Corporation
Hawaiian Pineapple Company, Ltd.
Idaho Potato Growers
Irradiated Evaporated Milk Institute
John F. Jelke Company
The Junket Folks

Kalamazoo Vegetable Parchment
  Company
Kraft Cheese Company
Mandel Brothers
Mirro Aluminum
National Association Service
National Dairy Council
National Live Stock and Meat Board
Northwest Cherry Bureau
Northwestern Yeast Company
The Palmer House
Peoples Gas Light and Coke Company
Poultry and Egg National Board
Reed and Barton
Rumford Baking Powder Company
Shrimp Canners Association
Sterling Silversmiths Guild of America
Swift and Company
The Borden Company
Towle Manufacturing Company
U. S. Bureau Home Economics
West Bend Aluminum Company
Wheat Flour Institute

●

All color plates, end papers and illustrations on the jacket are
by courtesy of
CARNATION MILK COMPANY
LAND O' LAKES CREAMERIES
LIBBY, McNEILL & LIBBY
JOHN F. JELKE COMPANY
THE ALUMINUM COOKING UTENSIL COMPANY

USEFUL FACTS ABOUT FOOD

USE OF RECIPES

TO become a good cook requires more than the blind following of a recipe. This is frequently illustrated when several women living in the same community, all using the same recipe, obtain widely differing results. It is the reason so many cooks say, "I had good luck with my cake to-day," or "I had bad luck with my bread yesterday." Happily, luck causes neither the success nor the failure of a product. To become a good cook means to gain a knowledge of foods and how they behave, and skill in manipulating them. The recipe by itself, helpful as it is, will not produce a good product; the human being using the recipe must interpret it and must have skill in handling the materials it prescribes.

Some of the lessons which the person desiring to become a good cook should learn are given in the following pages. They will not be learned all at once; but if they are mastered gradually, luck will play a less important part in culinary conversation.

Methods of Cooking Food

BAKE—To cook by dry reflected heat. See Oven Temperatures for Baking, page 5.

BARBECUE—To roast an animal slowly either whole or cut in pieces, on a spit or rack over direct heat, basting with a special highly-seasoned sauce.

BOIL—To cook in liquid, at a temperature of 212° F. at sea level. The boiling point decreases about 1° F. for every 500 feet of elevation. At the correct boiling temperature large bubbles rise rapidly and continually, so that all of the liquid is agitated.

BRAISE—To brown meats or vegetables, in a small amount of hot fat, and then cook slowly, in a covered utensil, on top of stove or in oven with a very small amount of liquid.

BROIL—To cook by direct heat.

CANDY—To cook fruit in heavy sirup until plump and transparent, then drain and dry; to cook vegetables in sugar or sirup and fat; to glaze.

CARAMELIZE—To heat dry sugar or foods containing sugar until a brown color and characteristic flavor develops.

CODDLE—To cook slowly just below the boiling point.

FIRELESS COOKING—To cook by heat that has been retained in a fireless cooker or insulated oven. It is accomplished by surrounding the thoroughly heated food with some insulating material to keep the heat from being lost rapidly.

FRICASSEE—To braise small pieces of fowl, game or meats, and then cook slowly in stock, gravy, or sauce.

FRY—(1) To cook in small amount of fat, also called sautéing or pan-frying. (2) To cook immersed in hot fat, also called deep-fat frying. (3) To cook in 1 to 2 inches of fat.

PAN-BROIL—To cook on a hot surface, greased only enough to prevent sticking, pouring off fat as it accumulates.

PAN-FRY—To cook in a small amount of fat. See FRY.

PARBOIL—To boil uncooked food until partially cooked.

PARCH—To brown by means of dry heat. Applied to grains.

PASTEURIZE—To preserve food by heating to 140° F. to 180° F. for 20 to 30 minutes or sufficiently to destroy microorganisms and arrest fermentation. Applied to milk and fruit juices.

POACH—To cook food by slipping into hot liquid to cover.

PRESSURE COOK—To cook in steam at a pressure of 5 to 30 pounds and at temperatures of 228° F. to 274° F.

ROAST—To cook by dry heat, usually in an oven or tightly covered kettle.

SAUTÉ—To cook in small amount of fat. See FRY.

SCALD—To heat liquid to temperature just below the boiling point. Scald milk over boiling water until foamy.

SCALLOP—To bake food, usually in small pieces, in a casserole with sauce, broken crackers, bread or cake; topped with crumbs.

SCRAMBLE—To cook while mixing.

SHIRR—To bake eggs in cream, vegetables or purée.

SIMMER—To cook in water at a temperature of 180° F. to 210° F., or below the boiling point of water.

STEAM—To cook in the steam generated by boiling water.

STEW—To cook slowly in a small amount of liquid.

Methods of Preparation of Food

BASTE—To moisten meat with spoonfulls of pan drippings or other liquids while cooking.

BEAT—A brisk regular motion that lifts mixture over and over to make it smooth and introduce air.

BLEND—To mix two or more ingredients thoroughly so that each loses its identity.

BREAD—To dip in bread crumbs until completed covered.

COAT—(1) To dip food into flour, bread or cracker crumbs. (2) To dip food into slightly beaten egg, then into crumbs.

CREAM—To mix one or more foods together until soft and fluffy. Usually applied to shortening and sugar.

DEVIL—To mix with hot seasoning as pepper, mustard, etc.

DREDGE—To coat with flour or other finely divided food.

FOLD—To blend two foods by cutting the spoon or egg whip vertically down through the foods, turning it under and bringing it up vertically; repeating until mixing is complete.

GLACÉ—To coat with a thin sugar sirup that has been cooked to the crack stage.

GLAZE for pies, certain breads and meats may be thickened slightly; or it may be uncooked.

GRATE—To reduce to small particles by rubbing on anything rough and indented.

GRIND—To reduce food to particles by cutting, crushing, or by forcing through a food chopper.

JULIENNE—To cut vegetables into thin matchlike strips.

KNEAD—To manipulate with a pressing motion plus folding and stretching. Usually applied to bread dough.

LARD—To insert matchlike strips of fat, called lardoons, into gashes in side of meat, or into lean meat by means of a larding needle or skewer; or to place on top of meat.

MARINATE—To saturate with vinegar or French dressing.

MELT—To liquefy by heat.

MINCE—To cut or chop very fine.

PARE—To cut away outside covering. Applied to fruits and vegetables.

SKEWER—The use of metal or wooden pin to keep meat or poultry in shape while cooking.

STIR—To mix ingredients with a circular motion for the purpose of combining, or blending.

WHIP—To incorporate air and produce expansion by beating rapidly such as cream, eggs and gelatin.

COOKING BY TEMPERATURE

For best results in cooking, exact temperatures should be known and followed. This requires the use of thermometers: an oven thermometer or an oven-heat regulator for all sorts of baking and broiling and special thermometers for sugar cookery, deep-fat frying, and roasting meats.

AUTOMATIC MECHANICAL OVEN-HEAT REGULATORS which control temperature automatically by regulating the supply of heat are available in both gas and electric ranges, providing oven and broiler are served by the same heating unit. This device not only insures proper roasting, broiling or baking temperatures, but also prevents needless use of fuel.

HEAT REGULATORS OR TEMPERATURE CONTROLS must always be built into electric and gas ranges at the factory. For both types of stove they may be set to a desired temperature for automatic control. Be sure that the oven is properly preheated, and when once set, it will maintain the temperature to within a few degrees Fahrenheit of that indicated, for an indefinite period. The oven heat is uniform throughout. No "hot or cold spots." An oven heat regulator is your guide to better cookery.

TIME CONTROLS are now quite common on electric ranges, electric fireless cookers, and gas ranges. In combination with the temperature controls, they will turn heat on at the time set and off again at another specified moment. This makes it possible to put a meal in the oven or cooker in the morning and leave it, with the assurance that it will start to cook at the time specified and that the heat will be turned off again at the time you set. As electric ovens and cookers are thoroughly insulated, the heat retained in the oven wall and in the food will complete the cooking. Moreover, since they are cooking on a decreasing heat, there is little or no danger of burning food, even if serving is delayed beyond the time planned.

THERMOMETERS THAT CAN BE SET IN THE OVEN may be used where an oven-heat regulator is not available. A small flash light is useful for reading them in a dark oven.

IF THESE DEVICES ARE NOT AVAILABLE the next best thing is to seek to develop delicacy of feeling and knowledge of practical tests which will detect differences in temperatures.

Cooking Periods and Temperatures

Oven Temperatures for Baking	
	Degrees Fahrenheit
Slow oven	250 to 350
Moderate oven	350 to 400
Quick or hot oven	400 to 450
Very hot oven	450 to 550

When two degrees of temperature or two periods of time are given, separated by a dash, (e.g. 350—375 or 30—40) it means that the temperature of the cooking medium or the length of the cooking period may range between these two extremes.

When the temperature figures are separated by the word "to" (e.g. 400 to 350) it means that cooking is to be started at the temperature first given and that the heat is afterward to be reduced to the second figure.

TABLE I

BREAD, CAKES, COOKIES, MERINGUES AND PASTRY

Baking Times at Preheated Oven Temperatures

Breads	Temperature Fahrenheit	Time in Minutes (Approximate)
Baking powder biscuits........	450°	12—15
Bread	400°	20
	to 350°	40—50
Coffee bread	375° — 400°	20—25
Coffee cake	400°	30
Corn bread	400°	30
Fruit or nut bread..........	350°	60
Muffins	425°	20—30
Popovers	450°	20
	to 350°	15—20
Rolls	400° — 425°	15—20
Spoon bread	350°	35—45
Cakes		
Angel Food	275°	30
	to 300°	40—45
Chocolate		
Layer	350°	25
Square	325°	60
Cup	375°	20—25

Cake (cont.) Fruitcake	Temperature Fahrenheit	Time in Minutes (Approximate)
Steamed 1 hour, then baked		
light	250°	1 hour
rich	250°	3 hours
Baked entirely	275°—300°	1½—4 hours
Gingerbread	350°	45—50
Jelly roll	350°	15—20
Layer	375°	25—30
Loaf (deep)	325°—350°	1—1¼ hours
Poundcake	275°—325°	1—2 hours
Spongecake	325°	1 hour
Square (shallow loaf)	350°	50
Tortes	350°	20—40
Upside-down cake	350°	50
Cookies		
Fruit, molasses or chocolate....	325°—350°	12—15
Other drop and rolled........	375°—400°	8—12
Other refrigerator (sliced)	400°	8
Ladyfingers	350°	10—12
Macaroons	300°	30
Meringues	275°	45—60
Pastry		
Pie shells	400°	15
Puff pastry	450°—500°	5—8
Puff shells		
Cream puffs and eclairs......	450°	15
	to 350°	20—25
Tarts	450°	10—15
Turnovers	450°	15
Pies		
Deep-dish pies	450°	10
	to 350°	30—35
Meat pies		
Biscuit top	450°	15—20
Pastry	450°	15
	to 350°	30
Meringues on cooked fillings...	350°	15—20
One-crust (unbaked)	450°	10
	to 350°	25—30

TABLE II

CUSTARDS, PUDDINGS, SOUFFLÉS AND SCALLOPED DISHES

For table of oven temperatures, see page 5

	Temperature Fahrenheit	Time Minutes (Approximate)
Au Gratin Dishes		
(to brown crumbs) ....400°		10
Custards ....300°		45—60
Puddings		
Batter, Cottage, etc............350°		35—45
Bread ....350°		45—60
Indian ....300°		3 hours
Rice ....325°		2 hours
Scalloped Dishes		
(not potatoes) ....350°		15—30
Soufflés ....300°		1¼ hours
Timbales		
(surrounded by water) ....250°—325°		35—45

MEAT, POULTRY AND FISH
ROASTED

For table of oven temperatures, see page 5

The number of minutes per pound which a roast requires for cooking at a given temperature is only an approximation. The accurate way of determining doneness is by the internal temperature shown on the meat thermometer inserted into the roast.

All boned cuts require longer cooking time than those with the bones left in. Allow about 10 minutes per pound longer for cooking boned cuts.

Many hams now on the market require shorter cooking time. For these hams, follow directions given with them.

Table III

Meat	Oven Temperature Fahrenheit		Roasting Period Total, hrs.
Braised meats	350°		2—2½
Meat en casserole	350°		2—2½
Meat pie with crust (meat previously cooked)	450°		Total, mins. 30

Beef	Oven Temperature	Internal Temperature	Minutes Per Pound
Rare	300°	140°	18—20
Medium	300°	160°	22—25
Well done	300°	170°	27—30
Pork			
Fresh (always well done)...	350°	185°	30—35
Smoked	300°	170°	25—30
Lamb and Mutton			
Medium	300°	175°	25—30
Well done	300°	180°	30—35
Veal	325°	170°	25—35
Poultry			
Chicken	325°—350°		22—30
Duck, Goose	325°—350°		20—25
Turkey	325°—350°		15—25
Fish			Total, mins.
Large	350°		15—20
Small or fillets	350°—375°		20—25
Lobster, stuffed	350°		15—20

SIMMERED OR BOILED

Simmering temperatures range from 180° F. to 210° F.

Meat		Cooking Period	
Fresh			
Pot roasts (3-4 lbs.)		Total, hrs.	2— 6
Swiss steak		" "	2
Corned or smoked (4-5 lbs.)		Mins. per lb.	30—40
Ham		Total, hrs.	4— 5
Ox tongue		" "	3— 4
Poultry			
Chicken (3 pounds)		" "	1— 1½
Fowl (4 to 5 pounds)		" "	2— 5
Turkey (10 pounds)		" "	3— 3½
Fish			
Small, thin		Mins. per lb.	5—10
Large, thick		" " "	10—15

Table III *(Continued)*

BROILED

Meat	Temperature Fahrenheit	Cooking Period in minutes
Chops, lamb or mutton..............550°		20—22
Ham patties or steaks..............550°		20—22
Liver, calves or lambs................425°		20—22
Steak, 1 inch thick (rare to medium)....550°		10
1½ inch thick (rare to medium)......550°		8—15

Poultry		
Chicken ....350°		45—60
Quail ....350°		35—45
Squab ....350°		35—45

Fish		
Fillets ....350°		15—20
Shad, whitefish, bluefish..............350°		20—25
Lobster ....350°		20
Oysters ....350°		25—30
Crabs, soft-shelled ....350°		8—10
Scallops ....350°		3

TABLE IV

DEEP FAT FRYING

	Temperature of Fat Degrees Fahrenheit	Cooking Period in minutes
Croquettes		
(cooked food) ....365°—382°		2—5
Doughnuts, Fritters		
(uncooked batter and dough)...350°—365°		2—3
Fish and Sea Food.............350°		5—10
Meat and Poultry..............382°—390°		5—8
Timbale Cases ....360°—370°		1—1½
Vegetables ....382°—390°		4—6

TABLE V
Candy and Boiled Frosting Temperature Chart
(Sea Level)

Product	Stage of Concentration	Degrees Fahrenheit	Behavior at Stage Desired
Sirup	Thread	230°—234°	The sirup spins a two-inch thread when dropped from fork or spoon.
Fondant Fudge Panocha	Soft ball	234°—240°	When dropped into cold water forms a soft ball which flattens on removal.
Frosting 1 egg white to 1 cup sugar	Soft to medium ball	238°—242°	
Caramels Frosting 2 egg whites to 1 cup sugar	Firm ball	244°—248°	When dropped into cold water forms a firm ball which does not flatten.
Divinity Marshmallows Nougat Popcorn balls Salt-water taffy	Hard ball	250°—265°	When dropped into cold water forms a ball which is hard enough to hold its shape, yet plastic.
Frosting 3 egg whites to 1 cup sugar	Hard ball	254°—260°	
Butterscotch Taffies	Soft crack	270°—290°	When dropped into cold water separates into threads which are hard but not brittle.
Brittle Glacé	Hard crack	300°—310°	When dropped into cold water separates into threads which are hard and brittle.
Barley sugar	Clear liquid	320°	The sugar liquefies.
Caramel	Brown liquid	338°	Liquid becomes brown.

TABLE VI

FRUITS AND VEGETABLES
BOILED

Fruits	Time in Minutes
Apples, cut	5—8
whole	15—25
dried	40
Apricots, dried	40
Berries	10—15
Cranberries	5—10
Currants	10—15
Figs, dried	20—30

Fruits	Time in Minutes
Peaches	12
Prunes, dried	45—60
Pears, summer	10—20
winter	25—30
Pineapple	20
Plums	12
Quince	15—40
Rhubarb	5

Vegetables	Time in Minutes
Artichokes	
French	20—30
Jerusalem	15—30
Asparagus	15—25
Beans, green	15—25
Lima, fresh	20—30
Lima, dried	hrs. 2— 3
Navy, dried	hrs. 2— 3
Beets	30—50
Broccoli	15—25
Brussels sprouts	10—15
Cabbage	5—15
Carrots	15—25
Cauliflower	10—15
Celery	20—30
Chard, Swiss	10—15
Chestnuts	20—30
Cucumbers	5—15
Corn	3— 6
Dasheen	15—30
Eggplant	10—15
Greens	
Beet tops	8—10
Collards	15—30
Dandelions	15—30

Vegetables	Time in Minutes
Endive, curly	15—25
Kale	15—30
Mustard	15—30
Spinach	8—10
Turnip tops	15—30
Kohlrabi	20—30
Leeks	15—20
Lentils, dried	hrs. 2— 3
Mushrooms	5— 8
Okra	15—25
Onions, white	20—40
Onions, scallions	8—15
Parsnips	15—30
Peas	10—15
Potatoes	
white	20—40
sweet	20—30
Rutabagas	20—40
Salsify	20—30
Soybeans, green	20—25
Squash	
summer	10—20
winter	20—25
Tomatoes	5—20
Turnips	20—40

BAKED

Fruits	Fahrenheit Temperature of Oven	Time in Minutes
Apples	350°—375°	20—40
Bananas	375°	15—18
Winter Pears.............	250°	1 hr.
Rhubarb	350° to 300°	30

Vegetables		
Beans, with pork	250°—350°	6—8 hrs.
Eggplant (stuffed)	325°	1 hr.
Mushrooms	400°—450°	15
Onions, whole (stuffed)	400°—450°	60
sliced	400°—450°	30
Peppers (stuffed)	350°—375°	30
Potatoes, white, in skins, large..	425°	30—60
small to medium	425°	30—45
scalloped................	350°—400°	1—1½ hrs.
Sweetpotatoes, in skins	350°	30—40
Squash	325°	1¼ hrs.

TIME FOR WATERLESS COOKING OF VEGETABLES

Time in waterless cooking varies somewhat with age of vegetable and size of pieces. Allow maximum period given in preceding tables. For fully matured vegetables, increase time from 10 to 20 minutes.

TABLE VII
EGGS

Cooked in Shell	Fahrenheit Temperature of Water	Time Minutes (Approximate)
Eggs, soft	212° to 185°	4
Eggs, hard	212° to 185°	15—20

Coddled		
Eggs, soft	180° to 200°	6—10
Eggs, hard	180° to 200°	30—45

Baked and Shirred	Temperature of Oven	
Eggs	325°	20

STRIKE UP A WARM ACQUAINT-
ANCE WITH YOUR OVEN AND
ITS SPECIAL TEMPERAMENT

FRUIT TARTLETS — CULINARY
GEMS IN MINIATURE

TIME AND YOUR OVEN AWAIT
THE OCCASION AND THE MAN

WHAT TO MAKE WITH EXTRA EGG WHITES

One

Desserts
Marshmallow Mousse, p. 572

Frostings, pp. 478-482
Boiled (1, 2, or 3 whites)
Chocolate
Chocolate, Seven-minute
Coffee, Seven-minute
Confectioners'
Honey Topping
Maple-Sugar
Seven-minute

Miscellaneous
Berry Sauces, p. 583
Fruit and Nut Filling, p. 476
Marshmallow Mint Sauce, p. 582

Two

Desserts
Chocolate Pudding, p. 633
Currant Sherbet, p. 574
Fruit Fluff, p. 535
Marzipan, p. 512
Meringues, p. 496
Peach Meringue, p. 571
Pie Meringues, p. 613
Prune Chiffon Pie, p. 603

Frostings, pp. 478-482
Caramel
Honey
Maple Marshmallow
Ornamental

Miscellaneous
Chicken Forcemeat, p. 189
Coconut Filling, p. 474
Divinity Fudge, p. 505
Walnut Filling, p. 478

Three

Cakes
Pineapple, p. 468

Desserts
Apple Meringue Pie, p. 593
Apricot or Prune Whip, p. 523
Baked Fruit Soufflés, p. 542
Cereal Flake Kisses, p. 497
Coconut Balls, p. 512
Dream Pie, p. 602
Fruit Snows, p. 520
Macaroons, Almond, p. 497
Maple Parfait, p. 572
New England Apricot Pudding, p. 553
Pineapple Fluff Pie, p. 601

Frostings
Lady Baltimore, p. 463

Miscellaneous
Orange Sauce, p. 582

Four

Cakes
Petits Fours, p. 500

Desserts
Baked Alaska, p. 568
Macaroons, Chocolate, p. 497
Meringues, Chocolate, p. 613

Miscellaneous
Nougat, p. 510

Five

Cakes
White, p. 461

Desserts
French Meringues, p. 614

Six

Cakes
Lady Baltimore, p. 463

WHAT TO MAKE WITH EXTRA EGG YOLKS

One
  Pies, p. 598
    Banana Cream
    Chocolate Cream
    Coconut Cream
    Fruit Cream
  Miscellaneous
    Chocolate Filling, pp. 473-474
    Mashed-Potato Balls, p. 413
    Glaze for Pie Crust

Two
  Cakes
    Dried Apricot, p. 467
  Desserts
    Coventry Tartlets, p. 607
    Vanilla Ice Cream, p. 563
  Pies, pp. 598-599
    Banana Butterscotch
    Black Walnut
    Butterscotch
    Coffee Cream
    Lemon Meringue

Two (cont.)
  Miscellaneous
    Green Soup, p. 615
    Hollandaise Sauce, p. 312
    Mayonnaise, p. 448
    Mock Hollandaise Sauce, p. 309

Three
  Desserts
    Mocha Pudding, p. 633
    Orange Tarts, p. 610
    Sour Cream Pie, p. 599
  Miscellaneous
    Boiled Salad Dressing, p. 450
    Lobster à la Newburg, pp. 720, 747

Four
  Desserts
    Biscuit Glacé, p. 572
    Custards, soft, p. 525

Five
  Desserts
    Nesselrode Pudding, p. 570

NUMBER PERSONS SERVED BY A POUND

Apples	3 to 4	Fish, fillets	4
Apricots, dry	10 to 12	Lettuce, head	5
Asparagus	3 to 4	leaf	8
Bacon	8 to 10	Onions	3 to 4
Bananas	3 to 4	Oranges	3 to 4
Beans, Lima, fresh	2 to 3	Peaches, fresh	5 to 6
Navy, dry	8 to 10	Pears, fresh	3 to 4
Snap, fresh	3 to 4	Peas, dry	8 to 10
Beets	3 to 4	fresh	2 to 3
Broccoli	2 to 3	Potatoes	3 to 4
Brussels sprouts	5 to 6	Poultry	2
Cabbage	3 to 4	Prunes	10 tc 12
Carrots	4	Rhubarb	4
Chops, lamb	3	Roasts with bone	2
pork	4	boneless	4
Cranberries	6 to 8	Spinach	2 to 3
Eggplant	5 to 6	Turnips	3 to 4

MEASUREMENTS

LEARN TO MEASURE ACCURATELY—All the measurements in this book are level. Do not heap or scant the measure.

HAVE ACCURATE EQUIPMENT FOR MEASURING, as follows:

A measuring cup holding ¼ quart and divided by ridges on one side into thirds and on the other side into fourths.

A quart measure divided by ridges into fourths. Each fourth is a cupful.

A standard tablespoon that holds ¹⁄₁₆ of a cup.

A standard nest of a teaspoon and its divisions.

A tested kitchen or sugar scale.

TO MEASURE DRY MATERIAL—Fill the cup, spoon or other measure to overflowing, then pass a spatula or the straight edge of a knife over the top, leveling the material. For an accurate half-tablespoon of dry material, fill spoon as above, then, owing to the difference in capacity of the tip and bowl of the spoon, divide the material lengthwise.

TO MEASURE FAT—An easy and accurate way to measure solid fat is by means of displacing water. For ½ cup of solid shortening, fill the cup half full of cold water, then drop in pieces of the shortening until the water reaches the top of the cup. Drain off water. The remaining shortening measures the correct amount. This method may be used for any fraction of a cup.

For spoonsful or divisions, pack the shortening into a standard measuring spoon and level off evenly with the straight edge of a knife as for dry material.

TO MEASURE LIQUIDS—Fill the measure until even with top of cup.

Equivalent Measures and Weights

3 teaspoons	1 tablespoon	4 cups	1 quart
4 tablespoons	¼ cup	2 pints	1 quart
16 tablespoons	1 cup	4 quarts	1 gallon
½ cup	1 gill	8 quarts	1 peck
4 gills	1 pint	4 pecks	1 bushel
2 cups	1 pint	16 ounces	1 pound

USEFUL FACTS ABOUT STARCH

Some of the foods which are used most frequently are rich in starch; for instance:

FLOUR—White enriched whole wheat, graham, buckwheat, rice, corn, rye, barley, potato, soy.

VEGETABLES—Potatoes, sweetpotatoes, hominy, corn meal.

LEGUMES—Dried peas, dried beans, lentils, Lima beans, soy beans, marrowfat peas.

BREAKFAST FOODS—Whole or cracked wheat, rolled oats, corn meal, rice, barley, cracked buckwheat.

MISCELLANEOUS—Chocolate, cocoa, macaroni, vermicelli, spaghetti, cornstarch, arrowroot, tapioca, sago, chestnuts, crackers, ginger snaps and other cookies.

STARCH-RICH FOODS MUST BE COOKED THOROUGHLY if they are to have fine flavor and be easily digested. This is because starch occurs in foods in the form of tiny, hard, dry, coated grains which are not soluble in cold water and upon which the digestive juices cannot act. When starch is cooked, it is easy to digest and develops fine flavor, because cooking changes its form.

WHEN STARCH IS COOKED IN LIQUID, the heat causes the starch grain to crack and absorb liquid, swell and soften. When flour or cornstarch or any other finely divided meal is cooked in a liquid, it thickens the liquid.

WHEN STARCH IS COOKED BY DRY HEAT, that is, with very little moisture, the heat, unless it is great enough to burn the starch, breaks down the starch grain and changes the starch to a valuable substance called dextrin. Dextrin does not thicken liquid, but, like starch cooked in water, it has a better flavor and is easier to digest than uncooked starch.

The baking of a loaf of bread illustrates both these changes. The starch in the dough inside the loaf absorbs the water used in making the dough, swells and softens. The water in the dough on the outside of the loaf evaporates and the starch in the outer layers of dough is partly changed to dextrin. As a result, the crust has more flavor, is sweeter than the crumb, and has a different texture.

In baking potato and sweetpotato the water for cooking the starch is supplied by the potato itself.

Points to be Observed in Cooking Starch-rich Foods

1. Use enough water to soften all the starch present. In cooking breakfast foods, follow directions carefully. Cook them for a long enough time to swell and soften the starch. A temperature as high as the boiling point of water (212° F.) is best for cooking until thick, then place over double boiler.

2. When flour or finely ground meal is to be mixed with a hot liquid, separate the particles before they reach the hot liquid, or gummy lumps with raw centers will be formed. Separation of particles of flour or meal can be accomplished by mixing the flour or meal with enough cold liquid to make a mixture as thin as cream, or by combining them with sugar or with fat before mixing with hot liquid. Lumpy gravies, sauces, mushes and puddings are caused by a failure to observe these precautions.

3. A double boiler is the best utensil to use in cooking cereals, mushes and starchy sauces because it does away with the danger of sticking and burning. The water in the lower part of the boiler should be boiling.

Thickening Power of Flour and Cornstarch

This is one of the most important things for a good cook to know. If the recipe and the directions are followed carefully, mixing and cooking these sauces and pastes to make them smooth, velvety and fine in flavor is easily accomplished. To keep thickened sauces and pastes hot, place over hot water until ready to use. Reheating or further cooking has a tendency to allow evaporation, which may make them thick and pasty.

WHEN THE LIQUID USED IS MILK, the recipe should call for a little more milk or a little less starch than when water is used. The solids in milk reduce the total liquid about 12 per cent.

WHEN THE LIQUID USED IS ACID, as vinegar, a tart fruit juice or tomatoes, the hot acid acts on the starch to form dextrin, just as dry heat does. Dextrin has not the thickening power of starch. Therefore, when an acid liquid is to be thickened, more starch may be needed, and the time for cooking may be shortened. No statement can be made as to exact differences, because acids differ greatly in dextrin-forming abilities.

WHEN FLOUR IS BROWNED, dry heat not only changes the color but part of the starch to dextrin, and the flour may lose a considerable part of its thickening power. More browned flour than uncooked flour must be used or browned flour may be used for color and uncooked flour for thickening.

Cornstarch Requires Longer Cooking than Flour. A quickly cooked cornstarch mixture always has a raw taste.

If a Sauce is Too Thick, it can be thinned by adding more liquid slowly, stirring constantly.

If a Sauce is Too Thin, it must be thickened by adding more of the thickening agent and recooking it. A starchy sauce or a cream soup is always thinner when hot than when cold. Even the amount of cooling which occurs in transferring a starchy sauce, gravy or soup from the cooking utensil to the serving dish perceptibly thickens it.

If a Sauce is Lumpy, because proper precautions have not been taken in mixing and cooking the thickening agent with the liquid, the sauce should be strained; but such a sauce never has the creamy, smooth texture of a well-made one.

With Each Cup of Liquid:

½ tablespoon flour or
½ teaspoon cornstarch

Makes a very thin sauce, which may be used in making thin cream soups.

1 tablespoon flour or
1 teaspoon cornstarch

Makes a thin sauce, which may be used in making cream soups of average thickness.

Makes a medium sauce, which may be used for creamed meats or vegetables, scalloped dishes, gravies or other sauces where a medium thickness is desired. It has about the thickness of heavy cream.

2 tablespoons flour or
2 teaspoons cornstarch

Makes a thick sauce, which may be used for creamed meats or vegetables, scalloped dishes, gravies or sauces where a thick sauce is desired. A sauce containing t h i s amount of flour has considerable body and spreads rather than runs.

3 tablespoons flour or
1 tablespoon cornstarch

Makes a paste when cold. This sauce may be used in making mixtures for croquettes, soufflés, blancmanges, and similar puddings.

4 tablespoons flour or
4 teaspoons cornstarch

Methods of Combining Flour or Cornstarch with Liquids

WHEN LITTLE OR NO FAT IS USED—Heat three-fourths of the liquid. Stir the remainder of the liquid gradually into the thickening agent. If sugar is used it may be mixed with the thickening agent before the liquid is stirred in. Stir into the thickening agent at first only enough of the cold liquid to make it thick. Stir constantly until smooth to prevent sticking, then add the rest of the cold liquid and continue to stir until smooth. The mixture should be about as thick as medium cream. Beat this gradually into the hot liquid and cook, stirring constantly, until the mixture is thickened. If some fat is used, it may be added at this time with continued mixing. After thickening, the sauce should be cooked in a double boiler with occasional stirring.

WHEN AMOUNT OF FAT EQUALS OR EXCEEDS AMOUNT OF THICKENING AGENT—(1) Melt the fat, add the flour or cornstarch and cook, stirring constantly, until thoroughly blended. Stir in the liquid, a little at first, then immediately enough to thin perceptibly and finally the remainder. Cook, stirring constantly until thick. This is called a roux. If roux is for gravy and meat soups, brown onion or other herbs in fat before adding flour, then proceed.

(2) Heat the liquid; cream together the fat and thickening agent; add this to the hot liquid and stir constantly while the fat melts and the particles of flour or cornstarch are being spread through the liquid and cooked. Complete cooking of roux, stirring constantly until thick.

Dishes That Have a Sauce Foundation

A WHITE SAUCE is one made from milk or white stock or part of each, seasoned, and thickened with plain flour or cornstarch. It is used as a sauce for fish, vegetables, creamed soups, and creamed desserts.

A BROWN SAUCE is one made from milk or water or brown stock, seasoned, and thickened with browned flour or part browned and part plain flour or cornstarch. It is used as a sauce for fish, meat, and poultry, and for soups.

USEFUL FACTS ABOUT SUGAR

Sugars are necessary in cooking (1) because of the body's need for them; (2) because of their flavor or the effect they have in modifying or intensifying other flavors; (3) because of the changes they make in the texture of other foods; (4) because they help preserve other foods, especially fruits.

THE NATURAL SUGARS are the best alternatives for granulated sugar—honey, maple sugar and sorghum when available are the first to use. Molasses and corn sirup, brown sugar, too, as long as it can be obtained, are favorites. Except for brown and maple sugar, all need special handling. Follow recipes carefully.

HONEY AND CORN SIRUP used in baking need special attention. Honey is ¼ water. Therefore in baking omit ¼ cup of liquid for every cup of honey that replaces a cup of sugar. Also honey browns more quickly than sugar, so all oven temperatures may be reduced 10° to 25° F. to prevent burning before baking is finished.

CORN SIRUP, too, carries water. It is advisable to follow the recipe carefully when corn sirup is used. One cup of corn sirup takes the place of ½ cup sugar, and for every cup so used the total liquids in the recipe must be reduced one-eighth. It is advisable to retain at least ½ the original sugar called for.

Ways in Which Sugar Affects Texture Foods

IN CAKES, sugar helps to make them tender and light.

IN BREADS, sugar helps to make them light.

WITH FRUIT JUICES, too much sugar makes jelly soft and sticky in texture. Too little sugar necessitates overcooking, invites spoilage, impairs flavor and gives a tough texture.

IN BEATEN EGG WHITES, sugar helps to hold air and stiffness.

Sirups for Freezer Storage of Fruits

With One Quart Water Use:		
1 cup sugar=20% sirup	4 cups sugar=50% sirup
2 cups sugar=30% sirup	6 cups sugar=60% sirup
3 cups sugar=40% sirup	6¾ cups sugar=65% sirup
	8 cups sugar=70% sirup

Caramel

1 cup granulated sugar   1 cup boiling water

Put the sugar into a pan and melt slowly over direct heat. Cook until dark brown, being careful not to scorch. Add the hot water and cook slowly until a thick sirup is formed. (Be sure that the water is hot. Cold water will make the hot sugar spatter.) This sirup will keep indefinitely in a covered glass fruit jar and is a popular flavoring for desserts, soups, meat sauces and confectionery. Brown or maple sugar may be used.

USEFUL FACTS ABOUT FATS

The cooking and table fats available for use in the modern household range from liquid oils to hard fats. The source may be vegetable, meat, milk or combinations of these. Fats are needed for health; they satisfy appetite and give energy.

Cooking and Table Fats Classified as to Sources

VEGETABLE OILS

Olive oil
Cottonseed oil
Peanut oil
Corn oil
Soybean oil
Salad oil combinations
Cream (milk)

SOLID FATS

Butter (milk)
Lard
Drippings of meat, poultry
Vegetable shortenings
Vegetable margarine
Meat and vegetable mixtures
Oleo and nut margarines

Cooking and Table Fats Classified as to Use

Fats are often classified as to their use: (1) for table use, (2) for shortening and (3) for frying. Many of them belong to 2 or all of these groups, while others are limited to 1.

OILS—Oils are both salad and cooking fats. As salad oils they are chosen for their mild flavor and texture in salad dressings. Those made of cottonseed, corn, peanuts and soybeans—alone or in combination with olive oil—are less expensive than pure olive oil. By reading the labels the purchaser will know just which type she is buying.

Oils for shortening are becoming popular because of their convenience. They are easily measured; they do not need to be creamed or melted.

For frying, particularly deep fat frying, cottonseed and corn oils are practical and inexpensive. They do not smoke and burn.

SOLID SHORTENINGS AND COOKING FATS—Lard and meat drippings for shortenings and cooking date from the time when all fats were prepared in the home.

Lard is solid without being hard to handle in doughs, and has an established reputation for pastry.

Fat from chickens and other poultry is often used for cake-making, as well as for cooking meats and vegetables. Use ⅔ cup for 1 cup butter, in baking.

Bacon, ham and sausage fats are too highly seasoned for any but limited use but are excellent for sautéing any food where their seasoning is desirable.

Drippings are not possible for deep fat frying, because they burn so easily; unless they are clarified and combined, when they become a good mixed fat. They may be used for sautéing or in seasoning. Use ⅘ cup for 1 cup butter.

In the solid vegetable compounds vegetable oils—cottonseed, corn, and sometimes peanut—are solidified by a special process. This gives certain characteristics of both the original oil and the solid fat, i.e.: they do not smoke or burn except at a high temperature. This makes them desirable for deep fat frying. Their high melting point makes pastry making easy at ordinary temperatures. Use ⅞ cup for 1 cup butter.

BUTTER—Butter's fine flavor keeps it the nation's favorite for eating, for some baking and for sauce making. To be assured of high quality when buying butter, see that the label states percentage of butterfat, manufacturer's name and address and if "made of cream from tuberculosis-tested cows."

VITAMIN-FORTIFIED MARGARINES—The addition of concentrated vitamins to margarine greatly increases its value to the homemaker. The concentrated vitamins allow a uniformity of vitamin content which does not vary with the seasons. Margarine, butter, lard and any other fats which melt below body temperature are all highly digestible. The food values of margarine, butter and other fats are equivalent. Margarine as a food for children and adults is equally as good as butter, provided the margarine is fortified with vitamin concentrates. Margarine's lower price makes it a valuable aid to a limping budget.

WHEN FINISHED, THE FAT IS CLARIFIED, STRAINED AND STORED TO BE USED AGAIN

BANANA FRITTERS CAN BE DONE IN A SHALLOW PAN

Testing Fat for Frying

Fats should never be brought to the smoking point as a test of heat. Use a thermometer or drop into the fat a one-inch cube of bread from the soft part of the loaf. Judge the heat of the fat by the length of time it takes the bread to brown.

1. If the fat is the right temperature for large pieces of uncooked food—breaded chops, etc.,—(382°-390° F.) it will take 20 seconds for bread to brown.

2. If the fat is the right temperature for smaller pieces of uncooked food or uncooked batters and dough (350°-365° F.) it will take 60 seconds for bread to brown.

3. If the fat is the right temperature for most cooked foods—croquettes, fish balls, etc., (365°-382° F.) the bread will brown in 40 seconds.

HAVE THE RIGHT TEMPERATURE IN FRYING—If fat is too hot, it scorches the food, or does not cook it thoroughly or spoils the fat. If it is too cool, the food becomes soaked with fat. Fats of low smoking temperature will naturally soak into food a little more than fats of high smoking temperature, because the food must remain longer in the fat.

Egging and Crumbing Foods for Frying

Except in the case of foods like doughnuts, fritters, potatoes and fried breads, foods are ordinarily either egged and crumbed or dipped in an egg batter before being fried. This is because the egg or egg batter hardens in the hot fat, making a case about the food which keeps it from becoming fat-soaked.

For crumbing, use dried bread crumbs rolled and sifted or soft crumbs forced through a strainer.

Break an egg into a shallow plate, add two tablespoons of water for each egg. Beat with a fork only enough to mix the yolk and white.

Place some crumbs on a board. Roll the food to be fried in crumbs, covering every part.

Dip the crumb-covered food into the beaten egg, being careful to cover completely.

Lift food from egg with broad-bladed knife and roll again in crumbs.

Let stand a few moments to dry. The food is then ready for frying. Foods may be egged and crumbed several hours or even a day before being fried.

USEFUL FACTS ABOUT EGGS

How to Buy and Care for Eggs

There is no difference between brown- and white-shelled eggs. A, B, and C are the U. S. government gradings for all eggs. If eggs are to be refrigerated for any length of time it is well to wash them, and let stand in cold water overnight. Then refrigerate at 45° to 55° F. This method will compensate for the evaporation which occurs in mechanical refrigerators.

Eggs Help to Bind Foods Together

Fats and liquids mixed together tend to separate very quickly. When an egg is added, it is possible, under the right conditions, to avoid this separation. A good illustration of this is the combination of oil, vinegar and egg in mayonnaise dressing, which produces a mixture that will keep for a long time. In the case of French dressing, the oil and acid can be held together for an hour or longer if a small amount of egg white is added.

Eggs Help to Combine Ingredients in Batters and Doughs—Although many batters and doughs such as cakes, muffins, pancakes, and breads, may be, and often are, made without egg, the use of egg materially improves them, and increases the lightness of texture.

Egg Increases Power of Batter or Dough to Hold Fat—Egg in batters and doughs allows the addition of more fat. If cake batter is too rich the addition of another egg will prevent the tendency of the too-rich cake to fall. If the cake batter is not sufficiently rich the addition of another egg will allow the use of more shortening. If richer muffins are desired, the same rule holds good; eggs as well as fat may need to be added if the product is to retain its lightness. In special yeast breads such as zwieback, brioche, rusks and fancy rolls, the large amount of fat present does not reduce the lightness of the mixture, in part at least because of the effects of the egg present.

Egg Increases Power of Batters or Doughs to Hold Liquid—Egg causes the liquid to be distributed in smaller particles throughout batters and dough. This makes possible a higher liquid content without interfering with lightness than would be desirable if the eggs were absent. The popover is the most interesting illustration of a batter that is very light in spite of the large amount of liquid.

Eggs Help to Give Lightness of Texture

This property is due to the presence in egg of albumin. Albumin has the power of holding air beaten into it, or gases formed in the mixture containing it, and of stretching as they expand.

AIR-HOLDING POWER OF EGG REDUCED BY FAT—Egg yolk is very rich in fat. For this reason egg white is better than the yolk for giving lightness of texture, and accounts for the direction, familiar to every homemaker, not to permit any of the yolk to escape into the white when separating eggs, if the white is to be beaten stiff. In cakes in which the air-holding quality of egg white needs to be used to greatest advantage, the egg white is beaten alone and is folded lightly into the batter at the last minute, so the shortening in the batter may not reduce its expansion.

AIR-HOLDING POWER OF EGG INCREASED BY SUGAR—In limited amounts sugar increases the tenacity and expanding properties of egg. This fact is interestingly illustrated in cakes, where the addition of sugar, within limits, increases the lightness of the cake. When sugar is added to beaten egg white, in limited amounts, it increases the air-holding property of the white and the meringue is lighter than the beaten white alone. When the sugar is added to unbeaten egg white, in limited amounts, and the two are beaten together, not only can the product be made very light but a meringue made in this way holds the air for a much longer time than when it is made by beating the white first.

How to Convert Dried Eggs

1 tablespoon powdered egg white
+ 2 tablespoons water = 1 liquid egg white.

1½ tablespoon powdered egg yolk
+ 1 tablespoon water = 1 liquid yolk.

2 tablespoons powdered whole egg
+ 2 tablespoons water = 1 liquid whole egg.

Effects of Temperature on Eggs

The texture of eggs cooked alone or in custards is directly affected by the temperatures at which they are cooked.

Cooked at 180° to 200° F. (below the boiling point of water), the egg white is firm but delicate and very tender and easily broken apart. The egg yolk is tender and waxy.

Cooked at 212° F. (at the boiling point of water), the egg white is firm, but somewhat tough. The egg yolk is mealy.

Cooked at 350° to 400° F. (the temperature of fat hot enough for frying), the egg white and yolk are leathery where touched by the fat.

Eggs Thicken Liquids, Making Custards

The value of eggs in custard making is due to the fact that uncooked eggs are fluid and readily mix with water or milk. When the mixture containing the egg is heated, the particles of egg become solid and the liquid is thus thickened.

Proportion of Egg to Liquid in Custard Mixtures

1 cup liquid 1 whole egg or 2 egg yolks	Makes a mixture that has sufficient body to bake in small cups or for a medium-thick soft custard.
1 cup liquid 1½ whole egg or 3 egg yolks	Makes a mixture that has sufficient body to bake in a large baking dish and hold its form while in the dish; or, when baked in small cups, to retain the form of the cup when turned into another dish. Good foundation for ice cream if less than ¼ to ½ its bulk of cream is to be used.
1 cup liquid 2 whole eggs or 1 whole egg and 2 egg yolks	Makes a mixture that has sufficient body, when baked in a large baking dish, to hold the form of the dish when turned into another dish. Good foundation for frozen custard where no cream is used. Good foundation for salad dressings.

DIRECTIONS FOR MIXING AND COOKING CUSTARDS

Scald the liquid. This saves time in making all custards.

Mix the eggs thoroughly, seasoning, and flavoring by stirring but not by beating.

Add hot liquid gradually to egg mixture.

FOR FIRM CUSTARDS, pour into baking dish, set baking dish in pan of hot water and bake in slow oven (300°-350° F.). Or put baking dish into steamer, keep water in pan constantly below the boiling point, and cook at 180° to 200° F. until firm. The custard is done when the blade of a knife inserted into the center comes out clean.

Why Custards Whey or Curdle

Custards usually whey or separate or curdle because they are cooked at too high a temperature or for too long a time. Milk that is a little sour may cause curdling of a custard.

The best way to prevent wheying, separating or curdling is to regulate the temperature and time of cooking all custards by cooking them over or surrounded by water slightly below the boiling point, by removing them from the heat when they are done, and by being sure that milk used in making them is sweet.

If a soft custard begins to whey, separate, or, as it is usually called in this case, curdle, it should be removed immediately from the heat. The pan containing it may be set into a pan of cold water, and the custard may be beaten vigorously to redistribute the particles of egg and milk solids.

PRECAUTIONS FOR CUSTARDS MADE WITH ACIDS—If a soft custard mixture is to be made with vinegar or acid juices, such as lemon juice or tomato juice, the custard should be removed from the heat the minute the mixture begins to thicken. Hot acid coagulates egg and then very soon begins to digest it. This process makes it thin instead of thick. If an acid custard mixture has become thinned by being cooked for a minute too long, it must be thickened by adding more egg or flour, following the directions for starchy sauces. Custards made with acid require more egg than other custards to get the same degree of thickness.

USEFUL FACTS ABOUT MILK

The value of milk in the daily meals is so great that every effort should be made to extend its use in cooking.

FRESH MILK, OR FRESH IRRADIATED-VITAMIN-D MILK, when it is available, is the most desirable form in which to procure the daily supply of milk. If fresh milk is not obtainable, some form of evaporated or dried milk may be used with excellent results from the standpoint of nutrition as well as of cooking and of cost.

HOMOGENIZED MILK is fresh milk in which the size of the fat globules is reduced so that the cream does not rise to the top.

IRRADIATED EVAPORATED MILK is irradiated unsweetened whole milk evaporated to double richness with the nutrition value of whole irradiated milk. When diluted with ½ water, it is used as fresh whole milk. It is also used undiluted as cream or in cooking.

CONDENSED MILK, which contains a large amount of added sugar, is used for making some desserts.

SKIM MILK may be used in cooking, but the fact must be remembered that the fat removed has carried with it important vitamins which must be returned as butter and cream.

SOUR MILK can be made from fresh milk by the addition of 2 tablespoons white vinegar or lemon juice to each pint of milk. Allow to stand at room temperature for ½ hour, then return to refrigerator. Use the same proportions for evaporated milk after it has been diluted ½ according to directions.

FOR SOUR CREAM add one tablespoon white vinegar or lemon juice to one cup cream or each cup evaporated or irradiated evaporated milk as it comes from the can.

BUTTERMILK, produced when the fat is removed as butter, is deficient in vitamins, as is skim milk, although valuable for its lactic acid.

CULTURED MILKS, such as acidophilus milk and fermented milks, are produced by the addition of desirable bacterial cultures.

DRIED MILK may be had as skim milk and whole milk powders. When mixed with water they come to the original composition of pasteurized milk.

What Milk Is

Milk is the fundamental human food for the very good reason that it contains calcium, phosphorus, protein, carbohydrates, and vitamins, A, B, D, G, and probably unknown quantities yet to be understood. Milk is a low-calorie food which makes it particularly valuable in helping to maintain a normal weight. Milk does more for the body than any other food and does it less expensively. The only nutritive elements in pasteurized milk too low for the daily requirements are vitamin C and iron. For that reason infants and adults must be provided with these from other sources. Since milk forms the basis of much cookery, it is fairly simple to assure every member of the family, young or old, his full daily quota.

To Pasteurize Milk

If there is any question about the cleanliness of fresh milk to be used for drinking, it should be pasteurized or boiled. Infants or small children should never be fed any milk about which there is the slightest doubt.

FLASH PROCESS—Put milk into a covered container and set over hot water. Heat until the milk reaches a temperature of 160° to 165° F. Hold at this temperature for one-half to one minute. Chill as quickly as possible and refrigerate.

HOLDING PROCESS—Heat until milk reaches 140° to 150° F. Hold at this temperature for about 30 minutes.

Pasteurized milk, if kept too long, is apt to spoil instead of becoming sour. If any pasteurized milk is left over and there is danger of its spoiling before it can be used, it may be mixed with a little sour milk and set in a warm place until it all becomes sour. Sour milk will keep for some days.

To Boil Milk

FLASH METHOD—Put milk into a shallow pan and cook quickly over direct heat so that the milk is brought as rapidly as possible to the boiling point. Stir constantly to prevent scorching, making the figure eight with the spoon, as this brings the spoon the greatest number of times in contact with the part of the kettle receiving the most heat.

When the milk has boiled up once, remove from the heat and chill as rapidly as possible.

Milk boiled by this rapid method is believed to be less affected in nutritive value than pasteurized milk.

Boiled milk, like pasteurized milk, spoils rather than sours.

A LITTLE LEMON
DOES THE TRICK
WHEN YOU'RE WHIP-
PING MILK OR CREAM
INTO SHAPE

Irradiated Evaporated
Milk Institute

HAVE EVERYTHING READY BE-
FORE YOU START

TO WHIP CREAM

To whip easily cream must be thick. This requires that it must contain not less than 20 per cent butter fat. Best results are obtained when it contains 25 to 40 per cent butter fat.

Fresh cream does not whip well even when it contains more than 20 per cent butter fat. This is because lactic acid is produced as cream ages, and the acid thickens the cream. The addition of ½ teaspoon commercial lactic acid to each pint of cream will do the same thing that is accomplished by twelve to twenty-four hours' standing.

Warm cream will not whip well because warmth thins cream. As cream is chilled, the fat congeals and the cream thickens. Cream refrigerated for two hours will whip easily, if it is rich enough and old enough. The best temperature for whipping cream is 35°-50° F. Cream is doubled in bulk after whipping.

If variety in flavor is desired add to ½ cup of whipped cream 2 tablespoons maple sirup, 4 tablespoons Chocolate Sauce, or 4 tablespoons jam. This will make 1 cup of sauce.

TO WHIP EVAPORATED MILK

Milk, bowl and beater should be thoroughly chilled to about 40° F. If the milk fails to whip, it is not cold enough. Scalding the milk prior to chilling causes it to whip a little more readily and somewhat stiffer, but scalding is not absolutely necessary. To scald the milk, cover the unopened cans with cold water. Bring water to a boil and continue boiling for five minutes.

Lemon juice can be added for even greater and "permanent" stiffness, when the lemon flavor is suitable to the food with which the whipped milk is to be combined. When lemon juice is used, first whip the milk until stiff. Then add two tablespoons of lemon juice for every cup of milk. Continue whipping long enough to blend in the lemon juice.

Evaporated milk has only about one-fifth of the amount of fat contained in whipping cream. Instead, it has a much greater content of whole milk solids. For that reason it is an ideal ingredient for a dessert which completes an already rich meal.

ALKALINE AND ACID-FORMING FOODS

Alkaline or Base-Forming Foods		Acid-Forming Foods
Olives	Berries	Bread, white and
Carrots	Broccoli	whole wheat
Turnips and tops	Brussels Sprouts	Barley
Beans, lima, kidney,	Buttermilk	Cheese, all but cream
navy, soy	Cabbage	Corn, fresh, canned
Beets	Cauliflower	and dried
Citron	Celery, Chard	Cornmeal
Dates	Cherries	Crackers
Potatoes	Chestnuts	Cranberries
Bananas	Chicory, Endive	Eggs, whole
Rutabagas	Cream	Fish, fresh
Cantaloupe	Cheese, cream	Fish, smoked
Sweet potatoes	Cucumbers	Lentils
Beans, pods, snap	Eggplant	Meats, fresh
Oranges or juice	Grapefruit	Meats, smoked
Radishes	Kohlrabi	Oatmeal
Tomatoes	Lettuce	Oysters
Lemons or juice	Milk	Peanuts
Pears	Molasses	Poultry
Watermelon	Parsnips	Prunes, Plums
Apples	Peaches, Figs	Rice
Almonds	Peas, fresh, canned	Walnuts
Apricots	and dried	Wheat, flour and
Asparagus	Pineapple	cereals

A KITCHEN COLLECTION TO GLADDEN THE HEART OF THE MOST ARDENT GADGETEER

HOW TO BUY FOOD

THOUGHT should be given to the expenditure of the money allotted to food, since a balanced diet, so necessary to health, depends on the wise apportionment of that allowance. The following rules apply to the average healthy family; they may be modified by each homemaker to meet her own special needs. For detailed guidance consult pages 39-46.

Milk

Spend as much for milk as is necessary to secure for each child ¾ quart to a quart of milk a day and for everyone else in the family from ⅓ to ½ quart of milk a day. Cheese or ice cream may replace a part of the milk for adults if they prefer it. Two ounces of cheese may be an alternate for ⅓ quart of milk.

Fruits and Vegetables

It is desirable to include fruit twice a day. Use fresh fruits in the height of their season. When they are cheapest, preserve them for winter use. Dried fruits, such as prunes, apricots, peaches and raisins, can usually be bought in the markets and are often the most inexpensive of all fruits. Oranges and other citrus fruits are particularly high in Vitamin C and minerals and should be used as often as possible unless replaced by tomatoes.

Women and little children will eat about two average potatoes and ¼ pound other vegetables daily. Adolescents and men at hard work can eat two to three times that amount.

Cereals

Buy cereals in variety. Be sure to include a generous proportion of cereals made from the whole grain. These contain elements of nutrition that are lost when the outer coat is removed, and also furnish part of the necessary roughage in the diet. Such cereals are especially desirable when it is difficult to obtain as great a quantity of vegetables and fruits as is necessary for good nutrition.

Fats

For each grown person, every day, allow at least 1½ ounces of fat (butter, cooking fat, cream, fat from meat, etc.). For children allow at least ½ as much, unless the child is getting a quart of whole milk daily; in that case, he is getting a large part of his fat allowance in the milk.

Meat and Other Protein Food

Ordinarily, do not try to serve flesh foods (meat, fish, and poultry) more than once a day. Milk, eggs, and cheese supply a desirable quality of protein or muscle-building foods and may be served often. The more milk one has, the less meat he needs, allowing for other sources of iron and vitamins. Peas, beans and cereals can not replace the high-quality protein found in meat, eggs, milk and cheese, but they have great value in supplementing the animal proteins. If they are used instead of meat, some milk, eggs or cheese should be included in the meal. The weekly allowance of meat foods need not be higher than 1¾ pounds for each person in the family, in order to furnish appetizing meals. This means an average daily portion of not more than ¼ of a pound.

A child under four or five years of age may have a little meat or poultry in addition to his milk allowance. He should have no more than a small serving (an ounce or less) each day of broiled or roasted lean beef, mutton, lamb, chicken, lean fish or oysters. If he has an egg every day in addition to his ¾ of a quart or quart of milk allowance, he will get adequate protein food.

The Pantry Shelf

Besides the usual supplies needed for everyday cooking a well-stocked emergency shelf proves a great time-and-labor saver. A long day away from home or unexpected dinner guests will be no problem at all when this shelf is kept supplied. Packaged cake and quick-bread mixes, canned fruits and vegetables that are not in everyday use, canned meats and fish in both large and small sizes to fit the number of guests, will greatly help hurdle an unexpected occasion.

How to Select Canned and Packaged Goods

If the average household is to be supplied with vegetables and fruits in the abundance necessary for good nutrition, some provision must be made to have a supply on hand during the months when fresh products are not available. In some households, these will be stored, canned or otherwise preserved at home. In others, they must be purchased fresh from the market or bought in preserved form from the dealer.

It would be profitable for every homemaker to learn sizes in canned goods and demand certain standards. She should keep a record of good and poor grades so that she may ask for the quality she prefers. Canned goods that are used frequently should be purchased in case lots, as a wholesale or reduced price can be obtained in that way.

Standard Sizes in Cans and What They Contain

No. $\frac{1}{4}$ cans—fish, sea food, potted meats, evaporated and condensed milk—contain 4 to $4\frac{1}{2}$ oz.; approximately $\frac{1}{2}$ cup.

No. $\frac{1}{2}$ cans—shrimp, lobster, salmon, pimiento, evaporated and condensed milk—contain 8 oz.; approximately 1 cup.

No. 1 cans (short or small)—fish, sea food, soups, milk, fruits, berries, boned meats and poultry—contain $9\frac{1}{2}$ to 13 oz.; approximately $1\frac{1}{4}$ cups.

No. 1 cans (tall or square)—fruit and vegetable juices, mincemeat, asparagus tips—contain 1 lb.; approximately 2 cups.

No. 2 cans—practically all fruits, berries, vegetables, fruit and vegetable juices—contain 1 lb. 2 oz. to 1 lb. 8 oz.; approximately $2\frac{1}{2}$ cups.

No. $2\frac{1}{2}$ cans—practically all fruits, berries, vegetables, fruit and vegetable juices—contain 1 lb. 10 oz. to 2 lb. 3 oz.; approximately $3\frac{1}{2}$ cups.

No. 3 cans—tomatoes, beets, sauerkraut, pumpkin and fruits —contain 2 lbs.; approximately 4 cups.

No. 10 cans—mincemeat, applesauce, marmalades, jams, pickles, sauerkraut, baked beans, corn on cob, fruits and vegetables, in fact, nearly all canned goods for large quantity use— contain 6 lbs. to 8 lbs. Approximately 13 cups.

While the size of can is standardized, there is a variation in weights of cans put up by different canneries. This difference in weight is probably due to a more solid pack or a greater density in sirup content in the heavier cans and, this being the case, the homemaker will find on the label not only the number but also the weight she can expect in the can.

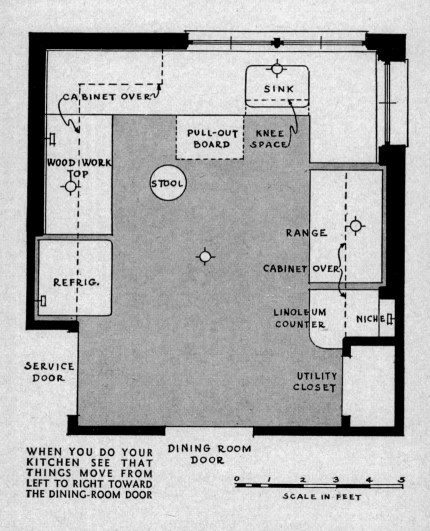

CABINET OVER

SINK

PULL-OUT BOARD

KNEE SPACE

WOOD WORK TOP

STOOL

RANGE

CABINET OVER

REFRIG.

LINOLEUM COUNTER

NICHE

SERVICE DOOR

UTILITY CLOSET

WHEN YOU DO YOUR KITCHEN SEE THAT THINGS MOVE FROM LEFT TO RIGHT TOWARD THE DINING-ROOM DOOR

DINING ROOM DOOR

0 1 2 3 4 5

SCALE IN FEET

FOOD VALUES AND MEAL PLANNING

TODAY the modern woman carefully plans her meals. She realizes that meals must appeal to the appetite and to the eye, but what is more important, they must be properly balanced to build healthy bodies, to stimulate vigor and energy, and to build up resistance against the elements and disease. The modern woman, in preparing a food budget, knows that bulky foods are essential, but not any more or less than the powerful, natural chemicals which we know today as vitamins. The modern woman has learned to distinguish between vitamins and calories. She knows that vitamins have to do with the chemical properties of many kinds of food, supplying the resistance-building and life-giving properties we shall discuss shortly at greater length. Calories, on the other hand, are units of heat formed during digestion of many foods and varying in a remarkable degree with the kinds of food eaten. Fresh vegetables and fruits provide little heat when digested and hence are said to be "low in calories," while fats, starches and sugars produce a high degree of heat and so are called "high calorie foods." When more of these are eaten than can be used up as energy, the remainder is deposited as fat. That is why we gain weight by eating foods of high caloric content and lose when their amount is reduced.

WHAT TO BUY TO BUILD HEALTHFUL MENUS

The food dollar will be used to advantage and serve all its necessary purposes, if it is divided into five, spent and served as follows:

ONE-FIFTH or more for whole milk, cream, cheese and cod-liver oil for growing children. Plan to give each child 1 quart and each adult at least 1 pint of milk in some form, per day.

ONE-FIFTH for vegetables and fruit, with emphasis on the green leaf and yellow fruits and vegetables. Serve at least 1 cooked vegetable, besides potatoes, and 1 fresh vegetable each day. Serve fresh fruit twice a day, with citrus fruit at least once.

ONE-FIFTH or less for meats, fish and eggs, serving liver in some form at least once a week.

ONE-FIFTH for breads and cereals, especially the whole grains.

ONE-FIFTH for fats, sugar and other groceries.

WHAT FOOD MATERIALS DO FOR THE BODY

The healthy body is built and maintained by:

Protein—helps make flesh and blood
Calcium—for bone, teeth, glands, nerve and muscle
Phosphorus—for bones, teeth, glands, muscle and nerve
Iron—with Copper and Manganese to help make blood
Iodine—for the functioning of the thyroid gland
Fat—heat, energy and padding for nerve and muscle
Sugars and Starches—supply heat and energy as well as fat—necessary for
    the proper functioning of the liver and the digestion of fat

Health can not be maintained nor the body function properly without abundant supplies of Vitamins. They are:

Vitamin A—promotes growth, increases resistance to infective
    diseases and prevents certain eye diseases
Vitamin B—promotes growth, stimulates appetite, protects nerve
    and brain tissue and function
Vitamin C—promotes growth, protects jawbone and teeth and the
    walls of the blood vessels
Vitamin D—promotes calcification of teeth and bones, hence
    protects against rickets and its deformities
Vitamin E—protects the growth and function of the reproductive
    glands and organs
Vitamin F—promotes growth and protects skin, hair and kidneys
Vitamin G—promotes growth and normal nutrition and prevents pellagra

WHERE TO FIND THESE BUILDING AND PROTECTING FOODS

PROTEIN	Milk, eggs, cheese, all meat, poultry and game, all fish and sea foods, peas, beans, corn, all nuts, all grains.
CALCIUM	Cheese, almonds, milk, green vegetables and tops, dried peas, beans, figs and dates, all sea food, egg yolk, olives, pecans.
PHOSPHORUS	Cheese, cashew nuts, almonds, dried peas, beans, lentils, Lima beans, all salt-water fish, liver, egg yolk, chocolate, unrefined grains, all meats and poultry, walnuts, peanuts, pecans.
IRON	Liver (calf, chicken, lamb), oysters, green vegetables and tops, egg yolk, dried peas, beans, lentils, Lima beans, raisins, currants, dates, prunes, avocados, almonds, fresh meats.
COPPER MANGANESE	Almonds, oysters, oatmeal, dried lentils, beans and peas, huckleberries, dates, pecans, shrimp, turnip tops, whole wheat.
IODINE	Sea foods and salt-water fish are the best sources of iodine, also iodized salt and cod-liver oil.
FATS	Butter, cheese, nuts, cream, fat meats, poultry and fish, margarine, lard, fish canned in oil, cottonseed oil, corn oil, olive oil, cod-liver oil, avocado, egg yolk, chocolate, olives.
SUGARS AND STARCHES	Sugar, molasses, honey, dried fruits, sweet chocolate, maple sugar and sirup, sorghum, jams, jellies, preserves, beets.
	Potato, sweet potato and yams, rice, corn, tapioca, cornstarch, arrowroot, all dried peas and beans, lentils, all grains, all flours, Jerusalem artichokes, winter squashes, pumpkin, okra, all nuts.

THE VITAMIN CONTENT
of
IMPORTANT FOODS

Food	Vitamin A	Vitamin B	Vitamin C	Vitamin G
Almonds	A	BB	—	GG
Apples	A	B to BB	CC	GG
Apricots	AA	—	CC	GG
Asparagus	A	—	CC	—
Avocado	AA	BBB	C	GG
Bacon	— to A	B to BB	—	GG
Bananas	A to AA	B to BB	CC	GG
Barley, whole	A	BB	—	G
Beans, dry or canned	A	BB	—	G
Beans, string	AA	BB	CC	GG
Beef	A	BB	— to C	GG
Beef fat	AA	—	—	—
Beets (roots)	A	B	C	G
Beet leaves	AA	BB	—	GGG
Brains	A	BB	—	—
Brazil nuts	A	BB	—	GG
Bread, white, water†	—	B	—	—
Bread, white, milk†	A	B	— to C	G
Bread, whole wheat, water†	A	BBB	—	G
Bread, whole wheat, milk†	AA	BBB	— to C	GG
Broccoli	AAAA	BB	C	GGG
Butter*	AAA	—	—	—
Buttermilk	A	BB	C	GGG
Cabbage, green, raw	AA	BB	CCC	GG
Cabbage, head, cooked	A	BB	C	GG
Cantaloupe	AA	BB	CCC	GG
Carrots	AAA	BB	CC	GG
Cauliflower	A	BB	C	GG
Celery, bleached stems	— to A	BB	CC	—
Celery, green leaves	AA	BB	—	—
Chard	AA	B to BB	—	—
Cheese, whole milk*	AA to AAA	—	—	G
Cheese, cottage	A	—	—	G
Cherries	AA	B	CC	—
Chestnuts	—	B	—	G
Chinese cabbage	AA	BB	CCC	G
Coconut	A	BB	—	GG
Cod-liver oil††	AAA	—	—	—
Collards	AAA	BB	CC	GG
Corn, yellow	AA	BB	—	G
Corn meal	A to AA	B	—	—
Corn oil	A	—	—	—
Cottonseed oil	—	—	—	—
Cranberry (or juice)	A	—	CC	—

* Supplies a small amount of Vitamin D
† When irradiated, an excellent source of Vitamin D
†† An excellent source of Vitamins A and D

Food	Vitamin A	Vitamin B	Vitamin C	Vitamin G
Cream	AAA	BB	C	GGG
Cress	AAA	BB	CCC	GG
Cucumber	— to A	B	CC	G
Dandelion greens	AAA	BB	C	GG
Dasheens	A	B	C	—
Dates	A	BB	—	G
Eggs	AAA	B to BB	—	GGG
Egg white	—	—	—	GG
Egg yolk*	AAA	BB	—	GGG
Eggplant	A	B	C	GG
Endive	AA	—	C	—
Escarole	AAA	—	C	GG
Figs	A	—	C to —	G
Filberts	—	BB	—	GG
Fish, fat*	A	B	—	G
Fish, lean	— to A	B	—	G
Grapefruit (or juice, fresh or canned)	A	BB	CCC	GG
Grapes	A	B	C to —	G
Grape juice	—	B to —	—	— to G
Ham	— to A	BB	—	GG
Heart	A	BB	C	GGG
Hickory nuts	—	BB	—	GG
Ice cream (regular)	AA	BB	C	GGG
Kale	AAA	B	CC	GGG
Kidney	AA	BB	C	GGG
Kohlrabi	—	B	C	—
Lemon juice	A	BB	CCC	GG
Lettuce	A to AA	BB	CC	GG
Limes (or juice)	—	—	CC	—
Liver	AA to AAA	BB	C	GGG
Mangoes	AAA	BB	CCC	GG
Milk, whole†	AAA	BB	C	GGG
Milk, "scalded"	AAA	BB	C	GGG
Milk, condensed†	AAA	BB	C	GGG
Milk, evaporated†	AAA	BB	—	GGG
Milk, dried, whole	AAA	BB	C	GGG
Milk, dried, skim	A	BB	C	GGG
Milk, fresh, skim	A	BB	C	GGG
Molasses	—	B	—	—
Mutton	— to A	BB	—	GG
Oatmeal	— to A	BB	—	G
Okra	AA	BB	—	—
Onions, raw	— to A	B	CC	G
Onions, cooked	— to A	B	C	G
Orange (or juice)	A	BB	CCC	GG
Orange peel	A	B	CC	—
Oysters	AA	BB	C	GG
Parsley	AAA	BB	CCC	—
Parsnips	— to A	BB	—	—
Peaches, raw	A to AA	B to BB	CC	G to GG

*Supplies a small amount of Vitamin D
† When irradiated, an excellent source of Vitamin D

Food	Vitamin A	Vitamin B	Vitamin C	Vitamin G
Peanuts	A	BB	—	G
Peanut butter	A	BB	—	G
Pears	—	BB	C	GG
Peas, green	AA	BB	CCC	GG
Peas, dry	A	BB	—	GG
Pecans	A	BB	—	—
Peppers, green	AA	BB	CCC	—
Pimientos	AAA	—	CCC	—
Pine nuts	A	B	—	—
Pineapple, raw	A	BB	CC	G
Pineapple, canned	A	BB	CC	G
Pork	— to A	BB	—	GG
Potatoes, white	A	BB	CC	G
Prunes	AA	BB	—	GG
Pumpkin	AA	B	C	G
Radish	— to A	BB	CC	—
Raisins	—	B	—	G
Raspberries	AA	B	CCC	—
Rhubarb	—	—	C	—
Rice, white	—	—	—	—
Rice, whole grain or brown	A	BB	—	G
Roe, fish	AA	BB	—	—
Romaine	AA	BB	—	GG
Rutabaga	— to A	BB	CCC	—
Rye, whole	A	BB	—	G
Salmon, canned	A	—	—	GG
Sauerkraut	A	B	C to CC	—
Shrimp	A	—	—	—
Spinach	AAA	B	CC	GG
Squash, Hubbard	AAA	B	—	G
Squash, summer	A	B	—	G
Strawberries	A	B	CCC	—
Swede	—	BB	CCC	—
Sweetbreads	A	B	—	—
Sweet potatoes	AAA	BB	CC	G
Tomato, raw or canned	AA	BB	CCC	G
Turnip	— to A	B	CC	G
Turnip greens	AAA	BB	CCC	GG
Veal	— to A	B	—	GG
Walnuts	A	BB	—	—
Water cress	AAA	BB	CCC	GG
Watermelon	A	B	CCC	G
Wheat bran	A	BB	—	G
Wheat embryo	AA	BBB	—	GG
Wheat, whole	A	BB	—	G
Yeast†	—	BBB	—	GGG
Yeast bouillon†	—	BBB	—	GGG

† When irradiated, an excellent source of Vitamin D

THE NUMBER OF CALORIES
in
YOUR USUAL SERVINGS

Food	Calories
Almonds, 12	100
Almonds, chocolate, 5	100
Apple, 1 large	100
Apple, baked, 2 tablespoons sugar	200
Apple, baked, 1 tablespoon sugar	150
Apple, brown Betty, ½ cup	250
Apple pie	300-350
Apple tapioca, ½ cup	205
Asparagus, 10 large stalks, no butter	50
Asparagus, 10 large stalks, with butter	150
Asparagus, 10 large stalks, with Hollandaise sauce	240
Avocado, ½ fruit	120-300
Bacon, broiled, four small slices	100
Banana, average size	100
Beans, dried, ½ cup uncooked	342
Lima beans, dried, ½ cup uncooked	273
Beans, string, ½ to 1 cup serving	22-44
Beef, round steak, lean, 4-ounce serving	170-220
Beet greens, ½ cup serving	22
Beets, red	50
Blackberries, fresh, ½ cup	50
Blackberries, cooked, with sugar, ½ cup	200
Blueberries, fresh, ½ cup	50
Bluefish, broiled, small serving	100
Brazil nuts, 2	100
Bread, white ½ inch thick slice	70
Bread, Boston brown	52
Broccoli, 1 cup	45
Butter, 1 tablespoon	100
Butter, ordinary serving	50-100
Cabbage, cooked	32
Cabbage, raw, shredded, ½ cup	13
Cantaloupe, ½	50
Carrots	30-40
Cauliflower	25
Celery	15
Cream of celery soup, per cup	200
Chard	36
Cheese, 1-inch cube	70
Cherries, 10 large ones	50
Chestnuts, 7 average	100
Chicken, roast, small slice	100
Chocolate cake	200
Chocolate cream candy, average piece	80-100
Chocolate cream mint, 1½-inch diameter	100
Chocolate drop cookie, 2-inch diameter	60
Chocolate éclair	260-400

Food	Calories
Chocolate fudge, 1-inch cube................................	80-90
Chocolate malted milk, large glass..........................	465
Coleslaw, ½ cup.....	50
Corn bread, average piece...................................	120
Corn flakes, ¾ cup....	100
Crackers, graham 2½..	100
Crackers, soda 2..	50
Cream, heavy, per tablespoon......	60
Cream, whipped, per tablespoon.............................	35
Cream, thin, per tablespoon................................	30
Cucumbers	12½
Cup custard, ½ cup...	100
Currants, dry, ¼ cup.......................................	126
Dates, 3 or 4..	100
Doughnut	200
Duck, small helping..	120
Egg	70-75
Eggnog, 1 cup..	200
Farina, cooked, ¾ cup......................................	100
Figs, 1½, dry..	100
Filberts, 8 to 10..	100
French dressing, 1 tablespoon..............................	67
Grapefruit, ½, average size................................	100
Grapefruit, ½, average size, with honey or sugar...........	140
Grapefruit juice, 1 cup....................................	100
Grape juice, ½ cup...	100
Grapes, large bunch..	100
Grapes, Malaga, 20 to 25...................................	100
Griddlecake, 4 or 5 inch...................................	100
Halibut	85-110
Ham, ¼ pound..	270-400
Hard sauce, 1 tablespoon...................................	100
Hominy, cooked, ½ cup......................................	62
Honey, 1 teaspoon..	25
Kale, cooked without fat, ½ cup............................	20
Kohlrabi, creamed, ½ cup...................................	100
Lemon	30
Lemon meringue pie...	450
Lettuce, ¼ head..	12
Lettuce, ¼ head, with salad dressing.......................	100-150
Liver, ¼ pound...	145-220
Macaroni, ¾ cup cooked.....................................	100
Macaroons, each..	50
Mackerel	85-100
Mayonnaise dressing, 1 tablespoon..........................	100
Milk, per glass..	110-170
Milk, irradiated evaporated, 1 cup, diluted to drink.......	175
Mince pie..	450
Muffin	125-150
Mutton, ¼ pound..	225-500

Food	Calories
Napoleon, average size	453
Oatmeal	150-250
Olives, each	15
Onions, cooked	50-60
Orange	100
Orange juice, 1 cup	133
Oysters, average size	6-16
Peaches, fresh	35
Peaches, canned, 1 with 3 tablespoons juice	100
Peanuts, shelled, ¼ pound	620
Peas, fresh, cooked, ⅜ cup	50
Peas, dry, ¼ pound, cooked	400
Pecans, 6 nuts	100
Peppers, green, average size	20
Pineapple, canned, 1 slice, 3 tablespoons juice	100
Pineapple, fresh	50
Plums, 3 or 4 large, fresh	100
Popover	100
Pork, ¼ pound	300-620
Pork, salt	1000
Potato, 1, average size	100
Potato chips, 8 to 10	100
Prunes, average size, 1	25
Pumpkin pie	225
Radish, average size	3
Raisin pie	450
Rice, steamed, ½ cup	70
Rice pudding, plain, ½ cup	200
Rice pudding, with egg, ½ cup	133
Salmon, canned, ½ cup	100
Shrimp, without oil, each	5
Spinach, ¾ cup	25
Squash pie	225
Strawberries, ½ cup	50
Strawberry shortcake	480
Strawberry shortcake, with whipped cream	530
Sugar, 1 teaspoon	17
Sweet potato	140
Tomato, fresh or canned, ½ cup	25
Tomato juice, ½ cup	25
Tuna, canned with oil	315
Tuna, canned without oil	140
Turnips, ½ cup	25
Turnip greens, ½ cup	35
Vanilla sundae with chocolate sauce	395
Veal, ¼ pound	115-200
Walnuts, 16 halves	100
Watercress, ½ bunch	10
Watermelon, ¾-inch slice, 6-inch diameter	100
Wheat breakfast food, 1 ounce	100

MENU MAKING

ALTHOUGH it is important that each meal should be well selected, cooked and served, the food for the entire day is the real measure of good nutrition. The facts on the preceding pages should be referred to for information on nutrition. There is a real art in combining these foods into wholesome, well-cooked, satisfying and attractive meals. This art is known as menu planning, the keynote of which is variety and a high degree of nutrition.

Every meal should be planned to meet the needs of the family group. The occupations and ages of the various members of the family, and the family income will determine to a great extent the kind of menus the homemaker will plan. If for example, the majority of the family are employed in occupations requiring a great deal of physical strength, that group will need menus which provide for more energy and muscle-producing foods than a family doing less active work.

Remember expensive foods are not necessarily the most nutritious. Each household is a problem in itself and printed menus can only offer suggestions.

Never serve food because it is "good for you." Prepare all food so attractively and season it so well that it will be irresistible. Teach children to like all foods served them. Adults should avoid in-between snacks and they will enjoy their meals more.

The following are suggestions which will assist in preparing menus.

THE APPEARANCE OF FOOD is important to civilized man. Beautiful color and dainty, attractive arrangement play a large part in a successful meal.

A combination of colors pleases the eye, stimulates the digestive juices and creates an appetite. Plan to use foods of different colors or use edible garnishes, such as parsley, watercress, pimiento, hard-cooked eggs and paprika. Avoid overcrowding of plates or table.

DESIRABLE COMBINATIONS—When planning combinations, follow the day's nutrition schedule and good combinations will result.

FLAVOR OF FOODS—Fine flavor in foods is developed by proper cooking. Additional flavors are provided by herbs: garlic, onion, celery, and by spices. Highly-seasoned foods whet the appetite while sweets satisfy it. For that reason well-seasoned foods are served for appetizers and sweets for desserts. Serve only one strongly-flavored food at each meal.

TEXTURE OF FOODS—A most important point is the serving of at least one each soft, solid and crisp foods at each meal. They give a meal necessary contrast.

TEMPERATURE OF FOOD—Serve hot foods hot and cold ones cold. Serve both at most meals, even in summer.

TIMING OF MEALS—Plan meals that do not have too many last minute touches. When entertaining, avoid serving food that will be ruined by a few minutes waiting.

USE OF EQUIPMENT—If planning to bake one dish, arrange your menu so that the whole oven may be used. This saves fuel, time and energy. Many times, one dish may be used later.

LEFTOVERS—Learn to buy so that there is a minimum of food left over. Serve leftovers differently from the originals. The liquids from cooked or canned vegetables are full of vitamins and minerals, and should be used in cocktails, soups, or gravies instead of going down the sink.

SEASONAL FOOD—In summer the market provides foods low in energy value but high in minerals or vitamins, such as fruits and vegetables. In winter high-energy foods, as fats and carbo-hydrates, are needed too.

Suggestions for the General Plan of a Day's Meals
Breakfast

Fruit, fresh, canned, dried, or fresh stewed.

Milk, or cocoa made with milk, for the children. Milk, cocoa, tea, coffee or other beverage for adults. Milk or cream on cereal for all the family.

Cereal, preferably whole grain, for all the family.

Bread, toast or muffins with butter.

If a heartier meal is needed, it may be desirable to add eggs, bacon or other fat meat, and potatoes, adapting the method of cooking to the children.

Doughnuts, cookies, jam, jelly, marmalade, and pancakes with sirup should be considered desserts, even at breakfast time, to be eaten only after more wholesome foods have been eaten.

Lunch or Supper

An egg, cheese or milk dish.

Succulent vegetable or salad.

Bread and butter, toast, muffins, or plain sandwiches.

Milk for children. Any preferred beverage for adults.

Sweets in moderation. Only light desserts such as fruit, simple pudding, and cookies should be served at supper.

The meal may be made more elaborate, if desired, but should always partake of simplicity.

Dinner

Meat or poultry, fish, egg or cheese dish. Dried beans may be used if milk or eggs are provided in the meal.

Potatoes, unless the meal includes dried beans, peas, Lima beans, soybeans, rice, or hominy.

Another vegetable. Two succulent vegetables (not potatoes) should be used with dried beans, macaroni or rice, etc.

Bread with butter or fortified margarine.

Salad may be served with the meal or in the place of dessert. Fresh vegetables that may be served as salad or relish are particularly desirable.

Sweets in moderation.

If all the milk that a person requires has not been used, the remainder may be served as a beverage.

If a more elaborate dinner is desired the meal may begin with soup, a variety of appetizers, sea food or fruit cocktail, or a canapé. The problem of the formal meal is discussed in the section that follows the simple menus given below.

SIMPLE MENUS
Breakfasts

Fruit Juice	Tomato Juice
Coddled Eggs Graham Muffins	French Toast Maple Sirup
Coffee Milk	Coffee Milk

Stewed Dried Apricots	Sliced Oranges
Corn-meal mush Buttered Toast	Scrambled Eggs and Bacon Toast
Coffee Milk	Coffee Milk

Applesauce	Grapefruit
Cracked Wheat	Codfish Balls
Oatmeal Gems Soft-cooked Eggs	Baking Powder Biscuits
Coffee Milk	Coffee Milk

BREAKFASTS—*Continued*

Broiled Grapefruit
Ham Omelet   Graham Biscuits
Coffee   Milk

——————

Prunes
Oatmeal
Corn Muffins   Baked Eggs
Coffee   Milk

Orange Juice
Whole-Wheat Cereal
Bacon and Eggs
Toast   Marmalade
Coffee   Milk

——————

Hot Baked Apples
Sausage Cakes   Popovers
Coffee   Milk

——————

Ready-to-Eat Cereal
Sliced Bananas with Cream
Poached Eggs on Toast   Toast
Coffee   Milk

Luncheons or Suppers

Bacon and Liver Sandwiches
Lettuce and Onion Salad Bowl
with Chiffonade Dressing
Baked Stuffed Pears

——————

Tomato Bouillon
Welsh Rarebit
French Fruit Salad
Hot Coffee

——————

Spinach in Egg Cups
Carrot Molds
Fruit Batter Pudding
Hot Tea

——————

Cucumbers Stuffed with Chicken
Potato Chips
Tomato Rose Salad
Individual Baked Alaskas
Iced Coffee

——————

Boiled Ham
Green Peas, Drawn Butter
Toasted English Muffins
Lemon Ice

Chilled Mixed Vegetable Juices
Shrimp Sandwiches
Watercress Sandwiches
Frosted Melon Mold Salad
Biscuit Glacé
Iced Tea

——————

Cheese Soufflé
Broiled Tomatoes
Watercress Salad Bowl
Little Baltimore Cakes
Hot Tea with Ginger

——————

Asparagus Goldenrod on Toast
Shredded Carrot,
Chinese Cabbage and
Romaine Salad
French Dressing with Orange
Juice
Sugared Berries

——————

Kidneys and Bacon en Brochette
Finger Rolls
Cardinal Salad Bowl
Rice Bavarian
Turkish Coffee

Baked Mushrooms on Toast
Pineapple and Nut Salad
in Tomato Baskets
Cheese and Crackers

Mixed Grill   Relish Tray
Raised Muffins with Chopped
Nuts
Baked Custard

Crab Rarebit on Toast
Tossed Greens Salad
with French Dressing
Fresh Fruit Bowl

Lobster à la Newburg
Spring Salad Bowl
with Roquefort French Dressing
Fruit Cup with Mint Ice

Cream-Cheese Sandwich Loaf
Frozen Fruit Salad
on Watercress
Iced Tea

Boston Baked Beans
Cabbage Salad
Boston Brown Bread
Baked Maple-Stuffed Apples

Planked Eggs with Ham Paste
Spicy Apple Coffee Cake
Vienna Coffee

Spaghetti with Tomato Sauce
Escarole Bowl
with Chicken Liver Dressing
Fresh Fruit   French Bread

Luncheons or Suppers Without Meat

Creamed Asparagus on Toast
Stewed Tomatoes
Cottage-Cheese Salad
Prune Whip   Custard Sauce

Tomato Soup
Rice Croquettes with Cheese
Sauce
Green Peas
Baked Apple with Raisins
and Nuts
Milk

Lettuce and Peanut Butter
Sandwiches
Banana Salad
Apple Sauce   Cookies   Milk

Stuffed Baked Potatoes
Cheese, Pickle and Pea Salad
Drop Biscuits
Pineapple   Ginger Snaps

Brown-Bread and Cream-Cheese
Sandwiches
Apricots   Vanilla Wafers
Tea or Milk

Scalloped Oysters   Waldorf Salad
Graham Muffins
Floating Island Custard
Tea

VEGETABLE PLATE
Potato, Green Beans, Squash
Beets   Carrots
Toasted Cheese Rolls
Fruit Salad
Coffee

Dinners

Roast Beef, Yorkshire Pudding
Toasted Carrots, Buttered Onions
Lettuce and Chicory Salad Bowl
Cheese Tray Toasted Crackers
Coffee

———

Pot Roast of Beef
Potato Pancakes String Beans
Molded Carrot and Cabbage Salad
Tipsy Pudding

———

Liver Piquante with Vegetables
Rice Border
Green-Bean Salad
Cheese Pie

———

Chilled Trout in Aspic
Saratoga Potatoes, Baked Squash
Tomato, Cucumber and
Watercress Salad Bowl
Lime Chiffon Pie

———

Onion Soup
Veal with Olives
Rice and Peas
Tomato and Celery Salad
Cottage Pudding with Jelly

———

Bouillon
Celery Curls   Carrot Sticks
Fricassee of Chicken
Dumplings   Succotash
Cranberry Pie

———

Roast Leg of Lamb
Potato Puff
Creamed Peas
Celery Salad
Fresh Pineapple with Kirsch

———

Barley Soup
Spiced Ham Loaf
Sweetpotato Casserole
Creamed Cabbage
Apple Charlotte

Oysters on the Half Shell
Roast Guinea Fowl with
Wild Rice and Mushroom Stuffing
Brandied Peaches   Broccoli
Avocado, Tangerine, Pecan salad
English Plum Pudding
with Foamy Sauce

———

Old-Fashioned Boiled Dinner
(Corned Beef, Potatoes, Turnips,
Cabbage, Onions, Carrots, Beets)
Horse-Radish
Baked Apricot Whip

———

Braised Pork Steaks
with Grape Apples
Scalloped Cauliflower
Potato on Half Shell
Steamed Date Pudding

———

Jellied Consommé with Sherry
Broiled Chicken
Potatoes Persillade
Asparagus, Watercress Salad Bowl
Glazed Strawberry Tarts

———

Baked Stuffed Whitefish
with Shrimp Sauce
Belgian Baked Potatoes
Spinach, American Style
Pickled Beets
Lemon Roll

———

Lamb Chops with Madeira
Stuffed Potatoes   Buttered Peas
Chicory, Escarole, Grapefruit
Salad
Chocolate Rennet-Custard

———

Stuffed Beef Heart
Glazed Sweetpotatoes
Buttered Turnips
Orange Salad
Tapioca Cream

Pork Chops Baked with Apples
Scalloped Potatoes
String Beans   Bread
Indian Pudding

Fish Chowder with Water Wafers
Grapefruit Salad
Graham Bread and Butter
Queen of Puddings

Broiled Chicken   Riced Potatoes
Corn Fritters   Rolls
Tomato Jelly Salad
Apple Pie with Cheese

Meat Pie with Potatoes, Carrots
and Turnips
Tomato Salad   Bread
Prune Whip   Custard Sauce

Broiled Halibut
Creamed Potatoes
Chili Sauce
Cole Slaw   Brown Bread
Rice Custard

Tomato Soup   Bread Sticks
Baked Ham
Southern Sweetpotatoes
Green Peas   Rolls
Lettuce Salad   French Dressing
Meringues with Fruit and
Whipped Cream
Coffee

Cream of Corn Soup
Baked Hash   Spinach with Egg
Chocolate Bread Pudding
Coffee

Salmon Loaf with Creamed Peas
Mashed Potatoes
Apple and Celery Salad
Banana Cream Pie

Fruit Cocktail
Stuffed Turbans of Flounders
French Fried Potatoes
Creamed Peas   Bread or Rolls
Tomato Salad
Fruit Ice   Cakes   Coffee

Dinners Without Meat

Cheese Soufflé
Mashed Potatoes
Buttered String Beans
Radish and Cucumber Salad
Strawberry Shortcake

Cream of Vegetable Soup
Scalloped Tomatoes
Stuffed Baked Potatoes with
Cheese
Waldorf Salad   Corn Muffins
Creamed Rice Pudding
with Apricots

Chilled Fruit
Stuffed Tomatoes
Parsley Potatoes
Creamed Asparagus
Pumpkin Pie   Milk

Baked Rice and Cheese
Buttered Beets
Stuffed Olive and Lettuce Salad
Nut Bread   Milk
Date Pudding   Lemon Sauce

Boston Roast
Spinach with Eggs   Rolls
Head Lettuce Salad
Bread Pudding with Cream Sauce

The Problem of the Formal Meal

The purpose of food is to satisfy hunger and to give pleasure. After hunger is satisfied, more food is a hindrance to health. After the appetite has been stimulated by a variety of foods, to stimulate it further jades it.

At one time it was the custom to serve long and elaborate dinners having many courses and much repetition of type foods. Gradually the realization has grown that elaborate meals are not justified from any point of view, social, physiological or economic, and that even the most formal meal must follow the rules of health.

Formal meals which conform to laws of health and good taste may be arranged according to the following general plan:

First Course

THE APPETIZER—Any *one* of the following types of dishes, with proper accompaniments, serves to whet the appetite:

Canapés or tiny open sandwiches made with highly flavored mixtures. Chilled oysters, clams, or shrimp; oyster or clam cocktail. Fruit cocktail; avocado served with lemon juice. Soup is preferably a clear stock.

Second Course

TO SATISFY THE APPETITE—For dinner, the *pièce de résistance,* or main course, may be roast of meat, poultry, baked fish or game, with the proper accompaniments of vegetables and a starchy food such as potato or rice.

For luncheon, the main course may be a small steak, chops, made dish or entrée of meat, fish, poultry, game, eggs, or cheese, served with a succulent vegetable, preferably a green vegetable, and rolls.

Third Course

LIGHT, REFRESHING AND CRISP—The salad course may be any simple vegetable salad with a suitable accompaniment of French dressing and wafers. Meat salads or heavy mixed or complicated salads should not be served in this type of meal.

Fourth Course

THE SWEET OR *Bonne Bouché*—This course may consist of any frozen dessert, whip, meringue with fruit, or any individual tart or pastry.

Fifth Course

TO KEEP THE SWEET FROM BEING TOO WELL REMEMBERED —This course includes a demi-tasse of coffee, with sugar if desired. It may include fruit or crackers and a cheese with a high flavor.

If the person giving a formal dinner or luncheon has not been converted to the new idea of simplicity and desires a more elaborate meal than the type just outlined, more courses may be introduced. An entrée may come between the appetizer and the main course. Soup may follow fruit, chilled oysters, broiled fruit, hot or cold canapés, cocktail of fruit or seafood. Fish may be served as a separate course, with meat to follow. An entrée may be introduced between the fish and meat courses. All of these procedures are correct by custom.

Order of Courses

The courses in a meal are served in the following order:
1. Appetizer
2. Soup
3. Fish
4. Roast
5. Game
6. Salad
7. Dessert
8. Crackers and Cheese with Coffee
9. Nuts and Raisins
10. Fruit

For the place of the entrée, see chapter, **ENTRÉES AND MADE-OVER DISHES.**

MENUS FOR SPECIAL OCCASIONS

St. Patrick's Day Luncheon

Cream of Spinach Soup

Fried Chicken   Parsley Buttered Potatoes

Green Pepper and Grapefruit Salad

Lemon Ice with Mint Leaves

Small Cakes

Green Mints   Coffee   Hard Green Candies

Thanksgiving Dinners

No. 1

Clear Soup   Bread Sticks
        Salted Almonds   Celery   Olives
Roast Turkey   Giblet Sauce   Chestnut Stuffing
        Mashed Potatoes   Brussels Sprouts
                    Cranberry Jelly
    Lettuce or Romaine Salad with French Dressing   Cheese Wafers
            Frozen Pudding or Hot Mince Pie
        Bonbons   Coffee

No. 2

                    Grapefruit Baskets
                        Olives
        Baked Guinea Hen with Gravy   Crabapple Jelly
            Candied Sweetpotatoes   Cauliflower au Gratin
    Tomato Jelly Salad   Graham Bread Canapés
            Individual Pumpkin Pie with Whipped Cream
                    Candied Orange Peel
                        Coffee

No. 3

                    Grapefruit
    Baked Loin of Pork with Gravy   Browned Potatoes   Apple Sauce
            or Baked Ham with Southern Sweetpotatoes
        Tomato and Celery Salad   French Dressing
            Thanksgiving Plum Pudding   Foamy Sauce
                        Coffee

Christmas Dinners

No. 1

            Oyster Cocktails in Green Pepper Shells
            Celery   Ripe Olives
    Roast Goose with Potato Stuffing
                                            Apple Sauce
                String Beans   Potato Puff
            Lettuce Salad with Riced Cheese and Bar-le-Duc
                French Dressing   Toasted Wafers
        English Plum Pudding
                                            Bonbons
                    Coffee

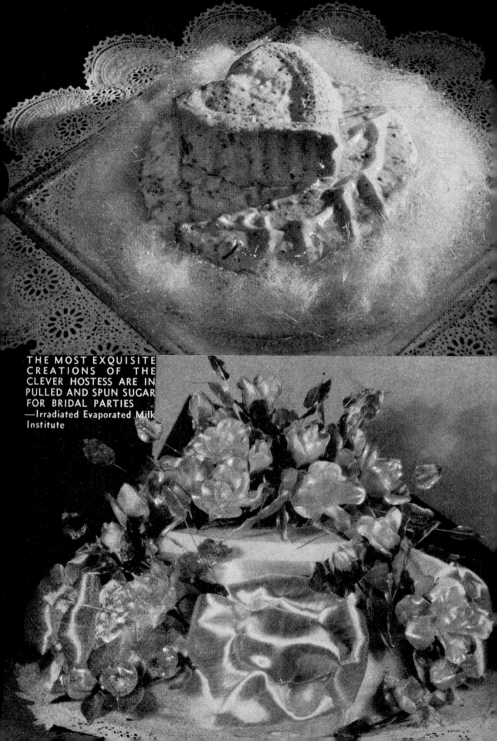

THE MOST EXQUISITE
CREATIONS OF THE
CLEVER HOSTESS ARE IN
PULLED AND SPUN SUGAR
FOR BRIDAL PARTIES
—Irradiated Evaporated Milk
Institute

No. 2

Cream of Celery Soup	Cheese Sticks
Salted Peanuts	Stuffed Olives
Roast Beef	Yorkshire Pudding
Potato Soufflé	Spinach in Eggs

White Grape Salad with Guava Jelly, French Dressing
Toasted Crackers

Plum Pudding, Hard Sauce   Bonbons
Coffee

Wedding Menus

No. 1

Bouillon

Chicken à la King	Buttered Rolls
Olives	Celery

Molded Fruit Salad

Ice Cream   Bride's Cake   Groom's Cake
Coffee   Candies

_____

No. 2

Creamed Sweetbreads in Ramekins

Buttered Rolls   Olives
Grapefruit Salad   Wafers
Ice Cream in Fancy Molds

Bride's Cake   Groom's Cake
Coffee   Candies

_____

No. 3

Hot or Iced Bouillon in Cups
Creamed Lobster or Shrimps in Croustades
Hot Buttered Rolls   Asparagus Tip Salad
Bride's Cake   Strawberry Ice Cream   Groom's Cake
Candies   Coffee

_____

No. 4

Molded Chicken Salad with Mayonnaise
Olives   Radishes
Buttered Rolls
Frozen Strawberries with Whipped Cream
Bride's Cake   Groom's Cake
Nuts   Coffee   Mints

Afternoon Tea

No. 1

Assorted Sandwiches   Small Cakes
   Tea with Sugar, Cream and Sliced Lemon
  Bonbons   Nuts

No. 2

Sweet Wafers   Toasted Sponge Cake
    Tea with Sliced Lemon
  Nougat Candy   Salted Nuts

Afternoon or Evening Refreshments

No. 1

Fruit Salad with Mayonnaise, Boiled Dressing or Whipped Cream
    Small Sandwiches
    Coffee or Chocolate
Candies   Small Cakes   Nuts

———

No. 2

    Chicken Salad
Olives   Rye and White Bread Sandwiches
   Ice Cream or Fruit Ice
  Maple Cake   Coffee

———

No. 3

   Chicken Salad Sandwiches
     Olives
  Ice Cream   Petits Fours
  Fruit Punch   Coffee

Chafing Dish Suppers

No. 1

    Fruit Cocktail
Creamed Crab Flakes   Bread and Butter Sandwiches
    Coffee

———

No. 2

Welsh Rarebit   Toast
  Watercress, Tomato Salad with French Dressing
    Coffee

Children's Party

Fruit Cocktails

Chicken Sandwiches   Fruit Butter Sandwiches
Vanilla Ice Cream   Small Cakes
Birthday Cake with Name, Date and Candles
Orange Juice   Candy

School Reception

Fruit Ice or Ice Cream   Small Cakes   Candies
Punch   Nuts

For Hikers

Camp Hamburgs to Broil

Whole Tomatoes   Potatoes to Bake
Olives   Carrot Sticks
Cup Cakes   Cans of Fruit or Vegetable Juices

Bridge Supper

Jellied Meat Loaf
Vegetable Platter with Sour Cream Dressing
Toast Melba   Clover Leaf Rolls   Saltines
Marron Mousse   Coffee
Crystallized Fruit   Salted Nuts

Men's Card Party

Platter Cold Meats and Strong Cheese
Potato Salad   Spaghetti Casserole
Rye Rolls   Poppyseed Rolls   Salt Rolls
Olives   Dill Pickles   Gherkins   Radishes
Rum Cake   or Beer without Dessert
Coffee

Cocktail Party

Assorted Cocktails and Dry Wines
Salted Almonds   Olives   Potato Chips
Assorted Canapés

THE LUNCH BOX

A S much care is needed in selecting and preparing the food for the lunch box as for the other meals served to the family. If the lunch is inadequate or lacking in food essentials throughout the year, the individual's whole nutrition will be seriously affected, and his work will suffer. The lunch box is one of three meals, not just a "snack," and should possess the following characteristics:

1. It should be abundant in amount for a hungry, healthy individual. A little too much is better than too little.

2. It should be chosen with regard to nutritive needs of the individual, and in relation to the whole day's food.

3. It should be clean, appetizing, wholesome and attractive.

FOOD SELECTION PLAN

Plan it the day before. Select from the following one food from each group. Make the lunch box bear its full share of responsibility for liquid as well as solid nourishment.

MILK, in food or drink.

BREAD, enriched or whole grain in sandwiches.

MEAT or cheese or eggs or fish. In sandwich fillings, salads or hearty main dishes.

FRUIT, at least one. Whole or in salads or desserts.

VEGETABLES, at least one, in sandwich filling, salads or in hearty main dishes. Use leafy green and yellow vegetables, and use them crisp and uncooked often.

Plan to have leftovers for the lunch box. Meat loaf or pot roast that will make good sandwiches, sliced cold. Gingerbread or stewed fruits. Don't specialize in starchy foods. Always include some kind of surprise such as: Whole tomatoes in season, radishes, celery, carrot or green pepper sticks, pickles, olives, dried fruits, nut meats, or cookies.

Keep in mind the season of the year in planning menus. In winter have something hot and invigorating in the thermos bottle: Hot soup, coffee, tea, baked beans, hot chocolate, or stew. Something cool and refreshing in the summertime, such as lemonade, tomato juice, fruit juices, chocolate milk shake, milk, iced tea or iced coffee, canned fruit juices. And do not forget the straws.

Be sure to include crisp, crunchy vegetables that will give the meal some contrast. In a packed sandwich lunch, texture and flavor are of great importance. Sandwiches have a tendency to be soft and too easily become soggy. Pack lettuce separately, to be added just before eating.

The men in the family will prefer spicy condiments and sauces on their sandwiches, while the school child will like a more mild, delicate flavor.

Plan for milk in every lunch box you pack. If in doubt whether milk can be bought or will be bought at work or school, send milk along in some form in food, or just cold or hot milk in the thermos bottle. Use evaporated milk in cooking if at any time fresh milk is scarce.

All too easily lunch box meals fall into a set pattern. It is only by the most careful planning that a lunch box is appetizing and has variety and balance each day.

MENU SUGGESTIONS

Cream of Spinach Soup
Crackers
Egg Salad Sandwiches with
Lettuce
Raw Vegetable Strips
Apple   Cup Cake

Cream of Tomato Soup
Ham Sandwich with Mustard
and Lettuce on Bun
Celery   Olives
Fresh Pear   Cookies

American Cheese Sandwich
with Catchup and Lettuce
Tossed Vegetable Salad
Dressing (in container)
Pickles
Cake   Orange
Cocoa

Peanut Butter, Bacon and Lettuce
Sandwiches
Cauliflowerlets   Carrot Sticks
Hard-Cooked Egg
Gingerbread   Grapes
Milk

Oven Baked Beans   Catchup
Boston Brown Bread Sandwiches
with Cream Cheese Filling
Cole Slaw
Applesauce
Milk

Beef Stew   Pickle Relish
Bread and Butter Sandwiches
with Lettuce
Whole Tomato   Crisp Radishes
Fruit Cup (in container)
Hot Coffee

Preparation of Food

SANDWICHES—Since sandwiches form a main part of the lunch box, their preparation is most important.

Whole grain breads should be used for sandwiches. Graham, whole wheat, oatmeal, brown, raisin, and nut bread are excellent. Cold bran or whole wheat muffins or filled rolls are often tempting.

Fillings for the sandwiches for the lunch box require some special preparation. The filling should be abundant in amount and should play an important part in the sandwich.

Cheese, meat, eggs, nuts, dried fruits or vegetables in combination may be put through the food chopper. Cream cheese, peanut butter and other compact substances should be thinned with cream. Ground meats, eggs, and vegetables should be moistened with a small amount of salad dressing or cream and vinegar. Succulent vegetables should be provided, if possible. Finely chopped celery, lettuce, watercress or sliced tomato may be used alone or with cottage cheese. Finely cut pineapple or orange often add greatly to the flavor of sandwiches.

Jellies, jams and conserves make sweet sandwiches or a container of sweetened fresh fruit may be tucked into the lunch box.

Dried figs, dates, raisins, thoroughly washed and steamed in a small sieve or strainer over boiling water for thirty minutes and then ground and moistened with a small amount of fruit juice or salad dressing, make excellent sandwiches.

Pickles, chowchow, relishes, and olives give variety to the lunch box.

The Chapter on Sandwiches pp. 131-155, gives full directions and recipes for a variety of sandwiches.

HOT DISHES—Special vacuum containers make it possible to include hot cocoa or hot soup in the lunch, also a creamed vegetable, a hot pudding or other hot food. These containers should never be filled the night before the lunch is prepared. If foods prepared for dinner are to be used for the lunch box, these foods should be refrigerated overnight and reheated in the morning.

MILK—Milk should be poured while cold into the vacuum container. Good milk properly refrigerated should be in good condition at lunch time.

LIQUID AND SEMI-SOLID FOODS—Stewed or canned fruits may be carried in any small screw-top container. Cold puddings, custards or similar desserts may also be carried in this manner.

Packing the Lunch

All foods not in containers should be wrapped separately in waxed paper before being placed in the box. The neatly wrapped articles should be placed, so far as is possible, in the order in which the food will be eaten, so that those found first may be eaten first without disturbing the remainder. The heaviest foods, however, should be placed at the bottom of the box.

Articles should be packed compactly in order to prevent the food from shaking about. Empty space may be filled with crushed paper. When space seems lacking, the difficulty may be overcome by more careful packing, by resorting to such expedients as cutting fruits or cookies in half, or by packing sandwiches the long way of the box. Fillings for sandwiches may be packed in small jars, and buttered bread in waxed paper included for spreading just before eating.

The Lunch Box

Select a box that can be kept clean. Lunch boxes should be washed, scalded and aired daily. Those made of lightweight metal are best. Many attractive boxes are now made with a vacuum bottle which fits the box. These are highly desirable. A lunch box should not be air-tight, as a circulation of air prevents the mingling of odors. All food should be protected by wrapping.

ACCESSORIES—A small vacuum container of cup-like shape for hot foods, a screw-top container for liquid or semi-solid food, plenty of waxed paper, paper cups some with tops, and paper napkins are essential for the lunch box.

WITHOUT THE HOT DISH—In many places the school, the Parent-Teacher Association or some woman's club provides milk and/or prepares one hot dish at school to be sold to children for a few cents. In this case the lunch box should supplement with sandwiches, vegetables and fruit. The greatest care should be exercised that vitamins and minerals are not sacrificed to bulk. Carrot sticks, parsley, whole tomatoes, radishes, cabbage leaves, oranges or grapefruit sections unpeeled will take care of this.

TABLE SETTING AND SERVICE

~~~~~~~~

THE social life of a household, whether the household is a simple one or an elaborate one, centers about its dining-table and whether that dining-table is simply or elaborately dressed, it should, by its harmony and unity of setting, indicate that it is arranged according to a definite artistic standard. Every accessory that builds the table-picture—the silver, china, glass, and linen—furthers the art of gracious living in the household.

CHINA

Perhaps in greater degree than any other domestic appointments, does china present an opportunity for indulgence of personal whim and the exercise of good taste on the part of the hostess. Today there are patterns for every occasion. Breakfast china is gay, sprightly; color runs rampant upon it; often whole gardens shine on its face. But it would not be used for a dinner, which demands fine china of exquisitely fine design. Luncheon is still another thing. Its china may vary as the season—or as the whim of the hostess.

Modern day impatience with formula and rite is nowhere more eloquently expressed than in the growing custom of using different patterns for different courses, all related by the thread of harmony. The hostess of today considers sameness identical with boredom. If she uses a cobalt and gold service plate, she may elect to use a simple gold-banded entrée plate. The fish plate perhaps may have yellow bands to match the flowers in the center. The roast plate may present a pattern border, touched with gold, and yellow, and blue. Her dessert plate will be utterly different from any of the foregoing: it may strike an entirely new note; but it will not be discordant or jarring. Obviously, all dishes used in one course should match.

Plates of Various Sizes and How They Are Used

In the following list the measurements, in inches, are from extreme rim to rim.

PLACE PLATE (also called cover plate, service plate, lay plate). 10 to 11 inches.

DINNER PLATE (roast plate). 10 inches, but seen as large as 10½ inches. The size of the dinner plate is fairly large, due to the current practice of placing attendant vegetables on the plate with the meat. The day of side dishes, each bearing a particular variety of vegetables, has definitely passed.

ENTRÉE PLATE. 8½ to 9½ inches. A most convenient size, for, in addition to its use in serving entrées, it is often employed as a salad plate, or a fish plate: even a dessert plate when the finger bowl is borne in with the dessert silver on the plate, the finger bowl being removed later.

DESSERT PLATE. 7½ to 8 inches. Used for miscellaneous desserts, and salads. It becomes the cake plate at tea.

BREAD AND BUTTER PLATE. 6 to 6½ inches. Universally used now: the butter chip, for individual butter service is extinct.

SOUP PLATE. 8 to 8½ inches at rim, for the usual type of soup plate with wide, flat rim. There is also a bowl soup plate, or "coup" soup, which has no rim at all. Soup plates are not as commonly used as at one time, due to the spreading favor accorded the cream soup cup and the bouillon cup for luncheons and informal meals.

Cups and Bowls

CREAM SOUP CUP. This is a low, broad cup, handled on both sides. Its width is from 4½ to 5 inches, and its depth about two. It is used for the serving of purées, bisques, cream soups, and is extremely popular for luncheons.

BOUILLON CUP. A tea cup with two handles. Clear soups, consommés, bouillons are served in it.

CHILLED COCKTAIL BOWL. This is distinctly an innovation in china service. It is a low, wide bowl, fitted with a separate small container. The space between the bowl proper and the inner cup is filled with crushed ice. Used for grapefruit, shrimp cocktail, and many other foods best served chilled.

GLASS

Of late years, an awakening appreciation of the charm of glass has taken place. Perhaps the appeal of glorious color, so striking in this substance, accounts for it. Blue in varying tones was some years ago in wide favor; then amethyst displaced it. Rapidly came amber, and green, which maintain a deserved respect, because of their adaptability. Rose, canary, sapphire, in quick succession—no color today is unrepresented.

Glass is often selected to "go with" certain tones of china. The hostess with a sense of fitness has a glass service for each of her dinner services. For her severely formal tables she uses glittering crystal, etched or cut, engraved or gold decorated.

But there is ample opportunity for her to indulge her love for color to the full, to arrange tables with an eye to the dining-room effects, or to build them according to her own color preferences.

Kinds of Glasses

GOBLET. The goblet is the aristocrat of table glass. In its usual form it is a flaring round bowl resting on a tall slender stem. In certain styles, however, the "stem" becomes a mere button. Goblets are always provided with a foot, however small. The goblet is the dominant member of the "place glass" group, and all glasses of a service take their shape from it, following its contours very closely.

OTHER PLACE GLASS. In addition to the goblet, there may be placed at each cover at least one other glass for the cup or other beverages. At very formal dinners two extra glasses are often placed, but never more.

The shapes and sizes of these supplementary glasses vary as their purposes. On the continent, for example, there is a definite type of glass placed for certain wines. Thus a glass for sherry is differently shaped from one for claret: it is more sharply tapered and considerably smaller.

For the most part the glasses of this type that we see in America are either the claret, or the tall shallow champagne glass. The claret, whose capacity makes it a fine utility glass, is used for almost any kind of cup. On the other hand the tall champagne glass is often placed for its high decorative value. Few glasses are as graceful as this shallow bowl on its slender shaft.

SHERBET. The sherbet glass is a medium depth broad bowl on a short stem. In it are served sherbets, ice-cream, frozen desserts. Much used now, however, for this purpose is the tall shallow champagne glass, perhaps because of its more imposing height and dignity.

HOLLOW STEM CHAMPAGNE. This glass is similar to the tall champagne glass, except that the stem instead of being solid is hollow to the very bottom. While its primary use was for serving champagne, today we often serve in it ginger ale, and other carbonated drinks. The hollow stem releasing a train of sparkling bubbles is picturesque indeed.

FINGER BOWL. The finger bowl is a low broad bowl, variously shaped. It is usually seen without a "foot," but certain styles have such supports. Finger bowls are fitted with matching under-plates, but their use is optional.

GRAPEFRUIT BOWL. This is a double bowl for chilled food cocktails. It consists of a large bowl on a stem. Within it is placed a smaller "cup" or "lining." The grapefruit or other cocktail is put in the small cup, and the space between the cups is filled with crushed ice.

TUMBLER. In its simplest form, a tumbler is simply a glass cylinder with one end closed. But the glass designer does wonders with it. He mounts it on a foot: he shapes its sides in lovely contours: often he makes it angular instead of round.

The sizes commonly used are:

Apollinaris Tumbler. This is a small, narrow tumbler used for liquids that are served in small quantities, such as orange juice, grape juice, mineral water. It is often used for water when space is at a premium, as on breakfast trays, or at bridge tables. It holds about five ounces.

Table Tumbler. Also called water tumbler. It is a low tumbler, containing about ten ounces, and is used to serve water informally, at simple meals.

There is also a water tumbler of about the same capacity, but narrower and taller, sometimes called the "Ale tumbler."

Highball Tumbler. A tall tumbler, used to serve "long drinks," or iced tea, iced coffee, iced chocolate, and so forth. It holds about 12 ounces.

Iced Tea Tumbler. A normal iced tea tumbler, sufficiently large to contain plenty of ice. Its capacity runs from 14 to 16 ounces.

BESIDES THE PIECES IN GENERAL USE DESCRIBED ABOVE, there are all manner of articles blown for special uses: trays for hors d'oeuvres; salad bowls, salt dips, saucers for berries, and plates of various sizes.

SILVER

The silver on your table is a declaration of your taste. Whether it is sterling or plate, there is, in an excellent pattern and in the perfect form and proportion of the utensils, an unmistakable aristocracy that gives distinction.

Modern methods of manufacturing silver plate have made it not only durable but beautiful as well. Plated silver ranges from the very durable triple-plated ware, (heavy weight) which lasts a lifetime, through the double plate (medium weight) which has good wearing qualities, to the single plate which is light weight.

When you choose a pattern of silver, examine all the pieces, to be sure that you approve of the shapes of all the pieces, that the pieces are perfectly balanced, that the handles are comfortable to hold, and that the tips of the handles of the knives and forks fit perfectly into the center of the palm of the hand. Find out how long the pattern has been on the market, and, if possible, how long it is to be made, so that you will not suddenly discover that the pattern has been "discontinued."

Place silver, or flat silver as it is sometimes called, consists of the knives, forks, and spoons necessary for general use at table.

Knives and Forks

The dinner knife and fork, although imposing members of the silver-family, are not the most important members, for their use is limited to the main course of dinner.

The luncheon knife and fork offer the greatest variety of uses. They may be used "around the clock," for breakfast, for luncheon, for supper, and for certain courses at dinner, such as hors d'oeuvres, entrée, fish, salad, for dishes served in a ramekin, for dishes served at informal entertaining, and for large and small sandwiches.

Smaller than the luncheon knife and fork are the tea knife and fork, with their increasingly-recognized number of uses.

Butter spreaders are necessary in your first list.

Later if you are not content to use the medium size knives and forks or the tea knives and forks for special courses like fish, entrée, salad, and fruit, you may buy fish knives and forks, entrée knives and forks, and salad knives and forks (or, if you prefer, individual salad forks,) and fruit knives, or preferably, fruit knives and forks.

Spoons

Accompanying the medium size knife and fork, and of a size between a teaspoon and a tablespoon, is the dessert spoon, the spoon of a variety of uses, from eating soup and cereals, to eating desserts such as pudding and compote of fruit.

Teaspoons have a great variety of uses, and while these are the first kind of small spoon to be bought you will want to add when you can, orange spoons, bouillon spoons, ice-cream spoons, coffee spoons, five o'clock teaspoons, and iced tea spoons.

A List of Useful Serving Pieces

2 or 3 Tablespoons

2 or 3 Dinner Forks (for serving)

Medium size Carving Set (or steak set) 2 pieces (or large size carving set)

Butter Knife or Butter Pick

Gravy Ladle

Sugar Tongs

Pie or Tart Server, long and flat

Cold Meat Fork

Olive Spoon (pierced) or Olive Fork

Berry Spoon. A very convenient serving-spoon which can be used in serving berries, large vegetables, casserole dishes, and puddings

Jelly Server, for jelly, marmalade, honey, etc.

Preserve Spoon

Long Handled Fork and Spoon, for serving salad from a central bowl

Pickle Fork, usually two-tined

Pierced server, usually called a tomato-server, useful in serving sliced tomatoes, fritters, poached eggs, sliced pineapple, etc.

Salad Dressing Ladle, smaller than gravy ladle. Can also be used for serving whipped cream

Lemon Fork

Asparagus Server

Entrée Server, wide and flat

Cake fork

Sardine Server

Ice Tongs

Ice Spoon

Sugar Spoon

Sugar Sifter for powdered sugar

Ice-cream Knife or Ice-cream Server

Cheese Server

Melon Knife

Grape Scissors

LINEN

White linen damask is the classic covering for the dinner-table. Linen and lace are often combined and sometimes elaborate all lace tablecloths are used. When a lace cloth is used, it is placed on a bare table.

In the colored damasks every woman will find an opportunity to vary her table setting effects occasionally with a harmonious combination of pastel shades in tablecloth, glass, china and centerpiece. But the conservative woman still uses white damask for her formal dinners, and undoubtedly will continue to do so.

Tablecloths

Before you buy your tablecloths, carefully measure your table, and allow a twelve- to fifteen-inch overhang for your dinner cloths, and an eight- to twelve-inch overhang for your luncheon cloths.

Tablecloths should be French hemmed, with the hem three-eighths of an inch to one-half an inch wide, and napkins, also French hemmed, have hems of from one-eighth of an inch to one-quarter of an inch wide.

A white linen damask cloth is as appropriate for the formal or informal luncheon as for the formal or informal dinner. Gay colored sets of damask or of less formal materials are often used. Linen runners, with small luncheon napkins to match, are popular, especially on long tables like refectory tables. An especially beautiful table is sometimes left bare except for the mats under the centerpiece, plates, and glasses. Damask napkins are used with these.

Luncheon sets are appropriate for use at breakfast, luncheon, an informal dinner, or supper.

For the tea table one may use an embroidered or hemstitched teacloth, or a simple or elaborate lace cover, or a combination of linen and lace.

Napkins

Tablecloths and napkins should match. For formal dinners an unusually large napkin is smart, but nowadays napkins, like most other "furnishings," have shrunk, and one rarely encounters dinner napkins larger than twenty-eight inches and usually not larger than twenty-four inches.

Luncheon napkins are from thirteen inches to eighteen inches square. White hemstitched luncheon napkins are often used with a white linen damask cloth.

Breakfast napkins, often colored or with a colored border to match the cloth, are usually a bit smaller than luncheon napkins but may be the same size.

Appropriate to the appointments of the tea table are the small tea napkins, sometimes of fine handkerchief linen with scalloped edges, sometimes of damask with hemstitched borders, and sometimes of heavy linen with drawnwork borders. In houses with Early American furnishings —and with excellent laundry technic—the old-fashioned damask napkins with fringe edges add a charmingly quaint touch. But with uncertain laundering these are very apt to be unattractive looking.

Monogramming

The pattern or design of the cloth and napkins and the type, design, and size of the monograms embroidered on them should make a perfect unity.

For table-cloths, the size of the monogram should be from two and one-half to five inches. For dinner napkins from one to two inches. For luncheon and breakfast napkins and doilies, from three-quarters of an inch to an inch and a half.

When the bride-to-be is marking her trousseau linens, it is best form for her to use the initials of her maiden name. However, there is no hard and fast rule for this marking, and she may if she prefers use the initials of the first and last names of her maiden name and the initial letter of the groom's last name.

If an initial is used instead of a monogram it should be the initial of your last name. When only one letter is used, it is usually a block letter—sometimes ornate—since a single letter in script is not very effective-looking.

How to Measure for the Placing of the Monogram

Spread the cloth on the table, place the end of your measuring stick at the corner of the table, and point it in the direction of the corner diagonally opposite. Measure from twelve to fifteen inches, mark this off, and place your monogram there unless it will, in this place, interfere with the design in the damask. In that event, raise it or lower it to make it artistically well-placed.

On a table-cloth of two yards square or less usually only

one monogram is placed. Larger sizes usually have two monograms diagonally opposite each other.

Dinner napkins should be marked with a smaller monogram of the same design as that used on the table-cloth. They are now usually embroidered in what is known as the "center of the side." Fold the napkin into thirds, and again into thirds in the opposite way. On the top of the center square with the selvedge toward you, place the monogram in the approximate center.

Tea napkins may be monogrammed with the two or three initials used on the other napkins. In very fine linen ones, cut-out monograms are often used.

TABLE DECORATION

Have in mind a definite plan.

Consider carefully the artistic height for your table decorations: table decorations that are too high are awkward, and those that are too low become monotonous to the eye.

No table decorations should obstruct the view of the guests (although at large, formal dinners, when the conversation cannot be general anyway, they may be tall).

All tall decorations should be narrow (e. g. candles).

Avoid over-decoration and inappropriate decorations. Don't crowd your table or make it look heavy.

Discriminate between a formal party and an informal party, and adapt your decorations accordingly.

Keep in mind the color-scheme of your room, and the colors of the food in your menu, and harmonize the color of your table decorations with these.

Adapt your flowers to the type and proportions of your flower-container.

Centerpieces

Centerpieces are of infinite variety, their beauty and distinction being limited only by one's imagination and one's budget. Flowers are still—and probably always will be—the most lovely decoration for the center of the table. The fashion of supporting a few flowers in flower-holders in low silver or glass bowls makes possible simple and very effective arrangements. Unusual effects may be obtained with central mirrors and with mirrored tables, with fruits, with formal combinations of flowers and fruits, with crystal trees and flowers, with delicate figurines, and even with amusing accessories of simple or elaborate kinds. But one must be careful that the designs built with unusual accessories are beautiful and appropriate and not simply bizarre.

Compote Dishes and Candles

To balance the centerpiece, decorative silver or glass—or gold!—compote dishes, two or four in number, are usually placed toward the ends of the table. These dishes, containing bonbons or mints or nuts, may be low, medium, or high, according to the proportion required by the other table decorations.

Four candles, or more if the table is very large, are used in candlesticks of glass or silver or fine china, and sometimes of pottery for an informal dinner on an Italian or Spanish table. Instead of candlesticks handsome silver candelabra may be placed on each side of the centerpiece.

The candles should be lighted before the guests enter the dining-room, and allowed to burn until they leave the dining-room, even if they stay so long in the dining-room that the candles burn down to their sockets!

The height of the candles should, of course, be adapted to the height of the candlesticks—very tall candles in low standards, and shorter ones in the standard of average height. Low candlesticks with tall slender tapers are interesting and effective, but their use is more appropriate to informal occasions. Formal functions seem to need the dignity of tall candlesticks.

Candles for formal dinner tables usually are the color of natural wax or, if that is not obtainable, of white. As a matter of fact, many hostesses use candles of this color on their tables for all their parties. Of course colored candles may be used to carry out a decorative scheme, and are festive and appropriate for special occasions.

Candles are now never shaded.

Service or "Cover" Plate

A service plate (sometimes called a "place plate" or "lay plate," and, most appropriately, a "cover plate"), which is about one inch larger than a dinner plate, is used in formal service. A service plate is a background plate on which other plates are placed. Since its function is largely decorative, it should be as handsome as your circumstances permit. Service plates are usually of beautiful china, though sometimes they are of gold or silver or silver plate or even glass. If they are of china, they do not match the rest of the china in design, since they are usually far more ornate. In advance of the meal, the service plate is set in the center of each cover, one inch, or sometimes two inches, from the edge of the table. No food is served directly on the service plate. On it are placed the plates containing the first courses of the meal, such as fruit, oysters, and soup. It is not removed until it is exchanged for the plate of the first hot course after the soup.

Large service plates are not used for breakfast, and it is usually inconvenient to use them in homes where there is no service, or in homes where the food is served at the table by the hostess or host or both.

Place Cards

Place cards are used at formal dinners and luncheons for convenience in seating the guests. A place card should be simple (plain white ones are best) of about the size of a visiting-card. It is sometimes engraved with the hostess' monogram or crest embossed in plain white. Sometimes at feature parties, such as Hallowe'en or Valentine's Day, decorative place cards are used to carry out the motif of the entertainment. The name of the guest is written on the card, the title—*Mrs., Miss,* or *Mr.*—before the name. Place cards are usually placed above the cover so that they do not conceal the beauty of either the place plate or the napkin.

Salts and Peppers

Salts and peppers may be tall, gold or silver ones, or they may be low silver or crystal ones, or a silver pepper shaker accompanied by a low salt cup lined with old blue glass. For breakfast use, they may be of china or pottery, consistent with the informality of the breakfast table or tray.

It is customary to place a set of salts and peppers between every two covers if the party is large, or a pair at each corner of the table, if few are dining, or at two corners of a small table. Individual sets are sometimes placed. Whether salt shakers or salt cups are used is a matter of choice, but with salt cups small salt-spoons should be provided.

Bread and Butter Plates

These convenient little plates are used at breakfast and luncheon, and at family and other informal dinners. Since butter is not served at formal dinners, bread and butter plates, are not usually placed. However, there is now a tendency to place bread and butter plates on the table, except at *the most* formal dinners, many hostesses maintaining, and quite rightly, too, that these plates are of great convenience, in affording a harbor for the roll or bread and for the celery, radishes, and nuts that are passed at dinner.

Bread and butter plates are removed after the salad course, with the salts and peppers.

The Napkin

The napkin is usually placed at the left of the forks and parallel with them. If the napkin is folded in a square or otherwise folded so that the corners are up, it is placed so that the open corners are toward the plate.

Often one sees the napkin placed on the service plate, but unless space demands this, it is not to be recommended. Service plates are usually of such loveliness that none of their beauty should be sacrificed.

It is no longer good form to put bread or a dinner roll in the napkin—too many embarrassing moments resulted from that custom, for it was most natural, when one was engrossed in conversation, to take up the napkin unthinkingly and discover the roll perversely flying for the regions under the table.

Finger Bowls

There are three methods of placing finger bowls:

FIRST, if the finger bowl is needed after fruits at the beginning of a meal, or after corn on the cob, artichokes, and other food that demands the use of the fingers, it may be placed to the left of the cover when the table is laid or it may be brought in toward the end of the course and placed to the left of the cover.

SECOND, if the dessert plate and finger bowl are served together, the finger bowl is placed on the dessert plate, usually with a small fine white or cream doily between it and the plate, and the dessert silver placed on the sides of the plate, the fork on the left and the knife or spoon (depending on what the dessert may be) on the right. The guest removes the silver, placing the spoon or knife to the right, and the fork to the left, of the cover. Then he removes the finger bowl and doily and places them on the left of the cover, leaving the plate ready to receive the fruit or dessert.

THIRD, if the dessert is served in individual portions, say in a sherbet glass or some other container, which precludes the placing of the finger bowl on the dessert plate, the finger bowl, on a doily on a plate, is placed in front of the guest after the last course.

If especially beautiful glass or silver finger bowls and plates are used, many hostesses now omit the doily between, maintaining that it destroys the harmony between the bowl and the plate.

The bowls, half-filled with tepid water, may be placed on the side table before the meal is announced.

SETTING THE TABLE

Precision and decision are demanded in table-setting: mathematical precision in laying the table-covering and in placing the silver and other table-appointments, and artistic decision in the choice and harmonious arrangement of the table-appointments.

Spreading the Cloth

When the table-covering is the conventional table-cloth, first place the silence-cloth, of white, thick, doublefaced material, which usually extends five inches over each side of the table. This is sometimes tied in place to prevent slipping.

Over this, spread the table cloth, perfectly laundered. There should be in the table cloth only one crease, the straight central crease, and the cloth should be most carefully adjusted so that this fold is placed *exactly* in the center of the table. The op-

THE BUFFET DINNER IS AN OPPORTUNITY
TO USE YOUR CHERISHED SILVER PIECES
—Sterling Silversmiths Guild of America

The service for dinner

APPETIZER—FIRST COURSE
THE NAPKIN IS ON THE PLATE OR LEFT OF THE FORKS. IF THE COCKTAIL IS FRUIT OR MELON, REPLACE OYSTER FORK WITH A SMALL SPOON. ALL GLASSES REMAIN THROUGHOUT DINNER

SOUP—SECOND COURSE
THE SOUP PLATE IS SET ON THE SERVICE PLATE AFTER THE APPETIZER AND ITS SILVER ARE REMOVED. THE SERVICE PLATE IS REMOVED WITH THE SOUP PLATE AND ITS SILVER

FISH OR ENTREE — THIRD COURSE
THE SERVICE PLATE IS REPLACED BY AN ENTREE PLATE— WARMED IN WINTER. USE THE OUTER KNIFE AND FORK

ROAST—FOURTH COURSE
THE LARGE DINNER PLATE FOLLOWS THE ENTREE SERVICE AND IS REMOVED WITH ITS SILVER

SALAD—FIFTH COURSE
BOTH SALAD PLATE AND SILVER ARE SMALLER THAN FOR THE MEAT COURSE AND THE PLATE SHOULD BE COLD

DESSERT—SIXTH COURSE
EACH PLACE SHOULD BE COMPLETELY CLEARED EXCEPT FOR THE GLASSES—AND THE TABLE CRUMBED — BEFORE THE DESSERT PLATE AND SILVER ARE PLACED

COFFEE—SEVENTH COURSE
WHEN COFFEE IS SERVED AWAY FROM THE TABLE, THE FINGER BOWL WITH ITS DOILY MAY COME IN ON THE DESSERT PLATE — DOILY AND BOWL SLIPPED OFF BY THE GUEST AS DESSERT IS SERVED. WHEN SERVED AT THE TABLE, THE COFFEE CUP AND SAUCER ARE PLACED AFTER THE DESSERT IS SERVED

ADDED TO GOOD TASTE, BEAUTY IS ACHIEVED BY THE MOST CAREFUL ORDER AND ACCURACY

posite edges of the cloth should fall at equal distances from the floor. The cloth should fall from twelve to fifteen inches below the edges of the table.

Placing the Decorations

Now having placed the background for your table-picture, focus your composition by placing the table decorations, the centerpiece, candlesticks or candelabra, and compotes.

For a table of six covers, four candles or two candelabra are sufficient. The candlesticks are usually placed about halfway between the center of the table and its edge, but their position depends on the general form and design of the decorations. The candles are unshaded.

Compotes, filled with bonbons or mints or nuts, are usually placed between the candlesticks and the edge of the table— their position too, depending on the general structural scheme.

Setting the Covers

Now you are ready to set the covers.

A "cover" is the place set for one person at the beginning of a meal. It consists of a service plate (called sometimes a "place plate," and most appropriately called, a *cover plate*), silver utensils, napkin, and water glass.

In setting a cover allow, if possible, the standard space of twenty-four inches, this space being measured from the center of one plate to the center of the next one. Allow fifteen inches for depth.

Place the cover plate in the exact center of the place, and so that the pattern is up, in other words so that the pattern-design is given its full beauty-value.

All the lines of the cover should go either across the table or lengthwise of it. Avoid diagonal lines because they attract the attention of the eye and take away from the harmony of the design.

Place the knives in a straight line, on the right of the plate, parallel to each other, and the spoons on their right. On the left place the forks, also in a careful straight line, and lay the napkin at the left of the forks with its edges parallel to the forks and knives and spoons. When the cover includes a bread and butter plate, lay the butter spreader on the edge of the plate so that it is parallel to the edge of the table with the handle toward the right. Salt and pepper sets should follow this rule of placing, as should the handles of dishes that are placed on the table, and if a piece of silver is placed on a dish at the table (for instance, the spoon on the plate under the fruit cocktail) it too should be placed parallel to the pieces of silver at the sides of the plate.

There are several other important rules for setting a cover, and the basic idea of these rules applies to informal meals as much as it does to formal meals.

KNIVES, since they are used in the right hand, are placed at the right of the plate, with the cutting edge toward the plate.

SPOONS, with the bowls up, are placed at the right of the knives.

FORKS are placed at the left of the plate, with the tines up. This is because the fork is held in the left hand when the knife is in the right hand. If an oyster fork is necessary, it is placed on the right of the knives and spoons —and parallel to them— or on the plate on which the oysters are served.

THE SILVER should be placed in the correct sequence—so that the person eating may use first the utensils *farthest* from the plate and "work toward the plate." Not more than three knives and three forks (not counting the butter knife or oyster fork) are laid at one cover. If necessary, additional pieces are laid just before the course is served. Usually the silver is laid for the courses through the salad course, and the dessert silver is either placed at the cover before the dessert is served, or brought in on the dessert plate. For every item of food in the menu the necessary piece of silver should either be placed at the cover or brought in before the service of the course.

THE NAPKIN is placed on the left of the forks. If it is folded in a square, the open corner is the lower corner, nearest the plate.

THE WATER GLASS is placed above the tip of the dinner knife. If there is a glass for another beverage, it is placed to the right of the water glass or in a line slanting down from the goblet to the right. If there are more than two glasses, they are grouped artistically.

THE BREAD AND BUTTER PLATE is placed above the tips of the forks so that it will be on a line with the water glass. The butter spreader is placed on the bread and butter plate parallel to the edge of the table, the handle toward the right and the cutting edge down.

THE PLACE CARD is best placed above the plate.

THE EDGE OF THE SERVICE PLATE, the tips of the handles of the silver utensils, and the lower edge of the napkin should be placed in exact alignment, usually one inch from the edge of the table. Some hostesses prefer that the silver be placed two inches from the edge of the table, so that there is a minimum of danger of its being brushed off the table.

SALTS AND PEPPERS are usually placed between every two covers, or individual sets may be placed, or, if there are only a few covers, sets may be placed at the ends of the table.

SALTED NUTS may be placed in small individual dishes above the covers, or in silver or glass compotes.

COVERS should be placed directly opposite each other.

THE CHAIRS are placed so that the line of the table-cloth is not broken.

TABLE SERVICE

Styles of Service

There are three styles of service:

RUSSIAN: In this style of service all the food is served from the kitchen, by attendants. The host and hostess take no part in the service. No food is put on the table except the decorating dishes of nuts, candy, and fruits. The food may be placed in individual portions before the guest, or may be separated into portions and arranged on serving-dishes for each guest to help himself.

ENGLISH OR FAMILY TYPE: In this service all the food is served at the table by the host, hostess, or both.

COMBINATION OR MIXED SERVICE: In this service the main course is usually served at the table, while the soup, salad, and dessert are served from the kitchen. Sometimes, the salad is served from a large salad bowl, and the hostess serves the dessert at table.

Service Suggestions

METHODS—There are three methods of table service. The one often preferred is the *left hand* service, that is, the placing, passing, and removing of all dishes at the left. Beverages are,

of course, an exception, and these are placed at the right. In
the left hand service, the waitress uses the hand farthest from
the guest, that is, the left hand. The left hand service permits
the guest to use his right hand in helping himself. In the *right
hand* service the waitress places and removes all dishes from the
right, using the right hand, but she passes a dish at the left,
using her left hand. Often a combination of these two services
is used: that is, the dishes are placed and passed at the left, and
plates are removed from the right. A hostess decides which
method seems to her the easiest and most practical for her
household, and directs her service accordingly.

ORDER OF SERVICE—In many houses the hostess is served first.
This is a relic of the old custom of taking it for granted that
the giver of the feast prove the absence of poison by first tasting of the food or drinking of the beverage! Some hostesses too
justify this custom by maintaining that, when complicated foods
are served, the hostess indicates to her guests the methods by
which they can most conveniently serve themselves.

However, the custom of serving the honor guest first is growing, and many hostesses now insist on giving the chief guest
this additional compliment.

The former custom of serving all the ladies first and the
gentlemen afterward is no longer in vogue, for this method
consumed too much time and delayed the service. Now guests
are served in the order in which they are seated, usually beginning with the honor guest or the hostess and proceeding to the
right.

THE EVER-PRESENT PLATE—It is an important rule of good
service that there must be a plate before each guest until the
salad course is removed. As soon as one plate is removed, another is put in its place. The first course—if a pre-soup course
—is either served from a large dish, in which case a plate is
placed for it on the cover plate, or is brought in on a plate which
is set on the cover plate already on the table.

When the first course is removed the soup plate is set on the
cover plate. Then, if the next course—an entrée, or fish, or
the main course—is, as usual, to be served on a heated plate, the
service plate is removed with the soup plate as this heated plate
is put before the guest.

THE "SERVICE NAPKIN"—On the palm of her left hand,
under the dish that she is passing, the waitress holds a napkin

folded in a square—the so-called "service napkin" or "serving napkin." She does not use a tray to bring dishes to the table or to remove them from the table.

USING A TRAY—When a waitress is passing two or three small articles such as the cream-pitcher and sugar-bowl, or extra pieces of silver, she uses a serving-tray, with a doily on it to keep the articles from slipping.

FILLING GLASSES—Water glasses are filled three-fourths full. The water pitcher should be three-fourths full. When a glass is being filled it should not be lifted from the table. If necessary, the waitress uses a napkin to catch the drip. Beverages are placed and glasses are filled at the right.

KNIVES AND SPOONS are placed at the right, and forks are placed at the left.

BREAD, in the form of plain or pulled bread, rolls, or toast, is passed after the soup has been served.

IF THE FIRST COURSE of an informal dinner or luncheon is a cold course, it may be on the table when the guests enter the dining-room. If it is hot, it is served after the guests are seated.

BEFORE PASSING A DISH TO A GUEST the waitress should see that adequate silver is placed on the dish—usually a serving-fork on the left and a serving-spoon on the right—in a convenient position. She should, if necessary, rearrange the silver before offering the dish to the guest.

FOOD SHOULD BE PLACED ON THE TABLE, passed, and removed in the order of its importance in the course.

IF A SALAD IS SERVED WITH THE MEAT COURSE, it is placed on the more convenient side of the plate. If there is no extra glass on the right side, it is usually more convenient to the guest to have the salad placed on the right.

HOT FOOD SHOULD BE SERVED HOT on heated dishes.

COLD FOOD SHOULD BE SERVED COLD on cold dishes.

WHEN THE HOST AND HOSTESS DO THE SERVING AT TABLE, the host serves the meat, and often the vegetables, and the hostess serves the soup, salad, dessert, and beverage.

IN THE MAID-LESS HOUSEHOLD, the hostess will find great convenience in the tea-wagon or any other kind of serving-table that may stand at her right, ready to help her.

BEFORE THE DESSERT COURSE, the table should be cleared and crumbed. The salts and peppers, the bread and butter plates, and all other accessories or dishes that will not be used in the dessert course, are removed on a tray. When the table is crumbed a small folded napkin and a plate should be used, and the crumb-clearing is done at the left of the guest.

WHEN THE DESSERT IS FINISHED, the dessert plate is exchanged for an after-dinner coffee cup, if the coffee is served at table.

AT THE END OF THE COFFEE COURSE, the cups are exchanged for finger bowls if these were not placed with the dessert.

THERE IS INCREASING INCLINATION to serve after-dinner coffee in the drawing room, living room or the library. The plan has many advantages. The original reason was to give guests more freedom and more luxury—dining-room chairs are stiff at best. But in large families, young adults and children are eager to be excused—the former for their own plans and the latter have school work to do, besides which they do not or should not drink coffee. The adults want to continue their discussions without interruption, while they have coffee, liqueurs and smokes at their leisure.

Besides, in many American homes, servants come in by the day or the hour. Serving coffee in the living room, in addition to the comfort it gives host and guests, allows maids to finish the cleaning-up process with more speed and care as well as more freedom. The coffee service can be done last or even left until morning without catastrophe. In the maidless home, the dining-room doors can be closed, the lights turned out and both hostess and guests forget the work that awaits the former, in the glow of the larger, more comfortable and less formal living room. Moreover, in many modern homes the dining room has disappeared and its function taken over by an enlarged living room, with or without a dining alcove or solarium but almost always when there is a garden, by the terrace used for meals out of doors. In homes with this arrangement there should be an appropriate screen to set around the table used for dining, when the guests move into the living room proper or onto the terrace. Often when there is a dining alcove, these screens are attached to opposing walls as permanent fixtures of the room, and need only to be swung out to meet around the disheveled table. For less formal entertaining see page 724.

CARVING

S KILL in carving depends upon two things: first, a knowledge of the anatomy of that which is to be carved, and
second, good tools with which to work.

EQUIPMENT FOR CARVING

FOR THE AVERAGE FAMILY, two carving knives are desirable,
one with a long blade for large roasts, and a smaller, lighter one
for steaks, cutlets and poultry. The smaller knife will be adequate for the small family where large roasts are not served. One
two-pronged fork can be used with both knives.

THE CARVING KNIFE SHOULD BE SHARP when it is brought
to the table. It should never be sharpened at the table.

THE CARVER SHOULD REMAIN SEATED while carving and
should carve enough for all who are at the table before he
begins to serve anyone.

THE PLATTER SHOULD BE LARGE ENOUGH not only for the
meat that is to be carved but also for the carved portions.

A SERVING SPOON should be provided for the gravy.

TO CARVE BEEF

Beefsteak

Separate the meat from the bone by cutting along the edge
of the bone with the thin point of the knife.

Beginning with the wide or bone end of a porterhouse or
sirloin steak, and following the grain of the meat, divide each
section into portions an inch or slightly more in width, depending on the number to be served.

In porterhouse and similar steaks, the tenderloin and wider
section are more tender with a better flavor and texture than
the narrow section. Each serving portion should contain a
part of both sections. Do not serve the small or flank end of a
porterhouse steak, but use for soup or stew.

Add to each portion a bit of garnish, a spoonful of gravy, and
if the steak is planked, a serving of vegetables.

Roast Beef

Carve all roasts across the grain of the meat. The thickness of the slices varies with the kind of roast that is being carved, and may be influenced by the personal preferences of the people for whom the carving is being done. Generally the slices should be thin, but whether thin or thick, they should be even and attractive looking.

FILLET OR TENDERLOIN ROAST—Hold the roast firmly with the fork and cut the meat squarely across the grain in slices slightly less than one-half inch in thickness. Begin with the thick or forward portion. Serve one slice to each person.

LOIN, ROUND OR RUMP ROAST—Cut across the grain, as with a tenderloin roast, but carve the slices as thin as possible, because the meat is less tender than the fillet.

STANDING RIB ROAST—Have the butcher separate the back-bone from the ribs. Place the roast cut side up on a platter with the rib side to the left. Insert the fork firmly between the two top ribs and draw the knife across the grain toward the fork until the bone is reached, cutting slices $\frac{1}{8}$ to $\frac{1}{4}$ inch thick. Cut several slices and then separate from the bone by cutting down with the point of the knife along the bone.

POT ROAST—Place the meat with the rib side toward the carver. Insert the fork straddling the narrow strip of cartilage running down the center of the meat and cut off the rib bone. Cut horizontally across the grain into slices $\frac{1}{4}$ inch thick, beginning at the right front corner and cutting up through the slice at the center of the roast. When one side is sliced, reverse and cut the other side.

SHORT RIBS—Place the meat so the ribs are at the back. Thrust the fork into the meat at the right end and cut down between the bones. A bone may be served with each slice, or it may be separated from the meat and left on the platter.

ROLLED ROAST—A rolled roast should be held together by skewers inserted before cooking directly through the roll across the grain of the meat. Set the roast on end and thrust the fork firmly into the side an inch or two from the top. Then, holding the knife horizontally, cut thin even slices across the entire roast.

Remove the skewers one at a time as you reach them in carving, and move the fork downward from time to time as necessary.

TO CARVE LAMB, MUTTON, VEAL
AND PORK

Leg of Lamb

Let the small bone extend toward your left and have the curved side of the meat uppermost. Thrust the fork into the center muscle and cut thin slices downward, across the grain of the meat, till the knife strikes the bone. To release the slices, insert the point of the knife beneath them and cut along the surface of the bone.

If the leg of lamb is boned, cut slices straight through, across the grain of the meat.

Loin Roast of Lamb, Veal or Pork

The backbone should be cut through at each rib before the meat is roasted. Let the roast lie on the platter with the bones down and the smaller end of the roast at your left. Carve down between the ribs and serve one rib to each person.

Crown of Lamb

Carve down between the ribs and serve one to each person.

Saddle of Mutton

Let the roast rest on the platter with the bone down and the end diagonally toward you. Make a cut through the center the entire length of the backbone, separating the meat into two similar parts. Remove the meat from the bone on each side by running the knife point between the meat and the bone. Carve the meat into slices slightly less than half an inch thick, cutting across the grain.

Baked Ham

Cut two or three slices from the thin side of the ham. Turn ham to rest on cut surface with shank end at right. Beginning at shank end, cut in thin slices slantwise down to leg bone. Run knife along bone at right angle to slices, to release from bone. Serve one slice to each person, including some of the crisped skin and the garnish with each portion. Meat lying beneath the bone is usually diced and used in other ways.

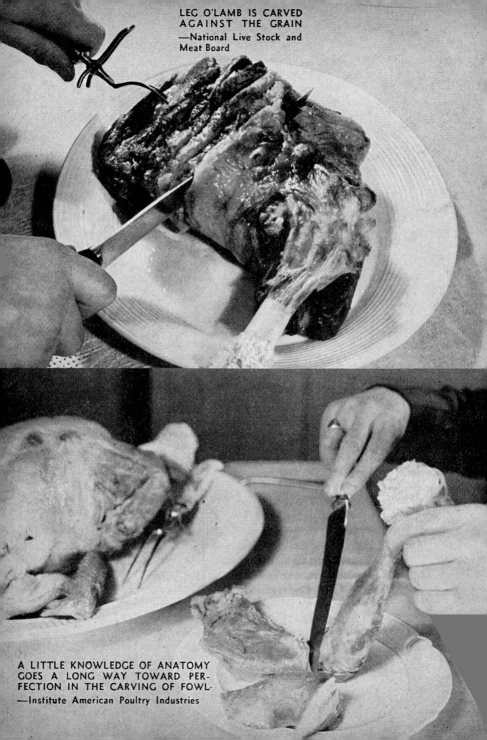

LEG O'LAMB IS CARVED
AGAINST THE GRAIN
—National Live Stock and
Meat Board

A LITTLE KNOWLEDGE OF ANATOMY
GOES A LONG WAY TOWARD PER-
FECTION IN THE CARVING OF FOWL·
—Institute American Poultry Industries

IN CARVING STEAK,
ROAST OR ANY MEAT,
GOOD FORM IS THE RE-
SULT OF PERFECT BAL-
ANCE AND MUCH PRAC-
TICE
—National Live Stock and
Meat Board

TO CARVE POULTRY

Roast Turkey or Chicken

Arrange the bird, breast side up, on a hot platter so the breast is at the carver's left and the legs at the right. Remove the leg, including the thigh and drumstick on the near side, by placing the knife between the thigh and body and cutting through the skin around the leg from left to right. At the same time, hold the leg bone with the left hand. Bend the leg back and cut smoothly through the skin down to the joint. Force the leg away from the body with the knife to dislocate the hip joint. Lift the leg to the side of platter, separate thigh from drumstick and cut each piece in slices parallel with the bone. The thigh and drumstick of chicken are often served whole. Remove the wing in the same manner as the leg, cutting the joint at the shoulder. It may be served or not, depending upon the number of guests and the size of the fowl.

Slice the breast meat by inserting the fork, held in the left hand, firmly astraddle the breastbone, just beyond its highest point. Or the fork may be inserted through the ribs from the near side. Start to slice the breast meat where the wing was removed. The slicing may be done downward from or upward to the breastbone. Cut in thin even slices parallel to the breast bone so each slice lies in place until it is carefully lifted down with the knife to be placed on the platter. Cut the other side as described above. Remove the stuffing from the vent side with a serving spoon. To remove dressing from the neck region, make an opening or cut a section of skin and fold it back. Serve on hot plates allowing a spoonful of white meat for each guest. Serve gravy separately.

Roast Duck or Goose

In ducks and geese, the thigh joint lies very near the backbone, and since it is more difficult to separate from the back, partial separation may be done before the bird is arranged on the platter.

Of Wild Duck, only the breast is served. Half a breast is usually removed in one portion and served to one person.

Broilers

Arrange the bird on the platter so that the neck is toward you. Insert the fork in the second joint; cut the flesh around the hip joint; bend the joint over sharply with the knife and separate it from the body. Separate the drumstick from the second joint or leave them together, as you prefer. Split the breast in two. Serve half the breast and a second joint or whole leg to each person.

TO CARVE FISH

Special carving sets are procurable for fish. If such a set is not available, a pie knife or ice cream server and a dinner knife with a silver or stainless steel blade may be used.

Baked or Planked Fish

If the fish has been slashed before baking, cut through these slashes, to, but not through, the backbone. If there are no slashes, cut the flesh crosswise at intervals of about two inches. Slip the server under each section and lift it from the bone. When one side of the fish has been served, lift up the backbone and divide the lower half.

Middle Cuts or Thick Pieces of Fish

Middle cuts or thick pieces of large fish, such as salmon, halibut, and cod, are placed on the platter with the skin down. Carve the fish in thick slices down to the bone, then slip the knife under the portions and remove them from the bone.

Split Fish

When fish are split down the back and broiled or sautéed, divide them through the middle, lengthwise, then divide each half into as many portions as are needed. Very small fish and fillets are served whole.

GARNISHES

~~~~~~~~~

GARNISHES serve two purposes. First, they make food more attractive to the eye, thus stimulating the flow of digestive juices and aiding digestion; second, they add bulk or "roughage" to the diet or increase the nutritive value of the dish.

GARNISHES SHOULD BE SIMPLE, appropriate and easy to prepare. They should not be used to disguise deficiencies or poor quality of any dish. Edible garnishes are more appropriate than those that are used merely for appearance. At least one-third of a dish should be left free of garnish and the garnish should be so placed that it does not interfere with the service.

WITH A FEW EXCEPTIONS, such as candied or maraschino cherries, sweet pickles, preserved whole currants, strawberries, cranberries, etc., sweets are not used to garnish savory dishes.

TOAST OR PUFF PASTES should not, as a rule, be used on the same dish with potatoes.

Garnishes for Soups

One of the simplest garnishes for soup is a tablespoon of salted whipped cream sprinkled with a dash of paprika or a little parsley chopped very fine.

Eggs are used as garnishes of soups in the form of a baked custard cut in fancy shapes, or as egg balls. (See Soup Accessories.) The whole yolks poached in salted water just below the boiling-point may be used; one yolk is served with each plate of soup.

Noodles, tapioca, spaghetti or macaroni cut in fancy shapes, or quenelles (See Soup Accessories) make simple and attractive garnishes for soup.

Cooked vegetables cut in thin strips or in Julienne style or in fancy shapes or slices, are often used to add color, flavor and nutritive value to a soup.

Soups may be garnished also with cubes of bread or puff paste buttered and browned in the oven or fried in deep fat.

Garnishes for Egg Dishes

Eggs are often served with toast in some form. They may be garnished with crisp slices of bacon and a spray of parsley or they may be served on a bed of chopped spinach, mashed potato or chopped meat. A sauce or purée is a very attractive garnish for poached eggs. Eggs are sometimes garnished with grated cheese or cooked egg-yolk put through a sieve.

Garnishes for Hot Vegetables

Mashed vegetables are sometimes garnished with bits of butter and a sprinkling of paprika or chopped parsley. Vegetables that are cooked and served whole are often covered with grated cheese and put into the oven long enough to brown the cheese. Slices of hard-cooked eggs or egg-yolk put through a sieve may be used as a garnish for spinach.

Garnishes for Meat, Fish, Game and Poultry

Garnishes often used with roasts of beef, lamb or mutton are browned potatoes, croquettes of potatoes or rice, mashed potato cups filled with green peas or diced vegetables, slices of carrot, parsnip or turnip sautéd or fried in deep fat, or boiled onions and sprays of parsley or cress.

Roast pork may be garnished with any of the above or with baked apple or sautéd apple rings filled with jelly.

Fried bananas make a suitable garnish for roast of mutton.

Chops and steaks may be served with a simple garnish of parsley or cress and a slice of lemon or in a border of French fried potatoes, Saratoga chips or lattice potatoes.

Creamed meat dishes may be served with triangles or rounds of toast, in borders of rice or mashed potato, in croustades of bread, in timbale cases or patty shells or in cups of rice or mashed potato.

Sausage, meat balls or chops are attractive arranged about a mound of rice, mashed potato, macaroni or spinach.

Roast or fried chicken may be served in a border of celery or of fried oysters or with a simple garnish of parsley or cress.

Roast duck is attractive with endive and slices of orange and olives or with rice cups filled with currant jelly; roast goose with broiled sausage, gooseberry sauce, apple or barberry jelly or cooked rings of apple; roast quail with squares of fried mush and cubes of currant jelly.

Fish steaks, broiled fish or baked fish are usually garnished with slices of lemon and parsley or cress. Slices of hard-cooked eggs are often used as a garnish for fish. Fat fish such as salmon may be garnished with slices of cucumber or of tomato or whole tomatoes stuffed. Fish may also be garnished with potatoes, peas, onions or tomato in any form.

Other garnishes that may be used are celery curls, olives, radishes, mushroom caps, small green pickles, strips of green pepper or pimiento.

Garnishes for Aspics and Salads

The best and simplest frame for any salad is a bed of lettuce leaves or shredded lettuce, cabbage or cress. Many salads are made more attractive by a sprinkling of chopped nuts or capers, minced green pepper or red pimiento or a grating of cheese. A half nut-meat, two or three radishes cut to resemble roses, dates or prunes stuffed with nuts or cream cheese, olives whole or sliced, tiny new onions or sliced green pickles all add flavor and color.

Truffles are wild, edible, subterranean fungi that are raised principally in France. They are too expensive to be used in large quantity but are highly prized as a flavorful garnish for aspics, salads and sauces. Because of their black color they make an effective contrast to the pale or vivid colors of the more common foods.

Very attractive decorations for meat, fish, salads or aspic are vegetables cut into simple flower designs. Cucumbers, beets, turnips, Russian radishes and carrots with chopped greens are the materials to have at hand. For a lily, cut a long cucumber in half crosswise. Stand up on this cut surface and with a sharp knife cut narrow strips, not too thin, from tip to within an inch of the base. Continue until all the white, too, is cut into strips resembling petals. Into the center insert a long narrow carrot, root end up, to simulate the yellow stamen. If necessary wrap base with a rubber band to hold tightly. Beets and round turnips can be peeled and cut to resemble budding roses. The turnips can be stained with vegetable coloring if desired. Flat slices of turnip or Russian radish cut to resemble daisies have a center of carrot and a sprinkle of chopped green. Calla lilies may be made of thin slices of larger turnips. Roll until the edges meet in cornucopia shape and fasten with a toothpick. Insert a long slender carrot or carrot strip for the stamen and fasten with another toothpick. Broccoli or spinach leaves may be attached. Make Easter lilies by rolling a second petal around the first.

FILLED BEETS—Use cooked small beets. Pickle or not as desired, or marinate in French dressing. Hollow out centers to make cups and fill with coleslaw.

TOMATO CUPS—Wash plum tomatoes, peel or not as desired, hollow out centers to make cups and fill with mayonnaise.

PICKLE RINGS—Hollow out centers of large dill or sweet pickles with apple corer and stuff with cream cheese. Chill and cut into slices.

CARROT CUPS—Cook large carrots until tender. Pare, cut into 2-inch lengths and chill. Hollow out center of each section to make cups and fill with pickle relish.

THE CALLA LILY IS ONLY ONE OF THE MANY EFFECTIVE DESIGNS TO BE MADE OF EDIBLE VEGETABLES

CEREALS

CEREALS or grains are the seeds of certain grasses, the most important of which are wheat, oats, rice, barley, corn, rye and buckwheat. To most persons "cereals" designate only breakfast cereals; and, while the term "cereal foods" actually does include also commercial products made from cereals such as macaroni and spaghetti, corn-starch and the different flours, the present chapter deals only with cereals in the breakfast-cereal sense. There are many kinds of breakfast-cereal products on the market. Most of them are made from the cereals listed above but they differ because of variety in the processes of their manufacture. The so-called breakfast-cereals have a wide usefulness in meals other than breakfast.

Storage of Cereals

With a suitable storage place, cereals and flour may be kept for several months. Unless there is a cool, dry place for storing them, they should be purchased only in amounts that can be used in a few days. This is especially true in warm weather.

Cereal products are liable to spoilage for two reasons: they may become wormy, or they may become rancid. Products made from the whole grain are more subject to spoilage than the refined products, because the whole products contain the germ, which is high in fat, and it is this that becomes rancid; it is this, also, that offers suitable material for the development of eggs laid by insects.

Cereals should be purchased from a merchant whose store is known to be kept in a sanitary condition. Closed glass jars are excellent for keeping cereals. If package cereal is purchased, it should be placed in closed glass jars after it is opened, thus insuring against infection by insects.

Whole or Refined Cereals

Seeds are made up of starchy material in a network of protein, and protected by several coats of fiber generally referred to as bran or cellulose. In the process of manufacture a part or all of the outer coats may be removed so that the actual composition of the cereal is a matter determined by the method of manufacture. If a large part is removed, the cereal is called highly refined; if a small part is removed, it becomes less highly refined; and if the coats are not at all, or but slightly removed, it is called "whole." Therefore, the terms "whole" and "refined" refer to the amount of outer coating which the cereal contains and not to the size of the particles into which the grain is ground.

One way to determine whether cereals are whole or refined is by the color. The less highly refined cereals are apt to be dark in color, and the more highly refined cereals are light in color.

Pre-Cooked Cereals

Cereals were formerly bought uncooked, but by modern methods of manufacture they may be partly or entirely cooked. Thus we have, in oats or wheat, a partly cooked product; and the long list of ready-to-eat cereals or entirely cooked products which need only a few minutes of reheating to be ready for the table.

Cooking Cereals

Two of the important secrets in cooking cereals so that they are acceptable are:

1. To allow enough water to swell and soften all the starch.
2. To cook them long enough to swell the starch and soften the cellulose present so that the starch may be exposed to the action of heat and water.

Cereals high in starch and low in cellulose or bran absorb more water than do cereals containing proportionately less starch and more cellulose or bran. Also, coarsely ground or unground cereals require more time to cook than the finely ground ones. These facts determine the method used in cooking. A refined cereal will require a proportionately larger amount of water than a whole cereal, though it will require less time in the cooking; a coarsely ground cereal will require longer time than a finely ground cereal.

Thorough cooking of cereals is necessary for two reasons: first, cellulose requires plenty of time to soften; and second, starch gains in flavor by cooking.

METHODS OF COOKING—Cereals may be boiled directly over the heat; steamed, as in a double boiler; or cooked in a fireless cooker. The first is the quickest process but requires attention in order to prevent sticking; and, even when stirred frequently, some sticking may occur. Since the slower cooking develops the flavor and more thoroughly softens the cellulose, the use of either double boiler or fireless cooker is recommended.

AMOUNT OF WATER NEEDED—Tastes differ greatly concerning consistency of cereals. Some persons like a thin cereal, almost a "gruel"; others prefer a thicker product, or "mush," while still others choose a thick "porridge." The following suggestions are only general. The directions on the packages are safe to follow in cooking any uncooked or partly cooked cereal, then if a thicker or thinner product is desired it is easy to determine the proportions that best suit the family and make your own rules.

In General:

1. Rolled cereals, such as rolled oats or rolled wheat, require about two parts of water to one of cereal.

2. Coarsely ground cereals from the whole grain, and unground whole grains require about four parts of water to one of cereal.

3. Finely ground refined cereals require from five to six parts of water to one of cereal.

Where directions are lacking for any cereal bought in bulk, the following table will serve as a fair guide.

Amounts of Water to Use with Various Cereals

TO ONE CUP	USE CUPS WATER	WILL MAKE CUPS PRODUCT
Cornmeal	5 to 6	5 +
Hominy Grits	4 to 5	4 +
Oatmeal	4 to 5	4 +
Oats, rolled	2 to 2½	2 +
Rice	4 to 5	4 +
Samp	4 to 5	4 +
Wheat, finely ground	5 to 6	5 +

AMOUNT OF SALT NEEDED—Tastes differ again here, but a safe rule from which to vary is to use one teaspoonful to each quart of water used.

SWELLING OF CEREALS—The amount of swelling is the same as the amount of water required; that is, rolled cereals swell about twice, coarsely ground or whole cereals swell about four times; and finely ground and refined cereals swell from five to six times.

TIME NEEDED FOR COOKING—Cereal products have a naturally delicious flavor, although not pronounced, which is brought out by long slow cooking, and the right proportion of water and salt.

Long slow cooking used to mean four to six hours, but manufacturing processes have cut the time considerably—to fifteen or twenty minutes in the case of some of the fine grained wheat products, and even three to five minutes for partially cooked cereals. However, a longer cooking only improves them.

In trying a breakfast cereal for the first time, follow the directions on the package; then if you wish, adapt them to the consistency and saltiness you prefer.

Some cereals may be boiled—notably rice, and those partially cooked products that need only three to five minutes cooking, and so demand but little constant attention. The standard ways of cooking cereals are steaming in a double boiler or baking in a slow oven, as in making creamy rice and Indian puddings. The baking method has obvious advantages, and can well be extended to include cereals for breakfast or entrées, omitting the sugar and flavoring.

If cereal is cooked in the evening for the following breakfast, it may stand in the double boiler all night and be heated in the morning. It is well not to stir it in the morning until it is thoroughly hot, because stirring when cold is apt to cause lumps which resist being made smooth.

Variations in Use of Cereals

Cereals may be cooked in milk instead of water, or a part of the water may be replaced by milk. This method offers an easy way of increasing the milk content of a meal and makes the cereal dish more nutritious. Raisins, dried fruit or fresh fruit supply a pleasing addition to cooked cereals. Dates or figs cut into pieces and stirred into the cereal before serving make a very appetizing change.

To prevent a hardening over of the cereal due to standing, two or three tablespoons of water may be poured over the top of the cereal after the cooking process at night is finished.

HOT TAMALES

Filling:

¾ pound chicken or
¾ pound veal or beef
1 small onion
3 cloves garlic

Bay leaves
3 tablespoons fat
3 ounces chili powder
2 teaspoons salt
1½ cups hot water

Envelope:

4 cups yellow corn meal
1 teaspoon salt
2½ cups stock

½ pound fat
1 pound cornhusks

The "redi-cut" cornhusks may be bought. Field cornhusks must have both ends removed; immerse in cold water while filling is prepared.

Boil both meats in water to which have been added one small onion, a clove of garlic and 2 bay leaves. When meat is tender remove and drain stock, setting it aside to use in making envelope. Cut meat into small cubes. Heat 3 tablespoons of fat, add meat and brown. Mash 2 cloves of garlic and add to meat. Stir the chili powder and salt with hot water and mix well with the meat. Cook mixture 10 minutes.

To make the envelope: Mix 4 cups yellow corn meal, salt, half the stock and all of fat. Beat well with a wooden spoon and then add remainder of the stock. It is very important that the mixture be well beaten to make it light. Dry cornhusks on the inside, spread thinly with mixture; add one teaspoon of chili meat filling and roll. Fold both ends down. Stack in a steamer and cook until well done. If a steamer is not available, place an ordinary kitchen pot lid on bottom of a deep kettle. Cover with husks and stack tamales over this in "pyramid" style. Pour four cups of boiling water over tamales, cover tightly and cook over a low heat for 45 minutes or one hour. Serve tamales hot. Makes 10 to 12 tamales.

VARIATIONS—Use leftover poultry or meats, chopped or ground; or ground leftover stew drained from its gravy. Place a green or stuffed olive in center of filling before rolling. Fresh green corn may be used with corn meal. Tie husks at ends with strings instead of folding if desired. Stand upright in steamer with ends down.

YEAST BREADS

THE age-old dependence of man upon bread as food has not been disturbed by the most recent researches in nutrition. Indeed it is considerably strengthened. Bread is not only an inexpensive source of carbohydrates and vegetable protein but carries minerals and the B vitamins, especially when whole grains are used. The use of yeast increases these vitamins. Bread can be made of flour, salt, water and yeast; more valuable bread results if sugar, shortening and milk are added.

Flours and Meals Used in Breadmaking

While flours and meals made from oats, rye, corn, rice and other seeds are used to some extent with wheat flour in making yeast breads, by far the larger amount of yeast bread is made from wheat flour only and most of it is made from white flour. This is because the gluten of wheat flour possesses properties which enable the dough containing it to stretch and hold the leavening gas produced by the action of yeast.

ALL-PURPOSE OR GENERAL-PURPOSE FLOUR is white flour containing the kind and quality of gluten which make it satisfactory for all types of household baking, for breads as well as pastries.

ENRICHED FLOUR is all-purpose flour which, according to government specifications, contains in each pound from 2.0 to 2.5 milligrams of thiamine, from 1.2 to 1.5 milligrams of riboflavin, from 16.0 to 20.0 milligrams of niacin and from 13.0 to 16.5 milligrams of iron.

WHOLE-WHEAT, ENTIRE-WHEAT AND GRAHAM FLOUR are ground from whole wheat and contain varying amounts of bran and germ. They do not make light-textured breads if used alone and are usually combined with an equal amount of white flour.

SELF-RISING FLOUR is all-purpose flour which contains salt and a leavening agent, usually bicarbonate of soda and calcium phosphate.

BUCKWHEAT, RYE AND SOYBEAN FLOUR may be used for yeast breads, but must be used in combination with wheat flour.

POTATO AND RICE FLOUR are often used to replace wheat flour in allergic diets.

CORN MEAL is a preparation of ground corn varying in degrees of fineness. It contains no gluten.

Yeast

The most satisfactory temperature for the development of yeast is from 75° to 85°F. It ceases to grow when the temperature is below 30°F. and is destroyed above 90°F. Yeast should be softened in lukewarm liquid.

COMPRESSED YEAST breaks with a clean edge and has a fresh odor. Only fresh yeast should be used in breadmaking. In compressed yeast the yeast plants are ready for action, hence breadmaking with compressed yeast takes less time than with dry cake yeast.

GRANULAR YEAST is yeast in a dry granular form which will keep without refrigeration for several weeks. It should be softened in a little lukewarm water (not milk) about five minutes and will then act as quickly as compressed yeast. Count the water used in softening as part of the liquid in the recipe.

DRY YEAST is yeast mixed with corn meal and dried. As dry yeast will live for some time and yet cannot grow without moisture, these cakes keep for many weeks. The dried plants are inactive but when warmth, moisture and food are supplied, gradually become active.

Amounts of Yeast

From one-sixth of a cake to two cakes of yeast may be used to one cup of liquid in making bread. With the minimum amount of yeast, the bread usually is allowed to rise overnight. With the maximum amount of yeast, the bread may be made and the baking finished three or four hours from the time it is started.

Liquids for Breadmaking

MILK is the best liquid to use because of its contribution to the food value as well as to the flavor and appearance of the loaf. It gives a creamy crumb and a rich golden-brown crust. The loaf retains its moisture better than when no milk is used.

WATER is cheap but has no food value. It is used in making the crusty types of bread such as French and Italian breads.

POTATO WATER hastens the action of the yeast and produces a characteristic crust excellent in flavor. It yields a loaf which retains its moisture and does not get stale as quickly as when water alone is used.

Miscellaneous Materials Used in Bread

SUGAR is added to hasten the activity of the yeast, to improve flavor and to produce a better bloom on the crust. Too much sugar retards the action of the yeast. In making large quantities of bread, the liquid is decreased if a large quantity of sugar is used.

SALT is used to improve the flavor of bread. Too much salt retards the activity of the yeast.

SHORTENING is added to give slight tenderness to both crust and crumb and to improve the keeping qualities of the loaf. Any soft fat or oil of mild flavor may be used as shortening in bread.

EGGS give a yellow color to the crumb and a rich brown bloom to the crust and add flavor and food value. Because of their leavening power, eggs add to the lightness of the loaf.

DRIED FRUITS AND NUTS add flavor and food value and help give variety to breads.

Preparation of Materials for Making Bread

Scald milk (unless evaporated milk is used) to destroy bacteria and enzymes which might cause injury to the dough during the rising process at a warm temperature. Cool to lukewarm.

Add the yeast, softened in a small amount of lukewarm water with one teaspoon of sugar to start yeast activity. Or crumble compressed yeast into the lukewarm liquid and let stand five minutes to soften. Mix well. Another method is to mix compressed yeast with two tablespoons sugar until it liquefies.

Sift flour before measuring, except graham and whole-wheat flours, which are not sifted but stirred lightly before measuring.

Methods of Making Bread

SPONGE METHOD—Add sugar and softened yeast to lukewarm liquid, then stir in half the flour and beat well. Cover and set in a warm place (not warmer than a warm room) until batter is bubbly and light. Add salt, melted shortening and enough more flour to make a dough of the desired stiffness. Turn onto a floured board and knead thoroughly until smooth and satiny.

STRAIGHT DOUGH METHOD—If scalded milk is used, add sugar, salt and shortening and cool to lukewarm, then add softened yeast. Otherwise, melt shortening and add to lukewarm liquid, then add sugar, salt and softened yeast. Add half the flour and beat well. Add enough more flour to make a dough of the desired stiffness, turn out onto a floured board and knead well until smooth and satiny. This method may be used with compressed or granular yeast.

KNEADING BREAD—Fold the dough over on itself and push it lightly away with the balls of the hands, exerting sufficient pressure to cause the part folded over to adhere to the part underneath. Turn dough one-quarter around and repeat motion. Continue turning, folding and kneading until dough is smooth and elastic and does not stick to an unfloured board.

FIRST RISING OF DOUGH—Put the dough into a greased receptacle large enough to hold at least twice the bulk of the dough. Grease the top of the dough, cover with a cloth and set in a warm place. Let rise until it doubles its bulk or until it retains the imprint of the finger when pressed.

SECOND RISING OF DOUGH—When dough is light, punch down by folding in the edges and pressing down in the center of the dough. Turn the dough smooth side up, grease lightly, cover and let rise again. This second rising is not essential but improves the texture of the bread.

SHAPING INTO LOAVES—Divide dough into portions for loaves, shape into smooth balls, cover and let stand 10 minutes. This rest period may be omitted but it allows the dough to rise slightly and become less compact and therefore more easily shaped. Flatten the ball of dough and fold lengthwise, pressing the edges together. Stretch the dough lengthwise to about three times the length of the pan. Overlap the ends across the center and press the edges together. Fold again lengthwise and place seam down in greased bread pan. For a tender crust, brush top with oil or melted shortening; for a hard crust, brush with water; for a bright shine, brush with egg white. Cover and let rise in a warm place.

SHAPING INTO BRAIDS—Divide dough for each loaf into thirds and allow to rest 10 minutes. Shape each piece into a long roll, press the three ends together and braid rolls. Press ends together, place on greased baking sheet, cover and let rise.

BAKING BREAD—The temperature for baking bread depends upon the type of crust desired. Baking a 1-pound loaf (containing about 1 cup liquid and 3 cups flour) at 425°F. for 35 minutes produces a thin dark crust; starting the baking at 400°F.

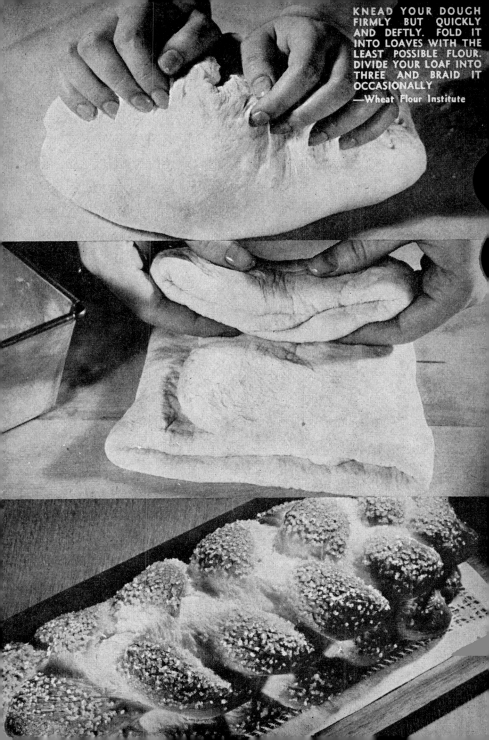

KNEAD YOUR DOUGH
FIRMLY BUT QUICKLY
AND DEFTLY. FOLD
IT INTO LOAVES WITH THE
LEAST POSSIBLE FLOUR.
DIVIDE YOUR LOAF INTO
THREE AND BRAID IT
OCCASIONALLY
—Wheat Flour Institute

ROLL YOUR OWN INTO
CLOVER-LEAVES, CRESCENTS,
POCKETBOOKS AND PARKER
HOUSE
—Wheat Flour Institute

and reducing the temperature to 375°F. after about 10 minutes produces a thicker, lighter crust. When the temperature is reduced, the total baking time should be 45 to 50 minutes. The latter method should always be used for breads containing eggs or extra sugar, since these rich breads tend to brown more rapidly.

When no oven regulator or thermometer is available, one may judge whether the baking is proceeding correctly by dividing the time into quarters and observing the bread at the end of each quarter.

First quarter: the dough rises quickly.

Second quarter: the dough crusts over and begins to brown.

Third quarter: the loaf continues to brown but does not become dark.

Fourth quarter: the loaf shrinks from the sides of the pan and is evenly browned over its entire surface.

Tests for Determining When Bread is Done

The color is a rich golden brown.

The loaf shrinks from the sides of the pan.

The loaf sounds hollow when tapped.

Characteristics of a Good Loaf of Bread

SIZE—A 1-pound loaf is a good household size. One cup of liquid and 3 cups of flour will make a loaf weighing about 1 pound.

SHAPE—A well-shaped loaf is symmetrical. The top is rounded but the middle is not appreciably higher than the ends. Its proportions are such that the slices cut from it will be approximately square. There is no bulge over edge of pan.

COLOR—Well-baked bread has an even golden brown color. The crumb is creamy in color with no streaks through it.

TEXTURE—A slice of bread with perfect texture feels silky smooth to the touch. The holes are small and uniform; there are no streaks or lumps. Perfect texture is the clearest indication of quality and depends upon a number of things: kneading the dough until it is smooth and elastic, allowing it to rise sufficiently and baking at the correct temperature.

CRUST—The crust of a good loaf is smooth and uniformly brown. It may be thick or thin, depending upon the preference.

FLAVOR AND AROMA—A good loaf of bread is fragrant and has a pleasing yet bland flavor.

Common Causes of Inferior Bread

POOR FLOUR—A cheap flour may be an expensive flour because it makes a loaf inferior in texture, color, flavor and volume.

OLD YEAST—Dead yeast plants cannot leaven bread. Old compressed yeast cakes or dry yeast which has been stored away until many of the yeast plants are dead will act very slowly if at all and will not give good results.

TOO MUCH OR TOO LITTLE KNEADING—Dough kneaded too much becomes sticky and will not rise well in the oven. Dough kneaded too little makes streaked bread, poor in texture, which sometimes contains lumps that might have been worked out in kneading.

TOO MUCH FLOUR—Too stiff a dough makes coarse-textured bread of small volume and dry crumb.

OVER-RISING—Too long rising gives a very porous loaf with little flavor, a pale crust and a porous crumb with broken, irregular texture. This bread crumbles badly. If the rising continues too long, the dough may become sour.

UNDER-RISING—Too little rising gives a loaf which is small and flat. It browns too quickly in the oven. The crumb is compact and dull.

TOO COOL AN OVEN—Bread will continue to rise too long if the oven temperature is too low. The result is bread that is very porous in the center and upper part of the loaf. The bread dries out before it begins to bake.

TOO HOT AN OVEN—The dough crusts over immediately and cannot continue to rise as it should the first ten or fifteen minutes it is in the oven. The crust becomes very brown before the crumb is baked.

ROPE IN BREAD—Rope may appear at any time but is most likely during hot, damp weather. It gives bread a ropy, stringy quality and a very disagreeable odor and makes it unfit for use. It is due to a type of bacillus which may be in any one or more of the ingredients used in bread.

If rope develops, all utensils used in making bread and containers in which bread is stored should be sterilized with boiling water and rinsed with water to which vinegar has been added. Since acid inhibits the growth of the bacillus, 1 tablespoon vinegar for each quart of liquid should be added to each subsequent batch of dough until all the materials in stock at the time the rope appeared are used up.

Care of Bread After Baking

Bread should be removed from the pans as soon as it is taken from the oven and placed on racks or crosswise of the pans so that air can circulate on all sides of it. Quick cooling prevents loss of moisture, but drafts of cold air on hot bread may crack the crust.

For a tender crust, brush with butter immediately upon removing from the pans and cover with a cloth.

As soon as the bread has cooled thoroughly, wrap carefully in waxed paper and store in a breadbox which has air holes for proper ventilation. The breadbox should be washed, scalded and aired once a week, oftener during hot weather.

MOLD—Bread wrapped while hot molds quickly. If mold is found, the bread should be thrown away and the container scalded immediately.

STANDARD RECIPE FOR WHITE BREAD

1 cake yeast	2 tablespoons shortening
1/4 cup lukewarm water	2 tablespoons sugar
1 teaspoon sugar	2 cups milk, scalded
1½ teaspoons salt	6 cups sifted flour, about

Add yeast to lukewarm water and 1 teaspoon sugar. Let stand 5 minutes. Add salt, shortening and remaining sugar to milk and cool to lukewarm. Add softened yeast and 3 cups flour. Beat well. Add enough more flour to make a soft dough. Place remaining flour on board, turn out dough on floured board and knead until smooth and elastic. Place in greased bowl, turn over, so that greased side is on top, cover with cloth and let rise until doubled in bulk. Punch down and let rise a second time if desired. Cut dough into halves, round into balls, cover and let stand 10 minutes. Shape into loaves and place in greased bread pans. Grease tops, cover with a cloth and let rise until doubled in bulk. Bake in hot oven (400° F.) 10 minutes, reduce temperature to 375° F. and bake 35 to 40 minutes longer. Makes 2 (1-pound) loaves.

For detailed directions for kneading, shaping the loaves and baking, see pages 100-101.

If dry yeast is used, mix by the sponge method, page 99.

LIQUID STARTER OR POTATO YEAST

3 medium potatoes
4 cups boiling water
1 cake yeast
1 cup lukewarm water

1 cup sifted flour
1/3 cup sugar
1 1/2 tablespoons salt

Pare and dice potatoes and cook in boiling water until very tender. Drain, saving liquid. Mash potatoes thoroughly and return to liquid. Cool to lukewarm. Soften yeast in lukewarm water and add to potatoes with remaining ingredients. Beat well. Cover and let stand at room temperature 24 hours. Pour into sterilized jar, cover and store in cool, dark place. Use 1 cup of the mixture to replace 1 yeast cake in recipes. Fresh starter should be prepared at least every 2 weeks, using 1 cup of the old or a fresh cake of yeast.

WHOLE-WHEAT OR GRAHAM BREAD

1 cake yeast
1/4 cup lukewarm water
1/4 cup brown sugar
1 1/2 teaspoons salt
2 tablespoons shortening

2 cups milk, scalded
3 cups whole-wheat or
  graham flour
3 cups sifted white flour

Mix and bake as for standard white bread. Makes 2 loaves.

RYE BREAD

6 tablespoons corn meal
1/2 cup cold water
1 cup boiling water
2 teaspoons salt
1 tablespoon shortening
1 cake yeast

1/4 cup lukewarm water
1 cup mashed potatoes
2 1/2 cups rye flour
1 1/2 cups sifted white flour
1/2 tablespoon caraway seeds

Mix corn meal with cold water, add boiling water and cook 2 minutes, stirring constantly. Add salt and shortening and cool to lukewarm. Soften yeast in lukewarm water. Add with remaining ingredients to corn mixture. Knead to a stiff dough. Dough will be sticky. Handle rapidly or too much flour is absorbed. Cover and let rise until doubled in bulk. Shape into 2 loaves, cover and let rise until doubled in bulk. Bake in 375° F. oven for 45 minutes.

COCKTAIL RYE—Shape into long loaves like French bread. Sprinkle with salt and seeds; let rise and bake as above.

CORN BREAD

½ cake yeast
¼ cup lukewarm water
½ cup corn meal
1¾ cups boiling water

1½ teaspoons salt
2 tablespoons sugar
1 tablespoon shortening
2¾ to 3 cups sifted flour

Soften yeast in lukewarm water. Cook corn meal in water 10 minutes; add salt, sugar and shortening. Cool until lukewarm, stirring occasionally to prevent a film. When cool add softened yeast and beat well. Add flour and mix well. Knead, using as little flour on board as possible. Put into a greased bowl and let rise until almost doubled in bulk. Knead down and let rise again. Shape into loaves, place in pan and let rise until it has almost doubled in bulk. Bake as for standard white bread. Makes 2 loaves.

RAISIN BREAD

½ to 1 cake yeast
¼ cup lukewarm water
2 cups scalded milk
2 tablespoons shortening
¼ cup brown sugar

1½ teaspoons salt
¾ cup raisins, chopped
6 cups sifted white flour, about

Soften yeast in water. Follow general directions for making bread, either sponge method or straight dough method (page 99). Add raisins with the flour. Makes 2 loaves.

MONTE CARLO BREAD

2 cakes yeast
½ cup lukewarm water
2 cups milk, scalded
1½ teaspoons salt
1 cup sugar

1 cup shortening
9 cups sifted flour, about
6 eggs, slightly beaten
1½ cups currants

Soften yeast in lukewarm water. Add milk to salt, sugar and shortening. When lukewarm add yeast. Add half the flour and beat well. Let rise until very light. Add eggs, currants and remaining flour. Knead lightly, let rise and when light place in greased bread pans. Let rise and when light bake as for white bread. When bread is 2 days old, cut into thick slices and toast. Makes 3 loaves.

GLUTEN BREAD

1 cake yeast
½ cup lukewarm water
2 cups scalded milk

1½ teaspoons salt
4 cups gluten flour
2 egg whites

Soften yeast in water. When milk is cool, add softened yeast, salt, gluten flour, a little at a time, and finally slightly beaten egg whites. The mixture should be of a consistency to drop from a spoon rather than to pour and should be baked in greased pans filled about half full. Follow general directions for rising (page 100). When light, bake in moderate oven (350° F.) 1 hour. If a less moist bread is desired, add enough white flour to make a dough, after beating in the gluten flour, and follow directions for straight dough method (page 99). Makes 2 loaves.

POTATO BREAD

1 cake yeast
½ cup lukewarm water
½ cup boiling water
1½ teaspoons salt
1 tablespoon sugar

1 tablespoon shortening
2 cups mashed potato
4 cups sifted flour (enough
to make medium dough)

Combine in order given, following general directions for straight dough method (page 99). Makes 2 loaves.

ROLLED OAT BREAD

1 cup rolled oats
2 cups boiling water
½ to 1 cake yeast
½ cup lukewarm water
½ cup molasses

1½ teaspoons salt
1 tablespoon shortening,
melted
4½ cups sifted flour

Combine rolled oats and boiling water, cover and let stand 1 hour. Soften yeast in lukewarm water. Add to cooled oats with molasses, salt and melted shortening. Add flour and let rise. When light beat thoroughly, place in greased bread pans, let rise again and bake as for white bread. For a less moist bread, add enough flour to make a medium dough and follow directions for straight dough method (page 99). Makes 2 loaves.

ROLLED CINNAMON BREAD

1 recipe Standard White   6 tablespoons brown sugar
Bread dough (page 103)   1 teaspoon cinnamon

When dough is light, divide into halves and roll each half into a sheet 9 inches square. Sprinkle with a mixture of brown sugar and cinnamon. Roll up like jelly roll and place, seam side down, in greased bread pans. Let rise until light. Bake in hot oven (425° F.) 15 minutes, then reduce temperature to moderate (375° F.) and bake 25 minutes longer. Remove from pans and cool. Makes 2 loaves.

SALT RISING BREAD

SPONGE—

1 cup milk   1 teaspoon salt
2 tablespoons corn meal   1 tablespoon sugar

SECOND SPONGE—

1 cup lukewarm water   2 tablespoons shortening
1 teaspoon salt   2 cups sifted flour
1 tablespoon sugar

DOUGH—

3¼ cups sifted flour
(about)

Scald milk, cool to lukewarm, add corn meal, salt and sugar, pour into fruit jar or pitcher, cover and place in pan of hot water (120° F.). Let stand 6 or 7 hours or until signs of fermentation (gas bubbles) appear. Add ingredients for second sponge, beat thoroughly and again cover and place in pan of hot water (120° F.). Let rise until very light; then add remaining flour gradually until dough is stiff enough to be kneaded. Knead 10 to 15 minutes, shape into 2 loaves, place in greased bread pans, brush top with melted shortening, cover and let rise until very light, more than doubled. Bake in moderate oven (375° F.) for 10 minutes, then lower to 350° F. and bake 25 to 30 minutes longer. If more than 2 loaves are to be made, for each additional loaf, add the amount of ingredients listed for "second sponge" except for the flour, at the time second sponge is made. Add 1 cup flour only for each additional loaf to be made and add 1⅝ cups more (about) when making the dough. Makes 2 loaves.

Rolls, Fancy Breads and Muffins

SOFT, LIGHT DOUGH—A softer dough is used for rolls than for loaves of bread, and rolls and fancy breads should be permitted to become lighter than loaves. This is because they are eaten fresh and should be very light and spongy in texture.

FOR PLAIN ROLLS, use the straight dough method. This saves time and they are just as good as when made by the sponge method.

FOR FANCY ROLLS when large quantities of fat, sugar and eggs are used, the best results are obtained by making a sponge of the yeast, liquid and one-half the flour, then adding the fat, sugar and egg after the sponge is light. However, very good results can be secured by adding all ingredients before the first rising and such a change may be made in any of the following recipes.

BAKING ROLLS—Bake in hot oven (425° F.). Rolls are so small in size that slow baking dries them out. For crusty rolls, bake in individual gem pans or place ½ to 1 inch apart in baking pan. To obtain a soft, bright crust, grease the rolls before baking; for a crisp crust, do not grease either before or after baking.

STANDARD ROLL RECIPE

1 cake yeast	4 tablespoons sugar
¼ cup warm water	6 cups sifted flour (enough
2 cups scalded milk	to make a tender dough)
1½ teaspoons salt	4 tablespoons shortening

If a greater amount of sugar is used the rolls will be sweeter. If a greater amount of shortening is used, the rolls will be richer and more tender. Not less than 2 or more than 8 tablespoons of sugar or shortening should be used, however.

Follow general directions for making bread (page 99) kneading in a little less flour and permitting the dough to become lighter during each rising process, both after it is shaped and before the rolls are placed in the oven.

PLAIN ROLLS—When dough is light, cut or tear it into pieces about the size of a small egg or a walnut. Fold sides under until top of roll is perfectly smooth. Brush top with fat. Place in greased bread pan, on baking sheet or in individual molds. When light, bake in hot oven (425° F.) 15 to 20 minutes. Makes about 30.

VARIATIONS OF STANDARD ROLL RECIPE

BOWKNOTS—See Brioche, page 112.

BRAIDS—Braid 3 narrow strips of dough; press ends to pan. Let rise and bake as for plain rolls.

BUTTERFLY—Roll out dough, brush with melted butter and roll up like jelly roll. Cut into 1½-inch slices and place on greased baking sheet 1 inch apart. Flatten across center with handle of spoon. Let rise and bake as for plain rolls.

BUTTER-LEAF ROLLS—Roll dough as thin as possible; brush with melted butter. Cut into strips 1½ inches wide and place strips in piles of 6. Cut into 1-inch slices and place in greased muffin pans with longer cut edge down. Let rise until light, then bake in hot oven (425° F.) about 20 minutes.

CINNAMON ROLLS—When dough is light, roll ¼ inch thick, brush with melted butter and sprinkle with sugar and cinnamon. Roll like a jelly roll and slice with very sharp knife. Place on greased baking sheet 1 inch apart. When light bake in hot oven (425° F.) about 20 minutes.

CLOVER-LEAF ROLLS—When dough is light, break off pieces about the size of marbles, brush with melted butter and place 3 or 4 together in greased muffin pans. When very light, bake in hot oven (425° F.) about 15 minutes. The success of these rolls depends upon having the 3 or 4 balls together equal only as much dough as would be used in 1 ordinary roll and in letting them rise until very light before baking them.

CRESCENT ROLLS—When dough is light, roll out and cut into triangles. Brush with melted butter. Roll each triangle, beginning at the base. Place on greased baking sheet with point underneath, curving ends toward each other. Let rise and bake as for plain rolls. When nearly done, brush with egg yolk mixed with milk and return to oven to brown.

DINNER ROLLS—Add 2 egg whites after adding half the flour. Add remaining flour, knead and let rise. Shape into small balls the size of a walnut and place on greased baking sheet 1 inch apart. Let rise, glaze with egg white mixed with a little water and bake as for plain rolls.

ENGLISH MUFFINS—Make a very soft dough. Knead lightly, let rise, punch down and let rise again. Roll out ¼ inch thick on lightly floured board. Cut into large circles and let rise until light. Bake on hot ungreased griddle, turning when one side is brown. When second side is brown, reduce heat and bake more slowly. Baking may be finished in oven.

A variation of this recipe may be made by adding only enough flour to make a drop batter. Let rise until light. Drop batter into large, greased English muffin rings, arranged on greased baking sheet. Bake in hot oven (425° F.) until nearly done. Turn rings upside down and complete baking.

FINGER ROLLS—Follow standard roll recipe. When light cut and shape into long pieces about the size and shape of a finger. Place on well-greased pan and brush with melted fat or egg white. When light bake in hot oven (425° F.).

LUNCHEON ROLLS—Follow standard roll recipe using 6 to 8 tablespoons of shortening. Add 2 well-beaten eggs after half the flour has been added. Add remaining flour and knead. When light shape into small biscuits. Place 1 inch apart in well-greased pan. When doubled in bulk, brush with egg yolk diluted with milk and bake in hot oven (425° F.).

PARKER HOUSE ROLLS (POCKET-BOOK ROLLS)—Follow standard roll recipe. Four tablespoons each of sugar and shortening give excellent results. When light roll dough ¼ inch thick. Cut with biscuit cutter, brush each circle with melted fat and crease through center of each roll with dull edge of knife. Fold each roll over double. Place 1 inch apart on well-greased pan, brush with melted fat and when very light bake in hot oven (425° F.).

ROSETTE ROLLS—Shape dough into very small balls, brush with melted butter and place 6 together in greased muffin pans. Let rise until very light and bake as for plain rolls.

Or shape dough into long slender rolls, tie ends in a knot and bring 1 end up through the center. Place on greased baking sheet 1 inch apart. Let rise and bake as above.

TEA ROLLS—Follow standard roll recipe. When dough is light, roll and cut with biscuit cutter. Place on greased pans ½ inch apart. When light bake in hot oven (425° F.).

TWISTED ROLLS—Follow standard roll recipe. When light break dough into small pieces and roll out with palm of hand into rolls about 7 inches long and ½ inch thick. Taking an end of each strip between the thumb and forefinger of each hand, twist in opposite directions and bring the ends together. Shape the 2 ends alike, place ½ inch apart on well-greased pans and brush with melted fat or egg yolk diluted with milk. When light bake in hot oven (425° F.).

REFRIGERATOR ROLLS

¾ cup shortening
1 cup boiling water or
    scalded milk
2 eggs, beaten
¾ cup sugar

2 teaspoons salt
1 cup cold water
2 cakes yeast
½ cup lukewarm water
7½ cups sifted flour

Combine shortening and boiling water; stir until shortening is melted. Combine eggs, sugar and salt and beat in cold water. Soften yeast in lukewarm water. Combine the 3 mixtures and add flour. Cover and chill overnight. Shape, let rise and bake as for standard rolls. Makes 36.

BREAD STICKS

1 cake yeast
¼ cup lukewarm water
1 cup milk
4 tablespoons shortening

1½ tablespoons sugar
½ teaspoon salt
1 egg white
3½ cups sifted flour

Follow standard bread recipe, adding egg white before the flour. When light shape into sticks the size of a pencil. Place far apart on greased baking sheet and let rise until light. Place in hot oven (400° F.) and reduce temperature to moderate (325° F.). Bake until dry and crisp. Makes 18.

If desired, brush rolls with egg white before baking and sprinkle with coarse salt or poppy seed.

RYE STICKS—Use rye bread dough (page 104) and shape as above. Place far apart on baking sheet sprinkled with corn meal. Before baking, brush with egg white mixed with water and sprinkle with coarse salt or caraway seeds. Bake until dry and crisp, as above.

RUSKS

1 cup scalded milk
½ to 1 cake yeast
¼ cup warm water
3½ to 4 cups sifted flour
    (to make a soft dough)

¾ teaspoon salt
2 tablespoons sugar
½ cup shortening
1 egg

Prepare dough as for fancy rolls (page 108). When light roll out and cut with biscuit cutter. Place on greased baking sheet, let rise; bake in hot oven (400° F.). Makes 24.

BRIOCHE

2 cakes yeast	½ cup sugar
¼ cup lukewarm water	4 eggs, well beaten
1 cup milk	4½ cups sifted flour
⅔ cup butter	Melted butter
1 teaspoon salt	

Soften yeast in water. Scald milk and add butter, salt and sugar; stir until butter melts. Cool to lukewarm, then add yeast and eggs. Beat in flour. Allow to rise in warm place 6 hours. Chill overnight or until ready to use. Form quickly into small balls and place in greased muffin pans. Brush tops with melted butter and let rise until doubled in bulk. Bake in hot oven (400° F.) 20 minutes. Makes 2 dozen.

TWISTS—Roll dough lightly to a rectangular sheet ½ inch thick. Brush with softened butter and fold lengthwise into thirds. Cut into 1-inch slices, place on greased baking sheet and let rise until light. Lift each roll by the ends and twist one end. Replace on baking sheet and let rise again. Bake as above.

BOWKNOTS—Twist strips of brioche dough lightly and tie in a bowknot. Bring the ends down and press to the pan.

HOT CROSS BUNS

1 cake yeast	½ cup shortening
¼ cup warm water	4½ cups sifted flour
1 cup scalded milk	(about)
¾ teaspoon salt	3 egg yolks
½ cup sugar	

Soften yeast in water. Add scalded milk to salt, sugar and shortening. When lukewarm add yeast and 1½ cups flour. Beat well and let rise until very light. Add egg yolks and remaining flour. Knead lightly and let rise until doubled in bulk. Roll out dough to 1-inch thickness and cut into rounds. Place 2 inches apart on greased baking sheets and let rise. Glaze the surface of each bun with a little egg white diluted with water. With a sharp knife cut a cross on top of each bun. Bake in hot oven (400° F.) about 20 minutes. Just before removing from the oven, brush with sugar and water. Fill the cross with a plain frosting. A cup of raisins may be added to the dough if desired. Makes 2½ dozen.

MAKE CRUMPETS OR MUFFINS
FOR YOUR ENGLISH COUSIN
AND HONEY SANDWICH BREAD
AS A TREAT FOR THE FAMILY
—Wheat Flour Institute

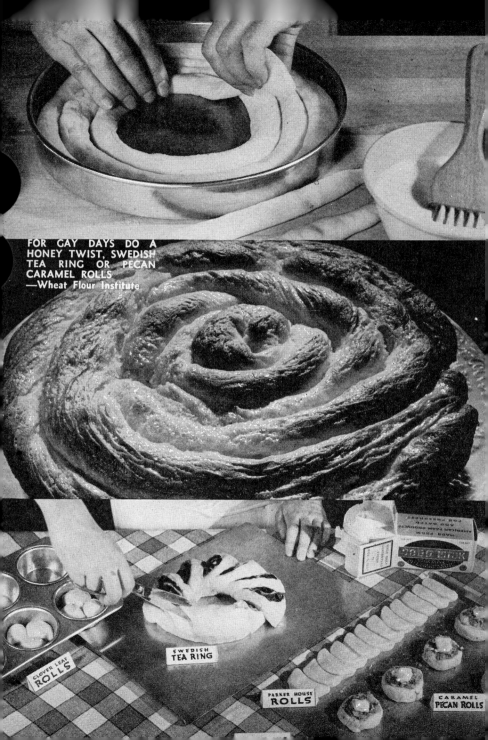

FOR GAY DAYS DO A
HONEY TWIST, SWEDISH
TEA RING OR PECAN
CARAMEL ROLLS
—Wheat Flour Institute

CLOVER LEAF
ROLLS

SWEDISH
TEA RING

PARKER HOUSE
ROLLS

CARAMEL
PECAN ROLLS

RAISED MUFFINS

1 cake yeast	4 tablespoons sugar
¼ cup warm water	2 tablespoons shortening
1 cup scalded milk	3½ cups sifted flour
¾ teaspoon salt	1 egg, beaten

Soften yeast in lukewarm water. Add scalded milk to salt, sugar and shortening. When lukewarm add yeast and 1½ cups flour. Beat thoroughly. When very light add beaten egg and remaining flour. Mix well and let rise until doubled in bulk. Shape into small balls and place in greased muffin pans. Brush tops with egg white, slightly beaten, and sprinkle with chopped nuts. Let rise and bake in hot oven (425° F.). Makes 2 dozen.

HONEY TWIST

1 cup milk, scalded	2 cakes yeast
¼ cup butter	¼ cup lukewarm water
½ cup sugar	2 eggs
1 teaspoon salt	5 to 6 cups sifted flour

Pour hot milk over butter, sugar and salt. Crumble yeast into lukewarm water to soften. Cool milk to lukewarm, add yeast and well-beaten eggs. Beat in flour to make a soft dough, then turn out on floured board and knead until smooth. Form into a ball and place in greased bowl. Cover and let rise until doubled in bulk. When light, shape into long roll about 1 inch in diameter. Coil roll into greased cake pan, beginning at the outside edge and covering the bottom. Brush with honey topping. Let rise until doubled in bulk and bake in moderate oven (375° F.) 25 to 30 minutes.

If desired, sprinkle with chopped nuts and chopped candied cherries and pineapple before baking.

HONEY TOPPING—

¼ cup butter	1 egg white
⅔ cup confectioners' sugar	2 tablespoons honey, warmed

Cream all ingredients together and brush over Twist before setting to rise.

COFFEE CAKE

1 cake yeast	2/3 cup sugar
1/4 cup lukewarm water	3/4 teaspoon salt
1 cup scalded milk	4 tablespoons shortening
2 cups sifted flour (about)	Sugar
1 egg, beaten	Cinnamon

Soften yeast in water. Cool milk and add yeast and half the flour. Beat well and let rise until very light. Add egg, sugar, salt and melted shortening, mix thoroughly and add remaining flour. Let rise until almost doubled in bulk. Pour into shallow greased pans. When light sprinkle thickly with sugar and cinnamon. Bake in hot oven (400° F.) 20 minutes. Serve hot. Makes 2 (9-inch) cakes.

SWEDISH TEA RING

1 cake yeast	6 tablespoons shortening
1/4 cup lukewarm water	3 1/2 cups sifted flour
1 cup scalded milk	1 egg, beaten
3/4 teaspoon salt	Melted butter
1/4 cup sugar	1/2 cup finely chopped nuts

Soften yeast in water. Combine scalded milk, salt, sugar and shortening. When lukewarm add yeast and half the flour and beat well. Let rise until very light, then add egg and remaining flour and mix well. Let rise. Roll dough into a rectangular sheet on a lightly floured board. Brush with melted butter and sprinkle with nuts. Roll up like a jelly roll and form into a ring on greased baking sheet. Using a large pair of scissors, cut ring around edge at 2-inch intervals, leaving inner edge intact. Turn each slice to lie flat on pan. Let rise until light and bake in hot oven (400° F.) about 30 minutes. Frost while hot with confectioners' sugar frosting. Makes 1 large ring.

CARAMEL PECAN ROLLS

1/2 recipe Standard Roll dough (page 108)	1/2 cup brown sugar
3 tablespoons butter	3/4 cup chopped pecans

When dough is light, roll out and spread with softened butter. Sprinkle with brown sugar and nuts and roll up. Slice and place cut side down on greased baking sheet. Let rise; bake at 400° F. about 25 minutes. Makes 12.

QUICK BREADS

QUICK breads are those breads or bread-like mixtures which are mixed and baked at once. The essentials of quick breads are a liquid and flour. When leavening agents are used, they are of the type which act quickly and make the mixture light without a long period of waiting.

Quick breads may be improved in flavor and texture by the addition of salt, sugar, eggs, shortening, etc. in various combinations and proportions.

READY-TO-USE FLOURS—Prepared flours which contain leavening and other ingredients require only liquid to make griddlecakes and biscuits. Follow directions on package. Added eggs, sugar and shortening produce a batter suitable for muffins, waffles, shortcake biscuits and similar quick breads.

Approximate Proportions of Liquid to Flour for Quick Breads

POUR OR THIN BATTER—Use 1 cup liquid with 1 to 1½ cups flour.

DROP OR THICK BATTER—Use 1 cup liquid with 1½ to 2 cups flour.

SOFT DOUGH—Use 1 cup liquid with 2 to 2½ cups flour.

STIFF DOUGH—Use 1 cup liquid with 3 to 5 cups flour.

Methods of Mixing Quick Breads

POUR OR THIN BATTER will pour easily from a spoon or a pitcher and varies in degree of thinness. Breakfast puff and popover mixtures are examples of the thinnest batter, while the griddlecake and the waffle mixtures are examples of a thicker pour batter. Thin batters are best combined with a rotary beater. Beat eggs, add milk and melted shortening, sift dry ingredients on top and beat until smooth. For waffle mixtures, the eggs are often separated and the beaten egg whites folded in last.

DROP OR THICK BATTER does not pour readily, but drops in a soft mass from a spoon or must be shaken or pushed free from it. Muffins and fritters are examples of the drop batter. They may be made with either solid or melted shortening. Solid shortening is added to the sifted dry ingredients and cut in thoroughly with a fork. Melted shortening or oil is added to the liquid mixture of milk and beaten eggs. In either case the dry and liquid mixtures are then combined with only enough stirring to dampen all the flour. The mixture will look lumpy. The cake method of mixing may be used if a large amount of shortening is included in the recipe. Cream shortening and sugar until fluffy; add beaten egg, then sifted dry ingredients and milk alternately.

SOFT DOUGH can be handled more or less easily. Biscuits are made from soft dough and are mixed as quickly and deftly as possible. Have the shortening and liquid cold. Cut the shortening into the sifted dry ingredients with two knives or a pastry blender. Stir in the liquid quickly and knead on a lightly floured board a few seconds.

STIFF DOUGH can be handled wthout sticking and some energy must be used to roll it out. The Southern beaten biscuits and noodles are examples of the stiff dough.

POPOVERS

1 cup sifted flour	1 cup milk
¼ teaspoon salt	1 tablespoon melted
2 eggs	shortening

Sift flour and salt together. Beat eggs and add milk, shortening and sifted dry ingredients. Beat until smooth with rotary beater. Fill greased muffin pans ½ full and bake in very hot oven (450° F.) 20 minutes. Reduce temperature to moderate (350° F.) and bake 15 minutes longer. Makes 8.

RYE—Use ¾ cup rye flour for ¾ cup white flour.

PLAIN MUFFINS

2 cups sifted flour	1 cup milk
½ teaspoon salt	1 egg
1 tablespoon sugar	2 tablespoons melted
4 teaspoons baking powder	shortening

Sift flour, salt, sugar and baking powder. Combine remaining ingredients and add to dry ingredients. Stir just enough to dampen the flour. Pour into greased pans filling pans ⅔ full. Bake in hot oven (425° F.) 20 to 25 minutes. Makes 12.

PINEAPPLE MUFFINS—Add ½ cup flour, 3 tablespoons sugar, 2 tablespoons shortening and 1 No. 1 can crushed pineapple. Mix and bake as above.

CORN-MEAL MUFFINS

1 cup corn meal	4 teaspoons baking powder
1 cup sifted flour	1 egg
½ teaspoon salt	1 cup milk
2 tablespoons sugar	2 tablespoons shortening

Sift dry ingredients together. Beat egg and add milk and melted shortening. Add dry ingredients, mixing only enough to dampen flour. Fill greased muffin pans ⅔ full and bake in hot oven (400° F.) 25 minutes. Makes 12.

JELLY CORN MUFFINS—Use recipe above. Fill greased muffin pans ¼ full, put a teaspoon of jelly on each, cover with more batter and bake in a hot oven (400° F.).

SOYBEAN MUFFINS

¾ cup sifted soybean flour	2 teaspoons baking powder
1¾ cups sifted white flour	¾ cup milk
1 teaspoon salt	1 egg, beaten
2 tablespoons sugar	1 tablespoon shortening

Sift dry ingredients together. Combine milk, beaten egg and melted shortening, add sifted dry ingredients and mix only enough to dampen all the flour. Fill greased muffin pans ⅔ full and bake in hot oven (425° F.) 20 minutes. Makes 12.

GRAHAM MUFFINS

2 cups graham flour	1 egg
2 tablespoons sugar	1½ cups sour milk or
½ teaspoon salt	buttermilk
¾ teaspoon baking soda	2 tablespoons melted
1¼ teaspoons baking powder	shortening

Sift dry ingredients together and return bran to mixture. Beat egg; add milk, shortening and sifted ingredients. Mix only enough to dampen flour. Fill greased muffin pans ⅔ full and bake in hot oven (400° F.) 25 minutes. Makes 12.

ROLLED OAT—Soak 2 cups rolled oats in sour milk overnight. Omit graham flour and add remaining ingredients and 1 cup white flour. Mix and bake as above.

RYE—Use 1 cup rye and 1 cup white flour instead of graham.

WHOLE-WHEAT—Use 1 cup whole-wheat flour and 1 cup white flour. Add ½ cup raisins, if desired.

RICE MUFFINS

¼ cup sugar	1 cup milk
¾ cup cooked rice	5 teaspoons baking powder
1 egg	1 teaspoon salt
2 tablespoons shortening	2¼ cups sifted flour

Mix sugar, rice, egg, melted shortening and milk. Sift baking powder, salt and flour together and add. Fill greased muffin pans ⅔ full; bake in hot oven (425° F.) 30 minutes. Makes 12. Use other cooked cereal instead of rice.

RAISIN BRAN MUFFINS

¾ cup sifted flour	1 egg
3 teaspoons baking powder	½ cup milk
½ teaspoon salt	1½ tablespoons molasses
1 cup bran	1 tablespoon melted
½ cup seeded raisins	shortening

Sift flour, baking powder and salt together; add bran and raisins. Beat egg and mix with remaining ingredients. Add dry ingredients, mixing only enough to dampen all the flour. Fill greased muffin pans ⅔ full and bake in hot oven (400° F.) 30 minutes. Makes 12.

BAKING POWDER BISCUITS

2 cups sifted flour	¼ cup cold shortening
3 teaspoons baking powder	⅔ cup cold milk
1 teaspoon salt	

Sift flour, baking powder and salt together and cut in shortening with 2 knives or a pastry blender. Add milk and mix quickly. Knead for a few seconds on lightly floured board. Pat out to ½-inch thickness and cut with biscuit cutter. Place in greased pan close together for crust on top and bottom only, far apart if crust is desired on sides also. Bake at once in very hot oven (450° F.) 12 minutes. Makes 12.

BISCUIT CRUST—Roll dough ¼ inch thick and cut to fit top of meat or chicken pie. Place on pie, pressing edges to dish. Cut opening in center to allow escape of steam.

DROP BISCUITS—Increase milk to 1 cup and drop mixture from spoon into greased muffin pans or onto greased baking sheet. Bake as above.

BUTTERMILK BISCUITS

2 cups sifted flour	¼ cup cold shortening
½ teaspoon baking soda	1 cup cold buttermilk or
2 teaspoons baking powder	sour milk
1 teaspoon salt	

Mix and bake as for baking powder biscuits.

Variations Using Baking Powder or Buttermilk Biscuit Dough

BUTTERSCOTCH—Roll dough to a rectangular sheet and brush with softened butter. Sprinkle with brown sugar and roll up like a jelly roll. Cut into 1-inch slices and place cut side down on greased baking sheet or in greased muffin pans.

CHEESE—Mix ½ cup grated cheese with dry ingredients.

CINNAMON—Follow directions for butterscotch biscuits, using granulated sugar and cinnamon instead of brown sugar.

GRAHAM—Use 1 cup graham flour and 1 cup white flour.

ORANGE—Dip cubes of sugar in orange juice and press 1 into the top of each biscuit.

Mix 1 tablespoon grated orange rind with milk and add 2 tablespoons sugar to flour.

PECAN CARAMEL—Follow directions for butterscotch biscuits, adding ½ cup chopped pecans to brown sugar. Mix butter and brown sugar and place a little of mixture in each muffin pan. Place slices of roll cut side down on top of mixture. Remove from pans as soon as baked.

SCONES—Roll dough into 2 circles ½ inch thick. Cut into wedges and bake on a hot griddle, turning to brown both sides. Split scones while hot, spread generously with softened butter and place in oven to melt butter.

BEATEN BISCUITS

3 cups sifted flour	⅓ cup cold shortening
1 teaspoon salt	½ cup cold milk

Sift flour with salt; cut in shortening. Add milk and mix to a very stiff dough. Place on floured board and beat with rolling pin or wooden potato masher 30 minutes, folding in edges after each stroke. Roll ⅓ inch thick and cut with biscuit cutter. Place on greased baking sheet and prick with a fork. Bake in hot oven (400° F.) 20 minutes. Makes 24.

SALLY LUNN

2 cups sifted flour
3 teaspoons baking powder
½ teaspoon salt
1 egg, beaten

1 cup milk
½ cup shortening
¼ cup sugar

Sift flour with baking powder and salt. Combine egg and milk. Cream shortening and sugar together and add flour alternately with liquid mixture. Place in greased loaf pan or muffin pans and bake in moderate oven (375° F.) 30 minutes. Makes 1 loaf or 12 muffins.

JOHNNYCAKE

2 cups corn meal
1½ teaspoons salt
1 teaspoon baking soda
2 tablespoons sugar

2 cups sour milk
2 eggs, beaten
2 tablespoons melted
shortening

Sift dry ingredients together and add milk, eggs and shortening. Mix well. Pour into greased pan and bake in hot oven (400° F.) 30 minutes. Makes 1 (8x10 inch) loaf.

SOUTHERN CORN BREAD

1½ cups scalded milk
1½ cups white corn meal
1 teaspoon salt
2 tablespoons shortening

2½ teaspoons baking
powder
1 egg, beaten

Mix milk with corn meal and stir in salt and shortening. Cool. Add baking powder and egg yolk and mix well. Fold in stiffly beaten egg white. Pour into greased pan and bake in hot oven (400° F.) 20 minutes. Makes 1 (8x8 inch) loaf.

BACON—Sprinkle with diced bacon before baking.

SOUTHERN SPOON BREAD

2 cups boiling water
1 cup white corn meal
1 teaspoon salt

1 tablespoon shortening
1 cup milk
2 eggs, separated

Mix water, corn meal, salt and shortening. Cool. Add milk and beaten egg yolks; mix well. Fold in stiffly beaten egg whites. Pour into greased baking dish and bake in hot oven (400° F.) 30 to 40 minutes. Serve from dish. Serves 6 to 8.

QUICK NUT BREAD

2 cups sifted flour
½ cup sugar
1 teaspoon salt
3 teaspoons baking powder
¼ cup cold shortening

½ cup chopped nuts
1 egg
1 egg yolk
1 cup milk

Sift flour, sugar, salt and baking powder together and cut in shortening with 2 knives or a pastry blender. Add nuts. Beat egg and egg yolk and add milk. Add to flour mixture and mix quickly, just enough to dampen all the flour. Pour into greased loaf pan and bake in hot oven (400° F.) 40 minutes. Makes 1 loaf.

HONEY SANDWICH BREAD

1 cup sifted flour
3 teaspoons baking powder
½ teaspoon salt
1 cup graham flour
½ cup bran

½ cup chopped nuts
1 egg
1 cup milk
⅓ cup honey

Sift flour, baking powder and salt together and mix well with graham flour, bran and nuts. Beat egg and add milk and honey. Add to dry ingredients and mix only enough to dampen all the flour. Pour into greased loaf pan and bake in hot oven (400° F.) 30 minutes. Makes 1 loaf.

WHOLE-WHEAT—Use 1½ cups whole-wheat flour instead of graham flour and bran. Use ¼ cup brown sugar for honey and add ¼ cup melted shortening.

PRUNE RYE BREAD

2 cups sifted rye flour
2 cups sifted wheat flour
6 teaspoons baking powder
1½ teaspoons salt
¾ cup sugar

1 egg, slightly beaten
1¾ cups milk
1 cup cooked prunes, chopped

Sift dry ingredients together. Combine egg and milk, and add to flour mixture, stirring only until well mixed; stir in prunes. Turn into greased loaf pans and bake in moderate oven (350° F.) about 1 hour. Makes 2 loaves, 6x3 inches, or 1 sandwich loaf, 11x3x3 inches.

QUICK COFFEE CAKE WITH CRUMB TOPPING

1½ cups sifted flour	1 egg
½ cup sugar	⅔ cup milk
2 teaspoons baking powder	3 tablespoons melted
½ teaspoon salt	shortening

Sift flour, sugar, baking powder and salt together. Beat egg and add milk and shortening. Stir liquids into dry ingredients, mixing only enough to dampen all the flour. Pour into greased pan, sprinkle with crumb topping and bake in hot oven (425° F.) 25 minutes. Makes 1 (9x9 inch) coffee cake.

CRUMB TOPPING

2 tablespoons butter	¼ cup dry bread crumbs
2 tablespoons sugar	½ teaspoon cinnamon
¼ cup sifted flour	

Cream butter and sugar together. Add flour, crumbs and cinnamon. Mix to consistency of coarse crumbs and sprinkle over coffee cake batter before baking.

SPICY APPLE COFFEE CAKE

2 cups sifted flour	⅔ to ¾ cup milk
1 tablespoon granulated sugar	2 or 3 apples
3 teaspoons baking powder	⅓ cup brown sugar
¾ teaspoon salt	½ teaspoon cinnamon
4 tablespoons shortening	1 tablespoon butter
½ cup grated nippy cheese	

Sift flour, sugar, baking powder and salt together. Cut in shortening and cheese. Add milk to make a soft dough. Turn out on lightly floured board and knead ½ minute. Pat out dough in ungreased 9-inch layer-cake pan. Pare apples, core and slice thin. Arrange apples in petal design over top. Sprinkle with brown sugar and cinnamon and dot with butter. Bake in hot oven (425° F.) 25 minutes. Makes 1 (9-inch) coffee cake.

Omit cheese if preferred. Use an oblong pan and arrange apples in rows on top of dough.

APPLE-FILLED FLAPJACKS OR WAFFLES HOT OFF THE GRID-DLE WILL GET EVERYBODY UP PROMPTLY
—Wheat Flour Institute

MAKE SEVERAL KINDS OF COFFEE CAKE AT THE SAME TIME, SUCH AS THESE STREUSEL, CHERRY AND FROSTED. POPOVER BATTER SHOULD HAVE A WARMHEARTED RECEPTION BY SIZZLING HOT BUTTERED PANS OR GLASS CUPS

—Wheat Flour Institute

BANANA BREAD

½ cup shortening	2 cups sifted flour
1 cup sugar	3 teaspoons baking powder
2 eggs	½ teaspoon salt
1 cup mashed ripe bananas	1 cup nut meats, chopped
1 teaspoon lemon juice	

Cream shortening and sugar together. Beat eggs until light and add. Press bananas through sieve and add lemon juice. Blend with creamed mixture. Sift flour, baking powder and salt together and mix quickly into banana mixture. Add nuts. Bake in greased loaf pan in moderate oven (375° F.) about 1¼ hours. Makes 1 (1-pound) loaf.

BOSTON BROWN BREAD

1 cup corn meal	1 cup graham flour
1 cup rye flour	¾ cup molasses
¾ teaspoon baking soda	2 cups sour milk or butter-
1 teaspoon salt	milk

Sift corn meal, rye flour, soda and salt together and mix well with graham flour. Add combined molasses and sour milk and mix well. Fill greased molds ⅔ full, cover closely and steam 3 hours. Remove covers and dry tops in moderate oven (375° F.). Makes 3 loaves.

RAISIN—Add 1 cup raisins.

DATE BRAN BREAD

2 cups sifted flour	⅔ cup sliced dates
1 teaspoon salt	1 egg
3 tablespoons sugar	1½ cups milk
3 teaspoons baking powder	2 tablespoons melted
2 cups bran	shortening

Sift flour with salt, sugar and baking powder. Stir in bran and dates. Beat egg and add milk and melted shortening. Add dry ingredients and mix only enough to dampen all the flour. Pour into greased molds, cover closely and steam 3 hours. Makes 3 loaves.

Griddlecakes, Waffles, Doughnuts and Fritters

GRIDDLECAKES

2 cups sifted flour
1 teaspoon salt
3 teaspoons baking powder
1 tablespoon corn meal
1 tablespoon sugar

2 eggs
1½ cups milk
1 tablespoon melted
shortening

Sift flour with salt, baking powder, corn meal and sugar. Beat eggs and add milk and shortening. Add sifted ingredients and beat until smooth. Drop by spoonfuls on hot griddle. When full of bubbles turn to brown other side. Makes 20.

SOUR MILK OR BUTTERMILK—Use 2 cups sour milk or buttermilk instead of sweet milk. Add 1 teaspoon baking soda to flour and use only ¾ teaspoon baking powder.

FLANNEL CAKES

2 cups sifted flour
1 teaspoon salt
3 teaspoons baking powder
2 eggs, separated

2 cups milk
1 tablespoon melted
shortening

Sift flour, salt and baking powder together. Beat egg yolks and add milk and shortening. Beat in flour mixture with rotary beater. Fold in stiffly beaten egg whites. Bake on hot griddle, turning to brown both sides. Makes 24.

CORN-MEAL GRIDDLECAKES

2 cups boiling water
1 cup corn meal
1 tablespoon sugar
1 teaspoon salt

1½ cups milk
2 cups sifted flour
3 teaspoons baking powder
2 eggs, beaten

Pour boiling water over corn meal, sugar and salt and mix well. Let stand until meal swells. Add milk and let stand until cool. Sift flour and baking powder together and add. Fold in beaten eggs. Bake on hot griddle, turning to brown both sides. The cakes should be small and well cooked. They require longer cooking than wheat cakes. Makes 36.

RICE GRIDDLECAKES

1 cup cooked rice
2 cups milk
1½ cups sifted flour
½ teaspoon salt
1 tablespoon sugar

2 teaspoons baking powder
1 egg
1 tablespoon melted
shortening

Mix rice with 1 cup milk and let stand overnight. Sift flour, salt, sugar and baking powder together. Beat egg and add shortening and remaining 1 cup milk. Add to softened rice alternately with sifted dry ingredients. Drop from spoon onto hot greased griddle and bake, turning once to brown other side. Makes 24.

FRENCH OR JELLY PANCAKES

3 eggs, separated
1 teaspoon sugar
½ teaspoon salt
1 cup milk

½ cup sifted flour
1 tablespoon melted
shortening
Tart fruit jelly

Beat egg yolks and add sugar, salt and ½ cup milk. Add flour and shortening and mix until smooth, then add remaining milk. Fold in stiffly beaten egg whites. Bake on hot griddle, making cakes larger than usual and very thin. Spread with jelly and roll up while hot. Serve with overlapping edges of cakes on bottom to keep them from unrolling. Sprinkle with confectioners' sugar if desired. Makes 12.

APPLE FLAPJACKS

1 tablespoon shortening
1 tablespoon sugar
2 eggs
1½ cups sifted flour

1 teaspoon baking powder
½ teaspoon cinnamon
1 cup apples, chopped fine
1 cup milk

Cream shortening and sugar, add beaten eggs, flour sifted with baking powder and cinnamon, and the chopped apples. Then add milk gradually to make a medium batter. Bake on griddle as for ordinary pancakes and serve in an overlapping row around a platter of pork chops or serve separately with roast pork, either hot or cold. Cooked apples may be used with batter in the same way. Makes 16.

QUICK NUT BREAD, DATE-BRAN BREAD, HONEY SANDWICH BREAD AND PRUNE-RYE BREAD, NOT TO MENTION THE EVER POPULAR GINGERBREAD AND CORN BREADS, WILL FIND THEIR PLACES AT YOUR TABLE

—Wheat Flour Institute

WHILE MARMALADE ESCORTS SCONES ON THEIR SHORT LIFE, SALLY LUNN IS TURNED OUT OF ITS PAN TO FACE A HUNGRY WORLD
—Wheat Flour Institute

BREAD-CRUMB GRIDDLECAKES

1½ cups dry bread crumbs
1½ cups scalded milk
2 tablespoons shortening
2 eggs

½ cup sifted flour
½ teaspoon salt
4 teaspoons baking powder

Soften crumbs in milk and melted shortening. Add eggs, well beaten, and dry ingredients, mixed and sifted. Bake on a hot greased griddle. The cakes are very tender and should be turned carefully. Makes 12.

BAKING POWDER BUCKWHEAT CAKES

1½ cups buckwheat flour
½ cup sifted white flour
5 teaspoons baking powder
½ teaspoon salt

1 tablespoon shortening
1½ cups milk
1 tablespoon molasses

Sift dry ingredients together. Combine melted shortening, milk and molasses, then add slowly to dry ingredients. Beat well and bake on a slightly greased, hot griddle. Makes 16.

RAISED BUCKWHEAT CAKES

2 cups boiling water
½ cup corn meal
½ cake yeast
¼ cup lukewarm water
1 tablespoon molasses

1 teaspoon salt
2 cups buckwheat flour
¼ teaspoon baking soda
⅓ cup hot milk

Pour boiling water over corn meal and let stand until it swells. Soften yeast in the lukewarm water. After corn meal is cool, add molasses, salt, yeast and flour. Beat thoroughly and set in warm place to rise overnight. It should rise and fall again by the morning. Add soda dissolved in hot milk, stir well and bake on a hot greased griddle. Makes 20.

When the cakes are desired frequently (say, three times a week), fresh yeast will not be required after the first making, if a little more than a pint of the batter is reserved each time and kept in a cool place to be used instead of the yeast. Molasses in buckwheat cakes helps to give them a good color. Without it, they may be gray and unattractive.

WAFFLES

1½ cups sifted flour
½ teaspoon salt
2 teaspoons baking powder
2 eggs, separated

1 cup milk
4 tablespoons melted
    shortening

Sift flour, salt and baking powder together. Beat egg yolks and add milk and shortening. Add flour and beat with rotary beater until smooth. Fold in stiffly beaten egg whites. Bake in hot waffle iron. Makes 4 waffles.

BUTTERMILK—Use 1¼ cups buttermilk instead of sweet milk. Reduce baking powder to 1¼ teaspoons and add ½ teaspoon baking soda.

RICE—Before folding in egg whites, add 1 cup cold cooked rice to either plain or buttermilk waffles.

CORN-MEAL WAFFLES

1½ cups boiling water
1 cup corn meal
1 teaspoon salt
4 tablespoons shortening
2 eggs, separated

1 cup sifted flour
½ teaspoon baking soda
2 teaspoons baking powder
½ cup sweet milk
⅔ cup buttermilk, about

Add boiling water to corn meal and stir in salt and shortening. Cook in double boiler 10 minutes, stirring occasionally. Cool. Add beaten egg yolks. Sift flour with soda and baking powder and add alternately with sweet milk. Add enough buttermilk to make a pour batter. Fold in stiffly beaten egg whites. Bake in hot waffle iron. Makes 6.

CREAM WAFFLES

2 cups sifted flour
1 tablespoon corn meal
1 teaspoon baking soda

½ teaspoon salt
2 eggs, separated
2 cups sour cream

Sift flour, corn meal, soda and salt together. Beat egg yolks and add cream. Add sifted dry ingredients and mix well. Fold in stiffly beaten egg whites. Bake in hot waffle iron. Makes 6.

DOUGHNUTS

SWEET MILK—

3 eggs
1 cup sugar
2 tablespoons shortening
3 teaspoons baking powder
1 teaspoon salt

½ teaspoon nutmeg
3½ cups sifted flour
1 cup milk
½ teaspoon lemon extract

Beat eggs until very light, beat in sugar, then add melted shortening. Sift baking powder, salt and nutmeg with 1 cup flour and stir into first mixture alternately with milk. Add lemon extract and just enough flour to make a very soft dough. Chill. Roll out ¾ inch thick on lightly floured board. A soft dough makes light, tender doughnuts when cooked. Fry in deep fat (360°-370° F.) and drain on unglazed paper. If you have no thermometer, test the fat for temperature as directed on page 26. Makes 2 dozen.

SOUR MILK—

1 cup sugar
2 tablespoons sour cream or
   shortening
3 eggs
½ teaspoon lemon extract
1 cup sour milk

½ teaspoon baking soda
1 teaspoon baking powder
½ teaspoon salt
½ teaspoon nutmeg
4½ cups sifted flour
(more or less)

Mix sugar with cream and add beaten eggs, lemon extract and sour milk. Sift remaining dry ingredients with 1 cup of flour and add to first mixture. Add additional flour to make a dough just stiff enough to handle. Toss on floured board, roll out and cut. Fry in hot deep fat (365° F.). Makes 2 dozen.

CRULLERS

¼ cup shortening
1 cup sugar
2 eggs
3½ teaspoons baking
   powder

¼ teaspoon nutmeg
½ teaspoon salt
4 cups sifted flour
1 cup milk

Cream shortening. Add sugar, then well-beaten eggs. Sift baking powder, nutmeg and salt with 1 cup of flour and add alternately with milk to the first mixture. Add additional flour to make a dough stiff enough to handle. Toss on floured board, roll ½ inch thick and cut into strips. Twist and fry in deep fat (365° F.). Drain on unglazed paper and when cold roll in confectioners' sugar. Makes 3 dozen.

RAISED DOUGHNUTS

1 cake yeast	2 tablespoons shortening
¼ cup lukewarm water	3½ to 4 cups sifted flour
1 cup scalded milk	1 egg
1 teaspoon salt	½ teaspoon nutmeg
¾ cup sugar	

Soften yeast in water. Add scalded milk to salt, sugar and shortening. When lukewarm add softened yeast. Add 1½ cups flour. Allow the sponge to stand in a warm place until it is so light that it will fall at the slightest touch. Add egg, nutmeg and remainder of the flour and knead. The dough should be softer than bread dough. Cover and set in a warm place to rise. Toss on a lightly floured board and roll ¾ inch thick. Cut with a doughnut cutter and let rise. Fry in hot deep fat (365° F.) 2 to 3 minutes. When frying put the raised side of the doughnut down in the fat. The heat will cause the top side to rise by the time the doughnut is ready to turn. Makes 2 dozen.

JELLY DOUGHNUTS—Cut doughnuts with cookie cutter and fry as above. Cut a hole in doughnut from side and fill with jelly. Replace cut-out section. Roll in sugar.

LONG JOHNS—Cut dough into strips and fry as above. Cut a slit in top and fill with jelly. Frost top with confectioners' frosting.

BANANA FRITTERS

1¼ cups sifted flour	⅓ cup milk
½ cup sugar	2 teaspoons melted
1¼ teaspoons salt	shortening
2 teaspoons baking powder	4 medium bananas
1 egg, beaten	

Sift 1 cup flour with sugar, salt and baking powder. Mix egg and milk and add to flour mixture gradually, stirring until smooth. Add shortening. Peel bananas and cut crosswise into halves or quarters. Roll in remaining flour, then cover with batter. Fry in hot deep fat (375° F.) 4 to 6 minutes. The batter is stiffer than for most fritters and requires longer cooking. Serves 8.

FRUIT FRITTER BATTER

1⅓ cups sifted flour
¼ teaspoon salt
2 teaspoons baking powder

2 tablespoons sugar
1 egg
⅔ cup milk

Sift dry ingredients and add well-beaten egg and milk. The batter should be just thick enough to coat the article it is intended to cover. If it is too thin, add more flour; if too thick, add more liquid. Makes 1½ cups.

PEACH FRITTERS

Peaches
Sugar

Fritter batter

Peel the peaches, split them in two, remove the stones, sprinkle sugar over them, dip each piece in fritter batter and fry in hot deep fat (365° F.) 2 to 3 minutes. Serve with confectioners' sugar or foamy sauce.

Apple Fritters

Pare, core and slice tart apples; dip in fritter batter, covering each slice with batter. Fry in hot deep fat (365° F.) 2 to 3 minutes. Serve with confectioners' sugar.

RASPBERRY FRITTERS

1 cup sifted flour
1 teaspoon baking powder
¼ teaspoon salt
2 tablespoons sugar

2 eggs
2 to 3 tablespoons water
1 cup raspberries

Sift flour, baking powder and salt together. Add sugar, egg yolks and water. Fold in stiffly beaten egg whites and the raspberries, leaving the fruit as nearly whole as possible. The amount of water may vary somewhat. The batter should be thin enough to fold in the fruit but thick enough to hold together well; otherwise, the fruit in cooking will soften it too much. Drop mixture from a tablespoon into hot deep fat (365° F.) and fry until brown, turning once. Serve with confectioners' sugar or foamy sauce. Makes 12.

SANDWICHES

A N encyclopedia published about 1900 defines a sandwich
as "an article of food consisting of a slice of meat, fish,
fowl or other food placed between two slices of bread, which
may be plain or buttered." No such simple definition could
be given today, for from these simple beginnings the sandwich
has developed in all directions, and has adapted itself to such
varied needs that it ranges from a fragile morsel served with
afternoon tea to an elaborate combination of toast, meat, lettuce, tomato, sauce, and any number of other things which
combine to make it a complete and satisfying meal.

Even the requirement of two slices of bread with something
between them is no longer in force. "Open-faced" sandwiches
offer almost unlimited opportunity for variety in both cold
and hot meals. In these the slices of bread or toast are laid
side by side. Sometimes, usually in hot meat sandwiches, both
slices are covered with beef or chicken, or whatever gives the
characteristic flavor, and the whole is covered with gravy.
Often, especially in cold sandwiches, one slice holds its chicken
or tomato or crab meat, while its companion is covered with
cole slaw and dill pickles or a lettuce leaf holding a spoonful
of mayonnaise. The possibilities are endless, and the suggestions given here can be combined and adapted to almost any
requirement where a sandwich can be called into service.

Serving Sandwiches

Garnishes of fine parsley, cress, celery plumes, stuffed or ripe
olives, or slices of lemon or pickle are effective on the serving-
dish. Barberries and leaves, fresh nasturtium leaves and
blossoms, or something to indicate the kind of sandwich may
be used as a garnish.

Making and Keeping Sandwiches

The bread for flat sandwiches should be a day old because
it can be cut more easily than fresh bread. For rolled sandwiches fresh bread should be used. Bread baked in special
tins which provide slices that are perfect squares or circles is

economical when the crusts are to be cut off, but any loaf of comparatively fine grain may be used.

The Bread

ALL SORTS OF BREADS are made into sandwiches—white, brown, rye, graham, whole-wheat, raisin, date, nut, etc. Sometimes two or more kinds are used together. Long narrow rolls are attractive when sliced lengthwise, buttered and filled. For picnics, where a substantial filling is desirable, the crumb of the roll may be removed and the hollow filled with sandwich material. Thin salt wafers and crackers are often used instead of bread for paste sandwiches.

FOR FANCY SANDWICHES, to be used for tea or receptions, or as an appetizer at the beginning of the meal, or to be served with the salad, the bread should be cut into slices as thin as possible and the crusts should be removed. Use a sharp knife, so that there will be no ragged edges.

PICNIC AND LUNCH-BOX SANDWICHES are cut somewhat thicker than fancy sandwiches, and the crusts are generally left on.

Butter and Filling

The filling and butter for sandwiches should be increased in proportion to the thickness of the slice of bread.

PREPARING THE BUTTER—The butter should be thoroughly creamed before it is used or it will not spread evenly over the bread. To cream butter, place it in a warm bowl and mash and beat it until it is soft. It will then spread well even on fresh bread. Sandwich butters are often made by creaming one cup of butter with one-half cup of cream. One-half cup of butter, creamed, will spread a two-pound sandwich loaf cutting forty to forty-five slices.

RELISHES such as mustard, salt, grated horseradish, chopped parsley, chives and curry may be added to creamed butter for use in sandwiches of meat, tomato, game, chicken, fish, cheese or eggs.

SPREADING BUTTER AND FILLING—A poorly buttered sandwich is very unpalatable. Spread the butter to the very edges of the slices, on the sides that are to be put together, being careful, however, not to let the butter spread over the edges so that it is untidy. If the slices need not be fitted together, it is often easier to spread the bread before cutting it from the

loaf. A pliable knife or small spatula is a help in spreading butter or filling.

Spread the filling on the buttered surface of one slice only of each sandwich. Have the filling come to the edge of the sandwich, if possible.

When mayonnaise is used, not combined with a filling, as in mayonnaise and lettuce sandwiches, it is more evenly distributed if it is spread on one of the slices of bread and the lettuce leaf placed upon it.

Shaping the Sandwiches

Sandwiches may be cut with a knife into triangles, oblongs and similar outlines, or shaped with cutters into hearts, circles, crescents or any preferred design. When sandwiches are shaped with these fancy cutters, the bread should be shaped before it is spread, to avoid waste of butter and filling. Care must be taken afterward, however, not to spoil the shape while spreading. Heart, club, spade and diamond shapes are popular for card parties. Heart shapes are attractive for valentine and announcement parties and for showers. Strips, triangles, circles, crescents and rolled and folded sandwiches are used for teas.

ROLLED SANDWICHES—Cut the crusts from a fresh loaf of bread (or if a stale loaf of bread is used, cut off the crusts and wrap for an hour in a cloth wrung from cold water). Spread a thin layer of butter on one end of the loaf and then cut from it as thin a slice as possible. If a filling is used, spread it on the buttered slice. Roll this slice with the spread side inward and lay it on a napkin, with the edge of the slice downward. When all the sandwiches have been prepared, draw the napkin firmly around the rolls and put them in a cold place until needed. The butter will harden and hold the rolls together.

Time Savers in Sandwich Making

In making sandwiches in quantity, route the work so that there will be no waste motions. Have a large enough space for (1) cutting the bread; (2) spreading the slices with butter and filling; (3) shaping and (4) wrapping the sandwiches.

Keeping Sandwiches

Sandwiches are best prepared just before serving, especially if the filling is of a kind that will become limp or soak into the bread. When it is necessary to make sandwiches several hours before they are to be used, they may be wrapped in paraffin paper or a slightly dampened cloth or placed in a stone jar.

Filling for Meat and Salad Sandwiches

When sliced meat is used, a sandwich is easier to eat and generally more palatable if the meat is cut as thin as a knife-blade with several tiny slices instead of one thick one in each sandwich. Fancy butters are excellent with sliced meat.

All kinds of potted and minced meats are used between slices of bread with or without mayonnaise. Salted meat and fish fillings are improved by lemon-juice, chopped pickles or capers. Pastes of fresh fish and meat require high seasoning.

All forms of meat may be used with lettuce or cress, between two slices of buttered bread, with or without salad dressing. The slices should be pressed together and the crust trimmed, if desired. Lettuce may be used in large, crisp leaves, or in "ribbons," to make the sandwich easier to eat. Where mayonnaise dressing is used, the sandwiches should be made at the last moment, and served promptly. Tomatoes and cucumbers with lettuce and mayonnaise make delicious salad sandwiches.

Filling for Tea Sandwiches

The tea sandwich is seldom made of meat, though such things as minced chicken, lobster, or crab meat, and sardines beaten to a paste, are sometimes used for it. The bread is cut very thin and the fillings may be a bit of lettuce spread with mayonnaise dressing, chopped olives, nasturtiums, watercress and similar morsels. An attractive sandwich is made from diminutive Vienna rolls split not quite through and spread with vegetable filling. Another tea sandwich is made by spreading jelly or preserves between two salt crackers. If the crackers are spread with a thin film of butter and crisped quickly in a hot oven, this form of sandwich is really worth eating. Almond sandwiches of all varieties are delicious for the tea-table

Filling for Sweet Sandwiches

Preserves of all kinds, drained from their sirup, marmalade, jam, jelly, crystallized and candied fruits are used for sweet sandwiches with graham or salt wafers, as well as with bread or sponge cake. The crystallized fruits may be sliced thin and dipped in cream, chopped fine, moistened in orange-juice, and spread between bread or lady-fingers.

Scraped or grated maple sugar mixed with chopped nuts is used with brown bread. Ice-cream is cut in slices and put between wafers or layers of sponge cake.

Tiny tea biscuits make an excellent foundation for sweet sandwiches. They are split and buttered while hot and filled with honey and almonds, cream cheese and jam, or chopped nuts and marmalade. They are best served warm.

Filling for Nut Sandwiches

Pignolias or pine nuts, butternuts, walnuts, hickory nuts, almonds and pecans may all be put through a meat-chopper, mixed, a very little salt added, and spread over thin, buttered slices of brown or white bread. Or, to the ground nuts may be added a little salt and paprika and either salad oil or creamed butter to make a smooth paste.

The salty taste of peanut butter is good with raisin bread. Peanuts may be rubbed to a paste with creamed butter and a layer of chopped preserved ginger added.

Butternuts, walnuts, hickory nuts, almonds, or pecans may be used in equal parts, ground fine, with cream cheese moistened with sweet thick cream and seasoned with salt. Grated American cheese may be used instead of cream cheese and melted butter instead of cream.

PETITE MARMITE

Yeast bouillon, on the market as cubes or paste, makes an excellent spread for sandwiches, hors d'oeuvres and appetizers. It may be used alone or mixed with butter or other pastes. Its strong flavor makes it especially desirable with milder flavored fillings.

PREPARED BUTTERS FOR SANDWICHES

ANCHOVY BUTTER

Yolks of 4 hard-cooked eggs	½ cup butter
4 boned anchovies	Paprika

Rub the yolks of the eggs to a smooth paste with the anchovies and butter and add paprika to taste.

HAM BUTTER

½ cup cooked ham	Yolks of 2 hard-cooked eggs
½ cup butter	Pepper

Grind the ham and pound smooth with the butter and the yolks of the eggs and season with pepper.

SHRIMP BUTTER

1 cup cooked shrimps	1 cup butter
Salt	About ¼ cup tarragon vine-
⅛ teaspoon cayenne	gar or lemon-juice

Pound the shrimps in a mortar with salt and cayenne. Add the butter and moisten the mixture with the tarragon vinegar or lemon-juice.

Sandwiches with Nut Fillings

PEANUT BUTTER, FIG AND RAISIN SANDWICHES

¼ cup figs	½ teaspoon salt
¼ cup raisins	½ cup peanut butter
2 tablespoons light corn-sirup	2 tablespoons lemon-juice

Wash figs and raisins and put through a food-chopper. Add salt, peanut butter, lemon-juice and corn-sirup, and mix well. Use between thin, buttered slices of bread.

PEANUT BUTTER AND ORANGE MARMALADE SANDWICHES

½ cup peanut butter	½ cup orange marmalade
¼ cup cream	

Mix peanut butter with cream or milk until it is smooth and light in color. Spread generously on thin slices of bread, and add a layer of orange marmalade. The marmalade may be mixed with the peanut butter, if preferred.

PEANUT BUTTER AND BANANA SANDWICHES

½ cup peanut butter	½ cup banana pulp or sliced
¼ cup cream or hot water	bananas
Lemon-juice	

Mix the peanut butter with the cream until it is smooth and light in color, then combine with the banana pulp and a little lemon-juice and use between thin, buttered slices of bread. Or place slices of banana over layer of peanut butter on bread.

PEANUT BUTTER AND PICKLE SANDWICHES

½ cup peanut butter   ¼ cup cream or hot water
½ cup chopped pickle

Cream peanut butter and water together and add chopped pickle. Use between thin, buttered slices of bread.

PEANUT BUTTER AND ONION SANDWICHES

1 cup peanut butter   1 small Bermuda or
¼ cup mayonnaise   Spanish onion

Beat peanut butter, add mayonnaise and spread sandwiches. Slice onion in very thin slices and put a layer of these over mixture on bread.

ALMOND SANDWICHES

No. 1

1¼ cups almonds   3 tablespoons lemon-juice
½ teaspoon salt

Chop the almonds fine, mix with the salt and lemon-juice and use with thin slices of bread, buttered. Cut into small ovals, pressing a blanched almond in the center of each sandwich.

No. 2

Use the same quantities as for No. 1. Toast the almonds a light brown and grate them. Form into a paste with the lemon-juice, add the salt and spread over the bread.

No. 3

⅓ cup almonds   ⅔ cup shredded celery
¼ cup mayonnaise

Chop the almonds fine and mix them with the celery. Spread between thin, buttered slices of bread. Sandwiches filled with this mixture are an excellent accompaniment to salads or cold meats. When served with meats the celery and almonds may be moistened with a few spoonfuls of mayonnaise.

MARRON SANDWICHES

Grind marrons glacés (candied French chestnuts) fine, spread on rounds of buttered bread and cover with rounds of bread from which the centers have been cut. Fill the centers with whipped cream, sweetened and flavored, and decorate with blanched and chopped pistachio nuts or tiny candied violets.

Sandwiches with Cheese or Egg Fillings
CHEESE SANDWICHES

No. 1

Place thin slices of American, Swiss or any preferred mild or snappy cheese between two slices of buttered bread. Add a dash of mustard if desired.

No. 2

Grate sapsago and Parmesan cheese and sprinkle thickly over a slice of buttered bread. Then dust with a mild red pepper and add another slice of buttered bread.

No. 3

Yolks of 3 hard-cooked eggs	Paprika Salt
2 tablespoons salad oil	1 tablespoon vinegar
Mustard	1 cup grated cheese

Rub smooth the yolks of the hard-cooked eggs. Add the oil, stirring it in very slowly with a fork, and mix thoroughly with a little mustard, paprika, salt and the vinegar. Add the grated cheese and use between thin buttered slices of white or brown bread.

No. 4

½ pound American full cream cheese, grated	¼ cup cream
	½ teaspoon dry mustard
2 tablespoons melted butter	Paprika Salt

Mix all the ingredients thoroughly and use between thin buttered slices of bread. This filling will keep indefinitely in closed jars in the refrigerator.

mustard, mixing thoroughly. Stir in the vinegar and spread between buttered slices of bread, crackers or pieces of oat-cake.

RUSSIAN SANDWICHES

½ cup cream cheese	¼ cup chopped pimiento
¼ cup chopped olives	¼ cup mayonnaise
Lettuce leaves	Boston brown bread

Spread the cream cheese on thin slices of Boston brown bread. Spread an equal number of buttered slices with chopped olives and pimientos mixed with mayonnaise dressing. Press together in pairs with a crisp lettuce leaf between.

EGG SANDWICHES

No. 1

Hard-cooked eggs	Salt	Paprika
Pepper	Capers or pickles if desired	

Slice the eggs and lay the slices between thin buttered slices of bread. Season to taste with salt, pepper and paprika and add a layer of chopped capers or pickles if desired. These are good for lunches for traveling or picnics.

No. 2

1 cup chopped, hard-cooked egg	Chopped capers or pickles
	¼ cup mayonnaise

Mix the chopped egg with the mayonnaise and add salt, pepper and chopped pickles or capers to taste. Use between thin buttered slices of bread.

Sandwiches with Meat and Poultry Fillings

CHICKEN SANDWICHES

No. 1

1 cup cooked chicken meat, white or dark	¼ cup mayonnaise

Chop the chicken meat very fine, mix with the mayonnaise, and spread thin slices of bread, buttered or unbuttered, with the paste.

No. 2

2 egg-yolks
1 teaspoon melted butter
1 teaspoon lemon-juice

1 cup minced, cooked chicken
Salt   Pepper
1 teaspoon stock

Cook the eggs thirty to forty-five minutes, in water just below boiling-point, take out the yolks, and mash as fine as possible. Add to these the melted butter and lemon-juice, the minced chicken, salt, pepper and stock. Mix all well together. A paste will be the result and with this very delicate sandwiches may be made.

No. 3

1 cup cooked white meat of
   chicken
1 tablespoon gelatin
1 tablespoon cold water

6 tablespoons thick cream
½ teaspoon salt
Dash of paprika

Chop the chicken very fine and pound to a paste, adding salt and a dash of red pepper. Soak the gelatin in the cold water for fifteen minutes, and add the thick cream. Dissolve the gelatin over boiling water, beat it slowly into the chicken and add salt and paprika. Set aside to cool, smoothing into an even mass. When cool, divide into squares, cut these squares into very thin slices and arrange on thin buttered slices of bread. Cut into fancy shapes, removing the crusts.

No. 4

¾ cup cooked chicken meat
¼ cup chopped stuffed olives

¼ cup chopped almonds
¼ cup mayonnaise

Cut the chicken meat into small bits and add the almonds and olives. Moisten with mayonnaise and spread on thin, buttered slices of bread.

CHICKEN, HAM AND CELERY SANDWICHES

1 cup cooked chicken meat
½ cup celery
1 tablespoon green pepper

¼ cup mayonnaise
¼ cup cooked ham

Mince the chicken, ham, celery and green peppers. Mix with the mayonnaise and spread on buttered bread.

CHICKEN AND DILL PICKLE SANDWICHES

Between buttered slices of white bread, use thin slices of white meat of roasted chicken and thin slices of dill pickle. Cut into triangles and serve on lettuce leaves.

CHICKEN LIVER SANDWICHES

1 cup cooked chicken livers
2 tablespoons chopped crisp bacon
Salt   Pepper

1 tablespoon lemon-juice
2 tablespoons sliced truffles
4 drops tabasco sauce
2 stalks celery, minced

Mash the chicken livers, add the chopped bacon, salt, pepper, tabasco sauce, lemon-juice and sliced truffles. Use between slices of bread spread with creamed butter mixed with minced celery.

CHICKEN AND TONGUE SANDWICHES

1 pint minced cold boiled chicken and tongue, mixed
½ cup melted butter
1 egg-yolk

Black pepper
1 teaspoon Worcestershire sauce

To cold boiled tongue and chicken add the melted butter, the yolk of the egg, beaten, a little black pepper, and the Worcestershire sauce. Spread this over buttered bread.

PÂTÉ DE FOIE GRAS SANDWICHES

No. 1

Moisten pâté de foie gras with cream to make a thin paste. Spread on lettuce leaves on white buttered bread and sprinkle with French dressing.

No. 2

1 tablespoon pâté de foie gras
¼ cup boiled chestnuts

2 tablespoons butter

Mash the butter and chestnuts to a paste, add the pâté de foie gras and mix well. Spread very thin on slices of buttered bread.

BEEF SANDWICHES

1¼ cups cold roast beef
1 teaspoon salt
½ tablespoon tomato catchup

½ teaspoon Worcestershire sauce
1 tablespoon melted butter

To minced cold roast beef add the salt, tomato catchup, Worcestershire sauce and melted butter. Spread on buttered bread, cover with a second slice, and cut into fancy shapes.

HAM SANDWICHES

No. 1

Slice boiled ham very thin and use several tiny slices between thin slices of buttered bread, adding a little mustard if desired.

No. 2

1 cup ham
1 tablespoon salad oil
1 tablespoon lemon-juice
Pepper

½ teaspoon mustard mixed with ¼ teaspoon water to a smooth paste

Chop the ham fine and season with salad oil, lemon-juice, a dash of pepper and the mustard. Spread between thin, buttered slices of bread.

No. 3

1 hard-cooked egg
1 small spiced cucumber pickle

1 cup boiled ham
¼ cup mayonnaise

Chop the hard-cooked egg, cucumber pickle and boiled ham and mix well. Moisten with the mayonnaise, season to taste, and spread between thin slices of buttered bread.

HAM AND ANCHOVY SANDWICHES

1¼ cups chopped ham
1 teaspoon onion-juice
Paprika

Few drops tabasco sauce
Anchovy paste
Creamed butter

Add to the chopped meat, onion-juice, paprika, a few drops of tabasco sauce and a little anchovy paste mixed with creamed butter. Use between thin, buttered slices of bread.

LIVER AND BACON SANDWICHES

½ cup chopped bacon
½ cup mashed liver

Salt and pepper
¼ cup cream

Mix chopped bacon and mashed liver, season with pepper and salt and mix with cream. Spread between slices of buttered bread. Decorate the plate with a border of lemon slices and hard-cooked eggs cut into halves lengthwise, with a sprig of cress or parsley on each half egg.

MUTTON OR LAMB SANDWICHES

1¼ cups cold mutton or lamb
1 teaspoon salt
1 tablespoon capers

1 teaspoon chopped mint
Dash of pepper
1 tablespoon lemon juice

Chop cold mutton or lamb very fine, add salt, capers, chopped mint, pepper and lemon juice. Spread between buttered slices of whole-wheat bread. Serve on a bed of lettuce leaves.

TONGUE SANDWICHES

½ pound cooked tongue
¼ cup mayonnaise

Salt, pepper
Cayenne

Chop the tongue and pound to a paste, or cut into thin slices and use, with the mayonnaise and seasonings, between thin buttered slices of bread.

TOMATO AND TONGUE SANDWICHES

12 slices rye bread
Butter
Mayonnaise

12 slices cooked smoked
tongue
3 tomatoes, sliced

Lettuce

Spread half of bread with softened butter and half with mayonnaise. Arrange slices of tongue on buttered slices of bread and slices of tomato on remaining bread. Arrange lettuce on plates and on each place a slice of bread with tongue and one with tomatoes. Serves 6.

VEAL SANDWICHES

1¼ cups chopped veal
1 teaspoon salt

1 tablespoon lemon-juice
Mustard   Pepper

Chop the veal, and season with salt, lemon-juice and a little pepper and mustard. Spread mixture between thin buttered slices of bread.

Sandwiches with Fish Fillings

Anchovies, sardines, or freshly boiled fish may be used for sandwiches. These are better pounded to a paste, with a few drops of lemon-juice added during the pounding. Fresh white fish, like cod, may be seasoned with salt and pepper, moistened with a little mayonnaise or even a plain white sauce, and then put between two layers of buttered bread.

FLAKED FISH SANDWICHES

1 cup flaked fish
2 tablespoons chopped celery
2 tablespoons chopped cucumber pickles, either sweet or sour

¼ cup thick mayonnaise
1 tablespoon Worcestershire sauce or catchup, if desired
Salt
Pepper

Delicious and appetizing sandwich fillings are made by mixing these ingredients. Season to taste with salt and pepper and spread between thin buttered slices of bread.

ANCHOVY AND OLIVE SANDWICHES

½ cup mashed anchovies or anchovy paste

½ cup olives
¼ cup cream or butter

Chop the olives and mix with the anchovy paste. Add the butter or cream and use between thin buttered slices of bread.

CAVIAR SANDWICHES

½ cup caviar

2 teaspoons lemon-juice

Flavor caviar with lemon-juice and spread thin on lightly buttered bread. A small quantity of chopped pickled beets may be added if desired.

CRAB OR LOBSTER SANDWICHES

1¼ cups crab or lobster meat   ¼ cup French dressing or mayonnaise

Butter thin slices of whole-wheat bread. Cover half of them thickly with flaked boiled crab meat or diced lobster meat and add a teaspoon of French dressing or mayonnaise. Cover with the other buttered slices of bread and cut into fancy shapes.

OYSTER SANDWICHES

Large oysters   Pepper
Salt   Tabasco sauce
Horseradish   Lemon-juice
Worcestershire sauce   Cress

Fry the oysters and place two or three between two buttered slices of brown or white bread. Sprinkle with pepper, salt, horseradish, lemon-juice, tabasco, Worcestershire or water cress, according to taste.

SALMON SANDWICHES

1 cup cold boiled or canned salmon   ¼ cup mayonnaise

Mix the salmon with the mayonnaise until a fine even mixture is obtained. Remove the soft crumb from French rolls and fill the space thus made with the salmon mixture.

SARDINE SANDWICHES

12 large sardines   ¼ cup mayonnaise or a little
1 hard-cooked egg   Worcestershire sauce, if de-
Pepper   sired
Lemon-juice   Salt
Shrimp butter, if desired   Creamed butter, if desired

Drain the oil from the fish, remove the skins and pound the fish to a paste with a little salt, pepper and lemon-juice. Use between thin buttered slices of bread. Shrimp butter may be mixed with the sardine paste and the flavor may be varied by the addition of Worcestershire sauce or mayonnaise or both.

The mashed yolk of the hard-cooked egg and three parts of creamed butter to one of the sardine mixture makes a delicious sandwich filling.

SHAD ROE SANDWICHES

1 shad roe
Yolks of 3 hard-cooked eggs
Butter
½ teaspoon paprika

3 drops tabasco sauce
1 teaspoon anchovy paste
Salt

Cook the roe and mash it together with the yolks of the hard-cooked eggs. Add an equal amount of creamed butter, the paprika, tabasco sauce, anchovy paste, and salt to taste. Spread between thin buttered slices of bread. Slices of lemon, peeled and salted, may be put between rounds of buttered bread and passed with the shad roe sandwiches.

Sandwiches with Vegetable Fillings
CUCUMBER SANDWICHES

No. 1

Soak thin slices of cucumber for one hour in good white vinegar seasoned with salt and pepper. Add one teaspoon of chopped chives, if desired. Drain the slices and use them between thin, buttered slices of brown or white bread. Each sandwich may be the size of a cucumber slice, if daintiness is desired.

No. 2

Chop a peeled cucumber and mix with mayonnaise. Use between thin buttered slices of brown or white bread.

ONION SANDWICHES

Pour salted water over thin slices of onion (or chopped onion) and let it stand for a time to extract the very strong flavor. Then drain the onion and use between buttered slices of bread, seasoning with pepper, salt, and a little mustard if desired.

PIMIENTO AND ANCHOVY SANDWICHES

¾ cup pimiento
Butter
½ teaspoon tabasco sauce

1 tablespoon lemon-juice
¼ cup anchovy paste
Salt

Rub pimientos to a paste with creamed butter and season with tabasco sauce, lemon-juice, anchovy paste and salt. Spread between thin buttered slices of whole-wheat bread.

RADISH AND HAM SANDWICHES

½ cup potted ham
¼ to ½ cup mayonnaise

½ cup sliced radishes

Peel and slice radishes, dip them in rich, thick mayonnaise, and lay on thin slices of bread covered with potted ham.

TOMATO AND LETTUCE SANDWICHES

4 tomatoes   Lettuce leaves   ¼ to ½ cup mayonnaise

Spread thin slices of buttered bread with mayonnaise, cover with a crisp lettuce leaf and spread with peeled, chilled tomatoes sliced thin. Cover with a second slice of bread, and cut into desired shape. Crisp bacon is a pleasing addition.

WATERCRESS SANDWICHES

1¼ cups cress
Paprika

2 tablespoons lemon-juice or
¼ cup mayonnaise

Sprinkle cress with salt, paprika, and lemon-juice, or mix with mayonnaise. Lay between slices of brown bread.

THE PIE CANAPÉ

An attractive canapé plate may be made by cutting twice horizontally, through a round loaf of rye bread. The slice should be ¾ inch thick and free of crust. Spread with softened butter and mayonnaise dressing. Mark in circles as guides with increasingly larger articles—a small cookie cutter at center, a large cutter, a bowl, a small plate, and decorate in concentric rings. Fill the center with caviar, piling chopped parsley or egg yellow at very center. Surround with circle of cream cheese tinted with vegetable coloring pressed from a pastry bag. Continue these rings of appetizer paste and colored cream cheese in accordance with your taste or color scheme. Use red salmon paste, sardellen paste, anchovy paste, shrimp paste, etc. When finished, use a very sharp knife to cut like a pie but do not separate. Serve cold within a few hours.

SANDWICH LOAF OR CAKE

Slice an uncut loaf of day-old white sandwich bread horizontally, making 3 or 4 long slices ¾ inch thick. Remove all crusts. Spread each slice with creamed butter and stiff mayonnaise, then each with a different chopped salad or sandwich mixture. Chicken, shrimp, salmon or tongue salad; deviled egg, sardine, anchovy, liver or cheese pastes may be used. Stack and cover the top and sides with soft cream cheese, garnish with flowers of colored cream cheese, paprika or chopped parsley. Chill. Illustrations page 139A and 160A.

Miscellaneous Sandwiches and Sandwich Fillings

1. Raisins worked into cream cheese.
2. Chopped raisins, figs, dates or prunes, mixed with chopped nut-meats and moistened with mayonnaise dressing or lemon-juice.
3. The well-whipped white of an egg mixed with a cup each of chopped raisins and nut-meats, seasoned with a little salt.
4. Peanut butter moistened with salad dressing and mixed with raisins, dates, figs or bananas.
5. Equal parts olives, peanut butter, celery, mixed with a little salad dressing.
6. Peanut butter mixed with chopped dill, sweet or sour pickles.
7. Cream cheese and chopped stuffed olives.
8. Chopped stuffed olives and chopped nuts, moistened with salad dressing.
9. Cream cheese and crushed pineapple between very thin slices of bread.

10. Tunafish mixed with parsley, lemon-juice, seasoning and a bit of onion.

11. Cream cheese and chopped nuts.

12. Ground boiled ham and chopped pickles or chopped peanuts.

13. Cottage cheese and pickles, olives, nuts or pimientos.

14. Currant jam with pounded walnut meats and creamed butter. Pass with cream cheese. Preserved currants may be substituted in this combination.

15. Boston brown bread with cream cheese or mayonnaise mixed with chopped nuts and raisins.

16. Rounds of brown bread spread with chopped olives, minced lettuce and water cress, tarragon, paprika, parsley and chives mixed with mayonnaise.

17. Pimientos, cucumbers and onion or chives, minced, mixed with mayonnaise and spread on buttered entire-wheat bread.

18. Green pepper, pimiento and olives with mayonnaise.

19. Boston brown bread with minced corned beef seasoned with mustard and rubbed to a paste.

20. Cream cheese used with chopped parsley, pimientos and mayonnaise, chopped nuts, sliced sugared bananas, crushed pineapple, chopped or sliced olives, shredded sliced apples. The cheese may be rubbed with butter or the creamed butter may be spread on the bread.

HOT SANDWICHES

The hot sandwich is now frequently used as a supper or luncheon dish with a salad. It is sometimes served as a breakfast dish and even a dessert may now be served in sandwich form, as, for instance, slices of ice-cream between slices of sponge cake.

There are several types of hot sandwiches. Some are made from plain bread and served with hot sauce; in others the framework of the sandwich is toast, sautéd slices of bread, French-fried toast or fresh slices of bread baked with the sandwich-filling; and in still others hot baking-powder biscuit or crisp toasted crackers are used.

Then besides the regulation kind of sandwich—a filling between two slices of breadstuff—there is the open-faced kind, in which the top slice is left off and a garnish of cut parsley, pickle, olive or grated cheese is used instead of the covering slice.

And, lastly, there is a third and novel type of sandwich in which the outer structure is of meat. This is cut in thin slices, dipped in fritter batter and fried in fat, and a filling of vegetables is placed between the slices.

GRILLED CHEESE SANDWICHES

Between two slices of medium thick bread, lay slices of cheese cut about one-eighth inch thick. Place in oven until cheese begins to melt. Then toast on both sides and serve hot. Or mash a soft cheddar cheese with cream. Spread this as a filling and toast the sandwich.

CHICKEN CLUB SANDWICHES
(For each sandwich)

3 slices toast	Crisped bacon
Mayonnaise	Tomato slices or
⅛ to ¼ breast of chicken	onion slices
Lettuce	Pickle or olives

For each sandwich remove the crust from three slices of toasted bread, buttered while hot. Spread the under slice with a thin layer of mayonnaise dressing. On this lay two small white lettuce leaves, allowing them to project beyond the edge of the toast. On the lettuce lay thin slices of breast of chicken spread with mayonnaise. Cover with a slice of toast, spread with mayonnaise and cover with slices of crisp bacon. A slice of tomato or onion may be placed over the bacon. Place the third slice of toast on this and garnish with pickles or olives. Serve while the toast and bacon are hot.

GRILLED TONGUE AND EGG SANDWICHES

1 cup chopped tongue	1 cup milk
1 egg	2 tablespoons mayonnaise
1 teaspoon onion-juice	dressing

Mix the tongue with the onion-juice and the mayonnaise and spread it on thin slices of unbuttered bread. Press the slices together and cut in two diagonally. Beat the egg, add the milk and dip the sandwiches in this mixture. Brown them in a small amount of butter, first on one side and then on the other. Garnish with parsley and serve at once on a hot platter.

COUNTRY CLUB SANDWICHES

Butter slices of toast. On each slice lay thin cuts of cooked sausage. Cover with a well-seasoned tomato sauce and sprinkle with grated cheese. Lay a strip of bacon on each sandwich and bake in a hot oven until the bacon is crisp.

TURKISH SANDWICHES

1 cup cooked chicken cut in small pieces	¼ cup cream
1 tablespoon butter	1 teaspoon onion-juice
½ cup stock	¼ cup walnut meats
1 tablespoon flour	Paprika Salt
	Thin slices of toasted bread

Make a sauce of the stock, cream, flour, and butter. Add the other ingredients, and heat thoroughly. Place on slices of toast. Brush with melted butter and garnish with thin rings cut from stuffed olives. Serve immediately on a hot platter.

HAM SWEET SANDWICHES

For each sandwich allow two medium-thin slices of cold boiled ham. Lay the ham in French dressing for a few minutes. Drain and dip in a plain fritter batter. Fry in deep fat and drain on soft paper. Place one of the slices of ham on a hot plate, add lettuce and cover with another slice of the fried ham. Pour orange-raisin sauce over the sandwich and serve at once.

HOT BISCUIT SANDWICH

Make plain baking-powder biscuits. Bake until the crust is crisp on both top and bottom. Break—do not cut—the biscuits apart and butter the halves. On one side place a thick slice of tomato, then a layer of mayonnaise dressing and then one of minced bacon. Cover with the other half of the biscuit, press lightly together and serve at once.

SAVORY SANDWICHES

Spread slices of whole-wheat or graham toast with butter. Over these place slices of crisply cooked bacon. Sprinkle generously with chopped pickle and horseradish. Serve with sliced tomatoes.

SARDINE AND TOAST SANDWICHES

1 cup sardines	Mayonnaise
Lettuce	Lemon-juice
Onion-juice	Graham bread

Sardines that have been prepared in oil are to be preferred for these sandwiches. Drain the sardines, tear them in pieces, add a few drops of lemon-juice, onion-juice and enough mayonnaise to moisten. Toast medium-thin slices of graham bread and spread with butter creamed with a few drops of lemon-juice. Cover with lettuce and add the sardines and another slice of toast. Serve with a garnish of lemon.

CHEESE AND TOMATO SANDWICHES

6 slices bread	6 slices bacon
6 slices tomato	Grated cheese

Butter the slices of bread. On each slice, place a slice of tomato, cover with grated cheese, and add a slice of bacon. Toast under the flame of a broiler until the bacon is crisp.

HAM OR BACON AND CHEESE SANDWICHES

Butter slices of toasted bread. Cover with a thin slice of boiled ham or bacon, spread with mustard, and cover with a layer of thinly sliced or grated cheese. Place the slices in the oven until the cheese is melted. Garnish with minced parsley and serve at once.

PEANUT AND CHILI SANDWICHES

Mix peanut butter with chili sauce to form a paste. Spread slices of hot brown bread or toasted graham bread with butter, add the mixture and put the slices together with crisp lettuce leaves between. Garnish with slices of dill pickle.

DEVILED TOMATO SANDWICHES

6 tomatoes	6 slices bread
Salt	1 cup ground boiled ham
Pepper	1 tablespoon French mustard
4 slices bacon	

Cut a slice from the stem end of each tomato. Sprinkle with salt, pepper and bits of bacon. Bake until the tomatoes are tender. Serve on slices of hot buttered toast spread with the ground ham mixed with the mustard.

Suggestions for Breakfast Sandwiches

Poached egg on toast is an open-faced sandwich. Rolls split, toasted, and buttered, with broiled tender bacon placed between them, or bacon between crisply toasted slices of well buttered corn bread are other forms of breakfast sandwiches.

Creamed oysters on toast, scrambled eggs on buttered toast spread with anchovy paste, creamed codfish between two slices of buttered toast are all in the breakfast category of sandwiches. To make a variation of French toast that takes it out of the sweet and puts it into the meat class, spread buttered slices of bread with deviled ham, put the slices together in twos, dip them into a mixture of egg and milk in proportion of two eggs to one cup of milk, and then sauté the slices in butter until they are nicely brown on both sides.

Old fashioned country sausage may be cut in thin rounds, fried a delicate brown and served between hot, savory pancakes of the same size as the sausage slices.

Suggestions for Hot Sandwiches

Hot sandwiches should be substantial and filling without losing the chief characteristic of all sandwiches—ease in handling. For this reason rolls and buns are often more satisfactory than sliced bread or toast.

Broiled Hamburger steaks on round rolls are always popular. The meat mixture may be varied by rolling a stuffed olive in each; by adding strips of bacon crosswise after the first turning, or by a slice of Bermuda onion on both sides. Chopped pickles, carrots, celery or radishes may be added to the meat before broiling.

1. Broiled pineapple with sliced hot chicken, hot turkey or hot duck, on whole wheat bread. 2. Broiled ham with a slice of pineapple, either fresh or canned, served on white toast. 3. Sliced roast lamb with grilled fresh pineapple on toasted English muffins. 4. Sliced hard-cooked egg with hot anchovy sauce on Boston brown bread. 5. Hot roast veal with anchovy sauce and grilled tomato on rye roll. 6. Grilled tomato with Cheddar cheese on rye toast. 7. Hot smoked tongue with fried apples on toasted English muffins. 8. Hot corned beef with grilled sweet potato and endive on finger rolls.

TOAST

B READ for toast should be cut in slices from one-eighth to one-half inch thick and toasted in oven or toaster until both sides are an even, rich golden brown. Unless a toaster with an automatic timing and turning device is used, the slices should be turned two or three times to avoid warping.

CRISP DRY TOAST

Cut the crust from stale bread. Slice the bread as thin as a wafer, dry it on a pan lined with paper, in the oven, leaving the door open. When it is entirely dry, close the oven door and brown slightly.

TOAST MELBA

Cut bread in one-eighth-inch slices and toast until it is crisp.

TOAST TIMBALES—Press crustless bread slices into muffin tins. Toast in oven at 350° F.

BUTTERED TOAST

Toast bread until crisp and a rich brown on both sides. Butter while hot and serve at once.

WATER TOAST

Toast bread until crisp and brown. Pour into a soup-plate one cup boiling water and one teaspoon salt. Dip the toast into this water and remove at once. Spread lightly with butter and serve immediately.

MILK TOAST

Toast bread, butter it well, sprinkle with salt and pour scalded milk over it.

TOASTED TREASURE CHEST

Cut top from loaf of bread. Slice around sides leaving wall ¼-inch thick and bottom crust. Scoop out crumb. Toast top and chest in oven at 350° F. Fill with hot entrées, Melba toast, scrambled eggs for breakfast, or soup croutons.

CREAM TOAST

6 slices buttered toast	1 cup scalded cream
1 tablespoon flour	Salt
1 cup scalded milk	1 egg

Make a white sauce of the milk, cream, flour and salt. Pour this hot liquid over the beaten egg. Pour over the toast and serve immediately.

TOMATO CREAM TOAST—Use 2 tablespoons flour and 1 cup tomato juice instead of cream.

FRIED TOAST OR FRENCH TOAST

12 slices bread ½ inch thick	½ teaspoon salt
3 eggs	2 cups milk

Beat the eggs, add the milk and salt. Dip slices of bread into the mixture and sauté in a little hot fat until a delicate brown on both sides. Serve hot. Sprinkle with confectioners' sugar or serve maple sirup with the toast.

BUTTERSCOTCH TOAST

Spread 6 slices toast with a mixture of 3 tablespoons butter and ½ cup brown sugar. Heat under broiler to melt sugar.

ORANGE TOAST—Use 2 tablespoons orange juice, 2 tablespoons grated orange rind and ½ cup granulated sugar as the spread. Heat under broiler until sugar is melted.

CINNAMON TOAST

Spread hot toast with butter and sprinkle generously with a mixture of sugar and cinnamon. Place on the top shelf of the oven or under the broiler just long enough to melt the sugar.

TOASTED LOAF AND CORNUCOPIA

Remove all but the bottom crust from loaf of bread. Cut through center, lengthwise, then into equal sections crosswise. Brush with melted butter and brown in 375° F. oven.

CORNUCOPIA—Remove crusts from sliced bread, lay thick cheese strip diagonally, fold bread to opposite corners, fasten with toothpick, brush with melted butter and brown in moderate oven (350° F.). Remove toothpicks to serve.

TOAST YOUR WHOLE LOAF IN
THIS FASHION AND USE THE
CRUST FOR AN ENTREE TREAS-
URE CHEST
—Wheat Flour Institute

USE THE SAME SANDWICH DE-
SIGNS FOR TOAST, OR ROLL A
CORNUCOPIA WITH A CHEESE
TONGUE FOR THE FESTIVE
OCCASION
—Wheat Flour Institute

APPETIZERS

STRICT convention in England and America at one time decreed that the formal dinner should begin with soup, but that custom is no longer binding even in the most formal household. Other dishes to introduce the meal have crept in and because of their savory qualities have found ready and general acceptance. Appetizers, they are usually called. Sometimes they are referred to as relishes or as *hors d'œuvres*, because they are often a glorified edition of the old side dish now given a conspicuous place as a separate course by itself.

Characteristics of the Appetizer

The appetizer must have distinct, piquant flavor and appetite-whetting qualities. Pickled and salted foods, acids, pepper and paprika play a conspicuous part in their manufacture. Raw oysters and clams, grapefruit, melons and fruit cocktails, canapés and small sandwiches spread with pastes of sardines, anchovies and caviar, lobster and crabmeat, pâté de foie gras, cheese, olives and other mixtures of high flavor, deviled eggs, small succulent salads, may all be included without prejudice in the list of appetizers. In parts of the United States, the dinner is always begun with the salad as the appetizer.

Serving the Appetizer

The appetizer should always be served in small portions because the purpose of this course is to whet but not to satisfy the appetite.

At formal dinners and luncheons, the same kind of appetizer is generally served to all the guests, but at more informal meals the hostess may give her guests an opportunity to choose their own appetizers. In that case a number of portions of various kinds are arranged on a regulation *hors d'oeuvre* tray or on a chop plate or small platter which is passed to each guest.

Each portion must be arranged so that it may be lifted from the tray by the guest and transferred to his plate without trouble. Suitable service silver—usually a tablespoon and large fork—must be laid on each tray.

The following combination will serve as a suggestion for the arrangement of an appetizer tray:

1. A crab salad
2. An onion and green pepper salad
3. Olives in lettuce cup
4. Watercress, brown bread and butter sandwiches
5. Aspic jelly with anchovies or sardines included
6. Deviled eggs in watercress nests
7. Cream cheese balls rolled in minced chipped beef or caviar
8. Large olives filled with cheese, wrapped in bacon; broiled
9. Celery stalks stuffed with cheese or anchovy paste
10. Small sweet pickles, rolled in cheese, then in smoked salmon and fastened with a toothpick
11. Rolled anchovies, caviar or tiny meat balls in broiled mushrooms
12. Chicken liver balls rolled in minced chipped beef

Shellfish

See pages 208, 210, 214, 223, 224 for shellfish used as appetizers.

Canapés

BREAD FOR CANAPÉS

Canapés are made from day-old white bread, cut into quarter-inch slices and then shaped with a cutter into circles two and one-half or three inches in diameter or cut into squares, strips, triangles or other fancy shapes. These portions of bread may then be fried in hot deep fat and drained on absorbent paper, or sautéed in just enough hot fat to keep them from burning, or toasted or set in the oven until they turn a delicate brown. When finished they should be nicely browned on both sides. They are then ready to be covered with the mixture preferred.

ANCHOVY CANAPÉS

6 portions prepared bread	2 hard-cooked eggs
3 tablespoons anchovy paste	Whole anchovies for garnish
3 teaspoons lemon juice	(may be omitted)

Anchovy paste, which comes in tubes, jars or bottles, may be utilized, or whole anchovies may be reduced to a smooth paste with a wooden spoon. Season with lemon-juice and spread the paste on the prepared pieces of bread. Split anchovy lengthwise and lay the halves diagonally across the canapé, marking the point where they cross by a little pyramid of riced yolk of hard-cooked eggs. Petal-shaped pieces of the hard-cooked white may radiate from this center pyramid. A large anchovy curved around a circle of hard-cooked egg in the center of a canapé is also effective. The anchovies may be omitted from the garnish.

SARDINE OR LOBSTER OR OTHER SEA FOOD CANAPÉS

6 portions prepared bread	Salt
6 large sardines or	Worcestershire sauce
6 tablespoons lobster or other sea food, chopped fine	Pickled beets
	6 large olives
Juice of 1 lemon	24 thin slices lemon

Remove skin and backbone and flake the sardines with a fork. Or chop cooked lobster meat very fine. Season with lemon-juice, salt and a few drops of Worcestershire sauce. Spread the prepared bread with the mixture and decorate by placing in the center of each canapé a small circle of pickled beet. Cut a slice from the end of a large olive so that it will stand firmly and place this in the center of the beet. A narrow border of minced beet may be placed around the edge of the canapé with good effect. Garnish the plate with four thin slices of lemon placed symmetrically.

Crab meat, shrimps or any smoked or canned fish, highly seasoned and attractively garnished, may be utilized for canapés instead of the sardines or lobster meat.

CAVIAR CANAPÉS

6 portions prepared bread	3 tablespoons white onion
3 tablespoons caviar	chopped fine
Garnish of green pepper or hard-cooked egg	

Caviar, which is the salted roe of the sturgeon, is highly esteemed by epicures as an appetizer. It is usually served with minced raw onion and decorated with hard-cooked egg and minced pickles. A favorite arrangement is to have an oblong canapé two by four inches, one half covered with the minced

raw onion and the other half with the caviar. The striking difference in the colors is very effective. A sliver of green pepper may lie just where the two mixtures meet and little points of the green pepper extend out on each side, or a circle of the white of hard-cooked egg may decorate the center of the half covered with caviar and a little mound of the riced yolk ornament the section covered by the chopped onion.

CHEESE AND OLIVE CANAPÉS

6 portions prepared bread
3 tablespoons cream cheese
Olives stuffed with pimientos

Garnish of red pepper or pickled beet

Spread on the prepared bread a paste made by mixing equal proportions of cream cheese and chopped stuffed olives. Garnish with a quarter-inch border of the chopped olives and a star of red pepper or pickled beet in the center of each canapé.

PÂTÉ DE FOIE GRAS CANAPÉS

6 portions prepared bread
3 tablespoons pâté de foie gras paste or pâté de foie gras de poulet

¼ cup cream
Cayenne pepper
Salt
Parsley

Add the cream and seasoning to the paste. Rub through a fine sieve and spread on portions of fried bread. Garnish with parsley.

PÂTÉ DE FOIE GRAS DE POULET

½ cup chicken livers
2 tablespoons chicken fat or butter

¼ onion, chopped
Salt and pepper
Mustard or celery salt

Carefully clean, cook and chop chicken livers and mash them to a paste with a wooden spoon. Chop the onion fine and fry in the fat until yellow. Place the livers, the fat and the onion in a cup, mix well and season with pepper and salt, and either mustard or celery salt, according to taste. Place at once on ice. This preparation makes excellent sandwiches.

Suggestions for Mixtures to Be Used in Making Canapés

1. Anchovy paste mixed with lemon-juice.
2. Shredded tuna fish mixed with lemon-juice and mayonnaise.
3. Chopped lobster meat mixed with cream and seasoned with salt, pepper and lemon-juice.
4. Cream cheese and chopped stuffed olives.
5. Minced red and green peppers mixed with mayonnaise and seasoned with salt, pepper and lemon-juice.
6. Sardine paste mixed with lemon-juice, salt and Worcestershire sauce.
7. A layer of anchovy paste covered with a paste of shredded crab meat, cream cheese and butter, seasoned with salt and pepper.
8. Devilled ham mixed with chopped hard-cooked egg and horseradish.

Fruit Appetizers

Fruit cocktails may be made from mixtures of almost any fruits, canned or fresh. As a rule, combinations of a sweet and a sour fruit are most piquant in flavor. All fruit appetizers should be thoroughly chilled. The trays of the mechanical refrigerator are excellent for this purpose.

GRAPEFRUIT COCKTAILS

No. 1—Grapefruit on the Half Shell.

Cut grapefruit in half, crosswise. With a pair of sharp shears or with a grapefruit corer, cut a circular piece from the center of each half, being careful not to cut through the skin. Then with a sharp knife loosen each section from the membrane and skin. Sprinkle with sugar and set in the refrigerator to chill. Pink the edges of the skin if you prefer, and remove the pieces of membrane between the sections of fruit if you have time. In this way the shell is left with only edible portions of the fruit. In any case each mouthful of fruit should be entirely detached from the shell. Serve a half grapefruit on a plate or in a special grapefruit glass, embedded in ice.

No. 2—Grapefruit and Orange Cocktail.

    1 cup diced grapefruit pulp   Sugar
    1 cup diced orange pulp   Lemon-juice or grape-juice
       Maraschino cherries or preserved pineapple

Mix the orange and grapefruit pulp. Sprinkle with sugar and a little lemon-juice or grape-juice. Chill, and have glasses chilled so that the whole, when served, may be very cold. At the last moment fill the glasses with the fruit mixture, garnishing with cherries or preserved pineapple.

No. 3—Grapefruit and Strawberry Cocktail.

    3 grapefruit   1 pint strawberries
    Sugar

Cut the grapefruit in half and carefully remove the pulp, leaving the inner white skin as lining. Place the shells in cold water to keep them firm. Mix the grapefruit pulp with the strawberries and sprinkle with sugar. Chill. At serving time, fill the shells with the mixture placing large handsome berries on top as garnish. The mixed fruit left over may be served at breakfast or used as a sauce for pudding or ice-cream.

STRAWBERRY AND PINEAPPLE COCKTAIL

    1 cup orange-juice   Sugar
    1/3 cup lemon-juice   1 cup strawberries
    1 cup diced pineapple

Combine the orange- and lemon-juice sweetened to taste, keeping the mixture rather tart. Chill. Wash and drain the strawberries and hull them. At serving time cut the berries in half (except six large ones), mix with the pineapple, place in glasses and cover with the fruit-juice. One large, perfect berry set on a tiny circle of pineapple may decorate the top of each cocktail.

ORANGE MINT COCKTAIL

    6 small, rather sour oranges   3 tablespoons lemon-juice or
    Powdered sugar   3 tablespoons pineapple-juice
    Fresh mint   2 tablespoons sugar

Separate the orange into sections and remove the thin skin with a pair of scissors. Chill thoroughly, place in glasses, sprinkle with powdered sugar and add the lemon-juice mixed with pineapple-juice or sugar. Sprinkle with chopped mint and garnish with an upright sprig of mint in the center of the glass.

WATERMELON COCKTAIL

2 cups watermelon balls	Powdered sugar
Fresh mint	2 tablespoons lemon-juice

(Lemon-juice and sugar may be omitted)

With a vegetable-cutter prepare small balls of bright pink watermelon. Sprinkle lightly with sugar and add lemon-juice. Chill thoroughly. Fill glasses. Garnish with sprigs of fresh mint. A pretty fancy is to moisten the edge of each cocktail glass and invert in chopped mint before filling. This will leave a line of green adhering to the edge of the glass. The glass may be lined with sprigs of mint before the watermelon is put in.

CHERRY COCKTAIL

1 pound cherries	6 tablespoons strawberry-juice
½ cup chopped almonds	6 tablespoons powdered sugar
3 teaspoons lemon-juice	

Pit the cherries, sprinkle with chopped almonds and pour over them a sirup made by mixing strawberry-juice with powdered sugar and lemon-juice. Chill and serve ice-cold in cocktail glasses. Decorate the plate with two or three whole cherries and a leaf or two.

MIXED FRUIT COCKTAIL

6 large oranges	Juice of 1 lemon
1 banana	Sugar
2 slices pineapple	

Slice off the tops of the oranges and scoop out the inside, being careful not to break the inside white skin of the orange-peel. Put the orange cups into a bowl of ice-water. Cut in small pieces the banana and pineapple, mix these with the orange pulp cut in small pieces, add the lemon-juice, sweeten to taste, and fill the orange shells. Set each one in a small bowl, filled with crushed ice.

The mixed fruit pulp that remains after the orange skins have been filled may be kept in the refrigerator and served as sauce with ice-cream or used in any other way that circumstances suggest.

VARIETY IS NOT ONLY THE SPICE BUT THE VERY LIFE OF A TRAY OF CANAPES, HORS D'ŒUVRES OR APPETIZERS

FOR THE HOSTESS WHO WOULD DEVELOP A SPECIALITE DE LA MAISON THERE ARE BACON-OLIVE-CHEESE, CREAM CHEESE COATED IN CHIPPED BEEF, OR THE INDIVIDUAL CHECKERBOARD LOAF

—Wheat Flour Institute

SOUPS

~~~

SOUPS may be roughly divided into two groups. In the first group belong the soups that are always made from meat stock. These are the various modifications of brown and white stocks, bouillons, consommés and broths. In the second group belong the soups that may be made either with or without meat stock. These are the various modifications of cream soups, purées and bisques, of chowders and stews and of vegetable soups.

The Value of Soup in the Dietary

The purpose of soup in the meal is two-fold; first, to improve digestion and stimulate appetite by introducing at the beginning of the meal a highly flavored liquid food which increases the flow of digestive juices; second, to increase the variety of nutrients in the meal, or even to furnish the main dish of the meal. Stock soups are chiefly valuable for the first purpose. Cream soups, purées, bisques, chowders and stews are more valuable for the second purpose.

A heavy meal should begin with an unthickened stock soup; a light meal may well begin with one of the cream variety.

Home Made and Ready to Use Soups

Not so long ago, all soups were made at home, and the stock pot was kept on the stove day in and day out; but with the gradual change from coal to gas and electricity as fuels, and with the perfecting of modern commercial canning and condensing methods, the long slow process of stock making has become less common in home kitchens.

However, in soup many valuable food materials that would otherwise be thrown out may be saved for the nourishment of the family, and some knowledge of the principles of soup making is worth while for every housekeeper. A home made soup which is lacking in strength or flavor may be easily improved by the addition of a can of soup or some of the various meat extracts obtainable.

For the small family, the canned soups are almost indispensable, and in the making of sauces and gravies, where only a small amount of stock is required, a can of soup supplies the required foundation at a minimum of trouble and expense.

Making Soup Stock

CUT MEAT IN SMALL PIECES and saw or crack bone. This is done to increase the surface exposed to the action of hot water.

BROWN FROM ONE-FOURTH TO ONE-HALF THE MEAT for brown stocks and consommés. This gives added color and improves flavor.

SOAK THE MEAT AND BONE IN COLD WATER for thirty minutes or more before cooking. This helps to extract the juices of the meat.

HEAT GRADUALLY TO THE SIMMERING-POINT (190°-210° F.). If stock is to be used for bouillon or consommé or any clear soup, skim at this time. Continue to simmer for three or four hours to insure as complete extraction as possible of the juices and flavor of meat. If the mixture boils, it is not so fine in flavor.

ADD THE SPICES, HERBS, AND VEGETABLES, and continue simmering from one-half hour to one hour. The seasonings are added at this time rather than earlier to prevent the disagreeable flavor of over-cooked vegetables.

STRAIN THE SOUP INTO A LARGE BOWL or other container. If the stock is to be used for clear soups, place several thicknesses of cheese-cloth over the strainer before pouring the mixture through it.

COOL THE STOCK QUICKLY, because quick cooling improves the keeping quality of the soup. Soup should, if possible, always be allowed to become thoroughly cold before being used, since the fat hardens and collects in a cake on top and can be removed easily. Do not remove fat from the top of soup stock until the stock is to be used. It protects the stock against spoilage.

KEEP STOCK IN A COLD PLACE, as it spoils quickly if it is not kept chilled. Spoiled stock, like spoiled meat, is dangerous food.

Using Soup Stock

When ready to use stock, loosen fat around the edges with the thin blade of a knife. Remove the cake of fat. If the stock is jellied, wipe off the remaining small pieces of fat and the edge of the bowl with a cloth wrung out of hot water. If the stock is very soft or liquid, pass small sheets of absorbent paper over the top of the stock.

WHEN STOCK MUST BE USED BEFORE COOLING, skim off all the fat possible. Most of the remainder of the fat may be removed in one of two ways. The first way is to pass over the top small sheets of absorbent paper or blotting paper. The second way is to cool the soup as much as possible beforehand, then to wrap a piece of ice in a cloth and let it down into the stock. Move the ice around just below the surface so that the fat on the surface is suddenly chilled, and it will gather on the cloth around the ice. This must be done quickly to prevent unnecessary dilution of the stock.

FOR CLEAR SOUPS, take the stock from the top of the bowl, being careful to avoid any sediment which may have escaped through the sieve and settled to the bottom of the bowl. This sediment is valuable as a food and should be reserved for gravies or soups which are not necessarily clear. Clarify this stock if a translucent, sparkling soup is desired.

TO CLARIFY SOUP—Allow 1 egg white and shell to 1 quart of stock. Wash egg well. Separate yolk and white. Crush the shell into small pieces and mix with the slightly beaten egg white. Heat the stock just enough to liquefy it if it is jellied. Stir the egg white and shell thoroughly into the stock. Heat slowly to boiling, stirring constantly, then boil without stirring 2 to 5 minutes. Remove from heat. Add ½ cup of cold water and let settle. Strain through 2 thicknesses of cheesecloth. The coagulated egg gathers around itself the particles of solid substance in the soup which otherwise would be fine enough to pass through a strainer.

Serving Soup

Serve clear soups in bouillon cups for lunch or supper and in shallow-rimmed soup plates for the formal dinner. Cream soups are served in soup plates or cream soup cups at luncheon or supper. Soups should always be served very hot.

INGREDIENTS NEEDED TO MAKE ONE QUART OF STANDARD STOCK

BROWN STOCK OR BOUILLON.

2 pounds beef (¼ to ½ bone)
1¼ quarts cold water
4 to 6 peppercorns
2 cloves
1 bay-leaf
1 blade mace
1 teaspoon sweet herbs
Sprig parsley
1 tablespoon, each, of carrot, onion, celery, turnip
1 teaspoon salt

A good stock can be made by using left-over meat scraps and bones instead of the beef specified, and by substituting any available vegetables, such as the outer leaves of lettuce, celery tops, etc., for those given above. After the stock is made, left-over vegetables, cereals, hard-cooked eggs, small pieces of meat, etc., may be diced or chopped and served in the soup.

CONSOMMÉ.

1 pound lean beef
1 pound veal
1¼ quarts cold water or
 1 pint cold water and
 1 pint chicken stock
2 peppercorns
1 clove
½ teaspoon sweet herbs
Sprig parsley
1 tablespoon each, celery, carrot, onion
1 teaspoon salt

MUTTON OR LAMB STOCK OR BROTH—Use the same ingredients as for brown stock or bouillon, using mutton or lamb instead of beef, and removing most of the fat from the meat.

WHITE STOCK.

2 pounds chicken or knuckle of veal
1¼ quarts cold water
2 peppercorns
1 clove
½ teaspoon sweet herbs
1 tablespoon, each, of onion and celery
1 teaspoon salt

The liquid in which a fowl or chicken is cooked is also a white stock or chicken broth.

FISH STOCK OR COURT BOUILLON.

2 pounds white fish or
   2 pounds head and trimmings
1¼ quarts cold water
2 peppercorns

1 clove
Sprig parsley
1 bay-leaf
1 tablespoon, each, carrot,
   celery, onion

Fish stock needs to be cooked for only half the time required for other stock.

VARIATIONS OF BROWN OR WHITE SOUP STOCK

VEGETABLE SOUP—If a clear soup is desired, follow the directions for clarifying soup stock, and then add, to each quart of brown stock, one cup of diced vegetables, raw or cooked. If the vegetables are cooked, the soup needs to be boiled for only a few minutes. When raw vegetables are added, simmer until the vegetables are all tender, adding boiling water, if necessary, to replace any that may have evaporated. Season to taste and serve.

SAGO, RICE OR BARLEY SOUP—For each quart of brown or white stock, use two tablespoons sago, rice or barley. Soak sago or rice one-half hour in enough stock or water to cover it. Barley should be soaked over night. Bring remainder of stock to simmering-point. Add soaked sago, barley, or rice and simmer in closed saucepan one-half hour.

MACARONI, VERMICELLI, SPAGHETTI, OR NOODLE SOUP—For each quart brown stock, use ¼ cup macaroni, spaghetti, vermicelli or noodles broken into small pieces. Simmer the pastes in the stock until tender, adding water if necessary.

VARIATIONS OF CONSOMMÉ

CONSOMMÉ PRINCESSE—Consommé served with shreds or small dice of cooked chicken and green peas.

CONSOMMÉ A LÁ ROYALE—Consommé served with tiny blocks of royal custard.

CONSOMMÉ JULIENNE OR JULIENNE SOUP—Consommé served with carrot, onions, turnips and celery cut into shreds about as thick as a match.

The vegetables should be boiled in clear water before being added to the consommé.

Unthickened Soups

Soups suitable for serving as the first course of a meal with a substantial main course are found in this group. Any of the variations of soup stock or consommé may be used for this purpose. The following recipes give directions for other soups of this variety.

CHICKEN OR TURKEY BONE SOUP

Never discard the bones of turkey or chicken as they always will make a delicious soup. Scrape the meat from the bones, break the bones, pack in a kettle, and cover with cold water, adding a small onion. Cover closely and simmer very gently for three hours. Strain and cool. One-half hour before it is to be served, return to the fire and for every quart of stock add one cup of the cold meat, season and keep hot till needed. This soup may be greatly improved by adding to it, three minutes before serving, ten oysters to each quart of soup.

CLAM BROTH

12 clams in the shell   2 cups water   Paprika

Purchase large clams in the shells. Scrub them thoroughly with a brush, place them in a kettle with cold water, closely covered, and bring water to the boiling-point. As soon as the shells have opened, remove them from the broth. The clams may be served at once, in the half-shell, or taken from the shells and kept to be served in any form desired. Let the broth settle, strain, being careful not to pour out the sandy sediment, reheat, add a little red pepper or paprika, and serve hot. Twelve good-sized clams should make enough broth for six persons, but if there does not seem to be sufficient, add a little boiling water or milk. Clam broth seldom needs added salt. Water wafers heated in the oven, or divided crackers toasted on their broken surfaces, buttered and heated for a few minutes in the oven, are generally served with this broth.

Clam broth may be served, hot or cold, in cups with a heaping teaspoon of whipped cream, into which has been beaten a little salt and pepper, placed upon the top of each cup. The cream adds richness to the flavor of the soup and increases its nourishing properties.

MODERN MILK PRODUCTS ADD
GREATLY TO THE SUCCESS OF
MAKING CREAMY THICK SOUPS
—Irradiated Evaporated Milk
Institute

SOUPS, HOT AND THICK, OR
JELLIED CONSOMME ARE
DOUBLY DELICIOUS WHEN
BEAUTIFULLY SERVED

CLEAR TOMATO SOUP

1 quart brown soup stock
1 can tomatoes
½ teaspoon peppercorns
1 small bay-leaf
3 cloves
3 sprigs thyme

4 tablespoons butter
2 sprigs parsley
¼ cup each, onion, carrot, celery, raw ham, cut in dice
Salt   Pepper

Cook onion, carrot, celery, and ham in butter five minutes. Add tomatoes, peppercorns, bay-leaf, cloves, thyme and parsley, cover and cook slowly one hour. Strain carefully, add hot stock, and season with salt and pepper.

This recipe may be used for jellied soup or for salad.

JELLIED SOUP

1 quart clear brown, or white stock, or tomato or chicken soup

2 tablespoons gelatin
½ cup cold water

Soften the gelatin in the cold water, add to the boiling hot soup, chill and serve in cups. The trays of the mechanical refrigerator are excellent for chilling soups.

Substantial Vegetable and Stock Soups

Soups in this group are suitable for serving as the first course of an otherwise light dinner or as the main course of an informal luncheon.

BEAN SOUP

3 slices bacon
2 cups baked or boiled beans
4 cups cold water

1 tablespoon flour
1 tablespoon butter
Salt, pepper, paprika

Cook bacon. Add to beans. Add cold water and cook until beans are soft, then rub through a strainer. Place on the fire and add a little more water, if needed, as the soup must not be too thick. Bind with the flour and butter. Cook two or three minutes. Season with salt, a dash of pepper, and paprika.

BLACK BEAN SOUP

1 cup black beans	2 tablespoons butter
1½ quarts water	2 tablespoons flour
1 onion	2 hard-cooked eggs
1 tablespoon fat for sautéin	½ teaspoon mustard
2 stalks celery	Pepper, salt, paprika
1 lemon	

Soak the beans over night. Next morning, drain them and cover with the cold water. Add sliced onion, which has been browned in the fat, also stalks of celery broken into inch pieces. Simmer until beans are soft, adding more water from time to time. Press through a sieve, again bring to the boiling-point, and then add seasoning of mustard, pepper, salt, and paprika to taste. Bind with roux of butter and flour to prevent the soup from separating. Cut the eggs and lemon in thin slices, and add these to the strained soup just before serving.

BORSCHT

(A Famous Russian Soup)

1 bunch beets	½ pound breast of beef
1 cup tomatoes, fresh or canned	1 tablespoon lemon-juice
4 cups water	¼ cup sugar
1 small onion	¼ teaspoon salt
	4 eggs

Pare the beets and cut them into long strips. Strain the tomatoes, over the beets, not letting any seeds through. Add water. Put in the onion and meat, cut into small pieces, and simmer for thirty minutes. Add lemon-juice, sugar, and salt. Boil one-half hour more. Beat the eggs with a pinch of salt. Add the hot borscht to this, a little at a time, stirring well to prevent the separating of the eggs. Serve at once, while very hot.

BARLEY SOUP

½ cup barley	½ cup diced celery
1 teaspoon salt	½ cup diced onions
1 quart boiling water	½ cup diced carrots
2 quarts soup stock	1 green pepper, diced

Wash barley in cold water and cook in boiling salted water until tender, about 2 hours, adding stock when water has evaporated. Add vegetables ½ hour before soup is done. For 6.

BOUILLABAISSE

2 large onions, chopped
2 cloves garlic, chopped
2 tablespoons flour
2 tablespoons butter
2 cups tomato pulp
2 cups water
8 cloves
3 bay leaves

1½ teaspoons curry powder
½ cup sherry
Dash of Tabasco sauce
1 teaspoon salt
4 pounds fish fillets
1½ quarts boiling water
½ pound mushrooms, sliced
Hot buttered toast

Use red snapper and redfish in equal amounts. Sauté onions, garlic and flour in butter. Add tomato, 2 cups water, 4 cloves, bay leaves, curry powder, ¼ cup sherry and Tabasco; simmer 30 minutes; add salt. Add fish and remaining cloves and sherry to boiling water; simmer 15 minutes. Add mushrooms and sauce and simmer 5 minutes. Place toast on large platter, add fish and pour sauce over fish. Serves 12 to 15.

CHICKEN GUMBO

This recipe, if followed as given, will provide the main dish for dinner. Chicken gumbo may be made by using leftovers, or the remainder after making chicken salad or boned chicken.

1 fowl (3 to 4 pounds)
½ cup salt pork fat
1 onion
1 quart okra, fresh or canned
5 tomatoes
1 cup cream

2 sprigs parsley
3 cups boiling water
½ teaspoon pepper
2 tablespoons salt
1 cup boiled rice

This is a noted Southern soup. Cut the chicken into convenient pieces and sauté until brown in salt pork fat, then place all the pieces in a saucepan. Cut a large onion into thin slices and sauté slowly for ten minutes in the fat. Add okra, cut fine, sliced tomatoes, and parsley sprigs. Sauté all of these ingredients one-half hour, quite slowly, and place them in the saucepan with the chicken. Add boiling water, pepper and salt. Simmer slowly two to four hours, or until the chicken is very tender, and then add boiled rice and cream. If more seasoning is needed, add it, and if necessary, thin with boiling water. Boil up once and serve. Cayenne pepper (one-fourth teaspoon) may be used instead of white or black pepper, if desired. Separate the bones from the chicken. Serve with pieces of chicken in the plate with the soup

CHICKEN SOUP

This recipe provides a large bowl of substantial soup, as well as a cooked fowl, and when the soup is served the rest of the dinner should consist of light dishes. For more economical recipes see Index for chicken or turkey bone soup, and chicken broth for invalids.

1 fowl (3 to 4 pounds)
½ pound ham
1 onion
2 to 3 quarts water
¼ cup rice

1 cup milk
1 tablespoon chopped parsley
Salt and pepper
1 tablespoon flour
1 tablespoon chicken fat

Cut up fowl into quarters, with the ham and onion, and add the water. Let this simmer until the meat is very tender, then strain, reserving the meat to be used in any way desired. Remove all possible fat, and to one and one-fourth quarts of this soup (the remainder can be used for sauce with the meat) add well washed rice, chopped parsley, salt and pepper. Simmer until the rice is tender, add milk, then add roux made of flour and chicken fat. Cook until the mixture is thickened (about five minutes), season and serve.

GREEN PEA SOUP

2 cups stock
1 quart water
1 quart green peas
1 celery stalk
1 onion
1 turnip

2 sprigs mint
1 tablespoon flour
1 tablespoon butter
Salt and pepper
Sugar

Reserve one-half cup of peas, and to the stock and water add the rest of the peas, the celery stalk, onion and turnip cut into pieces, and the mint. Stew until the mass is tender. Strain through a sieve or coarse cheese-cloth. Thin with stock or water, if necessary; bind with a roux of flour and fat and season with salt, pepper, and a little sugar. Add the half cup of whole peas, stew for a few minutes, and serve.

SPLIT PEA SOUP

This recipe provides the main part of a dinner, since the ham end will serve as the meat dish. A ham bone, left over from a boiled or baked ham, will flavor pea soup quite as well as a piece bought especially for the purpose.

2 or 3 pounds ham end	3 quarts boiling water
1 carrot	1 cup split peas
1 onion	Salt and pepper
2 potatoes	2 tablespoons catchup

Put the end of a moderately lean smoked ham into a kettle with carrot and peeled onion, whole potatoes, and boiling water. Boil one hour and strain. Now rinse the ham thoroughly in hot water and return to the strained stock, together with split peas which have been soaking all night, and boil for one hour. Season with salt and white pepper and add catchup. Serve at once. Thin with boiling water if too thick.

ONION SOUP GRATINÉE

4 onions	1 quart chicken stock
½ cup butter, melted	Salt
2 tablespoons flour	8 slices French bread
½ cup Parmesan cheese	

Slice onions very thin, add to melted butter and cook slowly until tender but not brown. Add flour and blend well; then add hot chicken stock slowly, stirring constantly. Season. Toast bread, spread with melted butter, sprinkle with Parmesan cheese and heat under broiler until cheese is slightly melted. Place slice on each serving of soup. Serve extra cheese in separate bowl. Serves 8.

ONION STEW OR DUTCH BROTH

6 onions	3 tablespoons flour
5 tablespoons butter	2 cups scalded milk
3 cups cold water	Salt and cayenne
1 egg-yolk	

Chop the onions and cook them in two tablespoons of the butter for five minutes, then add water and cook thirty minutes. Press through a sieve. Make a roux of the remaining butter and the flour, combine it with the scalded milk and add seasoning. Cook five minutes, stirring constantly. Add this milk mixture to the onion mixture. Mix thoroughly and add the egg-yolk, slightly beaten. Serve individually in Dutch bowls and place one teaspoon of grated Edam cheese on the top. Set for a few minutes in a hot oven to melt the cheese.

Thick Soups, Chowders and Stews

Cream Soups

Cream soups are made by combining a very thin white sauce, see page 308, with a suitable quantity of cooked, mashed, strained vegetable, fish or meat pulp. Irradiated evaporated milk used instead of white sauce will greatly increase the food value and when used for making white sauce will increase the flavor. Flavor is improved, too, by the use of some highly flavored vegetables or the addition of a proportion of soup stock.

Purées

Purées are made in the same way as cream soups, but are somewhat thicker. They are often served under the name of "Cream Soup."

Bisques

The name bisque is usually given to a cream soup made from fish, and the fish is often diced or mashed through a coarse strainer. A familiar example of an exception in the use of the word is mock bisque soup, or tomato bisque, as it is often called.

Chowders

Chowders were probably the common ancestors of the more refined cream soups, purées, and bisques. The word chowder comes from the French *chaudière*, meaning caldron. The chowder originated as a community fish stew to which each neighbor contributed something; milk, fish, potatoes, crackers, pork or some seasoning. These contributions were all cooked together in the common caldron, from which chowder derives its name, and each contributor withdrew his share of soup when it was ready.

The chowder of today is much the same as the old chowder, and consists of pieces of different vegetables or of fish and potatoes and various seasonings cooked in milk with crackers added just before serving.

Fish Stews

Fish stews are made of milk and the juice of the fish which gives flavor to the soup. They differ from the cream soups in that they need not be thickened, though they often are, and from the chowders in being less complex in composition.

Binding Thick Soups

When a vegetable, meat or fish pulp is combined with milk or stock in making soups, they separate and the solid substance sinks to the bottom of the liquid. Some flour or corn-starch cooked into the mixture will overcome this. With many of these soups the reason for using the flour or corn-starch may not necessarily be to thicken a soup which the vegetable, meat or fish pulp has already made thick enough, but to blend the liquid with the solid so that all parts of the soup will have the same consistency.

Flour or corn-starch may be mixed with enough cold liquid —milk, water, or stock—to make a creamy thickness and added carefully to the soup; or it may be combined with the soup by means of a roux (see Index). When a colored roux is desired the fat is browned before the flour is added and the mixture is cooked to a reddish brown color. When a roux is made in this way, the liquid is usually added to it gradually.

Preventing Skin on Cream Soups

A cream or milk soup has a tendency to form a skin on the top as it cools. If it is beaten just before it is served, the froth protects it against skin formation.

A spoonful of whipped cream or beaten egg-white served on top of each portion of cream soup aids in preventing the skin formation and adds to the delicacy and attractiveness of the dish.

DIRECTIONS FOR MAKING A STANDARD CREAM SOUP

4 cups milk or part milk and part stock	2 cups vegetable pulp or meat or fish pulp
2 tablespoons flour	Salt, pepper, other seasonings
2 tablespoons fat	

1. Make a white sauce of the liquid, flour, and fat.
2. Cook the vegetables or meat or fish until tender, drain, and mash through a sieve.

3. Combine the vegetable, meat, or fish pulp with the white sauce.

4. Season, beat with an egg-beater, and serve. A tiny portion of whipped cream or beaten egg-white may be served on top of each portion.

The amount of flour may be increased for purées and bisques.

VARIATIONS OF CREAM SOUP

CREAM OF ASPARAGUS OR CREAM OF CELERY SOUP—Follow directions for making a standard cream soup.

CREAM OF CORN SOUP

5 cups corn, canned or fresh	2 tablespoons butter
5 cups milk or part milk and part white stock	Salt and pepper
2 tablespoons flour	2 egg-yolks

Put the corn into a double boiler with one quart of the milk and cook for twenty minutes. Make a white sauce of the milk and corn, flour, and fat, add salt and pepper and cook five minutes. Rub the soup through a strainer, beat the yolks of the eggs well, and add to them the remaining cup of cold milk; stir this mixture into the soup, cook for a minute or two, stirring constantly. Beat and serve at once.

CREAM OF MUSHROOM SOUP

¼ pound mushrooms (or skin and stems of ½ pound)	2 tablespoons flour
2 tablespoons butter	1 teaspoon salt
	1 pint milk

Brush, wash and skin the mushrooms. Put the skins to simmer in a little water. Cut the mushroom caps and stems into very small pieces; add one pint of water and simmer until tender. Make a sauce of the fat, flour, salt and milk and add the water in which the mushroom caps, stems and skin were cooked.

CREAM OF ONION AND POTATO SOUP

3 cups scalded milk	4 medium potatoes
1 cup potato water	4 onions
2 tablespoons flour	1 tablespoon chopped parsley
2 tablespoons butter	Salt and pepper

Boil the potatoes and onions together, until tender. Drain. Save the water and rub the vegetables through a coarse strainer.

Make a white sauce of the liquid, flour, and fat and combine with the potato and onion pulp. Season with chopped parsley, salt and pepper. Beat with an egg-beater and serve with croutons.

CREAM OF PEA SOUP—Follow directions for making a standard cream soup, but keep one cup of the cooked peas whole and add them to the soup just before serving.

CREAM OF SPINACH SOUP—Follow directions for making a standard cream soup.

CREAM OF TOMATO SOUP

1 quart milk or half milk and half white stock	1 pint tomatoes
2 tablespoons flour	Salt and pepper
2 tablespoons butter	¼ teaspoon soda

Make a white sauce of the liquid, flour, and butter. Cook the tomatoes until tender, and mash through a coarse sieve. Just before serving, add the soda to the tomatoes and gradually add the tomatoes to the white sauce, stirring constantly. Season and serve at once. If soup begins to curdle, beat thoroughly with egg-beater.

Purées

PURÉE OF ONION

3 large or 6 small onions	2 or 3 tablespoons butter or other fat
2 cups white stock	Salt and pepper
2 cups milk	1 tablespoon chopped parsley
2 or 3 tablespoons flour	

Make a white sauce with stock, milk, flour, and butter. Cook onions in water until very tender. Drain, and rub through a sieve. Combine onion and sauce. Season with salt, pepper, and chopped parsley. Beat with egg-beater and serve.

Use three tablespoons flour when increased thickness is desired.

FISH PURÉE

1 quart milk	4 tablespoons butter or other fat
1 small onion, minced	2 cups cooked fish
4 tablespoons flour	Salt and pepper

Scald the minced onion in milk. Make a white sauce of the

milk, flour, and butter. Rub the cooked fish through a sieve.
Combine the fish and sauce. Season and serve.

PURÉE OF PEAS AND TOMATOES

½ pound dried yellow split
   peas
1 pint tomatoes
1 quart water
1 onion

1 or 2 celery tops
Salt and pepper
1 tablespoon flour
1 tablespoon butter

Soak peas over night in water enough to cover them three or
four inches. Drain, and put into a saucepan with the tomatoes,
water, sliced onion, and celery tops. Cook until the peas are
tender. Mash through a sieve. Season with salt and pepper.
Bind with a roux made of the flour and butter, and serve,
garnished with a thin slice of tomato or lemon and a few
canned peas if available. Serve with bread croutons.

SPLIT PEA OR LIMA BEAN PURÉE

1 cup split peas or dried lima
   beans
2 quarts water
1 tablespoon flour
1 teaspoon onion-juice

2 tablespoons butter or
   other fat
Salt and pepper
Celery salt

Soak peas or beans all night, then put them over the fire with
water and bring to a boil. Cook slowly, until soft. Rub
through a sieve, heat, and thicken with roux of flour and
fat. Season with salt, pepper, celery salt, and onion-juice.
Stir or beat until smooth and serve with croutons.

Cold Fruit Purées

In hot weather, cold fruit purées are sometimes preferred to
hot soups. They are always served in cups, usually of glass,
and with a few pieces of the fruit floating on the surface. They
should be thoroughly chilled. The trays of the mechanical
refrigerator are excellent for this purpose. These fruit purées
are really as closely related to the appetizers as to the soups.

CHERRY PURÉE

Juice from 1 quart of tart
   cherries, freshly stewed or
   canned

2 teaspoons arrowroot
Grated rind of 1 lemon

Heat the juice from the cherries. Add arrowroot moistened with cold water, stirring the mixture rapidly to prevent the forming of lumps. Flavor with the grated lemon-rind. Serve very cold, with a whole cherry floating on each portion.

ORANGE PURÉE

2 cups orange-juice
1 teaspoon corn-starch
2 tablespoons cold water

½ cup sugar
1 teaspoon grated orange-
   rind

Place orange-juice in saucepan and when it is thoroughly heated add the corn-starch mixed with the cold water. Cook slowly until clear. Add sugar and grated orange-rind. Serve ice-cold in glass sherbet cups.

RASPBERRY PURÉE

½ cup granulated tapioca
6 cups water
½ cup currant-juice

2 cups raspberries
Sugar

Boil tapioca in water and currant-juice. When tapioca is transparent, add raspberries and sugar to taste. Set aside to cool. Serve ice-cold in sherbet-glasses.

Bisques

BISQUE OF CLAMS

24 clams in the shell
2 cups rich milk or white
   stock or part of each
1 tablespoon butter
1 tablespoon flour

2 cups water
1 tablespoon chopped celery
1 teaspoon chopped parsley
Salt and pepper

Make a white sauce of the milk, flour, and butter. Scrub the clams thoroughly, then pack into pot with a tight-fitting lid, using ½ cup water to steam. When all have popped open, remove, cool in their own liquor. Detach clams from shells, put through food chopper and add strained liquor. Add water, chopped celery and parsley and cook ten minutes. Press through a sieve and add to the white sauce. Season, beat with an egg-beater, and serve.

BISQUE OF LOBSTER

1 medium-sized lobster
1 quart milk
4 tablespoons butter
4 tablespoons flour
1 cup cold water
Red pepper
Salt and pepper

Make a white sauce of the milk, flour, and butter. Remove meat from freshly boiled lobster. Reserve the coral and the green fat. Put the cold water into a kettle and add the broken claws and shell and the finely chopped tail meat. Bring to the simmering-point and simmer for twenty minutes. Drain, and stir into the white sauce. Add the remainder of the lobster meat, cut in dice. Season with salt, pepper, and cayenne. Just before serving, add the coral mashed to a paste with the green fat. Mix thoroughly, reheat, and serve with croutons.

BISQUE OF OYSTERS

1 pint oysters
2 cups milk
1 cup stale bread-crumbs
1 tablespoon flour
1 tablespoon butter
2 cups water
1 slice onion, chopped fine
1 stalk celery, diced
1 stalk parsley, chopped fine
1 bay-leaf
Salt and pepper

Scald the milk, add the bread-crumbs and cook in a double boiler for twenty minutes. Rub through a sieve. Make a white sauce of the milk and crumb mixture and the flour and butter. Chop the oysters, put them in a saucepan with their own liquor, the water and the chopped vegetables and herbs. Simmer for twenty or thirty minutes. Rub through a fine sieve and combine with the white sauce mixture. More milk or cream may be added if the bisque is very thick. Season and serve.

MOCK BISQUE OR TOMATO BISQUE SOUP

4 cups milk	2 cups cooked tomatoes
¾ cup dry bread crumbs	2 teaspooons sugar
½ onion stuck with 6 cloves	3 tablespoons butter
Sprig of parsley	1 teaspoon salt
½ bay leaf	⅛ teaspoon pepper

Scald milk with bread crumbs, onion, parsley and bay leaf. Remove onion and bay leaf and rub through sieve. Heat tomatoes with sugar to boiling; rub through sieve. Reheat milk mixture with butter, salt and pepper. Add tomatoes and serve at once with croutons or crisp crackers. If desired, garnish with whipped cream and a sprig of watercress. Serves 6.

VARIATIONS—Use cracker crumbs instead of bread crumbs if desired.

Add ½ teaspoon sweet basil to tomatoes.

Chowders

CLAM CHOWDER

¼ pound salt pork, cubed	½ teaspoon pepper
2 small onions, minced	3½ cups milk
1 quart shucked clams	6 to 8 common crackers,
6 to 8 medium potatoes	split
Water	Cold milk
Salt, if needed	

Brown salt pork in deep kettle. Add onion and cook 2 or 3 minutes. Remove stomach from clams, chop hard parts and leave soft parts whole or chop them, as preferred. Arrange potatoes and hard parts of clams in layers over onions, cover with cold water, heat to boiling and simmer until potatoes are tender. Add soft part of clams, seasonings and milk. Heat to boiling and add crackers which have been soaked in cold milk. Heat thoroughly. Serves 6 to 8.

MANHATTAN CLAM CHOWDER—Add ½ green pepper, chopped, and ½ cup chopped celery when browning the onion. Add tomato juice instead of milk. Season with a dash of cayenne, sage and thyme. Add tomato juice last; heat only to boiling before serving.

RHODE ISLAND CLAM CHOWDER—Omit milk and add 1 cup tomatoes instead. Crackers may be omitted.

CORN CHOWDER

3 slices salt pork
1 medium onion, sliced
4 medium potatoes, sliced
2 cups water
6 large soda crackers

2 cups milk
2 cups cooked corn,
   fresh or canned
1 teaspoon salt
¼ teaspoon pepper

Cut salt pork into cubes and brown in large saucepan. Add onion and cook until tender and lightly browned. Add potatoes and water and cook until potatoes are tender. Soak crackers in milk. Add corn, salt, pepper and soaked crackers to the cooked potato mixture. Heat to boiling. Serves 4.

VEGETABLE CHOWDER—Omit corn and milk and add ¾ cup diced cooked carrots, 1 tablespoon minced celery tops, 1 table-spoon minced green pepper and 4 cups cooked tomatoes.

FISH CHOWDER

¼ pound fat salt pork, sliced
2 cups diced uncooked fish
6 small potatoes, sliced
2 onions, chopped fine

3 cups boiling water
1 pint milk
3 pilot biscuits
Salt and pepper

Fry salt pork in a deep kettle. When crisp remove pieces of pork and put fish, potatoes and onions in kettle. Cover with the boiling water. Simmer one-half hour, or until the potato is tender. Add the milk and cook five minutes longer. Season with salt and pepper. Just before serving, add the pilot biscuit.

DOWN EAST FISH CHOWDER—Use salt cod or haddock for the fish in Fish Chowder. Cut potatoes into dice instead of slicing. Add 1 tablespoon minced parsley and ⅛ teaspoon pepper. Thicken with 1 tablespoon flour when milk is added.

FISH MULLIGAN—Omit pilot crackers and milk from Fish Chowder and add ⅓ cup uncooked rice and 2 tablespoons minced parsley with fish and vegetables. Add 3 cups water.

OYSTER CHOWDER—Use 1 quart oysters instead of fish in Fish Chowder. Use only 2 cups water and when potatoes and onions are tender, add oysters to boiling soup mixture and cook until the edges curl. Add milk and heat to boiling.

SHRIMP CHOWDER—Use 1 pound cooked shrimp instead of fish in Fish Chowder. Add the shrimp with the milk. Add 1 cup diced celery with the onions and potatoes.

CLAM STEW

Make in same way as oyster stew, using clams.

CRAB STEW

6 hard-shell crabs	1 pint rich milk
1 tablespoon butter	1 quart water
1 tablespoon flour	Salt and pepper
1 onion	Parsley

Boil the crabs. Remove the meat and sauté it in butter with one small onion. Cook until the onion is quite brown. Add flour, salt, and pepper, cook a little longer, then add water and minced parsley. Simmer ten minutes, add milk and reheat.

OYSTER STEW

UNTHICKENED

1 pint oysters	Salt, pepper, paprika
4 tablespoons butter	1 quart rich milk

Put cleaned oysters, strained oyster liquor, butter and seasoning into a saucepan and simmer gently until oysters begin to curl at the edges. At the same time, heat the milk, being careful not to scorch it. Add the hot milk to the oysters and oyster liquor and serve at once.

THICKENED—To the ingredients given above, add from four to eight tablespoons of flour, and, if desired, a little onion-juice and mace. Scald the oysters in their own liquor. Make a white sauce of the milk, flour and butter and season as desired. Combine the scalded oysters and oyster liquor with the white sauce and serve at once.

YEAST BOUILLON

In recent years several varieties of autolyzed yeast have appeared on the market to be used as bouillon or in sandwich pastes. They have the flavor of strong meat extract but have the advantage of being of pure vegetable origin. If purchased in jars use according to direction. When in cubes use like any other bouillon cube. Of peculiar value for the high content of vitamins B and G, it is also called petite marmite.

SOUP ACCESSORIES

SOUP may be served with many accompaniments, such as crisped crackers, cheese-sticks and pulled bread; and varieties of croutons, forcemeat balls, noodles, and vegetable pastes may be placed in the soup itself. Grated Parmesan cheese is passed with many kinds of soup to be sprinkled on each portion.

Recipes for some of the best-liked accompaniments for soup are given below.

CROUTONS

Cut stale bread into slices about one-third of an inch thick, and remove all crust. Spread with butter, cut in cubes and bake in the oven until delicately browned. If preferred, these cubes of bread may be fried in deep fat or sautéd in just enough fat to keep them from burning. Put into soup at time of serving, or pass in a separate dish, permitting each person to put as many croutons as he may wish in his portion of soup.

MOCK ALMONDS

These are merely croutons shaped to represent almonds.

CHEESE STICKS AND ROLLS

Cut bread in long, narrow strips, spread with butter, then with a thick coating of grated cheese. Brown in moderate oven (350° F.). Or cut crust from sliced bread, spread thickly with paste of grated cheese and butter, roll, fasten with toothpick and brown as above.

HOT CRISPED CRACKERS

Toast thin wafers or crackers for three minutes in a hot oven (400°-425° F.). They are better if spread with a thin film of butter before being put into the oven. If Boston crackers are preferred, split them, arrange the halves, rough side up, on a plate, lay a bit of butter on each, and brown them in the oven.

VARIATIONS

Use the cookie cutters in any small design to cut sliced bread for toasting on a cookie sheet or large pan. Or use the cutters on biscuit dough and bake or fry in deep fat.

NOODLES

1 egg   ½ teaspoon salt   Flour

Stir sufficient flour into a slightly beaten egg to make a very stiff dough. Add salt, knead, and roll as thin as possible. It should be of almost paperlike thinness. Cover with a towel and let remain untouched for half an hour. Then cut in small fancy shapes, and dry them. When needed, place in boiling water and cook rapidly for fifteen minutes. This dough may also be rolled into threads and used like macaroni in soup.

NOODLE BALLS—Roll the noodle paste as directed above, fold it double and with a tin cutter make circles about one-fourth inch in diameter. Toss these balls into hot fat, (360°-370° F.) using a wire frying-basket. In about a minute they will turn a delicate brown and puff into balls. Drain on soft paper and serve with soup. As these soften quickly, it is better not to put them in the tureen, but to pass them after the soup has been served.

EGG BALLS

No. 1.

    5 eggs   1 teaspoon salt
    ½ teaspoon pepper   Flour

Simmer four of the eggs in the shell twenty minutes and mash the yolks to a smooth paste in a bowl; then add the salt and pepper and the other egg, well beaten. Shape the mass into tiny balls, roll them in flour and sauté, tossing them about while frying to prevent their sticking to the pan. They may be made some time before needed. Use the hard-cooked egg-whites for a sandwich or a salad.

No. 2.

Mash the four cooked yolks to a paste, season, and mix with the uncooked egg-yolk. Form into small balls. Roll them in the uncooked egg-white, then in flour, and poach in hot water. These are attractive in consommé.

WITH A LITTLE TIME YOU CAN
ROLL YOUR CHEESE STICKS OR
SANDWICHES

FOR HURRY-UP ACCESSORIES FOR SOUPS AND SALADS, BUY THE MAKINGS AND PUT ON YOUR OWN FINISH

MARROW AND LIVER BALLS

2 tablespoons melted marrow   Paprika
1 egg   ⅛ teaspoon onion juice
Salt and pepper   ½ cup soft bread crumbs

Strain melted marrow through cheesecloth, beat until creamy and then add beaten egg. Season with salt, pepper, paprika and onion; add moist bread, and form into balls. Poach in boiling water. Use 1 cup chopped liver instead of marrow for liver balls.

PÂTÉ À CHOUX

1 teaspoon butter   1 egg
2½ teaspoons milk   Salt
¼ cup flour

Heat butter and milk together. When at the boiling-point, add the flour and a pinch of salt, stirring constantly. Remove from the fire, beat in the unbeaten egg, and continue beating until the egg is well mixed with the other ingredients. When cool, drop small pieces from the tip of a teaspoon into deep, boiling fat. When brown and crisp, drain on absorbent paper. If desired, two tablespoons of grated Parmesan cheese may be added to this recipe.

CUSTARD FOR GARNISHING

Allow two tablespoons of milk, cream, or consommé to each egg. Mix well, season with salt and pepper, and pour into a buttered mold, making the custard one-half inch thick. Set the mold in a pan containing hot water and place in a slow oven (300°-350° F.). When the custard is set, remove from the oven and cool. Cut it into small pieces or fancy shapes. The egg-white, the egg-yolk or the whole egg may be used in making this custard.

CUSTARD ROYALE.

2 egg-yolks   Salt and pepper
1 egg   Cayenne
½ cup beef stock

Beat the yolks of the eggs slightly and then beat into them the one whole egg. Add beef stock, a little salt, pepper and a few grains of cayenne. Pour the mixture into a shallow pan or dish, so that the custard will be about one-half inch deep. Set this pan into another holding water that is just below the boiling-point and place both in a slow oven (300°-350° F.). The custard should set without bubbling and without forming a brown crust on top. When cold, cut in fancy shapes with vegetable-cutter. Use care in placing these in the soup, so that they may not break. When used in consommé, they give the name "Consommé Royale" to the soup.

CHICKEN FORCEMEAT

WHITE—

2 breasts chicken (uncooked)	1 cup milk
½ teaspoon salt	½ blade mace
1 cup dry bread-crumbs	¼ teaspoon pepper
3 tablespoons butter	2 egg-whites

Chop, pound and rub through a purée-sieve, the uncooked breasts of chicken. There should be a full half-pint of meat. Add salt and pepper. Boil together the bread-crumbs (no crusts), milk and mace for ten minutes, or until cooked to a smooth paste. Remove from the fire, put in butter and then add the seasoned meat and the well-beaten whites of eggs. Stir until all ingredients are thoroughly blended.

DARK—Use dark meat instead of light and the yolks of the eggs instead of whites. Chicken livers, also, may be used for forcemeat.

FISH FORCEMEAT

Free any kind of delicate fish from skin, fat and bone. Pound, strain, use one-half pint fish and proceed as for chicken forcemeat.

OYSTER FORCEMEAT

12 oysters	Cayenne
2 cups dry bread-crumbs	1 teaspoon parsley
3 tablespoons butter	1 teaspoon lemon-juice
2 egg-yolks	3 tablespoons oyster-juice
1 teaspoon salt	Nutmeg

Chop the oysters fine and add the bread-crumbs, butter, salt, cayenne, minced parsley, lemon-juice, oyster-juice, the yolks of raw eggs and a grating of nutmeg. Pound to a smooth paste and rub through a purée-sieve. Add more salt if necessary. This is a fine forcemeat for timbales, or for stuffing poultry or fish. For use in soups, it may be made into balls, dipped in beaten egg yolks, then in bread crumbs and fried, or rolled into very small balls, dipped in egg yolks and browned in the oven.

QUENELLES—These are shapes made by forcing forcemeat through a pastry bag and tube into boiling water or stock. They are used to garnish entrées as well as soups.

COLORING FOR SOUPS AND SAUCES

To color brown, use browned flour or a little burnt sugar. (See Index for caramel recipe) or a few drops of commercial vegetable flavoring.

Spinach leaves give a fine green color. Pound the uncooked leaves, tie them in a cloth, squeeze out all the juice and add this to the soup five minutes before serving. The strained juice of tomatoes or the whole tomato if run through a sieve will color soup red. Grated carrots give an amber color. Okra imparts a pale green color as well as a delightful flavor.

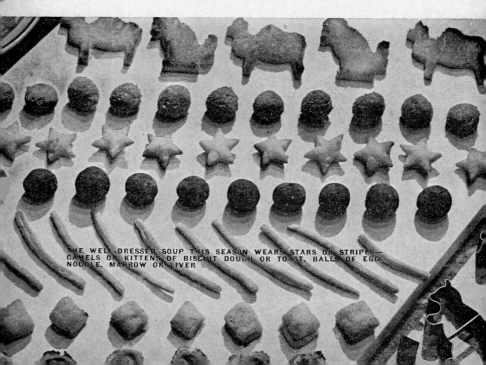

THE WELL-DRESSED SOUP THIS SEASON WEARS STARS OR STRIPES—CAMELS OR KITTENS OF BISCUIT DOUGH OR TOAST, BALLS OF EGG, NOODLE, MARROW OR LIVER

FISH

THE main difference between fish from fresh water and those from salt water, as food, is that the salt-water fish are an important source of bromine and iodine in the diet, and are considered desirable because of the value of iodine in preventing goiter. Some of the most common salt-water fish are cod, haddock, halibut, smelt, mackerel, salmon, shad, herring, oysters, clams, scallops, lobsters, crabs, shrimp and prawns, and some terrapins. Fish as food may be divided into:

WHITE FISH—Fish that have less than two per cent fat, examples of which are smelt, flounder, yellow perch, pike, pickerel, sea bass, cod and haddock.

MEDIUM FAT FISH—Fish that have two to five per cent fat, examples of which are weakfish, brook trout, mullet, and white perch.

FAT OR OILY FISH—Fish that contain five per cent or more of fat, examples of which are salmon, shad, herring, lake trout, bluefish, Spanish mackerel, butterfish, and eels.

SHELLFISH—Oysters, clams, scallops and mussels; lobsters, crabs, shrimp, prawns and crayfish or crawfish. Frogs, terrapins and turtles are usually included in this group.

Amount of Fish to Buy

If the fish bought is solid flesh, one-third of a pound should be allowed for each person. If fish is bought in the round (with bones, head, tail, etc.) at least one-half pound must be bought for each person.

Selecting and Caring for Fish

FRESH AND FROZEN FISH—Fresh fish, or fish that was frozen while fresh, has full or bulging bright eyes, bright red gills, firm and elastic flesh and fresh odor. Be sure that the flesh along the backbone smells fresh; it spoils there first. Fresh fish sink in fresh water. If it floats, it should not be used. As soon as fish comes from the market, clean it and put it into the refrigerator or other cool place until it is needed.

Fish that is frozen immediately after it is caught, and is kept frozen until the time for cooking does not lose its flavor. It is preferable to clean and draw it without thawing, but if it is too hard to handle soak in cold water or allow to thaw in the refrigerator overnight until just flexible. Skinning is sometimes easier than scaling. Then it should be cooked at once without further thawing. Quick frozen fish on the market today is cleaned and ready for use. Cook at once without thawing, allowing only slightly more than the usual cooking time allotted to broiling or baking as the case may be.

Cleaning and Dressing Fish

Although fish may have been cleaned and dressed at the market, they are likely to need additional cleaning before they are cooked. If any scales have been left on a fish that is to be cooked with the skin on, remove them with the back of a knife. Draw the knife over the fish, from tail to head, slanting it toward the body of the fish at an angle of about 45°. If the fish is to be split, remove the head and tail. Wash quickly under cold running water and wipe the fish thoroughly, inside as well as outside, with a wet cloth. Then wipe dry, sprinkle with salt and keep on a plate in a cold place until ready to use. When roe is found in the fish it should be saved and cooked separately.

To Skin a Fish

Remove the fins, cut off a strip of skin along the backbone, and cut the skin around the gills. Pull the skin off with the fingers. If the flesh is soft, work slowly and follow the skin closely with the knife, to avoid tearing the flesh.

To Bone and Fillet a Fish

Clean and skin the fish. Insert a sharp knife close to the backbone at the tail end, and cut the flesh from the bone, working toward the head and keeping the knife as close as possible to the bone. Small bones that adhere to the flesh or are embedded in it must be removed with the fingers.

Flounders are often boned, to form fillets, and are served as "fillets of sole." The English sole is seldom imported, and most of the "fillet of sole" that is served in America is made from the flounder, which has a white, delicate flesh similar to sole.

A fillet is merely a piece of fish without skin and bones. Fillets look better on the serving platter if they are approximately the same size. Rolled fillets are called turbans. They are fastened with wooden toothpicks to keep them in shape during cooking, but the picks are removed before the fish is served.

Salted, Smoked and Canned Fish

These may be had the year around. The following varieties are likely to be in any market:

DRIED SALT FISH—Cod, haddock, hake, pollack and whiting.

BRINE-SALTED FISH—Herring, mackerel, mullet, salmon, shad.

SMOKED FISH—Carp, catfish, eel, finnan haddie, hake, halibut, lake trout, pollack, salmon, sturgeon, whitefish.

CANNED FISH—Cod, haddock, herring, mackerel, salmon, sardines, tuna, oysters, shrimp, lobsters, clams.

PICKLED FISH—Sardines, eels, sturgeon, oysters, clams, scallops, lobsters and mussels.

To Boil or Steam Fish

To boil a large fish whole, place it in a wire frying basket or in the strainer of a fish kettle and lower it into water or Court Bouillon which is almost boiling. Add one teaspoon salt and one tablespoon vinegar or lemon juice for every two quarts of water. The acid whitens the flesh and helps to keep it firm. Heat to simmering and cook until flesh may be easily separated into flakes, 8 minutes per pound for the first 4 pounds and 5 minutes for each additional pound.

Fillets or slices of fish should be placed on a plate, tied in a piece of cheesecloth and lowered into the water or Court Bouillon (page 745). Cook about 10 minutes per pound.

To steam fish, oil upper part of steamer, place fish in it and set over boiling water. Sprinkle fish with salt and a few drops of lemon juice, cover and allow water to boil vigorously. Cook 10 to 15 minutes per pound.

Use cooking stock as a basis for sauce or chowder.

FISH COOKED IN PARCHMENT

2 pounds boneless fillets
2 tablespoons butter
2 tablespoons minced onion

1 tablespoon minced parsley
1 tablespoon lemon juice
Salt and pepper

Dampen 2 sheets of parchment paper and spread out flat. Brush with oil. Cut fish into serving pieces and place half the pieces on each sheet of paper. Place 1 teaspoon each of butter and onion on each serving and sprinkle with parsley, lemon juice, salt and pepper. Gather edges of papers and tie securely. Place in boiling water and cook 15 minutes. Remove fish to hot platter, taking care not to lose any of the juices. Serves 6.

Fish That Are Good Boiled, Steamed or Poached

FISH	SUGGESTED SAUCES	GARNISHES
Codfish	Butter, caper, oyster, shrimp	Parsley or cress
Flounder	Béchamel	Chopped parsley
Haddock	Egg	Parsley or cress
Halibut	Béchamel, creamy, egg, hollandaise	Parsley or cress
Mackerel	Caper, parsley	Cucumber, lemon
Red snapper	Mushroom, tomato	Parsley
Salmon	Egg, hollandaise, tartare	Cress, lemon
Sheepshead	Drawn butter	Parsley and lemon
Sole (flounder)	Béchamel	Parsley
Trout	Horse-radish	Lemon

BONED HERRING

6 large herring
Pepper
Salt

Parsley
Vinegar
6 slices buttered toast

Select fish with roes. Split, wash, scrape and remove heads, roe and backbone. Sprinkle generously with pepper, salt and minced parsley, then roll each piece tightly, beginning with the wide end, and tie with a string. Place in boiling water seasoned with pepper, salt and vinegar and simmer 10 to 15 minutes. Cut roe into pieces and fry. Place the fish and roe on buttered toast, garnish and serve. Serves 6.

PICKLED SALMON

4 to 5 pounds salmon
2 quarts vinegar
1 ounce peppercorns

1½ teaspoons nutmeg
6 blades mace
1 tablespoon salad oil

Wrap salmon in cheesecloth and simmer in salted water about 45 minutes. Drain, wrap in dry cloth and chill until ready to use. Combine 1 quart of the cooking water with vinegar and spices. Cover and cook 5 minutes. Cool. When quite cold, pour over salmon, then add oil. Cover closely and store in a cool dry place. This pickle will keep for several months. Serves 8 to 10.

POACHED FISH

Small fish and fish fillets are poached by simmering in a small amount of seasoned liquid. The liquid is then strained and used in making a sauce suited to the type of fish.

1 teaspoon salt
1 slice onion
1 slice lemon

½ teaspoon peppercorns
1 bay leaf
2 pounds fish fillets

Fill skillet half full of water and add salt, onion, lemon, peppercorns and bay leaf. Heat to boiling. Add fish and simmer 5 to 15 minutes, depending on thickness of fish. Remove carefully to serving plate. Strain stock and use in preparing sauce. Serves 6.

FISH POACHED IN TOMATO SAUCE

2 cups tomatoes
½ teaspoon salt
1 bay leaf
1 tablespoon minced onion

½ teaspoon peppercorns
2 pounds fish fillets
1 tablespoon butter

Cook tomatoes, salt, bay leaf, onion and peppercorns in greased skillet until reduced about half. Add fish and simmer 5 minutes. Turn fish carefully and simmer 5 minutes longer. Remove fish to hot platter. Strain tomato sauce, add butter and pour over fish. Serves 6.

In Milk—Use 1½ cups milk instead of tomatoes and do not cook down. Add 2 stalks celery, chopped, to seasonings. When fish is done, strain milk and use in preparing sauce.

Broiled Fish

To broil a whole fish, continue the slit made in cleaning the fish so that it can be opened flat. Dry and season with salt, pepper and lemon juice. Place skin side up on greased shallow pan and brown skin quickly under broiler. Turn carefully and cook flesh side 6 to 12 minutes, depending on thickness. Fillets are cooked 4 to 6 minutes on each side. Do not overcook. Fat fish need no basting but lean fish should be basted well with butter during broiling.

Fish That Are Good Broiled

FISH	SUGGESTED SAUCES	GARNISHES
Black Bass (split)	Melted butter	Lemon and parsley
Bluefish	Melted butter	Chopped almonds
Butterfish	Lemon	Watercress
Cod (sliced)	Melted butter	Lemon
Flounder (split or filleted)	Tomato, lemon	Parsley
Halibut (sliced)	Butter, hollandaise	Parsley, lemon
Mackerel (split)	Maître d'hôtel, lemon	Lemon, cucumber, parsley
Perch	Caper, anchovy	Parsley
Pompano (split)	Maître d'hôtel	Cucumber, cress
Red Snapper	Lemon butter	Cucumbers
Salmon (sliced)	Anchovy, caper	Chopped parsley
Shad (split)	Maître d'hôtel, butter	Parsley, radishes
Smelt (whole)	Remoulade, béchamel	Parsley
Swordfish (sliced)	Melted butter	Parsley
Trout	Melted butter	Lemon wedges
Whitefish	Mushroom	Watercress

BROILED SMELT

¼ cup butter, melted
1 tablespoon lemon juice
1 teaspoon salt

¼ teaspoon pepper
1 pound smelt
½ cup flour

Mix butter, lemon juice, salt and pepper. Clean smelt, splitting them open if they are large. Dip each in butter mixture, then roll in flour. Place in double broiler rack and broil 6 minutes, turning once. Serves 4.

TYING PLATE AND SALMON IN CHEESECLOTH WHEN BOILING, WILL PRESERVE ITS BEAUTY INTACT

WHETHER BAKED OR PLANKED, ONLY
CAREFUL HANDLING
WILL BRING FISH
TO THE TABLE
LOOKING
ITS BEST

THE LORDLY LOBSTER IS STILL THE ARISTO-
CRAT OF THE FESTIVE OCCASION

Baked Fish

Fish weighing from 3 to 5 pounds may be baked whole, either with or without stuffing. The head and tail may be removed or left on. Clean fish, dry and rub inside with salt. Stuff if desired and sew or skewer. Place a sheet of greased heavy or parchment paper in baking pan, having it large enough so that it can be used to lift fish from pan when done. Place a bay leaf and a few slices of onion and bacon or salt pork on the paper and lay the fish on top. If fish is lean, cut a few slashes down its back and place a strip of salt pork in each. Bake in quick or hot oven (425° F.) 10 minutes, then reduce heat to 350° F. and bake 15 to 20 minutes longer. Allow ten minutes per pound for the first 4 pounds and 5 minutes for each additional pound.

Small fish, steaks or fillets may be dipped in milk and rolled in bread crumbs. Sprinkle with melted butter or oil and bake in moderate oven (350°-375° F.) 20 to 25 minutes. Fillets are often rolled to form turbans and baked in muffin pans.

Fish To Bake Whole

Fish	Stuffings	Suggested Sauces	Garnishes
Bass (sea)	Bread stuffing	Tomato sauce	Tomato
Bluefish	Bread stuffing	Catchup	Parsley
Cod	Oyster stuffing	Egg sauce	Lemon
Haddock	Pickle-caper	Drawn butter	Lemon
Mackerel	Parsley		Lemon
Pickerel	Pickle-caper		Cucumber
Shad	Bread stuffing		Tomato
Tilefish	Bread stuffing	Maître d'hôtel	Parsley
Weakfish	Bread stuffing	Lemon juice	Watercress
Whitefish	Bread stuffing	Egg sauce	Egg

Fish To Bake in Steaks, Cutlets or Fillets

Fish	Suggested Sauces	Garnishes
Cusk	Creole	Lemon
Flounder	Egg	Egg
Haddock	Oyster	Lemon
Halibut	Brown, hollandaise	Tomato, parsley
Mackerel (horse)		Lemon
Salmon	Lemon	Parsley and lemon
Tilefish	Tomato	Parsley

Planked Fish

Select any fish suitable for baking. Large fish may be cleaned, split, boned, seasoned and planked flat; small fish may be cleaned, seasoned and planked whole. Oil plank and preheat thoroughly in hot oven. Place fish in center of plank; brush lean fish with melted butter or French dressing. Bake in very hot oven (425° F.) 10 to 15 minutes, reduce temperature to moderate (350° F.) and finish baking, allowing about 10 minutes per pound. About 15 minutes before fish is done, remove from oven and garnish with mashed potatoes pressed through a pastry tube and other vegetables as desired. Return to oven to finish baking and brown potatoes. Garnish.

FILLET OF FLOUNDER AU GRATIN

2½ pounds flounder fillets
1½ tablespoons butter
1 tablespoon flour
1 tablespoon chopped onion
½ bay leaf

1 cup chicken stock
Salt and pepper
½ tablespoon lemon juice
½ cup bread crumbs

Cut fillets into serving pieces and place in greased baking dish. Melt butter, add flour and onion and blend well. Add bay leaf and chicken stock and simmer 15 minutes, stirring until thickened. Remove bay leaf. Season with salt and pepper and add lemon juice. Pour over fish and sprinkle crumbs over top. Bake in hot oven (425° F.) 20 minutes. Serve at once. Serves 6.

HALIBUT CREOLE

2 tablespoons butter
1 tablespoon flour
1 tablespoon minced green
  pepper

1 tablespoon minced onion
2 cups cooked tomatoes
Salt and pepper
2 pounds halibut steaks

Melt butter and blend in flour. Add minced green pepper and onion and cook 3 minutes. Add tomatoes and cook until thickened, stirring constantly. Simmer 10 minutes longer, then rub through strainer and season with salt and pepper. Season halibut steaks with salt and pepper and arrange in greased baking dish. Pour Creole sauce over fish. Bake in hot oven (400° F.) 30 minutes. Serves 4.

Fried Fish

Small fish such as smelt, perch or herring are fried whole. Large fish are cut into steaks or fillets. Small fish and steaks are usually dipped in milk, then rolled in flour or corn meal. Fillets are cut into serving pieces and rolled first in fine bread or cracker crumbs, then in beaten egg and again in crumbs.

Fish steaks are best fried in a skillet with a small amount of fat; small whole fish are cooked either in a skillet or in hot deep fat; fillets are usually fried in hot deep fat.

Using browned butter as the frying medium diminishes the odor of frying fish.

See page 9 for time and temperature for deep fat frying.

Fish fried in deep fat should be drained on absorbent paper.

Oven-Fried Fish

Oven frying is a method of cooking fish which produces the characteristic flavor of fried fish but does not fill the kitchen with a frying odor. Use fillets, steaks or small whole fish. Dip in salted milk, then in bread crumbs. Flour, corn meal or cracker crumbs do not produce satisfactory results. Place in greased baking pan and sprinkle with oil or melted fat. Place high in a very hot oven (425° F.) and bake 10 minutes. Larger fish may be split to lie flat in the pan, covered with fine bread crumbs, sprinkled with oil and baked in the same way, allowing 10 minutes per inch of thickness. Do not add any water. The fish will not burn but will brown evenly on all sides.

Very thin strips of bacon may be used instead of oil.

Fish Roe

The roe (eggs) of many fish, which are available during the spring, make excellent and often delicate food. Shad roe are most frequently used, but the roe of mackerel and of flounder are palatable and usually much cheaper. The roe is a compact, granular mass covered with a thin film. It is either yellow and opaque or greyish and translucent. When fish are found to contain roe it should be removed, cooked and served separately.

Milt

The part of the male fish that takes the place of the roe of female fish is called the milt, and may be prepared and cooked in just the same way. The blue vein that runs through the center of salmon milt should be removed before cooking.

To Prepare Roe for Use

Small roe, as from smelt or shad, need not be parboiled before using in recipes. The larger roe should be simmered in water to which 1 tablespoon vinegar or lemon juice per quart has been added. Cook 8 to 10 minutes, drain and remove membrane.

Uncooked roe may be seasoned with salt, lemon juice and onion juice (if desired) and served in the same way as caviar.

BROILED ROE

Dry roe between paper towels, sprinkle with salt and pepper and place on greased broiler (not on rack). Broil 5 minutes on each side. Serve with maître d'hôtel sauce.

Or broil mushroom caps or small tomato cups lightly, fill with roe, brush with butter and season with salt and pepper. Broil about 8 minutes.

SCALLOPED ROE

1½ pounds roe	1 cup medium white sauce
1 tablespoon minced parsley	1 egg yolk
Salt and pepper	½ cup buttered crumbs
1 teaspoon lemon juice	

Parboil roe, drain and break into pieces. Place half the roe in greased baking dish and sprinkle with parsley, salt, pepper and lemon juice. Combine white sauce and egg yolk; pour half the mixture over roe. Repeat. Cover with crumbs. Bake in moderate oven (350° F.) 20 minutes or until browned. Serves 4.

ROE CAKES—Omit white sauce and use whole egg, beaten. Combine ingredients and shape into cakes. Roll in additional crumbs or in corn meal. Fry in butter.

SCALLOPED FISH

2 hard-cooked eggs
2 cups medium white sauce
2 cups flaked cooked fish

Salt and pepper
1 cup buttered bread crumbs

Rub egg yolks through sieve and chop egg whites. Mix well with white sauce. Arrange alternate layers of fish and sauce in greased baking dish. Season fish with salt and pepper. Cover with buttered crumbs. Bake in moderate oven (350° F.) 20 minutes or until crumbs are browned. Serves 4.

FISH TIMBALES

1 cup cooked fish
½ cup cooked mushrooms
1 cup bread crumbs
2 cups milk

⅓ cup butter
Salt and pepper
Few grains nutmeg
4 eggs, beaten

Remove skin and bones from fish, add mushrooms and chop very fine. Rub through sieve. Cook crumbs and milk in double boiler 10 minutes. Add butter and season with salt, pepper and nutmeg. Add fish and beaten eggs. Pour into greased molds or custard cups. Bake in moderate oven (350° F.) until firm, about 30 minutes. Unmold and serve with hollandaise sauce or tomato sauce. Serves 4.

This mixture may be baked in a large mold, about 60 minutes.

FISH SOUFFLÉ

1 teaspoon onion juice
½ teaspoon salt
⅛ teaspoon pepper

1 cup medium white sauce
2 eggs, separated
1 cup flaked cooked fish

Add onion juice, salt and pepper to white sauce. Stir in beaten egg yolks and flaked fish. Beat egg whites until stiff and fold into mixture. Pour into greased baking dish and place in pan of hot water. Bake in moderate oven (350° F.) 60 minutes. Serve from the same dish. Serves 4.

KEDGEREE

2 cups flaked cooked fish
1 cup cooked rice
2 hard-cooked eggs

4 tablespoons butter
Salt and pepper

Heat fish, rice and chopped egg whites in butter. Season and sprinkle with sieved egg yolks. Serves 6.

SCALLOPED SALMON

2 cups cooked salmon
2 tablespoons lemon juice
Salt and pepper

½ cup dry bread crumbs
1 cup thin white sauce

Flake salmon and place half of it in greased baking dish. Season with lemon juice, salt and pepper. Cover with half the crumbs. Repeat layers of salmon, seasoning and crumbs. Pour white sauce over the top and bake in moderate oven (350° F.) 20 minutes or until thoroughly heated and slightly browned on top. Serves 4.

Au Gratin—Season salmon, mix with white sauce and place in greased small molds. Cover with buttered crumbs. Add grated cheese if desired. Bake as above.

SALMON WIGGLE

2 cups flaked cooked salmon
2 cups cooked peas
2 cups white sauce

2 dozen crisp crackers
Paprika

Heat salmon and peas in white sauce. Serve on crackers and sprinkle with paprika. Serves 6.

SALMON LOAF

2 cups cooked salmon
2 eggs, beaten
½ cup soft bread crumbs

¼ cup butter, melted
Salt and pepper
1 tablespoon minced parsley

Flake salmon and add beaten eggs. Add remaining ingredients and place in greased loaf pan. Bake in moderate oven (350° F.) 40 minutes. Serve with egg sauce. Serves 4.

SALMON PUFFS

2 cups cooked salmon
½ teaspoon salt
⅛ teaspoon pepper

½ cup soft bread crumbs
1 tablespoon lemon juice
3 eggs, separated

Chop salmon fine and add salt, pepper, crumbs and lemon juice. Add beaten egg yolks, mixing thoroughly, then fold in stiffly beaten egg whites. Place in greased custard cups. Set in pan of hot water and bake in moderate oven (375° F.) 30 minutes. Unmold on a hot platter, garnish each with a sprig of parsley and serve with a sauce. Serves 6.

TUNA WITH CAPER SAUCE

1½ cups cooked tuna   1½ cups medium white sauce
3 tablespoons capers   Paprika
              1 tablespoon minced parsley

Heat fish thoroughly over boiling water. Add capers to hot white sauce. Place fish on platter, pour sauce over it and sprinkle with paprika and parsley. Serves 6.

TUNA AND MUSHROOM CASSEROLE

½ pound mushrooms   1¼ cups milk
3 tablespoons butter   1 cup flaked cooked tuna
2 tablespoons flour   3⅛-ounce package potato
¼ teaspoon pepper   chips, crushed

Slice mushrooms and sauté in butter. Blend in flour and pepper. Add milk and cook until thickened, stirring constantly. Add tuna and ¾ of the potato chips. Place in greased casserole and cover with remaining chips. Bake in moderate oven (350° F.) 30 minutes. Serves 4 to 6.

TUNA EN CASSEROLE

1 medium onion   ¾ teaspoon salt
4 tablespoons fat   Few grains cayenne
4 tablespoons flour   Juice 1 lemon
2 cups tomato juice   1 cup flaked cooked tuna
1 teaspoon sugar   2 cups seasoned mashed
1 teaspoon paprika   potatoes

Chop onion, add to fat and cook until tender. Blend in flour and add tomato juice, sugar, paprika, salt, cayenne and lemon juice. Cook, stirring constantly, until thickened. Add tuna and pour into casserole. Cover with potatoes. Bake in moderate oven (350° F.) about 20 minutes or until potatoes are browned. Serves 4.

SCALLOPED TUNA AND PEAS

2 cups cooked peas   ½ cup cream
2 cups flaked cooked tuna   ½ cup buttered crumbs
½ teaspoon salt

Place peas and tuna in layers in greased baking dish. Add salt to cream and pour over fish. Cover with crumbs and brown in moderate oven (350° F.). Serves 6.

CREAMED CODFISH

1 cup salt codfish	2 tablespoons flour
1 cup milk	⅛ teaspoon pepper
2 tablespoons butter	1 egg

Separate the fish into very small pieces and leave in cold water for 3 hours, changing the water 3 times. Heat milk in double boiler. Add well-drained codfish and cook for 10 minutes. Blend butter, flour and pepper and stir into milk. Cook 10 minutes, stirring constantly until thickened. Remove from heat, add beaten egg, stir well and serve at once. If the sauce is cooked after the egg is added, it is likely to curdle. The egg may be omitted. Serves 4.

NEW ENGLAND SALT FISH DINNER—Serve over opened baked potatoes and top with browned cubes of salt pork.

CODFISH BALLS

1 cup flaked salt codfish	2 tablespoons butter
3 cups sliced potatoes	⅛ teaspoon pepper
2 tablespoons milk	1 egg, beaten

Simmer fish and potatoes together in a large amount of water until potatoes are tender. Drain well and mash. Add remaining ingredients and beat until light. Shape into balls and fry in hot deep fat (380° F.) until brown. Serves 4.

CODFISH PUFFS

Follow recipe for codfish balls, using 2 eggs instead of 1. Beat with rotary beater until very light. Drop from spoon into hot deep fat (380° F.) and fry until brown. Serve with tomato sauce. Serves 4.

CODFISH SOUFFLÉ

Follow recipe for codfish balls, adding 2 beaten egg yolks instead of 1 egg. Mix well, then fold in 2 egg whites, stiffly beaten. Pour into greased baking dish and bake in moderate oven (350° F.) about 15-30 minutes. Serves 4.

CODFISH À LA MODE

Add 2 cups milk, ¼ cup butter and a second egg to recipe for codfish balls. Bake as for soufflé.

SALT FISH WITH EGG GARNISH

2 cups salt fish   2 cups white sauce
2 hard-cooked eggs

Soak fish overnight, drain and cover with fresh water. Simmer 10 minutes. Add to hot white sauce and pour onto hot
platter. Slice eggs and arrange around edge. Serves 4.

BROILED FINNAN HADDIE

2 pounds finnan haddie   2 tablespoons butter
1 teaspoon lemon juice   Pepper

Cover finnan haddie with boiling water and let stand 10
minutes. Drain and place on greased broiler rack. Sprinkle
with lemon juice and brush with softened butter. Brown under
moderate heat, turn and brush the other side with lemon juice
and butter. Brown. Sprinkle lightly with pepper and serve
with egg or pickle sauce. Serves 6.

CREAMED FINNAN HADDIE

2 pounds finnan haddie   2 cups medium white sauce
Paprika

Cover finnan haddie with cold water and let stand 20 minutes. Heat to boiling and simmer 30 minutes. Drain, separate
into flakes and add to hot seasoned white sauce. Sprinkle liberally with paprika. Serves 6.

FINNAN HADDIE CHEESE TOAST

2 tablespoons minced onion   1 cup grated American
1/2 cup butter   cheese
4 tablespoons flour   6 slices bread
1/2 teaspoon salt   1 cup flaked cooked finnan
Few grains cayenne   haddie
1/2 teaspoon paprika   Parsley
2 cups milk   3 hard-cooked eggs

Cook onion in 1/4 cup butter, blend in flour and seasonings,
add milk and cook until thickened, stirring constantly. Add
cheese, remove from heat and stir until melted. Toast bread on
one side, butter untoasted side and cover with fish. Heat in
broiler. Cover with cheese sauce and garnish with parsley and
quartered hard-cooked eggs. Serves 6.

Salt Mackerel

TO FRESHEN—Soak mackerel in running or in frequently changed water for 2 to 3 hours. Place fish on a rack, cover with water in a heavy skillet and heat to boiling. Drain. Cover again with fresh water and simmer until tender. Fish is then ready for use in any recipe. Allow ¼ pound per person.

BREAKFAST SALT MACKEREL—Simmer mackerel in milk for 5 to 7 minutes, brown in butter and serve very hot.

BAKED SALT MACKEREL—Place mackerel, skin side down, in a baking pan, cover with thin cream and bake in a moderate oven (350° F.) for 15 minutes.

BROILED SALT MACKEREL—Place well-drained fish on broiler rack and brush with butter. Broil in preheated broiler 3 inches from source of heat until fish is browned.

OTHER WHOLE SALT FISH may be prepared in the same ways.

Oysters

Oysters in the shell are sold by the dozen; shucked oysters by the quart or pint. Oysters in the shell should be alive when purchased as indicated by tightly closed shell. Shucked oysters should be plump with no sunken areas or evidence of shrinkage. The liquor should be clear and should smell fresh.

Opening and Cleaning Oysters

Scrub shells thoroughly with water and a brush. To open an oyster, hold it firmly with the thick part of the shell toward the palm of the hand. Push a strong, thin knife between the shells near the back and run it along until it cuts the strong muscle which holds the shells together. Drop the oysters into a strainer, set over a bowl, and save the liquor that drains through to be used in cooking the oysters or making soup or sauce. Then examine each oyster with the fingers and remove all particles of shell. They are then ready to be used in any way desired.

OYSTERS ON THE HALF SHELL

Open oysters and serve in the deep half of the shell. Arrange 5 or 6 oysters on a plate of cracked ice and place a small glass of cocktail sauce in the center. Place a wedge of lemon on one side and serve very cold.

OYSTER COCKTAIL

30 large oysters	3 tablespoons tomato catchup
COCKTAIL SAUCE	1 teaspoon salt
2 teaspoons prepared horse-radish	2 tablespoons vinegar
	4 tablespoons lemon juice

¼ teaspoon Tabasco sauce

Chill oysters. Mix remaining ingredients well and chill. Place oysters in chilled glasses and cover with sauce. Serves 6.

OYSTERS BAKED IN SHELLS

Scrub unopened oysters well and place, deep shell down, in pan. Bake in hot oven (450° F.) until shells open, about 10 minutes. Season with butter, salt and pepper; serve in shells.

PANNED OYSTERS

1 pint large oysters	¼ cup oyster juice
6 slices buttered toast	

Place oysters in a shallow baking pan and pour over them a small quantity of oyster juice, but not sufficient to raise or float them. Place dish carefully in hot oven (425° F.) and just heat the oysters through. Be careful not to bake them. Moisten hot buttered toast with hot juice from oysters and serve oysters on toast. Serves 6.

OYSTER CASINO

30 oysters in the shell	Buttered crumbs
Lemon juice	30 (1-inch) squares sliced bacon
Pepper and salt	

Wash and open the oysters. Into each shell put a half teaspoon of strained oyster liquor, a few drops of lemon juice, then the oyster. Sprinkle with pepper and salt and cover with buttered crumbs. On each place a square of bacon and bake in hot oven (425° F.) 10 to 12 minutes. Shallow ovenware dishes, with the half shells embedded in coarse salt, are excellent for this purpose. The salt keeps the shells from tipping during baking. Where shells are not available, arrange the oysters for each portion in a shallow ramekin or in mushroom or tomato cups.

SCALLOPED OYSTERS

6 tablespoons butter
2 cups fine cracker crumbs
1 pint oysters

Salt and pepper
½ cup milk
Parsley

Melt butter, add crumbs and mix well. Spread ⅓ of the mixture in a greased baking dish. Arrange half the oysters in one layer on top and cover with half the remaining crumbs. Season with salt and pepper and add a second layer of oysters and crumbs. Season. No more than 2 layers of oysters should be used, otherwise the top and bottom layers will be overcooked and tough before those in the middle are well heated through. Pour the milk over the top. Bake in moderate oven (350° F.) about 30 minutes or until top is brown. Garnish with parsley. Serves 6.

DEVILED OYSTERS

1 pint oysters
3 tablespoons butter
2 tablespoons flour
1 cup milk or cream
2 egg yolks

1 tablespoon chopped
parsley
1 tablespoon lemon juice
Salt and pepper
½ cup cracker crumbs

Drain oysters and chop slightly. Drain again. Melt 2 tablespoons butter and blend in flour. Add milk and cook until thickened, stirring constantly. Beat egg yolks slightly and add to sauce, mixing well. Add oyster liquor, parsley, lemon juice and oysters. Season with salt and pepper. Place in greased ramekins or scallop shells. Melt remaining butter and mix with crumbs. Sprinkle over creamed mixture. Brown in hot oven (425° F.) about 7 minutes. Serves 6.

OYSTERS EN BROCHETTE

30 large oysters
30 squares bacon

6 slices buttered toast

String oysters and bacon squares alternately on 6 skewers, taking care to put skewers through firm part of oysters. Place across deep baking pan so that oysters hang down but do not touch bottom of pan. Bake in very hot oven (475° F.) until bacon is crisp, about 5 minutes. Place a skewer on each slice of toast and pour juice over. Serves 6.

CREAMED OYSTERS AND MUSHROOMS

1 cup oysters
3 tablespoons butter
3 tablespoons flour
1 cup canned mushrooms

1½ cups milk, about
2 egg yolks
½ teaspoon salt
1 teaspoon onion juice

½ teaspoon lemon juice

Drain oysters and heat in shallow pan until edges begin to curl. Add liquid in pan to that drained from oysters. Melt butter in double boiler; blend in flour. Combine oyster liquor, mushroom liquor and enough milk to make 2 cups and add to flour and butter. Cook until thickened, stirring constantly. Add slightly beaten egg yolks and mix quickly. Add remaining ingredients and oysters and cook 2 minutes. Serve at once on crackers or buttered toast. Serves 6.

CREAMED OYSTERS—Omit mushrooms and mushroom liquor and use 2 cups oysters. Add enough milk to oyster liquor to make 2 cups. Proceed as above.

OYSTERS À LA POULETTE—Omit onion juice and add a few grains nutmeg. Serve with a border of baked puff paste, toast or baking powder biscuits.

OYSTERS AND SCALLOPS—Omit mushrooms and add 1 cup scallops. Cook scallops with oysters.

SAUTÉED OYSTERS

30 large oysters
Salt and pepper

1 cup fine cracker crumbs
Butter

Drain oysters, season with salt and pepper and roll in crumbs. Melt a little butter in hot skillet and brown oysters quickly. Turn and brown the other side. Add more butter as needed to prevent sticking. Serves 6.

FRIED OYSTERS

1 pint oysters
2 eggs

1½ cups milk
2 cups flour

1 teaspoon salt

Drain and dry oysters. Beat eggs, add milk and beat in flour and salt until smooth. Dip each oyster in batter and fry in hot deep fat (375° F.) until browned, 2 to 5 minutes. Drain on absorbent paper. Serve with lemon. Serves 6.

PIGS IN BLANKETS

24 large oysters   24 thin slices bacon
Salt and pepper   6 slices buttered toast

Season oysters with salt and pepper; wrap each in bacon and fasten with a pick. Fry quickly in a hot skillet until bacon is brown. Remove crusts from toast, cut into quarters and serve an oyster on each square. Serves 6.

OYSTERS ROCKEFELLER

4 dozen oysters in half shell   ¼ teaspoon pepper
8 slices crisp bacon   ¼ teaspoon paprika
2 cups chopped spinach   ⅓ cup lemon juice
3 tablespoons minced parsley   4 drops absinthe
½ cup chopped celery leaves   1 tablespoon white wine
2 green onion tops   ½ cup butter, melted
½ teaspoon salt   ½ cup buttered crumbs

Heat a 1-inch layer of rock salt in pans until very hot. Arrange oysters in shells on salt and heat in very hot oven (475° F.) until edges curl, about 5 minutes. While oysters heat, chop bacon, spinach, parsley, celery and onion tops very fine and add seasonings, lemon juice, wines and butter. Place a little of the mixture on each oyster, sprinkle with crumbs and return to oven to brown, about 2 minutes. Serve at once in the pans of salt. Serves 8.

Clams

There are two general types of clams, the soft clams and the hard or quahog clams. Hard clams include three classes: the littlenecks (small), the cherry stone (medium) and the large chowder clams. The littleneck and cherry stone clams may be used uncooked. Clams are purchased in the shell by the dozen, shucked by the quart or pint or canned.

If clams are purchased in the shell, discard any which are not tightly closed or which do not close when lightly tapped. They are unsafe for use. Cover with cold water and sprinkle corn meal over the top, using 1 cup for each peck of clams. Let stand 3 hours or overnight to allow the clams to take in the meal and work out any sand which might be in them, then scrub the shells well and open with a strong knife as for oysters. The larger clams are usually steamed open.

CLAMS COOKED IN THE SHELL

STEAMED—
    30 clams in the shell   Juice of ½ lemon
    6 tablespoons butter   Salt and pepper

The hard-shelled clam is used for steaming. Scrub the shell with a brush and wash free of sand in several waters. Steam the clams in a steamer for 10 minutes, or until opened. While the clams are steaming, melt the butter and mix with the lemon juice, salt and pepper. Lay a napkin on a hot platter and place the clams in their shells on this. Cover with a second napkin and serve. In eating, remove the clam from the shell and dip it in the sauce. The thin, tough part known as the neck or siphon is not eaten.

ROASTED IN THE OVEN—Prepare the clams as for steaming, place in a pan, set the pan in a hot oven (425° F.) and bake until the shells open. Remove the top shell, being careful not to spill the liquor. Arrange the clams in the half shell on plates and on each place a piece of butter and a little pepper and salt. Add lemon juice if desired. Serve immediately.

CLAMBAKE—The seashore is the natural place for a clambake, but it is possible to have one at any place where there is a flat open space. Preparations should begin several hours before the time set for the meal.

Make a circle of flat stones—from 2 to 4 feet in diameter, according to the size of the party—and on this circle build a hot fire of wood. Let this burn for 2 to 3 hours. Then rake off the fire and cover the hot stones with fresh seaweed. On this lay fresh clams in their shells; also, if desired, oysters, potatoes in the skins, corn in the husk, and any other food that may be steamed. Cover with a thick layer of seaweed, and over all spread a large piece of sailcloth, fastening down the edges with stones. Leave for 2 to 3 hours; remove the cloth and the top layer of seaweed, and rake out the clams and other foods as needed.

The same materials may be cooked in a large kettle with the bottom covered with water and wet cheesecloth between the layers, but will lack the fine flavor of the real clambake.

CLAMS ON THE HALF SHELL

Small clams are served raw on the half shell, just as raw oysters are served. (See Index.)

CLAM COCKTAIL

Follow recipe for oyster cocktail. (Page 207.)

CREAMED CLAMS

4 quarts clams
1 tablespoon minced onion
4 tablespoons butter
4 tablespoons flour
6 strips pimiento

1 to 1½ cups milk
Salt and pepper
6 slices buttered toast
Parsley

Steam clams and remove from shells, saving liquor. Cook onion in butter until yellow; blend in flour. Add milk to clam liquor to make 2 cups and add to flour and butter. Cook until thickened, stirring constantly. Add clams and season with salt and pepper. Serve on toast, garnished with parsley and pimiento. Serves 6.

DEVILED CLAMS

2 cups clams
½ cup clam liquor
2 tablespoons minced onion
2 tablespoons minced green pepper
¼ cup chopped celery

4 tablespoons butter
1 teaspoon salt
⅛ teaspoon pepper
3 drops Tabasco sauce
½ teaspoon prepared mustard

¾ cup cracker crumbs

Chop clams fine and simmer in their liquor 5 minutes. Cook onion, green pepper and celery in butter until tender. Mix with clams and remaining ingredients. Fill greased ramekins or scallop shells and bake in moderate oven (350° F.) 20 minutes. Serves 6.

CLAM CAKES

1 cup shucked clams
1 cup cracker crumbs

¼ teaspoon salt
2 eggs, beaten

Chop hard parts of clams; mix with soft parts, clam liquor, crumbs and salt. Let stand 5 minutes. Add eggs, shape into cakes and fry in hot deep fat (375° F.). Serves 4.

COLD LOBSTER EN COQUILLES WITH MAYONNAISE

Serve cold boiled lobster in the shell on a bed of lettuce. Color mayonnaise red with lobster coral and place on lobster. Canned lobster meat may be chilled thoroughly and served on lettuce with anchovy mayonnaise.

BROILED LIVE LOBSTER

1 large lobster   Salt and pepper
Melted butter

Kill lobster by inserting a sharp knife in its back between the body and tail shells, severing the spinal cord. Split lengthwise, remove the stomach and intestinal canal, crack the large claws and lay the lobster flat. Brush the meat with butter, season with salt and pepper, place in broiler with the shell side down, and broil slowly until browned. Serves 2.

A small lobster will cook in 15 minutes; larger ones may require 20 to 25 minutes. The lobster may be turned once, if desired, but this is not necessary and results in loss of juices. Serve a small dish of drawn butter with each lobster. A nut-cracker may be used at the table for further cracking of the claws. Serves 2.

BAKED LIVE LOBSTER

Prepare as for broiling. Place lobster in a baking pan, shell side down, and season with salt, pepper and butter. Bake in hot oven (400° F.) about 40 minutes, basting it twice with melted butter.

BAKED STUFFED LOBSTER

1 large live lobster   3 tablespoons butter, melted
1 cup soft bread crumbs   Salt and pepper

Prepare lobster as for broiling. Toast bread crumbs in the oven and mix with butter and green fat and mashed coral from the lobster. Season with salt and pepper. Fill cavities in lobster with mixture and cover exposed meat with a thin layer. Bake as above. Serves 2.

LOBSTER FARCI

2 lobsters	1 tablespoon minced parsley
1 tablespoon butter	Salt and pepper
1 tablespoon flour	Few grains nutmeg
1 cup milk	3 egg yolks, hard cooked
2 tablespoons bread crumbs	1/4 cup buttered crumbs

Boil lobsters and cut meat into small pieces. In opening the lobsters be careful not to break the body or tail shells. Melt butter, blend in flour, add milk and cook until thickened. Add crumbs, parsley, lobster, salt, pepper, nutmeg and egg yolks mashed very fine. Mix all together well. Wash shells, wipe dry and cut off the under part of the tail shells with a pair of scissors. Join the large ends of both tail shells to one body shell to form a boat-shaped receptacle. Place lobster mixture in this boat, sprinkle with buttered crumbs and bake in moderate oven (350° F.) 15 to 20 minutes. Serves 2 or 3.

LOBSTER THERMIDOR

1 boiled lobster	1/2 cup sherry
3 mushrooms, sliced	2 tablespoons flour
5 tablespoons butter	1 cup cream
Dash paprika	1/2 teaspoon salt
1/8 teaspoon mustard	2 tablespoons grated Par-
1 tablespoon minced parsley	mesan cheese

Cut lobster into halves, remove meat and break it into small pieces. Cook mushrooms in 3 tablespoons butter and add paprika, mustard, parsley and sherry. Heat to boiling. Melt remaining butter, blend in flour, add cream and cook until thickened, stirring constantly. Season with salt and add mushroom mixture and lobster. Fill shell with mixture. Sprinkle with cheese. Bake in very hot oven (425° F.) 15 to 20 minutes. Serves 2.

CREAMED LOBSTER, SALMON OR TUNA

2 cups diced cooked lobster, salmon or tuna	2 teaspoons lemon juice
2 cups medium white sauce	2 drops Tabasco sauce

Heat lobster in white sauce; add lemon juice and Tabasco sauce. Serve on toast or crackers. Serves 6.

LOBSTER BÉCHAMEL

1 boiled lobster	½ teaspoon salt
3 tablespoons butter	⅛ teaspoon pepper
3 tablespoons flour	1 teaspoon minced parsley
¾ cup chicken stock	1 teaspoon lemon juice
¾ cup cream	2 egg yolks
½ bay leaf	6 patty shells

Remove meat from lobster and cut into dice. Melt butter, blend in flour, add chicken stock, cream and bay leaf and cook until thickened, stirring constantly. Add salt, pepper, parsley and lemon juice and cook 5 minutes longer. Remove bay leaf. Add lobster and heat thoroughly. Add slightly beaten egg yolks and cook 1 minute longer, stirring constantly. Serve in patty shells. Serves 6.

DEVILED LOBSTER

2 cups diced cooked lobster	1 tablespoon flour
1 cup soft bread crumbs	1 cup milk
1 hard-cooked egg	½ teaspoon salt
2 teaspoons lemon juice	Few grains cayenne
1 tablespoon butter	½ teaspoon anchovy paste

Mix lobster with half the crumbs. Chop egg very fine and add to lobster with lemon juice. Melt butter, blend in flour, add milk and cook until thickened, stirring constantly. Season with salt, cayenne and anchovy paste. Mix well with lobster mixture and fill greased scallop shells or ramekins. Top with remaining crumbs. Brown in moderate oven (375° F.) about 15 minutes. Serves 6.

LOBSTER WITH CORAL SAUCE

1 boiled lobster	½ teaspoon salt
3 tablespoons butter	2 cups boiling water
2 tablespoons flour	2 tablespoons lemon juice

Dice lobster meat and mash coral with 1 tablespoon butter. Melt remaining butter, blend in flour and salt, add water and cook until thickened, stirring constantly. Add coral and cook 4 minutes. Strain, add lobster meat and lemon juice and heat to boiling. Serves 4.

Fresh Water Crawfish

Crawfish, or crayfish, look like lobsters, but are much smaller. They may be prepared and served in the same way as lobsters.

Add bay leaf, celery leaves, peppercorns and caraway seeds to boiling salted water, then drop crawfish into the water and cook 5 minutes. Drain, cool and remove shell. Take out the intestines by pinching the extreme end of the center fin and jerking it suddenly. This removes the gall cyst which is very bitter. Two pounds crawfish will serve 6.

Crabs

The blue crab, found on the Atlantic coast and in the Gulf of Mexico, is about 2½ inches long by 5 inches wide. The Dungeness crab of the Pacific coast is much larger. Crabs go through a molting season, in the spring and summer. During the few days between the shedding of the old shell and the hardening of the new one, they are called soft-shelled crabs. At other times, they are called hard-shelled crabs.

Oyster crabs are tiny, almost transparent, grayish-white crabs found in the shells with oysters. They are often served in oyster stews.

Dressing Crabs

All uncooked crabs should be vigorously alive when purchased, or the meat is not good.

SOFT-SHELLED CRABS—Place live crabs face down on a board; slice across just back of the eyes. Lift apron at opposite end of crab, scrape off spongy portion beneath and cut off apron. Remove sand bag. Lift each point at the sides and remove all the gills. Wash and dry.

HARD-SHELLED CRABS—Drop the live crabs head first into rapidly boiling salted water and boil 20 minutes. Drain and cool. Take the crab in both hands, with the thumbs at the tail end, and pull the upper and lower shells apart. Discard the material that sticks to the upper shell and pull off all the orange waxy material and white spongy substance between the halves of the body and at the sides. The edible part of the crab lies in the two compact masses remaining and in the small flakes that may be extracted from the large claws.

BROILED SOFT-SHELLED CRABS

6 soft-shelled crabs
¼ cup butter, melted
2 tablespoons lemon juice

¼ teaspoon salt
⅛ teaspoon cayenne
Flour

Clean crabs as directed. Mix butter, lemon juice, salt and cayenne and roll each crab first in this mixture, then in flour. Place on broiler rack and broil 4 minutes on each side. Serve garnished with toast triangles. Serves 6.

FRIED SOFT-SHELLED CRABS

6 soft-shelled crabs
Salt and pepper

2 eggs, slightly beaten
1½ cups fine bread crumbs

Clean crabs and sprinkle with salt and pepper. Dip in egg, then in crumbs. Fry in hot deep fat (375° F.) 3 to 4 minutes. Serves 3 or 6.

DEVILED CRABS

8 hard-shelled crabs
1 cup medium white sauce
1 egg, beaten
2 tablespoons tomato catchup

½ teaspoon prepared mustard
2 hard-cooked eggs
½ cup buttered crumbs
2 tablespoons minced parsley

Boil crabs as directed; remove and flake meat, saving claws for garnish. Add hot white sauce to beaten egg, then add catchup, mustard, crab meat and finely chopped hard-cooked eggs. Fill 4 crab shells with mixture and sprinkle with crumbs and parsley. Bake in hot oven (400° F.) until crumbs are browned, about 10 minutes. Serves 4.

CREAMED CRAB MEAT

2 cups cooked crab meat
2 tablespoons butter
2 tablespoons flour
Few grains pepper
½ teaspoon salt

½ teaspoon prepared mustard
¼ teaspoon paprika
1 cup milk

Remove spines from crab meat. Melt butter, blend in flour and seasonings, add milk and cook until thickened, stirring constantly. Add crab meat and heat thoroughly. Serve very hot in patty shells or on toast. Serves 6.

SCALLOPED—Add ½ cup crumbs, place in shells, top with buttered crumbs and bake in moderate oven (350° F.) 15 minutes.

CRAB MEAT IN SHELLS

½ cup butter
½ cup flour
Few grains cayenne
1 teaspoon salt
¼ teaspoon pepper

3 cups milk
½-pound can crab meat
½ cup minced parsley
4 hard-cooked eggs, chopped
½ cup buttered crumbs

Melt butter; blend in flour and seasonings. Add milk and cook until thickened, stirring constantly. Flake crab meat and remove spines. Add to sauce with parsley and eggs. Place in buttered shells and top with buttered crumbs. Brown in moderate oven (375° F.) about 10 minutes. Serves 8.

CRAB NEWBURG

½ pound cooked crab meat
¼ cup butter
¼ teaspoon salt
Dash cayenne

1 cup cream
2 egg yolks, beaten
1 tablespoon sherry
4 patty shells

Heat crab meat in butter; add salt and cayenne. Mix 1 tablespoon cream with egg yolks and add remainder to crab meat. Add egg yolks and sherry and heat until it begins to thicken, stirring constantly. Do not boil. Serve in patty shells or on hot buttered toast. Serves 4.

AVOCADO CRAB CUTLETS

2 cups cooked crab meat
3 tablespoons butter
4 tablespoons flour
½ teaspoon salt
⅛ teaspoon pepper

1½ cups milk
2 cups diced avocado
Fine bread crumbs
3 eggs, beaten

Remove spines from crab meat. Melt butter and blend in flour. Add salt, pepper and milk and cook until thickened, stirring constantly. Add avocado and crab meat and mix well. Shape into cutlets and roll in crumbs, then in egg and again in crumbs. Fry in hot deep fat (360° F.) until browned, 2 to 4 minutes. Serves 6.

Or add ½ cup cream, place mixture in casserole and cover with buttered crumbs. Brown in moderate oven (350° F.).

CRAB COCKTAIL

Follow recipe for oyster cocktail. (See Index.)

SHRIMP AND PRAWNS

Shrimp and prawns are very similar, but the prawn is larger than the shrimp. The shrimp is seldom more than 2 inches long, while the prawn is often 6 to 7 inches.

To Prepare Fresh Shrimp—Add bay leaf, celery leaves, peppercorns and caraway seeds (tied in cheesecloth if desired) to boiling salted water. Simmer a few minutes. Wash shrimp under running water, then drop into boiling seasoned water and simmer 10 to 15 minutes. Paprika is sometimes added to intensify the red color. Allow to cool in this liquor. When cold, remove shells carefully and remove the black line which runs the length of the back. Use in recipes as desired. If canned shrimp are used, they too must be cleaned by removing the black line, which is the intestinal tract. Strained liquor may be used in Court Bouillon or jellied fish salads.

SHRIMP COCKTAIL

Follow recipe for oyster cocktail, using cleaned cooked shrimp. (Page 207.)

CREAMED SHRIMP

2 cups cooked shrimp	¼ teaspoon celery salt
1 teaspoon lemon juice	1½ cups white sauce

Add shrimp, lemon juice and celery salt to hot white sauce and heat thoroughly. Serve on toast or on crisp crackers. Garnish with paprika and parsley. Serves 4.

SHRIMP WIGGLE

4 tablespoons butter	2 cups milk
4 tablespoons flour	Few drops onion juice
½ teaspoon salt	2 cups cooked shrimp
⅛ teaspoon pepper	1 cup cooked peas
½ teaspoon celery salt	Crackers

Melt butter and blend in flour, salt, pepper and celery salt. Add milk and onion juice and cook until thickened, stirring constantly. Add shrimp and peas and heat thoroughly. Serve on crisp crackers. Serves 6.

If desired, omit celery salt and cook ½ cup diced celery in butter before adding flour and seasonings. Add 1 tablespoon diced pimiento or sprinkle freely with paprika.

SCALLOPED SHRIMP

4 tablespoons butter
2 tablespoons minced onion
1 tablespoon minced green pepper
4 tablespoons flour

¼ teaspoon dry mustard
2 cups milk
2 cups cooked shrimp
1 cup buttered crumbs

Melt butter and cook onion and green pepper in it until tender. Blend in flour and mustard. Add milk and cook until thickened, stirring constantly. Add shrimp. Pour into greased casserole, cover with buttered crumbs and bake in moderate oven (350° F.) about 20 minutes. Serves 6.

CHARLESTON SHRIMP PILAU

1 cup diced bacon
2 tablespoons chopped onion
2½ cups cooked tomatoes

1 cup uncooked rice
1 pound shrimp, cooked

Fry bacon until crisp, remove and cook onion in bacon fat until a light yellow. Add tomatoes and rice, mix well, cover and heat to boiling point. Lower heat and simmer 20 minutes, occasionally stirring lightly with fork. Set in warm place where there is no danger of scorching for another 20 minutes, to allow rice to become fluffy. Add shrimp and bacon, place in casserole and bake in a 350° F. oven 15 minutes. Serves 6.

SHRIMP CREOLE

½ medium-sized onion, chopped
½ cup chopped mushrooms
2 tablespoons butter
2 tablespoons flour
1 cup mushroom broth
1 cup water
½ teaspoon salt
⅛ teaspoon pepper

Dash of cayenne
¼ teaspoon thyme
1 bay leaf
2 pimientos, chopped
2 cups cooked shrimp
4 wheat biscuits
Butter
3 sprigs parsley

Sauté onion and mushrooms in butter 3 minutes; stir in flour and cook 1 minute, then add liquid gradually and cook until thickened, stirring constantly. Add seasonings, pimientos and shrimp and cook 5 minutes. Remove bay leaf. Serve on wheat biscuits, which have been cut lengthwise into halves, toasted and buttered. Garnish with parsley.

SHRIMP PASTE

2 cups cooked shrimp
½ cup butter

Salt, celery salt, cayenne

Grind shrimp very fine; mix with softened butter. Season with salt, celery salt and cayenne, place in small pan and bake at 350° F. 30 minutes. Chill and slice. Serves 8.

SHRIMP GUMBO

6 green onions
2 cups chopped okra
1 tablespoon bacon fat
1 cup chopped tomatoes
6 cups stock
1 pod red pepper

1 green pepper
½ teaspoon thyme
1 bay leaf
1 teaspoon salt
1 pound shrimp, cooked

Clean onions, reserving green tops. Chop and sauté with okra in bacon fat. Add tomatoes and cook 5 minutes. Add stock, peppers, green onion tops cut into strips, thyme, bay leaf and salt. Heat to boiling and cook 10 minutes. Add shrimp, cut into halves, cover closely and simmer 1½ hours. Serve with rice. Serves 8.

JAMBALAYA SHRIMP

1 tablespoon fat
1 tablespoon flour
1 pound ham, cooked and
  chopped
1 cup cooked shrimp
1½ cups cooked tomatoes
1 onion, sliced
¼ teaspoon thyme
1 clove garlic, crushed

1 green pepper, chopped
1 tablespoon minced parsley
Salt, pepper and paprika
1 teaspoon Worcestershire
  sauce
1 red pepper, chopped
4 cups water
1 cup uncooked rice

Melt fat and add flour, stirring until smooth and slightly brown. Add chopped ham, shrimp and tomatoes and cook for 3 minutes. Add onion, seasonings and water. Simmer for 10 minutes. Add rice and boil until tender, 30 minutes. The mixture should not be stirred, although it may be necessary to lift it from the bottom of the kettle from time to time in order to keep rice from burning. Keep covered during cooking. Serves 6.

FROGS' LEGS

Frogs' legs (hindquarters only) are considered quite a delicacy. Turn the skin over and slip off the legs, like a glove taken off inside out.

FRIED FROGS' LEGS

6 frogs' legs	1 egg
Salt and pepper	Fine bread crumbs
Lemon juice	

Skin the legs and wash them in cold water; dry well on a towel or napkin. Season with salt, pepper and lemon juice. Beat the egg and season it with salt and pepper; dip the legs into egg, then into dried bread crumbs or fine cracker crumbs. Fry in hot deep fat (390° F.) 2 to 3 minutes. Use a wire frying basket if possible. Serve with tartare sauce. Serves 2.

EELS—Remove backbone, cut into 2-inch lengths and parboil 10 minutes. Proceed as for frogs' legs.

TURTLES AND TERRAPINS

Turtles and terrapins should be alive when purchased. If the large southern variety, the soft-shelled or snapping turtles are used, cut off the head and let the turtle lie in cold water ½ hour or hang on a hook with neck down until blood stops dripping. Then wash and drop into boiling water and cook for 10 minutes. Pour off the water and cover the turtle with cold water, letting it stand until cool enough to handle easily; then rub the nails and black skin from the legs with a towel.

Wash the turtle carefully, place it in a saucepan covered with boiling water and simmer until the flesh is tender. This will be when the joints of the legs can be broken with a slight pressure and the shell separate easily. It will take from 30 to 60 minutes, until the skin is like jelly. Remove the turtle from the water, cool slightly, place it on its back with the head end away from you and loosen and remove the under shell.

The liver, gall bladder and sand bag will be found near the head end, the gall being attached to the left side of the liver. Take out the gall as you would that of a chicken, being careful not to break it. Remove the entrails and throw them away.

Take out the eggs, if there are any, remove the slight membrane and drop them into cold water. Cut all the meat very fine, saving any water that may collect in the shells. The turtle is now ready to use in a stew or in other ways.

If terrapin is used, wash and plunge it alive into boiling salted water, and cook for about 10 minutes. Then plunge it into cold water, rub off the toe nails and dark skin, place it again in salted boiling water and cook until the legs are tender, from 30 to 60 minutes. Clean the terrapin according to directions for turtles, but instead of throwing away the small intestines, cut them in very small pieces and use them for food. Discard the thick, heavy part of the intestines.

TURTLE RAGOUT

1 onion, chopped	1 clove garlic
2 tablespoons butter	1 cup water
1 tablespoon flour	2 pounds turtle meat, diced
1 bay leaf	¼ cup sherry

Cook onion in butter; blend in flour. Add remaining ingredients and simmer 30 minutes. Serves 6.

TERRAPIN OR TURTLE À LA KING

6 hard-cooked egg yolks	Few grains allspice
2 tablespoons butter	Few grains nutmeg
2 cups cream	2 cups cooked terrapin or
½ teaspoon salt	turtle meat
⅛ teaspoon pepper	Patty shells or toast

Mash egg yolks and blend with softened butter. Heat cream in double boiler and mix gradually with egg yolks. Add seasonings and terrapin or turtle meat and cook 15 minutes in double boiler. Serve in patty shells or on toast. Serves 6.

TERRAPIN WITH MUSHROOMS

2 cups cooked terrapin meat	2 cups medium white sauce
1 pint chopped cooked	1 tablespoon sherry
mushrooms	6 slices toast

Heat terrapin and mushrooms in white sauce thoroughly. Add sherry and serve on toast. Serves 6.

MEAT

THE name meat is given generally to all edible flesh of animals used for food. The name beef is used for the flesh of adult cattle; veal for the flesh of calves under one year of age; pork for the flesh of swine; mutton for the flesh of adult sheep and lamb for the flesh of sheep from six weeks to one year old.

SELECTION OF MEAT

Beef

Good beef has a fresh red color, a smooth covering of brittle creamy fat and small streaks of fat distributed through the lean. In other words it is well marbled with fat. The lean is firm, fine-grained and velvety. The bones in young beef are porous and red, in older animals they are white and flinty.

Lamb

Good quality lamb varies in color from a light to a dark pink, since the color darkens as the animal grows older, and in mutton deepens to red. The fat of young lambs is quite soft and slightly pink in color. As the animal grows older it becomes harder and whiter, so that mutton fat is white and rather brittle.

Veal

Veal is light grayish pink in color. The meat is very fine-grained, velvety and fairly firm, with little surface fat and no marbling. The fat is clear, firm and white and the bones are porous and red.

Pork

Good quality pork is grayish pink, changing to a delicate rose in older animals. The flesh is relatively firm, fine-grained, well marbled and covered with firm white fat. Fresh pork must be thoroughly cooked, so should not be broiled or fried.

FROZEN MEATS

Frozen meat may be thawed and then cooked as any other fresh meat. Cooking may also be started while the meat is still frozen with successful results. Additional time must be allowed for cooking, however, and the approximate times for cooking various cuts by either method are indicated below:

CUT	MINUTES PER POUND Thawed	Unthawed
Standing Rib Roast (Roast at 300° F.)		
Rare	18	43
Medium	22	47
Well done	30	55
Rolled Rib Roast (Roast at 300° F.)		
Rare	32	53
Medium	38	57
Well done	48	65
Beef Rump (Braise)	30	50
Porterhouse Steak (Broil, rare to medium)		
1 inch	8–10	21–33
1½ inches	10–15	23–38
2 inches	20–30	33–43
Boneless Lamb Shoulder (Roast at 300° F.)	40	60
Leg of Lamb (Roast at 300° F.)	30–35	45–55
Pork Loin (Roast at 350° F.)		
Center cut	35–40	50–55
Rib or loin end	50–55	70–75
	Total Time Minutes	Total Time Minutes
Club Steak (Broil, rare to medium)		
¾ inch	16–20	24–28
1 inch	20	30
Round Steak (Pan-broil)		
½ inch	7	11
Beef Patties (Pan-broil)		
1 inch	8	10
Lamb Chops (Pan-broil)		
¾ inch	10	15
1½ inches	20	25
Shoulder Lamb Chops (Braise)		
½ inch	15	20
Pork Chops (Braise)		
¾ inch	45	55

Cuts of Meat

Animals dressed for market are divided lengthwise through the backbone into two parts, each of which is called a side. Each side is divided again into two parts, the forequarter and the hindquarter. Each quarter is then divided into smaller cuts which are sold in the retail market.

Comparative Cost of Various Cuts

As a general rule the price of the different cuts of meat is determined by considerations such as tenderness, grain, general appearance and convenience of cooking rather than by food values in terms of fat or protein, or the ease with which they are digested. The cheapest cuts for general use are the shanks, plates and chuck.

MEAT SPECIALTIES

LIVER—Calf and lamb liver are both very mild and tender. Beef and pork liver are somewhat stronger in flavor and coarser in texture, so are sometimes dipped into hot water for 5 minutes before using. All liver has a very high nutritive value, being particularly rich in iron and vitamins A and B. However, because of demand calf's liver is much higher in price.

KIDNEYS—Kidneys from veal, lamb, pork and beef may all be used for stews and pies. Lamb and veal kidneys should be selected for broiling.

SWEETBREADS—These are the thymus glands of calves and lambs. They are very delicate in flavor and texture. They should be cooked immediately since they are very perishable.

HEARTS—Calf, beef, lamb and pork hearts are all economical and nourishing foods with little or no waste. Beef heart is largest.

TONGUE—The tongues from various animals differ mainly in size. The beef tongue is largest and therefore slices best.

BRAINS—These are similar to sweetbreads in flavor and texture and may be obtained from calf, lamb, pork and beef. Brains are very perishable and should be used immediately.

TRIPE—Tripe is the muscular inner lining of the stomach of beef, sheep or pig. Veal tripe is most tender. Tripe may be honeycombed or smooth, the former being choicest.

MEATS AND HOW TO COOK THEM
lamb chart

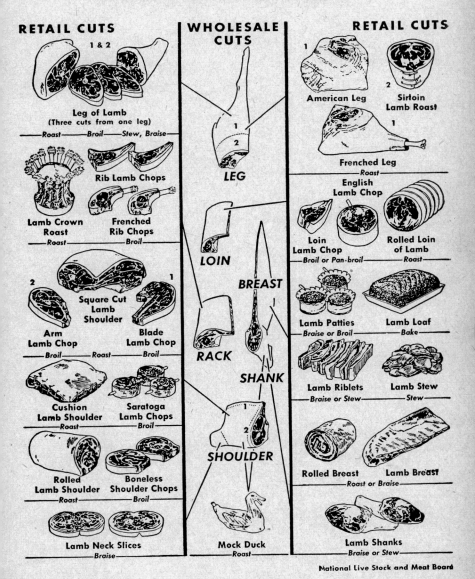

RETAIL CUTS

WHOLESALE CUTS

RETAIL CUTS

1 & 2

Leg of Lamb
(Three cuts from one leg)
—Roast——Broil——Stew, Braise—

Rib Lamb Chops

Lamb Crown Roast
—Roast—

Frenched Rib Chops
—Broil—

2 **Square Cut Lamb Shoulder** 1

Arm Lamb Chop
—Broil——Roast—

Blade Lamb Chop
—Broil—

Cushion Lamb Shoulder
—Roast—

Saratoga Lamb Chops
—Broil—

Rolled Lamb Shoulder
—Roast—

Boneless Shoulder Chops
—Broil—

Lamb Neck Slices
—Braise—

LEG

LOIN

RACK

BREAST

SHANK

SHOULDER

Mock Duck
—Roast—

1 **American Leg**

2 **Sirloin Lamb Roast**

1 **Frenched Leg**
—Roast—

English Lamb Chop

Loin Lamb Chop
—Broil or Pan-broil—

Rolled Loin of Lamb
—Roast—

Lamb Patties
—Braise or Broil—

Lamb Loaf
—Bake—

Lamb Riblets
—Braise or Stew—

Lamb Stew
—Stew—

Rolled Breast

Lamb Breast
—Roast or Braise—

Lamb Shanks
—Braise or Stew—

National Live Stock and Meat Board

MEATS AND HOW TO COOK THEM
beef chart

RETAIL CUTS

Ground Beef — Roast or Broil —

Heel of Round — Braise or Simmer —

Hind Shank — Soup or Simmer —

Rolled Flank — Braise —

Flank Stew — Stew —

Flank Steak Cubed

Flank Steak Fillets — Braise or Pan-broil —

Plate Boiling Beef

Rolled Plate

Short Ribs — Simmer or Braise —

Beef Brisket

Corned Beef — Simmer —

Knuckle Soup Bone

Cross Cut Fore Shank — Soup or Braise —

English Cut

Arm Pot Roast — Braise —

Arm Steak

WHOLESALE CUTS

ROUND

RUMP

LOIN END

SHORT LOIN

FLANK

PLATE

RIB

CHUCK

BRISKET

SHANK

RETAIL CUTS

Top Round

Round Steak

Bottom Round (Swiss Steak) — Braise —

Rolled Rump

Rump Roast — Braise or Roast —

Sirloin Steak

Pin Bone Sirloin Steak — Broil or Pan-broil —

Porterhouse Steak

T Bone Steak

Club Steak — Broil or Pan-broil —

Standing Rib Roast

Rolled Rib Roast — Roast —

Rib Steak — Broil —

Blade Steak

Blade Pot Roast

Triangle Pot Roast

Boneless Chuck Pot Roast

Shoulder Fillet — Braise —

Rolled Neck

Boneless Neck — Braise or Stew —

MEATS AND HOW TO COOK THEM
pork chart

RETAIL CUTS

2 Sirloin Pork Roast
—Roast—

1 Pork Tenderloin
Frenched and Whole
—Broil or Braise—

2 to 5 Canadian Style Bacon
—Broil—

Loin Chop

4 Rib Pork Chop

4 Frenched Rib Chop

2 to 5 Butterfly Chop
—Broil or Braise—

1, 2 Loin Roast Ham End

3, 4 Loin Roast Center Cut

5 Loin Roast Shoulder End

4 Crown Pork Roast
—Roast—

Fat Back
—Lard—Salt Pork—

Lard
—Shortening—

Blade Pork Steaks
—Braise—

Smoked Cottage Roll
—Bake or Pan-broil—

Boston Style Butt

Rolled Boston Style Butt
—Roast—

WHOLESALE CUTS

HAM

LOIN

SIDE

SPARE RIBS

BUTT

PICNIC

JOWL

Bacon Square
—Seasoning—Pan-broil—

RETAIL CUTS

Half Ham Butt End

Half Ham Shank End
—Bake or Simmer—

Ham Butt Slice

Center Ham Slice
—Broil or Pan-broil—

Fresh Ham Roast

Rolled Fresh Ham Roast

Bacon
—Broil—Pan-broil—

Salt Pork
—Seasoning—

Spareribs
—Simmer—Braise—Roast—

Fresh Picnic Shoulder
—Roast—

Smoked Picnic Shoulder
—Bake or Simmer—

Cushion Style Picnic Shoulder

Rolled Picnic Shoulder
—Roast—

Fresh Shoulder Hock
—Simmer—

Arm Pork Steak
—Braise—

National Live Stock and Meat Board

MEATS AND HOW TO COOK THEM
veal chart

RETAIL CUTS

Veal Rump Roast **Rolled Veal Rump Roast**
—*Roast or Braise*—

Sirloin Veal Steak (1) **Loin Veal Chop** (2) **Kidney Veal Chop** (3)
—*Braise*—

Veal Crown Roast **Veal Rib Roast** **Veal Rib Chop** (Frenched)
—*Roast*—*Braise*—*Roast*—

Blade Veal Roast (1) **Arm Veal Roast** (2)
—*Roast or Braise*—

Blade Veal Steak (1) **Arm Veal Steak** (2)
—*Braise*—

Rolled Veal Shoulder Roast **City Chicken**
—*Roast or Braise*—*Braise*—

WHOLESALE CUTS

ROUND

LOIN

RIB

BREAST

SHOULDER

SHANK

RETAIL CUTS

Heel of Veal Round **Veal Hind Shank**
—*Braise or Simmer*—

Veal Round Steak (Cutlet) **Veal Round Roast**
—*Braise*—*Roast or Braise*—

Veal Scallops **Veal Rosettes**
—*Braise*—

Veal Breast
—*Braise or Stew*—

Mock Chicken Legs **Veal Loaf**
—*Braise*—*Roast*—

Veal Riblets **Veal Stew**
—*Braise or Stew*—*Stew*—

Veal Fore Shank **Veal Patties**
—*Simmer*—*Braise*—

National Live Stock and Meat Board

Amount of Meat to Buy for Each Person

Meat shrinks from one-third to one-half in cooking. Therefore allow one-fourth pound of meat without bone for each serving, and one-half pound of meat consisting of lean, fat and bone as a minimum for each serving.

CARE OF MEAT IN THE HOME

As soon as meat comes from the market, the wrapping paper should be removed, and the meat should be put on a plate, covered lightly with waxed paper and placed in the refrigerator or other cool place.

Before cooking meat, wash quickly under running water, remove outer membrane and inspection stamp. In hot weather, if meat is to be kept any length of time and there is any danger of its spoiling, it may be seared on the outside on a hot griddle or may be plunged into boiling water and kept there for five minutes; lamb, mutton, or veal may be partly cooked. It should then be cooled as quickly as possible, uncovered, and put into the refrigerator or other cool place.

METHODS OF COOKING MEAT

Meat is cooked to soften connective tissue, to develop flavor, to improve appearance and to destroy bacteria or other organisms. The method of cooking depends on the kind and quality of the meat to be cooked. Only tender cuts of meat can be cooked successfully by dry heat. Less tender cuts of meat require moist heat and long, slow cooking.

BROILING—Broiling means to cook by direct heat and may be done over hot coals or under a flame or an electric unit. This method may be used for tender cuts of meat with adequate amounts of fat. Veal should not be broiled since it is too low in fat; pork should not be broiled. Preheat the broiler with the oven door closed, about 10 minutes. Slash the fat edge of meat in several places to prevent curling. If meat thermometer is used insert at the side and force bulb into center of cut. Place meat on broiler rack with surface of meat about 4 inches from source of heat. Turn when surface is browned and about half the total cooking time has been used. Sprinkle browned side with salt, turn meat and cook until brown or to same internal temperature as for roast beef.

PAN-BROILING—Place meat in sizzling hot skillet and brown on both sides. Reduce temperature, pour off fat as it accumulates and cook until as well done as desired, turning from time to time. Pork is not cooked by this method.

ROASTING—Place meat on rack in roasting pan, fat side up and cook in slow oven, uncovered and without water until as well cooked as desired. Basting is not necessary. The large tender cuts of meat are cooked by this method.

COOKING IN WATER—Cover meat with boiling water, season with salt and pepper and cook slowly at simmering temperature, not boiling, until meat is tender.

STEWING—Cut meat into cubes. Brown if desired, on all sides in hot fat, cover with boiling water and cook at simmering temperature in a covered kettle until meat is tender. Less tender cuts containing much connective tissue are best cooked by this method which softens both tissue and fiber.

The best cuts for stews are those containing both fat and lean and some bone. The shank is the most economical of all cuts for this purpose. Other cuts used are the neck, plate, flank, heel of the round and short ribs. The brisket and the rump are sometimes used. Occasionally a cut like the round is used, as in beef à la mode.

BRAISING—This method of cooking by moist heat is used for the less tender cuts of meat which require long slow cooking in the presence of moisture to bring out the full flavor and make the meat tender. Many pork cuts are cooked by braising rather than broiling or pan-broiling since pork requires thorough cooking. Brown meat in a small amount of hot fat, then cover tightly and cook slowly in juices from the meat or in added liquid such as water, milk, cream, stock, diluted vinegar, fruit or vegetable juices. Add only a small amount of liquid at a time and do not let boil, but keep at a simmering temperature. Pork chops, pot roasts, fricassees, casserole meats, smothered steaks and similar favorites are all cooked by braising.

FRYING AND SAUTÉING—Some meats, such as chops and cutlets, may be crumbed and fried in deep fat. Ham, liver, and some other meats are sometimes sautéed in a small amount of fat at low temperature, after the first searing.

PRESSURE COOKING—utilizes live steam in a special kettle.

BEEF

ROASTING

	WEIGHT POUNDS	OVEN TEMPERATURE	INTERIOR TEMPERATURE			TIME PER POUND Minutes		
			Rare	Med.	Well done	Rare	Med.	Well done
Standing ribs (3 ribs)	7–8	300°F.	140°F.	160°F.	170°F.	18–20	22–25	27–30
(1 rib)	2–6	350.	140.	160.	170.	33	45	50
Rolled ribs	6–8	300.	140.	160.	170.	32	38	48
Chuck ribs	5–8	300.		150–170			25–30	
Rump	5–7	300.		150–170			25–30	
Whole tenderloin	4–6	300.	140.	160.		25	30–35	

BROILING

	WEIGHT POUNDS	OVEN TEMPERATURE	TOTAL COOKING TIME Minutes		
			Rare	Med.	Well done
Filer mignon—1 inch	1/3	550°F.	5	6–7	
1 1/2 inches	1/2	550°F.	9–10	12	
2 inches	3/4	550°F.	15	18	
Club steak—1 inch	1	550°F.	9–10	12–14	
1 1/2 inches	1 1/4	550°F.	14–16	18–20	
2 inches	1 1/2	550°F.	18–22	24–30	
Sirloin steak—1 inch	3	550°F.	10–12	14–16	
1 1/2 inches	4 1/4	550°F.	15–20	20–25	
2 inches	5 3/4	550°F.	20–25	25–30	
Porterhouse steak—1 inch	2	550°F.	9–10	12–15	
1 1/2 inches	2 1/2	550°F.	14–16	18–20	
2 inches	3	550°F.	18–22	25–30	
Ground patties (1 x 3 inches)	1/4	550°F.	15	25	

BRAISING

	AVERAGE WEIGHT OR THICKNESS	COOKING TIME
Pot roast	3–5 pounds	3–4 hours
Swiss steak	1 1/2–2 1/2 inches	2–3 hours
Fricassee	2-inch cubes	1 1/2 hours
Beef birds	1/2x2x4 inches	1 1/2 hours
Short ribs	Pieces 2x2x4 inches	1 1/2 hours
Round steak	3/4 inch	45–60 minutes
Stuffed steak	1/2–3/4 inch	1 1/2 hours

BEEF

BROWNED BEEF BRISKET

6 pounds beef brisket	Salt and pepper
Dash celery salt	6 or more medium
Garlic	boiled potatoes

If the brisket has much bone, part may be removed to use in making soup or stock. Cover meat with boiling water, add celery salt and garlic and simmer 3 hours or until tender, turning it once during the cooking. Remove meat, place in shallow pan with skin side up, score several times across the top and season. Drop potatoes into kettle to take up some of the fat; then place around meat and brown in hot oven (400° F.) about 20 minutes. Make a gravy with the remaining liquid and serve. Serves 6.

BRISKET OF BEEF

3 pounds beef brisket	½ cup diced celery with
½ cup sliced onions	leaves
½ cup sliced carrots	1½ teaspoons salt

Cover beef with hot water, add vegetables and simmer, covered, until meat is tender, about 2½ to 3 hours. Do not boil. Add salt when half done and more water if necessary. Remove meat from broth, slice and serve with Horse-radish Sauce (page 324) or Onion Sauce (page 315). Allow ½ pound per serving.

TO CORN BEEF

Fresh-killed beef	½ pound brown sugar
1½ pounds fine salt	½ ounce saltpeter

Scrub a good oak barrel thoroughly. Put as much fresh-killed beef as desired to be corned in barrel and cover with cold water. Have the water 2 inches above meat. Let stand for 48 hours. Drain off the water and measure before discarding. Measure the same amount of cold water (spring water if possible) and to every gallon of water formerly used, add the above proportions of salt, sugar and saltpeter. Boil for 15 minutes and skim. When cold, pour over the beef. Place a heavy weight on meat to keep it under the brine. Store in cool cellar. The corned beef will be ready for use after 10 days.

BOILED CORNED BEEF

6 pounds corned beef   1 onion
1 carrot   Vinegar
                  Butter

Cover meat with cold water and let stand 1 hour. Drain and
put into kettle with carrot and onion and enough cold water to
cover. Add 1 teaspoon vinegar for each quart of water. Simmer
until tender, 30 to 40 minutes for each pound. Let stand in the
liquid 20 minutes, then drain and rub butter over the meat just
before serving if desired. Serves 12.

BAKED CORNED BEEF HASH

2 cups diced cold boiled $\frac{3}{8}$ cup cream
  potatoes   3 tablespoons butter
1½ cups chopped corned   Salt, pepper and paprika
  beef   6 eggs
1 small onion, minced

Combine potatoes, corned beef and onion. Add ¼ cup cream
and 1 tablespoon melted butter. Season and mix well. Place mixture in buttered oblong baking dish. With the bottom of a
custard cup, make 6 indentations in the hash and dot each with
bits of butter, using 1 tablespoon in all. Bake in very hot oven
(450°F.) 15 minutes. Remove from oven and into each indenta-
tion break one egg. Season and cover with 1 teaspoon of cream
to each egg and dot with remaining butter. Bake in moderate
oven (350° F.) until the eggs are set, 15 to 20 minutes. Serves 6.

RED FLANNEL HASH

9 cooked beets, chopped   ½ cup fat, melted
6 cooked potatoes, chopped   2 teaspoons salt
1½ cups chopped cooked   ⅛ teaspoon pepper
  corned beef   6 tablespoons water

Combine beets, potatoes, corned beef, fat, salt, pepper and
water. Place in greased baking dish and bake in moderate oven
(350° F.) about ¾ hour. Serves 6.

OLD-FASHIONED BOILED DINNER

6 pounds corned beef
  brisket
3 white turnips
1 cabbage

6 beets
6 onions
4 carrots
6 potatoes

Cover meat with cold water, heat rapidly to boiling, then remove scum, reduce heat and simmer until tender, 3 to 4 hours. Prepare vegetables, cutting turnips into quarters and cabbage into eighths. Cook beets in boiling water until tender. About 45 minutes before serving, skim fat from liquid. Add vegetables except beets and cook until vegetables are tender. Drain and add beets. Serves 10.

SCALLOPED CORNED BEEF

1 stalk celery, chopped
2 slices onion, chopped
1 cup Medium White Sauce

2 cups chopped cooked
  corned beef
Buttered bread crumbs

Cook chopped celery and onion in the sauce. Place corned beef in shallow baking dish and add the sauce. Sprinkle with buttered bread crumbs. Cook in moderate oven (350° F.) 20 to 25 minutes. Serves 5.

VARIATION—Heat corned beef mixture over direct heat instead of baking in oven. Serve on buttered toast. Omit bread crumbs.

BRAISED OXTAIL

1 oxtail (cut into 2-inch
  pieces)
2 tablespoons fat
2 small onions, sliced
1 carrot, chopped
1 tablespoon chopped celery

2 tablespoons flour
1 cup hot water
1 cup tomatoes
3 bay leaves
3 whole cloves
Salt and pepper

Brown pieces of oxtail in fat. Add onion, carrot and celery and cook until brown. Sprinkle with browned flour. Add hot water, tomatoes, bay leaves, cloves, salt and pepper. Place in casserole and cook in moderate oven (350° F.) until very tender. Serves 5 or 6.

VARIATION—Use beef stock instead of tomatoes and water, and omit cloves and garlic. Serve with noodles.

BEEF STEW WITH DUMPLINGS

1½ pounds shank, neck, plate, flank, rump or brisket
¼ cup flour
1½ teaspoons salt
¼ teaspoon pepper

1 small onion
⅓ cup cubed carrots
⅓ cup cubed turnips
4 cups potatoes, cut into quarters

Wipe meat, remove from bone, and cut into 1½-inch cubes. Mix flour with salt and pepper and dredge meat with it. Cut some of fat from meat and heat. When part of fat has fried out, brown meat in it, stirring constantly. Add enough boiling water to cover the meat or add a pint of tomatoes, stewed and strained and simmer until meat is tender, about 3 hours. Add onion, carrots and turnips during the last hour of cooking and the potatoes 20 minutes before serving. Add dumplings to stew, 15 minutes before serving. Cover kettle closely and do not remove cover for at least 12 minutes. Serves 6.

SAUERBRATEN

4 pounds beef (chuck, rump or round)
Salt and pepper
1 pint vinegar
4 bay leaves
12 peppercorns

4 cloves
1 bunch carrots, cut into strips
6 onions, sliced
1 tablespoon sugar
12 gingersnaps

Wipe meat with damp cloth and sprinkle thoroughly with salt and pepper. Place in an earthen dish and add vinegar and enough water to cover. Add bay leaves, peppercorns and cloves and let stand tightly covered in a cool place for 5 days. Drain meat, place in a Dutch oven and brown well on all sides. Add carrots, onions and 1 cup of spiced vinegar mixture. Cover tightly and cook over low heat about 3 hours or until meat is tender. When meat is cooked, add the sugar and crumbled gingersnaps and cook for 10 minutes. This makes delicious gravy. If necessary, more of the spiced vinegar may be added for cooking meat or making gravy. Serves 8.

VARIATION—Omit gingersnaps and thicken gravy with flour moistened with water.

HOT MARINADE—Combine salt, pepper, vinegar, peppercorns, cloves, 1 carrot, 1 onion and sugar. Add 2 cups water. Cook until vegetables are tender. Strain.

BRAISED SHORT RIBS

3 pounds short ribs of beef   Salt, pepper
Flour   1 cup water

Cut meat into serving portions. Dredge with flour and brown in a hot kettle or oven. Season with salt and pepper, add water, cover and cook in kettle at simmering temperature or in a slow oven (300°F.) until tender, 1½ to 2 hours. Allow ½ pound per serving.

VARIATIONS—Use Barbecue Sauce (page 260) for water.

2. Spread prepared mustard over ribs and use tomatoes or tomato juice in place of water.

3. Add sauerkraut during the last 45 minutes of cooking.

4. Add uncooked pared potatoes, carrots and onions to the ribs about 45 minutes before ribs are done.

BEEF GOULASH

8 onions   Vinegar
⅓ cup fat   Summer savory
3 pounds beef chuck   1 teaspoon salt
½ teaspoon paprika

Cook onions slowly in fat. Cut beef into cubes or slices and sprinkle with vinegar and savory. Add salt, paprika and cooked onions. Cover tightly and simmer about 2 hours. The liquid may be increased just before serving by the addition of beef stock or cream, either sweet or sour. Serves 6.

SAVORY BEEF

3 large onions, sliced   ¼ teaspoon black pepper
3 tablespoons fat   ¼ teaspoon ground cloves and
2 pounds beef, shank, plate   thyme or summer savory
    rump or round   1 pint brown stock or boil-
3 tablespoons flour   ing water and meat extract
1 teaspoon salt   2 tablespoons vinegar
1 tablespoon catchup

Brown onions slowly in fat. Cut meat into serving pieces, add to onions and brown. Mix flour and dry seasonings. Sprinkle over meat. Add stock, vinegar and catchup. Cover closely. Simmer until meat is tender, allowing 2 hours for shank or plate and 1½ hours for rump or round. Serves 6.

POT ROAST OF BEEF

4 pounds chuck, round or
  rump of beef
¼ cup flour

3 tablespoons fat
Salt and pepper
½ cup water

Dredge meat with flour and brown on all sides in hot fat.
Season with salt and pepper. Add water, cover and cook slowly
until tender, 3 to 4 hours. As the liquid cooks away add more,
as needed. Serve with gravy and vegetables. Serves 8.

VARIATIONS—1. Add uncooked pared potatoes, carrots, green
beans, celery and onions just long enough before serving to cook
them. They may be whole, quartered or sliced.

2. Use tomatoes or tomato juice in place of water.

3. After browning, pour ¼ cup horse-radish over meat.

4. Before cooking, cut slits in the meat and insert stuffed
olives, pushing them into the meat.

SMOTHERED BEEF

3 pounds rump
Flour mixed with salt and
  pepper
3 large onions, sliced
3 tablespoons fat

2 tablespoons mild prepared
  mustard
1 teaspoon celery seed
1 cup strained tomatoes or ½
  can tomato soup

Dredge the meat with flour and brown it in a heavy pan.
Brown the onions in the fat; add the mustard, celery seed and
tomatoes. Pour over meat and simmer 3 hours. Serves 6.

SWISS STEAK

½ cup flour
Salt and pepper
2 pounds steak cut 2½ inches
  thick from shoulder, rump
  or round

2 tablespoons fat
Few slices onion
½ green pepper, chopped fine
1 cup boiling water
1 cup strained tomatoes

Season flour with salt and pepper and pound it into the meat
with a wooden potato masher or the edge of a heavy meat mallet.
Brown the meat in fat. Add onions, green pepper, boiling water
and tomatoes. Cover closely. Simmer for 2 hours. This may be
cooked in casserole in moderate oven (350° F.) about 1 to 1½
hours. Vegetables may be added as desired. Serves 6.

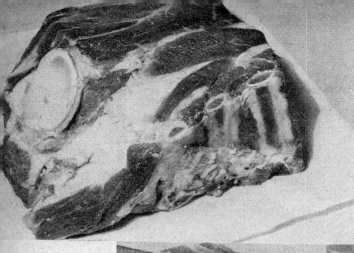

THE PROPER POT ROAST IS A SQUARE CUT OF CHUCK, RUMP OR ROUND

A HEAVY METAL POT WITH A TIGHT COVER AND GRILL IS THE PROPER SETTING FOR BRAISING THE ROAST

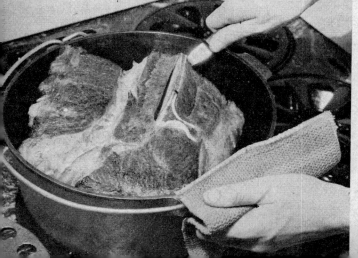

BROWN THE MEAT CAREFULLY ON ALL SIDES — SEASON AS YOU BROWN

SLIP THE GRILL UNDER THE ROAST AND ADD A SMALL AMOUNT OF WATER OR TOMATO JUICE

COVER CLOSELY AND SIMMER OVER LOW HEAT, RENEWING LIQUID OCCASIONALLY

ADD VEGETABLES, COVER CLOSELY AND PREPARE FOR A LUSCIOUS DINNER

—U. S. Bureau Home Economics

BEEF LOAF

1½ pounds chopped beef
1 egg
1½ cups bread crumbs
2 tablespoons chopped parsley
½ teaspoon pepper

2 teaspoons salt
2 tablespoons chopped onions
2 tablespoons chopped celery
  leaves
Dash thyme or savory

Mix meat thoroughly with egg, crumbs, chopped parsley, and seasonings. Place in bread pan. Bake in hot oven (350° F.) about 1½ hours, basting frequently with stock or butter melted in hot water. Garnish with parsley or watercress and serve with Mushroom Sauce or Onion Sauce. Serves 6.

MEAT CROQUETTES

1 tablespoon fat
4 tablespoons flour
1 cup milk
2 cups finely ground
  cooked meat
1 tablespoon chopped onion

½ teaspoon salt
⅛ teaspoon pepper
1 teaspoon minced parsley
Fine dry bread crumbs
1 egg

Melt fat, add flour and blend. Add milk and cook until very thick, stirring constantly. Add meat, onion, seasonings and parsley. Chill thoroughly. Form into cylinders, pyramids or patties. Dip into crumbs, then into slightly beaten egg mixed with 2 tablespoons water and into crumbs again. Chill. Fry in hot deep fat (380° F.) until brown. Serves 4.

BEEFSTEAK PIE

2 pounds rump, flank
  or chuck steak
1 recipe plain pastry
½ cup chopped onion

Salt and pepper
2 cups sliced cooked potatoes
Butter or other fat
Flour, egg

Cut meat into 2x1 inch strips. Cover meat and bones with water and simmer about 1 hour. Line sides of baking dish with pastry; put in a layer of meat and onion and sprinkle with salt and pepper; add a layer of sliced potatoes and dot with butter. Alternate steak and potato layers until dish is full. Thicken gravy with browned flour and pour into dish; cover with a top crust, brush with beaten egg and bake in hot oven (400° F.) about 30 minutes. Serves 6.

BRAISED BEEF

2 to 3 pounds brisket or round
   of beef
Drippings for sautéing
2 tablespoons butter
1 chopped onion

1 chopped carrot
1 tablespoon chopped parsley
½ cup diced celery
1 cup canned tomatoes
Salt and paprika

Cut the meat into cubes; brown in hot frying pan with drippings. Stir the meat so it will cook quickly and not lose its juices. Tender cuts can be cooked whole. Remove the pieces to a closely covered kettle that can be used either on top of the range or in the oven. Rinse the pan with a quarter cup of boiling water to save all browned bits, and pour this over the meat. Cover tightly and cook slowly for 2 hours.

FOR THE SAUCE, melt butter or other fat and brown the onion and carrot in it. Add parsley, celery and tomatoes. Heat thoroughly. Add seasonings. Pour the sauce over the meat and continue cooking for another hour.

BEEF MIROTON

6 onions
1 to 2 tablespoons fat
1 tablespoon flour
2 tablespoons vinegar

1 cup bouillon
Salt and pepper
12 slices cooked beef
½ cup bread crumbs

Slice onions and brown in fat. Add flour and brown. Then add vinegar and bouillon. Cook together until slightly thickened, stirring constantly. Season with salt and pepper. Heat slices of beef in the sauce for a few minutes. Pour into baking dish, sprinkle with crumbs and bake at 400° F. 10 minutes. Serves 6.

BEEF HASH

4 tablespoons butter
   or other fat
2 cups chopped cold
   roast beef or steak

2 to 4 cups chopped
   boiled potatoes
Salt and pepper
1 cup beef gravy or hot water

Melt butter and add remaining ingredients. Heat thoroughly stirring occasionally and brown hash.

VARIATION—Fry 2 or 3 slices of onion in fat before adding hash or mix a little chopped onion with hash.

ROAST BEEF WITH YORKSHIRE PUDDING

Wipe roast with damp cloth but do not wash. Rub with salt in proportion of 1 teaspoon per pound of meat. Rub with pepper, onion or garlic if desired. Place meat, fat side up, on rack of pan. If meat has little or no fat, place strips of bacon, salt pork or suet over it. This will baste the roast and no other basting is needed. Do not add water and do not cover pan. If meat thermometer is to be used, insert into center of thickest part of cut, being sure bulb of thermometer does not touch bone or fat. Roast at temperature given on page 233 for required length of time or until the thermometer registers the desired internal temperature. If a roast is not cut immediately upon removal from oven, it will continue to cook and the temperature at the center will continue to rise. This may continue 30 to 45 minutes. Allow about ½ pound per serving.

YORKSHIRE PUDDING

1 cup sifted flour
½ teaspoon salt
1 cup milk
2 eggs
Drippings from roast beef

Mix flour and salt. Combine milk and eggs, add to flour and beat well with rotary egg beater until smooth. Pour hot drippings into hot shallow pan to depth of 1 inch. Pour in mixture quickly and bake in hot oven (400° F.) ½ hour. The pudding may then be placed under the rack holding the roast beef and left for 15 minutes to catch the juices from the roast. If a rack is not used, cut pudding into squares and arrange in pan around roast. Serve with the meat.

FILET MIGNON

3 pounds beef fillet
Salt pork
Butter or other fat
Salt and pepper
Flour

The fillet is the under side of the loin of beef, the tenderloin. Remove skin, fat and ligament with a sharp knife. Lard the upper surface with strips of fat salt pork and rub the entire surface with soft butter or other fat. Dredge well with salt, pepper and flour, and place the fillet, without water, in a small pan. Bake in slow oven (300° F.), see page 233. Or cut tenderloin into steaks and broil. Serves 8.

BROILED STEAK

1 porterhouse or	Salt and pepper
sirloin steak	2 tablespoons butter

Select a steak at least 1½ inches thick. Heat broiler for 10 minutes with regulator set at 550° F. Arrange steak on a rack. Place rack 4 inches under heat. For rare steak broil 7 to 8 minutes, season with salt and pepper, turn and broil on other side for same length of time. Remove to a hot platter. Place butter on top of steak, sprinkle with salt and pepper and serve at once. Allow ½ pound of meat per person.

Other steaks may be broiled in the same way. See page 233 for broiling time.

PAN BROILED STEAK

1 porterhouse or	Butter
club steak	Salt and pepper

Heat a heavy skillet until sizzling hot. Place meat in hot pan and brown well on both sides. Reduce temperature and cook until the desired degree of doneness, turning from time to time, being careful not to pierce meat. Pour off fat as it accumulates in the pan. Place meat on a hot platter, spread with butter and season with salt and pepper. Allow ½ pound per person.

WITH MUSHROOMS

Use mushroom caps, whole or sliced. Sauté slowly in hot butter 5 to 10 minutes, stirring frequently. Allow 2 tablespoons butter for ½ pound mushrooms.

WITH ONIONS

Slice onions into water and drain. Place in shallow pan, cover closely, and cook over a slow heat 15 to 20 minutes, or until tender. Pan-broil the steak. Brown onions in pan in which the steak was cooked and serve with steak.

WITH OYSTERS

1 tablespoon flour	3 tablespoons butter
1 quart oysters	

Rub flour and fat together. Heat oysters to boiling in a little of their own liquid. Remove any foam and stir in flour mixture. Boil 1 minute, pour over steak and serve at once.

START WITH YOUR THERMOMETER AT THE HEART OF THE ROAST AND YOU NEED NEVER WORRY ABOUT THE PERFECT FINISH

—National Live Stock and Meat Board

THE ROLLED ROAST AND
THE PLANKED STEAK ARE
EASY TO DO AND VERY
FESTIVE
—National Live Stock and
Meat Board

PLANKED STEAK

1 steak, 2 inches thick	Butter
Duchess potatoes	Minced parsley
Cooked vegetables	Salt

Paprika

Trim the fat and make outline of the steak even. Broil (see page 233). Oil a heated plank (see directions for planked fish), place steak on plank, and arrange border of Duchess potatoes around it. Arrange other cooked vegetables, such as stuffed tomatoes or green peppers, small boiled onions, peas, string beans and cubes of carrot or turnip, around the steak, also, so that the board is entirely concealed. Place the plank in the oven until the potato border is browned and all the vegetables are heated through. After removing it from the oven, spread steak with butter and sprinkle with minced parsley, salt and paprika. Serve on plank. Serves 4 to 6.

STUFFED STEAK

2 pounds flank or round steak	¼ teaspoon pepper
1 cup crumbs	1 tablespoon chopped onion
½ cup stock or water	¾ cup chopped celery
1 teaspoon salt	1 small turnip, diced
	1 small carrot, diced

The meat should be cut from ½ to 1 inch thick. Wipe steak, remove skin and place meat flat on a board. Combine crumbs, stock or water, salt, pepper, chopped onion and ¼ cup celery. Spread on meat. Roll steak with the grain, so meat will slice across the grain when it is cut. Place remaining vegetables in roasting pan and place meat on top. Add 2 or 3 cups of water, depending upon size of pan. Cover and bake in moderate oven (350° F.) 3 hours, or until tender.

To cook on top of stove, melt ½ cup suet in flat-bottomed heavy kettle, flour roll thickly and place in kettle. Turn from side to side until it is well browned, then add hot water to nearly cover and simmer for 3 hours. When meat is cooked, remove from kettle and thicken broth, using 1 to 2 tablespoons flour to each cup of broth.

VARIATION—Omit stuffing suggested above. Stuff steak with Bread Stuffing No. 2, Sausage Stuffing, Potato Stuffing or Oyster Stuffing.

HAMBURG STEAK

2 pounds chopped beef
¼ pound suet
1 teaspoon salt

Dash pepper
3 tablespoons chopped onion
Flour, butter

Chop beef and suet together twice. Add salt, pepper and onion. Press into a flat steak ¾ inch thick and sprinkle with flour. Broil on a fine wire broiler or brown in a little fat. Spread with butter and serve. The steak may also be shaped into small flat cakes. When meat is browned, make a gravy by adding a little water to drip pan and thicken with flour. Serves 6.

BAKED HAMBURG STEAK

1½ pounds chopped beef
2 cups bread crumbs
    soaked in milk
1 small onion, minced
Salt and pepper
2 eggs, beaten

4 hard-cooked eggs
1 cup tomatoes
½ cup sliced onion
1 tablespoon butter or
    other fat
1 cup water

Press meat through food chopper twice. Combine with bread, onion, seasonings and beaten eggs. Pat out meat into a sheet. arrange hard-cooked eggs end to end across center of meat and roll meat mixture around them. Place roll in baking pan. Combine tomatoes, sliced onions, butter and water and pour over meat. Bake in moderate oven (350° F.) about 2 hours, basting frequently. In serving, slice the roll crosswise. The hard-cooked eggs may be omitted. Serves 6.

BEEF BALLS

1½ pounds beef from
    the shank
⅓ cup bread crumbs
Salt and pepper

1 teaspoon lemon juice
1 egg, beaten
3 tablespoons fat
1 cup stock

Put meat through food chopper twice; add bread crumbs, salt, pepper, lemon juice and egg. Shape lightly into balls and let stand for ½ hour or more, then roll in flour and brown in fat. Remove meat balls and add 1 tablespoon flour to the fat. Mix well and add stock. Season, add meat balls, cover pan closely and simmer for 1½ hours. Serves 6.

VEAL
Time and Temperature Charts
ROASTING

	Weight Pounds	Oven Temperature Constant	Interior Temperature When Done	Time Per Pound In Minutes
Leg roast	7–8	300° F.	170° F.	25
Loin	4½–5	300° F.	170° F.	30–35
Rack (4–6 ribs)	2½–3	300° F.	170° F.	30–35
Shoulder	7	300° F.	170° F.	25
Shoulder-Rolled	5	300° F.	170° F.	40–45

BRAISING

	Average Weight or Thickness	Cooking Time
Breast—Stuffed	3–4 pounds	1½–2 hours
Breast—Rolled	2–3 pounds	1½–2 hours
Birds	½x2x4 inches	45–60 minutes
Chops	½–¾ inch	45–60 minutes
Chops—Breaded	½–¾ inch	45–60 minutes
Steaks or Cutlets	½–¾ inch	45–60 minutes
Shoulder chops	½–¾ inch	45–60 minutes

STUFFED VEAL SHOULDER

5-pound veal shoulder
Salt and pepper

1 recipe Celery or Bread Stuffing

Melted fat or salt pork

Have bones removed from veal shoulder, season cavity and fill with stuffing. Sew or skewer edges together and place on rack of roaster. Brush with fat or cover with strips of salt pork. Bake uncovered in moderate oven (325° F.) allowing 40 minutes to the pound, or until meat thermometer registers 175° F. Serves 10.

VEAL COLLOPS

2 pounds veal
1 egg

1 cup cracker crumbs
Salt and pepper

Cut the veal in pieces the size of an oyster, dip in beaten egg, roll in cracker crumbs and season with salt and pepper. Fry in deep fat (375° F.). Serves 6.

STUFFED BREAST OF VEAL

4 pounds breast of veal	1/4 teaspoon pepper
2 cups bread crumbs	1/4 cup minced onion
1/4 cup salt pork drippings	1/2 cup diced celery
1 teaspoon salt	1/2 cup hot water

Have a pocket cut in veal breast. Make a stuffing by combining remaining ingredients and tossing together lightly. Pack stuffing into pocket and sew or skewer edges together. Brown the meat in hot fat, then add 2/3 cup water, cover and cook in a moderate oven (350°F.) 1 1/2 to 2 hours or until tender.

VARIATIONS—Add 1/2 cup cooked pitted prunes, apricots or seedless raisins to the stuffing.
Stuff breast with cooked and seasoned rice or noodles.

VEAL BIRDS

2 pounds veal steak (cut 1/4 inch thick)	Salt
	Flour, fat
1 cup Bread Stuffing No. 2	1 cup milk or water

Cut veal into 2x4 inch pieces. Place a mound of stuffing on each piece, fold veal over stuffing and fasten with toothpick. Season, roll in flour, brown in fat and add milk. Cover and simmer or bake in moderate oven (350° F.) 1 hour. Serves 6.

VARIATIONS—1. Wrap veal around sausages, cooked whole carrots, pickles or olives instead of stuffing.
2. Pour mushroom soup over browned meat instead of milk.

VEAL OR BEEF FRICASSEE, JARDINIÈRE

2 pounds veal or beef rump	2 carrots, sliced
2 tablespoons flour	1 cup water or stock
Fat	1/2 cup sliced celery
Salt and pepper	2 onions, sliced
1 teaspoon minced parsley	1 cup cooked peas or
2 bay leaves, minced	mushrooms

Cut veal into 1-inch cubes, dredge in flour and brown in fat; season and add parsley, bay leaves, carrots, water, celery and onions. Cover tightly and cook in moderate oven (350° F.) 45 to 60 minutes, or until meat is tender. Remove veal. Add peas and thicken liquid with flour mixed with a little cold water. Cook until thickened. Pour over veal. Serves 4 to 6.

VEAL STEW WITH DUMPLINGS

⅛ pound salt pork
2 tablespoons flour
2 pounds veal breast
   or shoulder

2 cups water
2 teaspoons salt
½ green pepper, chopped
1 cup peas

1 recipe Dumplings

Cut salt pork into cubes and fry until brown; add floured veal cut into pieces and brown well. Add 2 cups cold water, salt and green pepper and cover closely. Simmer 1½ hours. Add peas and drop in dumplings. Cover closely and steam 15 minutes. Do not remove cover until dumplings are done. Serves 5 to 6. For old-fashioned potpie, omit salt pork and use ¼ teaspoon ground pepper instead of green.

PAPRIKA CREAM SCHNITZEL

4 slices bacon, cut fine
1½ pounds veal steak
2 tablespoons chopped onion

1 teaspoon paprika
Salt
1 cup sour cream

½ cup tomato sauce

Fry bacon until crisp, add veal (cut into serving portions) and brown in hot bacon fat. Add onion and brown. Season with paprika and salt. Stir in sour cream and tomato sauce. Cover pan and cook about 30 minutes. Serve cutlets with the sauce and cover with boiled or fried noodles. Serves 6.

WIENER SCHNITZEL

6 veal chops or steaks
Salt and pepper
2 eggs, slightly beaten
Flour

3 tablespoons bacon drippings
Juice of 1 lemon
1 tablespoon flour
1 cup thick sour cream

Sprinkle veal with salt and pepper. Dip into eggs, then into flour. Brown on both sides in hot bacon drippings. Cover and cook slowly until chops are tender, about 1 hour. Sprinkle with lemon juice and arrange on hot platter. Blend flour with fat in pan, add sour cream and cook 3 minutes, stirring constantly. Season with salt and pepper and serve with chops. Garnish with lemon slices. Serves 6.

Melt currant jelly in liquid in which chops were cooked, instead of adding flour and cream.

VEAL CUTLETS WITH CREAM GRAVY

2 pounds veal cutlets
Salt and pepper
2 eggs, beaten

Bread or cracker crumbs
Drippings
1 cup milk or cream

1 tablespoon flour

Wipe cutlets and sprinkle with salt and pepper. Dip into beaten eggs, then into fine bread or cracker crumbs. Brown in drippings. Place on platter, add cream to liquid in pan and thicken slightly with mixture of flour and water. Serves 6.

VEAL PIE

2 pounds veal
2 tablespoons flour
1 recipe Puff Paste or Plain
    Pastry

2 tablespoons fat
1 teaspoon salt
Pepper

Cut meat into small pieces, stew until tender and dredge in flour. Line a baking dish with puff paste. Place a small inverted cup in center of dish, add meat, fat and seasonings. Add stock from cooking meat to nearly cover mixture. Cover with puff paste. Bake in very hot oven (450° F.) 30 minutes. When serving, remove the cup. Serves 6 to 8.

VARIATIONS—1. Cook ½ pound sliced salt pork or ham with the veal.

2. Cut hard-cooked eggs into slices and arrange in layers with the veal and ham.

VEAL LOAF

2½ pounds veal, knuckle
    or shin
¼ pound salt pork
2 teaspoons salt
1 teaspoon chopped onion

1 cup cracker crumbs
1 cup water or stock
1 egg
½ teaspoon sage
2 tablespoons butter

Chop veal and pork very fine and add salt, onion, crumbs, ½ cup water, the egg and sage. Mix well together. Pack into greased pan and cook in moderate oven (350° F.) 2½ hours, basting occasionally with remainder of water combined with butter. Garnish top of loaf with broiled or sautéed mushroom caps. Serves 6 to 8.

CURRIED VEAL

2 tablespoons butter	2 cups stock
2 tablespoons minced onion	1 teaspoon salt
¼ cup flour	Dash cayenne
1 tablespoon curry powder	1½ pounds veal shoulder

Melt butter, add onion and cook 2 to 3 minutes without browning. Combine flour and curry powder, add to butter and mix until smooth. Add stock, salt and cayenne and cook until thickened. Cut veal into 1-inch cubes, add to sauce, cover closely and simmer 1½ hours or until meat is tender. Add more liquid if necessary. Serves 5.

ROAST VEAL

4 pounds veal	Flour
Salt and pepper	Fat salt pork or bacon

A roast may be cut from the leg, the rump or the shoulder. Wipe the meat, dredge with salt, pepper and flour and place on rack of roasting pan with fat side up. If meat thermometer is used insert it into center of thickest part of meat. If cut has no fat or if layer is thin, place strips of salt pork or bacon over top. Place in slow oven (300° F.) and cook, uncovered and without water, until tender. See page 246 for time allowances for various cuts. Allow about ⅓ pound per serving.

VARIATION—Have bone removed from roast cut from leg and fill roast with Bread or Sausage Stuffing. Use bone for making soup or stock.

BRAISED VEAL STEAK WITH MUSHROOMS

2 pounds veal steak	2 cups crushed cereal flakes
1 egg, slightly beaten	4 tablespoons fat
2 tablespoons milk	1 small can mushrooms

Have veal steak cut 1 inch thick. Cut into pieces for serving. Dip into mixture of egg and milk. Roll in finely crushed cereal flakes. Brown in hot fat and cover with mushrooms and mushroom liquid. Cover tightly and cook very slowly until tender, about 45 minutes. Thicken liquid for gravy and serve with veal steaks. Serves 6.

LAMB

Very little mutton appears in the retail market for household use, since the majority of the sheep are sold for slaughtering while they are still young enough to be classified as lambs.

Time and Temperature Tables

ROASTING

	Weight Pounds	Oven Temperature Constant	Interior Temperature When Done	Time Per Pound In Minutes
Leg	6½–7½	300° F.	175–180° F.	30–35
Shoulder—Rolled ...	3–4	300° F.	175–180° F.	40–45
Shoulder	4½–5½	300° F.	175–180° F.	30–35
Cushion	3–4	300° F.	175–180° F.	30–35
Rack of ribs (6–7 ribs)	2	300° F.	175–180° F.	45–50
Crown (12–15 ribs) .	4	300° F.	175–180° F.	30–35

BROILING

	Weight		Cooking Time	
			Rare Minutes	Medium Minutes
Shoulder chops—1 inch	3	ounces	10	12
1½ inches	6	ounces	15	18
2 inches	10	ounces	18	22
Rib chops—1 inch	2	ounces	10	12
1½ inches	4	ounces	15	18
2 inches	5	ounces	18	22
Loin chops—1 inch	3	ounces	10	12
1½ inches	5	ounces	15	18
2 inches	6	ounces	18	22
Ground patties (1x3 inches) ...	4	ounces	15	18

BRAISING

	Average Weight or Thickness	Cooking Time
Breast—Stuffed	2–3 pounds	1½–2 hours
Breast—Rolled	1½–2 pounds	1½–2 hours
Neck slices	¾ inch	1 hour
Shanks	½ pound each	1–1½ hours

FRENCH LAMB CHOPS

French chops are made by scraping the meat and fat from the bones of rib chops for a little distance from the end. Broil, season with salt and pepper, and serve.

They may be sautéed or fried. When cooked in this way, they are breaded—that is, seasoned with salt and pepper and dipped in beaten egg and then into cracker crumbs.

PLANKED LAMB CHOPS

6 loin lamb chops (1½ inches thick)
Salt and pepper

Brussels sprouts, cooked
Mashed potatoes

Remove bones from meat and roll each chop by wrapping tail of chop around large "eye" of meat. Preheat oven to moderate (550° F.) and place chops 3 inches below broiler heat. Brown chops on both sides and season. Place chops on individual planks, with Brussels sprouts and border with mashed potatoes pressed through a pastry tube. Place under broiler heat until potatoes are browned and serve immediately. Serves 6.

Wrap a strip of bacon around each chop before broiling if desired.

MUTTON CHOPS

6 mutton chops   Oil   Salt and pepper

Mutton chops should be not less than one inch thick. The best way to cook them is to broil them. Sprinkle with salt and pepper, oil on both sides and broil, turning very often. Have them slightly rare and serve on a hot chop dish, with French fried potatoes and sprigs of parsley.

BROILED LAMB PATTIES

1½ pounds ground lamb
2 tablespoons grated onion

1 teaspoon salt
½ teaspoon pepper

Mix all ingredients thoroughly. Shape into thick patties. Place on a rack under preheated broiler, about 3 inches from source of heat so that by the time the patties are browned on the top they will be half done. Turn and brown on other side. Allow about 15 minutes. Serves 6.

BARBECUED LAMB

6-pound leg lamb
2 teaspoons salt
Flour
1 onion, sliced
1 cup water

½ cup catchup
2 tablespoons A-1 sauce
2 tablespoons Worcester-
    shire sauce
¼ teaspoon cayenne

Wipe leg of lamb with damp cloth, rub with salt and dredge with flour. Place in a roasting pan and surround with onion. Combine remaining ingredients, mix well and pour over meat. Roast in a 350° F. oven 30 minutes for each pound. Baste every 20 minutes with the sauce. Serves 8.

LAMB CURRY PIE

2 pounds lamb shoulder
1 onion, diced
1 tablespoon fat
3 cups hot water
¼ teaspoon thyme

2½ teaspoons salt
2 tablespoons flour
1 teaspoon curry powder
¼ cup water
3 cups cooked rice

Cut lamb into 1-inch cubes. Brown lamb and onion in fat; add water, thyme and salt; simmer 1½ hours or until meat is tender. Combine flour and curry powder; add cold water and mix to a smooth paste; add to lamb. Line greased baking dish on sides and bottom with rice, pressing rice firmly into place. Fill center with lamb mixture and bake in moderate oven (350° F.) 20 minutes. Serves 6.

SPICY LAMB SHANKS

4 lamb shanks
Salt and pepper
Flour
1 cup water
1 cup cooked prunes, pitted
1 cup cooked dried apricots

½ cup sugar
½ teaspoon cinnamon
½ teaspoon allspice
¼ teaspoon cloves
3 tablespoons vinegar
¼ teaspoon salt

Season meat with salt and pepper, dredge with flour and place in greased baking dish. Cover and bake in moderate oven (350° F.) until meat is tender, 1¾ to 2 hours. Combine remaining ingredients, heat to boiling and simmer about 5 minutes. Drain most of fat from cooked shanks, add fruit mixture to meat, cover dish and bake at 400° F. 30 minutes. Serves 4.

ROAST STUFFED SHOULDER OF LAMB

3-4 pound shoulder lamb
Salt and pepper

2 recipes Bread Stuffing
No. 2 (page 303)

Have shoulder bone removed from shoulder and sew on 2 sides, leaving 1 side open for stuffing. Season with salt and pepper. Fill cavity in meat with stuffing and sew or skewer edges together. Place fat side up on rack in an open roasting pan and roast in slow oven (300° F.) until tender, allowing 35 to 40 minutes per pound. Serves 6.

VARIATIONS—1. Add ½ cup chopped mint to stuffing.

2. Add ½ cup finely chopped dried apricots to stuffing.

3. Omit milk in stuffing and add 1 cup tomato pulp.

4. Sauté ½ pound sliced mushrooms in melted fat with onion and proceed with stuffing as directed.

5. Use Sausage Stuffing (page 305) in place of Bread Stuffing.

STUFFED PORK SHOULDER—Use boned pork shoulder. Prepare as above and roast in moderate oven (350° F.) 45 to 50 minutes per pound.

LAMB STEW

2 pounds lamb cubes, shank, breast, neck or shoulder
2 tablespoons flour
2 tablespoons fat
Salt and pepper
Hot water
6 potatoes

6 carrots
3 onions
4 white turnips
1 cup fresh peas
3 tomatoes
Flour

Dredge lamb with flour and brown well in hot fat. Season with salt and pepper, cover with water and simmer until nearly tender, 1 to 1½ hours. Add peeled vegetables, except tomatoes, whole or cut in cubes and simmer 30 minutes longer or until tender. Add tomatoes and simmer 10 minutes longer. Mix a little flour with water to a smooth paste and add enough to the liquid to thicken slightly. Serves 6.

SHEPHERD'S PIE—Use leftover stew. Line baking dish with hot mashed potatoes. Fill center with hot stew, cover with additional mashed potatoes and place in hot oven (425° F.) 15 minutes or until potatoes are browned.

STUFFED LAMB BREAST

Lamb breast and foreshank	1 cup cooked rice or barley
Salt and pepper	1 tablespoon grated onion

Have foreshank removed from breast and the meat ground. Have bones of breast cracked so that the meat may be carved between the ribs. Make a pocket lengthwise in the breast by cutting the meat close to the ribs. Sprinkle pocket with salt and pepper. Combine ground meat from the foreshank with cooked rice or barley. Season with onion, salt and pepper. Fill pocket with stuffing and sew or skewer edges together. Sprinkle outside with salt and pepper. Place uncovered in pan and bake in a slow oven (300° F.) for 1 hour, then cover and continue cooking until tender, about 1 hour longer. Serves 6.

ROAST LEG OF LAMB

1 leg lamb (5 to 6 pounds)	1½ tablespoons salt
	¼ teaspoon pepper

Have shank bone removed at the market, if desired. Do not remove the fell. Rub meat with salt and pepper. Place, fat side up, on rack in an uncovered roasting pan. Roast in a moderately slow oven (300°-325° F.) 30 to 35 minutes to the pound, or until a meat thermometer registers 175° to 180° F. Serve with sliced pineapple and garnish with sprigs of watercress.

1. Rub meat with the cut edge of a clove of garlic or place slivers of garlic into deep narrow gashes cut in meat, or insert clove of garlic into joint of leg and remove before serving.

2. Rub 1 teaspoon ginger over surface of meat.

3. Baste lamb with vinegar which has been seasoned with finely cut mint leaves.

4. Baste lamb with a mixture of ½ cup tomato catchup and 2 tablespoons Worcestershire sauce.

5. Rub meat with ½ cup finely chopped mint leaves. Baste meat frequently the last hour of roasting with ½ cup grape jelly melted in ½ cup hot water.

6. Rub 2 cups cooked apricots and juice through a sieve, add ¾ cup sugar and cook until thickened. Baste roast with this during last hour of roasting.

7. Cover meat with pineapple slices 1 hour before meat is done. Brush with butter so that pineapple will brown.

ROAST CROWN OF LAMB

1 crown of lamb or mutton	1 recipe Mushroom Stuffing
Salt and pepper	(page 305)
Sliced salt pork	

A crown is usually prepared at the market and is made by shaping the ribs (12-15) into a crown and frenching or scraping the rib ends. Season with salt and pepper. Fill center of crown with stuffing. Wrap rib ends with salt pork or bacon slices. Place crown on a rack in an open roasting pan and roast in a slow oven (300°F.) allowing 30 to 35 minutes per pound. To serve, remove salt pork from rib ends and slip paper frills over them. Allow 2 ribs to each serving.

VARIATIONS—Do not stuff. Roast crown upside down without wrapping ribs. To serve, turn right side up and fill center with vegetables: mashed potatoes, potato balls, peas, diced carrots or cooked whole cauliflower.

BRAISED LEG OF LAMB OR MUTTON

½ cup each finely chopped celery, carrot and onion	6 whole cloves
2 tablespoons drippings or other fat	1 clove garlic
3 cups vinegar	2 tablespoons chopped parsley
3 cups water	12 peppercorns
1 leg lamb or mutton	½ bay leaf
½ teaspoon each of powdered thyme and marjoram	1 tablespoon salt
	1 pint sour cream
	½ pint stock

Sauté celery, carrot, and onion in drippings until light brown, add vinegar and water and cook until vegetables are tender. Cool. Place meat in deep dish, pour first mixture over meat, being careful to have meat entirely covered. Add seasonings. Marinate meat in this mixture for 24 hours. Drain and dry thoroughly. Place in roasting pan, bake in slow oven (300° F.) for 30 minutes. Add sour cream and stock, cover and cook until tender, allowing 30 to 35 minutes per pound. Baste frequently. Boil liquor in which meat was marinated until only a small amount remains, strain and pour over meat when serving.

A CROWN ROAST OR LEG O'LAMB
HELPS CELEBRATE THE SPRING
—National Live Stock and
Meat Board

BREAST OF LAMB READY FOR STUFFING.

ROAST ON RACK, NO COVER, NO WATER. SERVE WITH STUFFED ONIONS
—U. S. Bureau Home Economics

PORK (Always cooked well done)
Time and Temperature Charts

ROASTING

FRESH	Weight Pounds	Oven Temperature Constant	Interior Temperature When Done	Time Per Pound In Minutes
Loin—Center	3–4	350° F.	185° F.	35–40
Whole	8–15	350° F.	185° F.	15–20
Ends	3–4	350° F.	185° F.	50–55
Shoulder—Whole ...	12–14	350° F.	185° F.	30–35
Boned and rolled .	4–6	350° F.	185° F.	40–45
Cushion	4–6	350° F.	185° F.	35–40
Spareribs	1½–1¾	350° F.	185° F.	40–45
Pork Butt	4–6	350° F.	185° F.	45–50
Ham	10–18	350° F.	185° F.	30–35
SMOKED				
Ham—Whole	10–12	300° F.	170° F.	25
Tenderized	10–12	300° F.	145–150° F.	15
Half	6	300° F.	170° F.	30
Tenderized	6	300° F.	145–150° F.	20
Shank end..........	3	300° F.	170° F.	40
Butt end	3	300° F.	170° F.	45
Cottage Butt	2–4	300° F.	170° F.	35
Picnic.............	3–10	300° F.	170° F.	35

BROILING

	Weight Pounds	Total Cooking Time
Ham slice—½ inch	¾–1	20
1 inch	1½–2	25–30
Ham slice—tenderized............		
½ inch	¾–1	10–12
1 inch	1½–2	16–20

BRAISING

	Average Weight or Thickness	Cooking Time Minutes
Chops	¾–1½ inches	45–60
Spareribs	2–3 pounds	90
Tenderloin		
Whole	¾–1 pound	45–60
Fillets	½ inch	30
Shoulder steak	¾ inch	30–45

CROWN AND CANDLE ROAST OF PORK

Crown of pork
1½ tablespoons salt

Pepper
Cubes of salt pork

Have crown prepared at the market. Rub salt and pepper into meat. Cover tip of each bone with salt pork. Roast in a moderate oven (350° F.) allowing 30 minutes per pound. To serve, replace salt pork with paper frills. If desired, center of roast may be filled with stuffing and baked. See Roast Lamb (page 256). For candle roast, do not roll ribs but leave loin in one straight piece. Roast with fat side up.

ROAST SPARERIBS

2 pounds of spareribs

Salt and pepper

Place spareribs in a shallow baking dish and sprinkle with salt and pepper. Roast in a moderate oven (350° F.) allowing 40 to 45 minutes per pound. Allow 1 pound per serving.

Cover spareribs with greased paper and roast for ¾ hour, then roast, uncovered, for remaining time. Just before taking meat from oven, sprinkle with 1 cup bread crumbs seasoned with ¼ teaspoon each of sage and minced onion. Baste with drippings in pan and return to oven 5 minutes longer.

STUFFED SPARERIBS—Use 2 matching sections of spareribs. Sew the edges together, except at 1 end. Fill with Bread Stuffing, Celery Stuffing (page 304) or apple stuffing, and sew or skewer the edges together. Bake in slow oven (325° F.) for 1½ hours.

BARBECUED SPARERIBS—Brown spareribs under broiler. Pour Barbecue Sauce (page 260) over ribs, cover pan and bake.

WITH SAUERKRAUT—Brown spareribs. Place sauerkraut in a greased baking dish. Sprinkle with brown sugar. Add ½ cup water and arrange spareribs on top. Cover dish and cook in moderate oven (350° F.) for 1 hour.

BRAISED SPARERIBS—Place spareribs in a baking dish and brown in very hot oven (450° F.). Season with salt and pepper, add ½ cup water, cover pan and return to oven. Reduce temperature to slow (325° F.) and continue cooking until tender, about 50 minutes longer. If desired, place cored apples around the ribs. Fill centers of apples with brown sugar and nut meats or raisins.

BRAISED PORK STEAKS WITH GRAPE APPLES

2 pounds pork shoulder steaks	Salt and pepper
2 tablespoons flour	3 large apples
2 tablespoons fat	½ glass grape jelly
	¾ cup boiling water

Dredge pork shoulder steaks in flour and brown in hot fat. Season with salt and pepper. Add ¼ cup water, cover tightly, and cook very slowly until tender, about 45 minutes. Pare apples, core and cut into halves. Dissolve grape jelly in boiling water, add apples and cook until tender. Serve around pork steaks. Serves 4.

BRAISED PORK CHOPS

Heat heavy frying pan until very hot. Add 1 tablespoon fat, or if the chops have a good covering of fat, place in the pan with fat edge down and cook out enough fat to grease frying pan. Brown chops on both sides. Do not add water. Reduce temperature, cover pan closely and cook slowly until chops are thoroughly done, about 45 minutes. Turn chops occasionally to cook uniformly.

STUFFED PORK CHOPS

6 double pork chops	1 teaspoon sage
2 cups bread crumbs	1 tablespoon grated onion
¾ teaspoon salt	3 tablespoons milk
¼ teaspoon pepper	Fat
1½ tablespoons minced parsley	

Cut a pocket on the bone side of each chop. Combine next 7 ingredients and mix well. Stuff each chop with mixture. Brown chops in fat, season, add a little water and bake in moderate oven (350° F.) about 1 hour or until tender. Serves 6.

FRESH PORK WITH VEGETABLES

1 pound pork butt	1 small red cabbage, quartered
4 large carrots	1 teaspoon salt
4 large parsnips	

Simmer pork 45 minutes. Add vegetables and salt and cook 45 minutes longer or until tender. Cut pork into thin slices and vegetables except cabbage into strips. Serves 3 or 4.

PORK CHOPS WITH BARBECUE SAUCE

6 pork chops   Flour   Barbecue sauce

Wipe the pork chops with a damp cloth and dust with flour. Sear on both sides until browned, then place 1 tablespoon sauce on each chop. Reduce heat, cover and cook slowly 5 to 8 minutes. Turn chops and place 1 tablespoon of sauce on other side. Cover and cook slowly until tender, about 40 minutes. Serve with sauce.

BARBECUE SAUCE

4 tablespoons minced onion
1 cup tomato purée
¾ cup water
3 tablespoons vinegar
2 tablespoons Worcester-
    shire sauce

1 teaspoon salt
1 teaspoon paprika
1 teaspoon chili powder
½ teaspoon pepper
¼ teaspoon cinnamon
Dash ground cloves

Combine all ingredients in order listed. Heat to boiling and use as directed above.

PORK PIE

2 pounds pork shoulder
2¼ cups boiling water or
    stock
1 teaspoon salt

1 bay leaf
2 cups cooked carrots
6 small cooked onions
1 recipe Plain Pastry

Cut pork into cubes, brown in fat and add water, salt and bay leaf. Cover and cook slowly until meat is tender, about 1 hour. Thicken gravy with flour mixed to a smooth paste with cold water. Add carrots and onions, pour into baking dish, cover with pastry and bake in very hot oven (450° F.) 20 minutes or until browned. Serves 6.

PORK TENDERLOIN

1 pound tenderloin
Flour

3 tablespoons bacon drippings
Salt and pepper

¾ cup sour cream

Cut tenderloin crosswise into 2-inch slices. Flatten out and dredge with flour. Place in hot skillet containing drippings. Brown on both sides; season with salt and pepper. Reduce heat, add cream, cover and simmer 30 minutes. Serves 6.

VARIATIONS—Place unflattened slices on a baking sheet. Spread with a thick layer of catchup and bake in a moderate oven (350° F.) until tender, about 45 minutes.

BOILED PIGS' FEET

6 pigs' feet   1½ tablespoons salt

Scrape feet, wash thoroughly and tie each separately in a piece of cheesecloth. Cover with boiling water and add salt. Heat to boiling, reduce heat and simmer 6 hours. Cool in the water. When cold, drain, but do not remove cloth. Chill. Use for broiling, frying or pickling. Serves 6.

BROILED—Split feet, dredge with salt, pepper and flour and broil for 10 minutes. Season with butter, salt and pepper.

FRIED—Split feet and season with salt, pepper and lemon juice. Dip into beaten egg, then into bread crumbs and fry in hot deep fat (375° F.) 5 minutes.

PICKLED PIGS' FEET (SOUSE)

4 good-sized boiled pigs' feet with uppers	1 tablespoon broken cinnamon
1 quart strong vinegar	¼ cup salt
4 bay leaves	2 teaspoons pepper .
1 tablespoon whole cloves	½ onion, cut into eighths
1 blade mace	

Clean feet carefully and cover with hot water. Simmer until meat will separate from bones, then remove carefully with skimmer. Place in stone jar, taking out the largest bones. Save water for later use. Heat vinegar with bay leaves, cloves, cinnamon, salt, pepper, onion and mace. Simmer slowly for 45 minutes, but do not boil at any time. Remove cake of fat from top of cooking water from feet. Add about 1 quart of the water to vinegar; if vinegar is not very strong, use less water. Strain liquid through a sieve and pour over meat in jar. Chill 2 days.

PIGS' KNUCKLES AND SAUERKRAUT

4 pigs' knuckles	2 quarts boiling water
3 teaspoons salt	1 quart sauerkraut

Place whole knuckles in boiling salted water. Cover and simmer until meat is tender about 2½ to 3 hours. Twenty minutes before serving, pour off most of the water and add sauerkraut. Heat thoroughly. Serve the meat on a bed of sauerkraut. Serves 4.

HEADCHEESE

1 hog's head   Salt and pepper
1 hog's tongue   Sage or chili powder

Clean and scrape hog's head and wash thoroughly. Wash and trim tongue. Cover head and tongue with slightly salted water and simmer until meat falls from bone. Drain meat, shred and season. Pack tightly in bowl, cover and weight it down. Let stand 3 days in a cold place. Slice. Makes 6 to 8 pounds.

FRIED SALT PORK WITH CREAM GRAVY

1 pound salt pork   1 pint milk
Flour   Salt and pepper

Slice pork thin, place in cold water and let stand 1 hour. Drain well and dry. Dip each piece into flour and fry in hot frying pan until crisp. Drain off all but 2 tablespoons of fat and stir 2 tablespoons of flour into that remaining. Cook 2 minutes, stirring well, then reduce heat and add milk slowly. Cook until thickened. Add salt and pepper, if needed. Serve over meat. Serves 3.

To serve with New England salt fish dinner, open hot baked potato, place cooked salt codfish on top and pour gravy over all. Arrange fried salt pork on top.

SCRAPPLE

1 hog's head   1 teaspoon powdered
4 to 5 quarts cold water   sage
4 teaspoons salt   Yellow corn meal
4 teaspoons pepper   (about 3 cups)

Separate one hog's head into halves. Remove eyes and brains. Scrape head and clean thoroughly. Place in a large kettle and cover with 4 or 5 quarts of cold water. Simmer gently for 2 to 3 hours, or until meat falls from bones. Skim grease carefully from the surface; remove meat, chop fine and return to liquor. Season with salt, pepper and sage to taste. Sift in corn meal, stirring constantly, until the mixture is thickened to the consistency of soft mush. Cook slowly for 1 hour over low heat. When sufficiently cooked, pour into greased oblong pans and store in a cool place until ready to use. Cut in thin slices and fry until crisp and brown. Makes 6 pounds.

BAKED HAM

1 smoked ham   Glaze
                       Whole cloves

Have ham warmed to room temperature and bake according
to directions given by packer, or as follows: Wipe ham with
clean cloth, wrap loosely in one of the papers wrapped around
ham or in clean wrapping paper and place fat side up on rack
of shallow pan. Do not cover pan or add water. For baking
allow 15 minutes per pound for hams, 12 pounds or over; allow
18 minutes per pound for hams, under 12 pounds; allow 22
minutes per pound for half hams; or bake to an internal temperature of 150° F., being sure bulb of thermometer is inserted
into center of thickest part of meat and does not touch bone.
Bake in slow oven (300° F.) until within 45 minutes of total
baking time. Remove paper and rind from ham, make a series
of shallow cuts across fat to cut into squares or diamonds, spread
with desired glaze and insert 1 clove into each square of fat.
Bake uncovered in 325° F. oven for remaining 45 minutes.

GLAZES—

One cup brown sugar, juice and grated rind of 1 orange.
One cup brown or white sugar and ½ cup maraschino cherry
juice, cider or sweet pickle juice from pickled fruit.
One cup honey.
One cup brown sugar, 1 tablespoon mustard.
One cup puréed apricots, rhubarb or applesauce.
One glass currant jelly, melted.
Use maraschino cherries and mint cherries fastened with pieces
of toothpicks instead of cloves.
Three-fourths cup pineapple juice, ¾ cup strained honey and
½ teaspoon mustard cooked until thick.
One-half cup maple sirup, ½ cup cider or apple juice and
2 tablespoons mustard.
One-half cup orange marmalade.
Cook ½ pound fresh cranberries with 1 cup maple sirup until
skins pop open. Press mixture through sieve and spread over
ham.
Instead of using cloves, make a flower on top of glaze, using
pineapple rings and apricot halves.

BOILED HAM

Wash ham thoroughly, cover with boiling water and simmer, partially covered, for 25 to 30 minutes per pound or to an internal temperature of 160° F. If ham is to be served cold, let stand in water to cool, peel off rind and slice. If it is to be served hot, peel off rind and glaze as for Baked Ham. Whenever possible follow packers' cooking directions.

BROILED HAM

Remove rind from slice of smoked ham and slash edges of fat. Arrange on broiling rack and place 4 inches from heat in the broiler preheated to 550° F. Broil half required time (see page 257). Turn meat and broil remaining time.

HAM BAKED IN MILK

1 teaspoon dry mustard
4 tablespoons brown sugar

1 slice ham (2 inches thick)
Milk

Mix mustard and brown sugar together and spread over ham. Place in casserole, add enough milk to barely cover ham. Bake in slow oven (300° F.) 1 hour. Center slice of ham will serve 6.

FRIED HAM WITH CREAM GRAVY

1 pound ham in ½ inch slices
1 cup milk

1 tablespoon flour
Pepper

Place meat in hot pan and cook without additional fat, unless ham is very lean, in which case a spoonful of drippings should be used. When ham is brown, place on platter and add milk to fat in pan. Add 1 or 2 tablespoons flour mixed smoothly with a little milk and cook until thickened. Season and pour over ham. Serves 4.

SPICED HAM LOAF

1 cup bread or cereal
   crumbs
½ cup milk
2 cups ground cured ham

½ pound ground fresh pork
1 tablespoon brown sugar
¼ teaspoon cloves
1 egg

Soften crumbs in milk. Combine meat, seasonings, crumbs and egg. Mix and pack into loaf pan. Bake in moderate oven (350° F.) 50 minutes. Serves 6.

THE CANDLE ROAST OF
PORK IS AN INTERESTING
VARIATION
—National Live Stock and
Meat Board

WHEN THE BONE IS A NUI-
SANCE, REMOVE IT AND
STUFF THE HAM BEFORE
BAKING

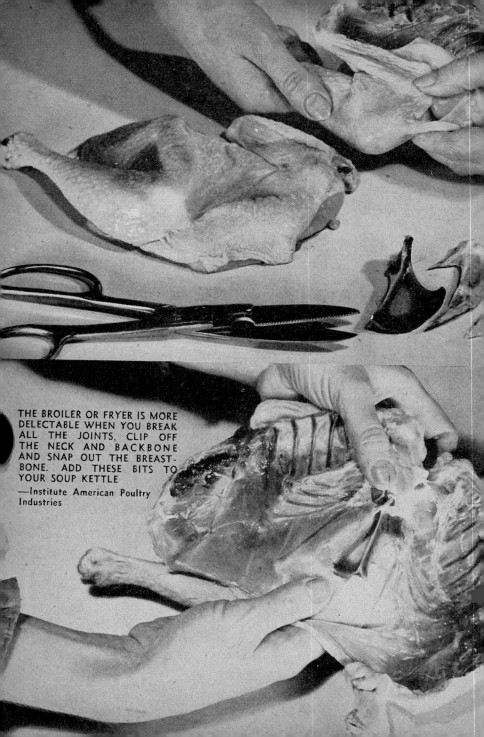

THE BROILER OR FRYER IS MORE
DELECTABLE WHEN YOU BREAK
ALL THE JOINTS, CLIP OFF
THE NECK AND BACKBONE
AND SNAP OUT THE BREAST-
BONE. ADD THESE BITS TO
YOUR SOUP KETTLE

—Institute American Poultry
Industries

POTTED HAM

1 cup minced cooked ham   Dash powdered mace
Cayenne   Mustard

Pound ham in mortar, and season with cayenne, mace and mustard. Place in baking dish and bake in moderate oven (350° F.) ½ hour. Pack into pots or little stone jars and cover with paraffin and paper. Use for sandwiches.

TO COOK BACON

BROILED—Place slices of bacon on rack of broiler, 4 inches below medium broiler heat. Broil about 2 minutes, turn and cook 2 minutes longer or to desired crispness.

A second rack placed on top of bacon will prevent curling.

FRIED—Place bacon in cold frying pan over low heat. Cook slowly to desired crispness, turning frequently. Pour off fat as it accumulates. Drain on absorbent paper.

BAKED—Place strips of bacon on wire rack placed over shallow baking pan. Bake in hot oven (400° F.) 12 minutes or to desired crispness. Do not turn.

BACON AND EGGS

Fry lean strips of bacon until crisp. Remove and lay them on a platter. Break the eggs separately, gently slide them into the bacon fat and cook until they are set. See page 373.

TO COOK PORK SAUSAGES

Broiling gives the most satisfactory results. To broil sausages arrange on wire rack and place 4 to 5 inches under broiler heat in unheated broiler. Broil slowly for 10 to 12 minutes. Turn several times while cooking to brown on all sides.

To pan-fry sausages, place in cold pan and cook slowly until browned. Pour off fat as it accumulates. Allow ⅓ pound per person. Serve with fried apples.

SAUSAGE ROLLS

12 link sausages   12 thin slices bread

Broil sausages. Remove crusts from bread. Roll each sausage in a slice of bread. Toast under broiler. Serves 4.

LIVER CASSEROLE

1 pound calf's liver
¾ cup tomato sauce
Dash salt and pepper

1 teaspoon Worcestershire
sauce

Wash liver, cut into 1½-inch cubes and place in casserole. Add sauce and seasoning, cover and bake at 350° F. ½ hour. Just before serving, add Worcestershire sauce. Serves 4.

BRAISED LIVER WITH STUFFING

1 calf's liver (about 2 pounds)
Bread Stuffing No. 2
    (page 303)
Salt and pepper

Flour to dredge
3 strips salt pork
½ cup water

Wipe liver with a damp cloth and dry. Make an incision in the thickest part using a sharp knife. Fill with stuffing, sew edges together, season with salt and pepper and dredge with flour. Place in a baking pan and place strips of salt pork on top. Add water, cover pan and cook in a moderate oven (350° F.) until tender, 1½ to 2 hours. About 10 minutes before serving remove cover so that salt pork may brown. Thicken gravy in pan and serve with meat. Serves 8.

VARIATION—Bacon may be used in place of salt pork.

LIVER AND BACON

½ pound sliced bacon
1½ pounds calf's liver, cut
    ½ inch thick

Flour
1 teaspoon salt
⅛ teaspoon pepper

Place a single layer of bacon in a cool frying pan and place over low heat. Turn bacon frequently and drain off excess fat so that the bottom of the pan is well greased. Cook slowly until bacon is light golden brown and crisped. Drain on absorbent paper. Keep in a hot place. Wipe liver with a damp cloth and dry thoroughly. Roll in flour to which salt and pepper have been added. Sauté in drippings at reduced heat 5 to 8 minutes, until browned on both sides and center is just done. Overcooking ruins liver. Serves 4.
Serve liver with slices of broiled corned beef instead of bacon.

LIVER LOAF WITH PAN GRAVY

1½ pounds beef liver
1½ cups boiling water
2 slices salt pork, ¼ inch thick
1 medium-sized onion
¼ cup chopped parsley
2 cups soft bread crumbs

2 eggs, slightly beaten
1 teaspoon salt
¼ teaspoon pepper
1½ cups cold water
2 tablespoons flour

Wash liver quickly under running water, cover with boiling water and let stand 10 minutes; drain. Grind with salt pork and onion; add parsley, crumbs, eggs, salt and pepper; mix thoroughly. Press into (8x4x3 inch) baking pan and bake in moderate oven (350° F.) about 1 hour, or until browned. Remove loaf to hot platter. Stir flour into drippings and brown; add water gradually and cook five minutes, stirring until thickened; season and pour over loaf. Serves 6.

SAVORY LIVER

¼ cup chopped onion
2 teaspoons chopped parsley
2 tablespoons butter
2 tablespoons flour
¾ teaspoon salt

Dash pepper
3 tablespoons vinegar
2½ cups bouillon
1½ pounds beef liver, sliced
  thin

Brown onion and parsley in butter; stir in flour, seasonings and vinegar, and add bouillon gradually, stirring constantly. Cook until thickened. Place liver in gravy and cook, covered, 15 minutes, turning once. Serves 6.

LIVER PIQUANTE WITH VEGETABLES

2 pounds liver
Fat salt pork
½ pound lean salt pork
2 cups boiling water

1 cup sliced carrots
½ cup sliced onion
1 tablespoon chopped parsley
Bit of bay leaf

Small sprig of thyme

Buy liver in solid piece, wash thoroughly, dry and lard with strips of fat pork (page 3). Cut lean salt pork into pieces and try out slightly; add liver and brown on all sides. Add hot water, vegetables and seasonings, cover and bake in moderate oven (350°F.) until liver is tender, or about 1 hour for veal liver and 2 hours for beef liver. Serve on hot platter surrounded by vegetables. Serves 8.

SWEETBREADS

PREPARING SWEETBREADS—Plunge sweetbreads into cold water and let stand 30 minutes. Parboil 20 minutes in acidulated, salted water (add 1 teaspoon salt and 1 tablespoon vinegar to 1 quart of water). Drain and plunge into cold water again. Remove any little strings and membranes.

BROILED—

2 pairs sweetbreads	Butter
Salt and pepper	Lemon juice

Prepare sweetbreads as above, cut into thin slices, sprinkle with salt and pepper, dot with butter and broil under moderate heat about 10 minutes. Serve with melted butter combined with a little lemon juice. Serves 4.

FRIED—

2 pairs sweetbreads	Bread or cracker crumbs
Salt and pepper	2 tablespoons flour
1 egg, beaten	1 cup milk

Prepare sweetbreads as directed above and cut into slices. Sprinkle with salt and pepper, dip into egg, then into crumbs and brown in hot fat. Place on platter. Add flour to 2 tablespoons of fat in which sweetbreads were fried, mix until smooth, add milk and season with salt and pepper. Serves 4.

CREAMED—

2 pairs sweetbreads	2 cups Medium White Sauce
1 teaspoon minced parsley	

Prepare sweetbreads as directed above, dice and heat in the white sauce, while stirring constantly. Add minced parsley. Serves 4.

LARDED—

2 pairs sweetbreads	2 cups seasoned stock
Salt pork for larding	6 slices toast

Prepare sweetbreads as directed above. Lard with salt pork, letting ends of strips curl over the edges of the sweetbreads. Place in roasting pan, pour stock over them, cover pan and cook in moderate oven (350° F.) 1 hour. Serve on toast. Thicken liquid in pan and serve with sweetbreads. Serves 4.

SWEETBREADS SUPREME

1 pound sweetbreads   ¼ cup flour
1 quart fresh mushrooms,   3 cups milk
   sliced   ½ pound dried beef
¼ cup butter   Toast

Precook sweetbreads and dice. Add sliced mushrooms to butter, cover and cook slowly 5 minutes. Sprinkle flour over mushrooms, blend and add milk, dried beef and sweetbreads and cook slowly until thickened, stirring occasionally. Serve on toast. Serves 8 to 10.

MIXED GRILL

Mixed grills consist of two or more kinds of meat broiled with vegetables or fruits. Combinations should be planned so that they will broil in about the same length of time. The meat may be liver, steaks, chops, kidneys, bacon, ground meat patties, precooked sweetbreads or sausages. Halves of tomatoes, mushroom caps, halves of boiled sweetpotatoes or white potatoes are suitable. The fruits may be sliced apples, whole or halved bananas, canned peach or apricot halves or sliced pineapple. The food should be basted with melted butter or margarine while cooking to keep it moist.

STEWED CALF'S HEART

2 calf's hearts   2 tablespoons flour
1 bay leaf   2 tablespoons butter
Salt and pepper   ½ lemon

Wash hearts carefully and remove veins, arteries and clotted blood. Cover hearts with boiling water and simmer 1½ hours. Remove all fat and set aside to cool. Cut hearts into small pieces, remove cords and artery cases and use only lean portions. Place chopped heart in saucepan, add water, bay leaf, salt and pepper and simmer for 10 minutes. Rub flour and butter together, add with sliced lemon, and cook 5 minutes stirring constantly. Serves 4.

WITH VEGETABLES—Dredge hearts with salt and pepper, brown in fat, then add water as above with ½ cup chopped celery, 2 tablespoons chopped onions, ¼ cup sliced carrots, 2 slices turnips, 1 bay leaf and ¼ teaspoon peppercorns. Cover and simmer 1½ hours or until tender.

STUFFED HEART

1 beef or 2 veal hearts	2 tablespoons flour
½ recipe Sausage Stuffing	2 tablespoons fat
1½ cups water	

Wash heart, trim and fill with stuffing. Tie firmly with string. Dredge with flour, brown in fat and season with salt and pepper. Add water, cover closely and simmer about 2 hours or until tender. Thicken liquid with additional flour. Serves 6.

1. BRAISED HEART—Reduce water to ½ cup. Prepare as above but cook, covered, in moderate oven (350° F.) instead of simmering. Allow 1½ to 2½ hours for lamb, pork or veal hearts, 2½ to 3½ hours for beef hearts.

2. Use Bread Stuffing No. 2 with braised heart. Cook vegetables in pan with heart.

SWEET-SOUR HEARTS

2 veal hearts	6 tablespoons vinegar
2 tablespoons flour	2 teaspoons sugar
2 tablespoons fat	¼ teaspoon pepper
1 teaspoon salt	3 cups water
1 small onion, chopped	

Clean hearts, remove membrane and large veins, and cut hearts into ½-inch cubes. Brown flour in fat and add meat and remaining ingredients. Cover and simmer for 1½ hours or until tender. Serve with noodles. Serves 4.

STEAK AND KIDNEY PIE

1½ pounds steak (beef or veal)	1 tablespoon chopped onion
½ pound kidney	1 tablespoon minced parsley
Salt and pepper	½ pound mushrooms, sliced
	Pastry

Cut steak and kidney into ½-inch cubes and dredge with flour. Season with salt and pepper. Arrange meat in greased casserole and add onion, parsley, mushrooms and sufficient water to cover meat. Cover casserole and cook in a moderate oven (350° F.) 1 hour or until meat is almost tender. Remove cover and replace it with pastry, pricking crust to allow steam to escape. Return to very hot oven (450° F.) and bake for 15 minutes or until crust is browned. Serves 4.

SAUTÉED KIDNEYS

Remove skin from kidneys. Cut into thin round slices, cover with cold salted water and let stand 30 minutes. Drain and dry. Sauté until tender in butter or other fat. Serve with Brown Sauce or Tomato Sauce.

If preferred, cut kidneys into halves after skinning, remove white tubes and fat and slice kidneys lengthwise.

SPANISH KIDNEY

1 beef kidney or 3 pairs   6 slices tomato
lamb or pork kidneys   Bacon

Cut beef kidney into 6 pieces or split open lamb or pork kidneys. Remove tubes and fat. Soak in cold water 30 minutes. Arrange tomato slices in greased frying pan, place a piece of kidney on each slice and a piece of bacon on each kidney. Broil under moderate broiler heat, 10 to 15 minutes or until kidney is tender. Cover and simmer over direct heat 4 or 5 minutes. Serve with parsley butter. Serves 6.

SMOKED BEEF TONGUE

1 smoked beef tongue   1 cup Spanish Sauce
10 chopped cooked mushrooms

Scrub tongue and let stand overnight in cold water. Cover with fresh cold water and simmer for 4 hours or until tender. Drain, place in cold water 2 or 3 minutes, remove skin and roots, and place in hot water for a few minutes. Drain. Place on serving dish. Add mushrooms to Spanish sauce and pour over tongue. Serves 6.

VIRGINIA BEEF TONGUE

1 fresh beef tongue   ¼ cup butter
1 cup brown sugar   1 tablespoon whole cloves
1 cup stewed cranberries   ½ lemon, sliced

Scrub tongue and simmer in water to cover until tender, 3 to 4 hours. Remove skin and trim root end. To 1 cup of liquid in which tongue was cooked, add remaining ingredients. Simmer tongue in mixture 15 minutes. Serves 6.

CALF'S BRAINS AND OYSTERS

1 set calf's brains
1 dozen oysters
1 cup water
1 tablespoon flour

½ cup cream
Salt and pepper
½ teaspoon soy sauce
1 teaspoon lemon juice

Place the brains in cold water for 30 minutes. Remove membrane and veins. Cook oysters in water 2 minutes. Remove oysters and cook brains in oyster broth 15 minutes. Place the brains on serving dish. Combine flour with cream, add to broth and heat until slightly thickened. Add salt, pepper, soy sauce, lemon juice and oysters. Pour over brains. Serves 4.

BRAISED BRAINS

1 set calf's brains
Salt and pepper

Flour or cracker crumbs
Fat

Soak brains in cold water for 30 minutes. Remove veins and membrane. Season, roll in flour or crumbs, brown in fat and cover skillet tightly. Cook slowly about 20 minutes. Serves 2.

VARIATION—Cook sweetbreads in the same manner.

TRIPE PATTIES

1 pound boiled tripe
1 egg
½ cup bread crumbs

½ teaspoon onion juice
1 teaspoon salt
Dash pepper

Grind tripe and combine with remaining ingredients. Shape into patties and fry in greased skillet until browned. Serves 4.

VARIATIONS—Make patties ½ inch thick and brown under low broiler heat.

BAKED TRIPE WITH BACON—Wrap each patty with slice of bacon and bake in hot oven (425° F.) 8 to 10 minutes, or until bacon is crisp.

TRIPE FRITTERS—Sift 1 cup sifted flour with ½ teaspoon salt. Combine 1 cup milk, 1 tablespoon melted shortening and 1 egg, slightly beaten. Add to flour and mix until smooth. Dip tripe patties into the batter and fry in hot deep fat (380° F.) until browned.

TRIPE

PREPARING TRIPE—Tripe is usually sold in the city markets already cleaned. If not so obtainable, wash well through several boiling waters, then put it in cold water and let it soak overnight.

STEWED WITH ONIONS

2 pounds tripe	1 cup hot milk
2 onions	Salt and pepper
	Butter

Simmer the tripe and onions in salted water for three or four hours. Drain. Chop the cooked onions very fine, place them in hot milk, and season with salt, pepper and butter. Pour this over the tripe and serve at once. Serves 6.

TRIPE STEWED WITH TOMATO SAUCE

2 pounds tripe	1 tablespoon butter
1 onion, cut into halves	2 tablespoons flour
2 cups cooked tomatoes	Salt and pepper

Choose honeycomb portions and thick section of tripe. Wash carefully, cover with hot water, add onion, cover pan and simmer 35 minutes. Cook tomatoes 10 minutes and strain through sieve. Melt butter, blend in flour, add tomatoes and seasonings and cook until thickened. Drain tripe well, cut into thin strips and drain again, pressing tripe gently to remove as much water as possible. Add sauce and heat thoroughly. Serves 6.

CREOLE—Cook clove garlic, 3 bay leaves, dash of thyme and dash cayenne with tomatoes.

REINDEER

Government breeding of reindeer has brought the meat back on the market in modern form. It is shipped frozen and may be thawed at low temperature or put directly under the broiler or in the oven, when additional time for cooking must be allowed. It is very much like beef or veal, with less fat, and has a pleasant gamy flavor. The round is the desirable cut and steaks, pot roast, oven roast, chops and cutlets are prepared like beef or veal except that they need larding more often.

POULTRY AND GAME

POULTRY includes all the domesticated birds that are used for food—chicken and fowl, turkeys, squabs and pigeons, geese and ducks. Game includes wild birds—ducks, geese, partridge, reed birds, quail, plover, etc., and animals suitable for food which are pursued and taken in field or forest, as the deer, moose and rabbit.

The flesh of game, except that of partridge and quail, is dark in color and has a fine strong flavor. The flesh of wild birds, except that of wild ducks and geese, contains less fat than the flesh of poultry.

Types of Poultry on Market

Several types of poultry are now available on the market. Fresh poultry is brought to market alive or dressed by scalding. A second type is dressed by producers and cooled. Another type is graded for feeding which makes the meat more tender and of a uniform flavor and texture. The dressed birds are again graded for size and quality, packed in boxes and frozen hard to preserve the freshness. Another type of poultry is of the quality described above, but before being hard-frozen, is fully drawn and cleaned, ready to be cooked. The birds are wrapped and may be kept in the home refrigerator until used. The giblets are wrapped separately and placed inside the body cavity.

Frozen poultry should be thawed only enough so the giblets can be removed. Prepare the chicken for roasting while in the frozen state. Fresh poultry should not be kept long uncooked. It should be drawn as soon as purchased and kept in the refrigerator, for the short time before cooking.

In many markets today, chickens are disjointed and the pieces sold separately. Halved or quartered chickens may also be purchased. Chicken feet are often sold and may be scalded, skinned and used for making soup, bouillon or clear gelatin, for aspic and poultry mousse.

Selection of Poultry and Game

Poultry should be plump, with smooth, soft legs and feet and smooth, moist skin. The lower end of the breastbone should be flexible, the skin should be easily broken when twisted and the joint of the wing should yield readily when turned backward. The eyes should be bright, the comb red, and there should be an abundance of pin feathers.

Birds with a yellow skin are likely to be plump; those with white skins are likely to be tender. Bruised, dry or purplish skin is an indication of careless dressing and of age. Hard, dry, scaly legs, hard breastbone and the presence of long hairs are all signs of an old and less-tender bird.

Avoid birds with a full crop. Buy dry-picked poultry whenever possible.

Unless hen turkeys are young, small and plump, cock turkeys are more satisfactory.

Geese should have an abundance of pin-feathers, soft feet and pliable bills.

There is more meat in proportion to the amount of bone in fowls weighing five to six pounds than there is in smaller birds. Broilers should weigh one to two pounds.

To Clean and Dress Poultry

Cut off the head and remove the pin-feathers with a sharp pointed knife or a strawberry huller. Singe by holding the bird over a flame, turning quickly on all sides until all down and hair have been burnt off. Wash with a weak solution of baking soda.

If the feet and tendons were not removed at the market, cut through the skin around the lower joint or "drumstick", one and one-half inches below the joint that connects the foot with the leg, but do not cut the tendons. Place the leg with this cut at the edge of the table and break the bone by pressing downward. Hold the bird in the left hand and with the right pull off the foot, and with it the tendons. In an old bird, the tendons must be removed one by one with a skewer or trussing needle.

To Prepare Poultry for Roasting

Make an incision lengthwise of body below the breastbone. Cut out vent, loosen and remove the entrails, gizzard, heart and liver. Reserve last three; these are known as the giblets. Care should be taken not to break the gall bladder attached to the liver. Discard quickly. Slit gizzard carefully just to the inside sac and remove the latter whole and discard. Remove the veins from the top of the heart and slit heart.

Remove the lung tissue and discard. Slit the neck skin down the back; remove crop, windpipe and gullet from the neck opening. This leaves the skin over the breast unbroken. Cut off the neck close to body, but leave enough of the neck skin intact to fold down under the back while roasting. Save the neck for soup stock. Cut out the oil sac above the tail. Discard.

Scrub bird inside and out in warm water to which a little soda has been added, but do not soak in water. Dry and rub inside with salt.

To Stuff Poultry—Loosen breast skin at the neck from the meat with the handle of a spoon and cover meat with a thin layer of stuffing. This helps to keep the breast meat moist. Fold the neck skin over back. Place remaining stuffing in body cavity lightly, allowing room for expansion. Place steel pins or toothpicks across the opening at regular intervals and lace cord around the pins to bring edges of skin together.

To Truss Poultry—Insert trussing needle with cord through the body below the knee joint at base of thighs and pull cord through. Continue cord across back and pull through triangular opening made by folding wing tips up and over back. Tie tightly to hold wings close to body. Tuck end of neck skin under cord and between wings. Using another piece of cord, insert needle through the legs near the end of drumstick and draw cord around tailpiece, tying legs down close to body. A skewer may be inserted through body under legs as an aid in tying legs close to body. After roasting, remove pins and cord before bringing to table to serve.

If the poultry has little fat, it should either be larded with thin strips of salt pork or bacon laid across the breast, or covered with a cloth dipped into melted fat, being sure breast, wings and legs are well covered. Remove cloth during last ½ hour for additional browning. To prevent the ends of the legs burning, wind them with strips of cloth which have been dipped into melted fat.

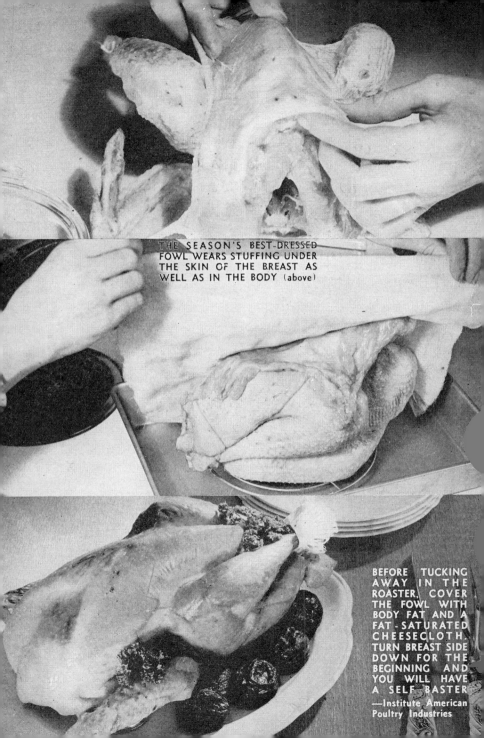

THE SEASON'S BEST-DRESSED
FOWL WEARS STUFFING UNDER
THE SKIN OF THE BREAST AS
WELL AS IN THE BODY (above)

BEFORE TUCKING
AWAY IN THE
ROASTER, COVER
THE FOWL WITH
BODY FAT AND A
FAT - SATURATED
CHEESECLOTH.
TURN BREAST SIDE
DOWN FOR THE
BEGINNING AND
YOU WILL HAVE
A SELF BASTER
—Institute American
Poultry Industries

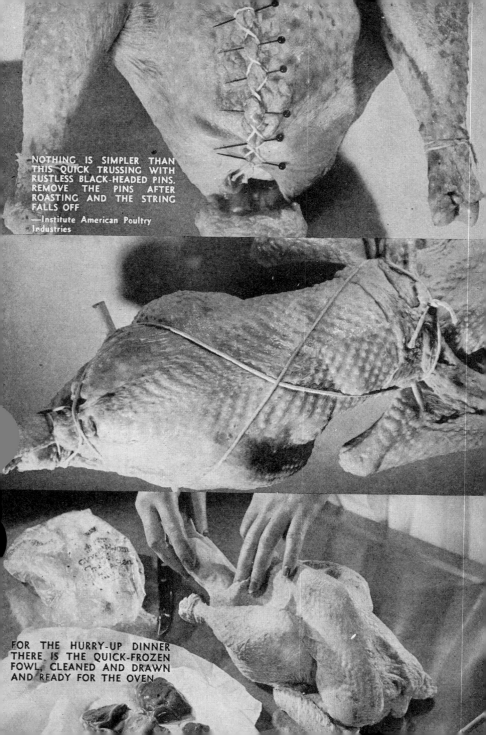

NOTHING IS SIMPLER THAN THIS QUICK TRUSSING WITH RUSTLESS BLACK-HEADED PINS. REMOVE THE PINS AFTER ROASTING AND THE STRING FALLS OFF
—Institute American Poultry Industries

FOR THE HURRY-UP DINNER THERE IS THE QUICK-FROZEN FOWL, CLEANED AND DRAWN AND READY FOR THE OVEN

To Dress Birds for Broiling and Frying

FOR BROILING—Cut off the head, neck and legs at the knee joints. Cut through backbone the entire length of bird. Lay the bird open and remove contents. Cut tendons or break the joints. Remove the ribs and breastbone to facilitate carving.

TO MAKE FILLETS—Remove skin from breast and make an incision close to breastbone, beginning at end nearest wishbone. Cut through entire length, following bone closely. Remove meat, cutting it away from wing joint. Separate large and small muscle to make "large fillet" and "fillet mignon".

TO CUT UP A FOWL—Remove head, tendons and oil sac. Cut off the legs at thigh joint and separate drumsticks from thigh. Cut the wings from the body, removing tips.

Separate the breast from back by cutting down both sides of bird below ribs. Remove heart, liver, gizzard, entrails and fat together. Remove windpipe, crop and lungs.

Cut back and breast crosswise. The back may be further divided by cutting lengthwise. Remove the wishbone by inserting knife under tip and cut downward, following the bone.

TO BONE A FOWL—Cut off head, wings to second joint and legs at knee joint. Cut downward along center back from neck, cutting on both sides of tail and around vent. Cut flesh and skin away from back and ribs down to breastbone. Remove flesh from keel bone by cutting and pushing with fingers. Break leg and wing joints by inserting knife tip into joints and turning. Loosen flesh from body on both sides and remove by pulling away from carcass. Cut and scrape flesh from leg and wing bones by working from inside body, leaving outside skin intact. Remove bones. Cut out wishbone. To stuff, place boned bird skin side down, sprinkle with salt and place stuffing in center. Fold over flaps of skin and tie cords around body across breast. Clip cords when bird is half-cooked so there are no marks over the skin after roasting.

To Clean Giblets

Cut the fat and membrane from gizzard. Make a gash in the thickest part, cutting carefully just to the inner lining. Discard the sac. Carefully separate gall bladder from the liver, cutting off any part that has a greenish color. Remove arteries and veins from top of heart and squeeze out clot of blood. Slit the heart.

Chickens

ROAST CHICKEN

Singe, draw, or clean chicken, wash and dry. Rub inside with salt, stuff lightly and truss. Rub surface with unsalted fat, place on rack in roaster, breast down. Cover with a layer of body fat from the chicken, if available. Roast uncovered in a moderate oven (325° F.) until tender. Season with additional salt when half done. A chicken from 4 to 5 pounds requires 35 to 40 minutes per pound; a smaller chicken, roast in a moderate oven (350° F.) 40 to 45 minutes. Weight should be taken before drawing or after stuffing. See page 8.

ROAST HALF CHICKEN—Arrange stuffing in outline of chicken in bottom of greased shallow pan. Press chicken, cut side down, on stuffing. Brush with melted fat. Roast uncovered at 350° F. 40 to 45 minutes.

BROILED CHICKEN

Cut small chicken into half and remove backbone and breastbone. Break hip, knee and wing joints. Brush both sides with melted fat, place on heated rack, skin side down and sprinkle with salt. Replace rack about 5 inches from heat. Cook with moderate heat (350° F.) from 45 to 50 minutes, until chicken is tender and browned on both sides, turning once.

PANNED CHICKEN

Prepare the chicken as for broiling. Place in a pan, cover with bits of fat and roast uncovered in a moderate oven (350° F.), allowing 15 to 20 minutes per pound. Baste with drippings every half hour. When nearly done, remove from the oven, season with salt and pepper, cover with additional fat, dredge with flour and return to oven to brown slightly on both sides.

When done, place on platter, skin side uppermost. Make gravy by pouring 1 cup hot milk into roasting pan and adding cracker or bread crumbs. Season with salt and pepper; add onion juice, if desired. Boil 1 minute and pour over chicken. Serves 3 to 5.

ROAST CHICKEN, MARYLAND STYLE

1 4-pound chicken	2 eggs, beaten
Salt and pepper	Bread crumbs
Flour	1/4 cup mild fat
	1 cup milk or cream

Clean and disjoint the chicken, leaving breast whole. Simmer neck and giblets to obtain a cup of stock for gravy. Season each piece of chicken with salt and pepper, dip in flour, beaten egg and soft crumbs and place in greased pan. Roast in moderate oven (350° F.) from 40 to 45 minutes, basting frequently with 1/2 cup of fat melted in 1/4 cup of hot water.

When the chicken is done, make a gravy from the fat left in the pan, stirring in 2 tablespoons of flour, 1 cup of milk or cream, and the cup of stock made from the giblets. Add a few button mushrooms, if desired. Serve the chicken with the gravy poured around it. Serves 6.

PLANKED CHICKEN

2 3-pound chickens	1 teaspoon minced onion
1/4 cup fat	1/4 cup oil or melted fat
1 teaspoon minced parsley	Salt and pepper
1 teaspoon minced green	2 cups sautéed mushrooms
pepper	4 cups seasoned mashed
1 teaspoon lemon juice	potatoes
	Garnishes for Plank

Make a savory fat by rubbing minced parsley, green pepper and onion into fat. Flavor with lemon juice, salt and pepper. Split the chickens, season with salt and pepper, and put in pan, pouring a little oil or melted fat over them. Roast until nearly done (about 30 minutes) at 350° F.

Prepare a plank of the proper size, oil it and garnish with a border of potatoes forced through pastry bag and tube. Place chicken in the center of plank, arrange sautéed mushrooms around it and spread the savory fat over chicken. Place plank in hot oven (400° F.) for 10 minutes to brown potato border and to give chicken final cooking. Serve on plank, garnished with stuffed tomatoes, green peppers and vegetables, cut as desired. Serves 6 to 8.

FRIED CHICKEN

No. 1—SOUTHERN STYLE

2 broilers	Flour
Salt and pepper	¼ cup fat

Cut each chicken into four or six pieces, dip each piece quickly into cold water, drain, season with salt and pepper, and roll in flour to make a thick coating. Sauté the chicken in a little fat until each piece is tender and brown on both sides. Drain the pieces well and arrange on a warm platter, setting dish in a hot place to keep the meat from cooling while the gravy is being made as on page 279. Serves 4.

No. 2—FRENCH FRIED

Cut the chickens into pieces and dip each piece into a fritter batter made of 1 cup milk, 1 cup flour, 1 tablespoon melted fat and 1 slightly beaten egg. Fry in deep fat (375°-390° F.) until brown. Transfer to a casserole or baking dish and bake in a moderate oven (350° F.) for 30 to 40 minutes.

For an interesting variation, roll the pieces of chicken in whole cereal flakes instead of flour before frying.

SMOTHERED CHICKEN

1 5-pound chicken	2 or more tablespoons fat
Salt and pepper	Flour

Remove neck and split chicken down the back. Season inside and out with salt and pepper and dredge thoroughly with flour. Lay the chicken, inside down, in a small roasting pan and add a small amount of water. The pan should be only slightly larger than the chicken so the gravy will not be too quickly evaporated. Cover and roast in a moderate oven (325°-350° F.) 2½ to 3 hours. If roasted without a cover, baste every 10 minutes after the first 20 minutes.

Add more fat, if necessary. When done, place the chicken on a hot platter, add 2 tablespoons of flour to the pan, stir until smooth, then add enough water to make 2 cups of gravy. Should chicken be too fat, remove all but 2 tablespoons of fat from pan before making the gravy. Season gravy with salt and pepper, pour over the chicken and serve at once. Serves 8.

SIMMERED CHICKEN

Simmering is an excellent way to prepare chickens that are large and less-tender. Singe and wash the chicken, then tie it into a wet cloth that has been generously sprinkled with flour. Plunge into boiling water and simmer gently until done, allowing about 20 to 30 minutes per pound. Remove cloth and serve with Oyster or Parsley Sauce, page 309.

STEAMED CHICKEN

1 5-pound chicken	1 onion
Salt and pepper	1 bay leaf
Flour	

A fat chicken a year or two old has a rich, fine flavor, and if steamed properly, will be perfectly tender. Singe and wash the chicken, draw and dress as for roasting, and wipe dry. Rub inside and out with salt and pepper, place a whole onion and a bay leaf inside and truss as for roasting.

Flour a cloth and wrap around the chicken. Lay the chicken, with cloth, back downward, in a steamer and allow to steam continuously from 3 to 4 hours, according to age and size. Serve with Celery, Olive or Piquante Sauce, pages 309 and 316.

STEAMED WHOLE SPRING CHICKEN

1 3-pound chicken	Minced herbs
Salt and pepper	1 tablespoon flour
1 cup oysters	½ cup cream or milk
1 tablespoon fat	3 hard-cooked eggs

Prepare full-grown spring chicken as for roasting, and season inside and out with salt and pepper. Stuff with whole, raw oysters and place in a steamer with a close-fitting cover, steaming until done. Place chicken on a warm dish in a warm place.

To make gravy, put the fat into a saucepan with minced herbs and flour and stir until mixture bubbles. Add the liquid from the bottom of steamer, cream or milk and heat to boiling, stirring constantly. Add the eggs, chopped fine, and let the mixture boil. Pour over chicken and serve at once. Serves 4.

CHICKEN AND DUMPLINGS

1 4-pound chicken
Salt and pepper
1 whole onion, if desired
1 stalk celery, if desired

3 tablespoons flour
1 cup milk
1 recipe Biscuit Dumplings,
page 336

Clean, singe and cut the chicken into serving portions. Place in a pot, season, and nearly cover with water. Cover the pot and simmer gently. An old fowl will require at least 3 or 4 hours slow cooking, but a young chicken should be done in 1½ hours. Remove the cover during the last half-hour of cooking, reducing the broth to about 1½ pints.

About 20 minutes before serving time, add Biscuit Dumplings. When dumplings are cooked and ready to serve, remove to hot pan. Make a gravy by adding to the broth in the kettle 3 tablespoons of flour stirred to a paste in 1 cup of milk. Skim out the chicken, lay it on a platter, place the dumplings on top and cover with gravy. Serves 6 to 8.

If desired, an onion and a stalk of celery may be cooked with the chicken before the dumplings are added.

PRESSED CHICKEN

1 4-pound chicken
Salt and pepper

1 tablespoon gelatin to
each pint broth

Clean, singe and cut up the chicken. Place in a kettle with a small amount of water, season, cover closely and simmer until the meat falls from bones. Skim pieces from the kettle and scrape remaining meat from bones, separating light and dark meat.

Soften the gelatin, using 2 tablespoons of water for each tablespoon of gelatin, and add to the boiling chicken broth. Place meat in loaf pan, laying white and dark meat in alternate layers, and moistening each layer with a little broth. When all of the meat is in the pan, cover with remaining broth; place a plate on top and weight with a heavy object. Refrigerate overnight. This makes an attractive luncheon dish when sliced and served with parsley. Serves 6.

For an interesting variation, chop whites and yolks of eggs separately and add in alternate layers with white and dark meat, or arrange sliced egg in bottom of pan or in ring mold. Unmold, slice and serve on lettuce leaves.

FRICASSEE OF CHICKEN

WHITE

1 3-pound chicken
2 tablespoons fat
Salt and pepper
1 tablespoon dry herbs
3 slices salt pork

2 cups chicken stock
2 tablespoons flour
1 cup milk or cream
1 egg yolk
Cooked rice or dumplings

Singe, clean and cut up chicken. Brown in pan with fat. Cover with boiling water, add salt, pepper, herbs and salt pork. Simmer 1 hour, or until tender, strain and thicken 2 cups of liquid with flour mixed to a smooth paste with a little cold water; add milk or cream beaten with yolk of egg. Heat again until slightly thickened, pour over chicken and serve with rice or dumplings, page 336. Serves 4.

BROWN

1 3-pound chicken
2 or 3 small slices salt pork
2 tablespoons flour

2 cups boiling water
1 teaspoon onion juice, if
    desired

Salt and pepper

Cut into pieces as for white fricassee. Place salt pork in a frying pan; when hot, brown chicken, turning frequently. Add flour to fat, stir well and cook 2 minutes. Add boiling water. When gravy is smooth and boiling replace chicken, season with salt and pepper, cover and simmer gently until chicken is tender. Add a teaspoon of onion juice, if desired, and serve at once. Serves 4. Fat from any smoked meat may be used instead of salt pork. If desired, top with biscuits cut into 1-inch squares, strips or diamonds. Bake at 450° F. for 12 minutes.

BROWN WITH MUSHROOM SAUCE

Cut the chicken into serving portions. Add cold water, 1 slice onion, 2 slices carrot, 1 stalk celery, salt and pepper. Bring to a boil and simmer until tender, about 2 or 3 hours. Drain off chicken stock. Roll pieces of chicken in flour seasoned with salt and pepper. Sauté in butter until brown. Arrange chicken for serving and cover with hot Mushroom Sauce, page 315. Serves 4.

CHICKEN PIE

1 4-pound chicken   Salt, pepper and flour
                 1 recipe Plain Pastry, page 587

Singe, clean and cut up chicken as for fricassee. Place in a kettle, season, adding hot water to cover. Cover kettle and simmer slowly until chicken is tender, adding more water if necessary. Make a gravy from stock, using 2 tablespoons flour for each cup of stock. Roll pastry a little thicker than for fruit pies and line sides of a deep baking dish. Invert a small cup in the middle of the dish, partially fill with chicken and season with salt and pepper. Add the remaining chicken.

Add about 2 cups of gravy made from the chicken broth and cover top of dish with pastry crust. The inverted cup will hold the crust up and prevent evaporation. Use a generous amount of gravy to avoid having the pie too dry. Bake in a hot oven (450° F.) ½ hour or until crust is done. After cutting first slice to serve, slip knife under cup and release gravy held there. Serve additional gravy in gravy dish. Serves 6.

To make a vegetable chicken pie, add cooked vegetables, such as carrots, celery, green beans or peas. Cooked rice may also be added. Cover with pastry rolled ⅛ inch thick; cut gashes in top to permit escape of steam, or arrange lattice of pastry strips on top.

CURRY OF CHICKEN

1 chicken (1½ or 2 pounds)   1 teaspoon to 2 tablespoons
1 teaspoon salt   curry powder
2 onions   1 tablespoon flour
2 tablespoons fat   1 egg yolk, beaten

Prepare the chicken as for fricassee. Place in a saucepan with salt and water to cover. Cover the pan closely and simmer until tender. Remove the chicken and pour broth from pan into bowl. Sauté onions in saucepan with fat until brown; skim out and fry the chicken 3 or 4 minutes. Sprinkle with curry powder. Pour in liquid from chicken, stew 5 minutes longer, and stir in flour mixed until smooth with a little cold water. Stir until thickened; add beaten egg yolk, with which has been mixed a little of the cooled broth. Serve with a border of hot boiled rice or in a rice ring. Serves 3.

SAVORY CHICKEN

¼ cup fat
1 tablespoon chopped onion
1 chopped carrot
1 slice turnip
¼ cup flour
1 cup boiling water

1½ cups strained tomatoes
Salt, pepper and paprika
1 3-pound chicken
Salt pork fat
1 cup button mushrooms
2 tablespoons chopped olives

Sauté chopped onion, carrot, and turnip in melted fat to make a savory sauce. Add flour gradually, boiling water and strained cooked tomato. Season with salt, pepper and paprika.

Cut up the chicken, dredge in flour and sauté in salt pork fat. Remove to a saucepan, cover with savory sauce and cook until tender. When done, add mushrooms, and chopped olives. Arrange the chicken on a platter; cover with savory sauce and garnish with hot spiced fruit and stuffed olives. Serves 4.

SCALLOPED CHICKEN

2 cups cooked chicken
2 cups chicken broth
2 tablespoons flour

3 tablespoons fat
Salt and pepper
Crushed crackers

2 cups cooked potatoes, sliced

Dice cooked chicken meat. Thicken broth with a paste made of flour and 2 tablespoons fat and season with salt and pepper. Fill a baking dish with alternate layers of crackers, chicken and potatoes. Cover with crumbs. Pour in the gravy, dot with bits of butter or other fat, and bake 15 to 20 minutes in a moderate oven (350°-400° F.). Serves 3.

CREAMED CHICKEN

2 cups cooked chicken
2 tablespoons fat
2 tablespoons flour

1 cup milk or cream
Salt and pepper
1 tablespoon parsley

1 egg yolk

Make a white sauce of fat, flour and milk. Season with salt and pepper. Add parsley and chicken and heat thoroughly. Beat egg yolk, add 2 tablespoons milk and pour into sauce. Cook 2 minutes, stirring constantly, and serve in croustades, or in ring of riced potatoes, noodles or vegetables. Serves 4 to 5.

Capons

Capons are large, plump, tender young castrated roosters weighing 6-7 pounds and especially fattened for the table. They are prepared for cooking in the same way as chickens. For stuffing, choose a mild dressing such as oyster, chestnut, mushroom, celery or nut, as the meat is very delicately flavored.

Turkeys

ROAST TURKEY

Dress as directed for roast chicken, stuff and truss. Place the turkey breast up, on rack of a shallow pan. Brush with melted unsalted fat and cover with a cloth dipped into melted unsalted fat, being sure breast, wings and legs are well covered; or cover with a layer of body fat, then with a clean cloth. Roast uncovered in a slow oven (300° F.) until tender. Allow 25 minutes per pound for birds under 12 pounds, or 20 minutes per pound for larger birds. Baste several times with melted fat, fruit juice, white wine, sugar in water, or drippings in pan. Season when half done. The cloth may be removed during last half-hour for additional browning. Serve with Giblet Gravy page 313. Allow ¾ to 1 pound per serving.

BRAISED TURKEY

1 8-pound turkey	½ cup chopped carrots
Stuffing	½ cup onion
½ pound salt pork	½ cup turnip
½ cup chopped celery	Salt and pepper
4 cups water or stock	

Stuff the body and breast of the turkey with a desired dressing and truss. Spread thin slices of salt pork over breast and legs and cover turkey with a sheet of heavy oiled paper, fastening paper on by passing string around body. In a large double roasting pan, spread sliced salt pork and chopped vegetables. Lay the turkey in the pan, breast up, sprinkle with salt and pepper, cover pan tightly and roast in a moderate oven (350° F.) allowing 25 minutes per pound.

At the end of 30 minutes, add water or stock. Uncover pan for last half hour and remove paper and pork from the turkey. This permits the meat to brown lightly. Serve with gravy for 10.

FILLETS OF TURKEY WITH RICE

Fillets of turkey breast
1 egg, slightly beaten
2 tablespoons water
Bread crumbs
3 cups turkey or chicken stock
1 cup cooked rice

½ teaspoon onion juice
1 teaspoon salt
2 teaspoons butter
1 tablespoon grated cheese
Pepper
6 tablespoons oil or melted fat

Skin the breast of a cooked turkey and separate into fillets about ½ inch thick and as uniform as possible. Beat the egg and add water. Dip the fillets into egg, then into crumbs, again into egg and into the crumbs. Chill. Heat stock with rice, onion juice and ½ teaspoon salt; cover and simmer until the stock is absorbed.

When the rice is tender, add butter and cheese; season with remaining salt and pepper. Cook the fillets slowly in oil until brown. Heap rice on a hot platter and arrange the fillets around it. Serves 6.

BROILED YOUNG TURKEY

Use a very young turkey or older bird steamed 1 hour. Cut the bird into serving pieces and use breast, thighs, and drumsticks. The other pieces are best cooked some other way, though they may be broiled, if desired. Brush the pieces with melted butter, place under a slow broiler, and cook until tender, 30 to 60 minutes, depending upon thickness of pieces. Turn frequently to brown on all sides. Serve with giblet gravy.

FRENCH FRIED TURKEY

Young turkey
2 teaspoons salt

2 eggs
2 tablespoons water

Bread crumbs

Cut turkey into serving pieces, season with salt and steam until nearly tender. Cool. Just before serving, roll in very fine crumbs, dip into eggs beaten with water and roll again in the crumbs. Fry in hot deep fat (370° F.) until brown, about 10 to 12 minutes or longer if not sufficiently tender.

TURKEY CURRY

1 cup mushrooms
1/3 cup minced onion
1 large apple, peeled and diced
3 cups cooked turkey, cut in pieces
6 tablespoons fat

1/2 teaspoon salt
3 tablespoons flour
1 to 1 1/2 teaspoons curry powder
1 1/2 cups turkey stock and top milk or cream

Sauté mushrooms, onion, apple and turkey in fat until the onion and apple are tender, 10 to 15 minutes. If fresh mushrooms are used, sauté several minutes before adding other ingredients. Remove from heat, add salt, flour and curry powder, and stir thoroughly. Add liquid and cook until thickened. Set over hot water, cover and cook 15 minutes longer to blend the flavors. Add more seasoning, if desired. Serve with hot boiled rice cooked with little or no salt.

Goose

ROAST GOOSE

1 8-pound goose
Potato Stuffing, page 304

Salt and pepper
Flour

Select a young goose, clean, singe, wash in hot water and dry on outside. Flatten breastbone by striking with a rolling pin. Fill body cavity lightly with Potato Stuffing, skewer the opening or truss. Roast in a slow oven (325° F.) for 45 minutes, on rack in uncovered roasting pan. Remove from oven, pour off fat, season with salt and pepper, dredge with flour and return to oven.

When the flour is browned, pour 1 cup hot water into pan and baste goose often, dredging each time with a slight sifting of flour to absorb fat. Allow 20 minutes per pound for a young goose, and 25 minutes for older goose. Remove from pan, add 1 cup hot water to gravy and thicken, if necessary, with browned flour. Garnish goose with parsley and serve with Giblet Gravy. Serves 5. Serve with applesauce, hot or cold spiced fruit, cranberry-orange relish, or coddled minted apples.

SALMIS OF GOOSE—Use leftover roast goose. To 4 cups sliced goose, add 2 tablespoons each of lemon juice and Worcestershire sauce, and 2 cups goose gravy; simmer 20 minutes. Add 1/2 cup sherry and 12 ripe, sliced olives, and reheat. Garnish with parsley and serve on hot buttered toast.

ROAST GOOSE WITH BAKED APPLE

1 8-pound goose
2 quarts bread crumbs
2 onions, chopped
2 tablespoons fat
1 teaspoon sage

2 teaspoons salt, dash pepper
6 to 8 apples
¼ cup brown sugar
3 cooked, mashed sweet-
potatoes

Cook giblets until tender, chop and mix with bread crumbs, onion, fat, sage, salt and pepper. Clean and wash the goose thoroughly. Rub inside of goose with salt, stuff with bread mixture and truss. Place in a roaster on rack and roast uncovered in a slow oven (325° F.) until tender, allowing about 25 minutes per pound. Every hour, skim off fat from broth in pan. Wash and core apples; sprinkle with brown sugar, stuff with seasoned sweet-potatoes and place in the pan with goose 1 hour before goose is done. Serves 6.

ROAST GOOSE STUFFED WITH SAUERKRAUT—Stuff goose with 2 quarts of drained sauerkraut instead of bread stuffing. Add 1 peeled whole apple to sauerkraut.

ROAST GOOSE AND CABBAGE—Clean and prepare goose for roasting. Cut into serving pieces, place in a roasting pan and roast in a slow oven (325° F.) until almost tender, about 2½ hours. Pour off most of the fat into large saucepan; sauté 3 sliced onions in fat and when brown, add 1 head of red cabbage, chopped. Cook for several minutes; season. Place pieces of goose on top of cabbage. Sprinkle with salt and pepper. Cover tightly and simmer for 1 hour or until goose is tender and cabbage cooked. Serves 6.

DEVILED GOOSE

1 8-pound goose
Potato Stuffing, page 304
¼ cup vinegar
1 teaspoon pepper

2 tablespoons prepared
mustard
1 teaspoon salt

Singe and clean goose. Cover with boiling water and simmer for 1 hour. Remove, drain and dry. Fill body and neck lightly with Potato Stuffing, skewer or truss. Roast in moderately hot oven (350°-400° F.), allowing 15 to 20 minutes per pound. Mix vinegar, pepper, salt and mustard and use to baste goose. Serve with Giblet Gravy.

An old, less-tender goose may be prepared this way, allowing 2 hours for simmering instead of 1. Serves 6.

Ducks

ROAST DUCK

Epicures prefer young ducks rare, and without stuffing. Some people consider that ducks have too strong a flavor, and to absorb this flavor lay cored and quartered apples inside the body. These apples are removed before the duck is sent to the table. Celery and onions also may be placed inside the duck to season it and improve the flavor, two tablespoons of chopped onion being used to every cup of chopped celery, which may consist of the green stalks that are not desired for the table. This stuffing is also removed from the bird before it is sent to the table. Most people prefer ducks that are stuffed for roasting.

Wash, singe, and clean a 5-pound duck; season with salt and pepper, rub with garlic and fill with apples mixed with raisins. Place in pan and roast uncovered in a slow oven (325° F.), allowing 20 to 30 minutes per pound. Baste every 10 minutes using 1 cup of orange juice, if the flavor is desired. Serve with currant or cranberry jelly. Green peas are usually served with roast duck. Serves 5.

Duck may be stuffed with Potato Stuffing, if desired, filling it while very hot.

BRAISED DUCK

1 4-pound duck	Salt and pepper
4 slices bacon	4 cups boiling water
1 onion, minced	1 small turnip, diced
1 carrot, diced	2 tablespoons melted fat
½ teaspoon powdered thyme	4 tablespoons flour
2 tablespoons minced parsley	¼ cup cold water

Prepare duck as for roasting and sauté in bacon fat until brown. Add onion, carrot, thyme, parsley, salt and pepper and cover with water. Simmer until the duck is tender, then remove from stock. Sauté turnip in fat until brown, then drain and cook in stock until tender. Strain stock. Blend flour and cold water together until smooth and add gradually to stock, stirring constantly. Pour gravy over the duck. Garnish with pieces of turnip. Serves 4.

BRAISED DUCK WITH MUSHROOMS—Omit bacon and carrot. Use ½ pound of mushrooms, sliced, and sauté in fat in place of turnips.

LAMB OR PORK
SHOULDER CAN BE
B O N E D   A N D
FILLED, WITH CAP-
TIVATING RESULTS
—U. S. Bureau Home
Economics

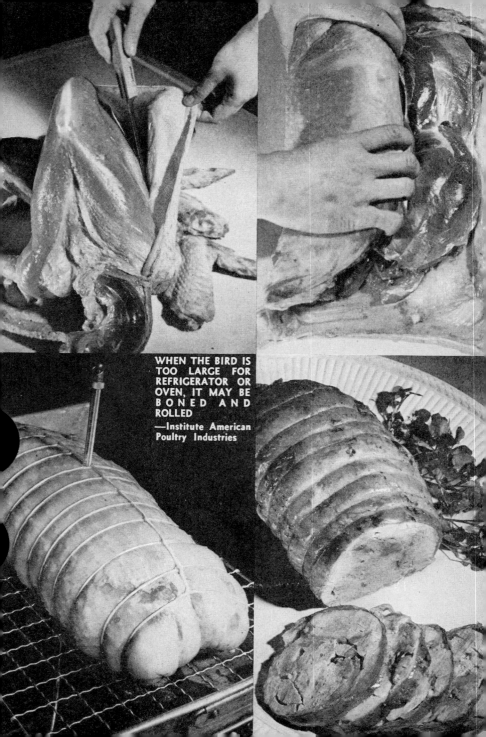

WHEN THE BIRD IS TOO LARGE FOR REFRIGERATOR OR OVEN, IT MAY BE BONED AND ROLLED

—Institute American Poultry Industries

DUCK À LA CREOLE

2 tablespoons fat
1 tablespoon flour
2 tablespoons chopped ham
Salt, pepper, and paprika
2 tablespoons minced onion
2 tablespoons chopped sweet
    pepper

½ cup chopped celery
1 tablespoon chopped parsley
1½ cups consommé
1 whole clove
¼ teaspoon mace
2 cups diced cooked duck

Melt fat, add flour and stir in ham. Season with paprika, salt, pepper, onion, sweet pepper, celery and parsley. Stir for 2 minutes, add the consommé, clove and mace. Simmer 1 hour. Strain the broth and stir in diced, cooked duck. Heat thoroughly and serve with fried hominy or mush. Serves 2.

Wild Ducks

Nearly all Spring wild ducks are likely to have a fishy flavor, and when dressed by an inexperienced cook are often unfit to eat. This flavor may be much reduced by placing in each duck a small peeled carrot, plunging the fowls into boiling water and simmering them for ten minutes before roasting. The carrot will absorb some of the unpleasant taste. An onion will have somewhat the same effect, but unless a stuffing with onions is used, the carrot is to be preferred. When there is an objection to parboiling (as when the ducks are young) rub them lightly with an onion cut in two and put three or four uncooked cranberries in each before cooking.

To pluck wild duck, remove large feathers dry. Melt ⅜ pound of paraffin in 7 quarts of boiling water. Dip the duck into the mixture several times and let the paraffin harden. Strip off the paraffin and feathers at the same time. Singe and remove any remaining pin feathers.

CANVASBACK DUCK, DELMONICO STYLE

This bird is in season from the last of November until March. As it feeds mainly on wild celery, it requires no spices in cooking. Dress in the usual way and wipe with a wet towel. Truss the neck under the wing, place in a dripping pan and roast in a moderate oven (350° F.), allowing 20 to 25 minutes per pound. Baste frequently. Season with salt and pepper and serve with gravy remaining in pan. Allow 1 pound per person.

ROAST WILD DUCKS

Clean, wiping inside and outside with a damp towel. Tuck back the wings and truss. Dust with salt, pepper and flour. If not fat, cover breast with 2 thin slices of salt pork. Place duck in a pan and add 1 cup of water and 2 tablespoons of fat. Roast uncovered and breast down in a moderate oven (350° F.), allowing 20 to 25 minutes per pound, according to rareness desired. Baste frequently. Turn breast up when half done. Serve with slices of lemon or orange and a brown gravy or with Olive Sauce, p. 317. Wild ducks are served rare and are seldom stuffed when roasted. Allow 1 pound per person.

MALLARD WILD DUCK

These ducks, in season during the Fall and Winter, are very dry when roasted, since they feed on grain. Braising is the best method of preparing them. Dress birds and stuff with a bread dressing. Truss and place in a covered roaster. Add water to the depth of 1 inch, a slice of onion and a small amount of thyme. Cover the roaster and cook in a slow oven, (325° F.) about 1 hour. Remove cover so the bird will brown and cook another 30 minutes. Use only enough water to prevent burning. Add water to pan and make a gravy to pour over ducks. Allow 1 pound per person.

Guinea Fowls
ROAST GUINEA FOWLS

1 guinea fowl	2 strips fat bacon
Salt	Stuffing, if desired

Clean and draw fowl. Rub inside with salt. Fowl may be roasted with or without stuffing. Cover breast with fat bacon which may be removed 5 minutes before serving. Roast, uncovered, in a slow oven (300°-325° F.) until tender, allowing 18 to 20 minutes per pound. Baste frequently. Season with additional salt when half done. Serve with currant jelly and Giblet Sauce. Serves 2 or 3.

FRICASSEE OF GUINEA FOWL

1 guinea fowl	2 tablespoons flour
4 slices bacon	Salt and pepper

Clean fowl and cut into serving pieces. Fry bacon to extract fat and sauté pieces of fowl in fat until brown. Add the flour, stir until thoroughly mixed; add 2 cups hot water, salt and pepper, and stir until gravy boils. Cover and simmer until tender, about 1½ hours. Serve with gravy for 2 to 3.

Peafowl

These fowls are cooked in the same way as wild turkeys. They should be larded with shreds of bacon, trussed and roasted about 30 minutes per pound at 325°-350° F. They are apt to be tough.

Pheasant, Partridges, Quail and Grouse

Game should not hang too long after being killed. In cold weather, birds may hang 10 days without becoming tainted, but during the warm season, they should be refrigerated at once. Hang in cool, dry room where air circulates freely. If birds are to be kept for several days, draw, but do not pick. Game is considered "high" when tail feathers are easily plucked. Game that is just slightly under the "high" stage has the best flavor. The inside of the bird is more susceptible to mold growth than the outside, because there is little fat covering. Placing a piece of charcoal in the body and sifting powdered charcoal into the feathers will delay tainting. Partridge taints first in crop, other birds around vent. At the first signs of tainting, dry-pick and cook bird.

A distinction must be made between white meat and dark meat in cooking game. Quail and partridges are white meat and, like chicken, must be thoroughly cooked, but not dry. Ducks, pigeons or squabs, grouse (prairie chicken), snipe and woodcock are dark meat and are cooked rare and served very hot.

All these birds are cooked by the same methods, varying only as to the degree of rareness desired. Pick out shot from birds with a sharp pointed knife. Wash quickly under running water. Small birds may be skinned when they are clean. The woodcock may or may not be drawn, as desired, the entrails being considered edible by some.

BROILED BIRDS

Clean the birds and split down the back. Season with salt and pepper and dust with flour to keep in juices. Broil in a wire broiler, placing inside of the bird near the fire first. Brown on both sides, allowing 8 to 12 minutes for quail, 25 to 40 minutes for partridges and pheasants. A strip of bacon, smoked ham butt, or salt pork may be placed over the top of each bird. When done, brush with melted butter. During broiling, if the breasts are quite thick, cover broiler with a pan and lengthen the cooking time, using lower temperature. Serve on toast with currant jelly.

PLANKED BIRDS—Prepare as for Broiled Birds; place on greased hot plank and brush with melted butter. Arrange a border around edge of plank of fluffy mashed potatoes, brushed with beaten egg. Bake in a hot oven (450° F.) 10 minutes, or until potatoes are browned. Garnish with parsley and buttered green peas.

PANNED BIRDS

Clean and draw birds and split down back. Dip quickly into hot water and season with salt, pepper and dredge with flour. Water causes the seasoning to adhere more thickly to the meat. Place the birds in a small baking dish inside up; place a teaspoon of fat in each bird, add 1 cup of water, and roast in a moderate oven (350° F.), allowing 15 to 20 minutes for quail, and proportionately longer for larger birds. Baste every 5 minutes after the first 15. Thicken gravy, add more salt and pepper, if necessary, and pour over the birds. Allow ½ to 1 bird per person.

WITH MUSHROOMS—Add 1 cup chopped cooked mushrooms to gravy.

ROASTED BIRDS

Clean, stuff and truss the birds. Brush with unsalted melted fat. If the birds are dry, lard by laying strips of salt pork across breasts. Roast uncovered in a moderate oven (350° F.) until meat is tender and bird is well browned. Baste every half hour with fat and water. Season bird with salt when about half done. Place on a warmed platter and cover with gravy made from pan drippings. Garnish platter with parsley and serve with Bread Sauce, p. 313. Allow ½ to 1 bird per person.

LARDED GROUSE

Grouse are rather dry birds and need to be larded to be palatable. Clean and wash quickly under running water. Cover bird entirely with thin slices of bacon, tying them in place with crossing of soft string. Place in a roasting pan and pour over enough boiling water to use for basting the birds. Roast in a moderate oven (350° F.) about 45 minutes. Baste frequently. When done, remove bacon strips, brush birds with oil and melted fat, dredge with flour and place in oven again until brown. The liquid in the pan may be thickened, seasoned, and used as gravy. Arrange the birds on a platter and garnish with rings of sautéed green pepper, and strips of bacon. Allow 1 grouse per person.

ROAST QUAIL

6 quail	Salt and pepper
6 large oysters	Flour
Strips of bacon	Butter or other fat

Dress, clean and stuff each bird with one large oyster. Truss, season and dredge with flour. Lard breast and legs with strips of bacon. Bake as directed for larded grouse, allowing 15 to 20 minutes for cooking. Serves 6. Serve with hot spiced crabapples.

GAME PIE

6 birds	2 whole cloves
4 cups water	¼ pound diced salt pork
Salt and pepper	2 tablespoons flour, browned
¼ cup minced parsley	2 tablespoons fat
½ chopped onion	1 recipe Plain Pastry, p. 587
2 cups diced cooked potatoes	

Clean the birds thoroughly and split into halves. Cover with water and heat to boiling. Skim top and add salt, pepper, parsley, onion, cloves and salt pork. Simmer until tender, keeping birds covered with water. When done, thicken the liquid with browned flour and let the gravy come to boiling. Add fat, remove from fire and cool. Line the sides of a greased baking dish with pastry. Fill dish with alternate layers of bird and potatoes. Pour in gravy and cover with top crust, slashed in center. Bake in a hot oven (450° F.) for 10 minutes, then in a moderate oven (350° F.) for 30 minutes. Serves 6.

Pigeons and Squabs

Domestic pigeons are the most desirable. Wild pigeons are likely to be tough. Squabs are the nestlings of pigeons, usually marketed at about 4 weeks of age. They are tender and delicately flavored. Both are prepared by the same methods as chicken, with pigeons taking a long, slow cooking time.

BROILED SQUAB

6 squabs
Salt and pepper

Butter
Toast

Wash birds quickly under running water, split the birds down back, flatten breast, season and broil. When browned, brush with melted butter and serve on toast for 6.

PIGEON AND MUSHROOM STEW

3 pigeons
1 tablespoon fat
2 cups stock or gravy
Salt, pepper, cayenne

2 tablespoons mushroom
  catchup
½ cup mushrooms
2 tablespoons cream

Clean and cut pigeons into serving portions. Sauté in fat, but do not brown. Add stock or gravy, salt, pepper, cayenne, and mushroom catchup. Simmer 1 hour, or until tender, add mushrooms, simmer 10 minutes more, and stir in cream. Serve on a hot platter with mushrooms arranged around pigeons. Serves 3.

POTTED PIGEONS

6 pigeons
Stuffing
3 slices bacon
1 diced carrot
1 diced onion

1 teaspoon minced parsley
4 cups hot water or stock
¼ cup melted fat
¼ cup flour
Buttered toast

Clean and dress pigeons; stuff, truss and place upright in pan upon slices of bacon. Add carrot, onion, and parsley, and cover with boiling water or stock. Cover pot closely and simmer from 2 to 3 hours, or until tender, adding boiling water or stock when necessary. Combine fat and flour and add to 2 cups of stock remaining in pan. Serve on toast with gravy for 6.

PIGEON PIE

6 pigeons
Bread Stuffing, p. 303
Salt and pepper

3 tablespoons fat
3 tablespoons flour
1 recipe Plain Pastry, p. 587

3 hard-cooked eggs

Stuff each pigeon with bread stuffing. Loosen joints with a knife, but do not cut them through. Simmer, with water to cover, until nearly tender; then season with salt and pepper.

Combine fat and flour with the liquid in which the pigeons have been cooked to make a gravy, and let cool. Line the sides of a greased baking dish with pastry. Cut eggs into slices and fill baking dish with alternate layers of egg, pigeon and gravy. Cover with a layer of pastry and bake at 450° F. for 10 minutes, then lower temperature to 350° F. and bake 30 minutes. Serves 6.

Venison

Venison differs little from beef or veal except that it is less fat. The flavor is gamey, but not strong, and the texture of the meat is fine. The most desirable cut is the round, which may be used for steaks, but which is most satisfactory for roasting. Other roasting pieces are the saddle and the leg.

Venison is shipped frozen and must be handled with the same care as any other frozen meat. It should be allowed to thaw slowly at a low temperature, and cooked at once, or cooked frozen, allowing the same additional time as for frozen beef. Most people prefer venison served rare, with a tart jelly.

ROAST LEG OF VENISON

Leg of venison
1/4 cup fat salt pork

Salt and pepper
Flour

Wipe carefully and remove dry skin. Lard the lean side of the leg with strips of pork. Soften fat, rub it over the meat and dredge with salt, pepper and flour. Lay the leg on rack of roaster, sprinkling bottom of pan with flour. Roast uncovered in slow oven (300° F.), allowing 20 to 22 minutes per pound. When flour in the bottom of pan is browned, add boiling water to cover bottom. Baste venison frequently, renewing water in pan as often as necessary. Serve with a gravy made from the juices in the bottom of the pan. Always serve a tart jelly like currant, wild grape or plum with venison. Allow 1/2 pound per person.

BROILED VENISON STEAK

2-pound venison steak
Salad oil and lemon juice

Cooking oil
Salt and paprika

If venison is strong, marinate in salad oil and lemon juice for 2 hours before cooking. Brush generously with oil. Place on preheated broiler rack and broil 7 to 10 minutes on each side at 550° F. Season with salt and paprika and serve on a very hot platter. Garnish with mushrooms, parsley and watercress. Serves 4.

Serve with slices of lemon, or spread with a mixture of butter and currant jelly, allowing half as much jelly as butter.

FRIED VENISON STEAK

2-pound venison steak
Salt and pepper
Flour

Cracker crumbs
½ cup fat
1 tablespoon currant jelly

Rub the steak with a mixture of salt and pepper, dip in flour or cracker crumbs and sauté in hot fat until browned on both sides. Place on a hot dish and cover to keep warm. Dredge 2 teaspoons of flour into fat in bottom of pan and stir until brown. Dissolve 1 tablespoon of currant jelly in 1 cup boiling water; add to gravy and stir a few minutes. Strain, pour over the meat and serve. Serves 4.

Rabbits, Hares and Squirrels

Avoid wild rabbits. Buy **ONLY** domestic rabbits, cleaned and dressed. Domestic rabbit meat is white and delicately flavored throughout. Most domestic rabbits are marketed at 8 to 10 weeks of age, and are then called "fryers." Since these rabbits are grown quickly, the bones are very brittle and in preparing for cooking, care should be taken to break them in such a way that they do not sliver. Because of their tenderness, young rabbits can be cooked by the quick methods of frying or broiling. Older rabbits need longer, slower cooking.

Choose rabbits with soft ears and paws—stiffness is a sign of age. Neither hares nor rabbits should be drawn before hanging, as they may become musty. In Winter, select a dry place for hanging, and they may remain for some time.

DRESSING AND TRUSSING

To skin and dress a rabbit, hare or squirrel, cut off the fore feet at the first joint, cut the skin around the first joint of the hind leg, loosen it and then with a sharp knife slit the skin on the under side of the leg at the tail. Loosen the skin and turn it back until it is removed from the hind legs. Tie the hind legs together and hang the rabbit to a hook by this fastening. Draw the skin over the head, slipping out the fore legs when they are reached. Cut off the head and thus remove the entire skin. Wipe with a damp cloth. Slit down the front and remove the entrails, saving heart and liver, and wipe carefully inside. Wash inside and out with acidulated water, using 1 tablespoon vinegar to each cup of water. Rinse and wipe thoroughly.

If blood has settled in any part, cut with the point of a knife where it is black and soak in warm water. Skewer firmly between the shoulders, draw the legs close to the body and fasten with skewers.

ROAST HARE OR RABBIT

1 hare or rabbit
Salt and pepper
Sausage Stuffing, p. 305

Poultry fat or oil
Currant jelly

Wash dressed hare or rabbit under running water and dry. Season with salt and pepper, stuff and sew up. Roast uncovered in moderate oven (325° F.) 1½ to 1¾ hours or until tender. Baste with fat. A thin piece of cheese cloth dipped in oil may be placed over the back for the first 45 minutes. Serve on hot platter with brown gravy and currant jelly. Garnish with parsley or watercress. Serves 4 to 6.

BROILED HARE OR RABBIT

1 hare or rabbit
Salt and pepper

Butter

Skin and clean the rabbit or hare, wipe dry, split down the back and pound flat. Wrap in heavy oiled paper. Broil at 350° F. until browned and tender, turning frequently. Remove the paper and serve on a hot platter, seasoned with salt, pepper and butter, turning over and over so it will take up the fat. Hare or rabbit may be broiled without the oiled paper, but it will not be so juicy. Serves 4.

FRIED HARE OR RABBIT

1 hare or rabbit
1 egg, beaten
Bread crumbs

Salt and pepper
1 cup milk or cream
2 tablespoons flour

Clean and dress as directed. Simmer 15 minutes and drain. When cold, cut into serving pieces, dip into beaten egg, then into bread crumbs, and season with salt and pepper. Sauté in hot fat until brown on all sides. Remove to warm platter. Brown flour in fat and add milk or cream. Bring to boiling and pour over rabbit. Garnish with sliced lemon and parsley. Serves 4.

HARE OR RABBIT SALMI

1 hare or rabbit
1 slice onion
1 stalk celery, minced
1 bay leaf
2 tablespoons oil
2 tablespoons fat
2 tablespoons flour

2 cups hot water
1 teaspoon salt
1 tablespoon Worcestershire
   sauce
1 tablespoon capers
12 pitted olives
Chopped parsley

Clean and dress as directed. Place in baking pan and add onion, celery and bay leaf; brush with oil and roast at 350° F. for 45 minutes. Remove meat from pan, add the fat and flour and stir until a rich brown. Add hot water, stir well, and when smooth, add salt, Worcestershire sauce, capers and olives. Replace meat, cover closely and roast in moderate oven (350° F.) for an additional 30 minutes or until tender. Arrange rabbit on platter, cover with strained sauce, arrange olives as a garnish and sprinkle with finely chopped parsley. Serves 6.

HARE OR RABBIT PIE

1 hare or rabbit
Lemon juice

Salt and pepper
1 recipe Southern Pastry, p. 588

Clean and dress as directed and cut into serving pieces. Back may be cut into three pieces. Cover with salted water and let stand for ½ hour. Dry and rub with lemon juice, salt and pepper. If the rabbit is plump, cut gashes in thickest parts to allow the seasoning to penetrate. Follow directions given for game pie. Serves 6.

HARE OR RABBIT EN CASSEROLE

Garlic, if desired
1 hare or rabbit
3 tablespoons fat

4 tablespoons flour
1 teaspoon salt
1/8 teaspoon pepper

Rub the frying pan with garlic if the flavor is desired. Dress and cut the hare or rabbit into serving pieces. Sauté in fat until brown. Remove from pan, stir flour into remaining fat, add 2 cups of hot water, salt and pepper and bring to boiling, stirring constantly. Place meat in casserole, add gravy, cover closely and bake in a moderate oven (350° F.) 1½ to 2 hours or until meat is tender. Serve in casserole. Serves 4 to 6.

HASENPFEFFER—Omit flour and garlic. Cover rabbit pieces in a jar with equal parts of vinegar and water. Add 1 sliced onion, salt, pepper, 4 cloves and 2 bay leaves. Soak 2 days. Remove meat and brown evenly in butter. Add gradually, about ½ sauce in which it was pickled. Let simmer about ½ hour. Before serving, stir 1 cup thick, sour cream into the sauce.

ROAST SQUIRRELS

3 small squirrels
¾ cup salad oil
¼ cup lemon juice or vinegar
2 cups bread crumbs
½ cup milk or cream
½ cup diced and sautéed
  mushrooms
½ teaspoon salt

1/8 teaspoon pepper
½ teaspoon onion juice
4 tablespoons olive oil or
  bacon fat
1 teaspoon Worcestershire
  sauce
Paprika

Dress and clean squirrels. Wash in several waters and dry. Cover with salad oil mixed with lemon juice and let stand for 1 hour. Combine bread crumbs, with just enough milk or cream to moisten, mushrooms, salt, pepper and onion juice. Stuff the squirrel with this mixture, skewer and truss. Brush with olive oil or bacon fat and roast uncovered in a slow oven (325° F.) 1½ to 1¾ hours or until tender. Baste every 15 minutes with fat from bottom of pan. When tender, make a gravy with remaining broth, adding Worcestershire sauce and paprika to taste. Serve gravy in a separate dish. Serves 6.

BRUNSWICK STEW

2 squirrels
1 tablespoon salt
1 minced onion
2 cups fresh Lima beans
6 ears corn
½ pound salt pork

6 potatoes
1 teaspoon pepper
2 teaspoons sugar
4 cups sliced tomatoes
½ pound butter

Cut squirrel into serving pieces. Add salt to 4 quarts of water and when boiling, add onion, Lima beans, corn cut from the cob, pork, potato, pepper, and the squirrels. Cover and simmer 2 hours, add sugar and tomato, and simmer 1 hour more. Ten minutes before removing from heat, add butter cut into pieces the size of a walnut and rolled in flour. Bring to a boil. Serve in soup plates for 6. The characteristic Brunswick Stew is made with squirrels. Chickens and rabbits are frequently used today in place of squirrels.

ROAST OPOSSUM

The opossum is a very fat animal with a peculiarly flavored meat. To dress, immerse in very hot water (not boiling) for 1 minute. Remove and use a dull knife to scrape off hair so that skin is not cut. Slit from bottom of throat to hind legs and remove entrails. Remove head and tail if desired. Wash thoroughly inside and out with hot water. Cover with cold water to which has been added 1 cup of salt and let stand overnight. Drain off the salted water and rinse with clean, boiling water.

STUFFING:

1 large onion minced
1 tablespoon fat
Opossum liver, chopped
1 cup bread crumbs

1 sweet red pepper, chopped
Dash Worcestershire sauce
1 hard cooked egg, chopped
Salt

Brown the onion in fat. Add liver and cook until liver is tender. Add bread crumbs, pepper, Worcestershire sauce, egg, salt and water to moisten.

Stuff opossum and place in roaster; add 2 tablespoons water and roast in a moderate oven. Baste every 15 minutes with drippings. Skim fat from pan gravy; serve gravy separately, with baked yams or sweetpotatoes for 10.

STUFFINGS FOR FISH, MEAT, POULTRY AND GAME

STUFFING does not necessarily have to be baked in the fowl or meat. If the bird is small or if there is some stuffing left over, it may be baked or steamed in a well-greased ring mold, loaf pan or individual molds. Fill center of ring with vegetables. Croquettes of stuffing, made by the usual method, are served in a circle around the bird.

BREAD STUFFING

No. 1

1½ cups soft bread crumbs
1 egg, slightly beaten
¼ cup butter

¼ teaspoon salt
Dash pepper

Moisten bread crumbs with egg and the melted butter. Season and mix well. This makes a rich, moist dressing. Makes 1½ cups.

No. 2

2 to 3 tablespoons melted fat
1 tablespoon chopped onion
1 cup dry bread crumbs
¼ teaspoon salt
Dash pepper

½ teaspoon each sage, chopped celery, parsley
1 to 2 tablespoons milk or stock

Melt fat in a frying pan; add onion and sauté until tender. Add bread crumbs and seasonings and mix well. Then add milk or stock. This makes a loose, light stuffing much preferred by many to the soft moist or compact type. It can be varied by omitting onion or sage, by adding chopped celery or by adding 2 tablespoons seeded raisins. Makes 1 cup.

No. 3

½ cup milk
2 cups grated bread crumbs
1½ tablespoons melted fat
1 egg, slightly beaten
½ teaspoon salt

¼ teaspoon pepper
¼ teaspoon thyme
½ teaspoon powdered sage
½ teaspoon chopped onion
¼ teaspoon summer savory

Pour milk on crumbs and let stand about 1 hour. Add remaining ingredients. Makes 2 cups.

CRACKER CRUMB STUFFING

2 tablespoons butter
1 cup cracker crumbs
¼ cup boiling water

⅛ teaspoon pepper
¼ teaspoon salt
¼ teaspoon poultry seasoning

Melt butter and mix with crumbs. Add water and seasonings. When this stuffing is used, a greater allowance than usual must be made for swelling. Makes 1 cup.

POTATO STUFFING

2 cups hot mashed potato
1 cup bread crumbs
½ teaspoon pepper
½ teaspoon salt

1 teaspoon sage
4 tablespoons melted butter
   or other fat
2 tablespoons onion juice

Mix the ingredients in order given. Makes 3 cups.

CELERY STUFFING

2 tablespoons butter
2 cups dry bread crumbs
2 cups finely chopped celery

1 teaspoon salt
½ teaspoon pepper

Melt butter, add crumbs and mix well. Add celery, salt and pepper. Makes 4 cups.

OYSTER STUFFING

2 cups oysters
2 cups dry bread crumbs
1 teaspoon salt

¼ teaspoon pepper
¼ cup melted fat

Mix oysters well with bread crumbs and seasoning and add the melted fat. Makes 4 cups.

PINEAPPLE NUT STUFFING

4 cups dry bread, ½ inch
    cubes
¾ cup finely chopped celery
½ cup chopped walnuts
¾ cup diced pineapple
1 pimiento, diced

1 teaspoon paprika
Dash cayenne
1½ teaspoons salt
¼ cup butter
2 eggs

Combine bread, celery, walnuts, pineapple, pimiento and seasoning. Melt butter, remove from heat, stir in unbeaten eggs
and add to bread mixture. Toss lightly. Use as stuffing for
turkey, chicken, duck, veal roll, lamb chops or pork chops. Use
crisp bacon cut into small pieces instead of nuts, reduce salt
one-third and add grated onion, or use red or green bell pepper
instead of pimiento. Makes 6 cups.

SAUSAGE STUFFING

½ pound sausage meat
2 cups dried bread crumbs
Salt and pepper

1 tablespoon onion juice
1 tablespoon minced parsley

Mix sausage and crumbs, then add seasonings. Makes 3 cups.

MUSHROOM STUFFING

3 cups dry bread crumbs
6 tablespoons melted butter
½ cup chopped mushrooms
½ teaspoon salt

½ teaspoon powdered
    thyme
1 teaspoon minced parsley

Mix ingredients in the order given. Makes 3½ cups.

RICE STUFFING

1 cup milk
1 cup soft bread crumbs
1 onion, chopped
1 tablespoon fat
4 cups cold boiled rice
½ pound sausage meat

½ teaspoon sage
1 tablespoon minced parsley
½ teaspoon thyme
1 teaspoon salt
⅛ teaspoon pepper

Pour milk over crumbs. Cook onion in fat until brown, then
add rice, soaked crumbs, sausage and seasonings. Makes 6 cups.

CORN-BREAD STUFFING

1 (1½-pound) loaf bread	⅛ teaspoon pepper
3 cups crumbled corn bread	1 large onion, minced
½ pound sausage meat	2 stalks celery, minced
2 eggs	1 teaspoon poultry seasoning

Slice bread and brown lightly in slow oven. Shred finely and mix well with remaining ingredients. Moisten with warm water until it will just hold together. Will fill a 16-pound turkey.

CHESTNUT STUFFING

1 quart chestnuts	2 tablespoons cream
¼ cup bread crumbs	Salt and pepper
2 tablespoons butter	½ teaspoon onion juice

Shell and blanch chestnuts and cook in boiling water until tender. While hot, rub through coarse sieve. Mix with remaining ingredients. Makes 2½ cups.

RAISIN-NUT STUFFING

2 cups dry bread crumbs	½ teaspoon salt
⅓ cup butter, melted	⅛ teaspoon pepper
½ cup chopped seeded raisins	½ teaspoon sage
½ cup broken walnut meats	

Mix ingredients together lightly with fork. Makes 2½ cups.

WILD RICE AND MUSHROOM STUFFING

⅓ cup chopped onion	¼ pound sausage meat
¼ cup butter	3 cups boiled wild rice
1 cup chopped mushrooms	1 teaspoon salt

Sauté onion in 2 tablespoons butter 5 minutes, or until lightly browned, and remove from pan; add remaining 2 tablespoons butter and mushrooms, and cook 5 minutes, then remove from pan. Fry sausage meat until lightly browned, stirring constantly; remove from heat and stir in onion and mushrooms; add wild rice and salt, mixing lightly. This makes a light goose stuffing. Makes 5 cups stuffing or enough for 1 (10-lb.) goose.

SAUCES FOR FISH, MEAT, POULTRY, GAME, AND VEGETABLES

S AUCES add variety to the diet, make foods more attractive to the eye and to the palate, and thus stimulate appetite, aid digestion and improve nutrition.

WHITE AND BROWN SAUCES

Methods of combining flour or corn-starch with liquids are given in the front of the book. (See Index.) The simplest method of thickening sauces is by means of a roux. Equal parts of fat and flour make the best roux. If much more fat than flour is used, the fat rises to the top of the mixture. If less fat than flour is used, the paste may burn. Therefore, if more fat than flour is required in the sauce, it should be beaten in in small pieces after the liquid is added and just before the sauce is served; if less fat than flour is required, it is better not to make it into a roux but to use another method of thickening the sauce.

All sauces thickened with corn-starch should be cooked for at least fifteen minutes. Standing over hot water in a double boiler for an hour or longer improves the flavor. Sauces thickened with flour are better if cooked for at least five minutes after thickening. The seasonings should be added just before the sauce is served.

To Make a Roux

FOR A WHITE SAUCE—The American method of making a roux for white sauce is to melt the fat, add the flour and cook only until the mixture bubbles before adding the liquid. This saves time, but at the expense of the flavor of the sauce. The French method is to melt the fat, add the flour and cook, with constant stirring, for five minutes, before adding any liquid. This removes the raw taste of the flour.

FOR A BROWN SAUCE—Melt the fat and allow it to brown

before adding flour, then stir in the flour and stir constantly, until the flour is brown. The color depends on this browning, but care must be taken not to scorch This long preliminary cooking is the secret of a successful brown sauce. Tomato juice or sauce may be used as liquid.

STANDARD RECIPE FOR WHITE SAUCE

Thin White Sauce.

For cream soups

1 tablespoon butter or other fat	1 cup milk
1 tablespoon flour	¼ teaspoon salt
	⅛ teaspoon pepper

Medium White Sauce.

For gravies, sauces, creamed and scalloped dishes

2 tablespoons butter or other fat	1 cup milk
2 tablespoons flour	¼ teaspoon salt
	⅛ teaspoon pepper

Thick White Sauce.

For cutlets, croquettes and soufflés

4 tablespoons butter or other fat	1 cup milk
4 tablespoons flour	¼ teaspoon salt
	⅛ teaspoon pepper

Use method 1 or 2 for making these sauces.

Method 1—Melt butter, blend in flour until smooth. Add milk gradually, stirring constantly until boiling point is reached. Reduce heat and cook for 3 minutes longer; add seasonings and blend. Place over hot water to keep hot and cover tightly to prevent film from forming.

Method 2—Heat milk. Blend butter or other fat and flour together and add to hot milk, stirring constantly until mixture thickens. Cook for 3 minutes longer, add seasonings and blend.

Method 3—When less butter than flour is used, heat ¾ of the milk; mix remaining milk with flour to make a smooth paste; stir into hot milk, heat to boiling and cook until thickened, stirring constantly. Add butter or other fat and seasonings and cook for 3 minutes.

VARIATIONS OF WHITE SAUCE

Use 1 cup medium white sauce as the basis for each sauce.

CAPER SAUCE—Add 2 to 4 tablespoons chopped capers.

CELERY SAUCE—Add ½ cup chopped cooked celery.

CHEESE SAUCE—Add 2 to 4 ounces grated cheese. Set over hot water and stir until the cheese is blended with sauce. Season to taste with mustard and paprika.

CREAM GRAVY—Use 2 tablespoons meat drippings for butter in white sauce recipe.

CREAM SAUCE—Use cream instead of milk in white sauce.

EGG SAUCE, No. 1—Add 1 hard-cooked egg, chopped.

No. 2—Beat an uncooked egg, dilute with 1 tablespoon of hot thin white sauce, then beat this into the remainder of a cup of sauce. If the egg white is beaten separately, the sauce will be foamy.

LOBSTER SAUCE—Add ½ cup finely flaked cooked lobster.

MOCK HOLLANDAISE SAUCE—Pour sauce over 2 slightly beaten egg yolks, 2 tablespoons each of butter and lemon juice, beat thoroughly and serve immediately.

MUSHROOM SAUCE—Add ½ to ⅓ cup chopped or sliced cooked mushrooms to sauce.

OLIVE SAUCE—Add ¼ cup chopped ripe or stuffed olives.

OYSTER SAUCE—Heat 1 pint small oysters in their own liquor to boiling point. Remove from heat after they have cooked ½ minute and combine with sauce. Season to taste.

PARSLEY SAUCE—Add 2 to 4 tablespoons chopped parsley.

PIMIENTO SAUCE—Add 2 tablespoons minced onion and 6 tablespoons minced pimiento. Onion may be browned in fat when making white sauce, if desired.

SHRIMP SAUCE—Add ½ cup chopped cooked shrimp.

SOUBISE SAUCE—Rub 4 boiled onions and 2 sprigs parsley through a coarse sieve. Combine with sauce.

TOMATO CREAM SAUCE—Cook 1 cup fresh or canned tomatoes, 1 stalk celery, 1 slice onion, ½ teaspoon salt and a few grains cayenne together for 20 minutes. Rub through a sieve. Add gradually, stirring constantly, to white sauce.

VELOUTÉ SAUCE—Use 1 cup well-seasoned white stock, milk in thin or medium white sauce.

YELLOW SAUCE—Add hot sauce to 1 or 2 slightly beat yolks and beat thoroughly.

BÉCHAMEL SAUCE

No. 1.

Use one-half cup of meat stock instead of half of the milk in medium or thin white sauce. If an acid flavor is desired, add one teaspoon of lemon juice to each cup of sauce.

No. 2.

1 small onion	4 tablespoons flour
2 tablespoons fat	1 pint milk
¼ cup chopped lean raw ham	Salt and pepper

Slice the onion, place the fat in a saucepan and slightly brown the onion and ham in it. Add the flour and, when well mixed, the milk. Stir until it boils, then cook over hot water for ten minutes or longer. Add seasonings, strain and use.

CHAUD-FROID SAUCE

WHITE—Soak one tablespoon gelatin in cold water and add to one cup of hot velouté sauce. Mix well; strain, if necessary; let cool and use to coat cold meats.

BROWN—Use a brown roux and brown stock in making the velouté.

YELLOW—Add the beaten yolks of two eggs to white chaud-froid sauce just before removing from the fire.

PINEAPPLE-ORANGE SAUCE

6 tablespoons sugar	1 cup orange juice
½ tablespoon cornstarch	Grated rind 1 orange
1 cup water	⅓ cup crushed pineapple

Combine ingredients in the order listed. Heat to boiling and cook for 3 minutes. Serve with ham or tongue.

Brown sugar may be used in place of granulated.

Add ¼ cup raisins and cook until they puff.

POULETTE SAUCE

1 cup velouté sauce	2 egg yolks
1 cup cream	

ly add, with constant stirring, the velouté to the egg eat in the cream and reheat over hot water. Beat well and serve at once. It is improved by adding, a little at a time, one tablespoon butter, the juice of half a lemon, a tablespoon of chopped parsley and a dash of nutmeg.

BUTTER SAUCE À LA CREOLE

1 cup cold water	½ tablespoon flour
4½ tablespoons butter	Juice of 1 lemon

Make a sauce of one-half cup cold water, one-half tablespoon butter and the flour. When the mixture boils, stir in quickly four tablespoons butter and add, by degrees, another one-half cup of cold water to keep the mixture from boiling. Stir in the juice of a lemon and strain. It must be served at once and hot. It becomes oily if kept long. One tablespoon of chopped parsley may be added.

DRAWN BUTTER SAUCE

⅓ cup butter	1 pint boiling water
4 tablespoons flour	¼ teaspoon salt

Make a roux of four tablespoons of the butter and all of the flour. Gradually add the boiling water, stirring constantly over hot water, until the sauce comes to the boiling-point. Simmer until it is thick and smooth. When ready to serve, add salt and the remaining butter in small bits, beating constantly.

MAÎTRE D'HÔTEL SAUCE

2 cups drawn-butter sauce	2 egg-yolks
1 tablespoon lemon-juice	Salt and pepper
1 tablespoon chopped parsley	

Add the lemon-juice and chopped parsley to the drawn-butter sauce. Let it cool slightly, add the beaten yolks and season with salt and pepper. Do not permit the sauce to boil after the addition of the egg-yolk.

CAPER SAUCE

Follow the recipe for maître d'hôtel sauce, omitting for parsley and adding three tablespoons capers. This is ex with fish.   en egg

(For another recipe for caper sauce, see Variations of White Sauce, pa

IMITATION CAPER SAUCE

½ cup chopped pickles   2 cups drawn butter sauce

To the drawn butter sauce add pickles, cut into tiny cubes of a uniform size and well drained. Boil for one minute. Serve with fish or chops.

HOLLANDAISE SAUCE

2 egg yolks   ¼ teaspoon salt
½ cup butter   Dash cayenne
        1 tablespoon lemon juice

Place egg yolks with ⅓ of the butter in top of a double boiler. Keep water in bottom of boiler hot but not boiling. Stir eggs and butter constantly; when butter melts add another portion and as it melts and the mixture begins to thicken add remaining butter. Keep stirring all the time. As soon as mixture is thick, remove from heat and add seasonings. The sauce is delicious served over vegetables. Should sauce separate, beat in 2 tablespoons boiling water, drop by drop. Makes 1 cup sauce.

Increase lemon juice to 1½ tablespoons.

WITH WATER—Cream butter, add egg yolks 1 at a time, blending each one in thoroughly. Add remaining ingredients and beat. Just before serving add ½ cup boiling water gradually, beating constantly. Cook over hot water, stirring constantly until thickened. Serve at once.

WITH ANCHOVY—Season sauce with anchovy paste.

WITH SHERRY—Just before serving sauce, add 2 tablespoons sherry, drop by drop, beating constantly.

BÉARNAISE SAUCE

4 tablespoons fat   1 tablespoon tarragon vinegar
Yolks 4 eggs   1 teaspoon onion juice
½ teaspoon salt   1 teaspoon chopped tarragon
½ teaspoon pepper   1 teaspoon chopped parsley

Stir the fat until perfectly soft and creamy. Place the egg yolks and the salt and pepper in the top of a double boiler and beat light with an egg beater, then add one-third of the fat and beat until smooth, add another third and beat again, and then add the remainder and beat until all is perfectly smooth. Add the vinegar and onion juice and beat again. Place over boiling

SAUCE SUPREME

2 tablespoons fat
2 tablespoons flour
1 cup chicken stock

2 tablespoons lemon-juice
2 teaspoons chopped parsley

Place the fat in a frying-pan, over the fire, and when it is hot, add the flour. Stir well. When it is turning brown, add the chicken stock and boil for several minutes, stirring constantly. Then add the lemon-juice and the parsley. After the sauce has boiled up once, it is ready to serve.

OLIVE SAUCE

2 dozen olives
2 tablespoons salad oil
1 slice onion
1 lemon

2 tablespoons flour
1 pint stock
Salt and pepper

Place the olives in an earthenware bowl, cover with hot water and let them remain for half an hour to draw out the brine. Place the oil in a frying-pan, and add the onion; when this commences to color, add the flour. Stir until smooth. After it has cooked for two minutes, add the stock, and regulate the heat so that the sauce will simmer gently. Pare the olives from the stones, round and round as though paring an apple, leaving the pulp in a single strip. If this is done carefully, the olives will coil back into shape. Place them in the sauce, add the seasoning and the juice of the lemon and simmer for twenty minutes. Skim carefully and serve.

SPANISH SAUCE

1 tablespoon minced lean raw
   ham
1 tablespoon chopped celery
1 tablespoon chopped carrot
1 tablespoon chopped onion
2 tablespoons fat

2 tablespoons flour
1/2 cup stock
1/2 cup tomato-juice
1/2 teaspoon salt
1/8 teaspoon pepper

Melt the fat. Add the ham and vegetables and cook until they are brown. Make a sauce of this mixture and the flour, salt, pepper and liquid.

CHATEAUBRIAND SAUCE

3 tablespoons fat
1 tablespoon lemon-juice
1 teaspoon salt

Pepper
1 teaspoon minced parsley
2 cups Spanish sauce

Whip together the fat, lemon-juice, salt, a pinch of pepper and minced parsley. Add the Spanish sauce, reheat, stir for a moment and serve.

TOMATO SAUCE

1 quart fresh or canned
   tomatoes
1 slice onion
8 cloves

3 tablespoons fat
3 tablespoons flour
Salt and pepper

Set the tomatoes, onion and cloves on the fire and cook for twenty minutes. Brown the fat in the frying-pan, add the flour, and cook until smooth and brown, stirring constantly. Add the tomatoes, cook for three minutes, season with salt and pepper and pass through a strainer fine enough to hold back the seeds. This makes a very thin sauce. Use more flour if you prefer a thick sauce.

TOMATO AND MUSHROOM SAUCE

2 slices bacon or small quantity uncooked ham
1 slice onion
6 slices carrot
Bay-leaf
2 sprigs thyme
Sprig parsley
½ No. 1 can mushrooms

2 cloves
½ teaspoon peppercorns
Few gratings nutmeg
½ No. 2 can tomatoes
5 tablespoons flour
1½ cups brown stock
Salt and pepper

Chop the bacon or ham, and cook with onion and carrot for five minutes. Add bay-leaf, thyme, parsley, cloves, peppercorns, nutmeg, and tomatoes, and cook five minutes. Mix the flour with five tablespoons of cold water and rub out all the lumps; then add enough water so that the batter can be poured in a thin stream. Add to the sauce, stirring constantly. As the sauce thickens, dilute it with the stock. Cover, set in the oven (300° F.) and cook one hour. Strain, add salt and pepper to taste and the mushrooms, drained and cut in quarters. Then cook two minutes over direct heat.

RAVIGOTE SAUCE

1 cup thin white sauce	1 tablespoon minced chervil
¼ cup lemon-juice	1 tablespoon minced tarragon
1 tablespoon tarragon vine-	leaves
gar	1 tablespoon minced chives
1 tablespoon minced shallot	1 tablespoon butter

While sauce is hot, add other materials, except butter. Keep hot five minutes, strain, beat in butter. Serve hot or cold.

BROWNED BUTTER

Place a piece of butter in a hot frying-pan and toss about until it browns. Stir browned flour into it until it is smooth and commences to boil. This is used for coloring gravies, sauces, etc.

BROWNED FLOUR

Spread flour on a pie-tin and place over heat or in a very hot oven (450°-500° F.). When it begins to color, stir constantly until it is evenly browned throughout. When cold, cork closely in jars.

GLAZING FOR MEAT

No. 1—Boil one quart of consommé until it is reduced to one cup. For half-glaze, reduce it to one pint.

No. 2—Simmer a small amount of jellied stock with burnt sugar until it becomes sirupy.

No. 3—To one cup brown stock, add one-half tablespoon gelatin soaked in four tablespoons water. The glaze should be melted over hot water and applied to meat, fish, game or poultry.

CRANBERRY SAUCE

No. 1.

1 quart cranberries
2 cups sugar

2 cups boiling water

Boil the sugar and water together for five minutes. Remove any scum that may have formed. Add the cranberries and cook without stirring until they are thick and clear.

No. 2—Cook the cranberries and water together until the skins of the berries are broken. Add the sugar and simmer for five or ten minutes. Chill before using.

No. 3—If a strained sauce is desired, cook the cranberries and water as in No. 2 and rub through a sieve. Return the strained portion to the fire, add the sugar and simmer for five or ten minutes.

SPICED CRANBERRIES

4 cups cranberries
5 cloves
3 cups sugar

5 allspice
2 sticks cinnamon
2 blades mace

Pick over and wash the berries. Place in a saucepan and cover with cold water. Tie spices in a cheese-cloth bag and drop in with the berries. Cook until the berries burst. Remove spices, add sugar, and cook until the mixture is clear. Chill.

MOCK WILD CHERRY SAUCE

1 quart cranberries
1 cup water

2¼ cups sugar
1 teaspoon almond flavoring

Add cranberries to boiling water, cover and cook until the berries burst. Add sugar and boil a few minutes longer. Add flavoring.

APPLE SAUCE

No. 1.

4 quarts sweet cider

2 quarts apples

By boiling it uncovered, reduce four quarts of new cider to two quarts. Pare, quarter and core the apples and simmer with the cider for four hours. Flavor with cinnamon, if desired.

No. 2.

| 1 quart apples | 1 cup sugar | 1 cup water |

Pare, chop and place apples in a deep pudding-dish; sprinkle with sugar, and pour water over them. Bake in a slow oven (250°-350° F.) two hours or more, until they are a rich red-brown. Serve with goose, pork or game.

MINT SAUCE

1 tablespoon powdered sugar   ¼ cup minced mint leaves
½ cup vinegar

Dissolve sugar in vinegar. Pour this over minced mint leaves and set where it will keep warm but not hot. Allow it to infuse for half an hour. If vinegar is very strong, dilute with water.

CURRANT MINT SAUCE

⅔ cup currant jelly   1 to 2 tablespoons chopped
Shavings from orange-rind   mint leaves

Separate jelly into pieces, but do not beat it. Add chopped mint leaves and orange-rind shavings. Serve around roast.

SOUTHERN BARBECUE SAUCE

½ cup butter or other fat   2 tablespoons chili sauce
1 sour pickle, finely chopped   4 slices lemon
2 tablespoons chopped onion   1 teaspoon brown sugar
2 tablespoons Worcestershire   1 green pepper, chopped fine
  sauce   1 cup vinegar

Combine all ingredients and mix thoroughly. Place in a saucepan and simmer until butter or other fat melts, stirring constantly. Place in the top of a double boiler and keep warm until ready to use on barbecued meats or as a sauce for barbecued sandwiches. Makes 1¾ cups sauce.

BARBECUED MEATS, beef, lamb, veal and pork in the form of roasts, chops or steaks are braised in this sauce. Chicken may also be used.

CUCUMBER SAUCE

2 cucumbers
½ cup stock
½ tablespoon vinegar

Salt and cayenne
Celery essence

Cut peeled cucumbers into very small pieces. Simmer until tender in a saucepan with stock, vinegar, salt, cayenne and a little celery essence. Celery-salt may be used instead of plain salt, if preferred. A bit of boiled onion and a little butter may be added also, if desired. Strain through a sieve.

ANCHOVY SAUCE

¼ cup fresh butter
1 teaspoon anchovy paste

Cayenne pepper

Melt the butter and stir in the anchovy paste and the cayenne pepper. Warm and stir thoroughly and serve with either boiled or fried fish.

BEURRE NOIR

2 tablespoons butter
1 tablespoon vinegar
1 teaspoon lemon-juice

1 tablespoon chopped parsley
½ teaspoon salt
¼ teaspoon pepper

Place the butter in a frying-pan and when it is browned add the other ingredients. Boil up once and serve. This sauce is poured over fried fish or boiled fish just before serving.

PARSLEY BUTTER

3 tablespoons butter
½ to 1 tablespoon lemon-juice

1 tablespoon chopped parsley
½ teaspoon salt
⅛ teaspoon pepper

Cream butter and add lemon-juice, chopped parsley, salt and pepper. This may be used to spread on fried or boiled fish or over potato balls. When intended for potato balls, one-half tablespoon of lemon-juice will be enough.

LOBSTER BUTTER

1 lobster coral
3 tablespoons chopped lobster

3 tablespoons butter
Seasoning

Lobster butter is used in lobster soups and sauces to give color and richness. Pound the coral of a lobster to a smooth paste with two tablespoons of butter, add chopped lobster and remaining tablespoon of butter and pound again until all is reduced to a smooth paste, then rub through a fine sieve. If coral is not obtainable, the small claws may be pounded with the butter.

MUSTARD SAUCE

1 tablespoon dry mustard
½ teaspoon sugar
¼ teaspoon salt

1 tablespoon vinegar
1 tablespoon melted butter
¼ cup boiling water

Mix dry ingredients, add liquids, mix well and serve.

MARMALADE SAUCE

1 glass orange or grapefruit marmalade

1 teaspoon dry mustard
1 teaspoon salt

Turn the marmalade out into a deep plate and beat it to a foam. Then add dry mustard and salt and beat again thoroughly.

ORANGE RAISIN SAUCE

1 cup boiling water
Juice and grated rind of one orange
¼ cup sugar

1 tablespoon flour
1 tablespoon butter
⅓ cup seeded raisins

Mix the dry ingredients, add boiling water and cook until clear. Add the orange juice and rind, the raisins and the butter.

REMOULADE SAUCE

2 hard-cooked egg yolks
1 raw egg yolk
3 tablespoons tarragon vinegar
3 tablespoons cider vinegar

2 cups oil
1 teaspoon mustard
½ teaspoon salt
1 teaspoon parsley

Put the cooked yolks of eggs through a coarse wire sieve, and then put them in a dish with the raw yolk and the seasoning. Add two tablespoons of the vinegar and beat thoroughly five minutes. Next add the oil, one teaspoon at a time, beating the mixture two or three minutes at a time after each addition of oil. When five teaspoons have thus been added, the rest of the oil may be put in in larger quantities, three or four teaspoons at a time. Whenever the sauce becomes so thick that the beater turns hard, put in one-half tablespoon of vinegar. This sauce may be used for meat, for salads, or for such vegetables as asparagus, broccoli and artichokes. It may be varied by adding capers, minced gherkins and a dash of cayenne. There is not a great deal of difference between remoulade sauce and mayonnaise.

TARTAR SAUCE

1 cup mayonnaise dressing
1 teaspoon onion-juice
1 tablespoon capers

1 tablespoon chopped cucumber pickle

Make the mayonnaise rather more sour and with a little more mustard than for salad, and mix into it the capers, pickle and onion-juice. Set in the refrigerator until needed. It should be quite thick when served.

HORSERADISH SAUCE

No. 1.

1 teaspoon mustard
3 tablespoons cream
1 tablespoon vinegar

Salt
Horseradish

Mix the first four ingredients and add as much grated horse-radish as needed to make it the desired thickness.

No. 2.

¼ cup heavy cream
3 tablespoons grated horse-radish

1 tablespoon vinegar
¼ teaspoon salt
Sprinkle of cayenne or pepper

Whip the cream stiff. Mix the other ingredients and beat them gradually into the whipped cream. Serve on baked ham.

BUTTER-ORANGE FLUFF

¼ pound butter
1 teaspoon grated orange rind
½ cup brown sugar

Cream the butter until light and fluffy. Add brown sugar gradually, beating the mixture to a light, fluffy mass. Stir in the grated orange rind. Use for waffles and pancakes.

VINAIGRETTE SAUCE

1 teaspoon salt
¼ teaspoon paprika
Few grains pepper
1 tablespoon tarragon vinegar
2 tablespoons cider vinegar
6 tablespoons olive oil

1 tablespoon chopped pickle
1 tablespoon chopped green pepper
1 teaspoon chopped parsley
1 teaspoon chopped chives

Mix the ingredients in the order given.

CREOLE SAUCE

2 tablespoons chopped onion
4 tablespoons minced green pepper
2 tablespoons butter
3 tablespoons flour

Salt and pepper
2 tomatoes or ½ cup canned tomatoes
1 cup bouillon
¼ cup sliced mushrooms

Sauté onion and pepper in butter 5 minutes; add flour and seasonings and stir until browned; add tomatoes and mushrooms gradually and cook 2 minutes; then add bouillon and heat to boiling. Serve with omelet, spaghetti and fish. Yield: 2 cups.

FRONTIER SAUCE

3 tablespoons flour
2 tablespoons butter
½ teaspoon salt
½ teaspoon paprika
Dash of tabasco

¾ cup tomato juice
¼ cup liquid drained from stewed or canned mushrooms
2 tablespoons heavy cream

Stir flour into melted butter; add seasonings and tabasco, then add tomato juice and mushroom liquor gradually and cook 5 minutes, stirring constantly until smooth and thick. Add cream and blend. Serve on macaroni or spaghetti. Yield: 1¼ cups sauce.

ENTRÉES AND MADE-OVER DISHES

~~~~~~~~

AN entrée is a dish that is served as an independent course between two main courses of a meal. In an informal meal, an entrée of protein food may be served as the main course.

An entrée is usually a "light" dish, small in bulk, and is often accompanied by a sauce which may or may not be an integral part of the dish. It may be served either hot or cold. Hot entrées are often accompanied by a hot sauce, such as Hollandaise or maître d'hôtel; and cold entrées by cold sauces, —vinaigrette, tartar, etc. Ordinarily the hot entrée precedes the roast and the cold entrée follows it.

Entrées may be made of a great number of foods—eggs in many attractive forms; fish of all kinds; meat, such as lamb, veal and tender cuts of fowl and beef, cooked by some method other than roasting; macaroni and spaghetti; some fruits; and many kinds of vegetables.

Increasingly in America today vegetables are served as entrées. This is undoubtedly due to the fact that the eating habits of the nation have changed, because we have a growing knowledge of and interest in the food-values of vegetables and fruits. For luncheon and dinner now one vegetable is often raised to the dignity of becoming a course by itself.

Hot Entrées

CREAMED MIXTURES—These are the most simple and easily prepared of the hot entreés. Any well-seasoned creamed mixture may be used. It must be kept hot and transferred at the last possible moment to the container in which it is to be served. This may be merely a slice of toast, an individual case such as a ramekin, patty shell or timbale case, or a border formed of bread, rice or potato.

FORCEMEATS—These should have a smooth, velvety texture. They call for more effort in preparation than any other type of entrée. They are made of cooked or uncooked meat or fish in finely divided form, those made of the uncooked material being considered the more choice. Such foods as chicken and

326

ham, shell fish and any fine white fish make typical forcemeats. Forcemeats may be used in combination with other materials or cooked alone to form cutlets and timbales. The cutlets are cooked in shallow, chop-shaped molds and the timbales in deep, straight sided molds.

CROQUETTES—Croquettes are made of cooked and chopped ingredients held together, usually, by means of a thick sauce. When the mixture is cold, it is made into shapes of uniform size, which are coated with flour or sifted crumbs, then rolled in an egg mixture so that the egg forms a continuous film, then rolled in crumbs again. The egg mixture is made by adding two tablespoons of water or milk to each egg required, and beating just enough to break up the white of the egg. The croquettes may be allowed to stand until dry or may be fried at once in deep hot fat. This is a good way to use left-over cooked foods.

Croquettes are made in the form of balls, rolls, cones, nests or cups, cutlets or flat cakes. Whatever shape is desired, it is usually easier to attain it by making the mixture into a ball first, thus insuring a compact mass from which the chosen form may be readily molded.

CUTLETS—This word, as used in this chapter refers to the form in which the food is cooked rather than to a distinct type of food. Sometimes cutlets are made by packing forcemeat into shallow, chop-shaped molds, but more often they are croquettes, cut or shaped to look like breaded chops or cutlets. The term may be extended to include boiled cereal, such as rice or cornmeal, which has been packed into a shallow dish, left until cold, and then cut into pieces, rolled in egg and crumbs and fried or sautéd.

FRITTERS—These may be composed of a piece of fruit enclosed in a batter, then fried in deep hot fat and served with an appropriate sauce; or chopped fruit, chopped vegetable, or other chopped food, such as clams or lobster, stirred into the batter and fried by spoonfuls.

TIMBALES—This term is sometimes used to describe forcemeat cooked in straight-sided deep molds. More frequently perhaps it refers to sugarless custards cooked in timbale molds. In timbales of this type, where egg is the thickening agent, savory seasonings are used, and the milk which ordinarily forms an important component of custard is replaced in part or entirely by meat stock or vegetable purée.

All timbales are cooked in molds of some sort; they are cooked by oven-poaching and are not browned. They are turned out of the molds before they are served. A circle of buttered paper laid in the bottom of the mold before it is filled insures perfect unmolding.

Hot Soufflés—These are the lightest of the entrées, being made so by well-beaten egg white folded into the seasoned foundation mixture. This may be simply a fruit purée or pulp; it may be a white sauce combined with egg yolks and the characterizing ingredient; or it may be a panada made by cooking either cracker or bread crumbs with milk and adding the prepared ingredient, this method being best for meat soufflés. Soufflés need the same careful baking given to egg timbales and are served in or from the baking dish. The top should be browned.

Fillets—This type of entrée is composed of a solid piece of meat or fish, and may comprise breasts or joints of poultry, chops, large oysters, scallops, crabs, fillets of fish and the first three cuts of beef tenderloin. These when used as entrées, may be cooked by broiling, sautéing, frying or oven-poaching, but never by roasting because the flavor and effect would be too much like that of the main course.

Vegetable Entrées—Hot or Cold

The following vegetables are suggested for service as entrées: asparagus, cauliflower and broccoli, hot with Hollandaise or butter sauce, or cold with vinaigrette; tomato surprise, stuffed, for instance, with mushrooms; corn on the cob; mushrooms; baked lima beans; long, thin string beans, not cut or split; large beets hollowed out and filled with bread crumbs and tiny peas or chopped carrots or both; stuffed peppers; eggplant; baked Hubbard squash, Brussels sprouts; braised celery or endive; cucumbers; and artichoke bottoms stuffed with forcemeat and baked.

Cold Entrées

Aspics—Aspic is a spiced tart jelly made from brown or white meat stock alone or in combination with gelatin. It is used to enclose a variety of foods in a mold or to give a transparent coating of shining, sparkling finish. Various foods may

be molded in aspic—for instance, stuffed olives, plain or stuffed tomatoes, eggs, birds, beef tongue, chicken salad or a mousse.

Aspics give ample opportunity to show inventiveness in design, for they are usually elaborately decorated. Decorative shapes may be cut from pimiento, green or red pepper, olives, pickles, hard-cooked egg-white, yellow custard, parsley, truffles or cooked vegetables. Green peas and capers, also, are frequently used.

CHAUD FROIDS—For these dishes, the sauce is made up hot but the finished product is served cold. The sauce, which may be white, yellow or brown, and stiffened with gelatin, is used to give a smooth, glossy surface to eggs, cutlets, breast or other choice pieces of chicken, fish fillets, etc., all of which must be plainly cooked and well seasoned. A decoration is usual, also a final coating of aspic.

MOUSSES—This term, used in connection with entrées, refers to a dish made of a meat, fish or vegetable purée stiffened with gelatin and made light by means of beaten cream. It is molded to give it shape, chilled, then unmolded for serving.

COLD SOUFFLÉS—It is difficult to differentiate these from the mousses. About the only difference is the manner of serving. The mixture may be put into individual dishes of china, or paper cases, having paper bands pinned about the top to give greater height. When the mixture is chilled, the bands are removed. The mixture, extending above the edge of the container, gives the effect of great lightness, thus simulating a soufflé.

SALADS—Salads are not usually thought of as entrées, but in a formal menu are so considered.

Borders and Cases

BREAD CROUSTADES

Cut slices of bread from one to two inches thick. Remove the brown part of the crust. Cut each trimmed slice into two oblongs or two triangles, for large croustades, or into four squares or four triangles, for small croustades. Or shape the bread with cookie cutters into circles, diamonds, etc. Insert the point of a sharp knife into the top of the shaped piece, one-half inch from the edge, and cut around the outline, running the knife down to within one-half inch of the bottom. Insert the knife point horizontally through one side of the slice, one-half inch from the bottom, and cut out and remove the center, leaving a box with half-inch walls and bottom. Fry these cases in deep fat, (375°-390° F.) or, if you prefer, brush them over with melted fat and set them in a moderate oven (350°-400° F.) to brown.

RICE CROUSTADES

Cook one cup of washed rice in white stock instead of in water. Drain well, mix with a thick white sauce, and spread in a greased pan to the depth of about two inches. Cover with oiled paper and place weights on top, so that the mixture may become very compact when cold. When it is perfectly firm, cut it in circles, make a cavity in the center of each, dip the case thus made in fine bread-crumbs, then in egg, and again in crumbs, and fry in deep fat (375°-390° F.).

POTATO BORDER

9 medium-sized potatoes
2 tablespoons butter
½ cup hot milk
1 tablespoon salt
2 eggs

Boil and rice the potatoes. Add remaining ingredients except ¼ teaspoon salt and the egg whites. Beat the mixture until very light. Pack into a border mold, well greased, and set in warm place eight minutes. Unmold onto an oven-proof platter. Beat egg whites, with remaining salt, to a froth, spread over the border and brown in a slow oven (300°-350° F.).

POTATO TIMBALES—Peel potatoes and cut into tiny strips lengthwise. Heat in a small amount of fat until slightly soft—don't brown. Remove, sprinkle with salt and arrange nests inside large deep muffin tins, pressing firmly against sides and bottom. Bake in hot oven (450° F.) for 15 minutes. Use carrots, parsnips, macaroni, spaghetti or fine noodles instead of potatoes.

RICE BORDER

1 cup rice
3 cups white stock
1 tablespoon salt
2 egg-yolks
2 tablespoons butter or other fat
3 tablespoons milk or cream

Cook washed rice in white stock for one-half hour, then add salt and butter or other fat and cook slowly twenty minutes more. Beat the yolks of the eggs with the cream or milk and stir in. Grease a border mold, pack the rice firmly into it, let it stand eight to ten minutes in a warm (not hot) place and turn out on a hot platter. Fill the center with any meat preparation warmed in sauce.

TIMBALE ROSETTES

1 egg	½ cup flour
10 tablespoons irradiated evaporated milk	⅛ teaspoon salt
	1½ teaspoons sugar

Beat egg slightly. Add milk. Sift flour, then measure. Re-sift with salt and sugar into the egg and milk mixture. Stir until batter is smooth. It should be about the consistency of heavy cream. Use a deep, heart-shaped timbale iron. Dip in the hot fat to heat, then in the batter, being careful that the batter does not come up over the top of the iron.

Have ready a small, deep kettle of fat, place the iron in it and heat until the fat is hot enough to brown a piece of bread while counting sixty (370° F.). The fat should be deep enough to cover the mold end of the iron. Take out the heated iron, remove surplus fat with a piece of absorbent paper and lower the iron into the batter until it is covered not more than three-fourths its height. This is necessary to allow for the rising of the batter during cooking. If only a thin layer of batter adheres to the iron, plunge it in again, and repeat if necessary until there is a smooth layer of partly cooked batter. Plunge it quickly into the hot fat and cook from two to three minutes. Remove from the fat, slip the case from the iron on to absorbent paper and continue until you have the required number of cases.

A fluted iron is easier to work with than a plain one, because the case does not slip off until thoroughly cooked. A properly cooked case, however, should slip easily from the mold. If the cases are not crisp, the batter is too thick and should be diluted with milk.

These cases may be filled with a creamed vegetable, creamed oysters, chicken or sweetbreads, or with fresh or cooked fruit topped with whipped cream or powdered sugar. When sweet fillings are used, they are served as a dessert. This recipe makes about 20 cases with an iron of average size.

RISSOLES

These are practically little turnovers, filled with a highly seasoned mixture of chopped chicken and ham or other delicate meat moistened with white sauce. Roll puff-paste very thin and cut in circles. Place a teaspoon of the mixture in the center of each circle, moisten half the circumference with cold water, and fold the other half over, pressing the edges closely together. Dip in slightly beaten egg mixed with a tablespoon of water. Fry in deep fat (360°-370° F.) and drain thoroughly.

BOUCHÉES

Small pastry shells or cases filled with creamed meat or game are called bouchées, and are much in vogue for entrées. They provide an excellent way of utilizing left-overs of chicken, sweetbreads, fish, etc. Paper cases, bought at the confectioner's, may be used instead of the pastry shells.

PATTY CASES

Roll puff-paste to the thickness of one-half inch and with a cookie cutter shape circles two and one-half to three inches in diameter. With a tiny cutter, remove the centers from half of the circles. Brush the edges of the complete circles with water and lay the rings on top. Chill thoroughly, then bake in a hot oven (400°-450° F.) from fifteen to twenty minutes. At the same time, bake the small centers removed from the upper layers of the cases, and use them as lids for the filled patties.

VOL AU VENTS

A vol au vent is a large patty. The French name signifies something that will fly away in the wind. Roll out puff-paste one and one-half inches in thickness, and cut a circle about six inches in diameter, using a cutter or, with a sharp knife, cutting around the edge of a plate laid on the paste. Place the circle on a baking-tin and, with a sharp pointed knife or a smaller cutter, cut a circle around the top about one and one-half inches from the edge and about an inch deep. Do not remove the center but bake the entire circle in a large, flat pan in a hot oven (450°-500° F.) from thirty to fifty minutes.

REMOVE ALL BUT BOTTOM CRUST.
CUT AND SCOOP OUT CENTER.
TOAST, FILL WITH CREAMED SAL-
MON MIXTURE. CRUMB AND BROWN
TO SERVE.
—Canned Salmon Industry

THE CLEVER HOSTESS WILL
MAKE TIMBALES OF SHREDDED
POTATOES, SPAGHETTI OR FINE
NOODLES AND FILL THEM
WITH SALMON A LA KING—
FOR INSTANCE
—Canned Salmon Industry

MAKE QUICK TIM-
BALES OF TOAST
OR FORMAL ONES
WITH THE FLUTED
IRON
—Wheat Flour
Institute
—Irradiated Evapo-
rated Milk Institute

THE RING MOLD IS THE DELIGHT OF FAMILY AND FRIENDS
WHETHER OF NOODLES, VEGETABLES OR CHICKEN MOUSSE

When the outer crust is cooked, lift out the center, remove the uncooked paste from below, and the shell is ready to be filled. It may be filled with lobster meat, oysters, chicken, or any kind of delicate meat or fish chopped and seasoned, and heated in Béchamel, white, brown or mushroom sauce, or with sweetmeats of any kind or fresh berries, sweetened. In using fish, always add one teaspoon of lemon-juice to the mixture after it is taken from the fire.

HOT ENTRÉES

Creamed Mixtures

PATTIES

Patty cases are usually made ahead of time and must be thoroughly heated before they are filled. To heat them, place them in a moderate oven (350°-400° F.) fifteen or twenty minutes before they are to be filled.

Chicken—Fill hot patty cases with creamed chicken.

Clam—Fill hot patty cases with creamed clams (See Index).

Lobster—Fill hot patty cases with creamed lobster.

Sweetbread—Fill hot patty cases with creamed sweetbreads.

CHICKEN OR SALMON À LA KING

2 tablespoons butter
1 green pepper, minced
1 cup sliced mushrooms
2 tablespoons flour
1 cup chicken stock
2 cups diced cooked chicken or boned canned red salmon

1 cup sour cream or evaporated milk
2 egg yolks
1 pimiento, diced
Salt and pepper
4 teaspoons sherry

Melt butter, add green pepper and mushrooms and sauté until tender. Lift out. Add flour to butter; add stock and cook until thickened. Add chicken or salmon, cooked pepper and mushrooms and heat thoroughly. Remove from heat and add cream mixed with beaten egg yolks and remaining ingredients. Serve at once or place over hot, not boiling, water to keep hot. Do not boil after adding egg yolks.

CHOP SUEY

2 pounds uncooked chicken-breast cut into pieces one-sixteenth inch by one inch by one-half inch

Bean sprouts equal in measure to the chicken

2 cups onions cut into threads

2 cups bamboo shoots cut into pieces the same size as the chicken

2 cups mushrooms sliced thin

Fat or oil

Put the chicken meat, bean sprouts, onions, bamboo shoots and mushrooms into a frying-pan with a little fat or oil to prevent sticking and sauté for ten minutes. Add hot water to cover and cook for fifteen minutes longer. Add Chinese gravy; season to taste; remove from fire and serve at once.

CHINESE GRAVY—

1 cup primary soup or chicken stock

1 teaspoon corn-starch

Sesamum seed oil

Sugar   Salt

1 teaspoon Chinese sauce (can be bought ready prepared)

Mix the corn-starch in a little cold water, stir in the primary soup or chicken stock and let it boil until it thickens. Add the Chinese sauce, a few drops of sesamum seed oil and sugar and salt to taste. Stir well.

PRIMARY SOUP—

½ pound lean pork

½ pound chicken

1 pint water

Chop the meat into small pieces and simmer in water 2½ hours, then strain through several folds of cheesecloth.

SWEETBREAD AND OYSTER PIE

1 pair sweetbreads

2 dozen oysters

1 tablespoon fat

1 tablespoon flour

1 cup cream or milk

2 egg-yolks, hard cooked

Pepper and salt

Puff or plain pie-paste

Prepare sweetbreads (see Index). Make a white sauce with fat, flour and cream or milk, and add the egg-yolks, chopped very fine. Add sweetbreads and prepared oysters to the sauce. Season, put into a deep baking-dish, cover with a layer of paste, and bake.

SHIRRED CLAMS OR OYSTERS WITH MUSHROOMS

12 toast rounds	1½ cups milk
12 large mushroom caps	1½ tablespoons butter
12 clams or oysters	1½ tablespoons flour
Melted butter	¼ teaspoon onion juice
Salt, lemon juice	1 or 2 teaspoons anchovy
Paprika	paste

Arrange toast in baking dish; place large peeled mushroom caps on the toast. Dip clams or oysters in melted butter seasoned with salt, lemon-juice and paprika and lay on mushrooms, using enough butter to season mushrooms also. Bake in a moderate oven (375° F.), until mushrooms are tender and clams are cooked. Make a thin white sauce of milk, butter and flour, season with onion and anchovy and color with vegetable bouquet. Pour around the toast and serve.

SCOTCH WOODCOCK

2 tablespoons fat	1 tablespoon anchovy paste
1 tablespoon flour	½ teaspoon salt
1 cup milk	6 slices of bread
5 hard-cooked eggs	

Prepare a white sauce with fat, flour and milk, add eggs chopped fine, anchovy paste and salt. Have the bread toasted and lay it on a hot dish. Pour the hot mixture over it and serve immediately.

Dumplings

IRISH STEW DUMPLINGS

1 cup sifted flour	1 teaspoon bacon
½ teaspoon salt	drippings
2 teaspoons baking powder	⅓ to ½ cup milk

Sift dry ingredients together, cut in fat and add enough milk to make a drop batter. Drop by spoonfuls over top of stew. Cover kettle and let dumplings steam 15 minutes without lifting cover. The stew should be kept boiling. Serves 6.

BISCUIT DUMPLINGS

2 cups sifted flour
2 teaspoons baking powder
1 teaspoon salt

¼ cup shortening
¾ cup milk

Sift flour, baking powder and salt together. Cut in shortening with 2 knives or pastry blender. Add milk, using more if necessary to make a soft dough. Pat out ½ inch thick and cut into 1-inch squares, strips or diamonds. Drop into boiling chicken stock. Cover and simmer 15 minutes. Serves 6.

WHOLE-WHEAT—Use 1 cup whole-wheat for 1 cup white flour.

FEATHER DUMPLINGS

2 cups sifted flour
1 teaspoon salt
4 teaspoons baking powder
¼ teaspoon pepper

1 egg, well beaten
3 tablespoons melted butter
Milk (about ⅔ cup)

Sift dry ingredients together. Add egg, melted butter and enough milk to make a moist, stiff batter. Drop by teaspoons into boiling liquid. Cover very closely and cook for 18 minutes. Makes 2 dozen dumplings.

EGG DUMPLINGS

1 teaspoon salt
½ cup milk

1 egg, beaten
1½ cups sifted flour

Add salt and milk to beaten egg and stir into flour to form a smooth batter. Drop by teaspoons into boiling salted water or soup, cover tightly and cook 15 minutes, being careful not to lift the lid during this time. Drain in colander. These may be served with hot fat poured over them or with meat gravy or stew. Makes 8 dumplings.

DUMPLINGS FOR PEPPER POT

1 cup finely chopped suet
2 cups sifted flour

¼ teaspoon salt
Water

Combine suet, flour, salt and enough water to make a stiff dough. Roll into dumplings about the size of marbles. Drop into hot soup and cook about 10 minutes. Sprinkle with parsley and serve at once. Makes about 24 dumplings.

DUMPLINGS FOR STEW

2 cups sifted flour
1¼ teaspoons baking powder
¾ teaspoon salt

1 tablespoon butter
Milk (about ⅔ cup)

Sift flour, baking powder and salt together. Cut in butter with pastry blender or 2 knives. Add sufficient milk to make a soft dough. Turn out on a well-floured board and roll about ½ inch thick. Cut into small squares, drop in hot liquid, cover closely and cook for 20 to 25 minutes. Cooking utensils must always have a tight-fitting cover or dumplings will be heavy. Makes 12 dumplings.

POTATO DUMPLINGS

9 medium potatoes
1 teaspoon salt
3 eggs, well beaten
1 cup sifted flour

⅔ cup bread crumbs or farina
½ teaspoon nutmeg

Boil potatoes in their jackets until soft, remove skins and press potatoes through a ricer. Add salt, eggs, flour, ⅔ cup bread crumbs and nutmeg. Mix thoroughly. Form mixture into dry balls about the size of walnuts (if mixture is too moist, add more bread crumbs). Drop balls into boiling salted water. When balls come to the surface, boil uncovered for 3 minutes. Remove one from liquid and cut open; if center is dry, they are sufficiently cooked. Remove balls from liquid. Serve with Mushroom or Onion Sauce (page 315). Serves 12.

LIVER DUMPLINGS

½ pound liver
½ onion
1 tablespoon minced parsley
½ teaspoon salt
Dash pepper

2 slices bread
1 egg
¼ cup flour
3 cups meat broth

Wash liver and force through food chopper with onion. Add parsley, salt and pepper. Crumble bread into mixture and add unbeaten egg and flour. Beat until thoroughly mixed. Drop by teaspoons into boiling broth, cover and cook 25 minutes. Serve in broth. Serves 2 or 3.

CROQUETTES

Croquettes are an excellent means of utilizing leftovers of meat, fish, poultry or vegetables. They are made by combining one of these cooked foods with thick smooth white sauce, mashed potatoes or eggs to bind it together. Cool and shape into balls, cones, cylinders, cutlets or as desired. Roll each croquette in sifted fine dry crumbs of bread, crackers or cereal flakes. Dip in slightly beaten egg diluted with 1 tablespoon water and again in the crumbs; fry in hot deep fat.

The cooked meat or poultry should be chopped fine enough that it can be held together but should not be pasty. Usually 1 cup white sauce is used to 2 cups cooked food though this proportion varies according to moistness of cooked food. Chicken or meat stock may be used instead of half the milk in making the white sauce. The mixture must be well seasoned. It should be as soft as possible, yet stiff enough to hold together when chilled. The coating of egg and crumbs must cover croquettes completely. If there are any small uncovered spots, the croquettes may break open in frying. Place in frying basket or drop into hot fat. Do not allow croquettes to touch one another. Fry until browned. Drain on absorbent paper. Serve very hot.

Croquettes are frequently served with some sort of sauce selected to blend with or enhance the flavor of the material used in making the croquettes. Tomato or Mushroom Sauce is good with meat croquettes. Fish croquettes are good with a Medium White Sauce, to which cooked peas have been added, or with Tomato Sauce. Medium White Sauce or Cheese Sauce may be used with vegetable croquettes.

PEA AND CARROT CROQUETTES

1 cup mashed cooked carrots	1 tablespoon melted butter
1 cup cooked peas	Salt and pepper
1 teaspoon minced parsley	Crumbs and egg
1 cup Thick White Sauce	

Combine carrots, peas, parsley, white sauce and butter, being careful not to mash peas. Season, cool and shape into croquettes. Roll in crumbs, then in egg and again in crumbs. Fry in hot deep fat (380° F.) 3 to 5 minutes. Drain. Makes 6.

CHICKEN CROQUETTES

No. 1

1 cup Thick White Sauce
1¾ cups minced cooked
  chicken
Salt and pepper
¼ teaspoon celery salt

1 teaspoon lemon juice
¼ teaspoon minced onion
1 teaspoon chopped parsley
Crumbs and egg

Combine white sauce, chicken and seasonings. Cool, shape and roll in fine crumbs, then in egg and again in crumbs. Fry in hot deep fat (380° F.) 3 to 5 minutes. Drain. Makes 6 croquettes.

No. 2

2 cups minced cooked
  chicken
¼ cup chopped cooked mushrooms
1 teaspoon salt
½ teaspoon pepper
1 teaspoon minced parsley

½ teaspoon minced onion
1 tablespoon lemon juice
2 tablespoons fat
1 tablespoon flour
1 cup milk or cream
4 eggs
Crumbs

Mix chicken, mushrooms, salt, pepper, parsley, onion and lemon juice. Melt fat, add flour and blend. Add milk and cook until thickened. Add chicken and cook 3 minutes. Stir in 2 of the eggs beaten until light. Pour into a greased flat dish and chill. Shape and roll in fine crumbs. Beat remaining 2 eggs in a deep plate. Dip croquettes in egg, then in crumbs and fry in hot deep fat (380° F.) 3 to 5 minutes. Drain. Serve with Béchamel Sauce (page 310) or Mushroom Sauce (page 309). Makes 8 croquettes.

SURPRISE HAM CROQUETTES

2 cups mashed potatoes
1 tablespoon fat, melted
3 egg yolks

Cayenne
1 cup chopped cooked ham
Crumbs and egg

Mix potatoes, fat, 2 egg yolks and cayenne. Beat until smooth, then cool. Mix ham with remaining yolk and cook until mixture thickens. Chill. Take a large tablespoon of the potato mixture, make a hole in center, put a large teaspoon of the chopped ham inside, close the hole and form a ball. Roll in crumbs, then in egg, again in crumbs and fry in hot deep fat (380° F.) about 5 minutes. Drain. Makes 8.

EGG CROQUETTES

2 cups chopped hard-cooked eggs
1 cup Thick White Sauce
½ teaspoon salt

⅛ teaspoon pepper
Dash cayenne
Crumbs and egg

Chop eggs fine and moisten with sauce until as soft as can be handled. Season and chill thoroughly. Shape, roll in crumbs, then in egg, again in crumbs and fry in hot deep fat (380° F.) 3 to 5 minutes. Drain. Makes 6 croquettes.

SWEETPOTATO CROQUETTES

2½ cups mashed sweet-potatoes
1½ tablespoons butter

Salt and pepper
2 tablespoons brown sugar
Crumbs and egg

Combine sweetpotatoes, butter, salt, pepper and brown sugar. Beat until fluffy. Chill. Shape, roll in crumbs, then in egg and again in crumbs. Fry in hot deep fat (380° F.) 3 to 5 minutes. Drain. Makes 6 croquettes.

SALMON CROQUETTES

No. 1

1¾ cups flaked cooked salmon
1 cup Thick White Sauce
Salt and pepper

Cayenne
1 teaspoon lemon juice
Crumbs and egg

Combine salmon, white sauce, seasoning and lemon juice. Chill and shape. Roll in fine crumbs, then in egg and again in crumbs and fry in hot deep fat (380° F.) 3 to 5 minutes. Drain. Makes 6 croquettes.

No. 2

1 cup hot mashed potatoes
1 cup flaked salmon
Salt and pepper

1 teaspoon lemon juice
Crumbs and egg

Combine potatoes and salmon. Season with salt, pepper and lemon juice. Shape, roll in crumbs, then in egg and again in crumbs and fry in hot deep fat (380° F.) 3 to 5 minutes. Drain. Makes 4 croquettes.

Any fish desired may be used instead of salmon.

MINCED HAM IN CIDER CUPS

1 cup boiled ham	½ cup celery
3 hard-cooked eggs	2 tablespoons gelatin
½ teaspoon salt	2 cups cider
Pepper	½ cup sugar
¼ teaspoon cayenne pepper	½ cup cold water
3 tablespoons lemon-juice	1 cup whipped cream

Soak gelatin in cold water, and pour over it boiling cider to which the sugar and lemon have been added. Strain into border molds. When firm, remove from the molds and fill with the mixture made of the other ingredients and serve immediately.

BRAISED TONGUE WITH ASPIC JELLY

1 beef tongue	1 blade of mace
2 onions	1 bunch thyme
1 stalk celery	1 bunch parsley
4 cloves	1 box gelatin
Salt and pepper	1 cup cold water
1 teaspoon sugar	

Wash and scrub the tongue well in salt water and simmer (180°-210° F.) it until tender. Remove the skin, and place the tongue in a stew-pan with onion, celery, cloves, salt and pepper. Cover it with the liquor in which it was boiled and add sugar, mace, thyme and parsley. Simmer for two hours. Take out the tongue. Add to the liquor gelatin, soaked in the cold water, boil for two minutes, stirring constantly, strain and pour over the tongue. Serve cold.

CHAUD FROID OF EGGS

6 hard-cooked eggs	Paprika
2 tablespoons butter	2 tablespoons chopped olives
Chaud-froid sauce	or pickles
Salt and pepper	

Cook eggs hard and cut in halves lengthwise. Remove yolks and mash to a paste with the melted butter, pepper, salt, paprika, and chopped olives or pickles. Refill whites and mask with chaud-froid sauce. Garnish each with a star cut from a truffle or from a green or red pepper. Let stand in a cold place till firm. These may be served at luncheon or supper.

CHICKEN MOUSSE

2 cups ground cooked chicken
½ cup salad dressing
2 tablespoons lemon juice
¾ teaspoon ground celery seed

¾ cup heavy cream whipped
Salt, pepper
1½ tablespoons gelatin
½ cup cold chicken stock
Lettuce, Brussels sprouts

Carrots and parsley

Blend the chicken, salad dressing, lemon juice and celery seed. Fold in the whipped cream. Season to taste. Fold in the gelatin which has been softened in the cold chicken stock, dissolved over hot water, then cooled. Pour into a ring mold and chill until firm. Unmold, on lettuce, fill the center with Brussels sprouts and garnish the platter with carrots and parsley.

HAM MOUSSE

Follow the directions for chicken mousse, substituting cooked ham for the cooked chicken. Chopped mushrooms are a delicious addition to this dish, and mushrooms may be mixed with the sauce when ready to serve, and also may be used as decorations.

SALMON MOLD PIQUANTE

1 tablespoon gelatin
¼ cup cold water
1½ teaspoons salt
1½ teaspoons mustard
Dash cayenne
2 egg yolks, slightly beaten

¾ cup milk
1½ tablespoons melted butter
4 tablespoons lemon juice
1 cup flaked salmon
Lettuce

Soften gelatin in cold water 5 minutes. Combine seasonings, egg yolks and milk in top of double boiler, and cook over hot water 6 to 8 minutes or until thickened, stirring constantly. Add butter, lemon juice and gelatin, stirring until gelatin is dissolved. Remove from fire and fold in salmon. Turn into fish mold; chill until firm. Unmold on bed of crisp lettuce and serve with cucumber cream dressing.

VEGETARIAN DISHES

~~~~~~~~~~

VEGETARIAN dishes make agreeable variations in the diet, and frequently reduce the food bill. They are welcome in any household where the program of using meat only once a day is being followed. Dishes containing a large percentage of milk, eggs or cheese, together with dried legumes, nuts or gelatin, are nutritious and typical vegetarian dishes.

People not accustomed to meatless menus may experience an unsatisfied feeling at the end of a meal that is entirely vegetarian. This is largely due to the fact that meat is a highly flavored food. The housewife will do well, therefore, to offer some well-seasoned dish in a vegetarian menu.

A ring mold is a decorative way of serving vegetarian dishes with no extra labor. The following recipes calling for a loaf form may be used for the ring mold. See page 344.

CHESTNUT CROQUETTES

2 cups hot mashed chestnuts
4 tablespoons fat
2 eggs
Salt and pepper

Few drops of onion-juice or
2 tablespoons minced onion
Egg and crumbs

Mix the chestnuts, fat, slightly beaten eggs and seasonings. Shape into croquettes. Roll in crumbs, then in beaten egg and again in crumbs. Fry in deep hot fat (375°-390° F.) until crumbs are brown (2-5 minutes).

This dish offers adequate protein and iron and a comparatively highly seasoned dish. The croquettes may be served with brown sauce or tomato sauce.

PEANUT BALLS

1 tablespoon fat
2 tablespoons flour
½ cup milk
½ teaspoon salt

Pepper
2 cups cooked rice
¼ cup ground peanuts
1 egg

Make white sauce from fat, flour, milk and seasoning. Mix rice, peanuts, white sauce and beaten egg, and shape into small

351

balls. Sauté in a greased frying-pan turning frequently so that the balls are browned all over. Or, roll in beaten egg, then in crumbs and fry in deep fat (375°-390° F.).

This dish is low in both iron and protein, therefore milk, eggs or cheese should appear elsewhere in the menu. These balls are good served with cheese sauce.

PEANUT SCRAPPLE

1 cup hot milk	1¼ teaspoons salt
1 quart boiling water	⅛ teaspoon paprika
1 cup yellow corn-meal	1½ cups chopped peanuts
¾ cup hominy grits	¼ to 1 cup grated cheese

Combine hot milk and boiling water, bring to boiling-point and add corn-meal, hominy grits and seasoning. Stir constantly until the liquid is thickened by the cereal. Place in a double boiler and cook one hour. Ten minutes before taking up, add the peanuts and cheese.

Place in a deep rectangular bread-pan and allow it to cool. When ready to use, cut in small slices (roll in egg and crumbs if desired) and fry in deep fat (375°-390° F.) until brown (2-5 minutes); or place in a greased baking-pan, sprinkle with grated cheese mixed with bread-crumbs and bake in a moderate oven (350°-400° F.) until brown.

This makes an excellent luncheon or supper dish.

PEANUT BUTTER CUTLETS

1½ cups peanut butter	Pepper
1½ cups hot milk	6 half-inch slices of bread
1 teaspoon salt	

Mix peanut butter with hot milk and seasoning, mixing together thoroughly. Dip slices of bread into the peanut-butter mixture. Sauté in hot fat. Garnish with pickles and olives.

This dish offers both adequate protein and iron.

BAKED PEANUTS

4 cups shelled raw peanuts	4 tablespoons salad oil

Cover peanuts with cold water and soak over night. In the morning, place them over the fire and boil ten minutes. Remove from water and dry. Add oil and mix well. Place the mixture in a greased baking-dish and bake (400° F.) until the peanuts are soft and well browned.

If extra seasoning is desired, a small quantity of catchup, salt, molasses and mustard may be added during the baking, as for baked beans.

PEANUT SOUFFLÉ

1 tablespoon fat	Few drops lemon-juice
6 tablespoons flour	1½ cups scalded milk
¾ cup peanut butter	4 eggs
1½ teaspoons salt	

Melt the fat and add the flour, peanut butter and seasoning. Cook for three minutes, stirring constantly. Add scalded milk, and continue cooking until the mixture reaches the boiling-point. Remove from the fire, pour the hot mixture over the well-beaten egg-yolks, mixing thoroughly. Cool, and fold in the egg-whites that have been beaten until stiff and dry. When the ingredients are thoroughly combined, place in a ring mold, set in a pan of water in a slow oven (375° F.) and bake thirty minutes. Serve immediately.

This is a hearty main dish, but, because of its texture, should have something crisp or solid served with it.

MOCK SAUSAGE

1 cup dried Lima beans or	3 eggs
3 cups cooked beans of any kind	2 tablespoons fat
⅔ cup bread-crumbs	½ teaspoon sage
	Salt and pepper

Pick over and wash beans, cover with water and let soak over night. Drain, cook in boiling salted water until tender, then force through a strainer. Add remaining ingredients, shape into the form of sausages, roll in crumbs, egg, and crumbs again. Sauté until brown. Serve with tomato sauce.

This recipe makes six to eight sausages, three inches long and three-fourths of an inch thick. It should be accompanied by some milk, egg or cheese dish.

PEANUT CHOPS

6 half-inch slices rye bread
1 cup peanut butter
¾ cup top milk
2 eggs

½ teaspoon salt
⅛ teaspoon paprika
Cracker-crumbs

Cut crust from bread and divide in lengthwise strips. Spread peanut butter on both sides of each strip. Add milk and seasoning to the eggs and beat thoroughly. Dip strips of bread into the mixture, remove and dip into sifted cracker-crumbs. Put into a greased bread-pan and bake in a hot oven (400°-450° F.) until golden brown. This is a good main dish.

BAKED COW PEAS

2 cups cooked cow peas
or split peas
2 cups boiled rice
2 cups stewed tomatoes

1 chopped onion
½ cup bread-crumbs
Salt, pepper, and butter

Put the cooked peas, rice, tomatoes and onion in layers in a greased baking-dish. Season well, cover with bread-crumbs and bake (400°) until brown. Serve with brown sauce.

This needs eggs, milk or cheese to accompany it, but it has excellent flavor.

BEAN ROAST

1 cup roasted shelled peanuts
2 cups seasoned mashed
potatoes
2 cups cooked Lima beans,
fresh or canned

¼ cup milk
1 egg
1 teaspoon salt
⅛ teaspoon paprika
1 teaspoon onion-juice

Grind the peanuts, using the finest blade of the food-chopper. In a greased baking-dish place a layer of potatoes, a layer of beans and a layer of peanuts. Continue making layers until all the ingredients are used. Blend milk with well-beaten egg and seasoning and pour over the top. Bake in a moderate oven (350°-400° F.) until brown. Serve with brown sauce or tomato sauce.

VEGETABLE LUNCHEON

1 pound kidney beans	2 cups cooked tomatoes, fresh
1 cup diced carrot	or canned
1 green pepper, chopped	½ cup rice
1 large onion	½ dozen large mushrooms

Soak the beans in cold water overnight; drain and cook in boiling water slowly for about four hours. A ham-bone or a piece of bacon cooked with them adds to the flavor. Drain, add carrot, pepper, tomatoes, and thin slices of onion. Simmer until tender. Boil rice separately in salted water, drain and add to the vegetables. (The rice water should be used in soups or gravies.) Garnish with sautéed green peppers and mushrooms.

CELERY, NUT AND POTATO LOAF

2 large stalks celery	1 egg
¾ cup chopped nuts	1 teaspoon salt
3 cups mashed potatoes	⅛ teaspoon paprika
3 tablespoons fat	2 teaspoons grated onion

Wash, cut in small pieces and cook the celery until tender in a small amount of boiling salted water. Drain off liquid. (This may be used for soup stock later.) Then add the other ingredients to the celery in the order in which they are given. Combine them carefully, pack in a loaf in a greased bread pan, and bake in a moderate oven (350°-400° F.) for thirty-five minutes. Serve with tomato sauce.

CARROT LOAF OR RING

2 cups ground carrot	2 cups strained tomatoes
2 cups bread-crumbs	1 teaspoon salt
⅔ cup chopped nuts	⅛ teaspoon pepper
3 eggs	2 teaspoons minced onion

Mix the ingredients in the order given. Shape the mixture into a loaf and put into a greased baking-pan. Steam the loaf for one hour and then brown it in the oven (400° F.). Or pour into greased ring mold, set in pan of hot water and bake in moderate oven (350° F.) until firm—about 40 minutes. Unmold on a hot plate; fill center with hot cooked peas.

PEANUT AND CARROT LOAF

1 cup chopped carrots	1½ tablespoons fat
1 cup coarse ground peanuts	4 eggs, slightly beaten
1 cup strained tomatoes	1 teaspoon chopped parsley
1 cup crumbs	Salt

Chop separately the carrots and peanuts, or put them through the food-chopper, using the coarse knife. Add the other ingredients and form in a loaf. Place in a greased pan and bake one hour and a quarter in a moderate oven (350°-400° F.).

NUT LOAF

2 cups soft bread-crumbs	2 eggs
1 cup milk	1 teaspoon salt
2 cups chopped nut-meats	1 teaspoon paprika

Soak bread-crumbs in milk, add nuts, slightly beaten eggs and seasonings. Turn into greased bread-pan, set into pan of water and bake (350° F.) forty minutes. Serve with tomato sauce. The loaf may be steamed instead of baked.

PEANUT ROAST

1 tablespoon chopped onion	1 cup bread-crumbs
1 tablespoon chopped celery	1 cup green pea pulp, fresh or canned
2 tablespoons fat	
½ cup hot water	Juice of half a lemon
1½ cups chopped peanuts	1 teaspoon salt
1 egg	Dash of pepper

Cook onion and celery in fat until golden brown. Add hot water and simmer until vegetables are tender. Mix other ingredients, adding the egg last. Combine the mixture with the celery and onion mixture. Pack into greased baking-dish and bake (350° F.) until golden brown. Serve with cream sauce.

BOSTON ROAST

1½ cups dry kidney beans	2 tablespoons chopped onion
3 tablespoons salt	1 cup bread-crumbs
1 to 2 cups grated cheese	½ cup milk

Soak beans twenty-four hours. Cook until soft in water in which the salt has been dissolved. Drain; chop; add onion, cheese, crumbs, more salt if needed, and enough milk to moisten. Form into a loaf. Bake in a moderate oven (350°-400° F.) for forty minutes. Baste occasionally with hot water and fat.

BAKED BEAN ROAST

2 tablespoons minced peppers
2 tablespoons minced onion
4 tablespoons fat
4 cups mashed baked beans
2 eggs, slightly beaten

2 cups crumbs
1 cup tomatoes
Salt and pepper
½ teaspoon paprika

Cook pepper and onion in fat. Add other ingredients in the order given. Bake (350° F.) in greased baking-dish for thirty minutes. Serve with brown sauce or tomato sauce.

A cheese or milk dish should be added to this meal.

LIMA BEAN LOAF

2 cups Lima beans
1 cup dry bread-crumbs
4 tablespoons peanut butter
½ teaspoon pepper

1 tablespoon poultry seasoning
2 tablespoons grated onion
1 tablespoon bacon fat
1 cup milk (more, if needed)

Wash and soak the beans overnight, then cook in boiling water until soft (about forty-five minutes). Drain, cool, then chop coarsely. Add crumbs mixed with peanut butter and seasoning, then fat, and milk to moisten. Put into a greased bread-pan and bake in a moderate oven (350°-400° F.) thirty minutes. Serve with brown sauce, cream sauce or tomato sauce.

COTTAGE CHEESE AND PEANUT LOAF

½ cup peanuts
1 cup cottage cheese
1 cup cold, cooked rolled oats
1 cup milk
1 egg, slightly beaten
1 tablespoon fat

½ teaspoon salt
Dash of pepper
1 teaspoon poultry seasoning
Few drops Worcestershire sauce
1 tablespoon chopped onion

Chop peanuts and add other ingredients in order given. When thoroughly combined, place in a greased bread-tin. Bake in a moderate oven (350°-400° F.) until brown. Serve hot with tomato sauce.

NUT AND CHEESE LOAF

1 tablespoon chopped onion	¼ teaspoon paprika
1 tablespoon fat	1½ tablespoons lemon juice
1 cup grated cheese	½ teaspoon Worcestershire
1 cup chopped nuts	sauce
1 cup cooked cereal	½ cup milk
1 teaspoon salt	Buttered crumbs
1 teaspoon sugar	

Brown onion lightly in fat. Mix with next 8 ingredients and moisten with milk. Cover with buttered crumbs and brown in hot oven (400° F.). Serve hot with tomato sauce. Serves 6. Serve with some crisp food such as celery.

BOILED MACARONI OR SPAGHETTI

1 cup broken macaroni or spaghetti	6 cups boiling water
	2 teaspoons salt

Break macaroni or spaghetti into 2-inch lengths, drop into rapidly boiling salted water and cook uncovered 15 to 20 minutes or until tender. Keep water boiling and stir occasionally with a fork. Pour into colander and rinse with hot water. Serve with butter, thin white sauce, tomato sauce or as desired. Makes 2 cups cooked macaroni or spaghetti.

To cook spaghetti in unbroken pieces, place ends in boiling water and coil it as it softens.

CHEESE MACARONI LOAF

¾ cup broken macaroni	½ cup grated cheese
1 teaspoon parsley	1½ cups milk
2 teaspoons chopped onion	1 egg
1 tablespoon green pepper	1 teaspoon salt
2 tablespoons fat	½ cup buttered crumbs

Cook macaroni in boiling salted water until tender. Cook parsley, onion and green pepper in fat until tender. Drain water from macaroni. Place a layer of macaroni in buttered baking dish, then add a layer of onion mixture and cheese. Repeat until dish is full. Pour over it the milk mixed with egg and salt. Cover with buttered crumbs and brown in hot oven (400° F.). Serve with tomato sauce. Serves 6.

VEGETABLE LOAF

½ cup cooked green peas	1 cup soft bread crumbs
½ cup cooked green beans	½ teaspoon salt
½ cup chopped cooked carrots	⅛ teaspoon pepper
1½ cups milk	½ teaspoon paprika
1 egg	

Press peas through a sieve, cut beans into small pieces, then combine all vegetables. Add milk, slightly beaten egg, crumbs and seasoning. Turn into greased baking dish and bake in moderate oven (375° F.) until firm, about 30 minutes. Serves 6.

PEA TIMBALES

1½ cups pea pulp	3 eggs, well beaten
2 tablespoons melted butter	Salt and pepper

Combine ingredients and pour into greased molds; set molds into pan of hot water and bake in slow oven (325° F.) about 30 minutes. Serve with medium white sauce. Serves 6.

RICE CROQUETTES

3 tablespoons butter	¼ teaspoon paprika
3 tablespoons flour	1½ cups cooked rice
½ teaspoon salt	Fine dry crumbs
1 cup milk	1 egg, slightly beaten
1 tablespoon minced parsley	Tart red jelly

Melt butter, blend in flour and salt and add milk and parsley. Cook until thickened. Add paprika and rice. Cool. Shape into cones and make a depression in top. Roll in crumbs, in egg and again in crumbs. Fry in hot deep fat (375° F.) until brown. Drain on absorbent paper and place spoonful of red jelly in top. Makes 6 croquettes.

CHEESE-FILLED—Blend grated cheese with a few drops Worcestershire sauce or onion juice or with minced pimiento. Shape into balls and coat with thick layer of rice mixture. Dip in crumbs, egg and crumbs and fry as above.

CRANBERRY-FILLED—Cut cranberry sauce into cubes, coat with chilled rice mixture and proceed as above.

TOMATO—Use tomato juice instead of milk and cook 1 tablespoon grated onion with flour mixture.

EGG DISHES

T O test an egg for freshness, place it in a glass of water. If the egg falls to the bottom of the glass and lies on its side, it is a fresh egg; if the large end rises slightly, the egg is somewhat stale; if it stands on end or floats, it is very stale. The shell of a fresh egg has a bloom; that of a stale egg is usually shiny. If the contents of an egg rattle when it is shaken, it is not fresh.

EGGS COOKED IN THE SHELL

HARD-COOKED (CODDLED)—Place the eggs in a saucepan of cold water and heat slowly until the boiling-point is reached. Set the container on the back of the stove or reduce the heat so that the water will not boil again and let stand twenty to thirty minutes before removing the eggs. Another method of regulating the temperature is to cook them in the double boiler.

SOFT-COOKED (CODDLED)—Use one pint water for each egg up to six eggs, one-half pint for each additional egg, and use a small deep saucepan so that the water will cover the eggs. Bring the water to the boiling-point in a vessel that can be covered closely. Put the eggs in at once, cover, set off heat and let stand in a warm place for four to six minutes, depending on consistency desired. In this way, the eggs will be cooked equally well in every part.

POACHED OR DROPPED EGGS

No. 1—Heat salted water to the boiling-point in a frying-pan or other shallow pan. Break an egg into a saucer, then slip it gently into the water. Repeat until all the eggs are in. Remove the pan from the fire, cover and keep hot until the eggs are set to the desired degree. If the yolk is not entirely covered, dip the water over it carefully until it is coated with white. Remove with a skimmer or perforated ladle and slip on to a thin piece of buttered toast. Buttered muffin rings may be placed in the water and each egg slipped into a muffin ring for cooking, or an egg-poacher may be used.

Poached eggs are often placed in clear soup, one egg being prepared for each person to be served. They are served also on thin slices of boiled ham, on mounds of corned-beef hash, on Welsh rabbit or on cooked spinach.

No. 2—Separate the yolk and white. Beat the white until stiff and put it in a glass ramekin. Drop the yolk in the center of the beaten white. Set the ramekin in hot water until the egg sets. Garnish with a bit of butter and sprinkle with salt and pepper. Serve in the ramekin.

FRIED EGGS

No. 1—Heat cooking-fat in a frying-pan and slip in the eggs. Cook as many eggs at one time as will fill the pan without touching one another. Baste with some of the fat, to cook the yolk. Cook slowly, for if the fat becomes very hot the eggs will be tough and hard to digest but if the temperature of the fat is kept down, the egg may be made as delicate as if poached in water.

Eggs may be fried very successfully by covering the pan as soon as the eggs have been added, and then placing it in the oven or over a very slow fire, so that the eggs will cook very slowly.

No. 2—With Brown Butter—

6 eggs	Salt and pepper
3 tablespoons butter	1 teaspoon vinegar

Sauté the eggs in one tablespoon butter until set, season with salt and pepper, and place on a platter. Brown two tablespoons butter in the pan, add one teaspoon vinegar, and when hot, pour over the eggs.

BAKED EGGS

No. 1—Use individual baking-dishes and melt one teaspoon of butter in each dish. Break the eggs into the dishes, allowing one or two eggs to a dish. Sprinkle with salt and pepper, and place a tiny piece of butter on each. Bake in a slow oven (250°-350° F.) until the eggs are set but not hard. Serve in the baking-dishes.

No. 2—SHIRRED—Use small ramekins or egg-shirrers. Grease each dish, put in a layer of buttered crumbs, break an egg over the crumbs, season with salt and pepper and cover with buttered crumbs. Bake in a slow oven (250°-350° F.) until the eggs are set and the crumbs brown. Serve in the ramekins.

No. 3—On Toast—Moisten the edges of the toast with hot water and spread with butter. Separate the yolks and whites of the eggs. Poach the yolks in salted water until soft cooked, and place one on each slice of toast, being careful not to break it. Beat the whites very stiff, spread around the yolks, season with salt and pepper, and brown in the oven (350° F.).

No. 4—In Tomato Sauce—Grease small ramekins and place two tablespoons thick tomato sauce in each. Slip a poached egg into each dish, cover with grated cheese, season with salt and pepper, and bake in a very hot oven (450°-500° F.) two or three minutes, to brown the cheese.

No. 5—In Bacon Rings—Curl long slices of bacon around the inside of muffin-cups or small ramekins. Break an egg inside each bacon-ring, season with salt and pepper and bake (350° F.) until set, but not hard. Remove carefully from the dish so that the egg will remain fastened to the bacon. Arrange on a platter and garnish with parsley.

No. 6—With Bacon Strips—Fry the bacon very crisp, but not hard, then arrange the slices in groups of two on a large plate or in individual baking-dishes. Break one egg over each two slices of bacon, season with salt and pepper and bake slowly (300° F.) until set, but not hard.

BATTERED OR SCRAMBLED EGGS

No. 1—In a frying-pan, place one teaspoon of butter for each egg. Beat the eggs until the whites and yolks are well mixed. Season with salt and pepper and add one to three tablespoons of milk or cream for each egg. Pour into the hot fat and cook slowly, stirring constantly until the eggs are of the desired consistency. Serve at once. A little onion-juice or chopped parsley may be added to the eggs, if desired.

No. 2—With Green Peppers—

8 eggs	2 sweet peppers
3 tablespoons cream	3 tablespoons fat
Salt and pepper	

Beat the eggs slightly, adding the cream, salt and pepper. Heat the fat and add the eggs. As the eggs begin to cook, add the chopped pepper, from which the seeds have been removed. Cook slowly, stirring constantly, until the mass is creamy.

One-fourth cup of chopped canned pimientos may be substituted for the pepper. It is often desirable to soften fresh peppers by placing in hot water for five minutes.

Eggs scrambled in the top of a double boiler will be more creamy than those cooked in a frying-pan.

PLAIN OMELET

Puffy—

4 eggs	Salt and pepper
4 tablespoons hot water	Butter or other fat

Beat the egg-whites until stiff. Beat the yolks until thick and lemon-colored, beat into them the hot water and add salt and pepper. Cut and fold together the yolks and stiffly beaten whites. Melt enough fat in an omelet-pan to grease the bottom and sides of the pan. Turn the egg mixture into the pan and cook over a slow fire until it is puffy and a light brown underneath, then place in the oven until the top is dry. Touch the top of the omelet lightly with the finger and if the egg does not stick to the finger the omelet is done. Do not overcook it or it will shrink or be tough.

Loosen the edges of the omelet, cut through the center, slip a spatula or flexible knife under the side next to the handle of the pan, fold one-half over the other and press slightly to make it stay in place, slip on to a hot plate and serve at once.

French—

6 eggs	2 tablespoons fat
Salt and pepper	

Beat the eggs just enough to mix the whites and yolks, and add salt and pepper. Heat the fat in an omelet-pan, pour a little of it into the beaten eggs and allow the remainder to get hot. Turn the eggs into the pan and as the mixture cooks on the bottom and sides, prick it with a fork so that the egg on top will penetrate the cooked surface, and run under the sides. The work must be done quickly and carefully so that the eggs are not all stirred up like scrambled eggs. While the eggs are still soft, but slightly thickened, fold over, let stand a few minutes to brown, and turn on to a hot dish.

Individual omelets may be cooked in a small frying pan.

FOR THE HOLIDAY BREAKFAST, SLIP YOUR POACHED EGG INTO A BREAD CROUSTADE THAT HAS BEEN HALF-FILLED WITH CHEESE SAUCE, OR DO A FLUFFY OMELET WITH MUSHROOMS AND ASPARAGUS

—Irradiated Evaporated Milk Institute

BEAUTY IS NOT ONLY IN THE EYE OF THE BEHOLDER WHEN THESE EGGS REACH THE BREAKFAST TABLE —Institute of American Poultry Industry

IN ANOTHER FEW MINUTES YOU CAN HAVE FLUFFY EGGS TO SERVE WITH THE BACON THAT IS BROILED FLAT BETWEEN RACKS

VARIATIONS OF PLAIN OMELET

Variations of the plain puffy omelet or the plain French omelet may be made by adding any of the following ingredients to the omelet before it is put into the pan to cook, or by spreading one of them on top just before the omelet is folded. Allow one tablespoon of mixture to each two eggs used.

Aux Fines Herbes—This favorite French omelet is made by adding a mixture of parsley, thyme and sweet marjoram to a plain omelet.

Cheese—Scatter grated or ground cheese over the center of the omelet while it is cooking.

Fish—Use any cooked fish. Chop it fine, season with salt and pepper and moisten with a little cream. Spread on the omelet before folding.

Ham or Other Meat—Scatter minced cooked meat over the center of the omelet while it is cooking. The meat may be browned in a small amount of fat before it is added.

Jardiniere—Stir into the beaten eggs, before cooking, a mixture of chopped parsley, onion, chives, shallots, and a few leaves each of sorrel and chervil, minced.

Jelly—Spread any jelly or jam over the omelet just before folding.

Onion—Mix one tablespoon chopped onion and one teaspoon chopped parsley. Add to the omelet mixture before cooking.

Parsley—Scatter minced parsley over the center of the omelet while it is cooking.

Vegetable—Use cooked left-over vegetables, one vegetable alone or two in combination. Mash the vegetable through a sieve, moisten with a little milk, cream or gravy, and season with salt and pepper. Lightly spread the mixture over the omelet before folding.

CHICKEN OR TONGUE OMELET

1 cup chicken or tongue
2 tablespoons fat
2 tablespoons flour
1 cup cream or milk
Salt and pepper
Plain omelet

Chop the meat until it is very fine. Make a sauce of the fat, flour, and milk or cream. Add salt and pepper and chopped meat. Make a plain omelet and spread the meat mixture on it just before folding.

MUSHROOM OMELET

1 cup mushrooms	½ teaspoon pepper
1 tablespoon fat	1 tablespoon flour
½ cup milk or cream	Plain omelet
1 teaspoon salt	

Use fresh or canned mushrooms cut into bits. Melt the fat in a saucepan, add the mushrooms, the milk or cream, salt, pepper and flour which has been mixed to a paste with a little cold milk. Cook for five minutes, then set aside until the omelet is made. Spread the mushroom mixture over the omelet just before folding.

MUSHROOM AND TOMATO OMELET

3 cups tomatoes	Salt and pepper
1 cup mushrooms	6 eggs
2 tablespoons chopped onion	½ cup milk
2 teaspoons sugar	

Strain the tomato, add the onion, sugar, salt and pepper and cook several minutes, then add the mushrooms, sliced very thin. Make a plain omelet of the eggs and milk. Pour part of the sauce over the omelet just before folding; fold; place on a hot plate; pour the remainder of the sauce around it and serve.

OYSTER OMELET

12 oysters	1 cup cream
½ tablespoon flour	6 eggs
2 tablespoons fat	Salt and pepper

Chop the oysters. Make a sauce of the flour, fat, and cream. Add the well beaten eggs, season with salt and pepper, stir in the oysters and cook as a plain omelet.

POTATO OMELET

4 cold boiled potatoes	⅛ teaspoon pepper
3 tablespoons bacon fat	2 eggs
½ tablespoon salt	2 tablespoons milk

Cut the potatoes into tiny cubes and cook in the bacon fat with the seasonings for five minutes. Beat the eggs slightly and add the milk, then pour over the potatoes. Cook slowly until set, fold, and turn on to a hot plate.

BAKED CREAMY OMELETS

2 slices bread　　　　　　Salt and pepper
1 cup milk　　　　　　　Chopped onion
6 eggs

Crumble the bread and allow it to soak in the milk while the eggs are being prepared. Beat the eggs until light, add seasonings and then the bread and milk mixture. Bake quickly (360° F.) in a well-greased shallow pan and when done roll as you would a jelly roll. Serves 6.

INDIVIDUAL OMELETS—Bake like pancakes on a griddle over low heat, turn and when lightly browned, remove to hot platter, fill and roll quickly. Makes 12-14.

CLAM OMELET

1 cup hard clams　　　　Paprika
2 tablespoons butter　　　6 eggs, separated
1 teaspoon salt　　　　　⅔ cup cream

After clams have been steamed and removed from their shells, put them through a food chopper and sauté in butter. Add salt and paprika to egg yolks and beat until light. Add cream and chopped clams and mix thoroughly. Fold in stiffly beaten egg whites, pour mixture into buttered omelet pan or skillet and bake in moderate oven (350° F.) about 25 minutes, or until brown. Serves 6.

SPANISH OMELET

1 medium tomato　　　　Olives
1 small green pepper　　　Mushrooms
½ onion　　　　　　　　Salt and pepper
2 sprigs parsley　　　　　4 eggs
1 stalk celery

Peel the tomato, add the pepper, onion, parsley, celery, olives, mushrooms, and chop all together in a chopping bowl. Place the mixture in a saucepan, add seasonings and cook for two to three minutes. Beat the eggs, put them in the omelet pan and, as soon as they begin to cook, add the chopped vegetables. Finish as for plain omelet. Serves 4.

TOMATO OMELET

3 tomatoes
2 tablespoons fat

4 to 6 eggs
Seasoning

Peel tomatoes, remove the seeds and cut into dice. Sauté in the fat until tender. Make the omelet in the usual way, first stirring the tomato into the beaten egg.

CUBAN EGGS

6 eggs
1/4 cup sausage meat
1 teaspoon chopped onion

1/2 teaspoon salt
Pepper

Cook the meat and onion together for five minutes. Beat the eggs until light, add the seasonings, and pour into the pan with the meat. Cook slowly, stirring constantly, until the eggs are thick and creamy. Serve with buttered toast or poured over slices of toast.

EGGS À LA CARACAS

1 tablespoon fat
1/4 pound dried beef
1 tablespoon grated cheese
1 cup tomatoes

Salt and pepper
4 eggs
Onion-juice

Melt the fat in a frying-pan and, when hot, add the dried beef and cheese. Toss lightly until the beef is slightly frizzled, add the tomatoes, the seasonings, and the eggs beaten until light. Stir and cook gently until of a creamy consistency.

EGGS À LA SUISSE

6 eggs
2 tablespoons butter or other
   fat
1/2 to 1 cup grated cheese

1 cup cream
Salt
Cayenne

Spread the bottom of a baking-dish with fat. Sprinkle a layer of grated cheese over it and break the eggs on the cheese, being careful not to break the yolks. Pour a little cream over the eggs, then more grated cheese. Season with salt and cayenne, and bake in a slow oven (250°-350° F.) until the eggs are set, but not hard. Serve in the baking-dish.

BAKED EGGS ESPAGNOLE

6 eggs	4 tablespoons fat
3 tablespoons chopped onion	¼ cup bread-crumbs
3 tablespoons chopped green pepper	½ cup grated cheese

Fry onion and pepper in the fat until slightly brown, then pour into a baking-dish. Break the eggs into the dish, being careful not to break the yolks. Mix the crumbs with the cheese and sprinkle over the eggs. Bake in a slow oven (250°-350° F.) until the eggs are set, but not hard. Serve in the dish in which they were baked.

PLANKED EGGS

1 cup minced cooked ham or corned beef	6 poached eggs
1 cup crumbs	Garnish of tomato slices
Cream	Green-pepper rings
	1 quart mashed potato

Mix the meat with the crumbs and enough cream to make a paste. Spread the mixture on a heated plank of suitable size. Around the edge of the plank make a narrow border of mashed potato and inside the border make six nests of the potato. Slip a poached egg into each nest and set in the oven until the potato turns a delicate brown. Garnish with alternate slices of tomato and green-pepper rings.

EGGS WITH CODFISH

1 cup salt codfish	2 uncooked eggs
4 tablespoons fat	Chopped parsley
2 tablespoons flour	3 hard-cooked eggs
2 cups milk	

Cover the fish with cold water and soak overnight. Drain, flake, and sauté with the fat for a few minutes; sprinkle with the flour; add the milk, and cook until smooth. Stir in the uncooked eggs, slightly beaten, and cook three minutes more. Serve on a platter garnished with the chopped parsley and the hard-cooked eggs cut in quarters.

Two additional tablespoons of flour may be substituted for the uncooked eggs, if desired. For creamed codfish, omit the hard-cooked eggs.

VARIATIONS OF WHITE SAUCE

Use 1 cup medium white sauce as the basis for each sauce.

CAPER SAUCE—Add 2 to 4 tablespoons chopped capers.

CELERY SAUCE—Add ½ cup chopped cooked celery.

CHEESE SAUCE—Add 2 to 4 ounces grated cheese. Set over hot water and stir until the cheese is blended with sauce. Season to taste with mustard and paprika.

CREAM GRAVY—Use 2 tablespoons meat drippings for butter in white sauce recipe.

CREAM SAUCE—Use cream instead of milk in white sauce.

EGG SAUCE, No. 1—Add 1 hard-cooked egg, chopped.

No. 2—Beat an uncooked egg, dilute with 1 tablespoon of hot thin white sauce, then beat this into the remainder of a cup of sauce. If the egg white is beaten separately, the sauce will be foamy.

LOBSTER SAUCE—Add ½ cup finely flaked cooked lobster.

MOCK HOLLANDAISE SAUCE—Pour sauce over 2 slightly beaten egg yolks, 2 tablespoons each of butter and lemon juice, beat thoroughly and serve immediately.

MUSHROOM SAUCE—Add ½ to ⅓ cup chopped or sliced cooked mushrooms to sauce.

OLIVE SAUCE—Add ¼ cup chopped ripe or stuffed olives.

OYSTER SAUCE—Heat 1 pint small oysters in their own liquor to boiling point. Remove from heat after they have cooked ½ minute and combine with sauce. Season to taste.

PARSLEY SAUCE—Add 2 to 4 tablespoons chopped parsley.

PIMIENTO SAUCE—Add 2 tablespoons minced onion and 6 tablespoons minced pimiento. Onion may be browned in fat when making white sauce, if desired.

SHRIMP SAUCE—Add ½ cup chopped cooked shrimp.

SOUBISE SAUCE—Rub 4 boiled onions and 2 sprigs parsley through a coarse sieve. Combine with sauce.

TOMATO CREAM SAUCE—Cook 1 cup fresh or canned tomatoes, 1 stalk celery, 1 slice onion, ½ teaspoon salt and a few grains cayenne together for 20 minutes. Rub through a sieve. Add gradually, stirring constantly, to white sauce.

VELOUTÉ SAUCE—Use 1 cup well-seasoned white stock for milk in thin or medium white sauce.

YELLOW SAUCE—Add hot sauce to 1 or 2 slightly beaten egg yolks and beat thoroughly.

ham may be added, or the yolks may be mixed with mayonnaise dressing. Refill the whites with the mixture; press two halves together, and wrap each egg in a square of waxed paper.

Hot—Omit vinegar, add nuts to the egg mixture, moisten with evaporated milk and refill whites. Cap with large sautéed mushrooms. Pack into greased baking dish, caps up, cover with rich white sauce, then buttered crumbs and brown in 350° oven.

EGG TIMBALES

1 tablespoon fat	3 eggs
1 tablespoon flour	Salt and pepper
⅔ cup scalded milk	Cayenne
1 tablespoon chopped parsley	Celery salt

Make a white sauce of the fat, flour, and milk, and add the egg-yolks, slightly beaten. Add all the seasonings, then fold in the stiffly beaten egg-whites. Fill greased baking-dishes two-thirds full of the mixture. Set dishes in a pan of hot water and poach in a slow oven (250°-350° F.) until firm. Arrange on a platter and serve with tomato cream sauce.

SAVORY EGGS

6 hot hard-cooked eggs	Chopped parsley
Salt and pepper	Anchovy paste
¼ cup hot cream	6 slices hot buttered toast
1 cup hot thin white sauce	

Cut the eggs in two lengthwise and remove the yolks. Mash the yolks, add seasonings, cream, parsley, anchovy or any desired relish, and refill the whites. Place on slices of toast and pour the white sauce over them.

EGG FARCI

6 hot hard-cooked eggs	¼ teaspoon pepper
½ teaspoon salt	1 tablespoon butter
1½ cups white, Béchamel,	4 tablespoons milk
curry or tomato sauce	Onion-juice

Remove the shells from the eggs and cut them in half crosswise, then cut an even slice from the end of each half so that it will stand up in a pan. Remove the yolks, mash, and add the salt, pepper, butter, milk and a few drops of onion-juice. Mix thoroughly and heap into the hollow of the whites. Set in a shallow pan and bake in a slow oven (250°-350° F.) for about six minutes, then arrange on a hot dish, and pour over them any preferred sauce.

EGGS À LA GOLDENROD

6 hard-cooked eggs	Salt and pepper
2 cups thin white sauce	Paprika
8 slices toast	

Separate the yolks from the whites of the eggs; chop the whites very fine, and add to the white sauce, with salt, pepper, paprika. Arrange six slices of toast on a platter and pour over them the white sauce mixture. Press the egg-yolks through a sieve and scatter over the top. Cut the two extra slices of toast into small triangles, or points, arrange on the platter and garnish with parsley.

CREAMED EGGS

6 hard-cooked eggs	2 tablespoons flour
2 tablespoons fat	2 cups milk
½ onion	1 teaspoon salt
6 slices hot buttered toast	¼ teaspoon pepper

Remove the shells from the eggs and cut each egg into six pieces. Heat the fat in a frying-pan, and cook the chopped onion with it for a few minutes until yellow, but not brown. Remove the onion, make a sauce of the fat, flour, liquid and seasonings. When it thickens, add the eggs, and when they are well heated, turn the mixture out on to the buttered toast and serve at once.

SCALLOPED EGGS

Butter	Salt and pepper
6 hard-cooked eggs	Milk or cream
Crumbs	

Grease a baking-dish and place in it a layer of crumbs, then a layer of slices of hard-cooked eggs. Dot with bits of butter, sprinkle with salt and pepper, and add another layer of crumbs. Repeat in this order until the dish is full, having a layer of buttered crumbs on top. Pour cream or milk over the whole until it comes about halfway to the top of the dish, and brown in a moderate oven (350°-400° F.).

EGG FRICASSEE

6 hard-cooked eggs	3 tablespoons fat
3 cups stock	3 tablespoons flour
Minced parsley	¼ cup cream
Chopped onion	Salt and pepper

Cut the eggs in slices. Make a sauce of the stock, fat, flour and seasonings. Add the sliced eggs, the cream and salt and pepper. Mix well and serve very hot.

EGGS AU GRATIN

6 hard-cooked eggs	2 cups medium white sauce,
Salt and pepper	or tomato sauce or yellow
Grated cheese	sauce
Buttered crumbs	

Remove the shells from the eggs and slice them. Arrange the slices in a greased baking-dish. Season with salt and pepper and pour the sauce over the top. Sprinkle with grated cheese and cover with buttered crumbs. Bake in a moderate oven (350 F.) until the sauce bubbles and the crumbs brown.

EGGS À LA DUCHESSE

1 onion	2 teaspoons chopped parsley
Fat	4 tablespoons grated cheese
1 cup milk	Paprika
6 hard-cooked eggs	Salt and pepper
2 uncooked egg-yolks	1½ tablespoons lemon-juice

Slice the onion and cook it in a very little fat until brown, then add to it the milk and the eggs cut in halves. Stir over the fire for three or four minutes, then add the slightly beaten egg-yolks, the parsley, cheese and seasonings. Stir over hot water for about eight minutes, add the lemon-juice and serve very hot.

PICKLED EGGS

24 cloves	½ teaspoon salt
6 hard-cooked eggs	½ teaspoon pepper
2 cups vinegar	½ teaspoon ground mustard

Shell the eggs and stick four cloves into each egg. Heat the vinegar and when boiling add the salt, pepper and mustard mixed with a little cold vinegar. Put the eggs in a glass fruit jar and pour the boiling vinegar over them. Cover and let stand two weeks before using. Serve with broiled steak.

FLUFFY EGGS

6 slices toast, square or round	½ teaspoon salt
Butter	⅛ teaspoon pepper
1 cup grated cheese	Paprika
6 eggs	12-18 strips bacon

Spread toast with butter and part of grated cheese. Separate eggs, place whites in mixing bowl and leave each separate yolk in shell till needed. Season whites and beat until stiff and fluffy. Heap onto toast and make a dent in center of each. Slip yolk into center of white, season and sprinkle liberally with cheese. Bake at 350° F. until cheese is browned and eggs are set. Garnish with paprika; serve with bacon. Serves 6.

EGGS ROMANOFF

Cut a small section from the pointed end of a hard-cooked egg. Remove yolk, fill with caviar, and replace the cap. Place on a slice of tomato on shredded lettuce and surround with pieces of cold boiled lobster. Serve with Russian Dressing, page 449, or Cucumber Cream Dressing, page 315.

EGGS ROBIN HOOD

Split and toast English muffins. Sauté circular pieces of boiled ham and place them on the halves of muffins with slices of broiled tomato. Arrange on each a poached egg and cover with cheese sauce.

POACHED EGGS, NEW STYLE—Spread buttered toast with deviled ham. Place poached eggs on toast. Pour Thin White Sauce on top and garnish with parsley.

CHEESE

~~~~~~~~

MANY of the well-known cheeses which originated in Europe are now reproduced in America with such success that they are considered as good as the European original. Moreover, the cheese manufactured in America is generally made on a much larger scale and under more carefully controlled conditions.

SEMIHARD CHEESE

Semihard cheese varies in flavor from very mild to sharp. Varieties also range in color from pale to deep yellow. In general they have a firm, rather elastic texture with or without holes. Most types may be used in sandwiches, for cooking or as dessert.

AMERICAN CHEDDAR CHEESE—Flavor ranges from mild to sharp, depending upon the time allowed for ripening. It may be made of whole milk (often called full cream), part skim or skim milk. This variety is sold in many shapes, such as daisies, longhorns and young Americas. IN RECIPES WHICH CALL FOR CHEESE WITHOUT SPECIFYING THE KIND, THIS CHEESE IS THE VARIETY USUALLY MEANT.

BRICK—An American Cheddar with a mild, sweetish taste, a rather elastic texture and many small round eyes or holes. It is a rennet cheese made from whole milk and molded into brick shape.

CHESHIRE—Hard rennet cheese somewhat like English Cheddar but with sharper flavor. Made from whole milk and colored with annatto. Made in England.

EDAM—Hard rennet cheese, round with red rind. Made from skim milk and from partly skimmed milk. Solid, dry, rather crumbly texture. Mild, slightly saline flavor. It was originally made in Holland, now some is made in the United States. Serve with salads, in rarebits or as dessert. To serve, cut off top and scoop out inside as needed.

EMMENTHALER—Hard rennet cheese with large holes and a mild, somewhat sweetish flavor. Holes should be uniform, very shiny and about the size of a quarter. It is made from whole milk. Use for cooking or with desserts or salads. Made in Switzerland.

ENGLISH CHEDDAR—Hard, sharp, white or yellow color. Made from sweet milk and sold as "full cream" (when whole milk is used), "part skim" or "skim," depending on the type of milk used.

GOUDA—Hard rennet cheese, round and flat. Made from whole milk. Similar to Edam cheese. Originally made in Holland but small quantities are now made in the United States.

GRUYÈRE—Originally the name applied to Emmenthaler cheese manufactured in France. Now made in United States where the name is generally applied to packaged processed Swiss cheese.

HERKIMER—Aged Cheddar with sharp flavor. It is used in rarebits, cheese sauces and as dessert. Made in the United States.

PINEAPPLE—Hard, highly colored Cheddar made in pineapple shape, then hung and dried in a net, making diamond-shaped corrugations on surface. The outer coat is rubbed with oil, making it very hard and smooth. Made from whole milk. It is grated and used like other Cheddars. Made in the United States.

SAGE—A Cheddar cheese formerly made by adding sage leaves to the curd. Now sage extract is usually used. Made in United States.

SWISS—Similar to Swiss made Emmenthaler. Much is made in the United States. When processed the characteristic holes are lost.

UNCOOKED SOFT CHEESE

COTTAGE—Soft curds. Made commercially from pasteurized sour milk with or without rennet.

CREAM—A soft rich cheese with mild flavor. Genuine cream cheese is made from pasteurized rich cream thickened by souring or from sweet cream thickened with rennet. It is also made from thin cream thickened with rennet and from whole milk. When fresh it has a mild delicate flavor. It must be refrigerated at all times. Used as a basis for mixtures with pimiento, crushed pineapple, etc.

NEUFCHÂTEL—The French cheese is similar to cream cheese but has been ripened by mold. It is a very soft rennet cheese made from whole or skimmed milk. Domestic Neufchâtel is similar to cream cheese but is made from various grades of milk ranging from cream to skimmed milk. It is not ripened.

PROCESSED CHEESE

Processed cheese is produced by grinding various lots of cheese, blending and pasteurizing at 140° to 160° F. to produce a standardized product, uniform in flavor and texture, without rind and with good keeping qualities. Among the types of cheese sold in this form are mild or sharp American Cheddar, Swiss, brick and Limburger.

SOFT CHEESE

Soft, creamy cheese is usually served as a dessert.

BRIE—A soft rennet cheese with a definite odor, sharp flavor and red color on surface. It is made from whole or partly skimmed milk. It originated in France but is now made in the United States. To serve as a dessert, cut off top so cheese may be dipped out with a spoon.

CAMEMBERT—A soft rennet cheese covered with a firm rind of molds and dried cheese. The interior is almost fluid in consistency. It is made from whole milk or slightly skimmed milk. It originated in France but is now made in the United States also. Serve as Brie.

LIVEROT—Soft rennet cheese, somewhat like Brie. It is made from partially skimmed milk and has a strong piquant flavor. Made in France.

PONT L'ÉVÊQUE—Soft rennet cheese, somewhat like Brie. It is made from whole milk with or without added cream, a mixture of whole and skim milk or from skim milk. Mostly imported from France.

SEMISOFT CHEESE

Most semisoft cheese has been well ripened and consequently has a sharp pungent flavor. This cheese is rarely used for cooking but is excellent for sandwiches, with crackers as dessert or appetizer.

LIEDERKRANZ—An American cheese originated in Ohio. It has a strong odor and pungent flavor somewhat like Limburger but has a slightly softer texture. It should be kept under refrigeration, then warmed to room temperature before using.

LIMBURGER—Soft rennet cheese with strong odor and flavor. Made from whole milk, partly skimmed or entirely skimmed milk. Originated in Belgium but is now made in large quantities in the United States.

PORT DU SALUT—Similar to brick but a little stronger in flavor and a little softer in texture. May show tiny gas holes. Originated in France by Trappist monks. The Canadian version is called Oka or Trappist.

MARBLED CHEESE

Marbled cheese includes those varieties which are delicately streaked throughout with blue or green veins of penicillium mold. Such cheese has a strong, rather salty flavor which is highly prized by cheese-lovers. It is used for dessert or in salads or salad dressings.

BLUE OR BLEU—Similar to Roquefort but made with cows' milk. Originally made in Denmark and France but now widely made in the United States in various dairy sections where limestone caves are available for ripening the cheese.

GORGONZOLA—Marbled cheese made in Italy. Semisoft with sharp flavor. Made from whole milk.

ROQUEFORT—Originally made in France from sheep's milk. It is a semihard rennet cheese with streaks of blue and green mold. The mold is produced by adding a special wheat and barley bread which has been allowed to mold before grinding and combining with the curd. It is ripened in limestone caves. Holes are punched in the cheese during curing to allow air, essential to growth of mold, to enter.

STILTON—Hard rennet cheese with green or blue mold and wrinkled or ridged skin or rind. It is made from cows' milk with cream added and is usually allowed to ripen at least 2 years before being marketed.

GRATED HARD CHEESE

Some types of cheese are so hard that they cannot be sliced, but must be used grated. These are used for cooking or as an accessory to cooked dishes, especially Italian. Most grated cheese is too dry to melt without added moisture. A considerable quantity of the Italian type is made in the United States and also imported from South America.

CACIOCAVALLO—A hard, beet-shaped rennet cheese. Made of whole or partly skimmed milk. Is lightly smoked. Originated in Italy.

PARMESAN—Hard, rennet cheese made from partly skimmed milk. Has a sharp flavor and a green or black rind. Will keep indefinitely.

PROVOLE OR PROVOLONA—Hard, round and held by a net. It is similar to Caciocavallo. Made from cows' milk. Originated in Italy.

ROMANO—Hard, dry, salty with black coating. Originated in Italy.

SAP SAGO—Small, hard and green in color. It is made from skim milk and flavored with leaves from an aromatic species of clover. Use as appetizer or dessert. Made in Switzerland.

SCANDINAVIAN CHEESE

APPETITOST—Semihard, made from sour buttermilk.

GJEDOST—Hard, made from goats' milk, chocolate-colored, sweet taste.

MYSOST—Semisoft whey cheese of light brown color, mild sweetish flavor. Used as a snack or as a dessert.

NOKKELOST—Hard, made from skimmed milk with spices added.

MACARONI AND CHEESE

1 cup broken macaroni	Dash salt
½ cup milk	Dash pepper
½ pound cheese, grated	Buttered crumbs

Boil macaroni in salted water until tender. Drain and rinse with hot water. Place in casserole. Heat milk, add cheese and heat until cheese is melted. Add seasonings and pour over macaroni. Mix with fork, cover with crumbs and bake in moderate oven (350° F.) 15 minutes. Serves 6.

FROMAGE

2 egg yolks	¼ teaspoon salt
1 cup milk	4½ cups grated cheese
Paprika	1 teaspoon butter, melted

Beat egg yolks light, add remaining ingredients, pour into buttered ramekins and bake in slow oven (300° F.) about 20 minutes or until set. Serves 6.

WELSH RAREBIT

No. 1.

2 tablespoons butter
1 teaspoon Worcestershire sauce
½ teaspoon salt
½ teaspoon paprika
1 egg, slightly beaten

¼ teaspoon prepared mustard
½ pound sharp cheese, grated
½ cup ginger ale

Melt butter and add seasonings and cheese. Stir in double boiler until cheese is soft. Add ginger ale, then add egg. Cook until thick. Serve on toast or crackers. Serves 3.

No. 2.

1 pound sharp cheese, grated
1 tablespoon butter, melted
1 teaspoon mustard
1 teaspoon cornstarch

¾ cup milk
1 egg, slightly beaten
½ teaspoon salt
1 tablespoon Worcestershire sauce

Melt cheese with butter in double boiler. Mix mustard and cornstarch, moisten with milk and add with remaining ingredients except toast. Cook until thickened. Serve on toast. Serves 4.

RINKTUM DITTY

1 small onion, chopped fine
1 tablespoon butter
2 cups cooked tomatoes
1 teaspoon salt

¼ teaspoon pepper
2 teaspoons sugar
½ pound cheese, grated
1 egg, beaten

Cook onion in butter until tender. Add tomatoes, salt, pepper and sugar and heat. Add cheese and cook until melted, stirring constantly. Add egg slowly, stirring constantly, and cook 1 minute longer. Serve on buttered toast. Serves 4.

GOLDEN GLOW CASSEROLE

½ cup corn meal
½ teaspoon salt
2½ cups boiling water

½ pound Cheddar cheese
½ cup milk

Add corn meal gradually to boiling salted water, stirring constantly; cook over boiling water 30 to 45 minutes. Pour into shallow pan. When cold cut into 1-inch squares. Melt cheese in top of double boiler. Add milk gradually, stirring constantly. Arrange layers of mush and cheese in casserole and bake in moderate oven (350° F.) 20 minutes. Serves 4.

CHEESE IN ANY FORM IS THE GOURMET'S DELIGHT WHETHER ON A SERVICE TRAY WITH FRUIT OR IN TANGY WELSH RAREBIT

TRY FILLING YOUR BISCUIT DOUGH WITH CHEESE AND CLIP IT INTO A SWEDISH TEA RING OR PILE UP STRIPS AND TUCK THEM, END UP, INTO BAKING CUPS

—Kraft-Phenix Cheese Corporation

CHEESE BISCUIT RING

1 recipe Baking Powder   ¼ pound cheese, grated
Biscuits (p. 118)

Roll dough into rectangle about ½ inch thick. Sprinkle with cheese, roll as jelly roll and bring ends together to form a ring. Place on baking sheet. With sharp scissors make cuts on outside of ring, about 2 inches apart and about ⅔ of the way toward the inside. Turn each section over so cut side is up. Bake in hot oven (400° F.) about 25 minutes or until browned. Serves 8.

CHEESE GEMS—Roll dough ⅓ inch thick, sprinkle with cheese and cut into 2-inch strips. Place 4 strips one on top of the other. Cut into pieces 1¾ inches long. Place each of these sections upright in buttered custard cup. Bake in hot oven (425° F.) 15 to 20 minutes or until browned. Makes 8 to 10.

CHEESE BALLS

1 cup grated cheese   Dash pepper
1 teaspoon flour   1 egg white, stiffly beaten
¼ teaspoon salt

Mix cheese, flour, salt and pepper; fold into beaten egg white. Form into small balls and fry in hot deep fat (375° F.) until brown. Makes 12 balls.

COCKTAIL—Shape sharp cheese into 1-inch balls, spread lightly with mustard and horse-radish and roll in salted cooked rice until completely coated. Fry in very hot deep fat (450° F.) until brown.

BAKED RICE AND CHEESE

3 cups cooked rice   1 cup milk
2 cups grated cheese   Crumbs
½ teaspoon salt   2 tablespoons butter
Cayenne

Arrange layer of cooked rice in greased baking dish, cover with a layer of grated cheese and season with salt and cayenne. Continue adding layers until the dish is almost full. Add enough milk to come half way to top of rice. Cover with crumbs, dot with butter and bake in moderate oven (350° F.) 30 minutes. Serves 6.

CHEESE CROQUETTES

3 tablespoons butter	1 cup milk
⅓ cup flour	2 egg yolks, slightly beaten
¼ teaspoon salt	1½ cups cubed cheese
¼ teaspoon paprika	

Melt butter, blend in flour and add seasonings and milk. Cook until thickened, stirring constantly. Add to egg yolks; when well mixed add cheese. Cool. Shape into balls and fry in hot deep fat (380° F.) until browned. Makes 12.

CHEESE AND RICE CROQUETTES

¼ cup butter	Dash pepper
⅓ cup flour	Dash paprika
1 cup milk	2 cups cooked rice
1 cup grated cheese	Fine dry crumbs
¼ teaspoon salt	1 egg

Melt butter, blend in flour and add milk. Cook until thickened, stirring constantly. Add cheese and heat until melted. Add seasonings. Chill. Add rice and shape into croquettes. Roll in crumbs, in slightly beaten egg and again in crumbs. Brown in hot deep fat (380° F.). Makes 12.

HOMINY AND CHEESE TIMBALES

2 cups cooked hominy	2 teaspoons chopped
⅔ cup grated cheese	pimiento
2 eggs	2 tablespoons chopped
¾ teaspoon salt	parsley
Dash pepper	1 cup milk

Combine ingredients, pour into buttered individual baking dishes, place in pan of hot water and bake in slow oven (325° F.) 30 minutes. Serves 6.

CHEESE AND SPINACH SOUFFLÉ

1 teaspoon chopped onion	1 cup Thick White Sauce
1 cup grated cheese	1 cup chopped cooked
Salt and pepper	spinach

3 eggs, separated

Add onion, cheese and seasonings to white sauce and heat until cheese is melted. Add spinach and well-beaten egg yolks. Mix well. Fold in stiffly beaten egg whites. Pour into buttered loaf pan, place in pan of hot water and bake in moderate oven (350° F.) 45 minutes or until firm. Serves 6.

CHEESE SOUFFLÉ

4 tablespoons butter
4 tablespoons flour
1½ cups hot milk
1 teaspoon salt

Dash cayenne
½ pound sharp cheese, grated
6 eggs, separated

Melt butter, add flour and blend. Add milk and cook until thickened, stirring constantly. Add seasonings and cheese; heat until cheese is melted. Add beaten egg yolks. Cool. Pour into stiffly beaten egg whites and mix well. Bake in 2-quart baking dish in 300° F. oven about 1¼ hours. Serves 6.

CHEESE FONDUE

5 eggs, separated
1¼ cups milk
2 cups soft bread crumbs
¾ teaspoon salt

½ teaspoon dry mustard
½ pound American cheese, shredded

Beat egg yolks and add next 5 ingredients. Fold in stiffly beaten egg whites. Pour into buttered custard cups, place in pan of hot water and bake in slow oven (325° F.) until firm. Unmold and serve at once. Serves 8.

SPAGHETTI LOAF

2 cups broken spaghetti
1 clove garlic
½ pound sharp American cheese
1⅔ cups milk

2 eggs, beaten
¾ teaspoon salt
¼ cup minced parsley
1 tablespoon grated onion

Boil spaghetti with garlic in salted water until tender. Remove garlic, drain spaghetti and rinse. Melt cheese in milk over boiling water; add to eggs. Add salt, parsley, onion and spaghetti; mix thoroughly. Pour into buttered loaf pan. Bake in moderate oven (350° F.) 1 hour. Serves 6.

CHEESE RICE RING

2 tablespoons chopped onion
1 green pepper, chopped
2 tablespoons butter
1½ cups cooked tomatoes

3½ cups cooked rice
¼ teaspoon salt
Dash pepper
1½ cups grated sharp cheese

Cook onion and green pepper in butter until tender. Add tomatoes and rice. Cook slowly until rice has absorbed liquid. Add seasonings and cheese. Pack into buttered ring mold. Unmold onto serving plate and fill with scrambled eggs. Serves 6.

SOUR MILK COTTAGE CHEESE

1 quart sour or clabbered milk   Salt
Cream

Heat milk over hot water until lukewarm (95° F.) and mixture appears to curdle and thicken. Remove from heat, let stand in warm place a few minutes for curd to collect. Turn into cheesecloth-lined strainer and let whey drain off thoroughly. If milk was very sour, rinse curd with cold water and drain again. Tie ends of cloth together and let curd hang until all whey has drained off. Moisten curd with cream and season with salt. Chill. Makes 1 cup.

Use skim or whole milk or buttermilk.

Add ½ teaspoon each grated onion, minced green onion tops and minced chives and a suggestion of garlic or caraway seeds.

SWEET MILK COTTAGE CHEESE

1 rennet tablet   Cream
1 quart milk   Salt

Crush rennet tablet to a powder and dissolve in a few tablespoons of the milk. Heat remaining milk to lukewarm (95° F.), stir in rennet, remove from heat and let stand in warm place until mixture thickens. Break curd, pour into cheesecloth-lined strainer and let drain very thoroughly. Moisten with cream, season with salt and chill. Makes 1 cup.

HOMEMADE CUP CHEESE

4 quarts thick sour milk   3 tablespoons butter
1 teaspoon salt

Cut through milk several times with a long sharp knife, then heat slowly to 90° F. or scald until curd is very dry. Remove from heat and place in a wet cheesecloth bag. Press under a heavy weight 12 to 24 hours or until cheese is dry. Force through a cheese sieve or grate fine. Place in a wooden bowl, cover with a heavy cloth and keep in a warm place 3 to 7 days or until soft and ripe, stirring occasionally. Then place in a skillet and cook, stirring constantly until smooth. Add salt and butter, mix well and pour into cups or bowls. Makes 3 cups.

VEGETABLES

ROOTS, stems, leaves, buds, seeds and fruits of plants used as food are called vegetables. They classify as follows:

ROOTS—Beets, carrots, parsnips, turnips, salsify, radishes, horseradish, rutabagas, celeriac, sweet potatoes, yams, cassava.

STEMS—Enlarged underground stems called tubers: Irish potatoes and Jerusalem artichokes, dasheen or taro, yautia, kohlrabi, fennel.

STEM AND BUD—Asparagus.

BULBS—Onions (green, called scallions), leek, garlic, shallot.

LEAF STALKS—Celery, rhubarb.

LEAVES—Lettuce, endive, spinach, romaine, watercress, chard, chives, chicory, tops of beets, turnips, dandelion, fennel, mustard, dill, and parsley, escarole, Chinese cabbage, collards, kale.

BUDS—Cabbage (terminal), Brussels sprouts (axillary).

FLOWERING HEADS—Cauliflower, French artichoke, broccoli.

FRUIT—Cucumbers, squash, eggplant, peppers, okra, pumpkin, tomatoes, string beans, green peas, green corn, vegetable marrow, zucchini, chayote, Lima beans.

SEEDS—Peas, beans, lentils, corn, rice, Lima beans, soybeans, grains, cereals.

FUNGI—Mushrooms, truffles.

Selection of Vegetables

Buy vegetables in their season. Many vegetables are in the market the year round, and modern agriculture has greatly extended the season for many others but some, when out of season, lack flavor and freshness.

Vegetables should be fresh, firm (not hard), and ripe. Do not buy vegetables that are old, withered, moldy or bruised, underripe or overripe; there is no saving in cost from purchasing such vegetables. Head vegetables should be solid, with few waste leaves. Cauliflower should be white and firm, with no blemishes. Leafy vegetables should not be wilted. Peas and beans should have crisp pods. Buy vegetables of medium size and regular shape.

Buy only the amount of summer vegetables you can use immediately, because they deteriorate in quality very quickly and are best when cooked soon after gathering.

Winter vegetables may be bought in larger amounts if there is a suitable dry, cool place for storage.

Get acquainted with vegetables that you or your family have never eaten. For the first time buy only enough for your own lunch and cook them after your favorite method. If that is successful, try them on the family. If not, try again with another recipe, until you find one you think they will like.

Care of Vegetables

SUMMER VEGETABLES—If these are not to be cooked at once, they should be put in the refrigerator or some other cool dry place. Peas and corn, especially, should be cooked soon after they are gathered, because they lose their sweetness on standing. Lettuce should be sprinkled and wrapped in a heavy cloth or paper, and put into the refrigerator until it is used. Salad greens keep a week or more in mechanically cooled refrigerators if they are washed and placed in closely covered enamel or porcelain containers after being well drained. Cloths or paper wrappings dry out too quickly in mechanically cooled refrigerators.

Cut the stems of wilted vegetables and plunge into cold water to freshen.

WINTER VEGETABLES—These should be in good condition, firm and uninjured and stored in a dry, cool, well ventilated place. Most of them keep better if they are piled up so that the air is excluded. Squash, however, keep better if they are spread out so that they do not touch one another. Squash and sweet potatoes require a warmer place than other vegetables. Vegetables cannot be kept successfully in an unpartitioned cellar containing a furnace. Vegetables should not be overripe when stored, but should be nearly mature. Parsnips improve in flavor if they are allowed to freeze before they are stored. They should be watched carefully and if they show signs of spoiling, should be used at once or removed from the other vegetables.

Preparation of Vegetables for Cooking

Wash all vegetables before cooking, even though they look clean. A vegetable brush is almost a necessity. Soak wilted vegetables before peeling them. Vegetables that are soaked after they are peeled lose some soluble food materials. Dry winter vegetables may be improved by soaking them for several hours. Scrape thin-skinned vegetables; pare thick-skinned vegetables or remove the skin after cooking. Make thin parings except in the case of turnips, from which a thick layer of corky material should be removed. Discard decayed vegetables.

Many vegetables, particularly of the bud, head and fruit groups, need to be immersed for a period in cold salt water. This freshens the fiber and drives out any insects that have taken refuge in crevices. Leaf vegetables need to be washed in several waters, the first of which should be salted for the same reason. The leaves should be lifted out of the water rather than the water poured off. This permits any sand to sink to the bottom of the pan. A tablespoon of liquid ammonia added to the last gallon of wash water will remove the last film that carries an earthy flavor.

What Vegetables Provide

The appreciation of vegetables as food has greatly increased in recent years with an extended understanding of their peculiar values. The modern woman realizes that these values, having been paid for at the market, must be retained in the preparation, if her family is to benefit by her intelligent purchases. Vegetables are one of the three groups of food that protect growth and vitality and preserve the characteristics of youth, the others being milk and fruits. The importance of these protective foods may be realized by the fact that scientists have found an astonishing relation between the early onset of old age and the food habits of persons involved. The modern woman knows that vegetables provide not only starches and sugars for energy, as well as several forms of protein, but what is most important they provide impressive amounts of Vitamins A, B, C, E, and G, in addition to mineral salts. (See pages 39 to 44.) These mineral salts are especially Calcium, Phosphorus, Iron, Copper, Manganese, and Sulphur, as well as Iodine, in vegetables grown along the seashore. Besides all this, she knows that the generous use of many vegetables helps to keep up the body's normal alkaline balance which contributes so very largely to sound health and vitality.

Cooking to Retain These Values

Many vegetables can be and are eaten uncooked with all their values intact. But many more need to be cooked before they can be served. Preparation by cooking should result in the least possible loss while it enhances values not otherwise available. For this reason cooking should:

1. Swell and burst the starch cell so that the center is softened and made digestible.
2. Sterilize the vegetable thoroughly.
3. Break up tough fiber so it is edible and digestible.
4. Release food proteins and minerals from their fiber cells.
5. Provide hot food.
6. Increase many flavors and some colors.

BAKING is the best method to secure all these results and still preserve Vitamins and minerals. Dry baking in their skins, generally used for potatoes, sweet potatoes, squash, turnips, carrots, onions, and parsnips, is a simple method whereby the vegetable is packed in a pan or laid on the rack of a hot oven to remain until just tender when pierced with a sharp fork. Baking, however, also includes the roasting of whole vegetables with meat, gravy, or fat, especially when potatoes or sweet potatoes are scraped, thus preserving mineral values just under the skin.

AU GRATIN AND SCALLOPING are other forms of baking, especially when fresh vegetables are used. In the latter method, layers of the vegetable are alternated in a baking dish or ring mold with white sauce, cream or milk, and seasonings, and in the former method a covering of buttered bread crumbs or buttered crumbs and cheese is added. Leftover cooked vegetables may be prepared by these methods also, but the Vitamin and mineral value will be determined by the first cooking. Only baking in the jacket will insure the preservation of the Vitamins.

BROILING is the exposure to direct heat and can be used for some vegetables. The minerals will be less injured than the Vitamins, for the high heat destroys most of the latter.

DEEP FAT FRYING, next to baking, is another satisfactory way to retain most of the food values. The vegetable is sliced or cut into convenient form, dipped in egg and crumbs or batter, and immersed in enough very hot fat to cover well. This permits quick cooking with little loss.

In SAUTÉING, the shredded or broken vegetable is turned into a shallow pan or skillet in which a small amount of fat has been heated. Cooking takes longer and more fat is absorbed by the food. hence, the process is not always advisable.

BOILING does the most damage to fresh vegetables, yet it is used most frequently by the largest number of homemakers. Although there are methods that reduce the losses to a minimum, the modern woman will remember that boiling is to be used least often, and always to be overbalanced by the better methods. Most of the mineral salts occurring in vegetables are easily dissolved in water and the loss of Vitamins during boiling takes place in several ways. They may be destroyed by overheating, by prolonged exposure to the air, and by dissolving out in the cooking water. When this is drained off and discarded, the principal food values gained by the intelligent buying of vegetables has been thrown away. In every case only the smallest possible amount of water should be used and it should be boiling rapidly when the vegetables are dropped in. They should be cooked only until just tender, and by this time most of the water has been evaporated. Greens such as spinach, chard, and dandelions need only the water that clings to the leaves. They go into a cold pot with the heat turned on after the vegetable is in the kettle.

To BOIL VEGETABLES THE PROPER WAY, four methods must be taken into account:

1. The green vegetables are best cooked in water that is slightly alkaline. In many sections of the country, drinking water may be decidedly acid. If there is any doubt, add a bit of baking soda the size of a pinhead. No drinking water would be acid enough to need more. Use an uncovered kettle and cook only until tender to the fork. If overcooked, green vegetables turn brownish because of chemical changes in the coloring matter, the fine flavor is ruined, while food values are lost.

2. White fresh vegetables such as cabbage, cauliflower, and onion are

strong flavored, due to their special oils. Hard water changes these oils so that the white color turns to yellow or brown. To prevent this, add 1 teaspoon of lemon juice or white vinegar. Drop the vegetable into enough rapidly boiling water to cover and cook with the kettle uncovered until just tender to the fork. Add the drained water, if any, to your soup stock.

3. The red color in vegetables is produced by acid and needs to be kept that way. Tomatoes usually have enough acid of their own to keep the color, but beets and red cabbage need a teaspoon of lemon juice or white vinegar. Cook in a small amount of water in a covered kettle.

4. Yellow vegetables are among the most valuable and stable. That rich yellow color is not only beauty but actually the foundation of Vitamin A. Not much damage can be done to it although the minerals and other Vitamins can still be destroyed if the vegetable is carelessly handled.

In general, the destruction of Vitamins is reduced when vegetables are boiled at high temperatures for the shortest possible time, in the smallest possible amount of water. Then the minerals, too, will be saved.

STEAMING as a method of cooking vegetables is valuable for those that can stand a high temperature for a long period, or those that are cooked in the meat pot so that the extracted minerals and Vitamins are used in the gravy. It is particularly good for dried and starchy ones. The long, slow process gives the starch cell time to swell and gelatinize. It is most valuable at high altitudes, because the extra pressure keeps the steam at 212° F. or more, while in the open-air cooking the high altitude reduces the boiling point below 212° F.

WATERLESS COOKING of fresh vegetables is any process in which no water is added. The water in the vegetable itself does the cooking. A thick-walled kettle with a tight-fitting lid is the necessary equipment. Very low heat is used, and the vegetable is tender in a very short time because neither heat nor steam escapes. No minerals are lost and the loss of Vitamins is almost as low as in baking.

All cooking of vegetables reduces the Vitamin C content, although tomatoes and the baked potato manage to retain most of theirs. To insure an adequate daily supply of Vitamin C, the modern woman never loses sight of the fact that some fresh fruits and vegetables must be served every day.

ARTICHOKES

The FRENCH artichoke is boiled in salted water, served hot with brown butter or Hollandaise sauce, or cold with mayonnaise. The spiny choke below the leaves and above the heart must be discarded. The JERUSALEM artichoke is washed, pared, boiled like a potato and dressed with seasoning, melted butter and minced parsley.

ASPARAGUS

Trim off hard stalks and scales to the head. Tie in bunches, stand upright in boiling salted water. After 10 minutes turn into loaf pan and continue with heat under the stems. Serve with browned butter or Hollandaise.

GOLDENROD ASPARAGUS

1 No. 1 can asparagus tips	2 cups Medium White Sauce
3 hard-cooked eggs	Buttered toast
12 stuffed olives	

Heat asparagus in juice. Chop egg whites and olives and add to sauce. Arrange hot asparagus on toast, cover with sauce and garnish with sieved egg yolks. Serves 6.

BOSTON BAKED BEANS

2 cups pea beans	½ teaspoon salt
1 small onion	½ teaspoon dry mustard
⅛ pound salt pork, scored	2 tablespoons molasses

Soak beans in cold water overnight. Simmer until skins begin to burst, turn into the bean pot over onion. Bury pork in beans, leaving only the rind exposed. Mix salt, mustard and molasses in a cup, fill with hot water, stir until well mixed and pour over beans. Add water to cover and bake in a slow oven (300° F.) 6 to 8 hours, adding more water to cover until the last hour. Remove cover and raise pork to the surface to brown.

QUICK METHOD—Use same ingredients as above but do not soak beans overnight. Cover with cold water and heat slowly to boiling. Simmer for 15 minutes, drain and cover with boiling water. Add onion and pork and simmer until beans are tender. Turn into bean pot and bake as above.

SOYBEANS

Of the many varieties of soybeans grown in this country, the yellow variety is the most popular for cooking purposes, though the black and green beans are used, and are particularly good in soup. Soybeans require longer cooking than white beans, but the length of time required is lessened if the beans are soaked for twelve hours before cooking.

BAKED SOYBEANS

2 cups yellow soybeans	2 tablespoons molasses
1 tablespoon salt	1 teaspoon mustard
1 small onion	¼ pound fat salt pork

Soak the beans for twelve hours, then heat to boiling and simmer until tender. Unless the beans are tender before they are baked, they will not be good. Prepare as directed for "Baked Beans." Eight to ten hours will be required to bake them.

BOILED LIMA BEANS

1 quart green Lima beans or 2 cups dried Lima beans	1 tablespoon fat
Salt and pepper	1 cup milk or cream if desired

If the green beans are used, put them into just enough boiling water to cover, and boil slowly until tender. Salt the water just before cooking is completed. Add fat and salt and pepper to taste. If desired, a cup of milk or cream may be added and the beans allowed to simmer in it for a moment.

If dried beans are used they may be soaked twelve hours in plenty of cold water, and boiled in the same water with one-eighth teaspoon of soda added for each quart of water; or the process may be hastened by soaking them for one hour and simmering them for two hours. If they are not soaked at all, they can be made tender by simmering for two and one-half hours. The water should be drained off before the milk or cream is added.

STRING BEANS

1 quart string beans	Salt and pepper	Butter

Wash beans, string and snap or cut into short pieces. Cover with least possible amount of boiling water and cook gently

TIE YOUR PUNGENT VEGETABLES SNUGLY INTO VEGETABLE PARCHMENT BEFORE PLUNGING INTO BOILING WATER. IT KEEPS THE HOUSE SMELLING SWEET

OR COVER WHITE VEGETABLES CLOSELY—A SMALL AMOUNT OF WATER AND PIECE OF BUTTER— COOK THEM IN THEIR OWN STEAM

POTATOES KEEP HOT WHILE WHIPPING IF YOU CARRY THE BEATER TO THEM.

ARTICHOKES WITH
HOLLANDAISE SAUCE
ARE WORKS OF ART

TENDER GREEN
ASPARAGUS WITH
CHEESE FONDUE AND
A STRIP OF PIMIENTO
FOR COLOR CON-
TRAST

until tender. Salt the water just before cooking is completed. When done, drain and season with butter, salt and pepper.

If the flavor of salt pork is liked cut slice of salt pork into small pieces and fry until brown, then add one tablespoon flour, one cup hot water, and the beans. Simmer for a few minutes and serve hot.

BOILED BEETS

Wash the beets thoroughly and remove the leaves, being very careful not to break off the little fibers and rootlets which retain the juices and coloring matter. Use plenty of water in cooking. If the beets are tough and withered, soak them for twenty-four hours in plenty of cold water before beginning to cook them.

Try with a fork, and when they are tender drop them into a pan of cold water and slip off the skins with the hands. If small, serve whole. If large, slice those to be used immediately, place in a dish and season with salt, pepper, and butter or savory fat. A teaspoon of sugar may be added also if the beets are not naturally sweet enough. Set them over boiling water to heat thoroughly and serve hot, with or without vinegar. Cold beets left over may be covered with vinegar and used as pickles.

BEET GREENS

Carefully wash and clean young beets, leaving roots and tops together. Put them into a kettle with very little boiling water and allow them to cook until just tender. Salt the water just before cooking is completed. Drain as dry as possible, in a colander. Chop, if desired. Serve hot with vinegar or with butter, salt and pepper.

BROCCOLI

Broccoli is a variety of cauliflower that is green instead of white. It was very popular in Colonial gardens and continued to be grown and sold along the east coast but gained popularity very slowly among native Americans. Within the last ten years growers on the west coast have promoted it and it is now as popular and often more abundant and lower priced than cauliflower. Shipped in ice from early cuttings, even the largest stalks are often tender. Choose heads and leaves that are bright green and crisp. Cut off only such portions of the stalk as are too hard and tough to admit the knife. Wash under running water and refrigerate, if not to be used at once. When ready to cook, use a deep kettle just large enough for the head or heads and bring salted water to a rapid boil. Insert carefully, stem end down, leave uncovered and when the water stops boiling add soda the size of a small pea to the water around the stems. The heads should not be submerged. When water boils up again they will cook more slowly than the stems and both will be tender in 15-25 minutes. If the heads are under water, they cook so much more rapidly that they will be mushy before the stems are tender. Broccoli heads, stems and leaves are valuable sources of vitamins A and G, as well as iron and calcium.

Serve with brown butter sauce, brown butter and crumbs, Hollandaise sauce or au gratin. Broccoli can be used instead of spinach for cream soup, especially when the green color is wanted.

BRUSSELS SPROUTS

Pick off the dead leaves from the sprouts, soak the sprouts in cold salted water for one-half hour, wash them and put them on the fire in plenty of boiling water. Boil in an uncovered saucepan until tender. Just before they are done, salt the water. Drain in a colander. Reheat; season with salt and pepper, and serve with cream sauce or melted butter.

BOILED CABBAGE

Cut the cabbage into desired shapes. Place it in a kettle with a generous amount of water. Cook uncovered until just tender. Add salt to the water just before cooking is completed. Drain, add butter or bacon fat, salt and pepper.

A little milk or cream may be added or it may be creamed or scalloped or served au gratin.

SCALLOPED CABBAGE WITH CHEESE

1 small head cabbage	1½ cups medium white sauce
2 cups grated cheese	½ to ¾ cup bread-crumbs

Cook the cabbage as directed for boiled cabbage. Into a greased baking-dish, put a layer of cabbage, then a layer of cheese, then a layer of white sauce, and continue to add layers until the ingredients are all used. Cover the top of the mixture with the crumbs, which may be mixed with a little melted butter, and bake in a moderate oven (350°-400° F.) for about twenty minutes, or until the crumbs are brown.

CARROTS, TOASTED

To serve carrots as a separate vegetable, scrape and wash; leave young carrots whole and cut old carrots in slices lengthwise or crosswise. Boil them until tender (15-30 minutes) in water containing one teaspoon sugar. Just before cooking is completed, salt the water. Drain, add butter, and seasoning or roll in butter, then in corn flakes and brown in oven at 350° F.

CARROTS AND PEAS

No. 1.

2 cups cubed, cooked carrots	3 tablespoons butter or other
1 cup cooked peas, fresh or	fat or
canned	Medium white sauce

Combine the carrots and peas, reheat and serve with melted butter or any savory fat such as bacon fat; or combine with a white sauce. Season to taste with salt and pepper.

No. 2—WITH GREEN MINT—Combine the carrots and peas, as directed above, add one-half cup mint leaves and a little boiling water and boil for five minutes. Drain, add salt and pepper, a generous amount of butter and a sprinkle of sugar. Set in the oven until the sugar melts. Serve with a garnish of fresh mint leaves.

CARROT MOLDS

.2 cups grated raw carrot	1 teaspoon salt
½ cup bread-crumbs	2 tablespoons melted fat
2 eggs	½ cup milk

Wash, scrape and grate the carrots and mix with the crumbs. Beat the eggs and add to them the salt, fat and milk. Add this mixture to the carrot and crumb mixture. Fill a greased ring mold or popover cups, set in a pan of hot water and bake in a slow oven (250°-325° F.) until firm.

BOILED CAULIFLOWER

Remove the green leaves from the cauliflower and cut off any bruised or dirty spots. Place it, top downward, in a deep bowl of cold, salted water and allow it to stay there about half an hour to draw out dust and other impurities. Cook it, whole or broken into flowerets, in boiling water, uncovered. Just before cooking is completed (15-30 minutes) salt the water. Lift out the cauliflower carefully and allow it to drain in a warm place. Pour medium white sauce over it or send the sauce to the table in a sauce-boat, or serve it with melted butter and paprika.

Sometimes hot boiled cauliflower is sprinkled with grated cheese and then with buttered crumbs and baked to a light brown in a moderate oven (400° F.), or it may be sprinkled with the grated cheese and served without baking.

SCALLOPED CAULIFLOWER

1 medium cauliflower
2 hard-cooked eggs or
4 tablespoons grated cheese

1½ cups medium white sauce
Bread-crumbs

Break the cauliflower into flowerets before boiling. Drain. Place a layer of the cooked cauliflower in a greased baking-dish, then a layer of egg slices or of grated cheese, then a layer of white sauce. Repeat until all the cauliflower is used. Put a layer of crumbs over the top and bake in a moderate oven (350°-400° F.) from fifteen to thirty minutes. A bit of cayenne pepper or paprika may be added for additional seasoning.

CREAMED CELERY

2 cups celery cut into 1-inch pieces
½ cup milk

2 tablespoons flour
2 tablespoons butter
Salt and pepper

Wash the stalks clean and cut them into pieces. Place the celery in a saucepan, cover with boiling water and boil until tender (about half an hour), by which time the water should be reduced to about one-half cup. Make a sauce with the celery water, milk, flour and butter. Add the cooked celery and season with salt and pepper.

SCALLOPED CELERY

Stew celery, as directed in the preceding recipe, using all milk in the sauce instead of part celery water. Turn the creamed celery into a greased ramekin, sprinkle with grated cheese and buttered crumbs and bake in a moderate oven (350°-400° F.) until it is a golden brown (15-30 minutes).

CELERIAC

Not every housewife knows celeriac, but it is well worth adding to her list of vegetable acquaintances. It is a variety of celery grown for its turnip-like root instead of for the blanched stalks. The flavor is similar to that of celery.

To prepare celeriac, trim off the tops, wash and pare the bulb, drop it into boiling water and cook about one-half hour, or until tender. Add the salt just before cooking is completed. It may then be prepared in the same way as creamed or scalloped celery, or may be used cold, sliced or diced, in salads.

BOILED GREEN CORN

To have this vegetable in perfection, the husks should be left on until just before it is to be served. Drop the ears into boiling water and cook 3 to 7 minutes, according to the size of the corn. Do not salt the water, as this toughens the corn. Or fit ears with only the clinging water into a closely-covered Dutch oven. Allow to steam at medium heat 15-20 minutes.

Lay a napkin on the serving-plate, pile the corn upon this, cover it with the corners of the napkin and serve.

CORN SOUFFLÉ

1 tablespoon fat	Pepper
1 tablespoon flour	1 boiled pimiento
½ cup milk	2 cups corn pulp
1 teaspoon salt	2 eggs
¼ teaspoon paprika	

Made a white sauce, using the fat, flour, milk and seasoning. Rub the pimiento through a sieve and add it to the sauce. Add the corn to the mixture. Cool slightly, then add the well-beaten egg yolks and fold in the stiffly beaten egg whites. Turn into a greased baking dish, set the dish in a pan of hot water, and bake in a moderate oven (375° F.) until the egg is set, about thirty minutes.

CORN OYSTERS

2 cups corn pulp
2 eggs
2 tablespoons flour

2 tablespoons fat
Salt and pepper

If fresh corn is used, grate it from the cob with a coarse grater. If canned corn is used, select one of the sieved varieties. Beat the egg-yolks and whites separately and add to the grated corn, with flour and fat, salt and pepper. Drop the batter from a spoon into hot fat (360°-370° F.) and fry light brown (2-3 minutes). Drain on soft paper. Serve hot.

CORN PUDDING OR DEVILED CORN

2 tablespoons fat
2 tablespoons flour
1½ cups milk
1 teaspoon salt
¼ teaspoon mustard
Paprika

2 cups corn pulp
1 egg
1 tablespoon Worcestershire sauce
Buttered crumbs

Make a sauce of fat, flour, milk, and seasonings, add corn, egg slightly beaten, and Worcestershire sauce. Pour into a baking-dish, cover with buttered crumbs and bake in a moderate oven (350°-400° F.) fifteen to thirty minutes.

BAKED CORN AND TOMATOES

2 cups cooked corn
2 cups tomatoes
1 teaspoon salt
Pepper

1 teaspoon sugar
1 cup fresh bread-crumbs
3 tablespoons fat

Mix seasonings with the corn and tomatoes and pour all into a greased baking-dish. Spread the crumbs over the top, dot them with the fat, and bake in a moderate oven (350°-400° F.) for one-half hour. This is a satisfactory way of utilizing left-over corn or tomatoes.

CUCUMBER CUPS

This makes a dainty dish for luncheon. Cut the unpared vegetables into sections two inches long and cook until tender in water salted just before cooking is completed. Scoop out the

A MIDSUMMER NIGHT'S DREAM COME TRUE IN THE DELICATE, TEMPTING FLAVOR OF CORN ON THE COB

—National Dairy Council

COOKED CARROTS ROLLED IN BREAD CRUMBS AND BAKED ARE EASY TO MAKE AND SERVE

A NEW PRESENTATION OF PEAS IN A CARROT RING, WITH SLICED CARROTS AND PARSLEY GARNISH

center of each section, leaving one-half-inch thickness all around the sides, as well as on the bottom, thus making green cups of the vegetable. These cups may be filled with creamed chicken, sweetbreads, mushrooms or any other filling held together with white sauce.

STEWED CUCUMBERS

3 cucumbers	1 cup boiling water
6 slices toast	½ teaspoon salt
2 tablespoons fat	Pepper
2 tablespoons flour	1½ tablespoons lemon-juice

Peel medium-sized cucumbers and cut them into quarters lengthwise. Place in a shallow pan, cover with the boiling water and stew gently for ten to twenty minutes. Add salt just before cooking is completed. When done, lay them carefully on toasted bread, make a sauce of the flour, fat, water in which cucumbers were cooked, and seasonings, cook until smooth, and pour the sauce over the stewed cucumbers.

CUCUMBER SAUTÉ

4 cucumbers	Salt and pepper
Butter	Minced parsley or chives
Flour	

Pare and quarter the cucumbers and boil them, without any water, for three minutes. Drain; season with salt and pepper; roll in flour and sauté in a little butter until tender. Sprinkle with parsley or chives just before the cooking is completed.

DANDELION GREENS

2 pounds dandelion greens	1 tablespoon butter
Salt and pepper	

Dandelions should be used before they blossom, as they become bitter after that time. Cut off the roots, pick the greens over carefully, and wash them well in several waters. Place them in a kettle, add a little boiling water, and boil until tender. Salt the water just before cooking is completed. When done, lift them into a colander, press them to drain off all the water, and chop. Add butter, salt and pepper.

FRIED EGGPLANT

1 eggplant	Cracker-dust or bread-crumbs
Salt	Egg

Cut the eggplant into one-half-inch slices, pare and sprinkle each slice with salt. Lay slice upon slice and place a plate upon the top. Let stand two hours. The salt will draw out the disagreeably bitter flavor. Half an hour before serving, wipe each slice dry, dip in beaten egg, then in cracker dust or fine bread-crumbs, and sauté in hot fat. Put a pan in the oven or in some other place where it can be kept hot; lay a piece of absorbent paper in the pan, and upon it place the slices as they come crisp and brown from the frying-pan. Serve on a hot platter with the slices overlapping.

STUFFED EGGPLANT

1 eggplant	½ cup water
2 tablespoons butter	2 cups crumbs
Salt and pepper	

Cut the eggplant in half lengthwise and scoop out the center pulp, leaving the rind about one-half inch thick so that the shape may be firm. Cover the shells with cold water. Chop the pulp fine, season it with salt, pepper, and butter, and cook in a frying-pan for ten minutes, stirring well, then add water and one cup of bread-crumbs. Drain the shells, sprinkle the interior of each with salt and pepper and fill them with the mixture. Spread the remaining crumbs over the tops. Place the halves in a baking-dish or deep pan, and pour enough hot water into the pan to come one-third up the sides of the plant. Bake in a moderate oven (350°-375° F.) one-half hour, and serve hot.

CREAMED CHICORY OR ENDIVE

Wash the plant carefully and pick off the outer green leaves, leaving only the white part. Boil until tender, drain well, return it to the kettle, and nearly cover with medium white sauce, which should be well seasoned.

BRAISED FENNEL

2 pounds fennel
1/3 cup butter
1 teaspoon salt

1 cup meat stock
Dash pepper

Wash and clean fennel. Cut into 1-inch pieces. Simmer in butter until lightly browned. Add salt, meat stock and pepper and simmer until tender, about 20 minutes. Serves 6.

BUTTERED FENNEL

2 pounds fennel
Boiling water
1 teaspoon salt

4 tablespoons butter, melted
Pepper

Wash and scrape fennel. Cut bulb and stalks into 1-inch pieces. Cover with boiling water, add salt and cook, covered, 15 to 20 minutes. Drain. Serve with butter and a dash of pepper. Serves 6.

BUTTERED KALE

4 pounds kale

Salt, pepper and butter

Wash kale and remove all the heavy stems. Cook uncovered in boiling water 25 to 35 minutes or until tender. (Makes about 3 1/2 cups.) Drain and chop. Season with salt, pepper and butter. Serves 6 to 8.

SCALLOPED KALE

3 cups cooked kale
3 hard-cooked eggs, chopped

1 cup Medium White Sauce
1 cup grated cheese

Combine kale with eggs and white sauce. Arrange in alternate layers with cheese and bake in hot oven (400° F.) 15 minutes. Serves 6.

CREAMED KOHLRABI

6 kohlrabi
Boiling water
1 teaspoon salt

Paprika
1 egg yolk
2 cups Thin White Sauce

Pare kohlrabi and cut into cubes or slices. Let stand in mixture of cold water and 2 tablespoons vinegar for 1 hour. Rinse. Cook uncovered in boiling salted water 20 to 35 minutes. (Makes about 4 cups cooked.) Drain. Add paprika and egg yolk to white sauce and pour over kohlrabi. Serves 6.

LEEKS AU GRATIN

2 bunches leeks
Boiling water
1 teaspoon salt

Pepper
½ cup grated cheese

Wash and trim leeks. Cook until tender, about 15 minutes, in boiling salted water to cover. Drain. Arrange in buttered baking dish and sprinkle with pepper and cheese. Heat under broiler until cheese is melted. Serves 8.

SAUTÉED LENTILS

2 cups lentils
2 tablespoons fat

Salt and pepper

Wash lentils and soak overnight in cold water. Drain and cook, covered, in boiling salted water, 2 to 3 hours or until tender. When they will crush quickly between the fingers they are done. Melt fat in frying pan, add lentils, salt and pepper and cook 15 minutes. Makes 4 to 5 cups.

Boil ham bone or small pieces of bacon or salt pork with lentils if desired.

Add 2 onions, minced, and fry with lentils if desired.

MACEDOINE OF VEGETABLES

2 cups mixed cooked vege-
tables
1 teaspoon beef extract or
½ cup stock

1 teaspoon sugar
½ cup water
Salt and pepper
2 tablespoons butter

Mix all the ingredients together and cook 8 to 10 minutes, shaking the pan now and then. Serve hot. Serves 6.

MUSHROOMS

To PREPARE cultivated mushrooms brush gently or rinse in cold water. Separate stems and caps for ease in cooking. Drop them into water containing the juice of ½ lemon or 1 tablespoon vinegar to prevent discoloration. Dice, slice, quarter or use whole.

SAUTÉED MUSHROOMS

Wash 1 pound mushrooms, dry and leave whole or slice. Combine 2 tablespoons butter, ¼ teaspoon salt, 1 tablespoon grated onion in frying pan, add mushrooms and cook on low heat for several minutes until slightly browned. Remove and serve hot.

CREAMED MUSHROOMS

No. 1.

2 tablespoons fat	1 teaspoon salt
1 tablespoon flour	½ cup boiling water
½ cup cream	2 cups mushrooms, fresh or
¼ teaspoon pepper	canned

Make a sauce of the fat, flour, cream and seasoning. Prepare mushrooms and stew them in boiling water until tender. Add, without draining, to cream sauce. Serve very hot.

No. 2.

1½ tablespoons fat	Salt and pepper
1½ tablespoons flour	1½ cups cooked mushrooms
1 egg-yolk	fresh or canned
1 cup milk	

Prepare a white sauce of the fat, flour, milk and seasonings. Add the cooked mushrooms to the sauce and cook gently for several minutes. Just before serving, add the beaten egg-yolk and reheat.

MUSHROOMS UNDER GLASS

2 tablespoons butter	1 slice toast
½ tablespoon lemon-juice	6 mushroom caps
Salt and pepper	¼ cup heavy cream
½ teaspoon minced parsley	

The quantities given allow for service of only one person.

Baking dishes with bell-shaped glass covers are obtainable at most house-furnishing stores. The mushrooms should be served with the covers on.

Cream butter and add lemon-juice, drop by drop, salt, pepper and minced parsley. Cover the bottom of an individual baking-dish with a circular piece of toast three-eighths of an inch thick, wetting the under side with half the sauce already made. Pile mushroom caps, cleaned and peeled, on the toast and pour over them the remainder of the sauce and the heavy cream. Cover with glass and bake in a quick oven (400°-450° F.) about twenty-five minutes. Save the stalks, if tender, or stew with skins in a little water to make stock for seasoning sauces and gravies.

BAKED OR ROASTED MUSHROOMS

36 mushroom caps   Butter
Salt and pepper   6 slices toast

Select mushrooms that are plump and are truly little cups. Prepare caps as directed. Place them upside down in a baking-dish, sprinkle with salt and pepper and place a bit of butter in each cup. Set the pan in a quick oven (400°-450° F.) and cook for fifteen minutes. The cups will be filled with their own liquor. Serve on toast, very hot.

BOILED OKRA

No. 1.

1 quart tender okra pods   3 tablespoons butter
Salt and pepper   1 tablespoon vinegar

Test the okra by breaking off the tips of the pods. If there are tough strings that will not break easily the pod is too old to be served as a vegetable and should be kept for a soup or sauce which is to be strained. The pods of okra are so sticky that special care is needed to avoid breaking them during the cleaning. Wash them well, and remove the stems, place in sufficient boiling water to cover them and boil until tender (20-40 minutes). Add salt just before cooking is completed. Okra should boil very slowly, as rapid boiling will break it in pieces. When it is tender, turn into a colander to drain, then lay it in a serving dish. Melt the butter, add the vinegar and a little salt and pepper; mix well, and pour the sauce over the okra.

No. 2.

2 cups okra   Salt and pepper
2 tomatoes   1 tablespoon butter

Test and wash the okra as above; remove stems and cut the pods into slices, crosswise. Place in a granite stew-pan, just cover with boiling water and simmer until tender (20-40 minutes). Add the tomatoes, peeled and chopped, and stew for ten minutes longer. Add butter, salt and pepper, and serve.

BOILED ONIONS

Peel the onions. If they are very large cut them in quarters. Cook in boiling water, uncovered, until tender (30-60 min-

utes). Just before cooking is completed, add salt to taste.
When cooked, drain well, season with butter and pepper and
serve hot.

CREAMED ONIONS

In peeling the onions remove all of the green leaves, for they
should be as white as milk when served. Drop them into boiling water and boil uncovered for ten minutes. Drain, add
freshly boiling water and continue cooking until tender (30-
60 minutes). Just before cooking is completed, add salt. Drain
thoroughly, place in a serving-dish and pour medium white
sauce over them. If the onions are large they may be quartered
before they are cooked.

STUFFED ONIONS

6 medium to large onions
½ cup chopped ham or
   chopped green pepper
½ cup soft bread crumbs
Pepper

½ teaspoon salt
1 tablespoon fat
Fine dry bread crumbs
½ cup milk

Remove a slice from the top of each onion and parboil the
onions until almost tender. Drain and remove the centers, leaving six little cups. Chop the onion that was scooped out and
combine with it the ham and soft crumbs. Add seasoning and
fat, refill the onion cups. Place them in a baking-dish, cover
with crumbs, add the milk, and bake in a hot oven (400°-450°
F.) until tender.

CREAMED PARSNIPS

12 medium-sized parsnips
1 cup milk
Salt and pepper

2 tablespoons flour
2 tablespoons fat

Young parsnips are most desirable, but old ones may be used
if the woody center is removed.

Wash and scrape the parsnips, and boil them until tender.
Drain and cut them into small pieces. Make a sauce of the
fat, flour, milk and seasonings. Add the cooked parsnips and
serve.

FRIED PARSNIPS

12 medium-sized parsnips   Salt and pepper
Flour or fine crumbs

Scrape and boil the parsnips until tender. If old, remove the woody centers. Drain, and when cold, cut them in long, thin slices about one-third of an inch thick, and season each slice with salt and pepper. Dip the slices in flour or fine crumbs and sauté in fat or oil until both sides are thoroughly browned. Drain well and serve very hot.

BOILED PEAS

2 quarts peas in the shell   2 tablespoons butter
Salt and pepper

Fresh peas should not be shelled until just before they are needed for cooking. Look them over carefully after shelling, taking out any tendrils that may be mixed with them. Wash and cook until tender in a covered pan in just enough boiling water to prevent scorching. Add salt just before cooking is completed. Young peas will cook in ten to twenty minutes but those that are more mature require a longer time. Most of the water should have cooked away. If any remains, drain carefully. Let the peas stand in the drainer over hot water. Melt the butter, add salt and pepper and the drained peas. Mix well, reheat, and serve.

CREAMED PEAS

2 cups cooked peas   1 cup medium white sauce

Mix peas with white sauce. Reheat and serve.

BHUGIA

2 cups peas   2 tablespoons oil or melted fat
4 medium potatoes   Salt
Chopped green peppers

This is a popular dish in India and is usually served with the dinner roast. Boil the peas and potatoes separately. When the potatoes are thoroughly done, drain and let them cool enough to be easily handled. Drain the peas. Heat the oil in a frying-pan. Slice the potatoes and sauté potatoes and peas together in the oil. Season with salt and sprinkle with chopped green peppers.

RICE AND PEAS

1 cup rice	2 onions	2 cups green peas

Boil the rice and peas separately. Chop the onions fine and fry them in oil until tender. Add the cooked rice and peas.

BOILED POTATOES

Select potatoes of uniform size. Wash, pare, if you wish, and drop into cold water. Cook in boiling water until tender when pierced with a fork. Just before cooking is completed, add the salt. The water should be kept boiling constantly. When done, drain and shake the pan over the fire to dry the potatoes. Serve in an uncovered dish or cover with a folded napkin. Old potatoes should be soaked in cold water for an hour or so before boiling. When they are pared, potatoes lose much vitamin and mineral content in boiling. It is better, therefore, from the nutritional standpoint, to wash them thoroughly, scrubbing with a brush, and boil them with the skins on. They may be peeled quickly before they are served, or served with the skins on.

RICED POTATOES

Force hot, freshly boiled potatoes through a ricer or coarse strainer. Sprinkle with salt and pile lightly into the serving-dish. Serve at once in an uncovered dish.

BAKED POTATOES

Select smooth, medium-sized potatoes, scrub, remove the eyes and any blemishes, place in a baking-pan or on the rack in a very hot oven (450°-500° F.) and bake until tender (30-60 minutes). Be sure to have the oven hot before the potatoes are put in. To test the potatoes, do not pierce them with a fork, but squeeze them with the hand wrapped in a towel. When soft, break the skin to keep them from being soggy, and serve.'

STUFFED POTATOES ON THE HALF-SHELL

Select large potatoes; scrub and bake. Remove from oven and cut potatoes in two lengthwise. Scoop out the inside, being careful not to break the shell. Mash very thoroughly or put them through the ricer—add butter, salt and milk, and beat well. Pile the mixture lightly back into the shells. Do not smooth down the top. Stand the filled shells in a shallow pan, return to the oven (400° F.) and brown lightly on top. Tuck in small wieners before serving if desired, or add ½ cup peanut butter and 2 egg whites to the potato mixture.

POTATO SALMON PIE

1 No. 1 can salmon	1 cup cooked peas
2 cups Thick White Sauce	2 cups mashed potatoes
1 tablespoon butter	

Bone and flake salmon; add hot sauce and drained peas. Place in baking dish; top with potatoes. Dot with butter; brown in hot oven (450° F.) 15 minutes. Serves 6.

POTATOES SUZETTE

6 medium-sized potatoes	Salt and pepper
½ cup hot milk	6 tablespoons buttered crumbs
2 tablespoons melted fat	1 tablespoon grated cheese
6 eggs	

Prepare as for potatoes on the half shell. Refill the shell almost to the top, break an egg into each opening, season with salt and pepper and sprinkle with buttered crumbs that have been mixed with grated cheese and bake in a slow oven (250°-350° F.) long enough to set the egg and brown lightly.

SCALLOPED POTATOES

6 medium-sized potatoes	4 tablespoons butter
Salt and pepper	Milk
2 tablespoons flour	

Pare raw potatoes and cut them into thin slices. Place in a baking dish a layer of the potato one inch deep, season with salt and pepper, sprinkle a portion of the flour over each layer, add a part of the butter in bits. Repeat and continue until required amount is used. It is best not to have more than two or three layers because of difficulty in cooking. Add milk until it can be seen between the slices of potato, cover and bake (350°-400° F.) until potatoes are tender when pierced with a fork (1-1½ hours). Remove the cover during the last fifteen minutes to brown the top. Serve from the baking-dish.

FRANCONIA POTATOES

Select medium-sized potatoes, pare and place them in the baking-pan with the roast, allowing an hour and a quarter for their cooking. Turn them often and baste with the gravy from the roast. Serve them arranged about the meat on the platter. If you wish to shorten the cooking time, parboil them for fifteen minutes before putting them into the roasting-pan, and allow forty-five minutes for the roasting.

DUTCH POTATOES

6 potatoes	6 slices fat salt pork or bacon
6 frankfurter sausages	Pepper

Scrub medium-sized potatoes; pare or leave the skins on as preferred. With an apple-corer cut a tunnel through the center of each, lengthwise. Draw through each cavity one of the frankfurters. Place in a dripping-pan and lay a blanket of fat salt pork or a thick slice of bacon on each potato. Pepper lightly and bake in a very hot oven (450°-500° F.) until the potatoes are tender, basting occasionally with the drippings and a little hot water.

POTATO PUFF OR SOUFFLÉ

2 cups hot mashed potatoes	2 tablespoons butter or other
2 eggs	fat
1 cup milk	

To the mashed potatoes add the fat, the egg-yolks which have been beaten until very light, and the milk. Stir until well blended and then fold in the stiffly beaten egg-whites. Mix lightly and pile the mass in a well-greased baking-dish. Set in a pan containing hot water and bake in a moderate oven (375° F.) twenty to thirty minutes. Serve at once.

DESIGN FOR EATING . . .
BRUSSELS SPROUTS IN
CHICKEN RING MOLD
FLANKED WITH WHOLE
CARROTS AND ACCENTS OF
PARSLEY AND PIMIENTO

WHOLE BOILED SQUASH SERVED
ON A PARSLEY BED, RINGED WITH
TOMATO AND CUCUMBER SLICES

THESE LITTLE PIGGIES CAME FROM MARKET TO NEST IN CRISPY BROWN AND FLUFFY WHITE "TATERS"

AN ATTRACTIVE NEW VEGETABLE PLATTER OF CAULIFLOWER WITH CREAM SAUCE, SURROUNDED BY PEAS IN POTATO CUPS AND CARROT STRIPS

SAVORY POTATO CAKES

1 egg
2 tablespoons butter or other fat
½ teaspoon salt
¼ teaspoon paprika

2 tablespoons chopped mint leaves
2 cups hot riced potatoes
Sifted bread crumbs

Add egg yolk, butter, seasonings and mint to potatoes. Shape into cakes, dip into the slightly beaten egg white, which has been diluted with two tablespoons water, roll in crumbs and fry in deep fat (375°-390° F.) until brown.

JULIENNE POTATO WITH SAVORY SAUCE

2 cups potato cut in strings
1 small onion
1 teaspoon mixed herbs
2 tablespoons fat
2 tablespoons flour

1 cup milk
1 teaspoon salt
Pepper
Grated cheese

Cut the raw, pared potatoes into long match-like strips. Cook them in boiling water until tender. Drain and turn into a warm dish. Brown the chopped onion and the herbs in the fat. Add the flour, stirring thoroughly, add the milk, salt and pepper and cook in a double boiler twenty minutes. Strain and pour over the cooked potato. Sprinkle with grated cheese and serve.

MASHED POTATOES

6 medium-sized potatoes
Hot milk or cream

2 tablespoons butter
Salt and white pepper

Pare and boil the potatoes. Drain, and set the saucepan in a warm place with the cover off for a minute or two to dry the potatoes thoroughly. Mash the potatoes in the saucepan in which they were boiled, or turn them out into a warm dish and put through the ricer into the same saucepan. Work quickly so that they will not get cold. Add the butter, season to taste, and beat, adding milk or cream a little at a time until the potatoes are light and moist.

FOR POTATO CUPS—Pile into a large teacup and make a hollow with the bottom of a smaller tumbler or bottle. Slip out carefully onto the serving plate. Keep hot until filled and served.

MASHED POTATOES AU GRATIN

6 potatoes riced	2 eggs
3 tablespoons fat	¼ cup grated cheese
½ teaspoon salt	½ cup buttered crumbs
½ teaspoon paprika	

Add fat, seasoning and eggs to the hot riced potatoes. Beat until light and mound on a baking-dish. Cover with grated cheese and then with buttered crumbs. Bake (400° F.) ten minutes, or until the crumbs are brown.

DUCHESS POTATOES

2 cups riced potatoes	2 egg-yolks
2 tablespoons fat	Salt and paprika

Mix riced potato, fat and beaten yolks of eggs, reserving a little of the yolk for brushing the cakes. Add a little salt and paprika. Shape by means of a pastry-bag and tube into leaves, crowns, pyramids, etc. Brush over with beaten egg-yolk to which one teaspoon of water has been added. Brown in a hot oven (400°-450° F.).

FRENCH FRIED POTATOES

No. 1—Wash and pare potatoes and cut into eighths lengthwise. Dry between towels and fry in deep fat (395° F.). Drain on soft paper, sprinkle with salt and serve in an uncovered dish.

No. 2—Cut uncooked potatoes into blocks measuring about three-fourths of an inch each way, and place them in boiling water. Cook until almost done, ten or eleven minutes being usually required. Then drain off all the water and allow five minutes for the escape of steam. Fry them a few at a time in deep fat (395° F.). Drain on soft paper placed on a hot plate. Sprinkle with salt and pepper.

BELGIAN BAKED POTATOES

Prepare potatoes as for French fried. Dip them in melted fat and lay them in a shallow pan, being sure that the pieces do not overlap. Bake in a quick oven (400°-450° F.) until brown on top, turn carefully and continue baking until they resemble

French fried potatoes. Baste them with more fat during baking, if necessary. When done, sprinkle with salt and serve piping hot.

POTATO CHIPS OR SARATOGA POTATOES

Wash and pare potatoes and shave into very thin slices. Soak them for one hour in cold water, then drain and dry on a towel. Fry in deep fat (395° F.) a few slices at a time until light brown, keeping them in motion with a skimmer. Lay them on soft paper to drain. Sprinkle lightly with salt, and serve.

In cool weather, enough potato chips may be cooked at one time to last a week or ten days. They should be kept in a cool dry place and should always be reheated in the oven until crisp, before serving.

AMERICAN FRIED OR BROWNED POTATOES

No. 1—Cut boiled potatoes into slices one-fourth of an inch thick. Heat a very little fat in a frying-pan and sauté the slices, browning on both sides. Season with salt and pepper.

No. 2—Chop the potatoes in a chopping-bowl until the pieces measure one-half inch or less, and add them to the hot fat in the frying-pan. Season with salt and pepper and sauté, stirring constantly, until the potatoes look yellow and are cooking well. Then cover the pan, set it in a slow heat for five minutes, and serve in a heated dish.

HASHED BROWN POTATOES

2 tablespoons oil or drippings	6 boiled potatoes
	Salt and pepper

Chop the potatoes, adding salt, and a dash of pepper. Heat the fat in a frying-pan, and add the chopped potatoes to the depth of one inch. Press the potatoes down in the pan, packing them firmly. Cook slowly, without stirring, until the potato is brown. Then begin at one side of the pan and fold the potatoes over on the other like an omelet, packing closely together. Turn out on to a hot serving platter and serve.

CREAMED POTATOES

2 cups diced cold cooked   1½ cups medium white sauce
   potatoes   Salt and pepper

Combine potatoes and white sauce and heat thoroughly. Season with salt and pepper. Serves 6.

Or use milk instead of white sauce. Dice potatoes into skillet in which 2 tablespoons butter have been melted. Season with salt and pepper and almost cover with milk. Simmer, uncovered, until milk is absorbed, tilting pan occasionally and basting top of potatoes with milk.

CREAMED NEW POTATOES

Scrape new potatoes and cook in a small amount of boiling salted water, closely covered, until tender. Place in serving dish and pour hot seasoned white sauce over them. Sprinkle with paprika or minced parsley.

POTATO PANCAKES

3 cups grated potatoes   ⅛ teaspoon baking powder
2 eggs, well beaten   1 teaspoon salt
1½ tablespoons flour   ½ teaspoon onion juice

Pare large potatoes and cover with cold water. Let stand 12 hours. Pour off water and grate potatoes. Drain well. Add eggs and mix lightly. Stir in remaining ingredients. Drop from tablespoon onto hot well-greased skillet and brown on both sides. Serve with applesauce. Makes 12 pancakes.

FLUFFY—Use 6 eggs. Add beaten egg yolks to grated potatoes, add remaining ingredients and fold in stiffly beaten egg whites last. Fry as above.

DELMONICO POTATOES

2 cups cooked potatoes, diced   Salt and pepper
2 cups Medium White Sauce   Buttered crumbs

Mix potatoes and sauce, add salt and pepper, and pour into a buttered baking dish; cover with crumbs and bake ten minutes in a hot oven (400° F.). Serves 6.

Add ¼ cup diced cooked pimiento to white sauce. The crumbs may be omitted and the potatoes sprinkled with grated cheese or grated cheese may be mixed with crumbs.

POTATOES AU GRATIN

Creamed potatoes No. 1
1 teaspoon minced parsley
1 cup buttered crumbs

2 to 4 tablespoons grated
cheese

Follow directions for creamed potatoes No. 1 adding the parsley. Turn into greased baking-dish, sprinkle with cheese, cover with buttered crumbs and bake in a hot oven (400° F.) until crumbs are brown.

POTATO DROPS

2 cups mashed potatoes
(without any milk)

2 eggs
Salt and pepper

Mix the mashed, seasoned potato and the beaten eggs. Drop the mixture from a spoon into the hot fat (375°-390° F.) and fry until a golden brown, (2-3 minutes) then drain on brown paper and serve with a garnish of parsley. If the spoon is dipped into boiling water after every using, each drop will retain the shape of the spoon.

POTATO O'BRIEN

6 medium-sized potatoes
Salt

Chopped pimientos
Onion-juice

Wash, pare and cut potatoes into half-inch dice. Dry between towels. Fry in hot fat (395° F.) until a delicate brown. Drain on soft paper, sprinkle with salt, then sauté them in just enough fat to keep them from burning, adding minced pimientos and a few drops of onion-juice. They should be tossed frequently during cooking, and not pressed close to the pan.

POTATOES PERSILLADE

12 small new potatoes or
6 medium-sized old potatoes

Butter
Juice of one-half lemon
½ cup minced parsley

These are dependent upon parsley, not only for their name but for their attractive appearance. Scrape new potatoes. Pare old potatoes and cut the size of a small egg or with a vegetable scoop cut them into balls. Boil until tender. Add salt just before cooking is completed. Drain, place in a saucepan with sufficient butter to coat all the potatoes, add the lemon-juice and sprinkle with minced parsley. The potatoes should be well coated with parsley when served.

LYONNAISE POTATOES

2 cups boiled potatoes, diced
Salt and pepper
1 tablespoon minced onion

2 tablespoons fat
1 tablespoon chopped parsley

The potatoes should be rather underdone to produce the best results. Season with salt and pepper. Sauté the onion in fat until yellow, add the diced potato and stir with a fork until all sides are brown, being careful not to break the potatoes. Add more fat if necessary. When done, turn the potatoes out upon a hot dish, sprinkle parsley over the top, and serve hot.

SPANISH POTATOES

1 tablespoon minced onion
2 tablespoons chopped green pepper
2 tablespoons chopped pimiento
4 tablespoons oil or cooking fat

2 cups cold boiled potatoes, diced
½ cup cold cooked ham, chopped
1 teaspoon salt
½ teaspoon paprika

Sauté the onion, pepper and pimiento in the fat until light brown, add the diced potatoes, the chopped ham and seasonings and cook until thoroughly heated through.

MASHED POTATO BALLS

2 cups cold mashed potatoes
1 egg yolk

Salt and pepper
Butter

Mix cold mashed potato with the beaten egg yolk, salt and pepper and shape the mixture into balls. Place the balls in a greased pan and make a depression on the top of each, put a bit of butter in each depression and brown in the oven (400°-450° F.).

PRINCESS POTATOES

2 cups cold mashed potatoes
1 egg

Melted fat

If the potato is cold and firm, cut into strips two inches long, one inch wide and one-half inch thick, otherwise shape into flat cakes one-half inch thick. Dip the strips or cakes first into the melted fat and then into the egg, which has been slightly beaten, and lay them carefully on a greased pan. Cook in a hot oven (400°-450° F.) until brown.

BOILED SWEET POTATOES

Follow directions for boiled white potatoes (See Index).

BAKED SWEET POTATOES

Follow directions for baked white potatoes (See Index).

GLAZED OR CANDIED SWEET POTATOES

No. 1.

6 sweet potatoes	1 cup brown or maple sugar
Salt and pepper	1/4 cup water
Butter	

Boil the potatoes without paring them, and when tender drain and strip off the skins. Make a sirup by boiling together the sugar and water. Cut each potato in half or in thick slices, dip each piece into the sirup and lay it in a greased baking-dish. Season with salt and pepper and bits of butter. When all the potato is in the dish, pour over it any sirup that remains and bake in a quick oven (400°-450° F.) until the potatoes are brown. They will brown quickly.

No. 2—Use the same quantities as for No. 1. Pare the potatoes and boil until about half done. Drain, cut in lengthwise slices, and lay in a shallow greased pan. Spread generously with butter and pour over all the sirup. Bake in a moderate oven (350°-400° F.) basting frequently with the sirup until the potatoes are transparent. It may be necessary to add more sirup during the baking. An hour or more is usually required for these potatoes.

SWEET POTATO PUFF

2 cups mashed sweet potato	Salt and pepper
2 tablespoons fat	1/4 cup milk or cream
1 egg	

To the mashed sweet potatoes add the melted fat, seasonings and milk. Beat the egg-yolk and white separately, add the yolk to the potato mixture, and then fold in the white. Put into a baking dish or individual molds, set in a pan containing hot water and bake (375° F.) until puffy and brown.

SWEET POTATO WITH PINEAPPLE

6 small sweet potatoes   ⅓ cup honey
⅓ as much pineapple as   ¼ cup water
   potato

Boil the potatoes with the skins on. When cool, peel and cut them in pieces one-quarter of an inch thick. Mix honey and hot water. Just cover the bottom of a baking dish with the mixture, add the sweet potatoes and sliced pineapple. Pour the remaining honey mixture over them and bake for ten minutes in the oven (400° F.).

CREOLE SWEET POTATOES

6 large sweet potatoes   Grated nutmeg
Salt   1 cup rich brown stock
Celery salt   Few drops of caramel
White pepper

Prepare potatoes by parboiling them for twenty minutes. Remove skins and cut potatoes in halves. Place the pieces in a shallow baking pan, sprinkle with salt, celery salt, white pepper and grated nutmeg. Pour into the pan the stock, to which a few drops of caramel have been added, and bake in a quick oven (400°-450° F.) until tender and slightly browned. Baste frequently with the stock. Serve around planked fish.

MASHED SWEET POTATO CARAMEL

2 cups mashed sweet potato   ½ cup maple sirup
Milk   ¼ cup butter
Pepper and salt

Left-over sweet potatoes, either baked or boiled, may be used for this dish. Mash potatoes and add sufficient milk or cream to make a smooth, soft paste. Season with pepper and salt. Put into a well-greased casserole. Pour in thick maple sirup heated with butter. Bake at 400° F. until the top is caramelized.

SWEET POTATO CASSEROLE—Omit maple sirup and butter. Cover potatoes with marshmallows and bake in a moderate oven (350° F.) until browned.

SWEET POTATO WAFFLES

4 tablespoons fat	¾ cup flour
1 tablespoon sugar	2 teaspoons baking powder
1 egg	1 cup milk
1 cup mashed sweet potato	Salt, cayenne, nutmeg

Mix the fat and sugar to a cream, stir in the well-beaten egg yolk, potato, flour, baking powder, milk and seasonings, and beat well until smooth. Fold in the stiffly beaten egg white. Bake in a heated waffle iron until golden brown. Serve, dusted with sugar and cinnamon, as an accompaniment to roast duck or turkey.

CREAMED RADISHES

1½ cups large, strongly flavored radishes	1 cup milk
2 tablespoons flour	2 tablespoons fat
	Salt and pepper

Wash, pare and slice the radishes. Boil until tender. Make a white sauce of the flour, fat, milk and seasonings. Combine radishes and sauce and serve. The flavor is not unlike spicy turnips and they make a pleasant novelty served with steak or chops.

BOILED RICE

1 cup rice	3 quarts water or more	1 tablespoon salt

Wash the rice; drop it into the salted boiling water; and boil rapidly, uncovered, for fifteen or twenty minutes, or until the kernels are soft when pressed between the thumb and finger. Place in a colander (saving the water for soup) and pour boiling water over the rice to remove the loose starch and separate the grains. Drain and place in the oven with the door open for a few minutes, to allow the cereal to dry out. The grains should be separate and distinct.

CURRY OF RICE

1 cup rice	1 to 2 tablespoons curry-powder
2 tablespoons fat	
1 teaspoon chopped onion	2 teaspoons salt
2½ cups boiling water	¼ teaspoon pepper

Wash the rice well. Place fat and onion in a stew-pan and cook them until the onion is yellow, add the rice and stir the whole over high heat for five minutes. Remove from heat, season with the curry powder, salt and pepper, stir well and pour in the boiling water. Cover the pan and boil rapidly for ten minutes, then cook for forty minutes over a double boiler.

Curry of rice is appropriate with any kind of meat dish that has been prepared with a sauce.

RICE À LA CREOLE

1 onion	2 cups cooked tomatoes
1 sliced cooked ham	Salt
1 tablespoon fat	Paprika
1 cup boiled rice	Bread crumbs

Chop onion and ham very fine. Add fat, boiled rice, and tomatoes seasoned with salt and paprika. Mix thoroughly, put into a baking dish, cover with bread crumbs and bake (400° F.) for fifteen minutes.

CREAMED SALSIFY OR OYSTER PLANT

Wash and scrape the salsify, drop it immediately into cold water to which a little vinegar or lemon juice has been added, to prevent discoloration. Cut in 1-inch slices and cook in boiling water until tender, adding salt just before cooking is completed. When tender, drain and combine with Medium White Sauce. Serve with tiny fried Beef Balls.

FRIED SALSIFY

Follow directions for fried parsnips (see index).

STEAMED OR BAKED SUMMER SQUASH

Cut the squash into pieces of medium size, remove the seeds and the soft mesh surrounding them. Steam or bake until tender. Serve in the shell or scrape from shell, mash, and place, uncovered, for ten minutes in a good heat to dry, stirring frequently. Season with butter, salt and pepper.

FRIED SQUASH

2 white squash	Egg and crumbs	Salt and pepper

The white "button" squash, about four inches in diameter, is best when fried. Pare and cut the squash into thin slices, dip in seasoned crumbs, then in beaten egg, then in more crumbs, and fry in deep fat (395° F.) from four to five minutes. When the slices are brown, drain on soft paper. Serve on a platter or other flat dish. Fried squash makes an excellent luncheon dish.

SQUASH IN THE SHELL

1 squash	Egg
3 tablespoons butter	Milk
Salt and pepper	

Cut off the top of a small squash, remove the seeds and stringy portion, place in a pan and boil, steam or bake about two hours, until tender. Remove the pulp from the shell, being careful to keep the large shell intact. Mash the pulp and season it with salt, pepper and butter.

Return the mixture to the shell, smooth the surface to a dome shape, score with a knife, brush over with milk and beaten egg, add bits of butter and place in a quick oven (400° F.) for a few minutes to brown. Or leave the pulp in the squash, season well and fill center with ham à la king, chicken à la king, creamed salmon or sausage mixtures.

BOILED SPINACH

No. 1—AMERICAN STYLE

2 pounds spinach	3 tablespoons butter
Salt and pepper	

Remove roots and wilted leaves of the spinach. Wash in several waters, until all trace of sand has disappeared. Place in a large kettle without additional water; the water which clings to the leaves is sufficient. Cover the kettle and cook with low heat until the spinach is tender. The time of cooking depends on the age of the spinach. Long cooking darkens it. Salt the water just before cooking is completed. When done, drain, chop, season with salt, pepper and butter and one tablespoon lemon-juice, if desired.

SPINACH MOLD—

1 peck spinach, cooked and chopped	¼ cup butter
3 unbeaten eggs	1½ cups bread crumbs
¼ cup milk	¼ teaspoon pepper
	1 teaspoon salt

Combine all ingredients, turn into a buttered ring mold and
steam 2 hours. Unmold and garnish with hard-cooked eggs and
carrots. Fill center of mold with mashed potatoes or creamed
mushrooms.

CREAMED SPINACH

2 pounds spinach
1 tablespoon butter
2 hard-cooked egg-yolks

Salt and pepper
2 tablespoons cream

Cook spinach according to directions for boiled spinach No. 1,
drain well, and chop fine. Return to fire, add butter, salt
and pepper, and stir until the butter is melted, then add cream
and chopped yolks and mix well.

SPINACH SOUFFLE

2 cups cooked spinach, fresh or canned   2 eggs

This is a satisfactory way to dispose of left-over cooked
spinach. To the spinach add egg-yolks beaten, place in a
granite saucepan, heat and stir over the fire until the egg sets,
then remove from the heat and when cold add the beaten egg-
whites. Fill individual baking-dishes one-half full of this mixture. Set the dishes in a pan of hot water and bake in a moderate oven (375° F.) from twenty to thirty minutes. Serve at
once to prevent falling.

SPINACH IN EGGS

2 cups boiled spinach
6 eggs
Salt
Red pepper

Mustard
Butter
Vinegar

While the spinach is cooking, cook the eggs hard. Cut eggs
in halves crosswise and remove the yolks. Cut a slice from the
bottom of each cooked egg-white so that it will stand on a
platter. Season the yolks with red pepper, mustard, butter and
salt. Mix thoroughly with vinegar to taste. Fill the egg-cups
with the spinach, mounding it high, and put the rest around
the egg. Put the prepared yolks in a ricer and squeeze over all.

SUCCOTASH

2 cups green corn or
1 cup dried corn
2 cups fresh Lima, string or
butter beans or 1 cup dried
Lima beans

Salt and pepper
1 cup milk
4 tablespoons butter

If fresh vegetables are used, cut the corn from the cob. Cover the beans with the least possible amount of boiling water, to prevent scorching, and cook until tender. Drain off the water, add the corn and the milk and cook slowly until the corn is tender. Add the butter and other seasoning.

When dried corn and beans are used, soak both separately over night. In the morning, cover the beans with fresh water, and boil them very gently until tender. Do not drain the water from the corn, but reduce heat so it will cook slowly. When the beans are tender, drain and add them to the corn, allowing only water enough to cover. Cook slowly until tender and drain off water to save for soup. Add the milk and seasoning.

STEWED TOMATOES

6 tomatoes, fresh or canned
2 tablespoons butter

Salt and pepper
Crumbs or flour

Pour boiling water on fresh tomatoes, and after they have remained covered one minute drain them and plunge them into cold water. Slip off the skins, remove the hard stem ends, and cut the tomatoes in pieces. Stew them in their own juice in a graniteware or porcelain-lined kettle until tender, add butter, salt, and pepper. Bread-crumbs or cracker-crumbs, or a little flour blended with the butter, may be added for thickening.

FRIED TOMATOES

6 tomatoes   Crumbs   Salt and pepper

Select firm, ripe tomatoes, wash them and cut in half-inch slices without removing the skins. Season fine crumbs with salt and pepper, dip each slice of tomato in the crumbs, and sauté in hot fat. Serve hot.

BAKED TOMATOES

6 tomatoes
4 tablespoons fat
Salt and pepper

1 cup bread-crumbs
1 teaspoon sugar

Peel the tomatoes and cut them in slices one-fourth inch thick. Place a layer of tomatoes in a pudding-dish, and sprinkle over them a little salt and pepper. Rub the fat into the crumbs with the sugar. Spread the mixture thickly upon the tomatoes, using all of it, and add another layer of tomatoes. Add bits of butter or other fat, sprinkle with dry crumbs, and bake (350°-400° F.) twenty minutes.

BROILED TOMATOES

6 tomatoes
Salt and pepper

Melted butter

Choose firm, round tomatoes, cut them into slices, three-quarters inch thick, dust each slice with salt and pepper, place in a greased broiler and broil tender. Turn once carefully. Add melted butter and serve at once.

SCALLOPED TOMATOES

6 large fresh tomatoes or
1 quart cooked tomatoes,
fresh or canned
Salt and pepper

Bread-crumbs
Butter or other fat
Grated cheese, if desired

Skin fresh tomatoes and cut them into slices. If using cooked tomatoes, drain off the juice, using only the pulp. Place a layer of tomato in a greased baking-dish, add a seasoning of salt and pepper then a thin layer of bread-crumbs. Cut the fat into tiny pieces and lay on the crumbs. Then add another layer of tomato and proceed until the materials are used, having crumbs for the top layer. Add bits of fat and bake for thirty minutes in a moderate oven (350°-400° F.). Serve in the baking-dish. Grated cheese may be added to each layer, or to the top one only.

STUFFED TOMATOES

No. 1.

6 tomatoes	2 tablespoons fat
1½ cups soft bread-crumbs	1 teaspoon salt
¼ teaspoon pepper	

The tomatoes should be very firm, smooth, and of equal size. Cut a piece from the stem end of each tomato, and remove the centers without breaking the walls. Make a stuffing of the centers of the tomatoes, crumbs, seasonings, and melted fat and mix well. Sprinkle each tomato well with salt and pepper and fill with the stuffing, packing it in quite solidly.

Place a small piece of butter on the top of each, arrange the tomatoes in a baking-dish and bake in a moderate oven (350°-400° F.) until tender. Serve hot in the baking-dish.

No. 2—INDIAN STYLE.

6 tomatoes	⅛ teaspoon pepper
3 tablespoons rice	⅛ teaspoon garlic clove
1 tablespoon fat	1 teaspoon chopped celery
1 slice bread	A little chopped parsley
2 tablespoons milk	Thyme
2 hard-cooked egg-yolks	½ teaspoon curry-powder
½ teaspoon salt	

Cut the tops from the tomatoes and remove the pulp. Wash the rice carefully, put it into a saucepan with one-half cup salted boiling water and the tomato pulp and cook until the rice is soft. Add the fat, the bread soaked in the milk, the mashed egg-yolk and seasonings. Stuff the tomato shells with this mixture, replace the tops and place in a baking-dish.

Bake in a moderate oven (350°-400° F.) until the tomatoes are soft (about twenty minutes). The curry-powder gives an unusual flavor to the tomatoes, but may be omitted.

MASHED TURNIPS

| 1 pound white or yellow turnips | 3 tablespoons butter |
| | Salt and pepper |

Wash, pare and slice the turnips and cook in boiling water until soft, adding salt just before the cooking is completed. Drain and mash the turnips in the stew-pan and stand the pan, uncovered, over a low fire for ten minutes to dry the turnips well, stirring them frequently. Add butter and pepper and more salt if needed.

TURNIPS IN CREAM

1 pound white or yellow
  turnips
2 cups milk

4 tablespoons flour
4 tablespoons fat
Salt and pepper

Pare the turnips, cut them in cubes; cook until tender. Make a white sauce of the flour, fat, milk and seasonings. Pour sauce over turnip cubes and serve.

TURNIP SHELLS OR CUPS

Pare the turnip and remove the center, leaving a shell one-half inch in thickness. Cook shell in boiling water until tender. Just before cooking is completed, add the salt. Cook the center in the same way and use for stuffing cup or serve as mashed turnips.

The turnip cups may be used as cases for creamed or buttered peas, carrots, beets, or any suitable vegetable or meat.

VEGETABLE MARROW, FRIED

Wash and pare a vegetable marrow, and scoop out the inside. Cook in boiling water for about fifteen minutes, and then drain and slice in inch slices, or cut in pieces of any desired size. Roll in flour, dip in beaten egg which has been diluted with water, roll in fine crumbs and fry in deep fat (395° F.). After frying, drain the pieces on absorbent paper, sprinkle with salt and pepper and serve hot.

To BAKE VEGETABLE MARROW, cut in half between the ends; peel each half, scoop out seeds and loose pulp. Fill each half with seasoned fresh Hamburg, diced onion and bread crumbs (beef loaf p. 246) or chopped leftover meats, chopped onion, green or red peppers and cooked rice. Fit halves together and truss with string or use skewers in opposite directions. Bake or simmer in deep pot or baking dish, covered with heavy seasoned tomato sauce, until marrow is transparent but not too well done. Serve by slicing through so each service is a complete circle.

SALADS

~~~~~~

FRUITS, nuts, uncooked and cooked vegetables and some cooked meats, fish and fowl, served cold and dressed with condiments, oils and acids, are known as salads.

Utensils Needed for Salad Making

A chilled earthenware bowl is excellent for mixing salad ingredients. Two forks or a fork and a spoon are better to use in folding together the ingredients than a spoon alone, because they do not crush the materials so much as a single utensil.

A sharp-edged knife or vegetable cutter is necessary for slicing vegetables or fruits. Where fruit pulp is to be removed from the thin white membrane enclosing it, a thin narrow knife slightly curved at the tip is useful. A pair of shears can be used for many of the processes of salad making, such as shredding lettuce, clipping off wilted or discolored edges, etc.

Various fancy shapes for molding individual salads may be bought, or tea-cups or small bowls may be used as molds. Gelatin salads may be put into pans and cut in square or fancy shapes after they have hardened. The cube trays of mechanical refrigerators are excellent for molding gelatin.

Materials for Salads

VEGETABLES—Leaf vegetables, such as head lettuce, curly lettuce, endive, chicory, romaine, water cress, celery and cabbage, make very attractive salads served alone with a dressing or in combination with other materials.

Tomatoes, cucumbers, celery, cabbage and ground carrots are excellent uncooked materials for salad, as are also Bermuda or Spanish onions in thin wafer-like slices or young spring onions marinated in French dressing.

Many cooked vegetables, such as peas, carrots, beans, beets, cauliflower, spinach, asparagus and potatoes, are used in salad making, alone or in combination.

FRUITS—The fruits most commonly used in the preparation of salads are oranges, bananas, apples, cherries, grapefruit.

grapes, peaches, pears and pineapple. Watermelon or cantaloupe adds a delicious flavor to a fruit salad.

DRIED FRUITS—Dates, figs and raisins give variety to fruit salads.

MEATS—Chicken always makes a delicious salad. Veal and pork may be combined with chicken and it is difficult to detect their use. They may be used alone in salads, also.

Crab, lobster, shrimp, oysters, salmon, tuna fish and sardines are most commonly used in fish salads. Any firm-fleshed cooked fish may be diced and combined with other materials.

CHEESE—Cream cheese or cottage cheese, served in mounds on lettuce leaves, makes an attractive salad, with bar-le-duc or other jelly or jam as a garnish. It can also be mixed with green peppers or pimientoes, rolled in nuts, served with pineapple or molded in a loaf and sliced.

EGGS—The most common egg salad is the "deviled egg," or salad egg. Hard-cooked eggs can be cut in slices or quarters or fancy shapes and served on a bed of lettuce leaves with a dressing or used with other ingredients in a vegetable or fish salad.

HERBS—Such herbs as chervil, mint, parsley, peppergrass, sorrel and tarragon may be added to salad to give a pungent flavor.

Fennel (finochio) tops, or root and stem of anise flavor, dandelion, chard, escarole, celery cabbage or cooked zucchini are used both as body of the salad and as flavoring. Those who have a garden will find dill, nasturtium leaves and seeds, catnip and rose geranium leaves usable.

Important Points in Salad Making

WASHING INGREDIENTS—Wash salad greens and examine to insure the removal of all aphids. Then soak in cold water for half an hour to crisp, and dry on a towel or by shaking in a wire basket.

CHILLING INGREDIENTS—All ingredients, fruits, vegetables, and dressing, should be chilled (see directions on next page for keeping materials) before being folded together. The bowl used should be chilled; also the plates upon which the salad is served.

FROZEN SALADS—This name may seem misleading because pieces of fruit or vegetable in salads should never be actually frozen. Combined with whipped cream and mayonnaise, the mixture is frozen like mousse, but it should not be frozen long enough to harden the fruit or vegetable. Salads made of vegetable or fruit pulp may be frozen. The freezing can be done by packing in ice and salt or by placing the mixture in the drawers of a mechanically cooled refrigerator.

KEEPING MATERIALS—Lettuce, most vegetables and many fruits may be kept for days by wrapping in a damp cloth or paper bag and placing on ice. In a mechanically cooled refrigerator, lettuce and other salad greens keep best if they are washed and placed in closely covered enamel or porcelain containers with a very little water.

CUTTING MATERIALS—Salad materials should be cut in uniform, well-defined pieces small enough so that they will not lose their shape in the folding process. If part of the celery to be used is tough, cut it in fine pieces and cut the tender parts in larger pieces. In this way the toughness will not be detected.

When both the dark and light meat of chicken are used, dice the dark in small cubes and the light in larger cubes. This gives a more pleasing appearance to the salad. If veal or pork is used to extend the chicken, dice it finer than the chicken and its presence will not be detected.

MARINATING SALADS—A marinade is used to give flavor to salad materials and is made by mixing oil, salt, and lemon-juice or vinegar (sometimes onion-juice). The vegetables, fish or meat may stand an hour or so in the marinade before using. When several vegetables are to be used, each one should be marinated separately. For serving, these vegetables may be combined, or placed on lettuce leaves in small individual mounds, as preferred.

ADDITION OF SALAD DRESSING—The dressing should never be folded into the salad until time for serving, except in the case of a salad like potato salad, when it is preferable for the dressing to soak in.

ARRANGEMENT OF SALAD—The lettuce leaf should have the stem end cut off so that this ragged part does not hang over the edge of the plate. Care should be taken that the garnish is carefully placed.

Place the salad on the lettuce leaf carefully so that it will not fall apart and spread ungracefully over the plate. No part of the salad should extend beyond the edge of the plate.

Garnishes for Salads

Chives, mint, chervil, parsley and similar small greens may be minced and sprinkled over a green salad.

Strips of pimiento and green pepper, or a dash of paprika may be used to give life to a colorless salad.

A chapon is a small piece of bread rubbed with garlic. When placed in a salad bowl it gives a delicious flavor to the salad.

The outside leaves of a head of lettuce may be used as garnish for a salad, reserving the heart for heart-of-lettuce salad.

MOLDED SALADS

Among the most decorative ways to serve jellied salad are the form mold and the ring mold. The latter lends itself to many additional touches since the center may be used for decorative vegetables, a pile of cut jelly of contrasting color or the bowl of salad dressing. Of exact size to fit, the bowl may be of glass, china or silver. Be sure the plate onto which the ring is unmolded is large enough for the decoration planned. See page 344.

COLD MARINADE

3 tablespoons oil	1 teaspoon salt
6 tablespoons lemon juice or vinegar	½ teaspoon pepper
	½ teaspoon onion juice

For fish, use three tablespoons vinegar and three tablespoons lemon juice. Mix ingredients in order given.

Vegetable Salads

ASPARAGUS SALAD

6 rings cut from green pepper or lemon	Lettuce leaves
24 stalks cold boiled asparagus, fresh or canned	French dressing
	½ tablespoon tomato catchup

Cut rings about one-third inch wide. If lemon is used, remove the pulp, leaving only the peel. Slip four stalks of cold asparagus through each ring and arrange each serving on crisp lettuce on salad plates or all on a platter. Serve with French dressing mixed with catchup. Serves 6.

A RUBY RING OF TOMATO ASPIC FOR THE ENCHANTMENT OF YOUR GUESTS

VEGETABLES ARE COOKED AND CHILLED TO THE QUEEN'S TASTE THEN SERVED WITH MAYONNAISE FOR LUNCH

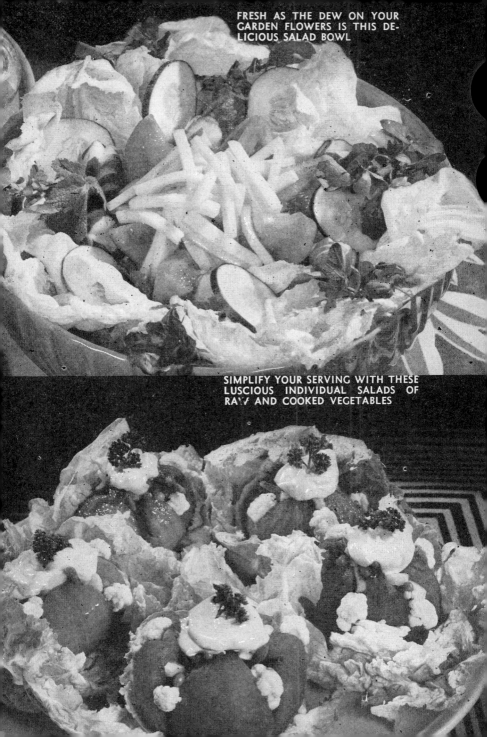

FRESH AS THE DEW ON YOUR GARDEN FLOWERS IS THIS DELICIOUS SALAD BOWL

SIMPLIFY YOUR SERVING WITH THESE LUSCIOUS INDIVIDUAL SALADS OF RAW AND COOKED VEGETABLES

GREEN BEAN SALAD

2 cups cooked green beans,
   cut or whole
1 tablespoon minced onion
½ cup French Dressing

Lettuce
1 hard-cooked egg yolk,
   minced

Marinate green beans and onion in French dressing for 1 hour or longer. Drain beans and arrange on lettuce. Sprinkle minced hard-cooked egg yolk over beans. Serves 4.

CABBAGE SALAD

Select a small firm head of cabbage. Cut into halves and slice it from the cut edge with a sharp knife or slaw cutter. Combine with any desired dressing and serve immediately.

To retain the vitamins, cabbage should be sliced as near serving time as possible and should never be soaked in water.

IN ASPIC—Fold cut cabbage into one package lemon gelatin made as directed on the package, chill and unmold. Garnish.

CALIFORNIA SLAW

1 small head of cabbage
2 tart apples, chopped
1 medium onion, minced
2 pimientos, minced
3 hard-cooked eggs
¼ teaspoon salt

1 tablespoon sugar
1 teaspoon dry mustard
1 tablespoon melted butter
⅓ cup lemon juice
½ cup cream, whipped
Parsley

Shred cabbage and combine with apples, onion and pimientos. Rub yolks of hard-cooked eggs to a paste and add salt, sugar, mustard and butter and mix thoroughly until smooth. Stir in lemon juice and mix. Add whipped cream. Combine with shredded cabbage mixture and garnish with the whites of cooked eggs and bits of parsley. Serves 6.

PENNSYLVANIA CABBAGE SALAD

2 cups shredded cabbage
1 green or red pepper,
   cut fine

1 teaspoon salt
½ cup Sour Cream Salad
   Dressing (page 450)

Mix shredded cabbage, pepper and salt; pour dressing over cabbage and mix well. Serve at once. Makes 6 portions.

CARDINAL SALAD

2 large beets
2 tablespoons vinegar
½ cup wax beans
½ cup peas
½ cup asparagus tips

Mayonnaise made with vine-
gar from beets
Lettuce .
Radishes for a garnish

Boil beets until tender, slice, cover with vinegar and let stand
until the following day. Drain off the vinegar and use it in
making the mayonnaise. Arrange beans, peas, asparagus tips
and mayonnaise in little rose-like nests of lettuce leaves, and
garnish with radishes.

CARROT SALAD

1 cup grated raw carrot
1 cup chopped raw cabbage
or celery, or cabbage and
celery combined

1 tablespoon lemon-juice
½ teaspoon salt
Mayonnaise or boiled dressing
Lettuce leaves

Mix the ingredients well and serve on crisp lettuce leaves.
The grated carrot may be served alone on lettuce or may be
combined with cold boiled peas, with chopped nuts and apples,
or with onions and radishes.

CAULIFLOWER AND SHRIMP SALAD

1 cauliflower
Mayonnaise dressing

Lettuce
Cooked shrimps

Cook the cauliflower in boiling water, drain, and put it, head
down, into a bowl. When cold, place it, stem down, on a shallow dish and cover with mayonnaise. Garnish with lettuce arranged to resemble the leaves of the cauliflower, and add little
clusters of shrimps.

CELERY SALAD

2 cups celery
½ cup mayonnaise

Strips of pimiento or green
pepper and celery curls

After thoroughly washing the celery allow it to crisp in cold
water. Then wipe it dry, cut it into inch lengths and these
into lengthwise strips. Place them in a salad-bowl, and add
sufficient mayonnaise dressing to moisten the whole. Garnish

with the pimiento or pepper and the celery curls. Serve at once. Celery salad admits of a wide range of additions, any cold meat, fish or fowl left from a previous meal being palatable served in it.

CELERY CURLS—These are made from the tender inner stalks. Cut in lengths of two or three inches and slit in narrow strips almost to the end. Place in water with plenty of ice. As the slit stalks chill, the ends curl.

CRESS SALAD

1 pint water cress   1 onion   French dressing

Pick over the leaves of the cress carefully, removing all bruised or wilted ones, wash and drain, and with the fingers break the stems into two-inch lengths. Lay the cress in a salad bowl, chop the onion very fine, strew it over the cress, add French dressing and serve.

CRESS AND DANDELION SALAD

1 cup water cress   6 thin slices raw onion
1 cup dandelion greens   French dressing

The dandelion should be fresh and young. Wash the leaves carefully and drain well. Arrange them in a salad bowl with the cress. Add the slices of onion and pour the French dressing over all.

CRESS AND WALNUT SALAD

½ cup walnut meats   1 pint water cress
1 lemon   French dressing

Crack walnuts and remove their meats as nearly as possible in halves. Squeeze over them the juice of the lemon and let them stand for a short time. Pick over the water cress and wash it carefully. Drain it on a napkin and at the last moment drench it with French dressing. Spread the nuts over it and give them also a generous sprinkling of the dressing.

CUCUMBER SALAD

3 cucumbers   Salt   French dressing

Cut about an inch off the point of each cucumber, and pare carefully. Slice very thin, sprinkle with a little salt, and let stand ten minutes. Serve with French dressing.

CUCUMBER JELLY SALAD

1 pint grated cucumber	2 teaspoons cold water
Salt and paprika	6 halves of walnut-meats
2 tablespoons vinegar	Mayonnaise
1 tablespoon oil	Lettuce leaves
1 teaspoon gelatin	

Peel cucumbers, removing most of the white as well as the green skin. Grate enough to give one pint and season with salt, paprika, vinegar and oil. Add gelatin mixed with cold water. Place over the fire until warm and well mixed. Do not boil. In the bottom of an individual mold put a half kernel of walnut, then pour in the cucumber mixture and when it has cooled, chill. When ready to serve, turn each mold on to a nest of young lettuce leaves, and add a spoonful of mayonnaise.

LETTUCE SALAD

Choose for this the crisp center of the lettuce. Wash it, dry it well, pull to pieces or cut it into four or six sections, and arrange it in a salad bowl. Pour over the center of the dish any dressing preferred. Mayonnaise is frequently used, and Russian dressing is used even more frequently, perhaps, but with a heavy dinner the French dressing is to be preferred to any other.

The following vegetables may be used instead of or with lettuce: endive, peppergrass, water cress, nasturtium leaves, spinach, chicory, sorrel, dandelion, escarole, and romaine.

LETTUCE AND ONION SALAD

2 lettuce hearts	French dressing	1 Spanish onion

Strip off, and set aside for some other purpose, the green leaves of lettuce. Wash the hearts, pull them to pieces or cut into sections, and drop into ice-water to crisp them. Peel the Spanish onion and cut it into thin shavings. Shake the lettuce in a colander or wire basket to free it from water or dry on a towel. Fill the salad bowl with alternate layers of the lettuce and onion slices, sprinkling on each layer a little French dressing.

POTATO SALAD

No. 1.

1 quart potatoes	2 tablespoons grated onion
2 tablespoons chopped parsley	French dressing to moisten

Boil the potatoes with skins on and allow them to cool before peeling, as it is considered a good thing to have potatoes waxy rather than mealy for salad. Peel potatoes, cut into small pieces or thin slices, and mix with parsley, onion, and French dressing. Set in a cool place for two hours before serving.

No. 2.

1 quart new potatoes	1 tablespoon chopped parsley
1 tablespoons oil	Salt and pepper
2 tablespoons vinegar	Thin mayonnaise or boiled
1 onion	dressing
2 stalks celery	Cut beets
1 tablespoon capers	Lettuce, lemon

Boil potatoes until done, but not too soft, slice them when cooled and add oil and vinegar. Chop onion and celery very fine, and add, with capers, parsley, and salt and pepper to taste. Pour a thin mayonnaise over all, mixing thoroughly with a wooden spoon and fork. Garnish with lettuce, a few pieces of lemon and cut beets.

POTATO AND PEA SALAD

2 cups boiled potatoes, diced	½ cup French dressing
1 cup boiled peas	Lettuce, mayonnaise

Pour two-thirds of the French dressing over the diced potatoes, and the other third over the cold peas, and set where they will be chilled. After an hour, combine them and arrange on lettuce leaves. Garnish with mayonnaise.

SPINACH SALAD

1 pint spinach	2 hard-cooked eggs	French dressing

Wash spinach carefully. Select only thick, tender leaves (save others and stems for cooking). If too large, tear to size. Shake off excess water. Chop whites and yolks of eggs separately and turn into bowl with leaves. Moisten with tart French dressing. Add any mild-flavored vegetable.

TOMATO AND LETTUCE SALAD

No. 1.

3 tomatoes   Lettuce leaves   6 tablespoons French dressing

Scald the tomatoes, remove the skins and chill the tomatoes. Just before serving time, cut them in halves, crosswise, and place one piece, with the outside upward, on each serving-plate with one or two leaves of white, crisp lettuce underneath. Pour over each portion a tablespoon of French dressing.

No. 2.

3 tomatoes   .   ⅓ to ½ cup French dressing
Lettuce   1 tablespoon capers

Select smooth tomatoes about two inches in diameter. Scald, peel and chill. Cut in quarters or in slices and arrange on a plate with lettuce leaves or sections of lettuce hearts. Add the capers to the dressing.

TOMATO AND CELERY SALAD

6 tomatoes   ⅓ to ½ cup mayonnaise
2 cups celery, diced   Lettuce leaves

Select firm tomatoes of a good size, scald, peel and chill, cut a slice from the top of each, and scoop out all the seeds and soft pulp, being careful not to break the sides. Cut celery into small dice, mix it with mayonnaise dressing, fill the shells with mixture, place one teaspoon of the dressing on top of each tomato and serve individually on a bed of lettuce leaves, placing three or four small leaves on each plate and the tomato in the center.

TOMATO SURPRISE SALAD

6 tomatoes   ¼ cup mayonnaise dressing
¾ cup diced cucumber   Lettuce
½ cup diced, cooked chicken   Parsley, cauliflower buds
¼ cup chopped nuts

Select medium-sized smooth tomatoes. Scald, peel and chill. Carefully scoop the inside out of the tomatoes. Remove the seeds from the pulp. Chill all ingredients, and when ready to serve, mix the chicken, cucumber, tomato pulp, and nuts with the mayonnaise dressing. Add more salt if needed. Fill the tomatoes. Arrange on lettuce leaves. Garnish with mayonnaise and decorate each tomato top with parsley and cauliflower buds.

TOMATO JELLY SALAD

3 cups stewed tomatoes, fresh or canned	1 teaspoon sugar
	Salt
¼ cup chopped onion	1 tablespoon gelatin
½ cup chopped celery	½ cup cold water
1 bay leaf 1 clove	Lettuce
¼ green pepper	Mayonnaise

Cook tomatoes with seasonings. Soak gelatin in cold water, add to boiling tomatoes, strain and pour into cups about the size of a tomato. Make a nest of small green lettuce leaves for each mold when serving, and place one tablespoon of mayonnaise on top of each tomato as it is turned from the mold.

TOMATO ASPIC RING SALAD—Pour into ring mold and fill center with crisp greens, cottage cheese, chicken or fish salad.

TOMATO ROSE SALAD

Firm Tomatoes	Hard-cooked egg yolk
Cream cheese	Watercress or lettuce
Milk	French dressing

Peel tomatoes and chill them. Slightly soften cream cheese with milk. Form two rows of petals on each tomato by pressing level teaspoons of the softened cheese against the side of the tomato, then drawing the teaspoon down with a curving motion. Sprinkle center of each tomato with hard-cooked egg yolk pressed through a strainer. Serve on crisp watercress or lettuce with French dressing.

FROZEN FRUIT SALAD

1 teaspoon unflavored gelatin	2 cups heavy cream
2 tablespoons cold water	1½ cups cut fruit (fresh canned or candied cherries, peaches, pineapple, etc.)
¾ cup mayonnaise	
1 teaspoon sugar	Lettuce

Soften gelatin in the cold water, melt it over steam and beat it into the mayonnaise. Add the sugar to the cream and

whip it, then combine with mayonnaise. Stir in fruit. Freeze
as directed on page 425. Serve on lettuce. The mayonnaise may
be omitted and served separately.

ALLIGATOR PEAR SALAD

2 alligator pears   French dressing
Lettuce leaves

The alligator pear, or avocado, is now available in all markets
at very reasonable prices throughout the greater part of the
year. Cut each pear into six pieces, giving wedge-shaped sections, and if these are too large, cut each section again lengthwise. Peel and arrange wedges on beds of lettuce leaves. Either
French dressing or Russian dressing may be used, but the fruit
is so rich that French dressing is preferred by most people.

APRICOT AND BANANA SALAD

2 cups lettuce leaves, shredded   Whipped cream or boiled
1 cup sliced bananas   dressing
6 stewed apricots

On each plate arrange a bed of shredded lettuce, and on it
place a layer of sliced ripe bananas, topped by the halves of an
apricot. Serve with whipped cream or boiled dressing.

BANANA AND NUT SALAD

3 well ripened bananas   ½ cup mayonnaise or boiled
½ cup chopped nuts   dressing
6 leaves lettuce

Peel bananas and cut in two lengthwise. Roll each half in
nut-meats. Place on lettuce leaf and garnish with dressing.
Equal parts of dressing and whipped cream may be used.

COCONUT, CELERY AND APPLE SALAD

1½ cups mixed diced tart   4 tablespoons orange-juice
   apples and celery   Salt
½ cup shredded coconut   Paprika
1 tablespoon lemon-juice   Lettuce leaves
4 tablespoons oil   Currant or plum jelly

Mix the apples, celery, and coconut. Sprinkle with the
lemon-juice. Add a French dressing made from the oil and

PEELED MELON FILLED WITH
TOMATO ASPIC AND FROSTED
WITH CREAM CHEESE

NATURE IN THE RAW IS EN-
TICING WHEN IT'S A SALAD
OF SUN-RIPENED FRUITS

AS IF BY MAGIC A STUFFED TOMATO WITH SPOONED PETALS OF CREAM CHEESE BECOMES A ROSE—LOVELY TO LOOK AT, DELIGHTFUL TO EAT

NOT PLUCKED FROM AN ITALIAN VINEYARD BUT FASHIONED WITH PEAR, FROSTED WITH CREAM CHEESE AND STUDDED WITH HALF GRAPES FOR INDIVIDUAL SALADS AT FORMAL OCCASIONS

orange-juice, with salt and paprika to taste. Line a salad-bowl with lettuce leaves and pile chilled salad in center. Dot with currant or plum jelly.

FRENCH FRUIT SALAD

1 orange	1 dozen walnuts
1 banana	Lettuce
½ pound Malaga grapes	French dressing

Peel the orange and cut the sections from the membrane with a sharp knife or a pair of shears. If the fruit is allowed to stand in cold water after peeling, the bitter white membrane will come off easily.

Peel the banana and cut in quarter-inch slices. Remove the skins and seeds from the grapes. Break walnuts into small pieces, but do not chop. Mix these ingredients thoroughly and place on ice. Serve on lettuce leaves with French dressing.

GRAPEFRUIT SALAD

Peel grapefruit and free the sections from all membrane and seeds. Cut sections in half, crosswise; lay on bed of lettuce leaves and serve with French dressing. Sprinkle with tarragon leaves or with mint if desired.

GRAPEFRUIT AND GRAPE SALAD

2 cups grapefruit sections	½ cup Malaga grapes, peeled
2 tablespoons grape-juice	and seeded
2 tablespoons French dressing	

Peel fine large grapefruit and separate the sections, removing every particle of the bitter white inner skin. Peel and seed the grapes and mix with the grapefruit. Set, covered, in the refrigerator until very cold. Pour over them the grape-juice and French dressing.

WHITE GRAPE SALAD

1 pound Malaga grapes   Lettuce   French dressing or mayonnaise

Peel grapes and remove the seeds by cutting the grapes almost in two, with a thin sharp knife. Arrange on lettuce leaves and serve with French dressing or mayonnaise.

ORANGE SALAD

Peel oranges and free the sections entirely from the membrane. Remove seeds, cut sections in halves crosswise, lay on bed of lettuce leaves, and serve with French dressing. Sprinkle with tarragon or with minced green pepper, if desired. Minced celery may be added.

LIME FRUIT SALAD IN MOLD

1 package lime gelatin
1 cup boiling water
1 cup cold water
4 slices canned pineapple

½ cup canned white cherries
¼ cup red seeded grapes, cut into fancy shapes
4 pears, halved

Dissolve gelatin in boiling water and add cold water. Set aside to cool slightly. Add fruit and pour into mold. Chill until firm. Serves 12.

GARNISH:—

Head lettuce and endive
Pimiento cream cheese
1 No. 2½ can pears
Cream cheese

Raisins
Nuts
Preserved ginger
Sliced pineapple

Mix cream cheese with chopped nuts, raisins and ginger and stuff pears. Use as garnish around lime mold. Top with pimiento-cream-cheese flower. Place slices of pineapple topped with pimiento cream cheese between pears. Garnish with endive. Serve with mayonnaise.

PEAR AND CHERRY SALAD

6 halves of stewed pears, fresh or canned
Lettuce leaves

36 white cherries
French dressing or mayonnaise

Place the half pears on crisp lettuce leaves. Stone the cherries and arrange them around the pears. Serve with preferred dressing. Omit cherries and garnish pear halves with pimiento.

PINEAPPLE AND NUT SALAD IN TOMATO BASKETS

1 cup crushed pineapple
1 cup broken nut-meats
French dressing

6 tomatoes
Mayonnaise

Mix pineapple with nut-meats and stand in French dressing in the refrigerator. Peel and cut off the top of each tomato leaving a strip to form a handle. Carefully scoop out the center and fill with the pineapple and nuts. Place one teaspoon of mayonnaise on top of each basket.

PINEAPPLE AND CREAM CHEESE SALAD

6 slices canned pineapple
1 cup cream cheese
Purple grape-juice

French dressing
Lettuce leaves

Work enough grape-juice into the cream cheese to soften it so that it can be made into balls with the hands or with butter paddles. Place a slice of pineapple on a lettuce leaf, put a cheese ball on top and pour grape-juice and French dressing over all.

TROPICAL SALAD

1 cup cantaloup balls
6 slices tomatoes
Garnish of red pepper

Any desired dressing
Lettuce leaves

With a vegetable cutter, cut small balls from a cantaloup that is fairly firm in texture. Arrange several balls on a slice of tomato which has been placed on a nest of lettuce leaves. Garnish with pieces of red pepper or green pepper cut in diamond shapes. Serve with any desired dressing.

WALDORF SALAD

1 cup diced apple
1 cup diced celery
½ cup broken walnut-meats

French dressing
Lettuce leaves
Mayonnaise

Fold together the apple, celery, and nuts with French dressing and serve on lettuce leaves with mayonnaise. Do not allow

FISH SALAD

1 pound flaked, cooked fish
2 tablespoons oil
1 tablespoon vinegar

1 cup chopped celery
Lettuce
Mayonnaise

The remains of almost any cold fish may be used in salad very satisfactorily, but the salad is more successful when made of fish that will flake nicely, such as salmon, cod, haddock, or halibut. Remove the bones, pick the fish into flakes, turn over it oil mixed with vinegar and set away in a cold place. When about to serve, chop celery and add to the fish. Arrange crisp white leaves of lettuce in cup shapes on a platter, using one or two leaves for each, then lay one spoonful of the mixture in each cup and pour over it one spoonful of mayonnaise.

LOBSTER SALAD

1 ½ cups diced lobster meat
½ cup diced celery
Vinegar

Mayonnaise
Lettuce

Prepare lobster as directed (see Index). Remove the meat and the coral. Cut the meat into pieces of convenient size for eating. Sprinkle a very little vinegar over the lobster, but keep the celery crisp until it is time to make the salad. Then mix the lobster meat and celery together, stir in enough mayonnaise to moisten and flavor the whole. Arrange the salad on the center of a bed of crisp white lettuce bordered with green lettuce leaves laid under the outer edges. Pour on the remainder of the mayonnaise and sprinkle over it the coral, well pounded, and, if liked, a few capers. Garnish with the claws. Sometimes lettuce leaves are arranged on a platter in cup-like clusters of two or three each, and the salad is divided equally among the clusters. The salad may be served in the cleaned lobster shells.

OYSTER SALAD

1 quart oysters
1 tablespoon oil
½ teaspoon salt
⅛ teaspoon pepper

2 tablespoons vinegar
1 tablespoon lemon-juice
1 pint celery
½ cup mayonnaise

Clean the oysters (see Index) and place them in a stew-pan on the fire, adding no water. When they are boiling, drain them in a colander; place them in an earthenware dish, and add the oil, salt, pepper, vinegar and lemon-juice. When cold, set in the refrigerator for at least two hours. Cut the white part of the celery into very thin slices, and place it in a bowl in the refrigerator. When ready to serve, drain the celery, mix with the oysters and half of the mayonnaise. Turn the whole into a salad-bowl, and pour over it the rest of the dressing. Garnish with white celery leaves and serve at once.

If preferred, lettuce leaves may be arranged on a large platter in groups of two or three to form cups and in each cup may be dropped four or five oysters with one spoonful of mayonnaise poured over them. A tiny spray of parsley may be thrust into the sauce at the center of each cup.

SALMON SALAD

1 cup cold boiled salmon, fresh or canned	1 cup shredded cabbage or chopped celery
Mayonnaise	Lettuce leaves

Combine salmon, broken in flakes, and shredded cabbage or celery. Serve with mayonnaise on lettuce leaves.

SARDINE SALAD

¾ cup sardines	Lettuce leaves
¾ cup hard-cooked egg	Mayonnaise or French dressing
1 cucumber	

Remove the skin and bones from sardines and mix with chopped hard-cooked eggs. Cut cucumber in thin slices and arrange on lettuce leaves. Add sardine and egg mixture. Serve with mayonnaise or French dressing.

SHRIMP SALAD

1 pint cooked shrimps or prawns	Lettuce, shredded celery, or shaved cabbage
Marinade	Maynonaise or other dressing

Marinate the shrimps and serve whole on lettuce, shredded celery, or shaved cabbage, and cover well with a mayonnaise or other dressing. Canned shrimps are excellent for salads.

SPINACH AND HAM SALAD

2 cups cooked spinach
Salt and pepper
Juice of 1 lemon

6 slices cold boiled ham
Any desired dressing
Lettuce leaves

Drain the spinach and season with salt, pepper, and lemon juice. Pack into 12 small molds. Place ham on lettuce and place two molds of spinach on opposite sides of each slice of ham. Serve with dressing.

SWEETBREAD SALAD

1 pair sweetbreads
1 tablespoon vinegar
½ tablespoon oil
½ teaspoon salt

⅛ teaspoon pepper
6 heart leaves lettuce
1 cup celery, thinly sliced
1 cup mayonnaise

Prepare sweetbreads (see Index); cut in cubes, add oil, vinegar, salt and pepper, and place in the refrigerator for one hour. Prepare the lettuce and celery, and put them also in the refrigerator. Just before serving time, fold the celery and sweetbreads together and add half the dressing. Arrange the lettuce leaves on a flat dish, divide the sweetbread mixture into six parts, and place one part on each leaf. Put the remainder of the dressing upon the salad and serve at once.

TUNAFISH SALAD

Follow directions given for fish salad, on page 443.

ESCAROLE BOWL—CHICKEN LIVER DRESSING

Wash a head of chicory and a head of escarole, pick over carefully, soak in cold water and dry thoroughly. Make the following dressing: Wash two chicken livers and boil until tender with a carrot, an onion, a piece of celery and a bunch of parsley. Add the bouillon to your soup stock. Rub the livers and yolks of 2 hard-cooked eggs through a sieve. Add 1½ teaspoons French mustard, pepper, salt and mix to a paste. Add 2 tablespoons olive oil, drop by drop, a teaspoon red wine vinegar and a tablespoon red wine. Pour this over the greens and toss well. Serve cold.

SALAD DRESSINGS

THERE are three kinds of salad dressings which are the foundation for practically all others used: French dressing, mayonnaise dressing and boiled dressing.

French Dressing

French dressing, made from oil and acid, is the most widely used dressing. Vinegar is the acid generally used with the oil in vegetable and meat salads, while in fruit salads the juice of lemons, grapefruit or oranges is used.

The choice of oils to be used in dressing is an individual matter. Olive oil has the most distinct flavor. With cottonseed or corn oil the amount of condiments used may be slightly increased if desired.

Serve French dressing with chicken, fish, meat, vegetable and fruit salads.

FRENCH DRESSING

1 clove garlic (optional)	1 tablespoon salt
1 cup vinegar	1 teaspoon paprika
2 teaspoons dry mustard	½ teaspoon pepper
1 tablespoon sugar	2 cups salad oil

If using garlic, soak it in vinegar ½ hour before mixing the dressing. Mix dry ingredients together and place in a covered jar or bottle. Remove garlic from vinegar and add vinegar to dry ingredients. Pour on the oil slowly. Place in refrigerator until ready for use. Just before serving, shake vigorously for 2 minutes. Makes 3 cups dressing.

VARIATIONS—TARRAGON DRESSING: Tarragon vinegar may be used. Mustard, sugar and paprika may be omitted.

FOR FRUIT SALADS: Use ¼ cup each of lemon or lime and orange juice in place of half the vinegar. Reduce mustard to ½ teaspoon, salt to 1 teaspoon and paprika to ½ teaspoon. Increase sugar to ¾ cup. Add ½ teaspoon Worcestershire sauce and omit pepper and garlic.

VARIATIONS using ½ recipe French Dressing as foundation—

ANCHOVY: Cream 2 tablespoons anchovy paste with seasonings. Add 1 tablespoon each of minced onion and parsley.

CHIFFONADE: Add 2 tablespoons each of chopped green pepper, olives, parsley, pimiento and 1 hard-cooked egg, chopped. Add chopped red peppers and cooked beets, if desired.

CURRY: Add ½ teaspoon curry powder and a few drops onion juice.

HORSE-RADISH: Add 4 tablespoons grated horse-radish (juice pressed out) ½ clove garlic, crushed and a dash of cayenne.

MINT: Add 2 tablespoons chopped mint.

OLIVE: Add ½ cup chopped ripe or stuffed olives.

PARMESAN: Add 4 tablespoons grated Parmesan cheese.

PICKLE: Add ¼ cup minced pickles.

ROQUEFORT: Add 4 tablespoons crushed Roquefort cheese, 1 to 1½ teaspoons onion juice or finely chopped chives and a dash of Tabasco sauce or cayenne pepper.

LEMON FRENCH DRESSING

½ cup lemon juice	1 teaspoon paprika
½ cup salad oil	2 tablespoons sugar or
1 teaspoon salt	honey

Combine ingredients in the order listed. Shake well before serving. If desired, add ½ teaspoon celery seed and clove of garlic. Makes 1 cup dressing.

If a clear dressing is desired, omit paprika and substitute a dash of pepper.

HAWAII FRENCH DRESSING

¼ cup pineapple juice	1 teaspoon sugar
2 tablespoons lemon juice	½ teaspoon salt
½ cup salad oil	½ teaspoon paprika

Combine ingredients, chill. Shake or beat thoroughly before serving. This recipe is adapted for use with mixed fruit salads. Makes ⅞ cup.

VARIATIONS—BANANA FRENCH DRESSING: Add 2 thoroughly mashed ripe bananas and ¼ teaspoon nutmeg.

RUBY FRENCH DRESSING: Add 1 to 1½ teaspoons grenadine or maraschino cherry juice.

MAYONNAISE DRESSING

No. 1.

2 uncooked egg yolks
½ teaspoon salt
¼ teaspoon pepper
¼ teaspoon paprika

⅛ teaspoon mustard
3 tablespoons vinegar or
    lemon juice
2 cups salad oil

To yolks, add dry seasonings, beat thoroughly, add vinegar or lemon juice and beat again. Add oil gradually (drop by drop at first) beating hard between additions. The mixture should be thick and creamy. Should mayonnaise curdle, begin with a third egg yolk, add a small quantity of oil to the egg, and then by very small quantities, add the curdled dressing. At times a dressing may be quite firm when left, only to be found curdled and disappointing when the time comes to use it. This third egg process will, however, usually restore it. Equal proportions of vinegar and lemon juice may be used. Tarragon vinegar is sometimes used to give an interesting flavor.

No. 2.

1 egg yolk, hard cooked
1 egg yolk, uncooked
½ teaspoon sugar
½ teaspoon salt
¼ teaspoon pepper
½ teaspoon prepared mustard

¼ teaspoon Worcestershire
    sauce
1 cup salad oil
3 tablespoons vinegar
    or lemon juice

Place hard-cooked egg yolk in a bowl and mash it fine. When the yolk is like powder, add uncooked yolk and stir until mixture is smooth, then add sugar, salt, pepper, mustard and sauce. When the whole is well mixed, add oil gradually, stirring constantly, and thin as necessary with vinegar or lemon juice. Chill for 1 hour before using.

Originally, only a spoon was used in beating this dressing, however, now a wire whisk, small wooden spoon, rotary egg beater or a four-tined fork may be used.

COLORED MAYONNAISE: To color mayonnaise red, add lobster paste, raspberry or cooked beet pulp or juice from raspberries or beets; for green color add chopped fresh spinach, parsley or concentrated liquor from boiled artichokes.

MAYONNAISE VARIATIONS—Foundation 1 cup mayonnaise.

APPETIZER MAYONNAISE: Rub bowl with garlic and beat in 2 cups French Dressing (page 446).

CHILI SAUCE MAYONNAISE: Add ½ teaspoon lemon juice, 2 teaspoons chili sauce, ½ teaspoon confectioners' sugar and 1 teaspoon horse-radish.

CORONATION MAYONNAISE: Add 1 tablespoon each of lemon juice and red Bar-le-Duc and a dash of paprika.

FRUIT JUICE MAYONNAISE: Add 3 tablespoons fruit juice, ½ cup confectioners' sugar and 1 cup heavy cream, whipped.

LEMON CREAM MAYONNAISE: Add ½ cup confectioners' sugar, ¼ cup lemon juice, a few grains salt and 1 cup heavy cream, whipped.

ROQUEFORT MAYONNAISE: Add 2 tablespoons Roquefort cheese, mashed, 1 teaspoon lemon juice and ¼ teaspoon salt.

SOUR CREAM MAYONNAISE: Add ⅓ cup confectioners' sugar, 2 tablespoons lemon juice and 1 cup sour cream, whipped.

THOUSAND ISLAND DRESSING: Add ⅓ cup chili sauce, 1 tablespoon each chopped olives and pimientos and 1 hard-cooked egg yolk, chopped or rubbed through a sieve.

WHIPPED CREAM MAYONNAISE: Add 4 teaspoons confectioners' sugar and 1 cup cream, whipped.

RUSSIAN DRESSING

1½ tablespoons lemon juice
2 tablespoons thick chili
   sauce
1 tablespoon Worcestershire
   sauce
½ cup mayonnaise

Mix the lemon juice, chili sauce and Worcestershire thoroughly and add the mayonnaise.

THOUSAND ISLAND DRESSING

1 cup mayonnaise
4 tablespoons chili sauce
1 tablespoon chives
3 tablespoons catchup
1 teaspoon tarragon vinegar
1 tablespoon chopped green
   pepper
3 tablespoons chopped red
   pepper
1 teaspoon paprika

Add chili sauce, chives, catchup, peppers, paprika and vinegar to mayonnaise.

BOILED DRESSING

1½ tablespoons sugar
¼ teaspoon salt
1 tablespoon flour
1 teaspoon dry mustard

3 egg yolks
¾ cup cold water
¼ cup vinegar
2 tablespoons butter

Mix sugar, salt, flour and mustard together. Beat egg yolks slightly; add dry ingredients, water and vinegar and mix to a smooth paste. Cook over low heat, stirring constantly, until thickened. Remove from heat and blend in butter. When ready to use thin with cream or fold in whipped cream. Makes 1 cup dressing.

CREAMY EGGLESS MAYONNAISE

1 tablespoon sugar
½ teaspoon paprika
½ teaspoon salt
Few grains white pepper
½ teaspoon dry mustard

½ cup evaporated milk, undiluted
2½ tablespoons vinegar
1¼ to 1½ cups salad oil

Mix dry ingredients with milk; beat in vinegar, add oil gradually, beating thoroughly. Use less oil for a thinner mixture or thin with evaporated milk before serving. Makes 1 pint.

SOUR CREAM SALAD DRESSING

1 teaspoon salt
1 tablespoon sugar
⅛ teaspoon cayenne

1 tablespoon lemon juice
2 tablespoons vinegar
1 cup sour cream

Combine all ingredients and mix thoroughly. Makes 1 cup.

WHIPPED CREAM FRUIT DRESSING

⅔ cup sugar
2 tablespoons flour
2 eggs, beaten
2 tablespoons salad oil

3 tablespoons lemon juice
4 tablespoons orange juice
1 cup pineapple juice
½ cup heavy cream, whipped

Mix sugar and flour; add remaining ingredients except cream and cook over low heat until thickened, stirring constantly. When cold fold in whipped cream. Makes 2 cups.

CAKES

CAKES are of two general types depending upon the basic ingredients they contain. In one group are the cakes made with fat—the various butter cakes, pound cakes, and fruit cakes; and in the other group are those that are made without fat—sponge and angel cakes. Either kind of cake may be baked in many different forms—oblong or round loaves, sheets, layers, or individual cakes of various shapes, depending somewhat upon the kind of cake but also upon the way they are to be served. The butter cakes are most frequently baked in layers, pound cakes in round or oblong loaves, and sponge and angel cakes, in sheets or in the tube pans which give round loaves with a hole in the center.

Materials Used in Cake Making

SUGAR—Fine grained granulated sugar is the standard sugar for cake. A coarse grained sugar may produce a coarse grained cake with a hard crust. Light brown or dark brown sugar is preferred by most people for fruit cake or any dark cake. Brown sugar is lighter and more moist than granulated and when it is used instead of granulated sugar the substitution should be weight for weight, not measure for measure.

SHORTENING—Any fat that has a mild flavor may be used for the shortening in cake. Butter is the first choice with many cooks because of its flavor, but it is the most expensive of fats. Tasteless vegetable or animal oils or hardened fats produce perfect results, aside from the flavor. Since these fats are unsalted the amount of salt should be increased by one-half.

Hard fats should be creamed with the sugar. If they are melted and added while hot, the cake is likely to be tough. If melted fat is called for, it should be cooled before it is added.

EGGS—Eggs for cake need not be newly laid, but they should be of good quality, free from taint and fresh enough to beat up well. Two yolks or two whites may be used instead of one whole egg, or a yolk may be substituted for a white or the other way around. The substitution of yolks for whites or vice versa makes a difference in the color and to some extent in the texture of the cake. In recipes calling for egg whites alone or for more whites than yolks, the number of whites cannot be reduced without changing the texture of the cake. If an egg white is used instead of a yolk, one teaspoon of shortening should be added. When fewer whole eggs are to be used than a recipe calls for, add one-half teaspoon of baking powder instead of each egg omitted, after the first one. Eggs improve the quality of the texture of batters, and while a fairly good plain cake can be made with only one egg, additional eggs give a lighter, more delicate texture, improve the flavor and produce a smoother crust.

FLOUR—In the cake recipes given in this book, cake flour has been used. Cake flour has a low gluten content and therefore makes a finer textured cake. Although cake flour is preferred for cakemaking, successful cakes are made with all-purpose flour. If all-purpose flour is used for cake flour, reduce the amount of flour used by 2 tablespoons per cup of flour called for and do not beat the batter as long as when using cake flour. Always sift flour before measuring. Fill cup lightly. Resifting with dry ingredients as directed.

LEAVENING AGENTS—The most usual leavening agents in cakemaking are eggs and baking powder. When 1 egg is omitted from a recipe the baking powder should be increased by $\frac{1}{2}$ teaspoon. If the liquid used is sour milk or cream, use $\frac{1}{2}$ teaspoon baking soda for each cup of liquid. Then decrease baking powder slightly. It is best to sift the baking soda with the dry ingredients. If the soda is dissolved in the sour milk it must be added to the mixture immediately or some of the gas to be used in leavening will be lost.

No chemical leavening agent is used in true spongecakes. The air incorporated by means of the beaten egg whites, and the steam generated in cooking make the cake rise as it is baked.

FLAVORINGS—A cake shortened entirely with good butter needs no additional flavoring though most people add some flavoring extract. Vanilla and lemon extracts are used more commonly than others, but almond, orange, pineapple, and rose give a variety in flavors. Very often the juices of fresh fruit such as lemon or orange, or the grated peel or rind, are used in certain types of cake. Too much flavoring is a common mistake. The amount given in recipes is for an extract of average strength. Where an extract of greater strength is used the amount should be decreased.

Standard Method of Mixing Butter Cakes

There are several methods of combining ingredients for butter cakes, but the method described below is considered the standard.

CREAM THE BUTTER OR OTHER SHORTENING by continued rubbing against the sides of the bowl until it is soft and light. Some people prefer to use a wooden spoon for this, but a fork does the work more quickly. If the shortening is too hard to cream easily, warm the bowl slightly by setting it in warm water, but do not melt the fat.

ADD THE SUGAR GRADUALLY and work well after each addition.

SEPARATE THE WHITES FROM THE YOLKS of the eggs. Beat the yolks until they are thick and lemon-colored, then add them to the creamed shortening and sugar. If the egg is not separated, beat the whole egg well and add here.

SIFT THE FLOUR, measure it and add to it all other dry ingredients, such as baking-powder, salt and spices, and then sift again.

ADD THE DRY INGREDIENTS AND MILK to the first mixture, alternately, keeping the batter of the same consistency throughout the mixing process. Beat just enough to make the mixture smooth.

ADD THE FLAVORING, then fold in the stiffly beaten egg-whites, unless the whites were added with the yolks.

WHEN FRUITS OR NUTS ARE USED, save out a little of the flour to sift over them, and add them to the cake mixture just before the egg-whites are added.

MELT CHOCOLATE OVER HOT WATER and add just after the egg-yolks. Add cocoa as one of the dry ingredients.

Baking Butter Cakes

For any cake made with fat, grease the pans with a melted, unsalted fat, using a pastry brush or a piece of soft paper, then dredge the pans with flour, and shake them to distribute the flour over the surface. Invert the pans and shake them to remove all surplus flour, leaving only the thin film which adheres to the fat. This helps to give the cake a smooth under crust.

If the oven temperature is difficult to control, if the cake pan is not smooth, or if the cake contains only a small amount of fat, it is advisable to line the pans with smooth paper. Cut the paper to fit the bottom of the pan, plus an allowance to cover the sides. For a rectangular pan, cut out the corners of the paper so that it will fit against the sides of the pan without overlapping or wrinkling. For a round or oval pan, cut gashes along the edge of the paper as far as the part which is to cover the bottom. The paper will then overlap smoothly on the sides of the pan. Grease the paper after it is fitted into the pan. The grease will hold the paper against the sides as the cake batter is poured in.

If you want the cake to rise to the top of the pan, fill the pan about two-thirds full. Spread the batter well into the corners and against the sides of the pan, leaving a slight depression in the center. As cake tends to rise more in the center than at the edges, this will help to make it flat on top when it is done.

BAKING TEMPERATURES—Place the pan in the center of the lower grate so that the greatest amount of heat will reach it from underneath. A moderate temperature, varying from 350° to 375°, is best for baking a butter cake. If the oven is too hot, a thick brown crust will form on the outside before the cake has fully risen and before the inside has thoroughly baked, resulting in a cracked surface.

THE TIME FOR BAKING depends on the thickness of the cake. Cup cakes take from twenty to thirty minutes, layer cakes about twenty minutes, and loaf cakes from forty-five to sixty minutes.

Divide the time of baking into quarters: (1) During the first quarter, the cake should rise and little bubbles form on the top; (2) in the second quarter, it should continue to rise and to form the crust; (3) in the third quarter, it should begin to brown, and (4) at the end of the fourth quarter it should be browned sufficiently and shrink from the tin.

TESTING THE CAKE—When the cake is fully baked, it will shrink from the sides of the pan. When touched lightly with the finger it will spring back. If the finger leaves a depression, the cake is not done.

Another test is to insert a clean wooden toothpick into the middle of the cake. If no particles of batter adhere to it when it is drawn out, the cake is done.

CARE AFTER BAKING—After removing the cake from the oven, allow it to remain in the pan about two minutes. Then, with a spatula or knife, loosen the edges. If there is any tendency for the cake to stick on the bottom, wring a cloth out of water and place it on the bottom of the pan for a few seconds. Turn the cake out on a wire cake-cooler and allow it to stand until cool.

Standard Method of Mixing Cakes Without Fat

Cakes without fat depend for leavening largely upon the air beaten into the eggs. The whites and yolks of the eggs may or may not be separated, depending upon the kind of cake. If using the whole egg, beat it till thick and lemon-colored; if using only the yolk, beat till thick and light in color, add the sugar gradually and beat after each addition until the sugar dissolves.

Add the flavoring and liquid, if there is any, and fold in the sifted dry ingredients.

When the whites have been beaten separately, they are added last, using the folding motion. Do not beat the mixture after the whites have been added. Place at once in a moderate oven (325°—350° F.).

General Directions for Baking Cakes Without Fat

Use an ungreased pan for sponge or angel cakes. If they are greased the batter cannot cling to the sides of the pan as it bakes and thus the cake does not reach its full height. Greasing also causes the cake to fall out of the pan during cooling, making it flat and soggy.

BAKING TEMPERATURES—True sponge and angel food cakes in which eggs are the only leavening are baked in a moderate oven (325°—350° F.) to insure the best volume and texture. If baked too slow the results will be a coarse uneven cake; if oven is too hot the cake will be small in volume, fine grained and tough. It can be truly said of such a cake, "half the making is the baking." When baking-powder is used, a slightly higher temperature is desirable. The division of baking time is the same as for butter cakes.

When the cake is a light brown, and springs back when

pressed with the finger, it is done. Remove it to a wire cake cooler, invert the pan and allow it to stand till the cake is cool. Then remove the cake from the pan. When serving, break it apart with two forks; cutting with a knife tends to crush the cake and make it appear heavy.

FOUNDATION OR PLAIN CAKE

1½ cups sifted cake flour	¾ cup sugar
2 teaspoons baking powder	2 eggs, well beaten
¼ teaspoon salt	½ cup milk
⅓ cup shortening	1 teaspoon vanilla

Sift flour, baking powder and salt together. Cream shortening, add sugar and cream until fluffy. Add eggs, then dry ingredients alternately with milk and vanilla, a small amount at a time. Beat after each addition. Pour into greased pans and bake in moderate oven (350° F.) 25 minutes. Frost as desired. Makes 2 (8-inch) layers.

CHEESE CAKE

2 cups fine zwieback crumbs	1½ teaspoons lemon juice
1½ cups sugar	1½ teaspoons grated lemon rind
1 teaspoon cinnamon	
½ cup melted butter or other shortening	1 cup cream
4 eggs	1½ pounds cottage cheese
⅛ teaspoon salt	3 tablespoons flour
	¼ cup chopped nut meats

Mix zwieback with ½ cup sugar, cinnamon and butter or shortening. Set aside ¾ cup to sprinkle over top, press remainder of crumbs into a 9-inch spring form pan, lining bottom and sides. Beat eggs with remaining 1 cup sugar, until light; add salt, lemon juice and rind, cream, cheese and flour, beat thoroughly and strain through a fine sieve. Pour into lined pan, sprinkle with remaining crumbs and nut meats. Bake in a moderate oven (350° F.) about 1 hour or until center is firm. Turn off heat, open oven door, let stand in oven 1 hour or until cooled. Serves 10 to 12.

Use 1 teaspoon vanilla instead of lemon juice and rind.

to lukewarm. Sift soda and flour together and add alternately with milk and eggs, beating thoroughly. Pour into greased muffin pans. Bake in a 350°F. oven 15 minutes. Makes 16 cakes. Cover with boiled frosting and coconut.

NUT CAKE

½ cup shortening	2 teaspoons baking powder
1 cup sugar	½ cup milk
2 eggs, separated	1 teaspoon vanilla
1½ cups sifted cake flour	1 cup chopped nut meats

Cream shortening and sugar, add egg yolks and beat well. Sift flour and baking powder and add alternately with milk and vanilla. Add nuts and fold in stiffly beaten egg whites. Bake in a greased loaf pan in a 350°F. oven 50 minutes.

WHITE MOUNTAIN CAKE

½ cup shortening	¼ teaspoon salt
1½ cups sugar	1 cup milk
2½ cups sifted cake flour	1 teaspoon vanilla
3 teaspoons baking powder	4 egg whites, stiffly beaten

Cream shortening, add sugar gradually and cream until light and fluffy. Sift flour, baking powder and salt together 3 times and add alternately with milk and vanilla a small amount at a time, beating until smooth after each addition. Fold in egg whites. Pour into a tube pan lined with waxed paper. Bake in a moderate oven (350° F.) 45 to 60 minutes. When cake is cold, cover with Boiled Frosting, page 479.

WHITE CAKE

⅔ cup shortening	½ teaspoon salt
2 cups sugar	1 cup milk
3 cups sifted cake flour	1 teaspoon vanilla
3 teaspoons baking powder	5 egg whites, stiffly beaten

Cream shortening, add sugar gradually and cream until light and fluffy. Sift dry ingredients together 3 times and add alternately with milk and vanilla to creamed mixture. Fold in egg whites. Pour into greased pans and bake in a moderate oven (350°F.) 30 minutes. Makes 3 (9-inch) layers.

GOLD CAKE

¾ cup butter or other
  shortening
1¼ cups sugar
8 egg yolks, beaten

2½ cups sifted cake flour
3 teaspoons baking powder
¼ teaspoon salt
¾ cup milk

1 teaspoon vanilla

Cream shortening and sugar until light and fluffy. Add egg yolks and continue creaming. Sift dry ingredients together 3 times; add alternately with liquids to creamed mixture. Beat until smooth. Pour into cake pans lined with waxed paper. Bake in a moderate oven (350°F.) 18 to 20 minutes. Makes 3 (9-inch) layers.

ORANGE CAKE

¾ cup shortening
1½ cups sugar
3 eggs
Grated rind of 1 orange
3 cups sifted cake flour

4 teaspoons baking powder
¾ teaspoon salt
½ cup orange juice
1 tablespoon lemon juice
½ cup water

Cream shortening, add sugar gradually, creaming until light and fluffy. Add eggs one at a time, beating thoroughly after each addition. Add orange rind. Sift dry ingredients together 3 times and add alternately with liquids to creamed mixture. Pour into cake pans lined with waxed paper. Bake in a moderate oven (350°F.) 25 to 30 minutes. Makes 2 (9-inch) layers. When cold spread Orange Filling (page 477) between layers and Twice Cooked Frosting or Seven Minute Frosting (page 479) on top and sides.

LAYER CAKE

½ cup shortening
1 cup sugar
2 eggs, separated
2 cups sifted cake flour

¼ teaspoon salt
2½ teaspoons baking powder
⅔ cup milk
1 teaspoon vanilla

Cream shortening, add sugar gradually and beat until fluffy, then add beaten egg yolks. Sift dry ingredients together 3 times and add alternately with milk and vanilla to creamed mixture. Fold in stiffly beaten egg whites. Bake in 2 layers in a moderate oven (350°F.) 20 minutes. When cold fill and frost as desired.

LADY BALTIMORE CAKE

¾ cup butter or other
    shortening
2 cups sugar
3 cups sifted cake flour
3 teaspoons baking powder

½ teaspoon salt
½ cup milk
½ cup water
1 teaspoon vanilla
6 egg whites

Cream shortening and sugar together until fluffy. Sift flour, baking powder and salt together 3 times. Combine milk, water and vanilla. Add small amounts of flour to creamed mixture, alternately with milk mixture, beating until smooth after each addition. Beat egg whites until stiff but not dry and fold into mixture. Pour into cake pans lined with waxed paper. Bake in moderate oven (350°F.) 25 minutes. Makes 3 (9-inch) layers.

LADY BALTIMORE FROSTING AND FILLING—

3 cups sugar
1 cup water
¼ teaspoon cream of tartar
3 egg whites, stiffly beaten

1 teaspoon vanilla
½ cup chopped figs
1 cup chopped raisins
1 cup chopped nut meats

Boil sugar, water and cream of tartar together to 238°F. or until a small amount of sirup will form a soft ball when tested in cold water. Pour hot sirup gradually over beaten whites, beating constantly and continuing to beat until mixture is of spreading consistency. Add vanilla. Divide mixture in half. Add fruit and nuts to 1 portion and spread between layers of cake. Frost top and sides with remaining frosting.

MARBLE CAKE

⅓ cup butter or other
    shortening
1 cup sugar
2 eggs, well beaten
½ teaspoon vanilla
1¾ cups sifted cake flour

2 teaspoon baking powder
½ teaspoon salt
½ cup milk
1 ounce (1 square)
    chocolate, melted

Cream shortening, add sugar gradually and cream until light and fluffy. Add eggs and vanilla and mix thoroughly. Sift dry ingredients together 3 times and add alternately with milk to creamed mixture, beating until smooth. To ⅓ of the batter add chocolate and blend thoroughly. Place by spoonfuls in a greased tube pan, alternating light and dark mixtures. Bake in a moderate oven (350°F.) 1 hour.

BLITZ TORTE

½ cup shortening
½ cup sugar
⅛ teaspoon salt
4 egg yolks, beaten light
1 teaspoon vanilla
3 tablespoons milk
1 cup sifted cake flour

1 teaspoon baking powder
4 egg whites
¾ cup sugar
½ cup sliced blanched
   almonds
1 tablespoon sugar
½ teaspoon cinnamon

Cream shortening; beat in sugar and salt, then egg yolks, vanilla, milk and flour (sifted with baking powder). Spread mixture in 2 round greased cake pans. Beat egg whites until very light, add ¾ cup sugar gradually and spread on the un-baked mixture in both pans. Sprinkle with almonds, 1 table-spoon sugar and cinnamon and bake in a moderate oven (350°F.) about 30 minutes. Let cool and put together with cream filling. Makes 1 (9-inch) 2 layer cake.

CREAM FILLING—

⅓ cup sugar
3 tablespoons cornstarch
¼ teaspoon salt

2 egg yolks
2 tablespoons butter
2 cups milk, scalded

1 teaspoon vanilla

Combine sugar, cornstarch, salt and egg yolks; beat thor-oughly. Add butter and enough milk to make a smooth paste. Add paste to remaining hot milk and cook over boiling water, stirring constantly until mixture is thickened. Cool and add vanilla. If desired add ½ cup chopped nut meats.

OLD-FASHIONED POUNDCAKE

1 pound butter (2 cups)
1 pound sifted cake flour
   (4 cups)

10 eggs, separated
1 pound sugar (2 cups)
1 teaspoon vanilla

Cream butter, work in flour until mixture is mealy. Beat egg yolks, sugar and vanilla until thick and fluffy. Add first mix-ture gradually, beating thoroughly. Fold in stiffly beaten egg whites. Beat vigorously 5 minutes. Bake in 2 loaf pans lined with waxed paper, in a moderately slow oven (325°F.) 1¼ hours. Makes 2 loaves (8 x 4 inches).

SPICE CAKE

½ cup shortening
2 cups brown sugar
3 eggs, separated
2 cups sifted cake flour
¼ teaspoon salt

1 teaspoon baking soda
2 teaspoons cinnamon
1 teaspoon cloves
½ teaspoon nutmeg
1 cup thick sour cream

Cream shortening and sugar together until fluffy, add beaten yolks. Sift dry ingredients together 3 times and add alternately with cream to first mixture, beating thoroughly after each addition. Fold in stiffly beaten egg whites. Pour into cake pan lined with waxed paper. Bake in moderate oven (350°F.) about 50 minutes. Makes 1 cake (9 inches square).

FIG LOAF CAKE

1 cup shortening
2 cups brown sugar
4 eggs, well beaten
3 cups sifted cake flour
3 teaspoons baking powder
¼ teaspoon salt

1 teaspoon cinnamon
½ teaspoon ground cloves
1 teaspoon nutmeg
1 cup water
½ pound figs, finely cut
2 cups chopped raisins

Cream shortening, add sugar gradually and cream until fluffy. Beat in eggs. Sift dry ingredients together 3 times and add alternately with water to creamed mixture. Blend in fruits. Bake in a waxed-paper-lined loaf pan (5½ x 10 inches) in a slow oven (300°F.) about 2 hours.

DELICIOUS FRUITCAKE

4 cups sifted cake flour
1 teaspoon mace
¼ teaspoon nutmeg
2 teaspoons cinnamon
½ teaspoon baking soda
3 pounds currants
2 pounds seeded raisins

1 pound citron, sliced
2 cups blanched almonds, sliced
1 pound butter
2 cups light brown sugar
9 eggs, separated
1 cup strong cold coffee

Sift flour, spices and soda together 3 times. Mix with fruits and nuts. Cream butter and sugar together until fluffy. Beat yolks until thick and whites until stiff; add to creamed mixture. Add flour-fruit mixture alternately with coffee. Pour into greased pans lined with greased paper. Bake in very slow oven (275°F.) 3 to 4 hours. Rich fruitcake is sometimes steamed 1 hour, then baked for remaining time.

WEDDING CAKE

2 pounds butter
1 pound granulated sugar
¾ pound brown sugar
20 eggs
2 oranges, juice and grated rind
1 lemon, juice and grated rind
1 teaspoon soda
½ cup molasses
1 cup black coffee
½ cup honey
2 pounds flour

1½ teaspoons salt
1 teaspoon cloves
2 teaspoons cinnamon
2 tablespoons nutmeg
2 tablespoons mace
1 glass tart jelly
3 pounds seeded raisins
2 pounds seedless raisins
5 pounds currants
1 pound almonds
2 pounds citron
2 cups flour (for the fruit)

Cream the butter till very soft, add the white sugar and the sifted brown sugar and mix thoroughly. Add the beaten yolks and the grated rind. Add one half the soda to the molasses, stir until foamy and add, with the coffee and honey, alternating with the two pounds of flour, sifted with remaining soda, salt and spices. Break the jelly into pieces and stir in. It is not necessary to have the jelly thoroughly mixed in.

Look over the raisins and currants, wash if necessary, drain and dry. Blanch the almonds and slice. Save half the nuts to sprinkle on the bottom and top of cake. Cut the citron in thin strips. Mix the two cups of flour thoroughly with this fruit. Candied orange or grapefruit peel may be used for citron.

Mix the prepared fruit with the batter. This may be added from time to time with the flour. When all is thoroughly combined fold in the stiffly beaten egg whites.

This amount makes about twenty four pounds of cake, and can be baked in small loaves or in one large one. Whatever size is chosen line the greased pans with three layers of paper (bottom and sides) having the top layer well greased. Sprinkle the bottom with about one third of the reserved nuts. Put the mixture into the pan making sure that the corners are well filled and that the top is level and smooth. Sprinkle the remaining nuts on the top. If made into one large cake steam four hours and then bake one hour in a very slow oven (250°-275° F.). If made into small cakes they can be baked without steaming first. Bake in a slow oven (250° F.) for two hours. Let cool in the pan, but have it stand on a rack so as to have a circulation of air underneath as well as on the top and sides.

Turn out and remove the paper. Cool and store in a cool dry place tightly covered. A few sound apples placed in the container where cake is stored will help keep the cake moist if it must be kept long, but they must be watched and replaced if they begin to show decay, or if they become shrivelled.

As there is so much preparation involved, the fruits and nuts can be gotten ready several days before the cake is to be baked. Even after the cake is entirely mixed and in the pan or pans it can stand overnight if kept in a cool place.

CHRISTMAS FRUITCAKE

1 pound butter	1 pound citron, sliced
1½ pounds brown sugar	1 pound dates, sliced
1½ pounds flour	10 eggs, well beaten
2 teaspoons nutmeg	1 cup molasses
1 teaspoon mace	1 cup strong cold coffee
1 teaspoon cloves	Juice and grated rind of
2 teaspoons cinnamon	2 oranges
1 teaspoon baking soda	Juice and grated rind of
3 teaspoons baking powder	1 lemon
3 pounds raisins	1 cup tart jelly
2 pounds currants	¼ pound almonds, sliced

Cream butter and sugar until fluffy. Sift dry ingredients together 3 times and mix with fruit. Add eggs to creamed mixture. Add flour-fruit mixture alternately with next 5 ingredients and beat thoroughly. Pour into pans lined with greased paper. Sprinkle almonds on top. Cover cakes with greased paper. Steam for 2 hours, then bake in slow oven (300°F.) 1½ to 2 hours, removing paper last ½ hour to dry surface.

DRIED APRICOT CAKE

1 cup dried apricots	1 teaspoon vanilla
2 cups water	1¾ cups sifted cake flour
6 tablespoons sugar	½ teaspoon salt
½ cup shortening	½ teaspoon baking soda
1 cup sugar	1 teaspoon baking powder
2 egg yolks	¼ cup water

Simmer first 3 ingredients together 30 minutes. Mash and measure ½ cup pulp. Cream shortening and sugar thoroughly, add yolks and vanilla; beat. Sift dry ingredients together and add alternately with water and pulp. Bake in a cake pan (8 x 8 inches), lined with waxed paper, at 350°F., 45 minutes.

APPLESAUCE SPICECAKE

½ cup butter or other shortening	2 cups sifted cake flour
1 cup sugar	1 teaspoon baking soda
2 eggs, beaten light	½ teaspoon nutmeg
½ cup chopped nuts	1 teaspoon cinnamon
1 cup chopped raisins	1 cup unsweetened applesauce

Cream shortening and sugar together until fluffy. Add eggs and mix thoroughly. Add nuts and raisins. Sift dry ingredients together 3 times and add alternately with applesauce to creamed mixture, beating thoroughly after each addition. Pour into a greased loaf pan and bake in a moderate oven (350°F.) for 1 hour. If baked in layers, bake only for 25 minutes. Makes 1 loaf (8 x 4 inches) or 2 (9-inch) layers.

PINEAPPLE CAKE

½ cup butter	¼ cup evaporated milk
1⅓ cups sugar	¼ cup water
2½ cups sifted cake flour	½ cup sirup drained from pineapple
½ teapsoon salt	
3 teaspoons baking powder	1½ teaspoons vanilla
3 egg whites	

Cream butter and sugar together. Sift dry ingredients. Combine milk, water and sirup and add alternately with dry ingredients. Add vanilla and fold in stiffly beaten egg whites. Pour into paper-lined layer-cake pans and bake in a moderate oven (350° F.) 35 minutes. Makes 2 (9-inch) layers. Fill with Pineapple Filling and frost with Seven-minute Icing.

TRUE SPONGECAKE

1 cup sifted cake flour	5 egg yolks, beaten until thick and lemon-colored
¼ teaspoon salt	
Grated rind ½ lemon	5 egg whites
1½ tablespoons lemon juice	1 cup sugar

Sift flour and salt together 4 times. Add lemon rind and juice to beaten yolks and beat until thick and light. Beat egg whites until stiff, but not dry. Fold in sugar, a small amount at a time, then add egg yolks. Fold in flour, sifting about ¼ cup at a time over surface. Bake in ungreased tube pan in moderate oven (350° F.) 1 hour. Remove from oven and invert pan 1 hour before removing cake.

FOR MARTHA WASHINGTON CREAM PIE, bake in 2 cake pans. Use the filling page 474 and top with whipped cream. When serving cut in wedges like a pie.

HOT WATER SPONGECAKE

1 cup sifted cake flour
1½ teaspoon baking powder
¼ teaspoon salt
½ tablespoon lemon juice

2 eggs, separated
1 cup sugar
6 tablespoons hot water

Proceed as for True Spongecake (page 468), adding water to egg and sugar mixture before adding dry ingredients.

MERINGUE SPONGECAKE

½ cup water
1¼ cups sugar
¾ cup egg whites (6)
1 teaspoon cream tartar

1 tablespoon lemon juice
6 egg yolks, beaten thick
1⅛ cups sifted cake flour
¼ teaspoon salt

Boil water and sugar together to soft-ball stage (238° F.). Beat egg whites until stiff, but not dry, pour sirup over whites, add cream of tartar and beat until cool. Add juice. Fold egg yolks into sirup mixture. Fold in flour sifted with salt. Bake in ungreased pan in a 350° F. oven 45 minutes.

ANGEL CAKE

1¼ cups sugar
1 cup sifted cake flour
1 cup egg whites
(8 to 10 eggs)

1 teaspoon cream of tartar
½ teaspoon salt
¾ teaspoon vanilla
¼ teaspoon almond extract

Sift ¼ cup sugar and flour together 4 times. Beat egg whites, cream of tartar and salt to a stiff foam. Add remaining sugar, a little at a time, beating it in, preferably with a rotary beater. Add flavorings. Fold in flour, sifting a little at a time over egg white and sugar mixture. Pour into a large ungreased tube pan; cut through batter with a spatula to remove large air bubbles. Bake in a slow oven (275° F.) 30 minutes. Raise heat to 300° F. and bake 40-45 minutes longer. Remove from oven; invert pan 1 hour.

ROLLED CAKES

5 eggs	½ cup sifted cake flour
⅔ cup sugar	3 tablespoons melted butter
¼ teaspoon salt	1 teaspoon vanilla
	1 cup jelly or jam, slightly beaten

Combine eggs and sugar and beat only until blended. Place over hot water and heat until mixture is slightly hot (140°F.). Remove from heat and beat until mixture holds a limp peak. Combine salt and flour and fold into egg mixture. Fold in butter a tablespoonful at a time. Blend in vanilla. Pour into a jelly roll pan (15 x 10 inches) lined with waxed paper. Bake in a moderate oven (350°F.) 15 to 20 minutes. Turn quickly onto waxed paper covered with confectioners' sugar. Remove bottom paper and trim sides. Spread quickly with jelly and roll; or roll cake and when cold unroll and spread with jelly. Wrap in waxed paper and cool. Just before serving sprinkle cake with confectioners' sugar. Makes 1 roll.

LEMON ROLL—Spread cake roll with Lemon Filling (page 476) instead of jelly or jam.

CHOCOLATE MARSHMALLOW ROLL—Spread with Marshmallow-Cream Frosting (page 482) and roll. Wrap in cloth to cool.
Unwrap and frost with coating made by adding 1 teaspoon melted butter to 1 square melted, bitter chocolate.

GRAHAM CRACKER CREAM CAKE

½ cup shortening	¼ teaspoon salt
1 cup sugar	1 cup graham cracker
2 eggs, beaten	crumbs
1 cup sifted cake flour	1 cup milk
2 teaspoons baking powder	1 teaspoon almond extract

Cream shortening and sugar together until fluffy. Beat in eggs. Sift flour, baking powder and salt together 3 times, add crumbs and add alternately with milk and almond extract to creamed mixture. Pour into 2 (8-inch) cake pans lined with waxed paper. Bake in a moderate oven (350°F.) 25 to 30 minutes. Put layers together with Cream Filling (page 464) and frost top and sides with a butter frosting.

WHIPPED CREAM CAKE

1 cup whipping cream	1 teaspoon vanilla
2 eggs, beaten until thick and lemon colored	1½ cups sifted cake flour
	¼ teaspoon salt
1 cup sugar	2 teaspoons baking powder

Whip cream until it holds its shape. Add eggs and whip until light as foam. Add sugar and beat again. Add vanilla. Sift flour, salt and baking powder together 3 times and add to egg mixture. Bake in greased layer cake pans in a moderate oven (350° F.) 25 to 30 minutes. Makes 2 (8-inch) layers. Cool and spread Seven Minute Icing (page 479) or whipped cream between the layers and on top.

SOUR CREAM CAKE

2 eggs	1½ teaspoons baking powder
1 cup sugar	
1 cup thick sour cream	½ teaspoon baking soda
1 teaspoon vanilla	¼ teaspoon salt
2 cups sifted cake flour	

Beat eggs very light, add sugar gradually and beat until fluffy. Add cream and vanilla and beat. Sift dry ingredients together 3 times and add to egg mixture, beating until smooth. Bake in a square pan (8-inch) lined with waxed paper, in a moderate oven (350° F.) about 35 minutes.

PRUNE AND APRICOT UPSIDE-DOWN CAKE

¼ cup butter	⅔ cup sugar
½ cup brown sugar	1 egg, beaten
½ teaspoon lemon rind	1 cup milk
Stewed apricot halves	2¼ cups flour
Stewed prune halves	4 teaspoons baking powder
5 tablespoons shortening	½ teaspoon salt

Cream butter and brown sugar; add lemon rind; spread on bottom of cake pan 8″ by 2″. Arrange apricot and prune halves to form design on top of sugar mixture. Cream shortening, add sugar slowly, then egg; beat well. Add milk alternately with flour, baking powder and salt sifted together. Mix thoroughly. Pour batter carefully over fruit in pan; bake 50 minutes at 350° F. Turn onto serving platter, upside down.

A FASCINATING VERSION OF THE EVER POPULAR UPSIDE-DOWN CAKE: APRICOT-PRUNE

DON'T RUN AROUND IN CIRCLES THINKING OF NEW DESSERTS—THIS CHOCOLATE MARSHMALLOW ROLL DOES IT FOR YOU

IT'S NO GIFT TO BAKE THIS BEAUTIFUL LAYER CAKE IF YOU FOLLOW THE SIMPLE DIRECTIONS

OUT OF THE OVEN AND READY TO SERVE WHEN YOU BAKE YOUR FRUITCAKE IN GLASS

CAKE FILLINGS AND FROSTINGS

A TABLE giving the temperatures of boiling sugar sirup at its various stages will be found on page 12.

FILLINGS—A filling is defined as "something that serves to fill up a space or cavity." In connection with cakes, the word is used to designate a soft, sweetened, cooked or uncooked mixture that will spread easily. It is usually put between layers to hold them together, or is put into a cavity in a cake; but occasionally it is spread over the top and sides of a cake. Sometimes a frosting is used between the layers instead of a filling.

FROSTING AND ICING—A frosting is a preparation of sugar and a liquid, which may or may not be combined with egg, and may be cooked or uncooked. The term is derived from the fact that the first sugar decorations of this sort were uncolored and gave the effect of hoar-frost. The word is now used to mean any sweet covering applied to cakes, whether white or colored.

Icing has been used interchangeably with the word "frosting" but more often in reference to the uncooked frostings. In the beginning the word was probably used because the substance looked like ice, being translucently white instead of frostily white. Therefore, it may be desirable to use the word "icing" to mean a thin mixture of confectioners' sugar and a liquid, spread on to give a glazed surface; and to keep the term "frosting" for a thicker, more opaque coating.

Applying Fillings and Frostings

Cakes should be cooled and the surface should be free from loose crumbs before a filling or frosting is applied, and the filling or frosting should be cool enough so that it will not soak in. Either the top or the bottom crust may be frosted, but the bottom crust is likely to be softer and more level than the top crust. This point should be considered also when fillings are to be put between layers. Fillings usually hold layers together better when the bottom crusts are placed together. A very soft filling should not be used for a cake that is to be kept any considerable time before it is eaten because the filling will soak into the cake and make it soggy. Sometimes the shape of a loaf cake makes it desirable to put the frosting on the bottom crust. The frosting may extend over the top of a cake only or may be spread over the sides. A well-made boiled frosting should be soft, but not soft enough to run. A frosting may be put on with a very smooth surface, may be left rough, or may be scored in ridges or designs.

Fillings

APPLE FILLING

2 apples	1 lemon	1 cup sugar

Pare two large, sour apples and grate them into a saucepan, add the juice and grated rind of the lemon, and the sugar. Cook for five minutes, stirring constantly. Cool before spreading on cake.

CARAMEL FILLING

1½ cups brown sugar
1 tablespoon butter
2 teaspoons corn-starch

1 cup milk
1½ teaspoons vanilla

Cook the sugar, corn-starch, milk and butter together in a double boiler until thick. Remove from the fire and beat vigorously until the mixture is stiff. Add flavoring. Cool before spreading on cake.

CHOCOLATE FILLING

No. 1.

1½ squares chocolate
¼ cup milk
1 cup brown sugar

1 egg-yolk
½ teaspoon butter
1 teaspoon vanilla

Melt the chocolate over hot water, in a double boiler; add the milk, and cook together, stirring until the mixture is thick and creamy. Add sugar and beaten egg-yolk, stir until smooth and cook five minutes. Add the butter. Beat well. Remove from heat and add flavoring. Cool before spreading on cake.

No. 2.

1½ squares chocolate	1 cup powdered sugar
⅓ cup cream	½ teaspoon butter
1 egg-yolk	½ teaspoon vanilla

Melt the chocolate over hot water, in a double boiler. Mix the cream and beaten yolk and add gradually, then the butter. Stir in the sugar and cook until thick. Remove from fire. Add flavoring. Cool before spreading on cake.

No. 1. COCONUT FILLING

1 tablespoon gelatin	½ cup sugar
½ cup cold water	3 egg-whites
½ cup boiling water	1½ cups moist coconut

Soak gelatin in the cold water until soft; then dissolve it in the boiling water. Add sugar and stir until it is dissolved. Allow gelatin to cool partly. When it begins to set, beat the egg-whites until stiff and beat in the gelatin. Fold in the coconut and spread upon the layers.

No. 2.

1½ cups moist coconut	4 tablespoons confectioners'
2 egg-whites	sugar

Beat the egg-whites stiff and add the sugar and coconut gradually. Spread the mixture thickly over the cake. If you like, sprinkle the surface with dry shredded coconut.

MARTHA WASHINGTON FILLING

1½ cups milk	¼ cup cold water
1 cup sugar	¼ cup rum, brandy or whisky
2 tablespoons flour	½ cup candied cherries, chopped
3 egg yolks	½ cup citron, chopped
2 tablespoons gelatin	1 cup whipped cream

Scald milk. Add sugar and flour to beaten egg yolks. Add to scalded milk and cook over hot water until eggs are done. Remove from heat. Add gelatin which has been soaked in the cold water. Chill. Add liquor, beat with rotary beater and chill again. Fold the fruit and cream into the mixture. Pile between layers of sponge cake. Top with whipped cream.

CHOCOLATE—Use 2 squares bitter chocolate, melted over hot water, omit liquor, add ⅛ teaspoon salt, dash cinnamon and increase sugar to 1½ cups.

COFFEE—Scald milk with two tablespoons ground coffee, strain, and make same as cream filling, omitting liquor.

ORANGE—Use half orange-juice and half milk and add two tablespoons grated orange rind to ingredients above, omitting the liquor. If you like, add one tablespoon lemon-juice.

WHIPPED CREAM FILLING

½ tablespoon gelatin
¼ cup cold water
2 cups cream

½ cup powdered sugar
1 teaspoon vanilla
¼ cup boiling water

Soak the gelatin in the cold water until softened. Whip the cream in a pan set in ice-water and sift the sugar over it. Add the vanilla. Pour the boiling water upon the gelatin and, when it is dissolved and cooled, strain it over the whipped cream. Then beat rapidly with a flat whip, turning the pan with the left hand while beating with the right. Beat until the gelatin is thoroughly blended with the cream. Set in a cool place. When the filling is nearly stiff, spread it on the cake layers.

WHIPPED CREAM MOCHA FILLING

½ pint cream
2 tablespoons sugar

1½ tablespoons Mocha
extract or strong coffee

Whip the cream in a bowl set in ice-water; add the extract or coffee and the sugar. Beat well.

If the top of the cake is spread with this filling, three-fourths cup of chopped nut-meats may be sprinkled over it.

FRUIT FILLING

½ pound single or mixed fruit
1 cup water

1 cup sugar
1 teaspoon vanilla

Chop the fruit fine and boil in the water, if necessary, until tender. Add sugar and cook slowly until smooth and thick. Remove from the heat, add vanilla and cool.

MIXTURE FOR UPSIDE-DOWN CAKES

2 tablespoons butter   Fresh or canned fruit
4 tablespoons sugar (white, brown or maple)

In a deep cake pan or heavy skillet, melt 2 tablespoons butter. Sprinkle 4 tablespoons sugar over bottom of pan and cover with well-drained sour cherries (or other canned or fresh fruit). Pour batter or light yeast dough over this layer and bake at 425° F. for 30 minutes.

FRUIT AND NUT FILLING

1 cup chopped raisins
½ cup chopped nuts
½ cup shredded coconut

1 egg-white
Currant jelly

Mix the raisins, nuts and coconut and add them to the stiffly beaten egg-white. Spread the layers of cake with a thin layer of currant jelly, then with a thick layer of the filling, and put together.

TUTTI-FRUTTI FILLING

¼ pound seeded or seedless
    raisins
¼ pound figs
½ pound dates

Chopped walnuts
¼ pound maraschino cherries
¼ pound maple sugar
½ cup water

Put raisins and figs in colander over a kettle of hot water and allow them to steam for about one hour. Then add dates, which have been pitted, and steam for fifteen minutes longer. Remove from steamer, add cherries, and chop all the fruit fine. Bring the maple sugar and water to a boil and pour it over the fruit. Mix well. When cool, spread between layers and on top of the cake and sprinkle with chopped walnuts.

No. 1.   LEMON FILLING

2 tablespoons flour
¾ cup cold water
1 egg-yolk
½ cup sugar

Juice and grated rind of
    1 lemon
2 teaspoons butter

Make a smooth paste of the flour and two tablespoons of the cold water. Cook the rest of the water, the sugar, grated lemon-rind and butter. When the sugar is dissolved and mixture boiling, stir in the flour mixture slowly. Cook until clear and smooth, about fifteen minutes. Add lemon-juice and beaten egg-yolk and cook two minutes. Cool before spreading on cake.

MAPLE CREAM FILLING

2 cups maple-sirup   1 tablespoon butter
¾ cup milk   Salt

Cook sirup, milk, butter, and salt together to the soft-ball stage (238° F.). Cool and beat until creamy. Use as a filling for cakes, cream-puffs or tarts.

ORANGE FILLING

2 tablespoons butter   1 tablespoon grated orange
¼ cup granulated sugar   rind
2 eggs beaten   1 tablespoon lemon-juice
½ cup orange-juice

Combine all ingerdients and mix well. Cook over hot water, stirring constantly, until well thickened, about ten minutes. Chill well before spreading on cake.

PINEAPPLE FILLING

2 tablespoons cornstarch   2½ cups drained crushed
¼ cup sugar   pineapple
4 tablespoons orange juice

Mix cornstarch and sugar. Add pineapple and cook until smooth and thickened. Add orange juice.

PRUNE FILLING

¼ pound prunes   ½ cup rhubarb-juice or
½ tablespoon gelatin   pineapple-juice
4 tablespoons cold water   ½ cup whipped cream
½ cup sugar

Wash the prunes, soak over night in water to cover, and cook slowly until soft. Remove pits and rub pulp through a coarse sieve. Soak the gelatin in cold water. When soft, add it to the hot prune pulp and stir until the gelatin dissolves. Add sugar and fruit-juice. When the filling has cooled, fold in the whipped cream.

WALNUT FILLING

2 cups brown sugar
½ cup water
2 egg-whites

½ teaspoon vanilla
½ cup chopped walnut-meats

Cook the sugar and water, stirring occasionally until the sugar is dissolved. Boil without stirring until sirup will form a thread when dropped from the tip of the spoon (234° F.). Remove from the fire and cool while beating the egg-whites stiff, then pour the sirup in a thin stream on the egg-whites, beating the mixture constantly until it is thick enough to spread. Add flavoring and nuts. Cool before spreading on cake. Chopped nut-meats may be sprinkled over the top of the cake.

Frostings

CONFECTIONERS' FROSTING

1 egg-white   ½ cup confectioners' sugar   ½ teaspoon vanilla

Beat the egg-white stiff and add the sugar gradually; continue beating until the mixture is smooth and light. Add flavoring.

EGGLESS CONFECTIONERS' FROSTING

2 tablespoons milk or water

1 cup confectioners' sugar
½ teaspoon vanilla

Stir the sugar gradually into the milk or water. Add vanilla. More sugar may be added if the frosting is not thick enough.

Any fruit-juice or flavored liquid such as strong coffee or maple-sirup may be used instead of milk or water.

Crushed berries mixed with the sugar give a pleasing frosting.

Two tablespoons cocoa may be mixed with the sugar.

One-half square of melted chocolate may be added.

BOILED FROSTING

1 cup sugar
½ cup water

1, 2, or 3 egg whites
½ teaspoon vanilla

Cook the sugar and water together, stirring until the sugar has dissolved. Then cook without stirring. For one egg white, cook to 238° F.; for two egg whites, cook to 244° F.; and for three egg whites, cook to 254° F. Remove from the fire and allow it to cool while you are beating the egg white stiff, then pour the sirup in a thin stream over the stiff white, beating the mixture constantly until thick enough to spread. Add vanilla.

ORNAMENTAL OR TWICE-COOKED FROSTING

1½ cups granulated sugar
½ cup water
2 egg-whites

1 teaspoon flavoring extract
⅛ teaspoon cream of tartar

Boil sugar and water without stirring until the sirup will form a soft ball in cold water (234° F.); add very slowly to beaten egg-whites; add flavoring and cream of tartar and beat until smooth and stiff enough to spread. Put over boiling water, stirring continually until icing grates slightly on bottom of bowl.

SEVEN-MINUTE ICING

1 unbeaten egg-white
⅞ cup granulated sugar

3 tablespoons cold water
½ teaspoon flavoring extract

Place all the ingredients in the top of a double boiler. Place over boiling water and beat with beater for seven minutes. Add flavoring, beat, and spread on cake.

CHOCOLATE—Add to above one and one-half ounces melted unsweetened chocolate two minutes before taking from fire.

COFFEE—Use cold boiled coffee in place of water.

CARAMEL FROSTING

1 cup brown sugar
½ cup water
2 egg-whites

1 teaspoon vanilla or
½ teaspoon lemon extract

Make a sirup of the sugar and water and cook to the soft-ball stage (238° F.). Remove from the fire and cool while the egg-whites are beaten, then pour the sirup in a thin stream on to the stiff whites, beating the mixture constantly until thick enough to spread. Add the flavoring.

Chopped nuts may be stirred into the frosting just before spreading.

CHOCOLATE FROSTING

1 square chocolate	1 egg-white
3 tablespoons granulated sugar	8 tablespoons confectioners' sugar
1 tablespoon water	½ tablespoon vanilla

Cook the chocolate, granulated sugar and water together, stirring until the mixture is smooth and glossy. Beat the white of the egg enough to thin it, but not to make it frothy; add the confectioners' sugar, stir until smooth and light, then add the chocolate mixture and vanilla. Cool before spreading on the cake.

COFFEE-BUTTER FROSTING

1½ cups confectioners' sugar	⅓ cup butter
1 tablespoon dry cocoa	1 tablespoon strong coffee

Cream the butter and add gradually the sugar and cocoa mixed together. Beat well. Stir in the coffee. Ornamental designs may be made by forcing the frosting through a pastry-bag or syringe, using the various tips to produce the desired designs.

FUDGE FROSTING

2 cups sugar	1 teaspoon vanilla
½ cup milk	6 marshmallows or 2 heaping
1½ tablespoons butter	tablespoons marshmallow
2 squares chocolate	whip
1 tablespoon corn sirup	

Put first five ingredients into a saucepan and boil to soft ball stage (234° F.). Remove from fire and stir in the marshmallows just until they dissolve. Cool and add vanilla and beat until right consistency to spread on cake.

REMOVE CRUMBS

FROST LOWER LAYER

.FROST SIDES.

FINISH TOP

TRANSFORMATION BEFORE YOUR EYES— THIS IS HOW IT'S DONE

SUIT BOTH SIDES OF THE HOUSE BY DOING TWO FROSTINGS ON THE SAME CAKE (ABOVE) "THE FLOWERS THAT BLOOM IN THE SPRING, TRA LA," ARE MADE FROM FROSTINGS OF DIFFERENT COLORS (BELOW)

HONEY FROSTING

1 cup honey   2 egg-whites

Boil the honey about ten minutes (238° F.). Remove from the fire and cool while the egg-whites are beaten stiff, then pour the honey in a thin stream over them, beating the mixture constantly until thick enough to spread. Cool before spreading.

MAPLE-SUGAR FROSTING

No. 1.

2 cups maple sugar   1 cup cream

Break the maple sugar into small pieces, put into a saucepan and heat slowly with the cream. Stir until the sugar is thoroughly dissolved, then boil without stirring until a soft ball can be shaped between the fingers when the mixture is tried in cold water (238° F.). Care must be taken not to have the heat too great, as this mixture will burn easily. Remove from the fire and beat until thick enough to spread.

No. 2.

¾ cup maple-sirup   1 egg-white
¼ cup sugar

Cook the sirup and sugar together until it spins a thread (220° F.) when dropped from a spoon. Pour this sirup slowly over the beaten egg-white and beat until cold. This icing is quickly made and may be used to give a maple flavor to simple, inexpensive cakes or cookies.

No. 3.

2 cups maple sugar   ½ cup boiling water
2 egg-whites

Make a sirup of the maple sugar and water and boil to the soft-ball stage (238° F.), remove from the fire and cool while the egg-whites are beaten stiff, then pour the sirup in a thin stream, over the stiff whites, beating the mixture until it is thick enough to spread. A rough surface may be obtained by spreading the top of the cake with the back of a spoon before the frosting is set.

MAPLE MARSHMALLOW FROSTING

1 cup maple sugar
½ cup boiling water
2 egg-whites

6 marshmallows or 2 tablespoons marshmallow cream
½ teaspoon vanilla

Cook the sugar and water together, stirring until the sugar is dissolved; then cook without stirring to the soft-ball stage (238° F.) add the marshmallow to the hot sirup, pressing it under the surface so that it will melt. If marshmallow candies are used, cut them into small pieces. Pour the sirup in a thin stream on to the stiffly beaten egg-whites, beating the mixture constantly with a spoon. Add vanilla. Cool before spreading.

MARSHMALLOW-CREAM FROSTING

¾ cup sugar
¼ cup milk
2 tablespoons hot water

6 marshmallows or 2 tablespoons marshmallow cream
½ teaspoon vanilla

Put the milk and sugar into a saucepan, bring slowly to the boiling-point and boil for five minutes. Place the marshmallow in a double boiler with hot water and vanilla. Stir until the mixture is smooth, then add the milk and sugar sirup gradually, stirring constantly. Beat until cool, then spread.

MILK FROSTING

1 teaspoon butter
1½ cups sugar

½ cup milk
½ teaspoon vanilla

Put the butter into a saucepan and, when it is melted, add the sugar and milk. Stir until the boiling-point is reached and then boil for ten minutes without stirring (235° F.). Remove from the fire, add vanilla, and beat until of spreading consistency.

MOCHA FROSTING

1½ teaspoons Mocha extract
or strong coffee

1 cup confectioners' sugar
2 tablespoons water

Mix the extract or coffee with the sugar and stir into the water, gradually, rubbing out all lumps. After the frosting is spread on the cake, three-fourths of a cup of chopped nut-meats may be sprinkled over the top.

COOKIES, GINGERBREAD AND SMALL CAKES

COOKIE doughs range from those soft enough to drop to those stiff enough to shape into a roll and slice for baking. Between these extremes are doughs which are spread in the pan and cut after baking, doughs just stiff enough to roll and those which are molded with a cookie press or pastry tube.

Shaping Cookies

Cookie doughs for rolling or slicing are more easily handled if they are well chilled; others may be chilled if time allows.

ROLLED COOKIES—Have dough as soft as it can be handled. Use only as much of the chilled dough as can be handled at one time and keep the remainder cold. Shape a portion of dough quickly into a smooth ball and place on lightly floured board or on board covered with canvas or heavy towel. Roll out from center to edges with light deft strokes of floured rolling pin, keeping the edges the same thickness as the center. Shift the dough frequently to be sure it is not sticking to board but do not turn dough over. Keep rolling pin and board free from any particles of dough. Work rapidly and lightly. Dust additional flour on board or pin when necessary but use as little as possible. Excess flour makes cookies tough.

Dip cutter into flour, shake to remove excess flour and cut cookies as close together as possible. Place on baking sheet with spatula, leaving 1-inch space between cookies. Save scraps from each rolling and combine all for chilling and rerolling. Cookies made from rerolled dough will be less tender.

Shortcut Methods—Shape cookie dough into small balls and place on cookie sheet. Flatten out with tines of fork, spatula or bottom of a tumbler, covered with waxed paper.

Roll dough on bottom of inverted baking sheet and cut into desired shape. Remove scraps between cookies. This method is especially useful when dough is a little too soft to handle well or if cookies are being cut into large shapes which would be difficult to move.

Cut cookies into squares, triangles or diamonds with knife or pastry wheel to eliminate rerolling of scraps.

REFRIGERATOR COOKIES—Press ½ the dough into a roll about 1½ inches in diameter and wrap tightly in waxed paper. Roll dough lightly back and forth to smooth outside and chill several hours or overnight. Make second roll in same way. Slice cookies very thin with very sharp knife, using very light pressure.

MOLDED COOKIES—Pack dough firmly in cookie press or pastry tube, being careful to leave no air spaces. Shape on cold baking sheet. Make cookies small and dainty.

ROLLED WAFERS—Bake only a few at a time. Shape at once into scrolls over rolling pin or handle of wooden spoon or roll into cornucopias. If last of cookies become too crisp to shape, warm in oven until softened.

Baking Cookies

Bake cookies on sheets with no sides or with very low ones. Or bake on inverted pans so that warm air can circulate freely over cookies and brown the tops.

Storing Cookies

Cool cookies thoroughly before storing. To keep soft cookies moist and crisp cookies dry, store each separately in tightly covered jars. If crisp cookies become soft they may be reheated until crisp.

Drop Cookies

ROLLED OAT COOKIES

2 cups sifted flour
½ teaspoon salt
½ teaspoon baking soda
2 teaspoons baking powder
1 teaspoon cinnamon
½ teaspoon cloves
1 cup shortening

1½ cups brown sugar
2 eggs, beaten
⅔ cup sour milk
1½ cups rolled oats
1 cup raisins or chopped dates
1 cup chopped nuts

Sift flour, salt, soda, baking powder and spices together. Cream shortening with brown sugar until fluffy. Add beaten eggs and mix well. Add sifted ingredients alternately with sour milk in small amounts. Add rolled oats, raisins and nuts. Drop from teaspoon onto greased baking sheet and bake in moderate oven (350° F.) until browned. Makes about 48.

DROP HERMITS

4½ cups sifted cake flour
2½ teaspoons baking powder
1 teaspoon salt
½ teaspoon baking soda
1 teaspoon cinnamon
½ teaspoon allspice

1 cup shortening
2 cups brown sugar
1 cup milk
2 eggs, beaten
1 cup nuts, chopped
1 cup raisins

Sift first 6 ingredients together. Cream shortening and sugar together. Add milk to beaten eggs. Add dry ingredients alternately with liquid to creamed mixture. Add nuts and raisins. Drop from teaspoon onto greased baking sheet and bake in moderate oven (350° F.) until browned. Makes 3 dozen (2-inch) hermits.

HONEY HERMITS

2¼ cups sifted flour
1 teaspoon baking soda
¼ teaspoon salt
½ teaspoon allspice
½ teaspoon cinnamon
½ cup shortening
1 cup honey

½ cup brown sugar
2 eggs, well beaten
3 tablespoons milk
1 cup seedless raisins
1 cup dried currants
1 cup chopped dates
½ cup chopped nuts

Sift flour, soda, salt and spices together 3 times. Cream shortening with honey and sugar. Add eggs. Add milk, dry ingredients, fruit and nuts and mix thoroughly. Drop from teaspoon onto greased baking sheet and bake in hot oven (400° F.) 10 to 12 minutes. Makes about 4 dozen.

RAISIN ROCKS

3 cups sifted cake flour
½ teaspoon salt
2 teaspoons baking soda
½ teaspoon cloves
½ teaspoon cinnamon
1 cup shortening

2 cups brown sugar
2 eggs, beaten
1 cup sour milk or buttermilk
1 cup nuts, chopped
1 cup raisins, chopped

Sift flour, salt, soda and spices together. Cream shortening and sugar until fluffy. Add eggs. Add sifted ingredients alternately with sour milk in small amounts. Add nuts and raisins and mix thoroughly. Drop from teaspoon onto greased baking sheet and bake in moderate oven (350° F.) until brown. Makes 48.

CHOCOLATE DROP COOKIES

1½ cups sifted flour
¼ teaspoon salt
1 teaspoon baking powder
2 ounces (squares) chocolate
½ cup shortening, melted

1 cup brown sugar
1 egg
½ cup milk
1 teaspoon vanilla

Sift flour, salt and baking powder together. Melt chocolate and add to melted shortening. Add sugar, egg, milk and vanilla, then add sifted ingredients. Let stand 10 minutes. Drop from teaspoon onto greased baking sheet and bake in moderate oven (375° F.) 12 to 15 minutes. Frost if desired. Makes 36.

CHOCOLATE CHIP COOKIES

1⅛ cups sifted flour
¼ teaspoon baking soda
½ teaspoon salt
½ cup shortening
¼ cup brown sugar
½ cup granulated sugar

1 egg, beaten
1 teaspoon vanilla
8 ounces semisweet chocolate (bar or pieces)
½ cup chopped walnuts

Sift flour, soda and salt together. Cream shortening and sugars together. Add egg and vanilla. Blend thoroughly. Add sifted ingredients. Cut chocolate into small pieces if bar is used. Fold in nuts and chocolate. Drop from teaspoon onto greased baking sheet. Bake in moderate oven (350° F.) about 10 minutes. Makes 50 cookies.

PEANUT COOKIES

1 cup sifted flour
¼ teaspoon salt
2 teaspoons baking powder
3 tablespoons shortening

½ cup sugar
1 egg, well beaten
2 tablespoons milk
1 cup unsalted peanuts

Sift flour, salt and baking powder together. Cream shortening with sugar until fluffy. Add egg, milk and sifted dry ingredients. Chop ⅔ cup peanuts very fine and add to dough. Drop from teaspoon onto greased baking sheet, top with remaining peanuts and bake in moderate oven (350° F.) 15 to 20 minutes. Makes 2 dozen cookies.

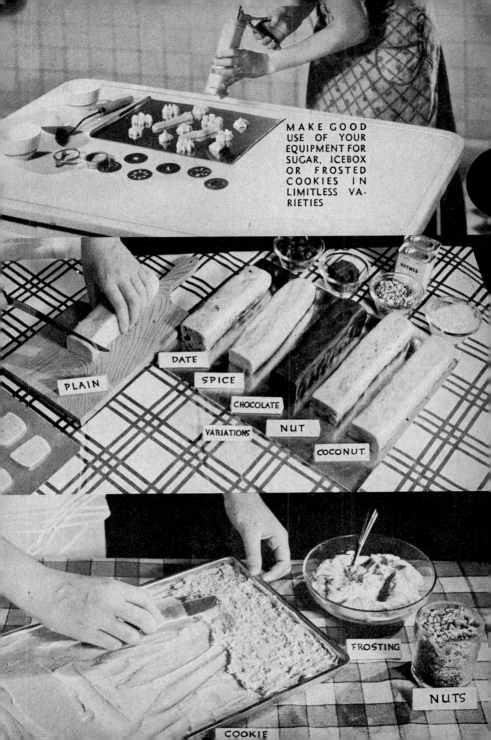

MAKE GOOD
USE OF YOUR
EQUIPMENT FOR
SUGAR, ICEBOX
OR FROSTED
COOKIES IN
LIMITLESS VA-
RIETIES

PLAIN

DATE

SPICE

CHOCOLATE

VARIATIONS   NUT

COCONUT.

FROSTING

NUTS

COOKIE

USE THE PASTRY TUBE
FOR MERINGUES AND
GAY LITTLE CAKES
FOR GALA OCCASIONS

FOR THAT CLEVER
TOUCH, COOKIE
CUTOUTS TO MATCH
THE MOOD OF YOUR
PARTY
—Wheat Flour Institute

SOUR CREAM SPICE COOKIES

3 cups sifted cake flour	1/3 cup shortening
1 teaspoon baking soda	2 cups brown sugar
1 teaspoon cinnamon	2 eggs, well beaten
1/2 teaspoon cloves	1 teaspoon vanilla
1/2 teaspoon nutmeg	2/3 cup thick sour cream
1/2 teaspoon salt	

Sift flour, soda, spices and salt together 3 times. Cream short-ening with sugar until light and fluffy. Add eggs and vanilla and mix well. Add dry ingredients alternately with sour cream in small amounts. Mix well. Drop from teaspoon onto greased baking sheet and bake in moderate oven (350° F.) 12 minutes. Makes 40.

ALMOND COOKIES

3/4 cup butter	1/4 teaspoon salt
3/4 cup sugar	1/2 cup blanched almonds,
1 egg, unbeaten	ground fine
1/2 teaspoon vanilla	1 1/2 cups sifted flour

Cream butter with sugar until fluffy. Add egg, vanilla, salt and almonds and beat thoroughly. Add flour, a small amount at a time. Blend thoroughly. Drop from teaspoon onto greased baking sheet and bake in moderate oven (375° F.) about 15 minutes. Makes 45 cookies.

SPONGE DROPS

2 eggs, separated	2 teaspoons cornstarch
1/2 cup sugar	1/2 cup sifted flour
1 1/2 tablespoons cold water	1/2 teaspoon baking powder
1/2 teaspoon lemon extract	1/8 teaspoon salt

Beat egg whites until stiff but not dry; then fold in 1/4 cup sugar gradually. Beat yolks together with cold water and flavoring until thick and lemon colored. Beat in remaining 1/4 cup sugar, then fold lightly into beaten egg whites. Sift dry ingredients together and fold into egg mixture. Drop from tablespoon onto greased baking sheet. Bake in moderate oven (350° F.) 12 minutes. Remove from oven and roll cookies into cones, securing each with a toothpick. When cool remove toothpicks and fill cones with whipped cream. Makes 12.

LACE COOKIES

½ cup butter
¾ cup sugar
2 eggs
1 teaspooon cinnamon

½ teaspoon soda
½ cup flour
1 cup chopped pecans
½ cup raisins

Cream butter with sugar; add eggs, well-beaten; sift in cinnamon and soda with flour. Add pecans and then raisins. Drop very small dabs on warm metal sheets and bake in a moderate oven (350° F.) 10 to 12 minutes. Makes 4 dozen.

GINGERSNAPS

1½ cups shortening
2 cups sugar
2 eggs
½ cup molasses
4 cups sifted flour

2 teaspoons baking soda
2 teaspoons cinnamon
2 teaspoons cloves
2 teaspoons ginger

Cream shortening and sugar together. Beat in eggs, add molasses and sifted dry ingredients. Roll into 1-inch balls. Dip in sugar. Place on baking sheet 2 inches apart. Bake in moderate oven (375° F.) 15 to 18 minutes. Makes 5 dozen.

Rolled Cookies

FILLED OAT CRISPS

2½ cups sifted cake flour
½ teaspoon baking powder
½ teaspoon salt
2½ cups rolled oats, ground fine

1 cup butter
1 cup light brown sugar
½ cup water
1 recipe Raisin Filling

Sift flour with baking powder and salt and add rolled oats. Cream butter with sugar until fluffy. Add dry ingredients alternately with water. Chill. Roll out a portion of dough about ⅛ inch thick on lightly floured board and cut into 2-inch rounds. Bake on greased baking sheet in moderate oven (350° F.) about 10 minutes or until browned. Cool and store. When ready to use, spread filling on one cookie and top with another. Makes about 2½ dozen.

SUGAR COOKIES

2¼ cups sifted flour	1 cup sugar
¼ teaspoon salt	2 eggs, beaten
2 teaspoons baking powder	½ teaspoon vanilla
½ cup shortening	1 tablespoon milk

Sift flour, salt and baking powder together. Cream shortening and sugar together, add eggs and vanilla, then add sifted ingredients and milk. Roll and cut. Sprinkle with sugar and bake on baking sheet in moderate oven (375°F.) 12 minutes. Makes 2½ dozen cookies.

BROWN SUGAR—Use brown sugar, firmly packed, instead of white.

CARAWAY—Sprinkle cookies with caraway seeds.

CHOCOLATE—Add 2 ounces (squares) chocolate, melted, to creamed mixture.

LEMON—Use lemon extract instead of vanilla.

MAPLE SUGAR—Use maple sugar instead of granulated.

SAND TARTS—Omit 1 egg and reduce flour to 1¾ cups. Brush cut cookies with egg white and sprinkle with sugar, cinnamon and blanched slivered almonds. Bake as above.

SPICE—Sift ¼ teaspoon each cinnamon, allspice and cloves with flour.

FILLED COOKIES

1 recipe Sugar Cookies	1 recipe Fig or Raisin Filling

Roll out dough and cut into circles. Place a teaspoon of filling on half the circles, keeping it away from the edges. Cover with remaining circles and press together around edges with tines of fork. Bake as for sugar cookies.

FIG FILLING

½ cup chopped figs	¼ cup sugar
½ cup water	1 tablespoon flour
Juice ½ lemon	Dash salt

Combine ingredients and cook until thick. Cool.

RAISIN FILLING

⅓ cup sugar	1½ teaspoons butter
⅓ cup hot water	Dash salt
1 cup raisins	

Combine ingredients and cook until thick. Cool.

SOFT MOLASSES COOKIES

3 cups sifted flour
1½ teaspoons baking powder
¼ teaspoon salt
½ teaspoon baking soda
½ teaspoon ginger

1½ teaspoons cinnamon
½ cup shortening, melted
1 cup molasses
2 tablespoons warm water
1 egg, beaten

Sift dry ingredients together. Combine remaining ingredients. Add sifted ingredients, mix thoroughly and let stand about 10 minutes. Roll out on floured board, cut and bake in hot oven (400° F.) about 15 minutes. Makes 4 dozen.

SCOTCH SHORTBREAD

1 cup butter
¾ cup brown sugar

2¼ cups sifted cake flour

Cream butter and sugar together and work in flour. Chill. Roll out about ¼ inch thick on lightly floured board. Cut with pastry wheel, small fancy cutters or cut into diamonds. Bake in slow oven (325° F.). Makes 70.

Molded Cookies

RICH CINNAMON COOKIES

2 cups sifted cake flour
¼ teaspoon salt
2 teaspoons baking powder
2 teaspoons cinnamon

½ cup butter
1 cup sugar
1 teaspoon vanilla
2 eggs, beaten

Sift first 4 ingredients together. Cream butter, sugar and vanilla together. Add sifted ingredients alternately with beaten eggs. Mold with cookie press on cold ungreased baking sheet. Bake in hot oven (400° F.) 10 minutes. Makes 3 dozen.

SPRITZ COOKIES

2½ cups sifted flour
½ teaspoon baking powder
1 cup butter
¾ cup sugar

Dash salt
1 egg, unbeaten
1 teaspoon vanilla

Sift flour with baking powder. Cream butter, sugar and salt, add egg and vanilla and mix well. Add sifted ingredients in small amounts. Mold with cookie press on cold ungreased baking sheet. Bake in 375° F. oven 12 to 15 minutes. Makes 45.

CHOCOLATE STARS

2½ cups shortening	6 cups sifted cake flour
1¾ cups confectioners' sugar	7 teaspoons cocoa
2½ ounces (squares) choco- late, melted	6 egg whites, stiffly beaten
	⅔ cup raspberry jam

Cream shortening with sugar until fluffy. Add chocolate and beat thoroughly. Sift flour with cocoa. Add to creamed mixture, a small amount at a time, blending well after each addition. Add egg whites and blend well. Press dough through cookie press, using star tip. Make tiny flat stars approximately ¾ inch in diameter on ungreased cookie sheet and bake in moderate oven (375° F.) about 8 minutes. Spread bottom of ½ of cookies with thick raspberry jam, cover with remaining cookies and dust with confectioners' sugar. Makes 100.

Refrigerator Cookies

STANDARD REFRIGERATOR COOKIES

6 cups sifted flour	3 cups brown sugar
4 teaspoons baking powder	2 eggs, well beaten
½ teaspoon salt	2 teaspoons vanilla
1½ cups shortening	

Sift flour, baking powder and salt together. Cream shortening and sugar until fluffy. Add eggs and flavoring and mix well. Add dry ingredients. Divide dough into 6 equal portions. Leave 1 plain and make the following variations of remaining dough. Shape each piece of dough into a roll. Chill. When firm slice very thin and bake in moderate oven (375° F.) 10 to 12 minutes. Makes 10 dozen.

CHOCOLATE—Add 2 ounces (squares) chocolate, melted, to 1 portion of the dough. Blend well.

COCONUT—Add ⅓ cup shredded coconut to 1 portion.

FRUIT—Add ⅓ cup chopped dates, raisins, currants, dried apricots, prunes or figs to 1 portion. Mix well.

NUT—Add ⅓ cup of finely chopped almonds, pecans, peanuts, Brazil nuts or walnuts to 1 portion of dough. Mix well.

SPICE—Add ½ teaspoon cinnamon and ¼ teaspoon nutmeg to 1 portion of the dough. Mix well.

BUTTERSCOTCH SLICES

3½ cups sifted cake flour
2½ teaspoons baking powder
½ teaspoon salt
1 cup butter
1½ teaspoons milk

1½ cups brown sugar
2 eggs
1 cup broken walnut meats
1½ teaspoons vanilla

Sift flour, baking powder and salt together. Cream butter with sugar until fluffy. Add eggs, 1 at a time, beating thoroughly after each is added. Add nuts, vanilla and milk, then add flour, mixing well. Shape into rolls. Chill and slice. Bake on ungreased baking sheet in hot oven (425° F.) 5 to 6 minutes. Makes about 8 dozen.

Spread Cookies

DATE BARS

2 eggs
1 cup confectioners' sugar
1 tablespoon shortening, melted
¼ cup sifted cake flour

¼ teaspoon salt
½ teaspoon baking powder
1 cup chopped dates
¾ cup nuts, chopped
1 teaspoon vanilla

Beat eggs until light. Add sugar and shortening. Blend well. Sift dry ingredients together and add. Add dates, nuts and vanilla. Blend well and pour into greased shallow cake pan. Bake in slow oven (325° F.) about 25 minutes. Cut into bars and roll in confectioners' sugar. Makes about 24.

FROSTED DELIGHTS

1½ cups sifted cake flour
½ teaspoon salt
1 teaspoon baking powder
½ cup shortening
1 cup granulated sugar

2 eggs, beaten
½ teaspoon vanilla
1 cup brown sugar, sifted
1 egg white, stiffly beaten
1 cup nut meats, chopped

Sift flour, salt and baking powder together. Cream shortening with granulated sugar until fluffy. Add eggs, vanilla and sifted ingredients and mix well. Spread batter very thin on baking sheet. Fold brown sugar into egg white, spread over cookie batter and sprinkle with nuts. Bake in slow oven (325° F.) 30 minutes. Cut into squares. Makes 30.

FUDGE SQUARES

¾ cup sifted cake flour
½ teaspoon baking powder
⅛ teaspoon salt
⅓ cup shortening
2 ounces (squares) chocolate

1 cup sugar
2 eggs, well beaten
½ cup chopped walnut
  meats
1 teaspoon vanilla

Sift flour with baking powder and salt. Melt shortening with chocolate. Beat sugar into eggs, add chocolate mixture and blend. Add sifted ingredients, nuts and vanilla and mix well. Bake in greased (8-inch) pan in moderate oven (350° F.) about 35 minutes. Cool and cut into squares. Makes 2 dozen.

BROWNIES

½ cup sifted cake flour
Dash salt
¼ teaspoon baking powder
3 tablespoons shortening
½ cup sugar
2 tablespoons strained honey
2 tablespoons corn sirup

1 egg, beaten
1 ounce (square) chocolate,
  melted
1 tablespoon hot water
1 teaspoon vanilla
½ cup pecans, chopped

Sift flour, salt and baking powder together. Cream shortening with sugar until fluffy. Add honey and sirup and continue creaming. Add egg and mix well. Add melted chocolate. Add dry ingredients, hot water and vanilla and blend well. Mix in pecans and spread mixture in 1 (8-inch) pan. Bake in moderate oven (350° F.) about 20 minutes. Makes 36.

MINCEMEAT BARS

Rolled oats
1¾ cups sifted flour
½ teaspoon baking soda

1 cup brown sugar (packed)
1 cup shortening
1½ cups moist mincemeat

Put rolled oats through food chopper, using coarse blade, and measure 2 cups. Add flour, soda and sugar and mix thoroughly. Cut in shortening until mixture is crumbly. Divide into 2 parts. Pack ½ firmly in bottom of oiled 7½x11 inch baking pan. Spread mincemeat evenly on top, then add remaining dough and pack firmly. Bake in moderate oven (350° F.) 40 minutes. Cool thoroughly and cut into 14 to 16 bars.

ALMOND BARS

½ cup shortening
1½ cups brown sugar
1 cup sifted cake flour
2 eggs, unbeaten
1 teaspoon vanilla
2 tablespoons sifted cake flour

1 teaspoon baking powder
½ teaspoon salt
1 cup shredded coconut
1 cup toasted almonds, chopped

Cream shortening with ½ cup brown sugar and work in 1 cup flour. Spread in very thin layer in square baking pan. Bake in moderate oven (350° F.) 10 minutes. Cool slightly. Beat eggs until light, then beat in vanilla and remaining sugar. Add remaining ingredients in order listed and blend well. Spread over partly cooled mixture. Return to oven and bake until browned, about 25 minutes. Cool slightly and cut into bars. Makes 24.

WALNUT STICKS

1 cup brown sugar
½ cup sifted flour
¼ teaspoon salt

½ teaspoon vanilla
2 eggs, well beaten
1 cup chopped walnuts

Add sugar, flour, salt and vanilla to eggs and mix well. Add walnuts. Spread in greased shallow (9x12½ inch) baking pan and bake in moderate oven (375° F.) 20 to 25 minutes. Cut into strips and remove from pan while warm. Makes 24.

FIG COOKIE SQUARES

½ cup dried figs
⅓ cup butter
1 cup sugar
1 teaspoon mace
1 teaspoon cinnamon
1 teaspoon nutmeg
¼ teaspoon salt

1 egg, beaten
⅓ cup drained crushed pineapple
1¾ cups sifted flour
¾ teaspoon baking soda
1½ tablespoons heavy cream

Pour boiling water over figs, cover and let stand about 5 minutes. Drain, dry on a towel, clip stems and slice fine. Cream butter with ⅔ cup sugar, spices and salt until fluffy. Add egg and beat well. Add pineapple and figs. Sift flour with soda and add, mixing well. Pour into greased (11x7 inch) pan. Smooth top with spatula and spread with mixture of remaining sugar and cream. Bake in hot oven (400° F.) 20 to 25 minutes. Cut into squares. Serve hot or cold. Makes 20 squares.

ENGLISH ROLLED WAFERS

2½ cups sifted cake flour   1½ cups sugar
½ teaspoon salt   2 eggs, beaten
2 teaspoons baking powder   ½ teaspoon vanilla
½ cup butter   ⅔ cup nuts, chopped fine

Sift flour, salt and baking powder together. Cream butter
with sugar. Add beaten eggs, flavoring and sifted ingredients.
Add a few drops of water, if necessary, to make dough of a
consistency to spread smoothly on chilled greased baking sheet.
Spread dough not more than ⅛ inch thick. Sprinkle with
chopped nuts. Bake in moderate oven (350° F.) until browned,
cut into 3x1½ inch strips and roll in small cylinders over
rolling pin or handle of wooden spoon. Makes about 40 wafers.

ROLLED VANILLA WAFERS

2 cups sifted cake flour   1 cup sugar
½ teaspoon salt   1 egg, beaten
2 teaspoons baking powder   ¼ cup milk
⅓ cup butter   2 teaspoons vanilla

Sift flour, salt and baking powder together. Cream butter
and sugar. Combine egg, milk and vanilla. Add liquid and
dry ingredients alternately to creamed mixture. Spread very
thin on greased baking sheet and bake in slow oven (325° F.)
until slightly browned. Cut quickly into 3-inch squares and
roll around handle of wooden spoon. Makes about 30.

ROLLED CHOCOLATE WAFERS

2¼ cups sifted flour   3 ounces (squares) choco-
½ teaspoon cinnamon   late, melted
1½ teaspoons baking powder   2 eggs, beaten
½ teaspoon salt   1 tablespoon milk
½ cup shortening   ½ teaspoon vanilla
1 cup sugar

Sift first 4 ingredients together. Cream shortening with sugar
and add melted chocolate. Add eggs, milk and vanilla. Add
sifted ingredients and mix thoroughly. Spread thin on greased
baking sheet and bake in slow oven (300° F.) about 12 to 15
minutes. Cut into squares and roll into cylinders. Makes about 30.

MERINGUES

2 egg whites
1/8 teaspoon cream of tartar
Dash salt

1/2 cup sugar
1/2 teaspoon vanilla

Beat egg whites with cream of tartar and salt until stiff but not dry. Add sugar, 1 tablespoon at a time, beating until stiff after each addition. Fold in vanilla. Heap in rounds or press through a pastry bag onto baking sheet covered with heavy ungreased paper. Bake in slow oven (275° F.) 40 to 60 minutes or until lightly browned. Remove at once from paper. Makes 18 large meringues.

BROWN SUGAR—Use brown sugar instead of white, fold in one-half cup chopped nuts.

PEANUT—Add 2/3 cup finely chopped peanuts.

COCONUT KISSES

1 1/3 cups (1 can) sweetened
condensed milk
1 teaspoon vanilla

3 cups (3/4 pound) shredded
coconut
1/8 teaspoon salt

Combine ingredients and drop from teaspoon onto greased baking sheet. Bake in moderate oven (375° F.) about 10 minutes. Remove from sheet while hot. Makes about 30.

CEREAL-FLAKE—Use 2 cups prepared cereal flakes with 1 cup shredded coconut.

CHOCOLATE—Add 2 ounces (squares) chocolate, melted.

FRUIT—Use 2 cups chopped dried fruit such as raisins, dates or figs and only 1 cup coconut.

NUT—Add 1 cup chopped peanuts, walnuts or pecans. Omit 1 cup coconut.

PEANUT-BUTTER—Add 1/2 cup peanut butter.

CHOCOLATE CHIP KISSES

1/2 cup sweetened condensed
milk
1 1/2 cups shredded coconut

1/2 teaspoon baking powder
1 cup chocolate pieces

Combine condensed milk, coconut and baking powder. Add chocolate pieces and drop from teaspoon onto greased baking sheet. Bake in slow oven (325° F.) 25 minutes or until browned around edges. Makes 2 dozen.

A GLAMOROUS
CREAM-FILLED
TORTE COMES
FORTH IN A BLAZE
OF GLORY TO SHED
ITS RADIANCE ON
YOUR ANNIVER-
SARY OR JUNIOR'S
BIRTHDAY
—Irradiated Evapo-
rated Milk Institute

GAY LITTLE
PLUM PUD-
DINGS TO
SPREAD HOLI-
DAY SPIRITS
AND CHEER

ANY KIND OF BER-
RIES TAKES THE
CAKE—MAKE IT
SHORT AND SWEET
—National Dairy Council

POTPOURRI OF SWEET-
TOOTH TEMPTERS, COLOR-
FUL AND DELECTABLE

CEREAL-FLAKE KISSES

3 egg whites
½ teaspoon salt
1½ cups sugar

½ teaspoon vanilla or
almond extract
1½ cups shredded coconut
3 cups cereal flakes

Beat egg whites with salt until stiff but not dry, add sugar in small amounts, beating after each addition until stiff. Mixture should be stiff enough to hold its shape by the time all sugar has been added. Beat in flavoring and fold in coconut and cereal flakes. Drop from teaspoon onto greased baking sheet and bake in slow oven (325° F.) 15 to 25 minutes, depending on size. Remove from pan as soon as taken from oven. Makes 4½ dozen.

ALMOND MACAROONS

½ pound almond paste
3 egg whites, slightly beaten
¼ cup sifted flour

½ cup granulated sugar
½ cup confectioners' sugar
⅛ teaspoon salt

Work almond paste with a wooden spoon until smooth. Add slightly beaten egg whites and blend thoroughly. Add flour, sugars and salt sifted together. Drop from teaspoon or press through a cookie press onto baking sheets covered with heavy paper. Bake in slow oven (300° F.) about 30 minutes. Remove from paper while still warm. If paper sticks to cookies, moisten it on the underside. Makes about 4 dozen.

CHOCOLATE MACAROONS

4 egg whites
¼ cup water
⅔ cup sugar
2 teaspoons vanilla
½ teaspoon salt

1 tablespoon flour
2 ounces (squares) chocolate, melted
2½ cups shredded coconut

Beat egg whites with cold water until stiff but not dry. Beat in sugar and vanilla. Add salt and flour and blend carefully. Fold in melted chocolate and coconut. Drop from teaspoon onto heavy paper on baking sheet and bake in slow oven (325° F.) 25 to 30 minutes. Makes about 2½ dozen.

GINGERBREAD

No. 1

2 cups sifted cake flour	1/3 cup shortening
2 teaspoons baking powder	1/2 cup sugar
1/4 teaspoon baking soda	1 egg, well beaten
2 teaspoons ginger	2/3 cup molasses
1 teaspoon cinnamon	3/4 cup sour milk or butter-
1/2 teaspoon salt	milk

Sift flour with baking powder, soda, spices and salt 3 times. Cream shortening with sugar until fluffy. Add egg and molasses; then add sifted ingredients alternately with milk in small amounts. Bake in greased (8-inch) pan in moderate oven (350° F.) about 50 minutes.

No. 2

2 1/2 cups sifted flour	1/2 cup shortening
1 1/2 teaspoons ginger	1/2 cup boiling water
1 teaspoon baking soda	1 cup molasses
1/2 teaspoon salt	

Sift dry ingredients together. Melt shortening in boiling water. Add molasses. Add sifted dry ingredients and mix well. Place in greased (8-inch) baking pan and bake in moderate oven (350° F.) 30 to 40 minutes.

TEA CAKES

1 2/3 cups sifted cake flour	1 cup sugar
1 1/2 teaspoons baking powder	2 eggs, well beaten
1/4 teaspoon salt	2/3 cup milk
1/3 cup shortening	1 teaspoon vanilla

Sift flour, baking powder and salt together. Cream shortening with sugar until fluffy. Add eggs. Add flour alternately with milk in small amounts. Add flavoring. Fill greased cupcake pans 2/3 full. Bake in hot oven (400° F.) 15 to 18 minutes. Makes 2 dozen.

SPICED TEA CAKES—Sift 1 teaspoon cinnamon, 1/4 teaspoon cloves and 1/4 teaspoon nutmeg with flour.

SNOWBALLS—Bake plain or spiced tea cakes in tiny pans. When cool spread on all sides with boiled frosting and roll in moist coconut.

LITTLE CHOCOLATE CAKES

1½ cups sifted cake flour
2 teaspoons baking powder
½ teaspoon salt
½ cup shortening
1 cup sugar

2 eggs, well beaten
3 ounces (squares) choco-
   late, melted
¾ cup milk
1 teaspoon vanilla

Sift flour with baking powder and salt. Cream shortening with sugar until fluffy. Add eggs and beat well; then add chocolate. Blend. Add sifted ingredients alternately with milk. Add vanilla. Fill greased cupcake pans ⅔ full and bake in moderate oven (350° F.) about 20 minutes. Makes 20.

FIG CUPCAKES

1 cup dried figs
2 cups sifted flour
3 teaspoons baking powder
1 teaspoon salt
1 teaspoon ginger

1 teaspoon cinnamon
½ cup shortening
1 cup sugar
2 eggs, beaten
½ cup milk

Pour boiling water over figs; cover, let stand 5 minutes, drain and dry. Clip stems and put through food chopper. Sift flour, baking powder, salt and spices together. Cream shortening and sugar until fluffy. Add eggs; beat well. Add sifted ingredients alternately with milk in small amounts. Add figs. Fill greased muffin pans about ⅔ full. Bake in hot oven (400° F.) about 20 minutes. Makes 15.

SPICE MARBLE CAKES

2 cups sifted cake flour
3 teaspoons baking powder
¼ teaspoon salt
½ cup shortening
1 cup sugar

2 eggs, well beaten
⅔ cup milk
1 teaspoon cinnamon
½ teaspoon cloves
½ teaspoon nutmeg

2 tablespoons molasses

Sift flour with baking powder and salt. Cream shortening and sugar until fluffy. Add eggs and beat thoroughly. Add sifted dry ingredients and milk alternately in small amounts, beating well after each addition. Divide batter into 2 parts. To one part add spices and molasses. Drop by tablespoons into fluted paper baking cups, alternating light and dark mixtures. Bake in moderate oven (350° F.) 25 minutes. Cool and frost. Makes 1½ dozen.

CHOCOLATE CHIP CUPCAKES

2 cup sifted cake flour
3 teaspoons baking powder
¾ teaspoon salt
½ cup shortening
1 cup sugar

1½ teaspoons vanilla
2 eggs
1 cup chocolate pieces
⅔ cup milk

Sift flour, baking powder and salt together. Cream shortening with sugar and vanilla. Add eggs one at a time, beating well after each addition. Mix chocolate pieces with part of flour mixture and add to creamed mixture. Add flour alternately with milk in small amounts. Bake in greased muffin pans in moderate oven (350° F.) 25 minutes. Makes 18.

LITTLE BALTIMORE CAKES

1 cup sifted cake flour
1½ teaspoons baking powder
¼ teaspoon salt
1 tablespoon grated orange rind

4 tablespoons shortening
½ cup sugar
4 egg yolks, well beaten
¼ cup milk

Sift flour with baking powder and salt. Cream orange rind, shortening and sugar until fluffy. Add egg yolks and beat well. Add sifted ingredients alternately with milk in small amounts. Bake in greased cupcake pans in moderate oven (375° F.) about 18 minutes. Cool. Makes 18.

PETITS FOURS

2 cups sifted cake flour
3 teaspoons baking powder
¼ teaspoon salt
½ cup shortening
½ teaspoon vanilla

1 cup sugar
½ cup milk
4 egg whites, stiffly beaten
2 recipes Fondant

Sift flour, baking powder and salt together. Cream shortening, vanilla and sugar together until fluffy. Add sifted ingredients and milk alternately. Fold in stiffly beaten egg whites. Pour into 2 greased (9-inch) pans. Bake in moderate oven (375° F.) about 25 minutes. Cool, then cut into 2-inch squares or triangles or use cookie cutters. Brush off crumbs, arrange on wire racks and place racks on waxed paper. Melt fondant slowly over hot water, tint with food coloring if desired and pour slowly over cakes. Decorate with nuts, candied fruit, small candies, coconut or ornamental frosting pressed into flower shapes with a pastry tube. Makes about 30.

CREAM PUFFS

½ cup shortening   1 cup sifted flour
⅛ teaspoon salt   4 eggs, unbeaten
1 cup boiling water

Add shortening and salt to boiling water and heat to boiling.
Reduce heat, add flour all at once and stir vigorously until
mixture forms ball around spoon, leaving pan clean. Remove
from heat. Add 1 egg at a time, beating very thoroughly after
each addition. Continue beating until mixture is thick and
shiny and breaks from spoon. Shape on ungreased cookie sheet,
using 1 teaspoon or 1 tablespoon of pastry for one puff (depending upon size desired). Bake in very hot oven (450° F.)
20 minutes. Reduce heat to moderate (350° F.) and bake
about 20 minutes longer. Cool. Make slit on one side of each
puff and fill with whipped cream or Cream Pie Filling (page
598). Makes 1 dozen large or 4 dozen small puffs.

CREAM PUFF SWANS—Press part of batter through a paper
funnel onto baking sheet into form of figure 2. Bake these
with the other puffs to form heads and necks of the swans. The
necks should be removed as soon as delicately browned. When
puffs are filled, make eyes on each side of the head, using dots of
chocolate and insert into base of puff.

ÉCLAIRS—Shape cream puff paste into strips 1 inch wide and
4 inches long. Bake as for cream puffs. When cool split, fill
with custard or sweetened whipped cream and frost with uncooked chocolate frosting. Makes about 12.

LADYFINGERS

3 eggs, separated   ½ teaspoon vanilla
½ cup sifted confectioners'   ½ cup sifted cake flour
   sugar   ⅛ teaspoon salt

Beat egg whites until stiff but not dry. Beat in sugar gradually. Beat egg yolks until thick, fold into egg whites, then fold
in vanilla, flour and salt. Shape into (4½-inch) fingers on
baking sheet covered with heavy paper. Sprinkle with additional confectioners' sugar and bake in moderate oven (350° F.)
10 to 12 minutes. Press together in pairs. Makes 12.

CANDIES

WHEN sugar and a liquid are boiled together, a sirup is formed which grows thicker as the boiling continues. The thickness of the sirup determines the general type of candy that will result.

Testing the Sirup

The simplest and most accurate method of determining whether the sirup is thick enough for your purpose is to measure its temperature, because the temperature rises steadily as the sirup thickens.

A CANDY THERMOMETER registering up to 350° F. is not expensive, and it will not only give you a higher average of success in candy making but will save you the time and labor that must otherwise be given to testing the sirup. A table giving the various stages of sugar cookery will be found on page 10.

IF YOU ARE NOT PROVIDED WITH A THERMOMETER, the following test will help you to determine when to take your candy from the fire.

Drop a little sirup into ice-cold water and pinch it between the thumb and finger:

Soft ball stage (for fondant and fudge) the sirup forms a soft ball which loses its shape immediately when removed from the water.

Stiff ball stage (for caramels and nougat) the sirup forms a stiff ball which retains its shape for a second or two when removed from the water and then flattens out.

Hard ball stage (for molasses taffy and soft candies to be pulled) the sirup forms a hard ball which will roll about on a cold buttered plate when removed from the water.

Light to medium crack stage (for toffee and butterscotch and hard candies to be pulled) the sirup forms spirals or threads which are brittle under water but which soften when removed from the water and stick to the teeth when chewed.

Hard crack stage (for clear brittle candies) the sirup forms spirals or threads which are brittle when removed from the water and do not stick to the teeth when chewed.

CREAMY CANDIES—Creaminess is desirable in soft candies. "Creamy" means that the texture should be very smooth, not grainy at all; soft but not sticky. This means that the sugar must not remain as a sirup, but must crystallize. The crystals, however, must be very fine, so that they can not be felt by the fingers or in the mouth.

Creamy candy should not be overcooked. If it reaches too high a temperature, accidentally, a little water may be added and it may be recooked to the correct temperature. This does not give as good a result as one cooking to the correct temperature, but it improves a poor product.

Creamy candy should be cooled before it is beaten. Beating candy while it is hot causes large crystals to form and grainy candy results. If crystals that form on the side of the pan in which candy is cooked fall back into the candy, they tend to cause large crystals to form and to make grainy candy.

A small amount of corn sirup tends to prevent grainy candy. Creamy candies made with corn sirup will require longer beating before crystallization takes place than will candies made from all granulated sugar. They also soften more quickly on standing. If too much sirup is used, the candy will not crystallize at all and the best thing to do with it is to boil it until it reaches the proper stage for a pulled or brittle candy.

One-eighth teaspoon of cream of tartar or one-half teaspoon of lemon-juice or acetic acid to two cups of sugar may be used instead of corn sirup or glucose. They change part of the granulated sugar to glucose during the cooking process.

Ingredients Used in Candies

SUGARS—Granulated, confectioners', brown and maple sugar, corn sirup, molasses, honey and maple and cane sirups are all used in candy, according to the flavor and texture desired. The light-brown sugar should be chosen rather than the darker brown, for a candy of delicate flavor. The same thing is true if corn sirup or molasses is used; the lighter color gives the less strong flavor.

Brown sugar and molasses contain an acid, which if used in candies with milk causes the milk to curdle. Therefore, candy containing these two ingredients should be stirred while it is cooking. Crystallization does not readily occur here because the milk tends to prevent it.

OTHER INGREDIENTS—Nuts of all sorts, chocolate or cocoa, butter, milk, cream, egg whites and fruits such as dates, figs, raisins and candied cherries give special flavor or texture.

Butter is often used because of its flavor and because it tends to make a creamy product. Other mild-flavored fats may be used instead of butter, particularly in candies containing chocolate, brown sugar or molasses.

Chocolate contributes flavor and tends to make a smooth candy because of the fat it contains. Three tablespoons of cocoa and two-thirds of a tablespoon of butter may be used instead of one square of chocolate.

Fresh milk, dried milk or canned milk, sweetened or unsweetened, may be used in candies.

CHOCOLATE FUDGE

2 cups sugar
1 or 2 squares chocolate
1/8 teaspoon cream of tartar
   or 2 tablespoons corn sirup
2/3 cup milk
1 teaspoon vanilla
2 tablespoons butter

Mix the sugar, milk, grated chocolate, cream of tartar or corn sirup and boil rather slowly, stirring until the ingredients are well blended. Boil to the soft-ball stage (238° F.). Remove from the stove, add the butter, but do not stir it in. When lukewarm, add the vanilla and beat until it creams; that is, until the shiny appearance disappears and the fudge will hold its shape when dropped from the spoon. Spread it in a buttered pan and when it hardens mark it into squares.

MARSHMALLOW FUDGE

To the recipe for Chocolate Fudge add three tablespoons of marshmallow cream just after taking it from the heat. Beat well and pour into buttered pans.

MAPLE FUDGE

2 1/2 cups maple sugar
1 cup cream or milk
1/2 cup boiling water
1 cup broken nut-meats

Break the maple sugar into small pieces and heat it in a saucepan with the water. When it is dissolved, add the milk. Boil to the soft-ball stage (238° F.). Remove from the heat and cool. When it is lukewarm, beat until it creams and add the nut-meats. Spread it in a buttered pan and when it hardens mark it into squares.

DIVINITY FUDGE

2 cups sugar	2 egg-whites
½ cup corn sirup	¾ cup blanched almonds
½ cup water	1 tablespoon almond or
¾ cup candied cherries	lemon extract

Put the sugar, water and corn sirup into a saucepan. Stir it while it dissolves over the fire, then let it boil without stirring to the light crack stage (265° F.). While it is cooking, beat the whites of eggs stiffly and when the sirup is ready pour it over them, beating constantly. Beat until creamy, add nuts, cherries and extract, and pour into buttered tins.

MAPLE DIVINITY FUDGE

Follow preceding recipe, using in addition one-half cup maple sirup.

OTHER VARIATIONS OF FUDGE

Brown sugar may be used partly or entirely in place of white or maple sugar. If brown sugar is used, the cream of tartar or corn sirup should be omitted.

Condensed milk may be used instead of fresh milk. It should have water added according to the directions on the can.

Peanut butter may be used instead of chocolate, using two tablespoons of the butter to each cup of sugar in the recipe. Like butter or other fat it should be added after the fudge is cooked.

Marshmallows or marshmallow cream may be added to any fudge after it has been taken from the fire. One cup of marshmallow to two cups of sugar is a good proportion.

Any kind of broken nuts, including coconut, may be added to the fudge just before it is turned into the pan.

Candied cherries, or other fruits, chopped candied orange-peel or citron may be added. Dates and raisins are often used.

Flavoring may be varied to suit. Orange extract is good with brown sugar, chocolate or molasses. Lemon extract or lemon-juice is good in a white-sugar fudge from which the chocolate is omitted.

FUDGE-COVERED DATES

Cut dates in half, lengthwise; remove the pits and lay the halves at intervals on a greased dish. Make fudge according to any fudge recipe and drop a teaspoonful on each half date. This must be done quickly, to avoid letting the fudge harden in the pan. The hardening may be delayed by standing the pan in a larger one containing hot water.

PANOCHA

3 cups brown sugar
1 cup milk
2 tablespoons butter

1 teaspoon vanilla
1 cup nut-meats

Put the sugar and milk into a saucepan and cook to the soft-ball stage, or 238° F. Remove from the fire, add butter and vanilla, and cool without stirring. When it is lukewarm, beat until it is creamy. Stir in the broken nut-meats. Hickory nuts, walnuts or pecans are especially nice. Pour into a buttered pan and when it hardens mark into squares.

MAPLE PRALINES

2 cups sugar
⅔ cup milk

1 cup maple sirup
2 cups pecan-meats

Boil the sugar, milk and maple sirup until the mixture reaches the soft-ball stage (238° F.). Remove from the fire and cool. When it is lukewarm, beat until it is smooth and creamy. Add any kind of broken nut-meats and drop on buttered paper from the tip of a spoon, making little mounds.

FONDANT

2 cups granulated sugar
1 cup water

2 tablespoons corn sirup or
⅛ teaspoon cream of tartar
1 teaspoon vanilla

Put the sugar, corn sirup and water in a saucepan and heat slowly. Do not let it begin to boil until the sugar is dissolved. Wash down the sides of the pan with a fork wrapped in a damp cloth or else cover and cook for two or three minutes so that the steam will carry down the crystals that have been thrown on the side of the pan. Remove the cover and continue to boil slowly without stirring to the soft-ball stage (238° F.). While cooking, keep the cover on part of the time so the steam can help to keep the crystals washed down.

Remove from the fire and pour at once on large platters or slabs which have been dipped into cold water, and let it stand until it is lukewarm. Add vanilla. Stir with a fork until creamy; then knead with the hands until it is smooth and free from lumps.

Fondant is better if allowed to ripen for several days before being used. It may be wrapped in waxed paper and put into a tightly covered jar. When it is to be used for centers of dipped bonbons the centers should be shaped by hand or in molds and allowed to stand in the air until the surface loses all stickiness. Then the shapes may be dipped into the coating.

HONEY FONDANT

2 cups granulated sugar   ⅓ cup honey   1 cup water

Proceed as for plain fondant.

CANDIES MADE FROM FONDANT

TUTTI-FRUTTI—Knead fondant and flavor with cherry or almond extract. Knead into it one-third its amount of a mixture of raisins, dates, figs, candied cherries, citron, orange-peel or other candied fruits, which have been chopped together. Shape into a flat cake and cut after it stands for an hour.

WINTERGREEN CREAMS—Melt a portion of fondant in the upper part of a double boiler until it is soft enough to drop from a spoon. It may be necessary to add a few drops of hot water. Color it with red vegetable coloring to a delicate pink. Flavor with oil of wintergreen. Stir until it is creamy. Drop from a teaspoon on oiled paper.

PEPPERMINT CREAMS—Follow instructions given for wintergreen creams, but leave the fondant uncolored and flavor with oil of peppermint.

NUT CREAMS—Knead fondant and flavor with almond or coffee extract. Knead into it a mixture of chopped nuts or moist coconut. Shape into balls, squares or other shapes attractive for dipping into chocolate.

STUFFED DATES, AND PRUNES—Stone dates or prunes and stuff them with fondant which has been colored pink and flavored with rose water. A whole nut-meat should be inserted with the fondant.

CHOCOLATE BONBONS—Melt very slowly a good quality of specially prepared dipping chocolate, sweetened or unsweetened, in the top of a double boiler. Do not heat the water under the chocolate above 120° F., for overheating spoils chocolate for dipping. Stir it constantly while it is melting to keep an even temperature, and after it has melted, beat it thoroughly. Keep the heat very low during the dipping process. To dip centers, use a fork or confectioner's dipper. Drop centers in one at a time and when covered place on oiled paper. The room in which dipping is done should be cool, so that the chocolate may harden quickly.

MARSHMALLOWS

2 tablespoons gelatin	⅛ teaspoon salt
¼ cup cold water	1 teaspoon vanilla
¾ cup boiling water	Confectioners' sugar
2 cups sugar	

Soak the gelatin in the cold water until it has taken up all the water. Boil the sugar and water to the soft-ball stage (238° F.). Add vanilla and salt to gelatin. Pour the sirup slowly over the gelatin, beating constantly with a whisk until cool and thick. Butter a shallow pan slightly and dust with confectioners' sugar. Turn the marshmallow mixture into the pan and smooth the top evenly. Dust with confectioners' sugar. Let it stand over night. In the morning cut it into small squares and roll in confectioners' sugar.

VARIATIONS FOR MARSHMALLOWS

Chopped nuts, dates, figs, raisins or candied cherries may be added to the recipe for marshmallows. Plain marshmallows may be rolled in coconut before being rolled in sugar, or they may be dipped in melted chocolate. Marshmallows may be tinted any desired color.

CARAMELS

VANILLA—

2 cups sugar
½ cup corn sirup
½ cup milk
1 teaspoon vanilla

4 tablespoons butter
1 cup cream or condensed milk

Cook the ingredients, except the vanilla, to the stiff-ball stage, or 246° F. Remove from the fire, add the vanilla and pour into a buttered pan. When it is cold, turn it out of the pan and cut it into squares.

CHOCOLATE—Use the same ingredients as for vanilla caramels but reduce the cream or condensed milk to one-half cup and add three squares of chocolate. Break the chocolate in small pieces, add to the other ingredients and proceed as for vanilla caramels.

MOLASSES TAFFY

2 cups molasses
1 cup granulated sugar
¾ cup water
⅛ teaspoon soda

4 tablespoons butter or other fat
½ teaspoon vanilla

Cook the molasses, sugar and water slowly to the hard-ball stage (260° F.) stirring during the latter part of the cooking to prevent its burning. Remove from the fire, add the fat, soda and vanilla and stir enough to mix. Pour into a greased pan and, when cool enough to handle, pull it until it becomes light in color. Stretch it into a long rope and cut with scissors into small pieces.

WHITE TAFFY

2 cups granulated sugar
½ cup water
1 teaspoon glycerin

2½ tablespoons vinegar
1 teaspoon lemon or vanilla extract

Boil the sugar, water, glycerin and vinegar to the hard-ball stage (260° F.). Add flavoring. Pour on to a greased platter. When cool enough to handle, pull until very white, stretch into a long rope, and cut into short pieces.

NOUGAT

2 cups sugar	1 teaspoon vanilla
⅓ cup corn sirup	1½ cups nut-meats
1 cup water	½ cup candied cherries
4 egg-whites	

Boil together half of the sugar, half of the water and half of the corn sirup to the stiff-ball stage (246°-250° F.). Remove the sirup from the fire and pour it slowly over the well-beaten whites and continue beating until it is cool. While beating, cook the remaining half of the ingredients to the stiff-ball stage. Remove and add at once to the first mixture, beating while adding. When cool, add the vanilla, nut-meats and candied cherries and pour into buttered pans. Smooth over the surface and let it stand over night before cutting. In the morning cut and wrap in waxed paper.

BUTTERSCOTCH

1 cup granulated sugar	1 cup water
1 cup brown sugar	⅓ cup butter
¼ cup light corn sirup	1 teaspoon vanilla

Put sugar, sirup and water into a saucepan and set over direct heat. Stir until the sugar is dissolved, then cook without stirring to the stiff ball stage (250° F.). Add butter and cook to the medium-crack stage (280° F.), for soft butterscotch, or to the hard-crack stage (300° F.) for brittle candy. Remove from heat, add the flavoring and pour on a greased slab. Mark while still warm and when cold break into pieces.

MAPLE SCOTCH

1 cup maple sugar	1 teaspoon vinegar
½ cup water	4 tablespoons butter

Boil together the maple sugar, water and vinegar to the stiff-ball stage (246° F.). Then add the butter and cook to the medium-crack stage (280° F.). Turn into a well-buttered pan. Mark while still warm, and when cold break into pieces.

POPCORN BALLS

No. 1.

3 quarts popped corn
1 cup sugar
⅓ cup white corn sirup

1 cup water
¼ teaspoon salt
1 teaspoon lemon or vanilla

Discard all imperfect kernels and put the popped corn into a large pan. Cook sugar, sirup and water to the medium-crack stage (280° F.). Add flavoring and salt. Pour over the corn, stirring with a spoon so that all kernels will be evenly coated. Shape the corn into balls, lay on waxed paper, and wrap in waxed paper.

No. 2.

3 quarts popped corn
1 cup honey
1 cup sugar

⅔ cup water
2 tablespoons butter
¼ teaspoon salt

Proceed as for No. 1.

MAPLE NUT BRITTLE

1 cup light brown sugar
1 cup maple sugar
½ cup water
2 tablespoons butter

1 teaspoon vanilla
¼ teaspoon salt
1 cup broken nut meats

Boil the sugar and water to the stiff-ball stage (246° F.). Add butter and cook to the brittle stage (290°-300° F.). Add the vanilla and salt and pour over the nut meats, which have been placed on a buttered pan. When cold, break into pieces.

PEANUT BRITTLE

2 cups granulated sugar
1 pint chopped peanuts

1 teaspoon salt

Put the sugar into an iron frying-pan and heat slowly, stirring constantly, until the sugar is melted and turns a light brown color (slightly above 300° F.). Spread the chopped peanuts in a buttered tin, sprinkle them with the salt, warm the tin slightly and pour the melted sugar over the peanuts.

TURKISH DELIGHT

3 tablespoons gelatin
2 cups sugar
½ cup cold water
Grated rind and juice of
1 orange

½ cup hot water
Grated rind and juice of
1 lemon
Red or green coloring

Soften gelatin in cold water. Combine sugar and hot water and heat to boiling. Add gelatin and simmer 20 minutes. Add citrous juice and rind and red or green coloring. Strain into loaf pan. The pan should be large enough so that mixture is ½ to 1 inch deep. Add chopped nuts if desired. Chill until firm.

When it is cold, turn it on to a board. Cut into cubes or other shapes and roll in confectioners' sugar.

If you prefer other flavors, such as peppermint, wintergreen and clove, omit the fruit juice and rind, add one-half cup of water, and flavor with a few drops of oil of peppermint, oil of wintergreen, oil of cloves, etc.

COCONUT BALLS

2 cups sugar
⅔ cup water
½ teaspoon vanilla

3 egg whites
2 cups moist coconut

Boil the sugar and water together to the soft-ball stage (238° F.). Add the vanilla and pour it slowly over the stiffly beaten whites of the eggs beating constantly until light and foamy. Stir in the coconut and drop on buttered pans by teaspoonfuls. Shape each confection like a ball. Bake in a slow oven (300° F.) for about twenty minutes.

MARZIPAN

2 egg whites
1 cup almond paste
½ teaspoon lemon or vanilla

1 cup confectioners' sugar,
more or less

Beat the egg whites and mix with the almond paste. Add the flavoring and enough sugar to make the mixture stiff enough to handle. After it has stood overnight, it may be molded into small shapes of fruits or vegetables such as pears, apples or carrots and colored with vegetable colors, or it may be cut into small pieces and dipped in chocolate or other coating, or used as the center for candied cherries, dates, prunes, etc.

The almond paste may be bought at a confectioner's, or the almonds may be blanched and pounded. Two and two-thirds cups shelled almonds make one cup of paste.

STUFFED SPICED PRUNES

½ pound prunes	⅛ teaspoon grated nutmeg
½ cup sugar	½ teaspoon cinnamon
⅛ cup corn sirup	5 allspice berries
⅛ cup water	⅛ teaspoon maple flavoring
3 to 6 cloves	Chopped nut meats

Soak the prunes overnight, after washing them thoroughly. Drain off the water; add the sugar, sirup, water, spices and flavoring and simmer slowly until the sirup is all absorbed by the prunes. Cut a slit along one side of each prune, slip out the stone and fill the cavities with chopped nut meats moistened with a little sirup or with cream. Roll in confectioners' sugar.

TUTTI-FRUTTI CANDY

1 pound raisins	1 pound figs
¾ pound walnut-meats	½ pound prunes
1 pound dates	Confectioners' sugar

Soak the prunes over night. Steam until they are soft and remove stones. Wash the figs, and steam them twenty minutes. Wash the dates and remove the stones. Put the fruit and nuts through a food-chopper. Put confectioners' sugar on the board and with the hands work the fruit and nuts until well blended. Roll to about one-quarter inch thick, using the sugar to dredge the board and rolling-pin. Cut in any desired shape, roll in sugar, pack in layers in a tin box, using waxed paper between the layers.

HOLIDAY COCONUT BALLS

⅓ cup corn sirup	¼ cup currants
¼ teaspoon maple flavoring	½ cup raisins
	1 cup moist coconut

Stir the ingredients together to make a stiff loaf. Pack in a small cake-tin. Chill in the refrigerator and roll into small balls. Dust with confectioners' sugar.

SALTED ALMONDS OR PEANUTS

Blanch the almonds or remove the thin brown skin from the peanuts. Dry the almonds well. Put a small amount of oil into a dripping pan, pour in the nuts and stir them until they are well coated. There should be no excess oil in the pan; just enough to give an oily surface to each nut. Set the pan in the oven, and stir the nuts often until they become light brown. Drain them in a colander, spread on a platter and sprinkle with salt.

To BLANCH ALMONDS—Shell the nuts and pour boiling water over them. Let them stand from two to five minutes, until the brown skin can be slipped off with the fingers. Pour off the water and remove the skins.

GLACÉ FRUITS OR NUTS

2 cups sugar	Small fruits or sections of larger fruits or whole nut-meats
1 cup water	
⅔ cup light corn sirup	

Make a sirup of the sugar, water and corn sirup. Boil, without stirring, to the hard crack stage (300° F.). Remove the saucepan from the fire and put it into an outer pan of boiling water to keep the sirup from hardening. Drop in the well drained fruit or the nut-meats, a few at a time. Skim out and place on heavy waxed paper to dry.

CANDIED FRUITS

SIRUP FOR CANDIED FRUITS—

2 cups sugar	⅓ cup light corn sirup
1 cup water	

Boil together until the sirup spins a thread when dropped from the spoon (234° F.).

CANDIED PEARS, PEACHES, PLUMS, AND CHERRIES—Pare, core, slice or otherwise prepare the fruits to be candied. Have them drained clear of all juice and add them to the boiling sirup, being careful not to have them crowded. Simmer until the fruits are clear. Skim from the sirup, drain, spread on a screen and allow them to dry until they are no longer sticky. Pack between sheets of waxed paper and place in a tin box or a glass jar.

CANDIED QUINCES, PINEAPPLES AND FIGS—Prepare fruits by washing, paring or slicing as desired, then simmer in clear water until tender. Drain and use the water in which the fruits were cooked to make the sirup. Proceed as in the preceding recipe.

CANDIED ORANGE, LEMON OR GRAPEFRUIT PEEL—Cut the peel into halves or quarters. Let them stand over night in salted water (one tablespoon salt to one quart water). Drain and wash thoroughly. Simmer in clear water, changing the water several times until it has no bitter taste. When the peel is tender, drain, cut into strips or add whole to the sirup and simmer until it is transparent. Drain, roll in granulated sugar, and allow the peel to dry well before packing.

FRUIT PASTE CANDIES

FRUIT PASTE—Paste may be made from most kinds of fruit-pulp after the juice has been drained off for jelly, or it may be made from fresh or canned fruit. A combination of the pulp of two or more kinds of fruit gives a delicious result.

Press the pulp through a rather fine strainer, measure it and to one pint of pulp add one and one-third cups of sugar. Cook this mixture, stirring it and taking care not to let it scorch. When the paste is thick and clear, turn it out on a platter which has been brushed with unsalted fat. Let it stand and dry until a film forms over the top. Then turn it on to a wire screen and dry until it loses its stickiness. To get the best results, dry it as quickly as possible in the open air. Roll the dried paste in thick paraffin paper and pack it in tin boxes or glass jars for future use. For finish, dip in fondant or chocolate.

SPUN SUGAR

2 cups sugar   1 cup water
                    ⅛ teaspoon cream of tartar

Dissolve sugar in water, bring slowly to boiling point and

boil to 280° F. Add cream of tartar and continue boiling without stirring until the sirup reaches 310° F. In the meantime, have prepared 2 oiled wooden spoon handles securely anchored in kitchen-cabinet drawers, with a clean paper spread on the floor below. When the sirup reaches 310° F. remove quickly to a pan of cold water to stop the boiling, then to pan of hot water. Tint with food colors if desired. Dip the spinner (a spoon, large knife or egg whip will serve) into the sirup and swing back and forth over the handles. The sugar falls in long threads. If the sirup thickens as you work, heat the water in the lower pan until the sirup melts and continue spinning. Use at once as decorative nests for ice cream, meringue glacé, Baked Alaska or Easter eggs.

PULLED SUGAR

2 pounds loaf sugar	1 teaspoon glucose
1 cup water	¼ teaspoon cream of tartar

Add water to sugar in a saucepan and when completely dissolved turn on heat, add glucose and cream of tartar and boil as quickly as possible to 312° F. Remove at once to pan of cold water to stop boiling, then pour sirup onto a lightly oiled slab. If different colors or flavors are wanted, divide the sirup as desired. As edges cool, lift with knife and turn in to the center. When sugar is cool enough to handle, pull from sides, turning in to the center, and roll into a ball. Work in a warm place so sugar does not cool too quickly as you work and be sure that all parts are pulled equally. When it becomes quite satin-white and china-like in appearance, start your design. Ribbons are made by pulling a straight piece, cutting the edges quickly and then arranging in knots or bows. Set aside to cool slowly so they will not crack.

For flowers and leaves, pull a small end into petal shape, pinch off the end, work the edges thin and curve into desired shape. Put the petals together as you work to form the flower, then pinch the lower ends together and attach to a new tin wire, or attach to a green pulled-sugar stem. Detached leaves may be mounted on wire and left uncovered.

FRUIT DESSERTS

Fresh Fruits

FRESH fruits are the simplest and easiest of all desserts to prepare, and furnish one of the most wholesome sweets. They are at their best when served ripe and in season. When fruit comes from the market it should be looked over and kept in a cool place. All fruit should be washed before it is served.

FRESH BERRIES

Turn the berries out of the container and spread them on a platter or board so that they are not piled up on one another. If there are any noticeably soft or moldy, remove them and set the rest in the refrigerator or other cool place until they are to be prepared for serving. Then pick them over carefully, wash and drain. Strawberries are usually hulled, but when very large and perfect they may be served with the hulls on and dipped into powdered sugar when they are eaten.

MELONS

All melons should be served very cold. They may be laid on chopped ice when served but the ice should never be placed in or on the edible parts of the melon.

CANTALOUP—Cut the cantaloup in half and with a spoon remove the seeds without injuring the flesh. Each half may be served alone or it may be filled with fresh berries or other fruit or with ice-cream. When used as an appetizer at the beginning of a meal, a quarter of a large cantaloup is enough. Chilled melon balls are often served.

HONEYDEW AND CASABA MELONS—These are usually cut lengthwise and served in sections two or three inches wide.

WATERMELON—To serve a whole watermelon at the table, cut it in half, crosswise, and cut a slice from each end to make it stand on a platter. Garnish the platter with green leaves.

The melon may be served in round slices, or in half or quarter slices from which the rind may or may not have been removed; the pulp may be shaped in balls or dice and served in glasses, or it may be scooped out in large spoonfuls and served in a watermelon tub shaped from the rind.

For other suggestions for serving melons, see Index.

GRAPEFRUIT

See Index.

ORANGES

Cut oranges in half crosswise. With a sharp knife, loosen the pulp from the center and from the dividing fiber. Serve two halves to each person.

An attractive dessert is made by cutting oranges crosswise in quarter-inch slices and laying the slices in an overlapping row on a glass plate, allowing about four slices to each person. The slices may be sprinkled with sugar and moist coconut or served plain.

ICED ORANGE JUICE

Fill small glass cups with strained orange-juice and set each in the center of a plate filled with cracked ice. This makes a delicious and beautiful fruit course for breakfast.

STUFFED PEACHES

Pare large peaches and cut a slice from the top of each. Remove the pits without breaking the fruit and fill the hollow with nuts or with any chopped fruit, such as apples, citron or raisins. Sprinkle with sugar and a little cinnamon or nutmeg. Pour custard over the peaches and bake. Or serve cold soft custard with the uncooked chilled fruit.

SLICED BANANAS

Chill and slice well ripened bananas, serve with cream or lemon-juice and sugar.

No. 1.   FRESH FRUIT CUP

½ pineapple
1 cup strawberries
3 well ripened bananas

3 oranges
2 tablespoons lemon-juice
Sugar

Peel and dice the pineapple, bananas and oranges. Wash and hull the strawberries. Mix all together, with the lemon-juice and sugar, and set in the refrigerator until very cold.

No. 2—Peel and slice oranges and arrange in a glass dish alternate layers of oranges and sugar until all the fruit is used. Whip some sweet cream very stiff, sweeten and flavor it and spread it over the oranges. Serve very cold.

Crushed pineapple and sliced bananas may be added, if desired.

No. 3.

3 oranges	3 well ripened bananas
1 cup diced pineapple	1 cup moist coconut

With a sharp knife cut the orange and pineapple into thick slices, then cut them into bits free from seeds and membrane. Slice the bananas thin. Arrange alternate layers of the different fruits in a deep dish and sprinkle each layer with sugar and coconut. Over the whole pour any fruit-juice. Serve very cold.

MACÉDOINE OF FRUIT

3 peaches	½ cup diced watermelon
3 pears	1 cup raspberries
½ cup diced pineapple	⅓ cup sugar

Pare and slice peaches and pears, cut pineapple and melon in small pieces, mix fruit and sugar, and chill for one hour. Serve in glasses, adding one tablespoon whipped cream to each glass just before serving. A berry or piece of pineapple placed on the cream gives color to the dish.

VERMONT QUARTERED APPLES

6 firm, tart apples	3 tablespoons butter
4 tablespoons shaved maple sugar	1 cup boiling water

Pare, quarter and core the apples, and place on an earthenware pie-plate. Mix the maple sugar, butter and boiling water and boil for five minutes. Pour this sauce over the apples, place in a moderate oven (350°-375° F.) and bake until the apples are soft. Baste occasionally with the hot sirup. This makes a delicious dessert served with cream. It may also be served in the baking-dish with duck or goose.

APPLE SAUCE

No. 1—Wash, pare, quarter and core sour, juicy apples. Place them in a porcelain kettle with just enough water to keep them from burning and boil until tender. Add sugar to taste and boil a few minutes longer. Serve hot or cold.

A few whole cloves or a dash of cinnamon or nutmeg or a little lemon-juice or a few seedless raisins may be cooked with the apples. Brown or maple sugar may be used instead of white.

No. 2—Prepare as for No. 1 but place in a baking dish with just enough water to start them cooking. Sprinkle with sugar. Cover and bake in a moderate oven (350°-375° F.) until the apples are soft but not broken. Add more sugar and a little boiling water if necessary, and cook, uncovered, until the top is slightly browned.

No. 3—Wash, quarter and core but do not pare apples. Cut out any bad spots. Stew until tender with just enough water to keep them from sticking to the pan. Rub through a colander or coarse strainer, add sugar to taste, and stir until the sugar is dissolved.

APPLE OR OTHER FRUIT SNOW

¾ cup sour apple pulp   Lemon-juice
Sugar   3 egg-whites

Pare, quarter and steam enough apples to make the required amount of apple pulp. Press through a sieve. Add sugar and lemon-juice to taste and fold into stiffly beaten whites very gradually. Pile on a glass dish, chill and serve with custard sauce or cream.

Other fruits may be used in the same way. Uncooked fruit pulp may be used by grating fresh fruit and covering it at once with lemon-juice to prevent discoloration.

BLUSHING APPLES

6 red apples   1½ cups water
1½ cups sugar   Juice of 1 lemon
Juice and grated rind of   Whipped cream
1 orange

Wash and core the apples. Cook until they are tender in sirup made of the sugar and water, turning so that they will

cook evenly. Carefully remove the skin, scraping the red pulp
from it and pasting it back on the sides of the apple. Put the
apples in a serving dish. Boil the sirup down to one cup and
add the grated rind and the juice of one orange, the juice of
one lemon, and, if desired, nuts, candied orange peel or raisins.
Pour sirup over the apples and serve with whipped cream.

JELLIED APPLES

Pare and core the required number of apples and bake, steam
or boil in sirup until tender. Cool. Cover the bottoms of individual molds with lemon jelly, put in apples and cover with
jelly. Unmold and serve with meringue or whipped cream.

BAKED APPLES

Select sound apples; core them and place from one teaspoon
to one tablespoon of sugar in each cavity. Place the apples in
a baking dish, add water to cover the bottom of the dish, and
bake in a moderate oven (350°-375° F.) until tender.

Sour apples cook more quickly than sweet ones, and summer
or fall apples take less time to cook than winter apples.

Baked apples may be varied by filling the centers with brown
sugar and raisins, sections of bananas, red cinnamon candies,
marshmallow, marmalade or jelly, honey or corn sirup and
lemon juice, nuts, candied orange peel, candied pineapple, preserved ginger, canned or fresh berries, peaches and other fruits
or leftover fruit juice. Meringues, custard sauce, whipped cream
or marshmallow sauce may be used as garnish.

BAKED STUFFED APPLES

6 large tart red apples	1 cup brown, or maple sugar
1 cup chopped bananas	1 teaspoon cinnamon
1 cup chopped cranberries	Chopped nut meats

Whipped cream

Cut off the stem end of the apples, but do not peel them.
Remove all the core and part of the pulp, leaving the walls of
the cup about ¾ inch thick. Mix bananas, cranberries, sugar,
and cinnamon. Fill the cavities in the apples with this mixture,
cover with chopped nut meats, and bake in the oven (350°-
375° F.) until tender. Serve cold with a spoonful of whipped
cream on top of each apple.

STEAMED APPLES

Core the apples, fill cavities with sugar and put in a saucepan with hot water about an inch deep. Cover and cook slowly, turning the apples over once. This will steam the apples and, if they are red, will preserve their color.

BAKED STUFFED PEARS

Pare and core large pears and stuff with seeded dates, raisins or chopped nuts with some tart marmalade or shredded coconut. Place close together in a baking-dish, cover bottom of pan with water and bake slowly until tender.

SNOW PEAKS

1 tall can evaporated milk
    with ¼ cup water
⅓ cup sugar
1 teaspoon cornstarch
⅛ teaspoon salt

3 eggs, separated
3 tablespoons Angelica wine
1 No. 2½ can peaches
6 tablespoons confectioners'
    sugar

⅛ teaspoon almond extract

Scald diluted evaporated milk in double boiler. Mix sugar, cornstarch, salt and beaten egg yolks. Add to milk and cook, stirring constantly until mixture coats spoon. Remove at once, cool and add wine. Pour custard into sherbet glasses, add peaches and top with meringue made by beating egg whites with confectioners' sugar and almond extract. Serves 6.

STEWED RHUBARB

Wash, but do not peel, the rhubarb and cut it in one-inch pieces. Add one-half as much sugar as rhubarb, put in a saucepan with just enough water to keep the fruit from burning, as rhubarb provides its own moisture. Cook until tender.

BAKED RHUBARB

Prepare as for stewing, using same proportion of sugar and rhubarb, and bake in a moderate oven (350°-375° F.).

Dried Fruits

If prepared carefully, most dried fruits retain their flavor. Except for some of the vitamins, none of the food values of

the product are lost in drying, for this method of preservation only drives off the moisture of perishable foods through evaporation. The modern method of drying fruit makes it unnecessary to soak the present day product. Dried fruits are edible as they come from the package, or may be plumped slightly by immersing in hot water.

Quick cooking without soaking saves the sugar of the fruit, allows a firmer texture and improves the flavor. Rinse the fruit, cover generously with water and boil briskly until very tender. Apples and apricots require 40 minutes, figs 20-30, peaches 50, pears 40, prunes 45-50 and raisins 10. Add sugar to taste during the last 5 minutes of cooking to all fruit except figs which must be cooked with sugar for at least 15 minutes.

Stick cinnamon, cloves or lemon juice may be added for flavor variety.

There are endless ways in which dried fruit may be used for garnishes, salads, cakes, cookies, breads and desserts.

APRICOT OR PRUNE WHIP

1½ cups sweetened apricot or prune pulp	⅛ teaspoon salt
1½ tablespoons lemon juice	⅓ cup sugar
	3 egg whites, stiffly beaten
Chopped nuts	

Mix pulp, lemon juice and salt together. Beat sugar into egg whites, fold in fruit mixture and serve garnished with chopped nuts. If desired this mixture may be piled lightly into a buttered baking dish and baked at 275° F. 30 to 45 minutes.

STEAMED FIGS

18 pulled figs	3 teaspoons confectioners' sugar
2 tablespoons water	¾ cup heavy cream
1 orange	

Wash the figs and cut out the stem end. Soak several hours, then drain. Add water and cook in a double boiler slowly until tender. Arrange the hot figs in individual dessert dishes around a central small mound of orange portions which have been skinned and sprinkled with sugar. Border with sweetened whipped cream slightly flavored with orange juice.

KNICKERBOCKER FIGS

½ pound figs
Maraschino cherries
Pecan meats

¼ cup orange-juice
3 tablespoons sugar
2 teaspoons lemon-juice

Stuff the figs with cherries and broken nut-meats, allowing two cherries and five nut-meats to each fig. Mix the orange-juice, sugar, and lemon-juice, add the figs, cover and simmer until the figs are tender. Drain, cool and serve in individual paper cases.

RHUBARB SCALLOP WITH MERINGUE

½ pound rhubarb
1 cup granulated sugar
Grated rind of 1 orange
2 tablespoons powdered sugar

¼ teaspoon salt
1 small sponge cake
2 egg whites

Wash and peel rhubarb and cut in 1-inch pieces; add sugar, orange rind and salt, mixing well. Cut sponge cake in thin slices; line bottom of greased baking dish with 3 or 4 slices; cover with ¼ of rhubarb. Continue to make alternate layers of cake and fruit until material is used. Cover and bake in moderate oven (350° F.) for 30 minutes. Beat egg whites until stiff; add sugar slowly, beating until blended. Pile on baked pudding and bake 15 minutes longer, or until meringue is slightly browned.

SOUTHERN FRIED APPLES

Core but do not peel, medium-sized Jonathan or Spitzenberg apples. Slice ½ inch thick to make perfect rings. Heat ⅓ cup butter in thick-walled skillet—aluminum, chrome or steel—until light brown. Fit in the apple slices to cover bottom without breaking. Mix ⅔ cup sugar with 1 tablespoon ground cinnamon and dash of salt. Cover apples with ½ the mixture. After 5 minutes turn the slices with pancake turner to avoid breaking. Cover with remaining sugar mixture. Fry over low flame until almost transparent. If too well done, they break easily. Serve hot.

CUSTARDS, GELATIN AND CREAM DESSERTS

M OST desserts made with eggs, cream and gelatin, or with any one or two of these ingredients, are best served very cold. The mechanical refrigerator is excellent for chilling such desserts.

Custards

A custard is a mixture of cooked egg and milk, flavored. Starchy material is sometimes used to replace part of the eggs. Custards are classified according to the method used in cooking them; those cooked over hot water and stirred throughout the cooking process are known as soft or stirred custards—erroneously, as boiled custards; those set in hot water and cooked in the oven (oven-poaching) are firm or baked custards.

The firmness of a custard depends on the proportion of eggs to milk. (See "Useful Facts about Eggs.") The finest-grained custards are those in which the yolks predominate.

If fresh milk is not available, an unsweetened canned milk or milk powder may be used with excellent results.

No. 1. **PLAIN SOFT CUSTARD**

2 cups milk	1/8 teaspoon salt
2 whole eggs or	4 tablespoons sugar
4 egg-yolks	1/2 teaspoon vanilla

Scald the milk in the top of the double boiler. Beat together slightly the eggs, sugar and salt. Add the hot milk to the egg mixture, mix thoroughly and return to the top of the double boiler. Cook over hot water, stirring constantly until the egg coats the spoon. Add vanilla.

No. 2—If eggs are expensive, modify the recipe for soft custard by substituting one teaspoon of corn-starch for one egg-yolk or two teaspoons for two egg-yolks or one whole egg. Make the milk and starch into a sauce and cook over hot water twenty to thirty minutes before adding any eggs.

VARIATIONS OF PLAIN SOFT CUSTARD

COFFEE—Use recipe for soft custard, substituting one cup of very strong coffee for one of the cups of milk.

CARAMEL—Caramelize one-fourth cup sugar and add to one cup scalded milk.

Follow recipe for soft custard, using this milk with caramel as part of the milk, and using in addition the full amount of sugar called for in the recipe.

CHOCOLATE—Melt one ounce of chocolate and add to it two tablespoons of sugar dissolved in two tablespoons of boiling water. Mix thoroughly. Add this chocolate mixture to two cups of scalded milk and use as the milk in a plain soft custard.

WAYS OF SERVING SOFT CUSTARD

Soft custard may be served in sherbet cups, frappé glasses or deep sauce dishes, garnished with whipped cream and pieces of tart jelly.

It may be poured over fresh fruit.

It may be poured over lady fingers or sponge cake and may then be garnished with meringue or whipped cream.

It may be served as a sauce for most gelatin dishes.

It is an excellent foundation for ice-creams.

FLOATING ISLAND

2 cups milk
3 eggs
⅛ teaspoon salt

6 to 8 tablespoons sugar
½ teaspoon vanilla

Follow directions for soft custard, using two egg-yolks and one whole egg. Cool and turn the custard into a glass dish or into custard cups. Beat the two egg-whites until stiff and beat into them two to four tablespoons of fine granulated or powdered sugar. Drop this meringue by spoonfuls on the custard and chill thoroughly. A candied cherry or a small bit of red jelly placed on each spoonful of meringue adds to the attractive appearance of the dish.

CARAMEL PUDDING

1 cup brown sugar	¼ cup flour
2 cups milk	2 eggs

Mix sugar and one and one-half cups of milk. Scald in double boiler until sugar is dissolved. Mix flour with beaten egg-yolks and the remaining half cup of milk and add to the hot milk, stirring constantly until it thickens. Remove from fire and fold in stiffly beaten egg-whites. Chill and serve with whipped cream.

ORANGE FOOL

6 oranges	Sugar
3 eggs	Nutmeg
2 cups cream	Cinnamon

Squeeze and strain the juice from the oranges. Beat the eggs and add to them the cream and the orange-juice. Sweeten to taste. Add a sprinkle of grated nutmeg and powdered cinnamon, and cook in a double boiler, stirring constantly until the mixture coats the spoon. Pour into glass dishes and chill thoroughly before serving.

PLAIN BAKED CUSTARD

2 cups scalded milk	⅛ teaspoon salt
3 eggs	½ teaspoon vanilla
4 tablespoons sugar	

Scald the milk. Mix sugar, eggs, salt and flavoring and combine with scalded milk. Pour into custard cups or baking-dish set in pan of hot water and poach in a slow oven (300° F.) until firm. A knife blade run into the center of the custard will come out clean.

VARIATIONS OF BAKED CUSTARD

CARAMEL.

No. 1—Caramelize one-fourth cup of sugar and add to two cups of scalded milk. Use as the liquid in a plain baked custard.

No. 2—Caramelize one-half cup of sugar. Pour into a mold or pour a little into each of six custard cups. Before it hardens, move the mold about so that the caramel will coat the sides. When the caramel is hard, fill the molds with plain baked custard mixture and bake as directed for baked custard. These custards are unmolded and served either hot or cold. The caramel melts during the cooking process and when the custard is turned into a dish forms a sauce around it.

Cocoa—Substitute cocoa, made as for drinking, for scalded milk in baked custard recipe.

Chocolate—Melt one and one-half ounces of chocolate and add to milk. Use in a plain baked custard.

Coffee—Substitute one cup of strong coffee for one cup of milk in baked custard recipe.

Gelatin and Cream Desserts

ONE QUART STANDARD GELATIN JELLY

1 ounce (2 tablespoons) granulated gelatin
½ cup cold water
½ cup boiling water
3 cups other liquid or fruit-juice

¼ cup to 1 cup sugar (lemon-juice requires more sugar than orange-juice, and orange-juice more than coffee or cream)

Soak gelatin in cold water until soft. Add to boiling water and stir over hot water until thoroughly dissolved. The object of heating only part of the water is to hasten the cooling and solidifying of the gelatin mixture. Add sugar and stir until dissolved. Remove from heat. Add remaining liquids or fruit pulp and mix thoroughly. Pour into molds that have been dipped into cold water.

STANDARD FORMULA FOR WHIPS

Use recipe for standard gelatin jelly but leave the mixture in the bowl in which it was mixed until it begins to congeal. Then whip until it becomes light and frothy. Fold in 1½ cups fruit pulp, as prune or apricot. Turn into molds and chill.

STANDARD FORMULA FOR SPONGES

Use recipe for standard gelatin jelly with these exceptions: use three-eighths cup instead of one-half cup cold liquid; whip the congealing jelly and add beaten whites of two eggs after jelly begins to congeal.

Any Fruit Sponge may be made into a delicious semi-frozen dessert by substituting cream for egg-white and chilling two to three hours. Three tablespoons cream should be substituted for each egg-white in the recipe, the other quantities remaining the same. Whip the cream and fold in, following directions given for egg-white.

STANDARD FORMULA FOR CHARLOTTE OR BAVARIAN CREAM

Use recipe for standard gelatin jelly with these exceptions: Use one-quarter cup instead of one-half cup cold liquid and add one-quarter cup cream, which should be beaten and folded in after the mixture begins to congeal. Part cream and part whipped egg-white may be used if you prefer.

LEMON JELLY

1 ounce (2 tablespoons) granulated gelatin	2¼ cups ice-water
½ cup cold water	1 cup sugar
½ cup boiling water	¾ cup lemon-juice
	A little lemon-rind

Combine as directed for standard gelatin jelly. Serve with cream or soft custard.

SNOW PUDDING OR LEMON WHIP

When lemon jelly begins to congeal, beat it thoroughly with an egg-beater. Mold. When cold and jellied, serve with soft custard.

LEMON SPONGE

Reduce the ice-water in lemon jelly to two cups. When the jelly begins to congeal, whip until light and frothy and fold in the stiffly beaten whites of two eggs. Serve with cream or soft custard.

ORANGE JELLY

1 ounce (2 tablespoons) granulated gelatin	1 cup ice-water
½ cup cold water	1½ cups orange-juice
½ cup boiling water	3 to 4 tablespoons lemon-juice
1 cup sugar	A little grated orange-rind (may be omitted)

Combine as directed for standard gelatin jelly.

ORANGE WHIP

When orange jelly begins to congeal, whip until light and frothy. Mold.

ORANGE SPONGE

Reduce the ice-water in orange jelly to one-half cup. When the jelly begins to congeal, whip until light and fold in the stiffly beaten whites of two eggs.

ORANGE CHARLOTTE OR BAVARIAN CREAM

Omit the ice-water in orange jelly. When the jelly begins to congeal, fold in one cup of whipping cream beaten to a stiff froth. The jelly may be whipped before adding the cream, if desired. It makes a more delicate product.

FRUIT JELLIES, WHIPS, SPONGES, CHARLOTTES OR BAVARIAN CREAMS

Use recipe for orange jelly, orange sponge, or orange charlotte or Bavarian cream, substituting one and one-half cups of any other fruit pulp or juice for one and one-half cups of orange-juice. If stewed sweetened fruit pulp is used, reduce the amount of sugar proportionately. Fresh raspberries, strawberries and peaches make particularly good sponges and Bavarian creams.

COFFEE JELLY

1 ounce (2 tablespoons) granulated gelatin	½ cup boiling water
½ cup cold water	1 cup sugar
	3 cups strong coffee

Combine as directed for standard gelatin jelly. Particularly good served with whipped cream.

FIG AND GINGER PUDDING

½ pound crystallized ginger	½ ounce (1 tablespoon) granulated gelatin
1½ pounds figs	
2 cups sugar	½ cup cold water
5 cups water	Whipped cream
½ teaspoon powdered ginger	

Cut the crystallized ginger and figs into tiny pieces. Dissolve the granulated sugar in the water, and add the powdered ginger, the crystallized ginger and the figs. Place all in a double boiler and simmer slowly all day. The entire mass must form a soft pulp so that the ingredients will scarcely be recognized. Soften the gelatin in the cold water and stir into the mixture while hot. Turn into high-stemmed glasses and serve ice cold with whipped cream.

GRAPEFRUIT À LA ST. PATRICK

1 ounce (2 tablespoons) granulated gelatin	¾ cup sugar
½ cup cold water	1 cup ice water
½ cup boiling water	2 cups grapefruit pulp and juice
Fresh mint	Maraschino cherries

Cut the grapefruit in half, crosswise, and scoop out the pulp being careful not to cut the skins. Drop the shells into cold water until needed. Simmer a few sprigs of fresh mint in the boiling water until the flavor is extracted. Follow the standard directions for making jelly. When jelly is firm, cut it into cubes, pile the cubes in the grapefruit shells and garnish with sprigs of mint and cherries.

PINEAPPLE SQUARES

1 package lemon gelatin	1 drop oil of peppermint
2 cups boiling water	½ cup drained crushed canned pineapple
2 cups cold water	
1 package lime gelatin	1 cup dry cake crumbs
1 cup heavy cream, whipped	

Dissolve lemon gelatin in 1 cup boiling water, add 1 cup cold water and chill. Do the same with lime gelatin, adding peppermint with cold water. When lemon gelatin is slightly thickened, fold in pineapple. Pour into shallow pan; chill until firm. Fold cake crumbs into whipped cream and spread on lemon gelatin. When lime gelatin is slightly thickened, place in bowl of cracked ice and whip until thick. Pour on cream mixture. Chill until firm, cut into squares. Serves 10.

Decorating Jelly

Have the mold thoroughly chilled. Pour in a layer of jelly about one-half inch deep. Chill. When firm, arrange a design of fruit or nuts or both, dropping a few drops of jelly on each piece to hold the design while the jelly hardens. When the jelly holding the design in place has congealed, add enough jelly to cover the design and let this harden. A single design may serve or alternate layers of fruit and jelly may be arranged in this way. Each layer must congeal before the next is added.

REFRIGERATOR CHEESE CAKE

½ cup melted butter
¾ cup sugar
2 cups fine zwieback crumbs
2 teaspoons cinnamon
2 tablespoons gelatin
1 cup cold water

3 eggs, separated
2 cups cream cheese
3 tablespoons lemon juice
1 tablespoon grated lemon rind
¼ teaspoon salt
½ cup whipping cream

Blend butter, ¼ cup sugar, crumbs and cinnamon. Press ¾ of this mixture on the bottom of a 9-inch spring form pan. Soak gelatin in ½ cup cold water for 5 minutes. Cook egg-yolks, remaining sugar (½ cup) and water (½ cup) in a double boiler, stirring constantly, until mixture coats a metal spoon. Add gelatin and stir until dissolved. Add gradually to cream cheese, add lemon juice, rind and salt, beat thoroughly. Cool, when beginning to congeal, beat several minutes with an egg beater. Whip cream and fold in with stiffly beaten egg-whites, blend thoroughly. Pour onto crumbs. Sprinkle remaining crumbs over top. Chill until firm. Serves 10 to 12.

For variety use crumbs made from graham crackers, vanilla wafers, gingersnaps, chocolate cookies, browned dried bread crumbs, crushed cornflakes or other suitably prepared breakfast foods in place of zwieback.

GELATIN BLANC MANGE

1 pint milk
1½ teaspoons granulated gelatin
1 tablespoon water

¼ cup sugar
1 teaspoon vanilla

Heat the milk in the top of a double boiler. Add the gelatin softened in the cold water. Stir constantly, adding the sugar a little at a time. Cook over hot water for fifteen minutes stirring frequently. Add vanilla. Strain into molds that have been dipped in cold water and chill. Serve with cream.

CHOCOLATE—Dissolve one square bitter chocolate, add the milk and sugar, using one-third cup sugar, before adding the gelatin.

CHOCOLATE CREAM

6 tablespoons cocoa	3 tablespoons water
1/3 cup sugar	1 pint heavy cream
1/2 teaspoon salt	1 egg

Mix cocoa, sugar, salt and water, and cook, stirring until thick and smooth. Cool slightly and pour over stiffly whipped cream, and beat thoroughly with a spoon. Add egg and again beat well. Chill in refrigerator, allowing an hour and a half or two hours for a mechanical refrigerator and longer for an ice-cooled refrigerator.

VELVET CREAM

No. 1.

1/2 ounce (1 tablespoon) granulated gelatin	4 tablespoons powdered sugar
1/4 cup cold water	1 pint cream
1/4 cup boiling water	1 teaspoon vanilla

Follow standard directions for making the jelly. As soon as it begins to congeal, add the cream. Flavor with vanilla. Turn into a mold and place on ice to harden. Serve with maple sauce.

No. 2—Use same ingredients as for preceding recipe. Whip the cream and fold into it the dissolved gelatin and sugar mixture. Mold.

SPANISH CREAM

1 ounce (2 tablespoons) granulated gelatin	1/4 teaspoon salt
1/2 cup cold water	2 eggs
1/2 cup hot milk	2 1/4 cups cold milk
1/3 cup sugar	1 teaspoon vanilla

Make a custard of the egg-yolks, sugar and hot milk. Add the softened gelatin. Proceed as for standard sponge mixtures. Mold, chill and serve with whipped cream.

PLAIN BAVARIAN CREAM

1 ounce (2 tablespoons)
    granulated gelatin
½ cup cold water
1 pint scalded milk
4 egg-yolks

½ cup sugar
Salt
1 teaspoon vanilla
1 pint heavy cream

Soak the gelatin in cold water until soft. Make a soft custard of the milk, egg-yolks, sugar and flavoring. Stir the softened gelatin into the hot custard. When the gelatin has dissolved, strain and cool. Whip the cream and fold it in as the mixture congeals.

RICE BAVARIAN

1½ pints milk
Lemon-peel
½ cup rice
¼ teaspoon salt
½ cup sugar
1 teaspoon flavoring

1 ounce (2 tablespoons)
    granulated gelatin
½ cup cold water
1 cup heavy cream
Strawberries

Put the milk and a few thin cuts of lemon-peel into a double boiler. When it is hot, stir in the well-washed rice and salt. Cook until the rice is perfectly tender. The milk should be nearly absorbed, leaving the rice very moist. Add to the hot cooked rice the flavoring, the sugar and the gelatin, which has been soaked in the cold water, and mix carefully. When the mixture is beginning to set, fold in the cream, whipped stiff. Pour into a mold and chill. Serve with sweetened crushed strawberries. The white mold with red sauce makes a charming combination.

MONT BLANC

1 pound large chestnuts
½ teaspoon salt

¾ cup sugar
Whipped cream

Put the chestnuts into the oven for a moment, until the shell and inner skin can be easily removed. Boil the skinned chestnuts in water with the salt and three tablespoons of the sugar, until they are very tender. Add one-half cup sugar to the water and chestnuts and let stand until thoroughly cold. Remove chestnuts from this sirup and run them through a potato-ricer on to a platter, mounding it high. Save a few of the finest whole pieces to decorate the dish. Top the mound with a spoonful of sweetened whipped cream, and put a border of whipped cream around the edge of the dish, dotting it with the whole nuts here and there.

MACAROON BISQUE

1 cup heavy cream	18 macaroons
Powdered sugar	6 maraschino cherries
Vanilla	

Whip a cup of cream until stiff, sweeten with powdered sugar and flavor lightly with vanilla. Stir in six macaroons broken in small pieces, but not powdered. Pile in sherbet glasses with a border of the whole macaroons and decorate with marshmallows or maraschino cherries. This is an excellent emergency dessert.

PINEAPPLE AMBROSIA

1 fresh pineapple or	1 cup heavy cream
1 can crushed pineapple	2 tablespoons sugar
½ pound marshmallows	1½ tablespoons lemon-juice

Shred the pineapple with a fork. Cut the marshmallows into small pieces, using a pair of scissors. Mix the pineapple and marshmallows and let stand on ice until thoroughly chilled. Just before serving, whip the cream and add the sugar to it. Add lemon-juice to the pineapple mixture and then fold in the whipped cream. Serve immediately in individual glasses or in a large dessert dish.

FRUIT FLUFF

1 cup powdered sugar	4 cups sliced peaches or
1 cup thick cream	apple sauce or berries
2 egg-whites	

Add half the sugar to the cream, stir until the sugar is dissolved, and then add the whites of the eggs beaten stiff. Place the sliced peaches in a dish, sprinkle them with the remainder of the sugar, pour on the cream mixture, and serve at once. The success of this depends upon its being thoroughly chilled when served. The cream, egg-whites and fruit should be chilled for at least two hours before the dish is to be prepared, and the finished dessert should be kept in the refrigerator until needed.

VARIATIONS ON A FAMILIAR THEME— BRING YOUR PASTRY GUN INTO PLAY AND CUT YOUR HARD SAUCE IN STRIPS TO DECORATE CUSTARDS

A COOL CREAMY SLICE OF CHARLOTTE RUSSE RISES TO THE OCCASION ON A HOT SUMMER DAY
—Irradiated Evaporated Milk Institute

SMOOTH, CHILLED MELON MOLD OF BAVARIAN CREAM IS THE FITTING CLIMAX TO A WARM-WEATHER MEAL

FIG PUFF

1 cup cream	2 tablespoons powdered sugar
1 egg-white	Chopped figs
1 tablespoon grapefruit marmalade	Maraschino cherries
	Shredded almonds

Whip the cream until thick. Beat the egg-white until stiff, then combine with the cream and add the sugar and marmalade. Stir chopped figs into the mixture until it becomes very thick. Pack in long-stemmed glasses. This may be garnished by sprinkling the top with macaroon crumbs. Arrange a half maraschino cherry with radiating strips of almonds in the center of each.

CHARLOTTE RUSSE

No. 1—Line a number of small molds, or one large deep mold, with a thin layer of cake. Thin sponge cake that has been cut with a sharp knife, when cold, into two layers of equal thickness is considered attractive, but halved lady fingers or pieces of any plain cake cut one-half inch thick may be used. Charlottes are made with and without tops, according to taste or convenience.

Fill the forms with whipped cream sweetened with powdered sugar and any desired flavoring. To make sure that the cream is sufficiently stiff, fold into it lightly the stiffly beaten whites of two eggs to each pint of cream. Keep the charlottes on ice until needed, and serve on chilled plates.

No. 2—Substitute velvet cream (See Index) for the whipped cream mixture in the preceding recipe.

MAPLE CHARLOTTE RUSSE

½ ounce (1 tablespoon) granulated gelatin	½ cup maple sirup
½ cup cold water	1 teaspoon vanilla
½ cup scalded milk	1 pint heavy cream
¼ cup brown sugar	Lady fingers

Follow standard formula for charlotte or Bavarian cream (See Index). Line molds with lady fingers and fill with the cream mixture. Chill, unmold and serve.

ICEBOX CAKES

GENERAL DIRECTIONS—Line the bottom and sides of a spring form melon mold or deep cake form with lady fingers, separated and placed with the rounded side toward the pan. Place them as close together as possible. Prepare any of the fillings and proceed as follows:

Place a layer of the filling on the lady fingers at the bottom of the form. On top of this arrange another layer of lady fingers, then another layer of filling, and so on, placing lady fingers on top like the spokes of a wheel.

Set in the refrigerator or other cold place and let it stand twenty to twenty-four hours. When ready to serve, remove the rim of the form, place the cake with the tin bottom on a platter, cover the top with sweetened and flavored whipped cream. Decorate, if desired, with pistachio or other nut meats, with candied cherries or fresh strawberries.

QUANTITIES REQUIRED—To encase and garnish the fillings given below, unless an exception is noted, the quantities required are as follows:

2½ dozen lady fingers	½ cup confectioners' sugar
½ pint thick cream	½ teaspoon vanilla

CHOCOLATE FILLING

4 eggs	3 tablespoons water
½ pound sweet chocolate	3 tablespoons sugar

Melt the chocolate in a double boiler, add the sugar and the water with the yolks of the eggs, well beaten. Cook slowly until thick and smooth, stirring constantly. When cool, add the stiffly beaten egg-whites.

MOCHA FILLING

1 cup hot milk	½ cup sugar
¼ cup ground coffee	3 eggs
2 tablespoons cornstarch	1 teaspoon vanilla
⅛ teaspoon salt	

Pour the hot milk over the coffee and let stand where it will keep hot for ten minutes. Strain. Mix cornstarch, salt and sugar in a double boiler, add the egg yolks, well beaten, stir in the coffee infusion gradually. Cook slowly until thick and smooth, stirring constantly. Remove from fire and cool slightly. While warm, fold in vanilla and stiffly beaten egg whites.

ALMOND OR PECAN FILLING—With this filling macaroons are combined with the lady fingers usually used.

1 cup unsalted butter	6 eggs
1⅓ cups powdered sugar	18 lady fingers
½ pound blanched and grated almonds	30 macaroons

Line the bottom of the mold with stout waxed paper. Separate the lady fingers and place the halves close together on the sides of the pan, rounded ends cut off and rounded sides toward the pan. Lay macaroons close together on the bottom, flat side down. Fill the small spaces between macaroons with the ends cut from the lady fingers.

Cream butter and sugar, add three eggs, one at a time, and stir well. Add the yolks of the remaining eggs, well beaten, then the nuts, then fold in the beaten whites. Place one-half of this mixture over the macaroons. Add another layer of macaroons and top with the rest of the filling.

Set in the refrigerator and leave for thirty hours. Serve as outlined in General Directions.

LEMON FILLING.

1 cup rich milk	½ cup sugar
1 tablespoon butter	3 eggs
1 teaspoon corn-starch	Juice of 1 lemon

Place corn-starch, sugar, egg-yolks, slightly beaten, milk and butter in a double boiler. Cook slowly until thick and smooth, stirring constantly. Add the lemon-juice. Remove from the fire and cool slightly. While still warm, fold in the stiffly beaten egg-whites.

RICH LEMON CREAM.

5 eggs, separated	1 cup powdered sugar
	½ cup lemon juice

Mix egg yolks, sugar and lemon juice and cook over hot water 5 minutes, stirring constantly until mixture thickens. Fold gently into stiffly beaten egg whites. Chill.

HOT AND COLD PUDDINGS

THE temperature at which a pudding is served depends somewhat upon the nature of the pudding. However, soufflés,
must be served hot because they begin to fall as soon as they are
taken from the oven; and certain others, such as the steamed
puddings and baked batters or doughs, become soggy when cold.

Some puddings may be chilled almost to the point of freezing, and for these the automatic refrigerator is excellent.

Puddings That May Be Served Either Hot or Cold

BREAD PUDDING

2 cups dry bread crumbs	¼ teaspoon salt
4 cups milk, scalded	¼ teaspoon nutmeg
2 eggs	1 teaspoon vanilla
½ cup sugar	½ cup raisins, if desired

Soak bread crumbs in milk until soft. Beat eggs until light;
add sugar, salt, nutmeg, vanilla and raisins. Mix thoroughly
with bread mixture. Pour into greased baking dish and set in
pan of hot water. Bake in moderate oven (350° F.) 1 hour or
until a knife inserted in center comes out clean. Serve warm or
cold with any desired sauce. Serves 6 to 8.

Chopped dates, figs or nuts may be added if desired.

CHOCOLATE BREAD PUDDING—Melt 2 ounces of chocolate
over hot water and add this to the soaked bread and milk.

COCONUT PUDDING

½ cup bread crumbs	3 tablespoons sugar
½ cup moist coconut	½ teaspoon salt
2 cups milk	1 tablespoon butter, melted
1 egg, separated	

Soak bread crumbs and coconut in milk. Beat egg yolk and
add sugar, salt and butter. Add to milk mixture. Fold in beaten
egg white. Pour into greased baking dish; set in pan of hot
water; bake in moderate oven (350° F.) 45 minutes. Serves 6.

ORANGE AND RICE

1 cup rice
8 cups boiling water
1 tablespoon salt
2 cups sugar

2 cups water
1 tablespoon lemon juice
3 oranges

Wash rice thoroughly and add slowly to boiling, salted water. Boil 20 minutes, or until rice is tender when pressed between the fingers. Drain, rinse with hot water, cover with clean cloth and let stand in warm place to separate grains. Boil sugar, water and lemon juice together for 10 minutes to make a sirup. Peel oranges, cut into halves crosswise and remove core. Add oranges to sirup and cook until tender but not broken. Place rice in a mound on serving dish. Arrange oranges around rice and pour sirup over the whole. Serve with plain or whipped cream or Custard Sauce. Serve hot or cold. Serves 6.

QUEEN OF PUDDINGS

1 cup fine bread crumbs
2 cups milk, scalded
2 eggs, separated

½ cup sugar
¼ teaspoon salt
Currant jelly or jam

Soak crumbs in milk. Beat egg yolks; add ¼ cup of the sugar and salt and add to milk mixture. Pour into greased baking dish, set in pan of hot water and bake in moderate oven (350° F.) 1 hour, or until firm. Spread a thick layer of jelly over top. Beat egg whites with remaining ¼ cup sugar until stiff. Spread meringue over top of pudding. Bake 10 minutes longer or until browned. Serve hot or cold. Serves 6.

SPICE PUDDING

1 egg, beaten
½ cup sugar
2 cups milk, scalded
1½ cups bread crumbs
1 teaspoon cinnamon
½ teaspoon cloves

½ teaspoon allspice
¼ teaspoon nutmeg
⅛ teaspoon salt
1 cup raisins
1 tablespoon melted butter

Combine ingredients in order given; mix thoroughly. Pour into greased baking dish; set in pan of hot water. Bake in moderate oven (350° F.) 45 minutes or until firm. Serve hot with Coffee or Raisin Sauce. Serves 6.

APPLE OR OTHER FRUIT TAPIOCA

¾ cup sugar
2 cups water
½ teaspoon salt
⅓ cup quick-cooking tapioca

2 cups fresh or dried fruit
½ teaspoon cinnamon
2 tablespoons butter

Mix sugar, water, salt and tapioca and heat to boiling. Arrange fruit and tapioca in alternate layers in greased baking dish. Sprinkle with cinnamon, dot with butter and bake in moderate oven (350° F.) 1½ hours. Serve hot or cold with cream or any desired sauce. Serves 6.

Fresh fruit such as apples, peaches, apricots, tart cherries or cranberries or any dried fruit may be used.

Pudding may be topped with Meringue if desired.

CREAM TAPIOCA

2 eggs, separated
4 cups milk, scalded
⅓ cup quick-cooking tapioca

½ cup sugar
¼ teaspoon salt
1 teaspoon vanilla

Mix egg yolks with small amount of milk. Add tapioca, sugar, salt and remaining milk. Cook in double boiler 10 to 12 minutes, stirring frequently. Remove from heat. Do not overcook the mixture as it thickens when it cools. Beat egg whites until stiff, but not dry. When mixture is slightly cooled, fold in whites and vanilla. Chill. Serves 6.

Serve plain, with whipped cream, or any desired sauce.

Fresh, dried or canned fruits, coconut or chopped nuts may be added to the tapioca after it has cooled.

Chocolate or Butterscotch Sauce may be folded into tapioca.

CREAMY RICE PUDDING

¼ cup rice
4 cups milk, scalded
¼ cup sugar

½ teaspoon salt
½ teaspoon cinnamon
½ cup raisins

Wash rice thoroughly, add remaining ingredients and pour into greased baking dish. Bake in slow oven (325° F.) 2 hours, stirring several times during baking. The mixture should not boil. Serve hot or cold. Serves 6.

This is the old-fashioned creamy pudding which has such a delicious flavor because of the long, slow cooking.

SCALLOPED PEACHES

1 cup sliced peaches
4 cups sliced apples
¼ teaspoon salt
¼ cup brown sugar
¼ cup bread or cake crumbs
¼ cup water

Arrange a layer of peaches on bottom of greased baking dish. Place half of apples over the peaches. Sprinkle with salt. Add remainder of peaches and apples and sprinkle again with salt. Spread sugar over the top, then crumbs, and add water last. Cover baking dish first 30 minutes so crumbs will not brown too rapidly. Bake in moderate oven (350° F.) 45 minutes. Serve hot or cold. Serves 6.

Other fruits may be used such as rhubarb, apricots, etc.

Puddings That Should Be Served Hot

SOUFFLÉS

FRUIT—

1 cup fruit pulp
1 tablespoon lemon juice
⅛ teaspoon salt
Sugar
3 egg whites, stiffly beaten

Any kind of fruit, fresh, canned or preserved may be used. If canned fruit is used, first drain sirup. Rub fruit through a sieve; add lemon juice, salt and sweeten if necessary; heat. Fold stiffly beaten egg whites into hot fruit pulp. Pour into greased baking dish or individual molds, filling them only ¾ full. Set in pan of hot water. Bake in moderately hot oven (375° F.) 20 minutes if a soft soufflé is desired. If a firmer soufflé is preferred bake in slow oven (325° F.) 40 minutes. Serve as soon as baked or mixture will fall. Serve plain or with whipped cream or a pudding sauce. Serves 6.

VANILLA—

¼ cup butter, melted
¼ cup flour
1 cup milk, scalded
¼ cup sugar
3 eggs, separated
1 teaspoon vanilla

Make a white sauce of butter, flour, milk and sugar. Add to beaten egg yolks and vanilla. Mix thoroughly. Fold in stiffly beaten egg whites, pour into greased baking dish, set in pan of hot water and bake in moderate oven (350° F.) 45 to 50 minutes or until soufflé is firm to the touch. Serve immediately with Lemon Sauce or cream. Serves 6.

CHOCOLATE—

1 tablespoon butter	⅓ cup sugar
3 tablespoons flour	2 ounces chocolate
1 cup milk, scalded	3 eggs, separated

Make a sauce of butter, flour, milk, sugar and chocolate. Proceed as for vanilla soufflé. Serves 6.

COFFEE—

Substitute coffee for milk in vanilla soufflé and omit vanilla.

CUSTARD—

2 tablespoons butter	2 tablespoons sugar
2 tablespoons flour	½ cup crumbled macaroons
1 cup milk	4 eggs, separated

Make white sauce of butter, flour and milk. Stir in sugar and macaroons; allow mixture to cool slightly. Add egg yolks which have been beaten until thick; mix thoroughly. Fold in stiffly beaten egg whites. Pour into greased baking dish and bake as directed for vanilla soufflé. Serve at once. Serves 6.

LEMON—

5 eggs, separated	3 tablespoons lemon juice
⅔ cup sugar	¼ teaspoon salt
Grated rind of ½ lemon	

Beat egg yolks until light. Add sugar and beat again; add lemon rind and juice. Beat egg whites with salt until stiff. Fold lemon mixture into beaten whites and bake as directed for vanilla soufflé. Serve at once. Serves 6.

OMELET—

6 eggs, separated	½ teaspoon salt
½ cup confectioners' sugar	1 teaspoon vanilla

Beat egg yolks until thick, add sugar, salt and vanilla. Beat whites until stiff. Fold whites into yolk mixture. Pile the mass as high as possible in a greased baking dish. Smooth the top and bake as directed for vanilla soufflé. The top may be sprinkled with additional confectioners' sugar before or after baking. Serve at once. Serves 6.

COTTAGE PUDDING

1¾ cups sifted flour	1 cup sugar
2½ teaspoons baking powder	1 egg
½ teaspoon salt	1 teaspoon vanilla
¼ cup shortening	⅔ cup milk

Sift flour, baking powder and salt together. Cream shortening and add sugar gradually. Beat in egg and vanilla. Alternately add flour and milk to sugar mixture, beating after each addition until smooth. Pour into 8 x 8 x 2 inch greased pan and bake in moderate oven (350° F.) 30 to 45 minutes. Serve with Lemon Sauce or jelly. Serves 6.

BLUEBERRY PUDDING

Add 1 cup blueberries to cottage pudding batter and bake in greased baking dish or muffin pans.

FRUIT BATTER PUDDING

Place a thick layer of fruit in bottom of greased baking dish and pour vanilla soufflé or cottage pudding batter over it. Bake in moderate oven (350° F.) 45 minutes, or until done. Any fresh, dried or canned fruit that is not too juicy may be used. Serve hot. Serves 6.

BROWN BETTY

This pudding is usually made with apples, but almost any other fruit may be used instead of, or in combination with, them. Serve hot with cream or with any preferred sauce.

No. 1

⅓ cup butter, melted	¼ teaspoon nutmeg
2 cups bread crumbs	½ cup sugar
2 cups sliced apples	½ cup water
¼ teaspoon cinnamon	1 lemon, rind and juice

Mix butter and crumbs. Arrange layers of crumbs and apples in greased baking dish. Sprinkle each layer with spices and sugar. Add water mixed with lemon rind and juice. Sprinkle top with crumbs; cover dish. Bake in moderate oven (350° F.) 30 minutes, remove cover and bake 45 minutes longer. Serves 6.

No. 2

1 cup bread crumbs
4 cups chopped apples
¾ cup honey

1 cup water
2 tablespoons lemon juice
1 apple

Mix crumbs and chopped apples and place in greased baking dish. Heat honey and water to boiling, add lemon juice and pour over fruit mixture. Sprinkle a few dry crumbs over top. Wash, core and slice apple. Arrange apple rings over top. Bake as directed for No. 1. Serves 6.

APPLE CHARLOTTE

2 recipes Mürbe Teig
4 cups diced apples
¾ cup chopped almonds
½ cup raisins

½ cup sugar
1 teaspoon cinnamon
1 lemon, rind and juice
¼ cup fruit juice

Line greased baking dish with ⅔ of mürbe teig. Mix remaining ingredients and pour into shell. Cover with remaining mürbe teig. Bake in hot oven (425° F.) 10 minutes, reduce temperature to moderate (350° F.) and continue baking about 35 minutes, or until fruit is tender and top browned. Serves 6.

Raisins may be omitted and currants used.

Red or white wine may be used and fruit juice omitted.

PEACH PUDDING

¼ cup sugar
½ teaspoon salt
½ teaspoon vanilla
2 cups milk

3 eggs, beaten
Sliced dry bread
6 peaches, sliced

Mix sugar, salt and vanilla with milk and stir in well-beaten eggs. Dip slices of bread into egg mixture. Line greased baking dish with bread slices. Arrange alternating layers of bread and sliced peaches to fill dish. Pour any remaining liquid over the top. Set dish in pan of hot water and bake in moderate oven (350° F.) about 30 minutes or until firm. Serve hot with any desired pudding sauce. Serves 6.

Use canned or cooked dried peaches. Or other fruits may be used if desired.

Omit bread and use dry cake slices or ladyfingers.

APPLE RICE PUDDING

1 cup rice	½ cup raisins
1 tablespoon salt	½ teaspoon cinnamon
8 cups boiling water	¼ teaspoon salt
2 eggs, separated	3 large apples
¾ cup sugar	¼ cup butter, melted

Wash rice and drain; boil in salted water until tender. Drain. Beat egg yolks, add sugar, raisins, cinnamon and salt. Pare and dice apples. Combine rice, eggs and apples. Add melted butter; mix thoroughly. Beat egg whites stiff but not dry. Fold into rice mixture. Pour into greased baking dish and bake in moderate oven (350° F.) 30 to 40 minutes, or until apples are tender. Serve hot. Serves 6.

NEW ENGLAND PANDOWDY

2 cups pared, sliced apples	¼ teaspoon salt
⅓ cup sugar	½ cup hot water
¼ teaspoon nutmeg	½ recipe Drop Biscuits
¼ teaspoon cinnamon	

Place apples in greased baking dish; add sugar, spices, salt and water. Cover and bake in hot oven (425° F.) 20 minutes. Spread drop biscuit dough over apples. Bake in hot oven (450° F.) 15 to 20 minutes or until browned. Serve hot. Serves 6.

Other fruits may be used in place of apples. Cooked, dried fruit may be used and first baking omitted.

ORANGE AND MACAROON PUDDING

2 cups crushed macaroons	¼ cup sugar
2 cups milk, scalded	Grated rind of 1 orange
4 eggs	¾ cup orange juice
¼ teaspoon salt	

Soak macaroons in milk 5 minutes. Beat eggs slightly, add salt, sugar, orange rind and orange juice. Mix thoroughly and add slowly to macaroon mixture. Pour into greased baking dish, set in pan of hot water. Bake in moderate oven (350° F.) 35 to 45 minutes, or until firm. Serve hot or cold garnished with orange sections. Serves 6.

Cake crumbs may be used and macaroons omitted.

INDIAN PUDDING

No. 1

4 cups milk, scalded	1/3 cup sugar
1/3 cup corn meal	2 tablespoons butter
1/2 cup molasses	3/4 teaspoon cinnamon
1 teaspoon salt	1/2 teaspoon nutmeg

Scald milk in double boiler, slowly add corn meal and cook 25 minutes. Add remaining ingredients. Pour into greased baking dish and bake in slow oven (275° F.) 2 hours. Serves 6.

No. 2

6 thick slices whole-wheat bread	1/4 teaspoon salt
1/2 cup butter	4 cups milk
	1/2 cup molasses

Remove crusts from bread and spread generously with butter. Place bread in greased baking dish. Add salt, milk and molasses. Bake in slow oven (275° F.) 2 hours. Serve hot with plain, whipped or ice cream. Serves 6.

Dates, raisins, figs or nuts may be added.

OLD-FASHIONED STRAWBERRY OR OTHER FRUIT SHORTCAKE

2 cups sifted flour	1/3 cup shortening
4 teaspoons baking powder	3/4 cup milk (about)
1/2 teaspoon salt	Butter
1 tablespoon sugar	3 cups crushed strawberries

Mix and sift dry ingredients; cut in shortening with knife or pastry blender. Add milk gradually to make a soft dough. Turn out on lightly floured board and knead just enough to shape into smooth ball. Roll or pat lightly 1/2 inch thick. Cut with floured biscuit cutter or bake in large sheets or bake in muffin pans. Brush tops with butter and bake in hot oven (450° F.) 15 minutes. Split hot biscuits. Butter generously and put together again with filling of sweetened strawberries. Top with more fruit. Serve at once with plain or whipped cream. Serves 6.

Some delicious and tempting shortcake fillings are: crushed raspberries with diced oranges, sliced bananas with strawberries, raspberries and pineapple, applesauce, peaches, blackberries, cooked blueberries, apricots etc.

APPLE DUMPLINGS

6 large apples
¾ cup brown sugar
¼ teaspoon salt
4 tablespoons butter

¾ teaspoon cinnamon
1 teaspoon grated lemon rind
1 recipe Plain Pastry

Pare and core apples. Combine next 5 ingredients. Roll pastry ⅛ inch thick and cut into squares large enough to cover apples. Place apples on pastry squares and fill each cavity of apple with sugar mixture. Bring corners of pastry together at top; moisten edges and pinch together to hold apple in place. Place in greased baking pan and bake in a moderate oven (350° F.) 30 minutes or until apples are tender. Serve with pudding sauce or cream. Serves 6.

Baking powder biscuit dough may be used instead of pastry.

APRICOT—Omit cinnamon and prepare as above.

PEACH—Prepare as apple dumplings.

ENGLISH PLUM PUDDING

¾ cup sifted flour
1 teaspoon salt
¾ teaspoon baking soda
1 teaspoon cinnamon
¼ teaspoon nutmeg
½ teaspoon mace
½ pound raisins, chopped
½ pound dried currants, chopped
¼ pound citron, chopped
⅛ pound lemon peel, chopped

⅛ pound orange peel, chopped
⅛ pound blanched almonds, chopped
¾ cup hot milk
½ cup fine bread crumbs
½ pound brown sugar
4 eggs, separated
½ pound suet, chopped
¼ cup fruit juice
½ cup jelly

Sift flour, salt, soda and spices together; stir in fruit and almonds. Pour milk over bread crumbs and let stand 10 minutes. Beat sugar with egg yolks until light and fluffy. Add suet and crumbs to egg yolk mixture; stir into flour-fruit mixture. Add fruit juice and jelly and mix thoroughly; fold in stiffly beaten egg whites. Fill greased mold, ⅔ full, cover tightly and steam for 3½ hours. Serves 12.

Use grape, plum or currant jelly.

Steamed Puddings

To steam puddings: generously grease molds and covers. Use steamer or deep covered kettle with rack. Have water, to half the depth of the mold, boiling rapidly. Keep water boiling constantly and add more boiling water as needed. If desired place in oven 5 minutes to dry top.

APPLE, OR OTHER FRUIT ROLY-POLY

2 cups sliced apples
¾ cup sugar
½ teaspoon cinnamon
2 teaspoons grated lemon rind

1 recipe Baking Powder Biscuit
2 tablespoons melted butter

Combine apples, sugar, cinnamon and lemon rind. Roll dough into a rectangle ¼ inch thick. Spread with butter and apple mixture; roll up like jelly roll. Wet edges and press together so that juice will not escape. Place roll in a cloth and tie loosely. Steam 1½ hours. Remove from cloth, slice and serve with a pudding sauce. Serves 6.

Cherries, peaches or other fruit may be used for apples.

CARROT PUDDING

1½ cups bread crumbs
¼ teaspoon salt
1 teaspoon baking powder
1 tablespoon shortening
½ cup grated carrots
1 cup molasses

½ cup chopped dates
½ cup raisins
½ cup chopped figs
½ cup ground nuts
2 tablespoons lemon juice
1 teaspoon grated lemon rind

Mix crumbs, salt and baking powder together very well. Add remaining ingredients and mix thoroughly. Fill greased mold ⅔ full and steam 3 to 4 hours. Serve with Lemon or Raisin Sauce. Serves 6.

FRUIT PUDDING

½ cup brown sugar
Cooked fruit, drained
1¼ cups sifted flour
¾ cup granulated sugar
3 teaspoons baking powder

¼ cup shortening
2 eggs
⅓ cup milk (about)
1 teaspoon vanilla

Grease a small pudding mold. Add brown sugar and arrange fruit over sugar. Sift dry ingredients. Melt shortening in a cup, add unbeaten eggs and milk to fill the cup. Add to dry ingredients and beat until smooth. Add vanilla. Pour over fruit. Steam 45 to 60 minutes. Serves 6.

TOP YOUR RENNET-CUSTARD WITH FLUFFY MERINGUE OR DELICATELY BROWNED COCONUT SHREDS

A HAPPY COMBINATION OF FRUITS MAKES THIS PUDDING COLORFUL AND TEMPTING
—Wheat Flour Institute

ALL DATED UP
AND DRESSED IN
WHIPPED CREAM
RUCHING, THIS
DATE PUDDING IS
READY FOR DINNER
—Wheat Flour
Institute

MONARCH OF ENGLISH
COOKERY, THIS PLUM
PUDDING ALSO HOLDS
COURT IN MANY AMERI-
CAN HOMES
—Wheat Flour Institute

STEAMED CHOCOLATE PUDDING

1½ ounces (1½ squares)
   chocolate
1 tablespoon butter
1 cup sifted flour
1½ teaspoons baking powder

⅛ teaspoon salt
1 egg
½ cup sugar
½ cup milk
1 teaspoon vanilla

Melt chocolate and butter together. Sift flour, baking powder and salt together. Beat egg; add sugar gradually and continue beating until mixture is creamy. Add melted chocolate and mix thoroughly. Add dry ingredients alternately with milk and vanilla, beating until smooth after each addition. Fill greased pudding mold ⅔ full, cover tightly and steam 1 hour. Serve hot with Coffee, Hard, Foamy or Marshmallow Mint Sauce. Serves 4 to 6.

STEAMED DATE PUDDING

1 pound dates
½ pound suet
3 cups bread crumbs
¾ cup sugar

1 egg, beaten
½ cup milk
4 tablespoons flour
2 teaspoons baking powder

Grind dates and suet very fine. Mix with bread crumbs and add sugar. Add remaining ingredients and mix thoroughly. Fill greased pudding mold ⅔ full, cover tightly and steam 2½ to 3 hours. Serve hot with Caramel, Custard, Orange or Vanilla Sauce. Serves 8 to 10.

STEAMED GRAHAM PUDDING

No. 1

½ cup raisins
1 tablespoon white flour
1 cup graham flour
¼ cup corn meal
2 teaspoons baking powder
¼ teaspoon baking soda
½ teaspoon salt

½ teaspoon cinnamon
¼ teaspoon each: mace, cloves,
   allspice, ginger
½ cup molasses
½ cup sour milk
¼ cup ground cracklings

Mix raisins and white flour. Mix dry ingredients thoroughly. Add molasses, milk, cracklings and raisins; mix well. Fill a greased mold ⅔ full, cover tightly and steam 3 hours. Serve with Caramel or Lemon Sauce. Serves 6.

No. 2

1 cup raisins	¾ teaspoon baking soda
1 cup sifted white flour	1 cup molasses
1 cup graham flour	1 cup sour milk
1 teaspoon salt	1 egg, beaten

Mix raisins with ½ cup of the white flour. Mix remaining white flour with dry ingredients. Add molasses, milk and egg and blend thoroughly. Add raisins. Fill greased pudding mold ⅔ full and steam 2½ hours. Serve hot with any desired pudding sauce. Serves 6 to 8.

Use dates, currants, nuts or coconut instead of raisins.

STEAMED MARMALADE PUDDING

1 cup sifted flour	½ cup sugar
¼ teaspoon salt	4 eggs, well beaten
2 teaspoons baking powder	4 tablespoons marmalade
½ cup shortening	

Sift flour, salt and baking powder together. Cream shortening and sugar together. Add flour and eggs and mix thoroughly. Spread marmalade in the bottom of a mold, place the batter on top, cover mold and steam 1½ hours. Serve with Custard, Honey, Lemon, Orange, Vanilla or Yellow Sauce. Serves 6 to 8.

Any kind of marmalade may be used.

STEAMED PEACH PUDDING

2 cups sifted flour	2 tablespoons shortening
½ teaspoon salt	1 cup milk
4 teaspoons baking powder	3 cups sliced peaches, fresh or canned

Sift flour, salt and baking powder together, rub in the shortening and add milk. The dough will be too soft to roll out. Place sliced peaches in a greased baking dish, spread dough over fruit and set the dish in a steamer over a kettle of rapidly boiling water. Cover the steamer tightly. Steam 1 hour. Turn the pudding out without breaking. Serve hot with Hard Sauce, whipped cream, Butterscotch or any desired Sauce. Serves 8 to 10.

Use individual molds, place peaches or any desired fruit on bottom, pour batter on top.

552

STEAMED SUET PUDDING

1 cup raisins
3 cups sifted flour
1 teaspoon baking soda
1 teaspoon cinnamon
1 teaspoon cloves

½ teaspoon grated nutmeg
1 teaspoon salt
1 cup ground suet
1 cup sour milk
1 cup molasses

Mix raisins with ½ cup of the flour. Sift remaining flour with dry ingredients. Combine suet, milk and molasses and add to dry ingredients. Add raisins and mix thoroughly. Fill greased pudding mold ⅔ full, cover tightly and steam 3 hours. Serve with Hard Sauce or any desired pudding sauce. Serves 8 to 10.

Cold Puddings

RICE PUDDING

½ cup raisins
2 cups milk, scalded
2 eggs, separated
¼ teaspoon salt

½ cup sugar
1¼ cups cooked rice
⅛ teaspoon cinnamon or nutmeg

Add raisins to hot milk and let stand 15 minutes. Beat egg yolks, salt and sugar until thick. Add hot milk, raisins, rice and cinnamon and cook in double boiler until thickened. Fold in stiffly beaten egg whites. Chill. If desired, serve garnished with sections of fruit. Serves 6.

RICE AND APPLE PUDDING

6 tart apples
⅔ cup water
4 tablespoons butter
⅓ cup sugar

¼ teaspoon salt
1½ cups cooked rice
½ cup marmalade

Pare apples, core and slice. Add water, butter, sugar and salt; simmer until tender. Line bottom and sides of a greased baking dish with part of rice, fill with cooked apples and spread marmalade over top. Cover with remaining rice. Bake in a moderate oven (350° F.) 15 to 20 minutes. Let stand until cold, then unmold and turn onto a serving plate. Serve with any desired pudding sauce. Serves 6.

Apricots or other fruit may be used instead of the apples.

NEW ENGLAND APRICOT PUDDING

½ pound dried apricots	1 cup boiled frosting, using 3
½ cup sugar	egg whites or 1 cup
Cinnamon toast	meringue
	Orange marmalade

Rinse apricots, cover with water and boil 30 to 40 minutes or until tender. Add sugar. It may be necessary to add more water as apricots should not be dry. Arrange slices of cinnamon toast in the bottom and around the sides of a greased dish. Pour in the hot apricots, cover the dish tightly so that no steam escapes and cool gradually. Chill. When ready to serve cover top with boiled frosting and garnish with bits of orange marmalade. Serves 6.

PEAR CONDÉ

1 cup rice	3 cups raspberries or straw-
2 cups boiling water	berries
1 teaspoon salt	⅔ cup sugar
1 cup milk	Whipped cream
3 pears	

Wash rice thoroughly, drain. Place rice in a double boiler, add water and cook until water is all absorbed. Add salt and milk and continue cooking until rice is tender. Turn into individual greased molds and chill. Unmold on a serving platter. Pare pears, cut into halves and remove core. Crush raspberries or strawberries and add sugar. Arrange pears around rice molds. Fill pears with raspberries or strawberries and pour remainder over rice molds. Top rice molds with whipped cream. Serves 6 to 8.

PEASANT GIRL WITH A VEIL

2 cups dried crumbs	1 cup tart jam
2 tablespoons sugar	Whipped cream

This is a delicious Danish pudding. Crumble bits of graham or rye bread to make fine crumbs. Add sugar to the crumbs and heat in a slow oven until they are very dry, cool and mix with any kind of jam, preferably a tart jam like apricot or plum. Mold and chill. Serve with whipped cream and garnish with additional jam. Serves 6.

FRUIT CHARLOTTE

Line cups with alternating triangular pieces of spongecake and chocolate cake. Fill center with slices of oranges and peaches. Chill, turn out on serving plate and surround with whipped cream and blackberries. Serve very cold topped with whipped cream.

SWEET STRAWBERRY OR OTHER FRUIT SHORTCAKE

1½ cups sifted cake flour	¾ cup sugar
2½ teaspoons baking powder	2 eggs, beaten
¼ teaspoon salt	½ cup milk or water
¼ cup shortening	Strawberries or other fruit

Sift flour, baking powder and salt together 3 times. Cream shortening and sugar until light and fluffy. Beat in eggs. Add dry ingredients and milk alternately, beating until smooth after each addition. Pour into 2 greased cake pans and bake in a moderate oven (350° F.) 25 minutes. Turn out and cool. Cover one layer with sweetened crushed fruit. Cover with other layer and cover with whole sweetened fruit. Top with whipped cream, if desired. Serves 6 to 8.

RENNET-CUSTARDS

1 rennet tablet	3 tablespoons sugar
1 pint milk (not evaporated or soft curd)	1 teaspoon vanilla

Set out 4 or 5 dessert glasses. Dissolve rennet tablet in 1 tablespoon cold water. Warm milk, sugar and vanilla slowly, stirring constantly, until lukewarm (120° F.)—not hot. A few drops of milk on the inside of the wrist should feel only comfortably warm. Remove from heat. If desired, add few grains of salt. Add dissolved rennet tablet and stir quickly for a few seconds only. Pour at once, while still liquid, into dessert glasses. Let set until it thickens—about 10 minutes. Chill rennet-custards in refrigerator. Serve in same glasses. Rennet-custards may be garnished in many attractive ways by the use of whipped cream with nuts, jams, or coconut.

VARIATIONS OF RENNET-CUSTARDS

CARAMEL—Caramelize the sugar, add ¼ cup hot water to dissolve the caramel and add to the milk.

CHOCOLATE—Melt 1 ounce of chocolate over hot water. Add 3 tablespoons hot water, cook until it is smooth and add to the milk before it is heated.

WITH EGGS—Beat yolks of 2 eggs with the sugar and mix with milk before it is heated. Proceed as for rennet-custard. Make a meringue of the whites by beating until stiff, then beating in ¼ cup sugar. Drop by spoonfuls onto a greased baking sheet and bake in a 350° F. oven until browned. Top each dish of rennet-custard with a meringue.

CORNSTARCH BLANC MANGE

3 tablespoons cornstarch	2 cups milk
2 to 4 tablespoons sugar	1 teaspoon vanilla
¼ teaspoon salt	

Mix cornstarch, sugar and salt with ½ cup cold milk. Scald remaining milk in top of double boiler. Add cornstarch mixture gradually to scalded milk, stirring constantly. Cook stirring constantly until thickened and smooth. Cover and cook 25 minutes, stirring occasionally. Cool and add vanilla. Turn into molds wet with cold water and chill. Serves 6.

VARIATIONS OF CORNSTARCH BLANC MANGE

COCONUT—Add 1 to 2 cups moist coconut to cornstarch blanc mange.

FRUITED—When cornstarch blanc mange begins to set, stir in one cup of fruit, such as cherries, crushed pineapple, raspberries, strawberries, apricots or orange sections.

ARROWROOT—Use 1 cup scalded milk and 2 tablespoons arrowroot mixed with ½ cup cold water. Cook in double boiler 30 minutes.

IRISH MOSS—Soak ⅓ cup Irish moss in cold water to cover, 15 minutes. Drain and add to 1 pint milk. Cook in double boiler 30 minutes without stirring. It thickens only on cooling. Serve with cream, pudding sauce or fruit.

CARAMEL—Add ¼ cup caramelized sugar sirup (page 457) to milk after scalding.

COFFEE—Use 1 cup strong coffee for 1 cup milk.

CHOCOLATE—

1 recipe Cornstarch Blanc Mange
2 eggs, separated
3 ounces (3 squares) chocolate

1 cup milk
5 tablespoons sugar
1 teaspoon vanilla

Prepare cornstarch blanc mange. Ten minutes before cooking is completed, add pudding to beaten egg yolks. Cook 10 minutes longer, then pour into molds. Melt chocolate over hot water, add milk and 3 tablespoons of sugar, and cook until smooth. Cool. Stir in vanilla. When pudding mold is cold, spread chocolate mixture over it. Beat egg whites until stiff, add remaining 2 tablespoons sugar and a few drops vanilla. Spread on top of chocolate. Bake in a moderate oven (350° F.) to brown top. Serves 6 to 8.

PEPPERMINT STICK—Add ½ cup crushed peppermint stick candy to cornstarch or chocolate blanc mange.

PRUNE—

3 tablespoons cornstarch
½ cup sugar
½ cup cold prune juice

1 teaspoon cinnamon
1½ cups hot prune pulp
2 tablespoons lemon juice

Combine first 4 ingredients. Add prune pulp, stirring constantly, cover and cook in double boiler 25 minutes or until thickened. Add lemon juice and pour into molds. Chill. Serves 6.

MOCK BUTTERSCOTCH CUSTARD

1 cup brown sugar
6 tablespoons flour
3 cups milk

3 eggs, separated
¾ teaspoon vanilla

Mix sugar and flour thoroughly; add milk slowly, stirring until smooth. Cook over boiling water 15 minutes. Stir small amount into beaten egg yolks, then return to remaining hot mixture and cook 2 minutes longer, stirring constantly. Remove from heat and fold gently into egg whites, beaten until stiff but not dry; add vanilla. Cool. Serves 6.

FROZEN DESSERTS

Ice Creams

ICE CREAMS are generally classified as cooked or uncooked. All ice-creams are stirred or beaten while freezing.

PLAIN OR PHILADELPHIA ICE CREAM—This is cream, or cream diluted with milk, sweetened, flavored and frozen. Plain ice-creams may be flavored with extracts or may have crushed nuts or fruits added. Rich, oily nuts do not combine well with ice-cream. Walnuts, almonds, pecans and pistachio nuts are most often used, and crushed peaches, pineapple, apricots or berries are particularly good for flavoring.

BISQUE ICE CREAM—This is made by adding to plain ice-cream such material as pulverized macaroons, ground nuts and stale sponge cake crumbs, to give variety in texture and flavor.

FRENCH AND AMERICAN ICE CREAMS—In these, the foundation is a custard made with cream, milk, eggs, sugar and flavoring, cooked, chilled and then frozen. In French ice-cream the custard mixture contains many eggs. In American ice-cream a plain custard is used.

NEAPOLITAN ICE CREAM—This may be made of any variety of ice-cream tinted in three colors and variously flavored. It is packed in layers after it is frozen. Sometimes it is made of a combination of ice-cream and water-ice.

FROZEN PUDDING—This is plain ice-cream plus a combination of fruit and nuts with bread-crumbs, cake-crumbs or powdered macaroons.

Mousses, Parfaits and Biscuits

MOUSSES—A mousse is whipped cream, sweetened, flavored, packed, and frozen without stirring. Gelatin is often used to give body to a mousse. In that case it is sometimes spoken of as a frozen soufflé. Chocolate, coffee, maple and fruit flavors of various kinds are used.

PARFAITS—A parfait is made by pouring a hot, thick sirup over beaten egg-yolks or beaten egg-whites, adding whipped cream, and packing and freezing the mixture without stirring.

Chocolate, maple and coffee are the most popular flavors for parfaits.

BISCUITS—A biscuit is a yellow parfait mixture to which beaten egg-whites are added. It is stirred until it is partly frozen and then packed in small paper serving cases. The cases are laid in the trays of the mechanical refrigerator or in containers which are placed in a freezing mixture.

Water Ices, Sherbets, Bombes and Punches

All these mixtures are stirred while being frozen.

ICES—A plain ice is a sweetened fruit-juice which may or may not be diluted with water.

SHERBETS—A sherbet is a plain ice plus egg-whites. Gelatin is sometimes used in sherbets. In milk sherbets, milk, instead of water, is used with the fruit-juice.

BOMBES—A bombe is a combination of two or more frozen mixtures, packed in layers in a covered mold.

PUNCHES—A punch is a water-ice frozen to a mush with some highly spiced fruit-juice or other flavoring added.

SORBETS—A sorbet is a sherbet made of several kinds of fruit.

Equipment for Making Frozen Desserts
The Crank Freezer

This type of freezer consists of a bucket of wood or metal for holding the freezing mixture, ice and salt, and a non-rusting metal container with a closely fitting cover for holding the mixture to be frozen. The mixture in the container is stirred by a paddle attached through the cover to a crank which is operated by hand or which may be attached to a small electric motor.

ICE CRUSHER—A bag of heavy muslin, burlap, canvas or sailcloth is required to hold the ice while it is broken into small pieces. Some implement is necessary for pounding the ice in the bag. A wooden mallet is generally preferred because it crushes the ice more thoroughly and quickly than a smaller implement. Very satisfactory mallets and bags for breaking ice can be bought.

THE FREEZING MIXTURE—One part salt to eight parts crushed ice, by measure, is a good proportion for home use. The ice should be crushed fine, to expose as much surface as possible to the action of the salt. Snow may be used instead of ice, but it is advisable to mix a small amount of water with the snow to hasten the melting process. Rock salt is best for use in freezing. Mix the ice and salt before putting them into the freezer, and fill the freezer well above the line of the mixture in the ice-cream container.

The Automatic Freezer

This variety of freezer requires no turning. The wall of the outer compartment is constructed with an air-space which helps to keep the warm air from entering and the cold air about the ice from escaping. The ice-cream is placed in the smaller container, covered and packed in ice and salt in the larger container. At intervals the cover is removed and the contents scraped from the side and beaten well with a spoon or paddle. It requires the minimum amount of ice and work to do the freezing and the frozen product is of a satisfactory quality, although not so smooth as that made by the freezer in which the mixture is stirred while freezing.

The Automatic Refrigerator

For speedy freezing, the temperature in the ice-making drawer of the refrigerator must be under twenty degrees. Your refrigerator is designed to keep foods at an even low temperature, and the freezing of desserts is an extra service. If yours will not freeze them, it is possible to have a switch added which will keep the motor operating continuously during the freezing period, or the valves may be readjusted to give the whole box a lower temperature.

No one, however, should be allowed to make adjustments or tamper with the valves except the electrician sent out by the salesman.

Preparation of Ingredients

USE MORE FLAVORING in all mixtures that are to be frozen than in mixtures that are to be served unfrozen, because the flavor freezes out to some extent. Stir well and thoroughly dissolve sugar before freezing.

CRUSH FRUIT for fruited creams or put it through a food-chopper. Large pieces of icy fruit are difficult to eat. Partly freeze the mixture before adding the fruit, otherwise the milk or cream may curdle and the fruit may settle to the bottom.

SCALDING (not boiling) at least part of the cream and milk will give greater body and finer grain to ice-cream than it will have if the cream and milk are used without this preparation.

CHILL THE MIXTURE before beginning to freeze. The best temperature is about 40° F. It should never be over 60° F. If it is too warm the cream may curdle before freezing.

Freezing Ice Cream

TO FREEZE ICE CREAM IN A CRANK FREEZER, have the ice-cream container not more than three-fourths full. The turning of the crank incorporates air in the mixture and the freezing causes expansion, so allow plenty of room for "swell." Place the can containing the mixture in the freezer pail. Cover the can and adjust the top. Turn the crank to be sure that the cover fits tight. Add the ice and salt mixture as directed. Turn the freezer slowly until the mixture begins to freeze; then turn it more rapidly. This beats up the cream and produces a swell.

Ice cream takes from twelve to twenty minutes to freeze in a crank freezer. Ices and sherbets take from twenty to thirty minutes.

TO FREEZE ICE CREAM IN A VACUUM FREEZER, pack in the same manner as when a crank freezer is used. Several times during the two hours that are necessary for freezing, remove enough ice so that you can uncover the can without danger of salting the cream; scrape the mixture from the sides of the can with a spoon or paddle and beat thoroughly.

FOR QUICK RESULTS WITH THE AUTOMATIC REFRIGERATOR, take these precautions:

1. Chill your mixture well before freezing.
2. Do not try to freeze pans of water at the same time with desserts.
3. Do not open and close your refrigerator doors often or place warm, steamy foods in the box while you are freezing desserts.
4. Do not have the mixture too sweet or it will not freeze.

Ice cream mixtures having a heavy custard base respond very well to the automatic refrigerator. It is best to cook only the yolks of the eggs, then chill, and finally fold in the beaten whites just before freezing. This method not only gives a better texture but a greater volume to the finished product.

Refreshing and palatable sherbets may be frozen in the automatic refrigerator, but they are likely to be granular even when gelatin and beaten egg-whites are added.

Ice-creams and sherbets, and all other frozen desserts having a custard or gelatin foundation should be very vigorously stirred one hour after being placed in the refrigerator to freeze, and several times subsequently at half to three-quarter-hour intervals.

The addition of whipped cream does much to make the texture fine and smooth. Crushed fruit, marshmallows, grape nuts and crumbled graham crackers will also make desirable textures.

Recipes which are especially good for refrigerator freezing are: rennet-custard ice cream, maple-fruit ice cream, peach ice cream—No. 2, prune ice cream, raspberry ice cream, chocolate ice cream, frozen pudding, peach meringue, maple mousse, strawberry mousse, maple parfait, biscuit glacé, charlotte glacé and marshmallow mousse.

In all of these recipes, except the rennet-custard ice cream, the cream must be whipped. In making chocolate ice cream, add the whipped cream when the mixture is half frozen.

Packing and Molding Frozen Desserts

Ice-cream is ready for packing when it has a dull appearance, adheres to a spoon and retains its shape for some time. By thermometer test it should be about 27° F. It should be firm and mellow, smooth and velvety, free from grains or lumps and neither tough nor mushy. Ice-creams and ices that are to be molded should be packed into the molds at this time.

To Pack Ice Cream in the Freezer, drain off the brine and pack the can in coarse cracked ice and salt. Use one part salt to four of ice by measure. Cover the top of the can with a layer of ice about six inches thick. Cover the top of the freezer with newspapers or burlap or any other covering that will exclude air. Set the freezer in a cool place and let it stand two or three hours, for the ice-cream to ripen.

When Frozen Mixtures are to be Molded, have the mold chilled and ready when the mixture is frozen to the point where it is ready for packing. If it is allowed to freeze too hard before it is packed into the molds, it is difficult to handle.

Pack the Mixture Into the Mold Carefully, so that all curves and corners are filled compactly without air spaces;

fill the mold to overflowing with the frozen mixture and cover with a sheet of white paper.

PRESS THE COVER DOWN TIGHT and seal the crack with a thick layer of some fat that is hard when it is cold. The crack must be completely covered. Bury the mold in cracked ice and salt, using four parts of ice to one part of salt, by measure.

IN PACKING A MOUSSE OR PARFAIT, use equal measures of salt and ice and let the mold stand from three to five hours, depending on its size.

WHEN USING THE AUTOMATIC REFRIGERATOR, pack the mixture into the trays. Allow four hours for freezing, until you find that your refrigerator will freeze more quickly.

PAPER CASES MAY BE FILLED with chilled or partly frozen mixtures. These may be placed in a closely covered receptacle and packed in ice and salt or placed in the trays of the automatic refrigerator.

DOUBLE MOLDING—Line the mold with a frozen mixture, making the layer equally thick in all parts. Fill the center with a mixture of contrasting color or texture or both. This mixture may or may not have been frozen first.

Unmolding Frozen Desserts

To unmold a frozen dessert, remove the mold from the ice mixture, rinse off the salt with cold water, break the seal, remove the cover and run a knife around the edge of the mold to a depth of not more than one-half inch. Invert the mold on a serving-plate. Let it stand for a few minutes and the contents will soon slip out. If it does not come out easily, dip a cloth into lukewarm (not hot) water wring as dry as possible and wipe quickly over the outside of the mold.

Suggestions Concerning Flavor and Texture

THE AMOUNT AND QUALITY OF FLAVORING EXTRACTS used are very apparent in the finished product. Some of the flavor freezes out, so an allowance must be made for this. The flavor should be delicately suggested rather than too pronounced.

THE AMOUNT OF FAT IN THE CREAM also affects the flavor. A rich cream has a better flavor than a thin cream.

SALT ADDED IN SMALL QUANTITIES—not more than one-half teaspoon to a gallon of the cream mixture—serves to give a "rounded out" or deeper flavor.

Ice Cream Should Stand Several Hours to ripen or blend the many flavors of the eggs, sugar, fruit, nuts, chocolate, and other substances found in the product. Each flavor may be distinguished in freshly frozen ice-cream.

If a Colored Product is Desired, only a small amount of coloring should be used. A delicate tint is all that is desired.

Texture is Affected by Whole Cream, egg-white, gelatin and cooked combinations such as milk and corn-starch or flour, and milk and eggs. A smooth velvety texture is desired. Other things being equal, a richer mixture gives a smoother product. A thin cream gives a coarse texture.

Texture is Also Affected by the Manner of Freezing. If the mixture is frozen too rapidly, it will be coarse and have a rough texture, while a slower freezing tends to improve its texture. This smoothness is not entirely due to the rate of freezing, however, but to the amount of whipping or beating which takes place before and during the freezing. If frozen without any beating, the product will be coarse even though made from a rich cream. The air that is beaten into the mixture in freezing produces a light smooth consistency.

A Certain Amount of Expansion is Desirable. If ice-cream is properly made, the volume increases at least one-third and the product is smoother in texture and richer to the taste than in a cream containing no air. Too rapid freezing prevents this increase of volume.

Ice Creams

VANILLA ICE CREAM

Philadelphia—

1 quart thin cream   ¾ cup sugar   ½ tablespoon vanilla
Dissolve the sugar in the cream, add the vanilla and freeze.

American.

1 pint milk	2 egg-yolks
2 tablespoons flour	1 cup heavy cream
2 tablespoons water	1 teaspoon vanilla
¾ cup sugar	

Scald the milk, stirring constantly. Mix the flour and cold water to a smooth paste and add to it slowly the scalded milk, continuing the stirring. When thickened, cook over hot water for about fifteen minutes. Add sugar and beaten egg-yolks and cook two minutes. Strain the custard through a fine sieve and, when cold, add the cream and vanilla and freeze. This makes a smooth, rich cream.

For variation, use dark-brown sugar or maple sugar instead of the white sugar.

FRENCH.

6 egg-yolks
5 cups medium cream

¾ cup sugar
Vanilla bean

Scald the cream with a piece of vanilla bean. Beat the egg-yolks, add the sugar and pour the cream slowly on the mixture, beating constantly. Cook in a double boiler until it thickens, watching it carefully. Cool, chill, and freeze.

APRICOT ICE CREAM

1 pint milk
2 tablespoons flour
2 tablespoons water
1 cup sugar

2 egg-yolks
1 cup heavy cream
1½ cups strained apricot-pulp
  and juice

Make custard as directed for vanilla ice-cream. When cool, add the apricot-pulp and juice, and freeze.

No. 2.

1 cup dried apricots
1 cup sugar

2 cups thin cream
1 cup milk

Soak the apricots over night and stew them until tender. Put them through a sieve. Add the sugar to the hot apricots, stirring until dissolved. When cold, add the cream and then the milk, stirring constantly. Freeze.

BANANA ICE CREAM

1 pint milk
1 tablespoon flour
1 tablespoon water
½ cup sugar
1 egg

2 bananas
⅛ teaspoon salt
1 pint thin cream
½ teaspoon lemon flavoring

Make custard as directed for vanilla ice cream, American (page 563). Peel and scrape bananas, rub through a sieve, add salt and add to the cold custard mixture. Add cream and flavoring. Freeze.

BERRY ICE CREAM

1 pint milk
2 tablespoons flour
2 tablespoons water
1 cup sugar

2 egg-yolks
1 cup heavy cream
1½ cups crushed berries

Make custard as directed for vanilla ice-cream, American (page 563). When it has cooled, freeze partly; add the crushed berries, and complete freezing.

CARAMEL ICE CREAM

2 cups milk
1 egg
½ cup sugar

1 cup thin cream
½ cup macaroons

Caramelize half the sugar (see Index). Combine the milk, beaten egg, sugar and caramelized sugar. Heat the mixture to the boiling-point. When cool, add the cream and the macaroons crushed fine. Beat well and freeze.

BISQUE ICE CREAM

Add one cup of macaroon-crumbs to caramel ice-cream.

CHOCOLATE ICE CREAM

1 pint milk
2 tablespoons flour
2 tablespoons water
1 cup sugar
2 egg-yolks

1 cup heavy cream
1 teaspoon vanilla
1½ squares unsweetened
    chocolate

Make custard as directed for vanilla ice-cream, American (page 563), adding the chocolate to the milk when scalding. Cool and freeze.

CINNAMON ICE CREAM

Use the recipe for vanilla ice-cream, American (page 563). When the milk is put on to scald, add a piece of stick cinnamon about one inch long and one square of chocolate, grated. Beat the custard thoroughly with an egg-beater to insure smoothness of color. The cinnamon imparts a rich, spicy taste that is as elusive as it is delicious.

GENERAL DIRECTIONS FOR MAKING FRESH FRUIT ICE CREAM

Prepare any desired fruit by sprinkling sugar over it. Let it stand one hour, press through a coarse sieve and stir into vanilla ice-cream, American (page 563), when the cream is frozen to a mush.

IF SEED FRUITS, such as currants or berries are used, strain through a fine sieve or a piece of cheese-cloth and use the pulp only. This can be put into the freezer with the cream and not reserved until later, as in the case of the mashed fruits.

CRUSHED PINEAPPLE with the addition of a little lemon-juice makes a particularly fine fruit cream.

VANILLA RENNET-CUSTARD ICE CREAM

2 rennet tablets	1 cup heavy cream
3 cups milk	1 cup sugar
2 tablespoons cold water	1 tablespoon vanilla

Dissolve rennet tablets in cold water. Warm the milk, cream, sugar and vanilla until lukewarm (110° F.). Remove from stove. Add dissolved tablets, stir a few seconds; pour at once into freezer can. Let set until firm and cool. Freeze.

MAPLE-FRUIT ICE CREAM

1 cup maple sirup	1 cup crushed pineapple, fresh
2 cups cream	or canned
½ cup candied cherries	

Combine all ingredients and freeze.

MARSHMALLOW ICE CREAM

1 pint milk	1 pint thin cream
1 egg	1 tablespoon vanilla
¾ cup sugar	½ cup marshmallows, diced
⅛ teaspoon salt	

Make custard of milk, egg, sugar and salt. Add remaining ingredients. Cool and freeze.

THREE EXCELLENT REASONS FOR ICE CREAM, STRAWBERRIES AND REFRIGERATORS

—National Dairy Council

PATTERNS OF ME-
RINGUE MOLDS—
FLAVORED WITH
CHOCOLATE OR
FRUIT — HOWEVER
YOU SERVE IT ICE
CREAM IS AMERI-
CA'S FAVORITE
DESSERT

AN IRRESISTI-
BLE SUMMER
SYMPHONY IN
FRUIT AND ICE
CREAM

GENERAL DIRECTIONS FOR MAKING NUT ICE CREAM

Add one-half cup of chopped nuts to a quart of vanilla, chocolate or caramel ice-cream when the mixture is frozen to a mush. Finish freezing.

ORANGE ICE CREAM

1 cup milk	2 egg-yolks
2 tablespoons flour	1 cup heavy cream
2 tablespoons water	1 cup orange-juice
1 cup sugar	

Make custard as directed for vanilla ice-cream, American (page 563). Cool, add the orange-juice slowly, then freeze.

No. 1.   PEACH ICE CREAM

1 pint milk	2 egg-yolks
2 tablespoons flour	1 cup heavy cream
2 tablespoons water	2 cups peach-pulp and juice
1 cup sugar	

Make custard as directed for vanilla ice-cream, American (page 563). When cool, add the peach-pulp and juice, and freeze.

No. 2.

1 cup fresh peach-pulp	¼ cup boiling water
½ cup sugar	2 cups cream

Make a sirup by boiling the sugar and water together for five minutes. Add the peaches and put the mixture through a strainer. Add the cream and freeze.

PISTACHIO ICE CREAM

Use the recipe for vanilla ice-cream, American (page 563). Scald three-fourths cup of blanched pistachio nuts with the milk. The mixture may be colored with green vegetable coloring, and the nuts may be put through a food-chopper, if desired. Cool and freeze.

PRUNE ICE CREAM

1 cup prune pulp	⅛ teaspoon salt
1 cup sugar	½ cup milk
Juice of 1 lemon	1 cup cream
Juice of 1 orange	

Rub cooked prunes through a sieve, to obtain the pulp. Add the remaining ingredients, the cream, whipped, last of all, mix thoroughly and freeze.

RASPBERRY ICE CREAM

1 quart raspberries	1 quart cream
2 cups sugar	

Mash the berries and sugar together, and let them stand for an hour. Rub through a strainer, add the cream and freeze.

ROSE ICE CREAM

4 cups light cream	1 to 2 teaspoons rose extract
3 cups heavy cream	¼ teaspoon salt
1 cup milk	Pink vegetable coloring
1 cup sugar	

Mix all the ingredients together thoroughly and freeze.

BAKED ALASKA

1 brick ice cream	4 tablespoons confectioners'
4 egg whites	sugar

Sponge cake

Freeze strawberry, vanilla and chocolate ice cream into brick form very hard. At serving time, beat the egg whites until light, add confectioners' sugar and whip until stiff and dry. Turn ice cream onto a sheet of sponge cake placed on a board and cover it completely with meringue. Sprinkle well with confectioners' sugar and place in very hot oven (450° F.) to brown. Place on a serving platter and serve at once. Serves 12 to 16.

SMALL INDIVIDUAL—Cut sponge cake into thick slices and cut out the center of each slice, leaving about half an inch on each of the four sides and on the bottom. Set these cake boxes on a board, put slices of well frozen ice cream inside, and cover with meringue, piling it up at the sides. Set in a hot oven

(400°-450° F.) for a moment to brown the meringue. Remove to a serving-dish and fill the hollows on top with any preserved fruit or nut mixture.

ICE CREAM SANDWICHES

Between thin slices of devil's food, angel cake, sponge cake or butter cake, or between halves of éclair or cream-puff shells, place a serving of ice-cream of a flavor to blend well with the cake. Cover with chocolate, butterscotch, marshmallow, maple or fruit sauce, either hot or cold, and top with whipped cream and nut-meats of various kinds, moist coconut, powdered or granulated chocolate or pieces of fresh or canned fruit.

For example: (1) Between thin slices of gold or white cake, place a slice of vanilla ice-cream; over the whole pour plain marshmallow sauce or whipped cream and garnish with several tablespoons of crushed strawberries. (2) Fill a cream-puff shell with peach ice-cream and pour over it a peach sirup, topped with whipped cream. (3) Place chocolate or vanilla ice-cream between layers of white or angel cake and cover with a thick fudge sauce.

SUNDAES

Vanilla, chocolate or any other ice-cream served in a low glass, with sweetened crushed fruit or any desired sauce poured over it, is known as a sundae. Whipped cream, nuts, marshmallow cream, etc., may be added as a garnish.

NEAPOLITAN ICE CREAM

1 pint strawberry ice-cream	(Any preferred combination
1 pint pistachio ice-cream	of flavors may be used in-
1 pint orange ice	stead of these)

Pack a mold in salt and ice and spread the strawberry ice-cream smoothly over the bottom. If it is not very firm, cover and let it stand for a few minutes. Spread a good layer of orange ice upon it, and as soon as this hardens, spread over it the pistachio ice-cream. Cover and freeze.

Frozen Puddings
FROZEN PUDDING

2 eggs
1 cup sugar
Pinch salt

2½ cups milk
1 cup heavy cream
1 cup candied fruit or nuts

Make a custard of the eggs, sugar, salt, milk and cream. Cool and freeze. Fill a mold with alternate layers of the frozen cream and candied fruit or nuts. Cover and freeze.

MOCHA BISCUIT

1 quart milk
½ cup pulverized coffee
6 eggs

½ cup sugar
2 tablespoons flour

Put the milk into a double boiler, drop into it a muslin bag containing the pulverized coffee and let it infuse for fifteen minutes, keeping the milk at the scalding point. Beat the eggs and sugar together until smooth. Remove the bag of coffee from the milk, add the flour stirred with a little cold milk or water and cook fifteen minutes. Pour over the egg mixture and return to the double boiler to cook until smooth and thick. When cold partly freeze, then fill paper cases with the mixture and complete the freezing. Serve garnished with whipped cream.

NESSELRODE PUDDING

3 cups milk
1½ cups sugar
5 egg-yolks
⅛ teaspoon salt
1 pint cream

3 tablespoons pineapple sirup
1 cup almonds
1 cup French chestnuts
¼ cup seeded raisins
¼ cup assorted fruits

Make a custard of the milk, sugar, egg-yolks and salt. When cool, add the cream and pineapple sirup. Blanch the almonds and chop them fine, then pound to a paste. Shell the chestnuts, blanch and boil until tender. Force through a sieve, and add to the custard. Freeze.

Line a two-quart melon mold with half the frozen mixture. To the remaining half, add a half-dozen large French chestnuts which have been boiled until tender, also the raisins and the assorted fruits cut in bits. Fill the mold with this mixture, cover and pack in ice and salt for two hours, or pack and freeze in the trays of the mechanical refrigerator. This is often served in individual paper cases with a bit of candied fruit on top of each.

PEACH MERINGUE

1/4 teaspoon gelatin	2/3 cup cream
1 tablespoon cold water	2 egg-whites
1/4 cup boiling water	1 teaspoon vanilla
1/4 cup sugar	Peach ice-cream

Soak the gelatin in the cold water and dissolve it in the boiling water. Add sugar and stir until it is dissolved. Add the cream. When it begins to thicken, pour slowly over the beaten whites of eggs and continue beating until it is the consistency of whipped cream. Add vanilla. Line a round mold with frozen peach ice-cream and fill the center with the meringue. Pack in ice and salt, and let stand three to four hours, or pack and freeze in the trays of the mechanical refrigerator.

Mousses and Parfaits

STRAWBERRY OR OTHER FRUIT MOUSSE

1 pint rich cream   1 cup fruit-pulp   Vanilla

Whip and drain the cream. Mix with it the pulp of any fruit drained free of juice and sprinkled well with powdered sugar. Add vanilla, mold, and pack in ice and salt for three hours, or pack and freeze in the trays of the mechanical refrigerator.

MAPLE MOUSSE

1 1/4 cups maple sirup	2 tablespoons gelatin
1/2 cup sugar	1/4 cup cold water
5 cups cream	

Combine maple sirup, sugar and one cup of cream and bring to a boil, stirring constantly. Add the gelatin softened in water and dissolved over heat. Strain, cool in ice-water until the mixture thickens, then add the remainder of the cream, whipped stiff. Place in a mold, pack in ice and salt and let stand for four hours, or pack and freeze in the trays of the mechanical refrigerator.

MAPLE PARFAIT

¾ cup maple sirup 3 egg-whites 1 pint cream

Cook maple sirup to the light crack stage (270° F.). Pour the sirup over the beaten whites of the eggs and beat until cold. Fold into the stiffly whipped cream. Mold and pack in ice and salt for four hours, or pack and freeze in the trays of the mechanical refrigerator. Serve in parfait glasses with whipped cream.

MARSHMALLOW MOUSSE

1 pint cream
1 cup top milk
6 marshmallows
½ cup chopped nut-meats
¾ cup powdered sugar

7 maraschino cherries, cut in pieces
½ teaspoon vanilla
1 egg-white, beaten

Warm the milk, add marshmallows and beat well to dissolve, then chill. Beat egg-white and fold in with the sugar and vanilla. Beat cream very stiff, and fold in, together with the nuts and cherries. Pack in ice and salt or freeze in the trays of the mechanical refrigerator not less than two and a half hours.

BISCUIT GLACÉ

1 cup sugar
¼ cup water
4 egg-yolks

3⅓ cups cream
1 teaspoon vanilla
Pulverized macaroons

Make a thick sirup of the sugar and water. Beat the yolks of the eggs and add the sirup and one-half cup of the cream. Place all in a saucepan over a slow fire and stir constantly until it forms a thick coating on the spoon. Empty into a mixing-bowl, set on ice, beat until it is cold and stiff, and then add the remainder of the cream beaten very stiff. Flavor with vanilla or any preferred extract.

Pack the mixture in small paper boxes, sprinkle with pulverized macaroons, and set in a covered container. Pack in ice and salt and let stand for four hours, or pack and freeze in the trays of the mechanical refrigerator.

MORE MOLD MAGIC IN THIS SUMPTUOUS BOMBE OF CHOCOLATE AND VANILLA ICE CREAM
—Irradiated Evaporated Milk Institute

YOU CAN BUY THE MAKINGS FOR THIS LUSCIOUS LOAF OF ICE CREAM AND DEVIL'S FOOD
—National Dairy Council

CHARLOTTE GLACÉ

¼ cup powdered sugar
1 pint thick cream
1 teaspoon vanilla
½ tablespoon gelatin
4 tablespoons cold water

Dissolve sugar in cream. Add vanilla. Soften the gelatin in cold water, dissolve over heat and combine the two mixtures.

Fill a cylindrical mold (a baking-powder can will do very nicely) and pack in salt and ice for two hours, or pack and freeze in the trays of the mechanical refrigerator. Turn out on a platter, surround with lady fingers, cover the top with whipped cream and serve.

Ices and Frozen Fruits

CRANBERRY ICE

1 quart water   1 quart cranberries   3 cups sugar

Make a sirup by boiling water and sugar together for five minutes. Boil the cranberries in a little water until soft, then press through a sieve. Add to the sirup, cool, and freeze.

LEMON ICE

1 quart water   2 cups sugar   ¾ cup lemon-juice

Make a sirup by boiling the water with the sugar for five minutes. Add the strained lemon-juice, cool and freeze.

ORANGE ICE

1 quart water
2 cups sugar
2 cups orange-juice
2 grated orange-rinds
¼ cup lemon-juice

Make a sirup as for lemon ice. Add the fruit-juices and grated rind. Strain, cool and freeze.

RASPBERRY AND CURRANT ICE

2 cups sugar
1¼ cups currant-juice
¾ cup raspberry-juice
1 quart water

At least one quart each of the berries and currants will be needed to give the required amount of juice. Sprinkle one-half cup of the sugar over them, stir well and let stand for one hour. Strain through a fine sieve or cheese-cloth. Make a sirup of the remaining sugar and the water. Add the fruit-juice, strain, cool and freeze.

GRAPE ICE

⅔ cup sugar
1 cup grape-juice
¼ cup orange-juice

1½ cups water
2 tablespoons lemon-juice

Boil the sugar and water together for five minutes. Mix all the ingredients together, strain and freeze.

COUPE SAINT JACQUES

Fruit cup
Lemon ice

Maraschino cherries
Angelica

Fill champagne glasses with fruit prepared by the recipe for fruit cup, No. 1 (See Index). Over the top spread a thick layer of lemon ice, decorating the center with one Maraschino cherry, and four leaves of angelica radiating from it.

FROZEN STRAWBERRIES OR OTHER FRUIT

Strawberries, raspberries, fresh peaches or crushed pineapple make delicious frozen fruit. Mash or crush the fruit very fine, add half as much sugar as there is fruit and allow it to stand until a sirup is formed. Freeze in a crank freezer or pack in the trays of a mechanical refrigerator and stir occasionally while it is freezing.

CANNED FRUITS, especially pears, and peaches in heavy sirup, may be frozen in the can. Pack in ice and salt, allow two or three hours for freezing, open the can and serve in slices.

Sherbets Made without Gelatin
CURRANT SHERBET

3 pints red currants
1 pint red raspberries
2 cups water

1½ cups sugar
3 tablespoons lemon-juice
2 egg-whites

Place currants, raspberries and a cup of the water in a kettle and simmer slowly together for a few minutes. Strain, add remaining water, sugar and lemon-juice. Dissolve sugar in the fruit-juice mixture, cool and freeze to a mush. Stir in the beaten whites of eggs. Pack and let stand several hours.

LEMON SHERBET

No. 1—WITH WATER.

1 quart water	¾ cup lemon-juice
3 cups sugar	2 egg-whites

Make a sirup by boiling sugar and water together for five minutes. Add lemon-juice, cool and freeze to a mush. Add the beaten whites of the eggs and continue freezing.

No. 2—WITH MILK.

½ cup lemon-juice   1½ cups sugar   1 quart milk

Mix together the lemon-juice and sugar and add to the milk slowly, stirring constantly. If the ingredients are cold, and the acid is added slowly to the milk, rather than the milk to the acid, there is little danger of the mixture curdling. However, if it does curdle slightly the quality of the sherbet will not be affected. Strain and freeze.

PINEAPPLE SHERBET

1 quart water	2 cups crushed pineapple,
2 cups sugar	fresh or canned
1 lemon	2 egg-whites

Boil water and sugar together for five minutes. Scald the pineapple in the boiling sirup, and rub through a sieve. Cool, add lemon-juice and freeze to a mush. Add the beaten whites of the eggs and continue freezing.

RASPBERRY SHERBET

1 cup sugar	1 tablespoon lemon-juice
1 quart raspberries	1 egg-white

Add sugar to the raspberries, and let stand in refrigerator for two hours. If the mixture does not seem sweet enough, more sugar may be added. Add lemon-juice and beaten egg-white and freeze. Serve in glasses garnished with whipped cream.

Sherbets Made with Gelatin

STANDARD RECIPE FOR SHERBETS MADE WITH GELATIN

1 tablespoon gelatin	1 cup sugar
1½ cups cold water	Fruit-juice
½ cup boiling water	

Soak the gelatin in one-half cup of the cold water. Add the boiling water and stir until disolved. Then add the sugar, remainder of cold water, and the strained juice of any fruit. Chill and freeze.

LEMON—Use the strained juice of six lemons.

ORANGE—Use the strained juice of six oranges and two lemons.

RASPBERRY—Use a pint of strained raspberry juice and the juice of two lemons.

STRAWBERRY—Use a pint of strained strawberry juice and the juice of two lemons.

CRANBERRY SHERBET

1 quart water	2 lemons
2 cups sugar	1 pint cranberry-juice
1 tablespoon gelatin	

Boil the water and sugar together for five minutes. Add the gelatin, which has been softened in cold water and dissolved over heat, the lemon-juice, and cranberry-juice. Strain, cool and freeze.

GINGER SHERBET

2 quarts water	¼ cup sirup from Canton ginger
3 cups sugar	
6 lemons	1 teaspoon powdered ginger
1 tablespoon gelatin	2 egg-whites, if desired

Boil water and sugar together for five minutes. Add lemon-juice, gelatin softened in a little cold water, the sirup and the powdered ginger. Freeze to a mush, then stir in the beaten egg-whites (these may be omitted). Serve in sherbet glasses.

PEACH SURPRISE SHERBET

2 cups sugar	2 cups peach pulp
1 quart water	1 lemon
1 teaspoon gelatin	2 oranges

Boil sugar and water together for five minutes, add the gelatin softened in cold water. When the mixture is cold, add the peach pulp, which has been pressed through a sieve, and the juice of lemon and oranges. Freeze.

RASPBERRY SHERBET

2 tablespooons gelatin	2 cups sugar
3 cups cold water	1 cup strained raspberry
1 cup boiling water	juice
3 tablespoons lemon juice	

Soften gelatin in ½ cup cold water; dissolve in boiling water, and add sugar, fruit juices and remaining 2½ cups cold water; strain and freeze (page 558). Yield: 2 quarts sherbet.

STRAWBERRY SHERBET

Use 1 cup strained strawberry juice; freeze.

RHUBARB SHERBET

Use 1 cup stewed, sieved, pink rhubarb, and omit lemon juice; freeze.

CARDINAL ICE

1 quart raspberries	3 cups sugar
1 quart currants	2 cups water

Wash, pick over berries. Add 1 cup sugar to each, mash slightly, cover and let stand in warm place 2 hours, or until juice is drawn out; strain through cloth. Make a sirup of remaining cup of sugar and water as for lemon ice (page 573);

add fruit juices, cool, strain and freeze (page 558). Yield: 3 pints ice.

AVOCADO PIQUANT CRÈME

1½ ripe large avocados	¼ teaspoon salt
¼ cup honey	¼ teaspoon celery salt
	⅓ cup lime juice

Peel and remove seed from avocados; force pulp through sieve; add remaining ingredients and blend well. Pour into freezing tray of automatic refrigerator with temperature control set at coldest point. Freeze 2 to 4 hours, or until firm, stirring once during freezing. Serve in sherbet glasses with lamb, turkey or game; or serve as dessert.

BOMBES

PEACH BOMBE—Line a melon mold evenly with peach ice cream; fill center with peach mousse mixture; cover, pack in ice and salt and freeze 3 hours (page 561).

COFFEE BOMBE—Line a melon mold evenly with vanilla or chocolate ice cream; fill with Mocha biscuit mixture (page 570); cover, pack in ice and salt, and freeze 3 hours (page 561).

PISTACHIO BOMBE—Line a melon mold evenly with vanilla ice cream; fill with pistachio cream (page 567); pack in ice and salt and freeze 3 hours (page 561).

CHOCOLATE-VANILLA BOMBE—

¼ cup sweet butter	⅛ teaspoon salt
½ cup sugar	1 egg
2 cups irradiated evaporated milk	1 teaspoon gelatin
	1 cup water
2 teaspoons vanilla	

Cream butter. Add sugar and cream until fluffy. Beat in egg. Soften gelatin in 2 tablespoons water. Scald 1 cup milk. Add gelatin to milk. Stir hot gelatin-milk mixture into butter-sugar mixture. Add remaining water, milk, salt and vanilla. Freeze.

TO MAKE CHOCOLATE—Heat 2 ounces finely chopped bitter chocolate with one cup of the milk, add softened gelatin and dissolve. Proceed as above, with ingredients as for Vanilla.

SAUCES FOR DESSERTS

APRICOT SAUCE

¾ cup apricot pulp   ¾ cup heavy cream   Sugar

DRAIN canned apricots from their sirup and rub through a sieve. Beat cream until stiff, add to apricot pulp, and sweeten to taste.

BUTTERSCOTCH SAUCE

1½ cups light brown sugar   ½ tablespoon lemon-juice
¼ cup water   ½ cup chopped nut-meats
4 tablespoons butter

Boil sugar and water together to the soft ball stage (234°-240° F.) Add butter, lemon-juice and nut-meats.

CARAMEL SAUCE

1 cup sugar   1 tablespoon corn-starch
1 tablespoon cold water   1 tablespoon butter
1⅓ cups hot water   1 teaspoon vanilla

Place the sugar and cold water in a pan and stir until the resulting sirup is a clear brown, but not so dark as caramel; then add the hot water and stir until the whole is well blended. Add the corn-starch mixed with a little cold water and boil for five minutes. Continue cooking over hot water for fifteen minutes, stirring all the time. Beat in the butter and vanilla.

CHERRY SAUCE

1 cup sugar   ½ cup water
½ cup butter   ½ cup cherry-juice
1 tablespoon corn-starch

Cream the sugar and the butter, add the corn-starch and the liquid, and boil over hot water for five minutes, stirring constantly. Continue cooking for twenty-five minutes.

CHOCOLATE SAUCE

No. 1.

1½ cups sugar
½ cup water
¼ cup rich milk or water

4 squares unsweetened chocolate
½ teaspoon vanilla

Let sugar and water boil in a saucepan for five minutes. Cool partly and gradually stir in the chocolate which has been melted over hot water. Add the vanilla. Place in a double boiler or in a pan over hot water until ready to serve. At the last moment, add the milk. (If to be used with ice-cream, use water instead of milk.)

No. 2.

1 cup sugar
½ cup water
½ teaspoon vanilla

1 square chocolate
1 tablespoon butter

Mix together the sugar, water and grated chocolate. Boil for five minutes. Cool slightly and add the butter and vanilla.

COFFEE SAUCE

1 cup clear black coffee   3 egg-yolks   ⅓ cup sugar

Make a soft custard of the three ingredients. This is delicious for vanilla or lemon ice-cream.

CUSTARD SAUCE

Use recipe for soft custard (See Index). If a thinner sauce is desired, the custard may be thinned with a little cream.

FOAMY SAUCE

½ cup butter
1 cup confectioners' sugar
1 egg

2 tablespoons hot water
1 teaspoon vanilla

Cream the butter and gradually add the sugar, the egg, well beaten, and the hot water. Heat over hot water, beating continually until it thickens. Add the vanilla and serve.

HARD SAUCE

⅓ cup butter
1 cup powdered, granulated,
  brown or maple sugar

1 teaspoon vanilla or other
flavoring

Cream the butter until very soft, then stir in the sugar and the flavoring. Set in a cool place until required for use. A grating of lemon-rind or nutmeg, or a sprinkle of powdered cinnamon may be used instead of the vanilla. Cream or milk may be added, with more sugar to make more sauce. This sauce may be used with a hot pudding of any kind.

HONEY SAUCE

1 egg
½ cup honey
1 cup hot water

1½ tablespoons butter
½ lemon, juice and grated
  rind

Beat the egg, and add the other ingredients in the order given. Cook over hot water for about fifteen minutes, stirring constantly.

LEMON SAUCE

½ cup sugar
1 tablespoon corn-starch
2 tablespoons lemon-juice

Nutmeg   Salt
2 tablespoons butter
1 cup boiling water

Mix the sugar and corn-starch, add the boiling water and a pinch of salt and boil until thick and clear. Continue cooking over hot water for twenty minutes. Beat in the butter, the lemon-juice and nutmeg. A grating of lemon-rind may be added.

MAPLE SAUCE

½ cup water
½ cup walnut-meats

1 pound (2 cups) maple sugar
or 2 cups brown sugar

Add the water to the maple sugar and boil until it reaches the thread stage (230°-234° F.). Add the walnut-meats broken into small pieces. This sauce is good with ice-cream, blanc mange or custard. It may be used hot or cold.

MARSHMALLOW SAUCE

¾ cup sugar	½ pound marshmallows
¼ cup milk	2 tablespoons water

Boil the sugar and milk to the thread stage (230°-234° F.). Cool and beat until thick and white. Set in boiling water and stir until thin enough to pour. Stir the marshmallows with the water in a double boiler until smooth. Pour the sirup over the melted marshmallows and beat together. Keep warm, but not hot.

FRUIT MARSHMALLOW SAUCE

Thin commercial marshmallow whip with fruit-juice.

MARSHMALLOW MINT SAUCE

½ cup sugar	1 egg-white, beaten stiff
¼ cup water	1 drop oil of peppermint
8 marshmallows	Green coloring matter

Make a thin sirup of the sugar and water (220°-230° F.). Cut the marshmallows in quarters and add to the sirup. Pour the mixture over the egg-white gradually, beating vigorously. Add the flavoring and tint a delicate green. This sauce is excellent served with chocolate ice-cream.

MOLASSES SAUCE

1 cup molasses	1 tablespoon lemon-juice or
1½ tablespoons butter	vinegar

Boil the molasses with the butter for about five minutes. Remove from the fire and slowly stir in the lemon-juice or vinegar. This sauce is especially good with brown betty or Indian pudding.

ORANGE SAUCE

5 tablespoons butter	3 egg-whites
½ cup sugar	Juice of 2 oranges
½ cup boiling water	1½ tablespoons lemon-juice

Cream the butter with the sugar. Put into a saucepan over hot water and add the boiling water. Then beat in the stiffly beaten whites of the eggs, the orange-juice and lemon-juice and continue beating until light and foamy.

PLUM PUDDING SAUCE

¼ cup butter	2 eggs
1 cup powdered sugar	½ cup rich milk or cream
2 tablespoons cider	

Cream the butter and powdered sugar. Add the cider and the well-beaten yolks of the eggs. When well mixed, stir in the milk or cream. Cook in a double boiler until it is as thick as a custard and then gradually pour it into the beaten whites of the eggs, beating constantly.

RAISIN SAUCE

½ cup seeded raisins	¼ cup chopped citron
1 cup boiling water	1 teaspoon corn-starch
¾ cup sugar	1 tablespoon butter
½ teaspoon lemon-juice	

Simmer the raisins and citron in the water until the raisins are tender (about one hour). Sift the sugar and corn-starch together and add to the raisin mixture. Mix well and continue cooking for ten minutes. Add the butter and lemon-juice.

SUGAR BRITTLE

Stir one-fourth cup of sugar without any water in a saucepan over the fire until melted and of an amber color. Turn on to an oiled pan. When cold, pound in a mortar or in several folds of cloth. This may be sprinkled over any ice-cream.

STRAWBERRY OR OTHER BERRY SAUCE

No. 1.

2 cups berries	1 tablespoon granulated sugar
1 tablespoon butter	1 egg-white
1½ cups powdered sugar	

The small fruits such as strawberries, raspberries and blackberries, make most satisfactory sauce for desserts. Place the berries in a bowl, add the granulated sugar and mash slightly. Refrigerate until time to serve. Beat the butter to a cream, add the powdered sugar gradually, working it in well. Then add the egg-white, beaten stiff. Just before serving, combine with the mashed berries.

No. 2—Crush ripe berries in sugar.

VANILLA SAUCE

Use the recipe for lemon sauce (page 581) substituting one teaspoon vanilla for the lemon-juice and grated rind.

YELLOW SAUCE

1 egg
3 tablespoons sugar

3 tablespoons milk
½ teaspoon vanilla

Beat the white of the egg stiff, add the sugar, mix well and add the yolk of the egg, then the milk and flavoring, beating after each is added until the whole is smooth. This sauce is delicious on almost any pudding.

NEW ENGLAND NUTMEG SAUCE

1 cup sugar
1 tablespoon flour
2 cups boiling water

1 tablespoon butter
1 teaspoon nutmeg, grated
Salt

Mix well the sugar, flour and a pinch of salt. Add boiling water gradually, stirring continuously. Then add the butter and cook for five minutes. Remove from the fire and stir in the nutmeg. Serve hot on apple dumplings, bird's-nest or berry puddings that have been made with biscuit dough.

AVOCADO CREAM SAUCE

1 cup cream, whipped
½ cup powdered sugar
3 drops green vegetable coloring

⅛ teaspoon salt
¾ cup sieved avocado

Peel an avocado, remove pit, and force the pulp through a fine sieve. Whip the cream until stiff and add the sugar. Mix well. Add the salt and strained avocado and blend. Then add the food coloring. This dressing is delicious on fruit salads, baked apples or any hot dessert.

PASTRY AND MERINGUES

PASTRY may be defined as a stiff dough made very short by means of some kind of shortening. It is used for pies and tarts and for some other dishes. There are two kinds of pastry; plain pastry and puff pastry.

PLAIN PASTRY is usually used for pies and tarts.

PUFF PASTRY is used for tarts of various kinds, for cases, such as patty shells and vol-au-vents, to hold creamed mixtures, and for various shapes which are frosted or otherwise decorated for serving with afternoon tea or as desserts. It is not used for under crusts of pies because it rises or puffs up too much. It is used for rims where height is desirable, or for upper crusts of rich pies.

Pastry Making

Good pastry is flaky, tender, delicate and evenly browned. It is not crumbly, but when broken, shows layers of flat flakes, piled one above the other with air spaces between.

To achieve this result the cook must be quick and "light-handed," since pastry cannot be good if handled roughly or slowly. The flakiness of pastry is caused by many particles of shortening which are surrounded and separated by flour. During baking each shortening particle melts to form a delicate flake. However, rough, slow handling may cause these particles to melt and blend with the flour to form a solid mass, which is tough and hard after baking. See Shortenings and Fats, pages 21-26.

Everything Must Be Cold

Chilled ingredients are important for success and for the beginner even the flour may be chilled. A cold, solid shortening and ice water are essentials. Baking powder is sometimes used but with skillful mixing and handling of the dough it is unnecessary.

Sift flour and salt together, then add cold shortening and cut in as quickly as possible. A pastry blender is one of the best utensils to use for this purpose, although a quick job can be done with 2 knives. The fingers may be used by those able to work rapidly enough to work in the shortening before it starts to melt from the heat of the fingers. Distribute the shortening evenly through the flour, being sure not to neglect that at the bottom of the bowl. It has been mixed sufficiently when the largest pieces of shortening are the size of small peas. These particles roll out and melt into crisp flakes. The mixture may be placed in a clean jar, covered and kept in the refrigerator.

How Much Water

The greatest care is required when adding water. No definite amount can be specified since this varies with the dryness of the flour and the amount of shortening used. Usually 2 to 4 tablespoons water are required for 1 cup flour. Sprinkle the water a tablespoon at a time over the flour mixture while tossing it quickly with a fork. Avoid stirring or mixing that would crush shortening particles and blend them with the flour. Push moistened portions to one side before adding more water so a dry portion can be sprinkled each time. If allowed to do so, the shortening-flour mixture will absorb a great deal more water than should be used, so care must be taken to keep the moisture well distributed. Too much moisture makes the crust hard and brittle. Too little makes a crust which cracks at the edges while being rolled; it may crack open while baking and the pie be difficult to serve.

Be Swift and Deft

When moist enough to hold together under slight pressure, divide into halves, press each into a ball, flatten out with the hands and chill. If too little or too much water has been used, nothing can be done about it, except to profit by experience next time. Sprinkle board and rolling pin lightly with flour and rub into wood. A canvas cloth or coarse linen kitchen towel to cover the board and a "stocking" for the rolling pin are aids to the rolling out process, by preventing sticking without the use of too much flour. Excess flour on board and pin make the crust hard. Roll quickly but lightly since heavy pressure makes the pastry stick and breaks the surface. Start each stroke at center of dough and roll to edge, keeping pastry in as circular a shape as possible and keeping edges as thick as the center. Lift and turn pastry occasionally to make sure it is not sticking and rub extra flour over board if necessary. Keep all particles of dough cleaned from uncovered rolling pin since the pastry being rolled will stick to these more readily than to the wood. Roll out to $\frac{1}{8}$-inch thickness for lower crust; roll top crust slightly thinner. Place pastry in pans and bake as directed.

Piecrust mixtures, containing all ingredients, except the water can now be purchased. They are valuable for the small family.

About the Filling

When filling for a two-crust pie is very juicy some precautions are necessary to prevent it from boiling over. The top crust should be well slashed to allow steam to escape. Some get good results by inserting paper funnels or several 3-inch lengths of uncooked macaroni through the slashes into the filling to act as "chimneys." The edge of the pie may be bound with an inch-wide strip of muslin dipped into water, or with paper pie tape used as directed on the package. A little flour paste will hold the ends together. Remove strip when pie is baked. Another method is to cut the top crust ½ inch larger than necessary and turn the excess under the moistened edge of the under crust. Or cut bottom crust ½ inch larger and turn it over the top crust. When these are firmly pressed together a tight seal is made. A little flour, cornstarch or tapioca mixed with sugar thickens the juice.

PLAIN PASTRY

2 cups sifted flour	⅔ cup shortening
¾ teaspoon salt	4 to 6 tablespoons cold water

Sift flour and salt together and cut in shortening with 2 knives or pastry blender. Add water, using only a small portion at a time, until mixture will hold together. Divide dough into 2 parts. Roll out on floured board to desired size. Line the piepan with one piece of dough, being careful not to stretch dough. After filling is placed in pastry, dampen edges of lower crust with cold water and cover with remaining dough which has been rolled out and slashed in several places to allow steam to escape while baking. Press edges together with prongs of fork and bake according to recipe for filling selected. Makes 2 (9-inch) shells or one 2-crust (9-inch) pie.

PASTRY SHELL—Roll ½ of the dough ⅛ inch thick, fold in half and lift into piepan. Do not stretch dough. After crust is fitted, trim edges evenly, leaving a 1-inch overhanging border, fold dough under and back to make an upright rim, then flute edges using thumb and index finger of one hand and the index finger of the other hand. Prick crust thoroughly with a fork and use one of the following methods to prevent shrinkage of crust.

OFF TO A GOOD START CUTTING IN THE SHORTENING AND ICE WATER

A LIGHT TOUCH AND NOT TOO MUCH OF IT, IN THE KNEADING AND ROLLING

FILLED WITH
JUICY FRUIT
AND COVERED
WITH A BLAN-
KET OF PAT-
TERNED CRUST

FINISHING
TOUCHES—
SNUGLY RUF-
FLED AND
LIGHTLY
BRUSHED

TO PREVENT SHRINKAGE OF CRUST

Place rolled dough in pan and set aside for 5 minutes, then fit into place with a ball of dough.

Line pastry shell with waxed paper and partially fill with rice or beans, remove paper after first 10 minutes of baking.

Fit a second pan inside on crust, remove pan after first 10 minutes. Bake in a very hot oven (450° F.) about 15 minutes or until delicately browned. (See illustration Page 594A.)

PASTRY FORMS

TARTS—Cut pastry into rounds to fit muffin or tart pans and proceed as for pies. Makes 4 (2-crust) or 8 single tarts.

TART SHELLS—Cut pastry into rounds to fit muffin or tart pans and proceed as for Pastry Shell, or shape pastry over the back of muffin or tart pans, trim edge and prick thoroughly with a fork. Makes 8 shells.

PASTRY WHEELS—Combine leftover scraps of dough; roll out, sprinkle with cinnamon and sugar and roll up tightly. Slice into tiny circles and bake in hot oven.

HOT WATER PASTRY

2 cups sifted flour
½ teaspoon baking powder
1 teaspoon salt

⅓ cup boiling water
⅔ cup shortening

Sift flour, baking powder and salt together. Pour water over shortening and mix with fork until creamy, add flour mixture and mix into a dough. Chill thoroughly and proceed as for Plain Pastry. Makes 1 (9-inch) double crust pie or 2 (9-inch) shells.

SOUTHERN PASTRY

2 cups sifted flour
½ teaspoon salt .

1 cup shortening
6 tablespoons ice water

Mix flour and salt, cut shortening into flour; add water a tablespoon at a time, using only enough to make a workable paste; too little will leave it crumbly. This pastry, being exceedingly rich, must be handled deftly. Roll out pastry and line piepan. Makes 2 (9-inch) pastry shells or pastry for 1 two-crust (9-inch) pie.

Thorough chilling before rolling makes pastry easier to handle.

DECORATIONS

Roll out Plain, Southern, Cheese or Hot Water Pastry according to directions and cut out any of the following designs with cookie cutters or cardboard patterns, leave plain or decorate as suggested below. Bake in very hot oven (450° F.) about 10 minutes. Top any open-faced pie or tart.

CAT OR OTHER ANIMALS—After baking, mark to suggest features, using melted chocolate, colored sugar, nut meats, candied or dried fruits.

CHICK—After pastry is baked, mark features using a toothpick and melted chocolate.

CHRISTMAS TREE—Mark to suggest branches and decorate with green sugar.

CRESCENT—Sprinkle with colored sugar.

CROWN—Cut rounds with large scalloped cutter and cut out out center with medium cutter.

FLAG—Mark to suggest stars and stripes and decorate with red, white and blue sugar.

HATCHET—Press cutting edge to make it thin and sprinkle red sugar over handle.

HEART—Sprinkle red sugar over all or only on edges. Arrange heart-shaped candies on pastry.

HEARTS, CLUBS, SPADES AND DIAMONDS—Sprinkle colored sugar over top.

PUMPKIN—Mark ribs and sprinkle stem with green sugar.

SANTA CLAUS—Mark features and decorate with red sugar.

SHAMROCK—Sprinkle green sugar over all or only on edges.

STAR—Use colored sugar.

TURKEY—Sprinkle with cinnamon and sugar.

WITCH—Mark features.

CHEESE PASTRY

½ cup butter
1 cup sifted flour

¼ pound cottage or cream
cheese

Cut butter into flour; add cheese and mix to a smooth dough. Chill thoroughly. Roll and proceed as for Plain Pastry. Makes 1 (9-inch) pastry shell.

PUFF PASTE

1 cup butter   ½ cup ice water
2 cups sifted cake flour

Wash butter in cold water to remove salt. Allow ⅔ of butter to become soft. Cut remaining butter into flour with 2 knives or a pastry blender; add ice water using only enough to hold ingredients together. Roll out to ¼-inch thickness on a lightly floured board, making a square sheet. Spread ⅔ of dough with ¼ of softened butter; fold unbuttered ⅓ over center ⅓ and fold remaining ⅓ over to cover first ⅓, buttered side down, making 3 layers of dough with butter between each layer. Turn dough ¼ of way around on board and roll to about ¼-inch thickness. Spread with butter. Fold as before and chill thoroughly. Roll, spread with butter, fold and chill 2 more times. Roll, shape and bake as directed in recipes using Puff Paste. Bake at once or wrap in waxed paper and chill 12 to 24 hours. Makes 15 to 24 fancy pastries.

PATTY SHELLS

Roll puff paste ¼ inch thick, cut into 3-inch rounds with floured cutter. Cut out centers from half of rounds with a small cutter; moisten underside of each ring with cold water and place one on each remaining plain round, pressing down lightly. Bake in very hot oven (450° F.) for 10 minutes, reduce to 400° F. bake 5 minutes, then reduce to 350° F. and bake 15 minutes longer.

VOL-AU-VENT

Roll puff paste 1½ inches thick and cut a circle about 6 inches in diameter, using a cutter or, with a sharp knife, cutting around the edge of a plate placed on the paste. Place circle on a baking sheet and, with a sharp pointed knife or a smaller cutter, cut a circle around the top about 1½ inches from the edge and 1 inch deep. Do not remove the center but bake entire circle in a very hot oven (450° F.) about 8 minutes, reduce temperature to 350° F. and bake 30 minutes longer. When the outer crust is baked, lift out center and remove uncooked paste from below. Place top upside down and place in oven a few minutes to dry.

Fill with any kind of sweetened fresh berries or fruit, creamed fish, fowl or meat. Replace top and sprinkle with confectioners' sugar, if using fruit.

CRUMB PIE SHELL

1½ cups fine crumbs   ½ cup butter, melted
¼ cup sugar

Mix crumbs and sugar together; stir in butter. Line piepan with mixture by pressing it firmly into place. Chill for 20 minutes or bake in moderate oven (350° F.) 10 minutes. Cool. Makes 1 (9-inch) shell.

CINNAMON—Add ½ teaspoon cinnamon to bread or graham cracker crumbs.

Use crumbs of the following: Chocolate Cookies; Cereal Flakes; Gingersnaps; Graham Crackers; Toasted Bread; Vanilla Wafers; Zwieback.

BRAZIL-NUT—Omit crumbs and butter and use 1⅔ cups ground Brazil nuts. Proceed as above.

ALMOND PASTRY

1½ cups sifted flour   ½ cup shortening
¼ cup ground almonds   1 egg, beaten
¼ cup sugar   Cold water
½ teaspoon salt

Mix first 4 ingredients and cut in shortening. Add egg and cold water to make stiff dough. Chill, roll and bake as for plain pastry.

MÜRBE TEIG FOR PIES

1 cup sifted flour   ¼ cup butter
⅛ teaspoon salt   1 egg yolk, slightly beaten
1 tablespoon sugar

Combine flour, salt and sugar. Cut in butter with 2 knives or a pastry blender. Add egg yolk and mix thoroughly. Press into a pie plate or spring-form pan to ¼-inch thickness. Fill with a fruit filling. Bake in hot oven (425° F.) 10 minutes, reduce temperature to 350° F. and bake until fruit is cooked. Makes 1 (9-inch) shell.

CHEESE STICKS

Use ½ recipe Plain Pastry. Roll out ¼ inch thick, sprinkle half with ⅓ cup grated cheese and fold over other half. Roll out 2 more times, sprinkling with cheese each time. Cut into strips and bake on an ungreased baking sheet in a hot oven, (425° F.) about 10 minutes or until delicately browned.

SUET PASTRY

1 teaspoon baking powder	1 cup chopped suet
2 cups sifted flour	1 cup cold water
½ teaspoon salt	

This pastry is excellent for boiled fruit pudding and dumplings or for baked or boiled meat pies. All the ingredients must be very cold. Sift baking powder with flour, add salt, suet and water and mix into a smooth, firm dough. Chill and roll out. Makes one 2-crust (9-inch) pie or 2 (9-inch) shells.

APPLE PIE

6 apples	2 tablespoons flour
½ to ⅔ cup sugar	1 recipe Plain Pastry
¼ teaspoon salt	1 tablespoon butter

Pare and slice apples. Sift dry ingredients together and mix with apples. Line piepan with pastry, fill with apple mixture, dot with butter and cover with top crust. Bake in very hot oven (450° F.) 15 minutes; reduce temperature to moderate (350° F.) and bake 45 minutes longer. Makes 1 (9-inch) pie.

VARIATION—Add 1 teaspoon cinnamon to dry ingredients.

ENGLISH DEEP-DISH APPLE PIE

1 recipe Plain Pastry	1 teaspoon cinnamon or
6 to 8 tart apples	nutmeg
⅔ cup sugar	¼ cup water
	1 teaspoon butter

Invert a heavy china cup or custard cup in the center of a baking dish, 2 or 3 inches deep. Line sides of dish with pastry, letting it extend a little above the dish. Do not line the bottom with pastry. Pare and core apples and cut into slices. Add sugar, spice and water and dot with butter. Cover apples with pastry, slash the top to let steam escape and pinch edges of pastry together. Bake in very hot oven (450° F.) for 10 minutes; reduce temperature to 350° F. and bake 45 minutes longer. When serving, slip the knife under cup to let the confined juice mix with apples. Serve in wedges with hard sauce. Serves 6.

VARIATION—Use 2 recipes Cheese Pastry or 2 recipes Mürbe Teig for Pies instead of Plain Pastry.

Use fresh peaches, apricots or pears instead of apples.

APPLE MERINGUE PIE

3 cups sweetened applesauce
1 teaspoon nutmeg
1 baked Cheese Pastry Shell
3 egg whites

3 tablespoons confectioners'
sugar
½ teaspoon vanilla

Combine applesauce and nutmeg. Turn into pastry shell. Beat egg whites until stiff; fold in sugar and vanilla. Cover applesauce and bake in a slow oven (325°F.) 20 minutes or until browned. Serve cold. Makes 1 (9-inch) pie.

DAINTY APPLE PIE

3 cups sliced tart apples
2½ cups canned grapefruit
juice
1 Graham Cracker Pie Shell
½ cup sugar

3 tablespoons cornstarch
Whipped cream
8 maraschino cherries,
chopped

Cook apples in grapefruit juice until tender. Arrange apples in pie shell. Mix sugar and cornstarch, add to juice and cook until clear and thickened. Pour over apples. Cool. Cover with whipped cream and sprinkle with cherries. Makes 1 (9-inch) pie.

BLACKBERRY PIE

3 cups fresh blackberries
1 cup sugar
2 tablespoons flour
2 tablespoons lemon juice

⅛ teaspoon salt
1 recipe Plain Pastry
1 tablespoon butter

Combine berries, sugar, flour, lemon juice and salt. Line piepan with pastry, add filling, dot with butter and cover with top crust. Bake in very hot oven (450° F.) 10 minutes; reduce temperature to moderate (350° F.) and bake 25 to 30 minutes longer or until berries are tender. Makes 1 (9-inch) pie.

BOILED CIDER PIE

Line piepan with Plain Pastry. Dissolve ⅓ cup grated maple sugar by heating with ⅓ cup rich boiled cider. Add eggs slowly, stirring constantly and cook until thickened. Add ½ teaspoon nutmeg, 1 teaspoon butter and ½ cup seeded raisins. Pour into pastry-lined pan, cover with meringue and bake as directed. Makes 1 (9-inch) pie.

BLUEBERRY PIE

4 cups blueberries
1 cup sugar
4 tablespoons flour

⅛ teaspoon salt
1½ tablespoons lemon juice
1 recipe Plain Pastry

Mix berries with sugar, flour, salt and lemon juice. Line pie-pan with pastry, pour in filling and cover with top crust. Bake in very hot oven (450° F.) 10 minutes; reduce temperature to moderate (350° F.) and bake 20 to 30 minutes longer. Makes 1 (9-inch) pie.

FRESH CHERRY PIE

1¼ cups sugar
2½ tablespoons flour
¼ teaspoon salt

1 quart tart red cherries,
    washed and pitted
1 recipe Plain Pastry

Mix sugar, flour, salt and cherries together. Line piepan with pastry, add cherry mixture and cover with top crust. Bake in very hot oven (450° F.) 10 minutes; reduce temperature to moderate (350° F.); bake 25 minutes longer. Makes 1 (9-inch) pie.

VARIATIONS—Decrease flour to 1 tablespoon and add 2 tablespoons quick-cooking tapioca. Dot cherries with 1 tablespoon butter.

For a pie with a clearer filling use 1¼ tablespoons cornstarch instead of the flour listed.

Use 2 recipes Cheese Pastry instead of Plain Pastry.

CRANBERRY PIE

4 cups cranberries
1½ cups sugar
2 tablespoons flour
¼ teaspoon salt

3 tablespoons water
1 tablespoon melted butter
1 recipe Plain Pastry

Wash berries, chop and mix with next 5 ingredients. Line piepan with pastry, pour in filling and arrange strips of pastry over top in lattice design. Bake in very hot oven (450° F.) 15 minutes; reduce temperature to moderate (350° F.) and bake about 30 minutes longer. Makes 1 (9-inch) pie.

CRANBERRY AND APPLE—Use 2 cups cranberries and 1½ cups chopped apples instead of 4 cups cranberries.

A DOUBLE PLATE, BEANS, RICE OR VEGE- TABLE TAPE WILL KEEP YOUR PIECRUSTS IN GOOD SHAPE WHILE BAKING

THIS PIE IS AIR CON- DITIONED WITH A LATTICEWORK TOP CRUST

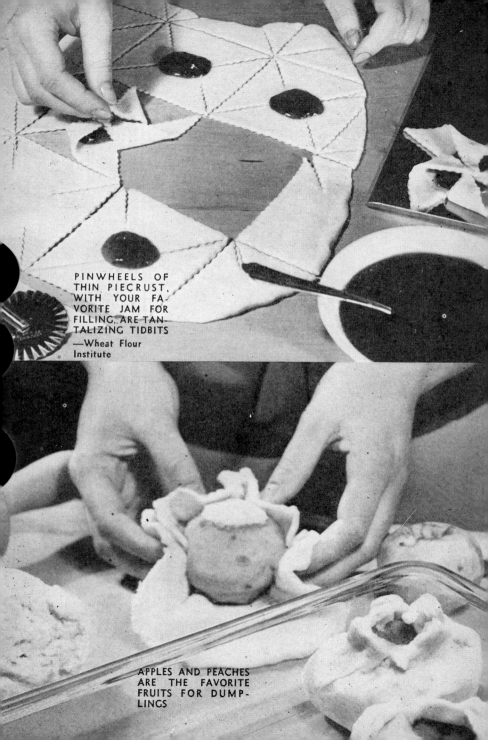

PINWHEELS OF
THIN PIECRUST,
WITH YOUR FA-
VORITE JAM FOR
FILLING, ARE TAN-
TALIZING TIDBITS
—Wheat Flour
Institute

APPLES AND PEACHES
ARE THE FAVORITE
FRUITS FOR DUMP-
LINGS

CURRANT PIE

1 cup fresh ripe currants	¼ cup flour
2 egg yolks	1 tablespoon water
1 cup sugar	1 recipe Cheese Pastry
¼ teaspoon salt	1 recipe Meringue

Wash currants and stem. Beat egg yolks slightly; add sugar, salt, flour, water and currants. Line piepan with pastry and pour in filling. Bake in moderate oven (350° F.) 35 minutes or until filling is firm. Cover with meringue and proceed as directed. Makes 1 (9-inch) pie.

GRAPE PIE—Use 2 cups seeded Concord grapes instead of currants; omit flour.

LOGANBERRY PIE

3½ cups cooked loganberries	½ cup loganberry juice
1 tablespoon butter	1 baked Pastry Shell
⅛ teaspoon salt	1 recipe Meringue
1½ tablespoons cornstarch	

Combine berries, butter and salt; heat to boiling. Mix cornstarch and juice together, add to berries and cook slowly until thickened, stirring constantly. Cool. Pour into pastry shell, cover with meringue; bake as directed. Makes 1 (9-inch) pie.

BLACK OR RED RASPBERRY—Use canned or cooked black or red raspberries for loganberries. Proceed as above.

YOUNGBERRY—Use cooked or canned youngberries for loganberries, omit meringue and cover with whipped cream.

MINCE PIE

1 recipe Plain Pastry	2½ cups mincemeat

Line piepan with pastry, fill with mincemeat and cover with top crust. Bake in hot oven (400° F.) about 35 minutes or until pastry is browned. Makes 1 (9-inch) pie. Serve hot.

MINCEMEAT TARTS—Line tart pans with pastry, fill with mincemeat, cover with pastry strips and bake.

MINCEMEAT TURNOVERS—Cut rolled pastry into squares and place tablespoon of mincemeat on each. Moisten edges, fold to form triangles and seal firmly. Prick with fork and bake.

PEACH PIE

1 cup sugar
2 tablespoons flour
¼ teaspoon salt

8 peaches, sliced
1 recipe Plain Pastry

Sift dry ingredients together and mix with peaches. Line pie-pan with pastry, fill with peach mixture and cover with top crust. Bake in very hot oven (450° F.) 15 minutes; reduce temperature to moderate (350° F.) and bake 35 minutes longer. Makes 1 (9-inch) pie.

PINEAPPLE PIE

2 eggs
1⅓ cups sugar
1 tablespoon lemon juice

2 cups shredded fresh pine-apple
1 recipe Plain Pastry
1 tablespoon butter

Beat eggs slightly, add sugar, lemon juice and pineapple. Line piepan with pastry, pour in filling, dot with butter and cover with top crust. Bake in very hot oven (450° F.) 10 minutes; reduce temperature to moderate (350° F.) and bake 35 minutes longer or until pineapple is tender. Makes 1 (9-inch) pie.

CANNED PINEAPPLE—Use 2 cups canned shredded pineapple instead of fresh and only ½ cup sugar.

PINEAPPLE AND STRAWBERRY—Use 1 cup grated fresh pine-apple and 1 cup sliced strawberries.

PLUM PIE

3 cups pitted fresh plums
1¼ cups sugar
2 tablespoons flour
2 tablespoons lemon juice

⅛ teaspoon salt
1 recipe Plain Pastry
1 tablespoon butter

Combine plums, sugar, flour, lemon juice and salt. Line pie-pan with pastry, add filling, dot with butter and cover with top crust. Bake in very hot oven (450° F.) 10 minutes; reduce temperature to moderate (350° F.) and bake 35 minutes longer or until plums are tender. Makes 1 (9-inch) pie.

PRUNE—Use 2½ cups quartered cooked prunes for plums. Reduce sugar to ½ cup. Omit flour and add 1½ tablespoons prune juice. Proceed as for plum pie.

RAISIN PIE

1/3 cup lemon juice	2 cups seeded raisins
1 teaspoon grated lemon rind	1 3/4 cups water
1/2 cup orange juice	6 tablespoons flour
2 teaspoons grated orange rind	1 recipe Hot Water Pastry
1 cup brown sugar	

Combine lemon juice and rind, orange juice and rind, sugar, raisins and 1 1/4 cups water and heat to boiling. Mix flour and remaining 1/2 cup water to a smooth paste and add to mixture gradually, stirring constantly. Cook 5 minutes. Line piepan with pastry, pour in filling and cover with top crust. Bake in hot oven (400° F.) 40 minutes. Makes 1 (9-inch) pie.

RHUBARB PIE

3 tablespoons flour	2 cups rhubarb cut into small
1 cup sugar	pieces
1 egg, beaten	1 recipe Plain Pastry

Sift flour and sugar together, add egg, beat thoroughly and add rhubarb. Line piepan with pastry and pour in filling. Cover with top crust or lattice and bake in very hot oven (425° F.) 10 minutes; reduce temperature to moderate (350° F.) and bake 35 minutes longer. Makes 1 (9-inch) pie.

FRUIT SALAD PIE

Soften 2 teaspoons gelatin in 3 tablespoons orange juice; dissolve over hot water. Mix with 3 cups diced, sweetened fresh fruits. Pour into chilled Crumb Pie Shell; cover with sweetened whipped cream. Makes 1 (9-inch) pie.

STRAWBERRY PIE

1 cup sugar	3 cups fresh strawberries
1 tablespoon cornstarch	1 recipe Plain Pastry
1/8 teaspoon salt	1 tablespoon butter

Mix sugar, cornstarch and salt together and add to berries. Line piepan with pastry, add filling, dot with butter and cover with top crust. Bake in very hot oven (450° F.) 10 minutes; reduce temperature to moderate (350° F.) and bake 30 minutes longer. Makes 1 (9-inch) pie.

RASPBERRY—Use fresh raspberries instead of strawberries.

BUTTERSCOTCH PIE

¾ cup brown sugar
5 tablespoons flour
½ teaspoon salt
2 cups milk
2 egg yolks, slightly beaten

2 tablespoons butter
1 teaspoon vanilla
1 baked Pastry Shell
Whipped cream

Combine sugar, flour and salt and stir in milk slowly. Cook over boiling water until thickened, stirring constantly. Cover and cook 10 minutes longer, stirring occasionally. Add mixture to egg yolks, stirring vigorously; cook 1 minute longer. Add butter and vanilla and cool. Place filling in pastry shell and cover with whipped cream. Makes 1 (8-inch) pie.

BANANA BUTTERSCOTCH—Peel and slice 3 bananas and arrange in layers with filling in butterscotch pie.

CREAM PIE

1½ cups milk
¼ cup sugar
¼ teaspoon salt
3 tablespoons flour
1 egg yolk

1 tablespoon butter
½ teaspoon vanilla
1 baked Pastry Shell
Whipped cream

Scald 1 cup milk over boiling water. Mix sugar, salt, flour and remaining milk together. Stir into hot milk and cook slowly until thickened, stirring constantly. Cover and cook over boiling water for 5 minutes. Add mixture slowly to egg yolk and cook 1 minute longer. Add butter and vanilla. Cool. Pour into pastry shell and spread with whipped cream. Makes 1 (8-inch) pie.

VARIATIONS—Any crumb pie shell may be used instead of baked pastry shell. For 9-inch pie use 2 cups milk and 3 egg yolks, or 1 of the following variations:

BANANA—Use 4 ripe bananas. Fill pastry shell with alternate layers of sliced bananas and cooled filling.

CHOCOLATE—Add 1 ounce (square) chocolate, melted, and 2 tablespoons sugar.

COCONUT—Stir 1½ cups moist shredded coconut into filling.

FRUIT—Stir 1½ cups drained canned fruit salad and a few slices of banana into filling.

BLACK WALNUT PIE

1 cup sugar
6 tablespoons flour
1/4 teaspoon salt
2 egg yolks, beaten
2 cups milk
1 teaspoon vanilla

2 teaspoons butter
1 cup black walnut meats chopped
1 Graham Cracker Pie Shell
1 recipe Meringue

Sift sugar, flour and salt together and add to egg yolks; add milk and cook over boiling water until thickened. Add vanilla and butter. Cool. Add nut meats and pour into crumb shell. Spread with meringue; bake as directed. Makes 1 (9-inch) pie.

COFFEE CREAM PIE

1/4 cup flour
1/8 teaspoon salt
2/3 cup sugar
1 cup strong coffee
1 cup milk

2 egg yolks
2 tablespoons butter
1 Brazil-Nut Pie Shell
1 recipe Meringue

Mix flour, salt and sugar thoroughly; add coffee and milk and cook until thickened, stirring constantly. Stir slowly into beaten egg yolks and cook 1 minute longer. Add butter. Cool. Pour into pie shell, top with meringue and proceed as directed. Makes 1 (9-inch) pie.

LEMON MERINGUE PIE—Omit coffee and milk. Use 1 1/2 cups boiling water and 1/3 cup lemon juice. Add 1 tablespoon grated lemon rind. Use 1/4 cup cornstarch instead of flour, increase sugar to 1 cup. Proceed as above. Use Baked Pastry Shell.

SOUR CREAM PIE

1/2 cup flour
3/4 cup sugar
1/2 teaspoon salt
2 cups sour cream

3 egg yolks
1/4 teaspoon almond extract
1 baked Cheese Pastry Shell
1 recipe Meringue

Mix flour, sugar and salt together; stir in cream and cook in top of double boiler until thickened, stirring constantly. Pour hot mixture slowly over egg yolks, stirring constantly. Return to heat and cook 3 minutes longer. Add flavoring and cool. Pour into pastry shell, top with meringue and proceed as directed. Makes 1 (9-inch) pie.

CUSTARD PIE

4 eggs, slightly beaten	½ teaspoon vanilla
¼ teaspoon salt	½ recipe Plain Pastry
½ cup sugar	Nutmeg
3 cups milk, scalded	

Combine eggs, salt and sugar; add milk and vanilla slowly. Line piepan with pastry, pour in filling and sprinkle with nutmeg. Bake in very hot oven (450° F.) 10 minutes. Reduce temperature to slow (325° F.) and bake 30 to 40 minutes longer, or until a knife inserted comes out clean. Makes 1 (9-inch) pie.

CARAMEL—Caramelize sugar and add to scalded milk before combining milk with egg mixture.

COCONUT—Add 1 cup shredded coconut to custard before baking.

MODERN CUSTARD—Use 1 baked Pastry Shell in place of pastry. Pour custard into well-greased piepan of same size as used for pastry shell. Bake in slow oven (325° F.) 45 to 55 minutes, or until knife inserted in center comes out clean. Chill thoroughly. Place waxed paper on top of custard, a cookie sheet on paper and turn upside down, leaving custard on sheet. Remove piepan and invert pastry shell and its piepan over custard. Turn right-side up. This method keeps crust crisp.

BARBARA FRIETCHIE PIE

½ recipe Southern Pastry	2 tablespoons butter
¾ cup granulated sugar	½ teaspoon vanilla
¾ cup brown sugar	⅛ teaspoon salt
½ cup heavy cream or evaporated milk	2 egg whites, beaten
2 egg yolks, beaten	Nutmeg

Line piepan with pastry. Cook next 5 ingredients in top of double boiler until thickened, stirring constantly. Remove from heat, add vanilla, salt and egg whites. Pour into pastry shell, sprinkle with nutmeg. Bake in hot oven (425° F.) 10 minutes, reduce temperature to slow (300° F.) and bake about 45 minutes longer or until a knife inserted in center comes out clean. Serve very cold. Makes 1 (9-inch) pie.

Omit pastry and use Brazil-nut Pie Shell.

DATE—Add 1 cup chopped dates and reduce granulated sugar to ¼ cup. Omit nutmeg and increase vanilla to 1 teaspoon.

NUT—Add 1 cup broken nut meats to filling.

ORANGE CHIFFON PIE

1 tablespoon unflavored
  gelatin
1/4 cup cold water
4 eggs, separated
1 cup sugar
1/2 cup orange juice

1 tablespoon lemon juice
1/2 teaspoon salt
1 tablespoon grated orange
  rind
1 Cereal Flake Pie Shell
Whipped cream

Soften gelatin in water 5 minutes. Beat egg yolks and add 1/2 cup sugar, orange juice, lemon juice and salt. Cook over boiling water until of custard consistency. Add grated orange rind and softened gelatin and stir thoroughly. Cool. When mixture begins to thicken fold in stiffly beaten egg whites to which remaining 1/2 cup of sugar has been added. Fill crumb shell and chill. Spread with whipped cream. Makes 1 (9-inch) pie.

CHERRY—Omit orange juice and rind and 1/3 cup sugar. Use 1/2 cup cherry juice and 1 cup drained canned tart cherries.

GRAPEFRUIT—Use grapefruit juice instead of orange juice.

GRAPEFRUIT AND ORANGE—Use 1/3 cup grapefruit juice and 1/4 cup orange juice instead of orange juice and lemon juice.

LEMON—Use 1/2 cup lemon juice and 1 teaspoon grated lemon rind instead of orange juice and rind.

LIME—Use 1/2 cup lime juice instead of orange juice.

PINEAPPLE—Use 2/3 cup canned pineapple juice and only 1/2 cup sugar. Omit orange rind.

STRAWBERRY—Omit orange juice and rind. Combine 1 cup diced strawberries with the first 1/2 cup sugar and allow to stand 1 hour. Strain juice and use instead of orange juice.

PINEAPPLE FLUFF PIE

2 1/2 tablespoons cornstarch
1/2 cup water
1 cup pineapple juice
3/4 cup sugar
1 cup drained crushed pineapple

3 egg whites
1/4 teaspoon salt
1 Chocolate Cookie Shell
Whipped cream

Blend cornstarch and water. Add pineapple juice and 1/2 cup sugar and cook slowly until thickened, stirring constantly. Add pineapple and cook a few minutes longer. Combine egg whites and salt and beat until foamy; add remaining sugar gradually, beating until stiff. Fold into pineapple mixture and pour into crumb shell. Cool. Spread with whipped cream. Makes 1 (9-inch) pie.

BANANA CHIFFON PIE

2 teaspoons unflavored
  gelatin
3 tablespoons cold water
1 cup mashed bananas
1 tablespoon lemon juice
½ teaspoon grated lemon rind

⅛ teaspoon grated orange
  rind
5 tablespoons sugar
2 eggs, separated
⅛ teaspoon salt
1 Brazil-Nut Pie Shell
Whipped cream

Soften gelatin in water 5 minutes. Combine banana, lemon juice and rind, orange rind, 3 tablespoons sugar, slightly beaten egg yolks and salt; cook slowly until consistency of soft custard, stirring constantly. Remove from heat, add gelatin and stir until dissolved. Cool until slightly thickened. Beat egg whites until stiff, beat in remaining sugar and fold into banana mixture. Pour into pie shell and chill until firm. Spread with whipped cream. Makes 1 (9-inch) pie.

PUMPKIN CHIFFON PIE

2 teaspoons unflavored gelatin
¼ cup cold water
3 eggs, separated
1 cup sugar
1¼ cups mashed cooked
  pumpkin
½ teaspoon salt

½ teaspoon cinnamon
¼ teaspoon nutmeg
½ teaspoon ginger
½ cup milk
1 Gingersnap Pie Shell
Whipped cream

Soften gelatin in water 5 minutes. Beat egg yolks and add ½ cup sugar, pumpkin, salt, spices and milk. Cook over low heat, stirring constantly until mixture begins to thicken. Add gelatin to hot pumpkin and stir until dissolved. Cool. When mixture begins to thicken, beat egg whites until almost stiff and beat in remaining sugar, 1 tablespoon at a time. Fold into pumpkin mixture, pour into pie shell and chill until firm. Cover with whipped cream. Makes 1 (9-inch) pie.

DREAM PIE

3 egg whites
¼ cup sugar
1½ cups chopped dates

1 tablespoon lemon juice
1 teaspoon vanilla
1 baked Toasted Bread Shell

Beat egg whites until stiff but not dry. Beat in sugar gradually. Fold in dates, lemon juice and vanilla and pour into crumb shell. Bake at 325° F. 25 to 30 minutes. Makes 1 (9-inch) pie.

RHUBARB WHIPPED CREAM PIE

2 tablespoons unflavored gelatin	1 cup sugar
½ cup cold water	1 cup heavy cream, whipped
2½ cups stewed rhubarb	1 Cereal Flake Pie Shell

Soften gelatin in water. Heat rhubarb and sugar to boiling, add gelatin and stir until dissolved. Cool; when mixture begins to thicken fold in whipped cream. Pour into pie shell and chill. Makes 1 (9-inch) pie.

TOFFEE CHIFFON PIE

1 tablespoon unflavored gelatin	2 eggs, separated
¼ cup cold water	½ teaspoon vanilla
2 cups hot milk	¾ cup crushed pecan toffee
⅛ teaspoon salt	1 Zwieback Pie Shell
⅓ cup sugar	Pecan toffee shavings

Soften gelatin in water 5 minutes. Combine milk, salt and 4 tablespoons sugar; stir until dissolved. Add to slightly beaten egg yolks and cook over boiling water until thickened, stirring constantly. Add gelatin and stir until dissolved. Cool. Add vanilla and toffee when custard begins to thicken. Beat egg whites until stiff, add remaining sugar and fold into custard. Fill crumb shell and chill. Sprinkle with toffee shavings. Makes 1 (9-inch) pie.

SHERRY—Use almond extract instead of vanilla; add 2 tablespoons sherry and use ¼ cup chopped almonds instead of toffee and toffee shavings.

PRUNE CHIFFON PIE

1 tablespoon unflavored gelatin	¼ teaspoon salt
¼ cup cold water	2 tablespoons lemon juice
1 cup chopped cooked prunes	1 teaspoon grated lemon rind
¾ cup prune juice	2 egg whites, stiffly beaten
½ cup sugar	1 baked Pastry Shell

Soften gelatin in water 5 minutes. Combine prunes, juice, sugar, salt, lemon juice and rind, and heat to boiling. Remove from heat, add gelatin and stir until dissolved. Cool. When slightly thickened, fold in egg whites. Pour into pastry shell and chill. Makes 1 (9-inch) pie.

PUMPKIN PIE

⅛ teaspoon salt
⅔ cup sugar
2 teaspoons pumpkin pie spice
2 eggs, slightly beaten

1⅔ cups milk
1½ cups mashed cooked
  pumpkin
½ recipe Plain Pastry

Sift dry ingredients together and stir into eggs. Add milk and pumpkin. Line piepan with pastry and pour in filling. Bake in very hot oven (450° F.) 10 minutes; reduce temperature to slow (325° F.) and bake 35 minutes longer or until knife inserted in center comes out clean. Cool. Makes 1 (9-inch) pie.

VARIATION—Use 1 teaspoon cinnamon, ¼ teaspoon nutmeg and ½ teaspoon ginger instead of pumpkin pie spice.

SQUASH PIE

1 cup sugar
¾ teaspoon salt
1 teaspoon cinnamon
1 teaspoon nutmeg
¾ teaspoon ginger
¼ teaspoon mace

1 cup steamed squash,
  strained
3 eggs
1 cup heavy cream or evaporated milk
½ recipe Plain Pastry

Add sugar, salt and spices to squash and mix thoroughly. Beat eggs, add cream and mix with squash. Line piepan with pastry and pour in filling. Bake in very hot oven (450° F.) 10 minutes, then reduce temperature to moderate (350° F.) and bake 40 minutes longer or until knife inserted in center comes out clean. Makes 1 (9-inch) pie.

SWEET POTATO PIE

½ cup sugar
¼ teaspoon salt
1 teaspoon cinnamon
1 teaspoon nutmeg
½ teaspoon ginger

2 cups steamed sweet potato,
  strained
1 cup milk
2 eggs, slightly beaten
½ recipe Plain Pastry

Combine dry ingredients and mix with sweet potato. Mix milk and eggs and combine with sweet potato mixture. Line piepan with pastry and pour in filling. Bake in a very hot oven (450° F.) 10 minutes, then reduce temperature to 350° F. and bake 35 minutes longer. Makes 1 (9-inch) pie.

CHEESE PIE

1½ recipes Zwieback Pie Shell
4 eggs
1 cup sugar
⅛ teaspoon salt
1½ tablespoons lemon juice

1½ teaspoons grated lemon rind
¾ cup cream
3 cups cottage cheese
4 tablespoons flour
¼ cup chopped nut meats

Line a deep dish or piepan with zwieback mixture, reserving ½ cup for the top. Beat eggs, add sugar and continue beating until light. Add salt, lemon juice and rind, cream, cheese and flour; beat thoroughly and strain through a fine sieve. Pour into pastry shell, sprinkle remaining crumbs and nuts on top and bake in moderate oven (350° F.) about 1 hour or until center is firm. Turn off heat, open oven door and let stand in oven 1 hour or until cooled. Serves 10 to 12.

STRAWBERRY ICE CREAM PIE

10 marshmallows
2 tablespoons crushed strawberries
Few drops red food coloring
2 egg whites
¼ cup sugar

¼ teaspoon salt
⅔ quart vanilla ice cream
1 Cereal Flake Pie Shell
1 cup fresh strawberries, sliced
8 or 10 unstemmed berries

Heat marshmallows with crushed strawberries slowly, folding over and over until marshmallows are half melted. Remove from heat and continue folding until mixture is smooth and fluffy. Add coloring and cool. Beat egg whites until they hold a peak; add sugar slowly, beating constantly. Add salt. Blend lightly with marshmallow mixture. Place ice cream in crumb shell, cover with sliced strawberries and top with marshmallow meringue, swirled attractively. Brown quickly in broiler or very hot oven (450° F.) ½ minute or until tips of the meringue swirls are browned. Remove pie from oven, tuck unstemmed strawberries into the swirls and serve immediately. Makes 1 (9-inch) pie.

PEACH—Use sliced ripe peaches instead of strawberries. Heat marshmallows with 2 tablespoons hot water instead of with crushed strawberries. Use baked Almond Pie Shell.

RED RASPBERRY—Use fresh red raspberries instead of strawberries. Use mint ice cream instead of vanilla ice cream. Do not slice berries. Garnish baked meringue with whole berries and mint leaves.

CHEESE PASTRIES

4 eggs	⅔ cup sugar
1 tablespoon cream	Puff Paste
3 ounces cream cheese	

Beat eggs until light, add next 3 ingredients and beat until mixed. Line shallow muffin pans with puff pastry and bake in very hot oven (450° F.) 10 minutes. Remove from oven, fill with cheese filling and bake again in slow oven (325° F.) 30 minutes. Makes 4 to 6 pastries.

DUTCH APPLE PIE

2 cups sifted flour	⅔ cup milk (about)
3 teaspoons baking powder	6 to 8 juicy apples
½ teaspoon salt	1 teaspoon cinnamon
2 tablespoons butter	¼ cup molasses
1 egg, beaten	3 tablespoons sugar

Sift flour, baking powder and salt together; cut in butter. Add egg and enough milk to make a soft dough. Roll ½ inch thick and line greased baking pan with it. Cover dough with sliced apples and sprinkle with cinnamon and molasses. Bake in hot oven (400° F.) 30 minutes or until browned. Sprinkle with sugar and bake 5 minutes. Serve hot. Makes 1 (9-inch) pie.

BANBURY TARTS

¼ cup chopped raisins	1 egg, slightly beaten
¼ cup chopped dates	3 tablespoons lemon juice
¼ cup chopped figs	1 tablespoon grated lemon
¼ cup chopped nut meats	rind
1 cup brown sugar	1 recipe Plain Pastry
1 tablespoon flour	

Combine first 7 ingredients and cook slowly for 10 minutes, stirring constantly. Remove from heat and stir in lemon juice and rind. Cool. Roll pastry to ⅛-inch thickness and cut into 3-inch squares. Place 2 teaspoons of filling on each square, moisten edges and fold over, making 3-cornered tart. Pinch edges together, make 3 short slits in top. Bake in hot oven (425° F.) about 20 minutes. Makes 12 tarts.

Use Puff Paste instead of plain pastry. Add ¼ cup each chopped candied cherries and pineapple to filling.

CHESS PIES

1 recipe Southern Pastry	1 cup chopped raisins
½ cup butter	1 cup chopped nut meats
1¼ cups sugar	1 teaspoon vanilla
3 eggs, separated	

Line individual pie plates with pastry. Cream butter with 1 cup sugar; add beaten egg yolks and 1 egg white, stiffly beaten. Blend well, add fruits, nuts and ½ teaspoon vanilla, pour into pastry shells and bake in a hot oven (400° F.) about 15 minutes or until fillings are set. Reduce temperature to 325° F. Beat remaining egg whites until stiff, fold in remaining sugar and vanilla. Cover pies with meringue and return to oven. Bake about 15 minutes longer until meringues brown. Makes 6 pies.

VARIATION—Instead of topping with meringues, bake pies as above, cool and top with whipped cream.

COVENTRY TARTLETS

½ pound cream cheese	½ teaspoon salt
½ cup sugar	¼ teaspoon nutmeg
¼ cup butter	1 tablespoon orange juice
2 egg yolks	1 recipe Plain Pastry

Mix cheese with next 6 ingredients until creamy. Line 12 tart pans with pastry. Prick and fill with cheese mixture. Bake in a hot oven (450° F.) 10 minutes. Then reduce temperature to 325° F. and bake 15 minutes longer or until brown and firm. When done, turn upside down on sheet of paper to cool. Spread each tartlet with apricot or currant marmalade, quince or apple jelly or greengage plum jam. Makes 12.

DAINTY TARTS

1 cup sweetened rhubarb sauce	8 small baked Tart Shells Whipped cream
½ cup diced pineapple	Pineapple wedges and straw-
½ cup sliced strawberries	berries

Combine first 3 ingredients. Pile into tart shells, cover with whipped cream and garnish with pineapple wedges and whole strawberries. Makes 8 tarts.

Fill tart shells half full with Cream Pie filling. Cover with fruit and whipped cream as described above.

FRENCH PASTRY SANDWICHES

1 recipe Puff Paste	1 cup sugar
1 lemon	1 egg

Roll puff paste about ¼ inch thick and cut into circles. Dip in ice water and bake. Serve 2 of these put together with filling made as follows: Remove rind and seeds from lemon and chop lemon fine. Add sugar and egg and beat together thoroughly. Cook until thickened. This filling is sufficient for 12 pastries.

GLAZED STRAWBERRY TARTS

1 quart strawberries	1 tablespoon cornstarch
½ cup confectioners' sugar	Red food coloring
1 cup water	8 baked Tart Shells
½ to ¾ cup granulated sugar	Whipped cream

Wash and stem berries, mix 3 cups of them with confectioners' sugar and let stand at least 1 hour. Cook remaining cup of berries with water until tender and rub through a sieve. Mix granulated sugar and cornstarch, add to strained strawberry juice and cook until clear. If not red enough, add food coloring. Arrange whole berries in tart shells and pour hot glaze over top. Cool. Garnish with whipped cream. Makes 8 tarts.

VARIATIONS—Use 1 quart cherries, ground cherries or gooseberries instead of strawberries. Omit coloring.

Fill tart shells ⅓ full with Cream Pie filling, cool and add berries and glaze.

GOOSEBERRY TARTS

Combine 2 cups cleaned gooseberries, a few grains salt, ¾ cup sugar, mixed with 1 tablespoon flour and 3 tablespoons water. Heat slowly until berries break, then cool. Line tart pans with pastry, fill with cooled mixture, cover with pastry and bake in very hot oven (425° F.) 15 minutes. Makes 6 tarts.

MACAROON TARTS

Mix yolks of 2 eggs with ½ cup sugar and beat until light. Add 1 cup macaroon crumbs, 3 tablespoons lemon juice and 1 tablespoon butter. Fold in stiffly beaten egg whites. Place a teaspoon of marmalade in bottom of baked tart shells, cover with mixture and brown in a moderate oven (350° F.).

JAM MERINGUE

1 recipe Puff Paste
1 cup strawberry jam
1 recipe Meringue

¼ cup shredded blanched almonds
2 tablespoons confectioners' sugar

Roll puff paste to ⅛-inch thickness. Trim edges to make a sheet 10 x 7 inches. Place on cookie sheet and make a ½-inch rim around the edge. Prick with fork and chill thoroughly. Bake in very hot oven (450° F.) about 10 minutes or until lightly browned. Cool. Spread jam over all, cover with meringue, sprinkle almonds over top, then sugar. Proceed as directed for meringue. Serves 8.

MAMMY'S FRIED PIES

Stew dried apples, peaches or apricots. Drain off all juice, mash well and sweeten. Roll Puff Paste ⅛ inch thick and cut circles 3 inches in diameter. On one of the circles place a spoonful of the filling, having a clear margin of the pastry. Moisten this edge all around, place another circle on top and press edges firmly together. Fry in hot deep fat (370° F.) or sauté in a small amount of fat in a hot frying pan, turning pies so that they will brown on both sides. These are good with fillings of mincemeat, or any thick jam or preserve.

MARMALADE STRIPS

Place a thin layer of Plain Pastry on an inverted baking pan. Spread with thick marmalade. Cover with another thin layer of pastry. Cut into strips 4 x 1½ inches. Bake in a hot oven (400° F.). When cool, spread with a thin icing made of confectioners' sugar and water. Sprinkle with finely chopped nuts.

NAPOLEONS

Divide ½ recipe Puff Paste into three portions and roll each portion into a sheet as thin as possible without breaking. Prick thoroughly and chill. Bake in a hot oven (400° F.) until brown, cool and spread the pastry sheets with cream filling. Spread the top with confectioners' frosting. When ready to serve, cut into blocks 2 x 4 inches.

ORANGE TARTS

1 cup sugar
1/3 cup flour
1/4 teaspoon salt
1 cup orange juice
2 tablespoons lemon juice

Grated rind 1 orange
3 egg yolks, beaten
4 baked Mürbe Teig Tart Shells
1 recipe Meringue

Sift dry ingredients, add fruit juices and rind, then beaten egg yolks. Cook in double boiler, stirring until thickened. Cool. Fill tart shells, cover with meringue and bake in a moderate oven (350° F.) 15 minutes. Makes 4 tarts.

PEACH DUMPLINGS WITH WHIPPED CREAM

Pare freestone peaches, cut holes in stem ends and carefully remove stones. Wrap in circular pieces of puff paste rolled to 1/4-inch thickness and tuck in the paste where the stones were removed. Bake in a moderate oven (350° F.) 30 minutes. To serve fill centers with sweetened and flavored whipped cream.

PASTRY PINWHEELS

2 cups sifted flour
3 teaspoons baking powder
1/2 teaspoon salt
2 tablespoons sugar

4 tablespoons shortening
1 egg
2/3 cup milk
Jam

Sift dry ingredients together; cut in shortening. Beat egg, add milk and mix with dry ingredients. Turn onto lightly floured board; knead gently. Roll out 1/8 inch thick. Cut into 3-inch squares, then diagonally from each corner toward center, making cuts about 1 inch long. Place a teaspoon jam in center. Fold corners toward center, pinwheel fashion. Bake on cookie sheet in hot oven (400° F.) 15 minutes. Makes 15.

PEEK-A-BOOS

Cut thin piecrust into rounds about 3 inches in diameter. Prick 1/2 the rounds with a fork. In each of the other rounds cut 3 holes to form a triangle, using a thimble or some other small cutter. Bake in a very hot oven (450° F.) until browned. Spread jelly on the pricked rounds, cover with perforated ones. Sprinkle with confectioners' sugar.

PINEAPPLE TARTS

Roll Puff Paste about ½ inch thick. Cut half the pastry into rounds with large biscuit cutter and place in greased pan. Cut other half with biscuit cutter, then cut holes in centers of circles. Moisten underside of rings and place on rounds in pan. Place a small piece of butter in each center and bake in a very hot oven (450° F.) 15 to 20 minutes. Before serving, fill with crushed pineapple and cover with whipped cream. Makes 8 tarts.

APRICOT TARTS—Fill centers with dried apricots, cooked with sugar and a small amount of water to jam consistency.

PINEAPPLE PUFFS

1 recipe Puff Paste	8 slices canned pineapple,
1 recipe Cream Pie filling	drained
	Maraschino cherries

Roll puff paste to ⅛-inch thickness. Cut into rounds the size of pineapple slices, place on cookie sheet and chill thoroughly. Bake in very hot oven (450° F.) 10 to 15 minutes. Cool. Place 2 rounds together with cream pie filling between, place pineapple slice on top and garnish with a cherry. Serves 8.

ORANGE MARMALADE TARTS—Fill pastry rounds with orange marmalade and spread with icing.

RASPBERRY TURNOVERS

1 recipe Plain Pastry   Raspberry preserves

Roll pastry ⅛ inch thick and cut into 3-inch circles. Moisten the edge of half the circle and place a teaspoon of raspberry preserves in center. Fold ½ of the circle over the other, making the edges meet. Press edges together firmly and mark with the floured tines of a fork. Brush with beaten egg and prick the top. Chill, then bake in a very hot oven (450° F.) 12 to 15 minutes. Sprinkle with sugar before serving. Makes 15.

DAMSON PLUM TURNOVERS—Use plum preserves instead of raspberry preserves.

PRUNE TURNOVERS—Use cooked dried prunes with a small amount of butter and extra sugar added instead of preserves.

QUINCE MARMALADE TURNOVERS—Use quince marmalade.

RAISIN TURNOVERS—Use filling for Filled Cookies (page 486) instead of preserves.

SWEET RISSOLES

Cut circles of Puff or Plain Pastry 3 inches in diameter from a sheet rolled not more than ¼ inch thick. Wet the edges of each circle for ½ inch all around, place teaspoon of any thick stewed fruit or marmalade on one side of the circle and fold the other half over upon this until edges meet. Pinch edges together, brush over with beaten egg and fry in hot deep fat at 365° F. Sprinkle with sugar and serve.

PASTRY ROLLOVERS

Roll Plain Pastry ¼ inch thick and cut into 5-inch circles. Prick thoroughly, spread with jelly and sprinkle with chopped nuts. Roll closely over and over. Place on a cookie sheet with the lapped side underneath. Bake in hot oven (400° F.) 10 minutes. Brush with milk before removing from oven.

MERINGUES

A meringue is a very light, delicate preparation consisting of stiffly beaten egg whites, sweetened and generally flavored, then baked to a delicate brown.

EGG WHITES FOR MERINGUES—Use good quality egg whites so that they have no tendency to be too liquid to beat up well.

VARIETIES OF SUGAR FOR MERINGUES—The sugar for meringues may be confectioners', granulated or brown. It should be free of lumps.

PROPORTION OF SUGAR TO EGG WHITE—For pie and pudding meringues, use 1 to 3 tablespoons sugar to each egg white. For kisses and meringue shells, use from 4 to 5 tablespoons sugar to each egg white.

IN SPREADING MERINGUES over the surface of a pie, tarts or a pudding be sure that it touches the pastry rim or baking dish all around or it will shrink away from it while the meringue is baking.

TEMPERATURES FOR BAKING—All meringues should be baked in a slow oven. For meringues on pies, tarts and puddings the temperature should be 325° F. for 12 to 18 minutes, depending upon the thickness of the meringue. The meringue for kisses or shells should be baked in a very slow oven (250° to 275° F.) 40 to 60 minutes, depending upon the size.

PIE OR PUDDING MERINGUE

2 egg whites
4 tablespoons sugar
Few grains salt

½ teaspoon vanilla or ¼
teaspoon lemon extract

Method 1.

Beat egg whites until stiff, add sugar gradually and continue beating until the mixture is fine grained and will hold its shape. Add salt and vanilla and bake as directed.

Method 2.

Add sugar to unbeaten egg whites and beat mixture until stiff. Add salt and vanilla and bake as directed.

Methods of Using Meringues on Pies, Tarts and Puddings

These may be used in any of the following ways:

No. 1—Spread the meringue evenly over the surface, using a knife or the back of a spoon.

No. 2—Make the surface uneven by spreading in ridges or by making points.

No. 3—Make fancy shapes by using a pastry bag and tube.

No. 4—Put the meringue on by the spoonful. This is desirable for some puddings, for then it is easy when serving the pudding to have a nicely shaped meringue for each serving.

No. 5—Bake the meringue for puddings by itself. To do this, float spoonfuls of the mixture upon hot water in a shallow pan. Set the pan in a slow oven (325° F.) and bake until the meringues are lightly browned. Skim them off immediately and place upon the prepared pudding.

CHOCOLATE MERINGUES

4 egg whites
1 cup sugar

1½ ounces chocolate, melted
½ teaspoon vanilla

Beat egg whites until frothy and add sugar gradually, beating well after each addition. Fold in chocolate and vanilla. Drop from spoon onto cookie sheet covered with wet unglazed paper. Bake in slow oven (275° F.) 50 to 60 minutes. Makes 12 large meringues.

FRENCH MERINGUES

2 cups sugar
¾ cup water
5 egg whites

¼ teaspoon salt
¼ teaspoon cream tartar
1 teaspoon vanilla

Cook sugar and water to 238° F. or until a soft ball forms when a small amount of sirup is dropped into cold water. Beat egg whites until stiff, adding salt and cream of tartar when frothy. Pour sugar sirup over stiffly beaten egg whites gradually, beating constantly. Continue beating until cool. Fold in vanilla. Wet sheets of unglazed paper and arrange on cookie sheets. Shape meringues with a pastry tube or a spoon on wet paper and bake in a slow oven (275° F.) 1 hour or longer, depending upon the size. The soft inner portion may be removed and center filled with ice cream or fresh fruit or fruit sauce may be served over the ice cream filled meringues. Makes 15 meringues. These are often called MERINGUE GLACÉS.

NUT MERINGUE

1 recipe French Meringues or 2 recipes Meringues (page 499)

1 cup finely chopped nut meats (walnuts, pecans or toasted blanched almonds)

Prepare meringues and fold in nut meats. Shape into one large or several small meringues and bake as directed for each.

NUT BRITTLE MERINGUES—Use 1 cup crushed peanut brittle instead of nut meats.

DATE AND NUT MERINGUES—Add 1 cup finely chopped dates to Nut Meringues and drop from teaspoon onto wet unglazed paper. Bake as directed.

MARRON MERINGUES—Use ⅔ cup marrons instead of nut meats and use only 3 tablespoons sugar for each egg in meringue.

FRUIT FILLED MERINGUES

1 recipe French Meringues or 2 recipes Meringues (page 499)

Sweetened fresh fruit (sliced peaches, strawberries, or apricots)

Prepare meringues and bake in muffin pans, lined with unglazed ungreased paper. Bake in a slow oven (275° F.) 1 hour and 15 minutes. Remove from pans while warm and take out soft center from underside. Cool. Just before serving fill center with fruit and top with whipped cream. Serves 15.

FRENCH RECIPES

The Institute secured these excellent recipes directly from French kitchens. They have been selected for those who are interested in real French dishes. The secret of French cooking (except for sweets) is the use of a whiff of garlic. Even when it does not appear in the recipe, bowl, baking dish or food is usually rubbed with it.

PLAIN SOUP

6 tablespoons rice
Boiling water
½ teaspoon salt
1 medium-sized carrot
4 medium-sized turnips

2 large potatoes
1 large onion
2 sprigs water cress
1 tablespoon butter
2 cups milk

WASH the rice and add to rapidly boiling salted water. Clean and pare the vegetables, cut them in small pieces and add to the rice. Boil together for five or ten minutes, adding more water if necessary, then cover the pan and simmer the mixture gently until it is well cooked, and the water is reduced. Add the butter and milk and serve very hot.

GREEN SOUP

2 bunches water cress
2 diced potatoes
2 hard-cooked egg-yolks

2 slices bread
2 tablespoons butter or other fat

Cook the water cress until almost done, then add potatoes and cook until they are soft. Press through a sieve and add the purée to the water in which it was cooked. Brown the bread slightly in one tablespoon of the fat, and cut into small cubes. Add the minced egg-yolks and the remaining tablespoon of butter or other fat to the soup, season to taste, add the cubes of bread and serve hot.

ECONOMICAL VEGETABLE SOUP

Cut equal quantities of any left-over vegetables, such as carrots, turnips, green peppers, potatoes, celery, string beans, into small pieces. Brown them in a frying-pan with some butter or other fat, add enough hot water to cover, season with salt and pepper, and cook until tender. Drain, press through a sieve and return the pulp to the water in which the vegetables were boiled. Serve hot with small squares of toasted bread. Canned vegetables may be used.

CODFISH WITH BROWN SAUCE

2 cups salt codfish	1 clove garlic, chopped
6 tablespoons cooking-oil	1 tablespoon chopped parsley
3 tablespoons flour	Few grains nutmeg
1½ cups water	¼ teaspoon paprika

Soak codfish in cold water over night. Drain and fry in oil until slightly browned. Add flour and brown. Add water and seasonings, and cook slowly for fifteen minutes. Serve fish on platter surrounded by border of rice or potatoes.

CODFISH A LA BÉNÉDICTINE

1 pound fresh codfish	Butter or other fat
4 medium-sized sweet potatoes	Juice of 1 lemon
Salt	1 cup cream or milk
Pepper	Bread-crumbs

Boil the codfish, drain it and keep it warm.

Pare the sweet potatoes, cook them in salted water or steam them and let them dry, then mash and add salt and pepper, two tablespoons of butter or other fat, the juice of half a lemon, and one cup of cream or milk.

Skin the fish and remove the bones. Pound it rather fine; add a tablespoon of butter or other fat and the juice of half a lemon. Mix the hot mashed potatoes with this. Add more milk or cream, enough to make a rough dough. Grease a baking-dish, and put the dough into it. Cover the top with bread-crumbs and melted butter. Put small dots of butter here and there on the top and bake in the oven (350° F .) for twenty minutes. Serve in the dish in which it was cooked.

CODFISH, BRANDADE STYLE

1 pound salt codfish
1 diced potato
2 tablespoons table oil

1 cup milk
Salt and pepper
3 tablespoons lemon-juice

Soak the codfish over night, then put it in a saucepan of cold water, add the potato and cook on a quick fire. When it is on the point of boiling, reduce the heat and cook slowly, stirring constantly with a wooden spoon. Add the oil, drop by drop, and the milk. When it thickens it has been cooked long enough. Add the salt, pepper and lemon-juice, and serve hot.

CRAB A LA CREOLE

12 small live hard-shell crabs
   or ½ pound crab-meat
3 tablespoons lemon-juice
2 red peppers

4 tablespoons butter or other
   fat
1 teaspoon salt
⅛ teaspoon pepper

Boil the crabs twenty minutes; open and clean them and reserve the yellow fat. Pour the lemon-juice over the crab-meat. Melt the butter or other fat and the crab fat in a frying-pan and add the crab-meat, seasoning, and chopped peppers. Cook for twenty minutes.

CRABS WITH RICE

15 small crabs
1 cup rice
2 or 3 small onions
2 small carrots

1 tablespoon butter or other
   fat
Salt and pepper

Clean the crabs. Cut off and crush the legs, and cook in boiling salted water for about an hour. Strain the juice and pour it over the rice. Let stand for half an hour and then cook until rice is tender. Cook the chopped onion and carrots in the fat until slightly browned and then add the crab-meat. Season with salt and pepper, add the rice and cook together for several minutes. Serve hot.

This is an old provincial recipe and has a particularly delicious taste that makes it a favorite.

618

SALMON A LA MORNAY

4 cooked potatoes	Buttered crumbs
½ cup Swiss cheese	1 cup medium white sauce
1 egg-yolk	2 cups boiled salmon

Mash the potatoes and line a greased baking-dish with them. Add the cheese and egg-yolk to the white sauce and pour half of it over the potatoes. Add the fish and cover it with the remaining sauce and buttered bread-crumbs. Bake in the oven (350° F.) for twenty minutes.

FISH FRITTERS

1 pound of small fish	Salt and pepper
3 eggs	Minced garlic
3 tablespoons flour	Minced parsley

Cook the fish and mash them. Beat the yolks of the eggs until light and thick then add, little by little, the flour, salt, pepper, the minced garlic and parsley, and the fish. Lastly add the whites of the eggs beaten to a froth. Drop spoonfuls of this mixture into hot fat (360°-370° F.) and fry to a golden brown.

CREOLE FISH

1½ pounds fish	Salt and pepper
1 lemon	½ cup tomato-juice
1 teaspoon butter or other fat	Grated lemon-rind
Finely chopped onion	1 small pimiento
	6 tablespoons rice

Select a fish with firm flesh, clean the skin and rub well with a slice of lemon. Melt the fat, add the onion and the fish and cook to a golden brown. Season with salt and pepper, add the tomato-juice, a bit of lemon-rind, and the pimiento finely cut. While the fish is cooking, cook the rice in boiling salted water until tender. Make a crown of rice on a platter, place the fish in the center, pour the gravy over it, and garnish with thin slices of lemon.

FISH LOAF

2 cups cooked fish	2 eggs
1 teaspoon salt	1 cup thick white sauce

Drain the fish and tear into small bits. Add the salt, the beaten egg-yolks, the white sauce, and the beaten egg-whites.

Pour into a greased baking-dish and bake in a moderate oven (350°-400° F.) for twenty or thirty minutes.

FISH EN COQUILLES

1 cup left-over fish
8 mussels or clams
½ cup bread-crumbs
10 tablespoons milk
1 clove garlic
1 teaspoon chopped parsley

1 chopped onion
Salt and pepper
3 tablespoons butter or other fat
Buttered crumbs

Chop the fish with the mussels or clams. Add the crumbs which have been soaked in two tablespoons of milk, and the garlic, parsley, onions, salt and pepper. Melt the fat and when hot add the mixture and cook several minutes. Stir in one-half cup of milk and fill small ramekins or scallop shells. Cover with buttered crumbs and bake in a moderate oven (350°-400° F.) about fifteen minutes. Serve the dishes on a platter or on individual plates.

CASSEROLE OF SAUSAGE AND CORN

7 Vienna sausages
1 No. 2 can whole grain corn
½ green pepper

1½ cups cracker crumbs
2 cups medium white sauce

Cut sausages in short lengths and mix with corn and chopped pepper, season to taste. Make sauce by melting ¼ cup butter, adding ¼ cup flour and 2 cups milk. In a baking dish place layers of crumbs, corn mixture and sauce. Top with buttered crumbs and bake in a moderate oven for 20 minutes. Serves 5.

PORK LIVER LOAF

1 pound pork liver
1 onion
Parsley
1 cup milk

1 egg
1½ tablespoons flour
Salt and pepper
Nutmeg

Chop the liver, onion and parsley together until they are minced very fine. Add the milk and egg, flour and seasonings. Mix well, shape into a loaf, place in a baking-pan and bake in a moderate oven (375° F.) for an hour and a quarter.

RÉCHAUFFÉ

No. 1.

2 cups cold cooked meat
2 cups boiled rice
Butter or other fat

Grated cheese
Salt and pepper
Milk or soup stock

Any pieces of left-over meat may be used for this dish. Cut the meat in small pieces and moisten with a little milk or stock. Spread a layer of rice in a greased baking-dish. Put several small pieces of fat on top and sprinkle with grated cheese. Season with salt and pepper. Then add a layer of chopped meat and again add several small pieces of fat and a little grated cheese. Spread the rest of the rice on the meat, then put fat and grated cheese over it more abundantly than before. Put in a moderate oven (350°-400° F.) for fifteen or twenty minutes. Serve very hot.

One can improve this dish by mixing some good tomato sauce or cream sauce with the meat.

No. 2.

1 large onion
1 tablespoon fat
Salt and pepper
1½ cups uncooked rice

1 cup tomatoes
Left-over pork, beef, mutton
    or chicken

Slice the onion and brown it with the fat. Wash the rice well and add it, with salt and pepper, to the onion. Cook slowly, stirring constantly until the rice is slightly brown. Press the tomatoes through a sieve and add to the rice mixture, together with the meat. Cover with boiling water and simmer for about one-half hour.

No. 3.

3 small onions
2 tablespoons butter or other
    fat
1 cup stock
½ cup gravy
1 cup left-over meat

½ teaspoon salt
⅛ teaspoon pepper
3 diced potatoes
½ cup carrots
½ cup prune-juice
½ cup stewed prunes

Slice the onions and fry in the fat until brown. Add the stock, gravy, meat, salt and pepper and vegetables. Cook slowly until the vegetables are tender. Add the prune-juice and boil five minutes. Turn the stew on to a platter and surround with cooked prunes.

PORK LIVER WITH RICE

1 pound pork liver	2 or 3 sliced carrots
¼ pound sliced bacon	2 sliced onions
½ cup rice	Salt and pepper
3 tablespoons chopped parsley	

Fry the liver with the bacon until brown, then add the rice which has been soaked in water for one-half hour. Cover with hot water or stock, add the parsley, carrots and onions, salt and pepper. Simmer slowly until tender, about forty minutes.

HAM LOAF

¼ pound lean ham	¼ pound grated cheese
2 tablespoons flour	3 eggs
2 cups milk	Salt and pepper

Cook the ham and chop it fine. Mix the flour with the milk and cook for a few minutes; then add the ham, cheese, the egg-yolks slightly beaten, and the stiffly beaten egg-whites. Season with salt and pepper, pour into a mold, set the mold in a pan of hot water and bake in a moderate oven (375° F.) until firm (20-30 minutes). Serve with garnish of orange slices, with pear halves filled with mint jelly and topped with cherries.

BEEF HASH A LA NORMANDIE

3 onions	½ cup cooked potatoes
1 tablespoon fat	½ cup meat stock
2 cups cold boiled beef	Salt and pepper

Cut the onions into cubes and fry in the fat until brown. Slice the beef and add to the onions, then add the potatoes and stock. Season and cook about fifteen minutes.

FRENCH RISSOLES

2 cups chopped veal or chicken (white meat)	1 cup water
1 onion	1 tablespoon melted butter or other fat
Salt and pepper	4 cups flour
1 egg	

Chop the onion and add it to the meat. Season with salt and pepper. Mix this well with the yolk of the egg.

HOLLANDAISE SAUCE WILL GIVE ASPARAGUS A FRENCH ACCENT

THERE'S A CONTINENTAL FLAVOR TO THESE LIMA BEANS NEUFCHATEL IN FRENCH CASSEROLE

FRENCH DISHES EN CASSEROLE
—RECHAUFFE OF LAMB

OR SAUSAGES AND
CORN AU GRATIN

Mix together the water, a little salt, the white of the egg and the melted fat. Pile up the flour, make a well in the center and pour in, little by little, the liquid mixture. Work the dough thoroughly until it is smooth, then cut it in slices and roll out into thin strips with a rolling-pin.

Place the chopped meat here and there on these strips and season with salt and pepper and a little chopped onion. Fold the strips in the center and press the edges together. Cut with a small biscuit-cutter, making small rissoles. Boil these in slightly salted water for five minutes, remove them from the water, drain, and put them in the oven (400° F.) for ten minutes to form a yellow crust on top. Serve hot.

SAUCE FOR COLD MEAT AND FISH

4 tablespoons salad oil	Mustard
4 tablespoons cream	Salt
3 tablespoons vinegar	Pepper

Mix the salad oil, cream, vinegar, a little mustard, salt and pepper. Beat together quickly, with an egg-beater. The sauce gets white quickly and looks like whipped cream. Soon it becomes as thick as the best-made mayonnaise. Eggs are not required, the sauce will not curdle, and can be made quickly.

CAMBRISSON SALAD

1 cup cooked beef	4 anchovies
2 hard-cooked eggs	1 small head lettuce
2 tomatoes	

Cut the beef into small pieces, add the sliced eggs and tomatoes, and the anchovies cut up into small pieces. Serve on lettuce with French or mayonnaise dressing.

RAGOUT OF DUCK OR CHICKEN

2 tablespoons butter	1 sliced onion
2 tablespoons cooking oil or fat	1 clove garlic
1 duck or chicken	Sprig of parsley
Salt and pepper	1 cup stock
	1 tablespoon vinegar

Clean and cut up the duck or chicken. Heat butter with oil or drippings in a frying-pan. When hot, add the meat.

Season with salt and pepper and cook until the meat is slightly brown. Remove the meat and add the onion to the fat in the pan and cook until brown, then add the garlic and parsley, the stock and vinegar. Return the meat to the pan and simmer slowly until tender.

Rabbit, hare, lamb or young partridge may be prepared in the same way.

CHICKEN VICTORY

1 chicken	Thyme
2 tablespoons salad oil	½ bay-leaf
9 onions	3 large tomatoes
½ pound bacon	1 cup stock
Parsley	½ pound mushrooms

Prepare the chicken for roasting. While it is roasting, heat the oil in a frying-pan, add three of the onions finely chopped, and cook until a light brown. Add half the bacon, cut in small pieces, the parsley, thyme, and bay-leaf. When brown, add the tomatoes cut in slices, and the stock. When all is cooked, press through a sieve.

In another pan, brown lightly the other half of the bacon cut in strips, the mushrooms and the six remaining onions, chopped. Cook until everything is tender, then add the previously made sauce and the gravy from the roasted chicken, and, if necessary, thicken with a little flour.

Cut up the chicken, arrange pieces in the center of a platter and pour the sauce, with bacon, mushrooms and onions, around it. Cut bread in diamond-shaped pieces, fry in the bacon fat, and place these also around the chicken.

ASPARAGUS WITH CHEESE

1 bunch asparagus	1 tablespoon butter
½ cup grated cheese	⅛ teaspoon pepper
1 teaspoon salt	

Cut asparagus in pieces and boil in salted water for ten minutes, then place it in a baking-dish. Sprinkle with the grated cheese and seasoning, and add the butter in small pieces. Bake in a moderate oven (350°-400° F.).

RED CABBAGE WITH CHESTNUTS

1 red cabbage	½ cup water
1 tablespoon drippings	Salt and pepper
½ cup melted grape jelly	French chestnuts

Select a nice red cabbage, discard the outer leaves and soak for a short time in cold water. Drain, and slice in thin shreds. Melt the fat in a saucepan, add the jelly and the cabbage, the water, salt and pepper. Cook very slowly until tender.

At the same time, boil some French chestnuts; take off the skin and add them to the cabbage. Cook all slowly for about two hours, until the liquid has evaporated.

STUFFED CABBAGE

1 cabbage	Spices
Cooking fat	1 cup bread-crumbs
Butter	3 eggs
Parsley	1 chopped onion

Place a thin piece of cheese-cloth in the bottom of a bowl and lay the large cabbage leaves in it. Chop the middle of the cabbage fine and sauté it in the fat until it is yellow. Remove it from the fire, add a little chopped parsley, spices, bread-crumbs, eggs and onion. Place this mixture inside the large cabbage leaves, and tie up the cabbage by tying together the four corners of the cloth.

Place in a pan of boiling salted water and boil until the cabbage leaves are tender (about thirty-five minutes). When done, remove from the cloth, pour a little melted butter over it, and some fine bread-crumbs, and bake for five minutes. Serve with tomato sauce.

EGGPLANT ORIENTAL

2 green peppers	6 ripe tomatoes
2 eggplants	3 teaspoons salt
3 tablespoons cooking oil	1 teaspoon paprika

Remove the seeds from the peppers, and cut the peppers into small pieces. Pare the eggplants and cut into small pieces. Cook the eggplant and peppers in the oil until slightly brown, then add the tomatoes and seasonings and continue the cooking until the eggplant is done. Serve very hot.

LEEKS AND POTATOES AU GRATIN

12 leeks	½ cup grated cheese
6 potatoes	Bread-crumbs
1 cup medium white sauce	Salt and pepper

Cook the leeks in boiling water; boil and slice the potatoes; arrange the vegetables in a baking-dish, and pour the white sauce over them. Add the cheese, bread-crumbs and seasoning, and bake (350° F.) for fifteen minutes.

LIMA BEANS, NEUFCHÂTEL STYLE

2 cups green Lima beans or 1 cup dried Lima beans, soaked in water over night	¼ cup butter or other fat
	1½ cups milk
1 teaspoon salt	2 egg-yolks

Cook beans in boiling salted water until almost tender. Drain; add fat, salt, milk and beaten egg yolks. Turn into casserole and bake in 350° F. oven, 20-30 minutes. Stir twice until beans begin to brown.

MUSHROOMS AU GRATIN

½ pound mushrooms	½ cup bread-crumbs
1 sliced onion	1/16 teaspoon pepper
2 tablespoons cooking oil	¼ teaspoon paprika
2 tablespoons flour	1 tablespoon butter
1 cup mushroom stock (made from stems)	½ teaspoon salt
	Juice of 1 lemon

Peel the mushrooms and sprinkle salt over them to extract the water. Fry the onion in the oil. Add the flour and brown; add the stock, the pepper, paprika, butter, salt and lemon-juice and cook the sauce until it is thickened. Drain the mushrooms and add them to the sauce. Put into a baking-dish, sprinkle with crumbs and bake until slightly browned.

POTATO PATTIES

6 potatoes	2 tablespoons butter
2 tablespoons flour	1 tablespoon grated Swiss cheese
Salt	Tomato sauce

Boil the potatoes in their jackets; peel and mash them and add flour, butter, grated cheese and salt. Mix well and shape in round patties, rather thick, making a hole in the middle. Cook in a well-greased baking-dish, in a hot oven (400°-450° F.). When they are nicely browned pour over them tomato sauce, and serve hot in the baking-dish.

POTATOES, PEASANT STYLE

3 cups potatoes
6 tablespoons bacon fat
2 cloves garlic
2 tablespoons parsley
½ teaspoon paprika
2 tablespoons flour
2 cups milk
1 teaspoon salt
⅛ teaspoon pepper

Wash, pare and cut potatoes in dice. Sauté in the bacon fat until brown. Remove potatoes and fry the chopped garlic and parsley in the fat remaining in the pan. Add flour, milk and seasonings, and cook until thickened (about five minutes). Add potatoes and cook three minutes.

POTATOES, JEANETTE COURRANGELLE STYLE

6 medium-sized potatoes
Left-over meat
1 clove garlic
1 small onion
1 teaspoon chopped parsley
½ teaspoon salt

Pare the potatoes, bake in the oven until tender, then cut in halves lengthwise. Scoop out the centers. Chop the meat, garlic, onion and parsley together; add the salt, fill the potatoes with the mixture and reheat. The pulp removed from the potatoes may be seasoned with salt, pepper, and butter, and baked in the oven with tomato sauce.

POTATO FRITTERS

3 large potatoes
¾ cup powdered sugar
Lemon or orange flavoring
¾ cup flour

Pare the potatoes and boil in salted water. Mash them; add the sugar and flavor with a little lemon or orange. Allow the mixture to cool. Then add the flour and knead the dough until it is very firm.

Spread the dough with a rolling-pin and cut it with a biscuit-cutter. Fry in deep fat (360°-370° F.) until brown, then drain on brown paper.

POTATOES A L'ARCHIODOISE

4 cups potatoes, sliced thin	1½ teaspoons salt
2 cups tomato sauce	1 teaspoon paprika
2 minced garlic cloves	

Wash, pare and slice potatoes into a baking-dish. Add other ingredients and bake (350°-400° F.) one hour and thirty minutes.

COOKED RADISHES WITH CHEESE

Boil small pink radishes from which the leaves have been removed. Drain, and cook in a saucepan with butter and grated cheese until the cheese is melted.

SPINACH WITH CHEESE

1 quart spinach	4 eggs
2 tablespoons chopped parsley	2 cups milk
4 tablespoons fat	1 cup Swiss cheese
½ teaspoon paprika	1 teaspoon salt

Wash and chop the spinach. Add the parsley and cook in the fat for ten minutes. Add well-beaten eggs to the milk, and pour over the spinach. Add cheese and seasoning; turn into greased baking-dish and bake in a moderate oven (350°-400° F.) one-half hour.

SPINACH À LA REINE

½ tablespoon chopped onion	Salt and pepper
½ tablespoon fat	3½ tablespoons grated cheese
1 quart spinach	3 eggs
1 tablespoon flour	6 cooked shrimps
1 cup milk	

Cook the onion in the fat, add the spinach, which has been washed and chopped, and fry quickly. Add flour and milk, and cook until it thickens. Season with salt and pepper and add the grated cheese. When it starts to boil remove from the fire and add well-beaten egg-whites, then the beaten yolks, turn into a baking-dish and bake in a very hot oven (450°-500° F.) for ten minutes. Garnish with the shrimps.

TOMATOES WITH BROWN SAUCE

4 tomatoes
½ teaspoon salt
Few grains pepper

1½ tablespoons butter or
  other fat
Brown sauce

Plunge tomatoes in boiling water for one minute. Peel, slice and put in baking-dish. Add seasoning and fat in small pieces. Bake in a moderate oven (350°-400° F.) for ten minutes. Add brown sauce and again bake for ten minutes.

STUFFED TOMATOES

8 tomatoes
5 medium-sized onions
4 cloves garlic
1 piece thyme
1 bay-leaf

½ teaspoon salt
⅛ teaspoon pepper
5 tablespoons fat
2 tablespoons flour
½ pound sausage-meat

Cut off the tops of the tomatoes and remove the pulp. Cook the pulp and four of the onions chopped fine, with the seasonings for twenty-five minutes, then add three tablespoons of the fat mixed with the flour. Cook the mixture for twenty minutes. Brown the rest of the fat in a pan and fry a chopped onion in it, add the sausage-meat to it, cook for ten minutes and add this mixture to the tomato pulp. Stuff the tomatoes with the mixture and bake (at 350° F.) for twenty-five minutes. Serve in the baking-dish.

TURNIP LEAVES

Select the leaves of young turnips, wash carefully and boil in salted water until tender. Drain, chop very fine, and season with salt, pepper and butter. Serve hot.

TURNIPS WITH CHEESE

3 medium-sized white or
  yellow turnips
2 tablespoons fat
2 tablespoons flour

1½ cups milk
1 teaspoon salt
⅛ teaspoon pepper
½ cup grated cheese

Peel the turnips, cut them in slices, and boil them for about fifteen minutes in boiling salted water. Make a white sauce with the fat, flour, milk, salt and pepper. Pour this over the turnips and sprinkle the grated cheese on top. Bake for ten minutes and serve hot.

DANDELION OMELET

1 cup dandelion hearts   4 eggs   Butter or other fat

Fry the hearts of very white dandelions in butter or other fat, and mix them with the well-beaten eggs. Cook like an ordinary French omelet. The taste resembles an asparagus-tip omelet.

EGGS FLORENTINE

2 quarts spinach	1 teaspoon salt
4 tablespoons butter	6 hard-cooked eggs
½ teaspoon pepper	½ cup tomato sauce

Wash, cook and drain the spinach and add the butter and the seasonings. Arrange a nest of spinach at each end of a small platter. Put three eggs in each nest and pour the tomato sauce between the nests.

EGGS IN FRENCH STYLE

6 eggs	½ teaspoon salt
2 tablespoons fat	½ teaspoon paprika
4 tablespoons flour	⅛ teaspoon pepper
1 cup milk	Bread-crumbs

Boil the eggs for five minutes; make a thick white sauce, using fat, flour, milk and seasonings. Dip the eggs into the sauce; cool and dip into fine bread-crumbs. Fry in hot fat (375°-390° F.) until golden brown. Serve with tomato sauce.

MOLDED EGGS WITH CHEESE

3 eggs	Salt
3 cups milk	Cayenne
½ pound grated cheese	Parsley

Beat the eggs and milk together and add the grated cheese and seasonings. Pour the mixture into a greased baking-dish, set in hot water, and bake at 375° F. until it is firm. Turn out on a platter, and garnish with chopped parsley.

MIMOSA EGGS

6 hard-cooked eggs
Lettuce

¾ cup boiled ham
Mayonnaise

Cut the eggs in halves lengthwise. Remove the yolks and stuff the whites with chopped ham. Lay the eggs on a plate lined with lettuce leaves and cover with mayonnaise dressing. Decorate with sifted yolks of the eggs.

EGGS AU GRATIN

1½ cups milk
1 teaspoon salt
⅛ teaspoon pepper

½ cup grated Swiss cheese
4 eggs

Add milk, seasoning and cheese to slightly beaten eggs. Turn the mixture into a greased baking dish, set the mold in a pan of water and bake (375° F.) twenty minutes, or until firm. Remove from the oven; let stand three minutes and unmold on a platter. Serve with tomato sauce.

CHEESE OMELET SOUFFLÉ

2 tablespoons butter or other fat
4 tablespoons flour
1 cup milk

Salt and pepper
¼ pound grated cheese
3 eggs

Put the fat and flour into a pan and when blended add the hot milk, the salt and pepper, and the grated cheese, stirring quickly to melt the cheese. When the mixture is getting cool, add first the yolks, then the stiffly beaten whites of the eggs. Put the mixture into a greased baking dish, set in a pan of hot water and bake in a moderate oven (350° F.) 45 to 50 minutes. Serve at once.

CHEESE TOAST

1 egg
1½ tablespoons cream
1½ tablespoons flour

¼ pound grated cheese
Salt and pepper
Slices of bread

Mix first five ingredients well together and work the mixture until firm. Spread this mixture on slices of bread two and one-half inches thick. Fry in deep hot fat (375°-390° F.) putting the cheese side down first; then turn over. Remove when the toast is a golden brown. This dish is quickly made, delicious and not costly.

GNOCCHI

4 tablespoons butter or other fat	3 eggs
1 cup milk	Salt and pepper
2 cups flour	2 ounces grated cheese
	1 cup medium white sauce

Melt the fat in a pan. Put in the milk, bring to a boil, and add the sifted flour. Stir six to nine minutes. Let it cool slightly, then work in the eggs, one at a time, beat well, and season to taste. Add the grated cheese. Put the dough on the board or on a platter and cut into squares or small fingers.

Drop these into boiling salted water and poach them for about ten minutes. When they are cooked, drain them and place in a baking-dish. Pour over them the white sauce to which may be added, if desired, one ounce of grated cheese, and put the dish in the oven (250°-350° F.) for fifteen minutes. Serve hot. The gnocchi can also be served with tomato sauce.

EGGS WITH BLACK BUTTER

(Oeufs au Beurre Noir)

2 eggs	1 tablespoon clarified
1 tablespoon wine vinegar	butter
1 teaspoon parsley, finely chopped	

Multiply the quantities given by the number of persons to be served. Poach the eggs in water to which a little vinegar has been added. Remove while still soft and place in a dish in the oven to finish cooking. Heat the vinegar until it is half its original quantity; then pour it over the eggs. Simmer the butter for a few minutes in a pan. Add parsley and continue cooking until both butter and parsley are browned. Pour over eggs and serve at once.

Cakes and Puddings

FRENCH CAKE

1 cup sugar
1 egg
2 teaspoons cocoa
1 teaspoon cinnamon
2 cups milk or cream

3 cups flour
1 teaspoon soda
1 tablespoon melted grape
   jelly
Nuts

Beat together the sugar and egg, then add the cocoa and cinnamon and the milk or cream very slowly. Stir in the flour, then add the soda, dissolved in the jelly. Pour into a loaf-pan and scatter some nuts over the top. Bake in a moderate oven (350°-400° F.) about forty minutes.

FONDANT CAKE

¾ cup cream
2 eggs
2 cups powdered sugar

2 cups flour
Chopped almonds or grated
   lemon-rind

Cover the bottom of a shallow cake-pan with oiled paper. Blend cream, eggs, sugar and flour and pour into the pan. Sprinkle some finely chopped almonds or some grated lemon-rind on top of the cake. Bake in a moderate oven (350°-400° F.) for twenty or thirty minutes. It is preferable served hot.

CHESTNUT DESSERT

2 pounds chestnuts
½ cup sugar
¼ cup water
1 tablespoon vanilla

4 or 5 apples
1 tablespoon butter
1 teaspoon cinnamon
2 tablespoons apricot jelly

Blanch and peel the chestnuts and cook until soft, then rub through a sieve. Make a sirup of the sugar and water, add the vanilla and chestnuts and stir until the mixture is smooth. Place in a ring on a plate. Cook the apples until soft, mash them, add the butter, cinnamon, and apricot jelly. Put this mixture in the center of the chestnut ring and garnish with preserved fruits.

APPLES BAKED WITH BREAD

Remove the cores from good-sized apples; fill with jam and butter. Place round slices of stale bread in a baking-dish and put an apple on each. Pour scalded milk and water over the bread. Bake until the apples are soft. Serve in the baking-dish.

MOCHA PUDDING

⅓ cup butter or other fat	¾ cup cold strong coffee
1 cup brown sugar	¼ teaspoon vanilla
3 egg-yolks	12 lady fingers

Cream the fat and add sugar gradually, then the egg-yolks. Add coffee little by little, and vanilla. If coffee is added quickly, the mixture will curdle. Line a mold with the lady fingers. Turn the mocha mixture into the middle, and chill. Unmold and serve on a platter.

SOUR MILK PUDDING

1 quart sour milk	1 tablespoon lemon-juice
3 eggs	4 tablespoons granulated
2 tablespoons powdered sugar	sugar

Heat the milk slowly until it separates, and drain the whey from the curd. Add the eggs, powdered sugar, and lemon-juice to the curd, and beat thoroughly. Caramelize the granulated sugar and pour it into a mold. Add the curd mixture and bake the pudding for twenty minutes.

MOLDED CHOCOLATE PUDDING

½ cake sweet chocolate or 3 squares bitter chocolate	2 tablespoons gelatin
2 tablespoons sugar	2 egg-whites
3 cups milk	Marshmallow whip
	Cherries

Melt the chocolate and sugar in the milk in a double boiler. Add the gelatin, previously soaked in three tablespoons of water. Pour the mixture into a wet mold and let it stand in a cool place until the pudding is firm. Turn the pudding on to a glass dish and garnish it with beaten egg-whites mixed with marshmallow whip. Place a cherry in the center of each mound of garnish.

RICE CROWN WITH APRICOTS

Cook rice in milk and put in a buttered ring mold. When cool, turn into a fruit-dish. Cook dried apricots and place halves around the top of the crown. Strain the remainder of the fruit through a fine sieve and pour in the hollow of the crown. If this dish is desired hot, put the mold in the oven for a few minutes before trimming it with the apricots.

BREAD PUDDING

6 or 8 slices stale bread	½ cup seeded raisins
Salt	1 quart milk
2 eggs	½ teaspoon cinnamon
¼ cup sugar	1 teaspoon lemon extract

Dip slices of stale bread in slightly salted water until they are soft. Drain and put into a bowl, adding the well-beaten eggs, the sugar, and the seeded raisins. Scald the milk, flavor it with the cinnamon and lemon extract, pour it over the bread, and fill a greased pudding-dish with the mixture. Set in a pan of hot water and cook in the oven (250°-350° F.) from forty-five to sixty minutes. Serve with hard sauce.

APPLE MERINGUE PUDDING

Toasted bread	Sugar
Hot milk	Nutmeg
1 dozen apples	3 eggs

Cover the bottom and sides of a baking-pan with toasted bread, wet with hot milk. Core the apples and cook them whole; sweeten with sugar and flavor with nutmeg. Beat the yolks of the eggs together with a little sugar and pour over the apples. Put the apples in the baking-pan over the bread, then cover with the stiffly beaten whites of the eggs. Bake in a slow oven (300°-350° F.) for a few minutes.

HOT AND COLD BEVERAGES

Coffee

THE standard kinds of coffee on the market today are Mocha, Java, Bogota, Rio and Santos. Although only about three per cent of the coffee used in the United States is actually from Mocha or Java, these names represent grades that are regularly for sale.

Buying Coffee

The size of the coffee bean is not important, since that differs with each variety; the color, however, may be, because this indicates the amount of roasting to which it has been subjected. A light-colored bean is likely to be mild in flavor; a medium one, somewhat stronger; while a very dark one may be bitter.

If possible, purchase unground coffee and grind it at home as it is needed. It is much more economical to use finely ground coffee, because more strength can be obtained from a given amount than from that which is coarser. If one has equipment for using pulverized coffee, that will be the most desirable.

CAFFEIN-FREE COFFEES—Coffees from which most or all of the caffein has been extracted are on the market. These are sold under trade names. Together with cereal beverages they are used by those who prefer them to coffee or who may find coffee too stimulating.

INSTANTANEOUS COFFEES consisting of finely pulverized coffee which may be dissolved in boiling water are available for campers and those who want a quick cup of coffee.

Storing Coffee

As coffee loses its strength when it is exposed to the air, it should be kept tightly covered, especially after it has been ground. When coffee has lost its flavor from exposure to the air, it can be improved by heating the dry coffee in a frying-pan, taking care not to let it burn. The flavor, however, will not be so good as the original flavor.

Methods of Making Coffee

The most delicious coffee is made with water just below the boiling-point. Many of the percolators and drip coffee-pots on the market are planned on this principle. Coffee should be served as soon as it is ready; if it has to stand, the pot should be tightly covered and the spout should be plugged with cotton or tissue, so that none of the aroma will be lost.

For weak coffee, use 1 level tablespoon coffee to 1 cup water. For medium coffee, use 2 level tablespoons coffee to 1 cup water.
For strong coffee, use 3 level tablespoons coffee to 1 cup water.

FILTERED OR DRIP COFFEE—There are many coffee-pots on the market for making filtered coffee. They all contain some sort of a strainer which allows the water to drip through the coffee very slowly. Pulverized coffee should be used for this method. Place the coffee in the strainer and pour boiling hot water over it. If the infusion is not strong enough, refilter it. Serve immediately. Glass tricolators of oven glass ware are excellent for making filtered coffee, as they hold the heat well.

BOILED COFFEE—Put the coffee into the pot with the white of an egg or some egg-shells and a little cold water and stir all together thoroughly. Pour boiling water over it and place on the stove. Cover the spout of the coffee-pot or stuff it with paper to preserve the aroma. As soon as it boils up, reduce the heat and allow it to settle. A quarter of a cup of cold water poured in will cause the coffee to settle more quickly. Do not allow it to become muddy by careless pouring. To avoid this, decant it into a hot serving-pot.

PERCOLATED COFFEE—Use the correct size percolator for the number to be served. Measure fresh-running cold water into pot to same number of cups. Measure coffee, finely ground or pulverized, into the basket, using 1 heaping tablespoonful to cup of water. Use medium heat or flame until percolating begins, then lower flame and continue for 8 to 10 minutes, when the liquid in the glass cap is light brown or deep amber. Serve at once. Prolonged percolating dissipates the fine aroma and flavor.

AFTER-DINNER COFFEE

The best after-dinner coffee is made with a filter. If really black coffee is desired, use three tablespoons of finely ground

coffee to each cup of freshly boiled water. Wet the strainer in cold water before adding the coffee. Pour the boiling water slowly upon the coffee, and leave the pot over the heat while the water is finding its way through the fine grains and absorbing their flavor. When all the liquid has dripped through, the coffee is done and should be served at once.

VIENNA COFFEE

Make after-dinner coffee and serve in demi-tasses topped with stiffly whipped cream. Sugar may be used if desired. This style coffee is best suited to afternoon or evening service, although it is adapted for after-dinner service as well. Serve with small cakes.

CAFÉ AU LAIT

Make medium or strong coffee by the drip or percolator method and while it is being prepared scald an equal amount of fresh milk. Pour the coffee and hot milk together into the cups in equal amounts, one pot in each hand.

TURKISH COFFEE

Use finely pulverized coffee. Mix one tablespoon of coffee for each demi-tasse with an equal amount of granulated sugar. When the water is boiling briskly, add the coffee, and when it looks frothy remove from the fire. In a moment or two, boil it up again and repeat a third time. It should be thick and foamy. Serve at once, without cream, as the last course at dinner or luncheon or as a refreshment in the evening with small cakes. It is too strong to serve in cups any larger than demi-tasse.

ICED COFFEE

Make coffee of desired strength—it should be fairly strong, as the ice dilutes it. Cool it and serve in tall glasses with cracked ice; or pour the hot coffee over cracked ice, in glasses, adding more ice if needed. Top the glass with whipped cream or vanilla ice-cream. Cream may be poured on the ice before the coffee is added, and the coffee may then be topped with whipped cream.

Cereal Beverages

Grains, roasted so that they produce a brown infusion, similar in appearance to coffee, are obtainable in several brands. These furnish a hot beverage for many who do not care for or cannot drink coffee or tea. They are excellent breakfast beverages for children and young people. Directions for preparing them are given on the packages.

Tea

A cup of tea with its delicately fascinating aroma is one of the most delicious beverages, but probably no other is attended with such doubtful results, chiefly because the average person knows little about the selection of teas, and methods of brewing it are uncertain.

Varieties of Tea

Teas divide into three groups according to the method used in preparing them for market.

UNOXIDIZED OR UNFERMENTED—These include the green teas, an example of which would be the Japan pan-dried tea. The leaves are greenish and the tea made from them is light colored and delicate in flavor.

PARTLY OXIDIZED OR PARTLY FERMENTED—These include the Oolong and Ceylon varieties. The leaves are brown and the tea made from them is darker in color than that made from the unfermented leaves and has a characteristic aromatic flavor.

OXIDIZED OR FERMENTED—These are known as black teas, such as English Breakfast or China Congou, and India teas such as Darjeeling and Pekoe. The leaves are black and the beverage has a rich dark color and a fruit flavor.

During oxidation or fermentation, chemical changes take place which improve the flavor and reduce the amount of tannin, the substance which gives tea its astringency. As green teas are not oxidized, they contain a larger proportion of tannin than the others and consequently have a more astringent flavor.

Buying Tea

Buy tea that has well-curled leaves and that is free from stems or dust. In preparing tea for marketing, the leaves are withered or steamed and then rolled by hand or machinery.

Tea with very large leaves, dusty tea or tea in which stems are found in abundance is of poor quality and even though offered at a reduced price is bad economy, as a large quantity must be used to produce even a fair flavor.

Storing Tea

Tea will absorb moisture and odors, and the volatile oil, to which it owes much of its flavor, will evaporate. Store tea, therefore, in tightly covered cans and in a cool place.

Best Method of Making Tea

Glass or earthenware pots are by all means to be preferred in making tea; avoid metal if the best flavor is desired.

THE QUALITY OF DRY TEA TO USE to 1 cup of water varies with the grade of tea and the strength desired. In general 1 teaspoon of tea to a cup gives good results.

THE METHOD OF MAKING is simple but important. Heat pot by filling with boiling water. Empty. Add tea leaves and freshly boiling water. Cover and allow it to brew for 3 to 5 minutes in warm place. Remove tea container or pour off the liquid into another warm pot or into cups. Serve at once. Do not boil tea while brewing or attempt to re-use leaves.

TEA MAY BE PUT IN A TEA BALL or a muslin bag and taken out when sufficiently steeped. These containers should be not more than half full, to allow the tea leaves room to swell.

MAKING TEA IN A CUP with the aid of a tea ball or strainer is not to be encouraged, as the tea does not steep long enough and the flavor and aroma are dissipated.

TEA MAY BE SERVED WITH SUGAR, cream or milk, lemon, cloves, candied cherries, orange peel or rose leaves and mint. Black teas are best to serve with cream.

ICED TEA

METHOD 1—Make hot tea double strength by using twice as many tea leaves as usual for each cup of water. Brew as usual and pour into glasses or pitcher filled with ice cubes.

METHOD 2—Make hot tea regular strength. Brew as usual and pour over tea cubes made by freezing regular strength tea in automatic refrigerator trays.

METHOD 3—Make hot tea regular strength. Brew as usual and cool. Add a little ice to chill and serve.

MATÉ

Maté is a beverage similar to tea, made from the roasted leaves of a South American tree. It has a refreshing and stimulating effect similar to that of tea and coffee but contains less caffeine and tannin and has no astringent qualities. The flavor is heavier than tea with a floral bouquet.

PREPARE MATÉ like tea, using only an earthenware or glass container for brewing. Let steep 5 minutes, then remove leaves at once. Do not boil. Strain and serve. Sugar, cream, lemon or crushed mint leaves may be served with maté if desired.

ICED MATÉ may be prepared like iced tea.

Chocolate and Cocoa

CHOCOLATE is made from cocoa beans that are ground under pressure. It is sold in the unsweetened form, such as we commonly use for a beverage, and also sweetened and flavored. If chocolate is stored in a warm room, the fat known as cocoa butter will melt and come to the surface, and when it hardens will give the chocolate a gray look, because the fat is practically white. The cake of chocolate, however, is as good to use as ever. The instantaneous chocolates found on the market are combinations of cocoa, flavoring, sugar and often milk powder.

COCOA is the ground bean from which part of the fat has been extracted. It should be a rich reddish brown in color. If it is very dark, it is usually because it has been artificially colored or made from imperfectly cleansed beans or those of a poor quality.

Cocoa is a valuable food and is an excellent medium by which to introduce milk into the diet. Because it contains a stimulant, it is best to use a minimum of cocoa and a maximum of milk when giving it to children.

Cocoa preparations, in which cocoa, sugar, powdered milk and malt are used, make quickly prepared beverages.

The method of making all beverages containing cocoa is based on the fact that cocoa is rich in starch; therefore cocoa boiled for five minutes has a much better flavor than that which is made by simply adding it to scalded milk, because cooking improves the flavor of all starches.

COCOA

2 to 3 tablespoons cocoa	1 to 2 tablespoons sugar
½ cup water	⅛ teaspoon salt
1 quart milk	

Stir cocoa, sugar and either hot or cold water together and boil over the fire for five minutes; add salt. Scald the milk in a double boiler; add to the cocoa mixture and stir until well blended. Or, add cold milk to the cocoa mixture after boiling for five minutes and let it stand over hot water until hot and well blended. Beat with a rotary egg-beater to make foamy before serving. Whipped cream or marshmallows may be served with cocoa.

CHOCOLATE

2 squares unsweetened chocolate	3 tablespoons sugar
	3 tablespoons water
4 cups milk	

Scrape the chocolate fine, mix it with the water and heat over hot water until the chocolate is melted. Bring the milk to the scalding point (in a double boiler), add the chocolate and the sugar, stir until dissolved and whip with an egg-beater until the beverage is light and frothy.

ICED CHOCOLATE

Make chocolate or cocoa as usual; cool and serve in tall glasses with chopped ice, topped with sweetened whipped cream.

RECEPTION CHOCOLATE

1 quart milk	½ cup sugar
½ cup cocoa	½ teaspoon vanilla
¼ cup flour	⅛ teaspoon salt
1 quart water	

Mix dry ingredients and make a smooth paste with some of the water. Pour on the remainder of the water and boil slowly for fifteen minutes. Combine with the milk, bring to the boiling-point. Add vanilla. Serve with whipped cream. This is a very thick, rich cocoa which is improved by standing over hot water an hour or more.

Fruit Beverages

Fruit beverages are particularly valuable in the diet. They should be served more frequently than any of the others except milk. The time has passed when we think of them as only for formal or semi-formal occasions or for the warmest Summer days. They offer most desirable minerals, are rich in vitamins, and, because of the sugar used to sweeten them, are fairly high in fuel value. Most of the fruit-juices have a wholesome laxative effect. In the Summer they make refreshing drinks; through the Winter, the juices that have been bottled during the warmer months plus the fresh juices available from the citrus fruits are a source of vitamins and minerals, which may be so lacking in the diet at that time; and in the Spring they are most valuable stimulants to the jaded appetite. The tang of their acid flavor and their attractive color make them welcome additions to the table.

Grape-juice, pineapple-juice, tomato-juice concentrated grapefruit-juice and orange-juice, etc., for making fruit beverages, may be bought in bottles or cans.

COMBINATIONS OF FRUITS—Any combination of fruit-juices will make a successful beverage provided some of the more tart juices, such as those from lemons, sour oranges, apple cider or rhubarb, are present to give the necessary acidity.

SUGAR SIRUPS—A beverage sweetened with a sugar sirup is better than one to which unmelted sugar has been added. The sirup gives a smoother texture and is easily mixed through the whole drink, while sugar has a tendency to sink to the bottom.

The amounts of sugar given in the recipes can not be exact, as the sugar must vary according to the acidity of the fruit and individual taste.

UTENSILS—It is best to use silver, glass or stainless steel in cutting fruit, or for pressing or stirring the juices. Some metals give a metallic flavor to the beverage. Utensils of glass, china, enamel or wood are the most desirable to use for holding the juices.

CHILLING—Fruit beverages may be chilled by putting cracked ice into the beverage or into a bowl in which the container holding the beverage is set. Ice cubes made in the trays of the mechanical refrigerator are excellent for chilling beverages.

SUGAR SIRUP

4 cups sugar   4 cups water

Boil sugar and water together for ten minutes. Pour into clean hot jars and seal. This sirup may be kept on hand and used as needed.

No. 1.   LEMONADE

6 lemons   3 cups water   1 to 1½ cups sugar sirup

Squeeze the juice from the fruit. Mix well with the sirup and water. Serve very cold.

No. 2.

6 lemons   4 cups water   ½ to ⅔ cup sugar

Squeeze the juice from the lemons and mix with the water and sugar. See that the sugar is well dissolved.

VARIATIONS OF LEMONADE

APPLE LEMONADE—Wash apples and dice, using everything, including skin and core. Cook with enough water to cover, strain through a cloth and add one cup sugar for each cup of juice thus obtained. Dissolve sugar in the juice and cool. Fill glasses half full of this apple sirup, add to each glass the juice of half a lemon and fill up with ice and water.

BERRY LEMONADE—To each glass of lemonade add two tablespoons of crushed fresh or canned berries—strawberries, raspberries, blackberries, loganberries or blueberries. Seedy fruits should be strained. Garnish with whole berries and serve with crushed ice.

CURRANT LEMONADE—

1 cup sugar   1 cup water
4 cups currants   Lemons

Cook the sugar with the currants until the fruit is soft. Add the water, strain and cool. Allow one-half lemon and one-half glass of currant sirup for each serving. Fill glasses with ice and water.

EGG LEMONADE, No. 1—For each glass use one beaten egg;

add the juice of one lemon and one-fourth teaspoon nutmeg. Fill glass with chilled water; shake well and serve.

No. 2—Into a tall glass half full of crushed ice put a spoonful of chopped fruit, pineapple, peaches or crushed berries. Beat in an egg, add juice of one lemon and sugar to taste. Fill glass with plain or effervescent water and shake or stir until very cold.

LEMON FROST—Fill a tall glass one-fourth full of cracked ice, add lemonade fill the glass three-fourths full and frost the top with a spoonful of stiffly beaten egg-white sweetened slightly and flavored with lemon-juice.

LEMON GINGER—For each glass allow two tablespoons ginger sirup, the juice of one-half lemon and two tablespoons pineapple-juice. Fill with cracked ice and water.

LEMON MINT—For each glass squeeze the juice of one lemon over six or seven crushed mint leaves. Sweeten to taste and add chopped ice, and water to fill the glass.

PINEAPPLE LEMONADE—

1 pineapple	1 cup sugar
1 quart boiling water	1 cup tea infusion
1 lemon	

Wash, slice and pare the pineapple, and take out all the eyes. Prepare the tender part to serve. Put the core, the rind and the grated rind of the lemon in a kettle and pour on the boiling water. Cover and simmer for half an hour. Strain through cheese-cloth. Add sugar, tea and lemon-juice. Serve cold. As some pineapples are much more sour than others, more sugar may be necessary.

LIMEADE

Limeade is made in the same way as lemonade, using limes instead of lemons and a little more sweetening. This is even more refreshing than lemonade in summer.

ORANGEADE

4 oranges	1 to 1½ cups sirup
1 lemon	3 cups water

Follow directions for lemonade given on the preceding page.

PINEAPPLE ORANGEADE

4 oranges   1 quart boiling water
1 pineapple   Sugar or sirup

Add the juicy parts of the pineapple, shredded, to the orange-juice. Pour the water over the fruit and sweeten to taste. Cover and set aside to cool. Strain and serve iced. Blood oranges will give the mixture an attractive pink color.

No. 1.   **MIXED FRUIT PUNCH**

1 quart blue grape-juice   Sugar or sirup to taste
1 pint white grape-juice   2 quarts ginger ale
Juice of 12 oranges   1 pint charged water
Juice of 12 lemons

Mix fruit and sugar or sirup. Add ginger ale and charged water and serve with chopped ice. This will serve twenty-five people.

No. 2.

1½ cups water   Juice of 6 lemons
1½ cups sugar   Juice of 6 oranges
1 quart grape-juice   1 pint tea
2 quarts chilled water   1 pint grated pineapple

Boil water and sugar ten minutes. Cool and add other ingredients and let stand one hour. Add chilled water and serve with chipped ice. This will serve twenty-five people.

No. 3.

2 cups water   1 cup white grapes
2 cups sugar   1 cup maraschino cherries
1 cup pineapple   Juice of 6 oranges
1 cup strawberries   Juice of 6 lemons
1 cup raspberries   2 quarts charged water
1 cup bananas

Boil water and sugar ten minutes. Cool and add crushed fruit and fruit-juice. Chill. Add charged water just before serving. This will serve twenty-five people.

GINGER ALE PUNCH

Juice of 4 lemons
1 pint grape-juice

Sugar or sirup to taste
1 quart ginger ale

Mix fruit-juices and sugar or sirup. Just before serving, add ginger ale.

GINGER PUNCH

1 quart water
1 cup sugar
¾ cup chopped Canton
    ginger

¼ cup ginger sirup
1 cup orange-juice
¼ cup lemon-juice
1 quart charged water

Boil water, sugar, ginger and ginger sirup for twenty minutes. Cool. Add fruit-juices and charged water gradually.

GRAPE JUICE PUNCH

1 cup sugar sirup
1 pint water
Juice of 3 lemons

Juice of 1 orange
1 pint grape-juice

Mix ingredients in order given. Chill and serve.

LEMON PUNCH

Juice of 6 lemons
Juice of 3 oranges
1 quart water

½ cup mashed strawberries
½ cup crushed pineapple

Mix fruit-juice, sweeten to taste with sirup, add water and crushed fruit. Garnish with very thin slices of orange.

PARADISE ISLAND PUNCH

½ cup sirup
1 quart pineapple-juice
Juice of 2 oranges
Juice of 1 lemon

Juice of ½ grapefruit
½ cup crushed pineapple
½ cup crushed strawberries

Proceed as for lemon punch.

RASPBERRY PUNCH

1 lemon
1 cup raspberries
1 cup currants

1 pint boiling water
1 cup sugar
1 cup tea infusion

Crush fruit and strain through a cloth. Without taking the pulp from the cloth, put it into another dish and pour the boiling water over it. Drain off, but do not squeeze or it will be muddy. Add the sugar and stir until it is dissolved. Cool thoroughly before adding the fruit-juice and tea.

VERANDA PUNCH

Juice of 3 lemons
Juice of 2 oranges
½ cup sugar sirup

1 cup tea infusion
1 pint ginger ale
1 pint charged water

Mix fruit-juice and sugar sirup. Add the hot tea. Cool, and, when ready to serve, add ginger ale and charged water. Thin slices of lemon and orange may be used for a garnish.

LOGANBERRY COCKTAIL

2 cups loganberry-juice
1 cup orange-juice
Juice of 1 lemon

1 cup water
¼ cup sirup

Proceed as in lemon punch.

MOCK CLARET CUP

Small stick of cinnamon bark
3 lemons
5 oranges
1 pint water

1 cup currant-juice
Sugar sirup
¼ cup currants
1 cup tea infusion

Boil cinnamon, lemon-rinds and orange-rinds in the water for ten minutes. Strain, and when cool add other ingredients including the juice of the lemons and oranges. Serve in a tall glass and garnish with currants.

CHILLED GRAPE JUICE

Wash purple grapes and boil until skin, pulp and seeds separate. Press through jelly-bag and to every pint of juice add one-half cup of sugar. Boil for twenty minutes, chill and serve with shaved ice.

GRAPE JUICE HIGHBALL

Use Niagara grapes. Proceed as for recipe for chilled grape-juice. Serve in tall glasses half filled with shaved ice and add an equal quantity of charged water. Lemon is an attractive addition.

GRAPE-JUICE RICKY

For each glass mix the juice of one-half lime with one-half glass of grape-juice and two tablespoons of sugar. Shake in a mixer with crushed ice. Fill glass with plain or charged water.

ORANGE LILY

½ cup white grape-juice   2 tablespoons orange-juice
1 teaspoon sugar

Fill glass half full of shaved ice. Add grape-juice, orange-juice and sugar and fill with chilled water. Serve with two straws thrust through a thin slice of orange.

QUAKER DRINK

3 sprigs of mint   Juice of 3 oranges
3 cups tea infusion   ½ teaspoon powdered ginger
Juice of 3 lemons   2 cups cold water

Bruise mint. Pour the tea over the fruit-juice. Mix ginger with two tablespoons hot water and the cold water. Mix all ingredients. Chill and serve.

EGGNOG

1 egg   1 tablespoon powdered sugar
Pinch of salt   2 tablespoons fruit-juice
Milk

Add salt to the egg-white and beat to a stiff froth. Add the sugar, the well-beaten yolk of the egg and the fruit-juice. Fill the glass with ice-cold milk. Sprinkle top with chopped nuts. The egg-yolk and white may be beaten together rather than separately, if desired.

MILK SHAKE

Fill a glass two-thirds full of ice-cold milk. Sweeten to taste and flavor with two tablespoons of fruit-juice, strained preserves, melted jelly or chocolate sirup. Fill the glass with finely chopped ice. Shake well. In the absence of a regulation "mixer" pour from one glass into another. When frothy, sprinkle with cinnamon or nutmeg.

MILK PUNCH

2 tablespoons sugar	1 cup milk
¼ cup charged water	½ teaspoon vanilla

Mix sugar, vanilla and milk. Stir well and add the water. Pour this mixture from one bowl to another to froth it. Hold the bowl high as you pour the liquid. When it is frothy, pour it into a tumbler and serve.

ICE CREAM PUFF

Break an egg into a mixing-glass and add four tablespoons of any preferred fruit sirup and a serving of vanilla ice-cream. Shake until well mixed, fill with carbonated water and sprinkle with nutmeg. Extra ice-cream may be added just before serving.

ORANGE MILK SHAKE

2½ cups orange juice	½ teaspoon salt
1½ cups grapefruit juice	¼ teaspoon almond extract
1 cup evaporated milk	¼ cup sugar
1 cup water	1 cup cracked ice

Combine all ingredients as listed, in a shaker; shake until well mixed.

COFFEE-EGG MILK SHAKE—Use 3 cups cold strong coffee, 3 eggs, well beaten, 6 cups chilled milk, 6 tablespoons cream, sugar to taste and dash of salt. Add enough iced carbonated water to each glass to foam mixture to the top.

COFFEE-CHOCOLATE MILK SHAKE—Use 1½ cups cold strong coffee, ¾ cup chocolate sauce (page 580) and 7 cups milk. Top each glass with 1 tablespoon whipped cream, if desired.

ICED COFFEE SHAKE—Use 3 cups cold strong coffee, 3 drops almond extract, 2 cups chilled milk, 2 cups Apollinaris water and powdered sugar to taste. Top each glass with sweetened whipped cream and dust with cinnamon.

For additional beverage recipes including wines see pages 737 to 757.

FOODS AND BEVERAGES
FOR INVALIDS

A DOCTOR'S advice is necessary in planning the diet for an invalid, as each case must be considered individually. The following general suggestions are intended to help the housewife who, in addition to her other work, has the duty of ministering to the needs of the sick and convalescent.

THE PROPER SELECTION AND PREPARATION of food for an invalid is important, but the best cooked and most palatable food may be spoiled in the serving. When possible, remove all bottles and suggestions of medicine from the room. Use a light tray, and serve everything as nicely as possible—the hot things really hot; the cold dishes cold, not lukewarm. In illness, even more than in health, care in serving is imperative, for appetite may be poor.

MEALS SHOULD BE SERVED AT REGULAR INTERVALS, and although the patient should not be consulted about the food to be brought to him, his likes and dislikes should be considered as far as possible.

BEFORE SERVING THE MEAL, be sure that the patient is ready for it, with hands and face washed; and that provision has been made for placing the tray where it will be convenient for him or his attendant to reach it. Special raised trays or bedside tables may be bought; or a rest may be improvised by placing a block of wood or a bundle of magazines on each side of the patient so that he will not have to bear the weight of the tray on his knees.

THE TRAY SHOULD BE COVERED with a clean napkin or tray cover, and the dishes and serving should be very dainty. A flower or sprig of green will often take an invalid's mind from the food, and the attractiveness of the whole will tempt him to eat what would otherwise remain untouched. Serving the meal in courses will add to the interest. Place the courses on the tray in the order in which they are to be eaten and within easy reach of the patient. Do not serve too much of any one food. Invalids will often take liquid diet through a straw and enjoy it after the glass has become tiresome.

REMOVE THE TRAY AND DISHES as soon as the patient has finished eating. In contagious diseases, sterilize everything used in the sick-room by boiling in water for ten minutes.

Milk and Egg Dishes

MILK

HOT—Heat the milk quickly over direct heat, stirring constantly, and serve at once. Heat the cup before pouring in the milk, and cover it with a saucer for carrying to the sick-room. Hot milk is a mild stimulant in cases of extreme fatigue. Cooked milk will agree with many persons who cannot take raw milk.

DILUTED—If milk disagrees with a patient it may sometimes be made more digestible by diluting it with barley water, oatmeal water or any good carbonated water, in the proportions of two tablespoons or more of the water to one cup of milk.

ALBUMENIZED—

1 egg-white	½ cup cold milk
2 tablespoons cracked ice	Pinch of salt

Beat the egg-white with a fork or egg-beater, add ice, milk and salt. Beat or shake enough to mix well.

ARTIFICIAL BUTTERMILK.

1 quart skimmed milk	¼ cup water
1 buttermilk tablet	

Pasteurize the milk (See Index) and cool it to body temperature. Dissolve the tablet in the water, and add this to the milk. Mix thoroughly and stand covered in a warm place for twenty-four hours, or until a solid curd is formed. Keep in a cool place until needed. Beat smooth with a rotary egg-beater or shake thoroughly just before serving.

KUMISS.

1 quart milk	1½ tablespoons sugar
¼ yeast-cake	

Heat the milk to 75° F., add the sugar and the yeast-cake dissolved in lukewarm water. Fill sterilized bottles to within one and one-half inches of top, cork tightly and shake. It may be necessary to tie the corks on the bottles, as the yeast causes the milk to ferment and if gas is produced in considerable amounts the corks are forced out. Invert the bottles and place where they can remain at a temperature of about 70° F. for ten hours. Place in the refrigerator inverted and let stand for twenty-four hours, shaking now and then to prevent the cream from forming in the mouth of the bottle. If left standing too long, it becomes less palatable. It should look like thick foamy cream when ready to serve. In opening the bottle care must be taken not to let the milk foam over.

WHEY

Whey is the water solution of milk sugar, salts and minerals which forms the basis of fresh whole milk and which is separated from the curd and fat as follows:

½ rennet tablet   1 cup fresh whole milk
                1 tablespoon cold water

Dissolve rennet tablet in water. Warm milk slowly, stirring until lukewarm—not hot (120° F.). A few drops of milk on the inside of the wrist should feel comfortably warm. Remove milk from stove. Add dissolved rennet tablet and stir quickly for a few seconds, then let stand unmoved until firm. While warm, cut curd gently into coarse pieces to separate from the whey and strain carefully through fine bleached muslin (72 to 76 mesh). Sweeten and flavor if desired. Serve as the doctor orders.

WITH LEMON-JUICE—
  1 cup hot milk   2 teaspoons sugar
  2 tablespoons lemon-juice

Add lemon-juice to hot milk and let stand over hot water until the milk separates. Strain through a double thickness of cheese-cloth and add the sugar to the whey.

WITH ORANGE-JUICE—Substitute orange-juice for lemon-juice and use one-half the sugar in the recipe for lemon whey.

EGGS

STEAMED—Put a piece of butter in an oatmeal dish, remove the tea-kettle lid and set the dish over the boiling water. When the butter is melted, break an egg into the dish, and cover with the tea-kettle cover. The egg will cook in a few minutes, will keep hot, and may be served in the same dish. This is also an easy way of scrambling eggs without changing the dish.

For Other Ways of Serving Eggs to Invalids look in the index for the following recipes: Coddled Eggs, Poached or Dropped Eggs, Battered or Scrambled Eggs, Shirred Eggs, Baked Eggs, Egg Timbales, Egg Toast, Scalloped Eggs, Creamed Eggs, Eggs à la Goldenrod, Plain Puffy Omelet, Plain French Omelet, Cream Omelet, Oyster Omelet, and others, depending on the condition of the patient to be served.

EGG DRINKS

Albumen Water—No. 1.

1 egg-white	Sugar
1 cup ice-water	1 tablespoon lemon-juice

Stir the white of an egg with a sliver fork, and add the water. Serve plain or sweeten and flavor with lemon-juice. Mix well.

No. 2.

2 teaspoons sugar	1 egg-white
½ cup warm water	Pinch of salt
2 tablespoons lemon-juice or	Crushed ice
3 tablespoons orange-juice	

Dissolve the sugar in the warm water. Add lemon-juice. Beat egg-white enough so that it will mix; add salt and put with remaining ingredients. Shake or beat the mixture. Strain, and serve with cracked ice.

See Index for Egg Lemonade, Egg Orangeade, Eggnog, etc.

Cereal Dishes

In preparing any of the grain foods for an invalid, take special care to see that they are well cooked. In some cases the cereal may be put through a sieve or purée strainer. Whole-grain foods are important laxative articles of diet.

BANANA GRUEL

Stir banana meal into hot milk, and add sugar to taste.

OATMEAL PREPARATIONS

For oatmeal gruel and oatmeal water when the prepared oat flour is used, follow the directions for barley gruel and water. They may, however, be made from either coarse oatmeal or rolled oats. If the latter are used, they should be prepared as described in the chapter on cereals, (See Index) using the following proportions:

OATMEAL GRUEL—
 ¼ cup rolled oats or ⅓ cup coarse oatmeal   1½ cups water

OATMEAL WATER—
 1½ tablespoons rolled oats or 2 tablespoons coarse oatmeal
2 cups water

OATMEAL JELLY—
 4 tablespoons rolled oats or 5½ tablespoons coarse oatmeal
1½ cups water

BARLEY PREPARATIONS

BARLEY GRUEL, NO. 1.
 1 tablespoon barley flour   1½ cups boiling water
 1½ tablespoons cold water   Salt

Mix the flour with the cold water. Add the boiling water gradually, stirring constantly, and boil hard for thirty minutes. Salt to taste. Strain through a very fine sieve.

No. 2—Use the same ingredients as for No. 1 but decrease the boiling water to one cup and add one-half cup of hot milk to the gruel when serving.

BARLEY WATER, NO. 1.
 2 teaspoons barley flour   2 cups boiling water
 1 tablespoon cold water

Follow directions for barley gruel.

No. 2.
 2 tablespoons pearl barley   1 quart cold water

Wash the barley, and soak for five hours or over night in the cold water. Cook until it has boiled down to a pint. Strain twice.

BARLEY JELLY—

| 2 tablespoons barley flour | 2 cups boiling water |
| 4 tablespoons cold water | |

Follow directions for barley gruel. Strain into a mold, chill, and serve with sugar and cream.

INDIAN-MEAL GRUEL

2 tablespoons corn-meal	1 quart boiling water
1 tablespoon flour	½ teaspoon salt
4 tablespoons cold water	

Mix the meal and flour with the cold water, rub smooth, and stir the paste into the boiling water. Stir well, and when the gruel boils, lower the heat so it will simmer gently for two hours. Add the salt, cook for one-half hour longer, and serve with cream or milk.

PANADA

| Boiling water | 2 soda or graham crackers |

Place the crackers in a bowl, and add just enough boiling water to soak them well. Set the bowl in a vessel of boiling water, and let it remain twenty or thirty minutes, until the crackers are quite clear, but not broken. Lift them out carefully without breaking and lay them on a hot saucer. Salt if necessary. Serve very hot with sugar and cream.

RICE JELLY

2 tablespoons rice flour	Salt and sugar
1 cup boiling water	Cinnamon or lemon-juice, if
Cold water	desired

Mix the rice flour with enough cold water to make a thin paste, and then add the boiling water. Sweeten and salt to taste, and boil until the rice flour is transparent. Add a little cinnamon or lemon-juice as flavoring, if desired.

Wet a mold with cold water, pour in the jelly, and when cold serve with milk or cream and sugar.

FLAXSEED LEMONADE

4 tablespoons whole flaxseed	4 tablespoons sugar
1 quart boiling water	Juice of 2 lemons

Simmer the flaxseed in the water for an hour or more. Strain, add sugar and lemon-juice, and serve hot.

CHICKEN BROTH

1 fowl (3 pounds)	2 tablespoons sago or tapioca
2 quarts cold water	or rice
1 teaspoon salt	

Wash the chicken and remove all the skin and fat. Cut it into small pieces, crack the bones well, and place it in a kettle with two quarts of cold water and let stand one-half hour. Set the kettle on the fire in a slow heat, add the rice, and gradually bring the water to the boiling-point. Keep it simmering for three hours, with the kettle tightly covered. Season with salt, skim off fat, strain off the broth, and serve. If made the day before using, the soup may be allowed to cool, when fat may be more easily removed.

BEEF JUICE

Broil one-half pound round of beef, cut about four inches square and an inch thick, until both sides are browned and the meat is well warmed through to start the juices. Two minutes should be sufficient. Sprinkle with salt, cut in pieces, place in a presser, lemon-squeezer or potato-ricer and squeeze out all the juice. One-half pound of beef yields two ounces or four tablespoons of juice.

Sufficient juice for two servings is generally prepared at one time. Warm the second serving over boiling water, stirring the juice constantly until it is a little more than lukewarm and serve at once.

BEEF TEA—Place 1 pound lean, ground beef in a fruit jar. Add 1 pint cold water, and let stand 1 hour. Place jar in a saucepan of cold water with a cloth on bottom of pan under the jar, and heat water slowly to 140° F. Do not let it boil. Continue two hours, then slowly increase heat until beef tea turns a deep chocolate color. Add ½ teaspoon salt.

HIGH ALTITUDE COOKING

THE boiling point of water is called 212° F. but actually that temperature is reached only at sea level. For every 500 feet ascent the boiling point drops one degree. As altitudes rise in this country from sea level to 12,000 feet, food boils at 202° F. in Denver, and 198° F. in Laramie.

Simple boiling processes are carried on by the use of a pressure cooker or a sealed steamer as indicated under vegetable cookery (pages 386 to 388). In the baking of meats and vegetables oven heat can be regulated without regard to altitude. Above 7,000 feet, additional time must be allowed. The little book called "Vegetable Cookery at High Altitudes" by Emma J. Thiessen of the University of Wyoming will be found valuable.

Candy and frostings can no longer be tested by temperature because the soft-ball stage, which is 236° F. up to 1,000 feet, is 226° F. at 3,000 feet, 223° F. at 5,000 feet, and 220° F. at 7,000 feet. The other stages also occur at lower temperatures as the altitude rises. Testing consistency of the sirup by the finger or the saccharometer is the way out.

High altitude does the greatest damage to the baking processes, particularly to those baked foods containing sugar, non-yeast leavening, and shortening.

Marjorie W. Peterson of Colorado State College has made a careful study entitled "Baking Quick Breads and Cakes at High Altitudes," giving recipes for sea level with their necessary variations for 3,000 to 11,180 feet. Miss Peterson calls attention to some general requirements for all high levels. Cake and bread flours should be used exactly as indicated and not interchanged. Reductions in the amounts of sugar and baking powder as well as fat must also be made as the altitude rises, and while these bear a certain ratio per thousand feet, they are not regular. The modern woman living in high altitudes would do well to buy Miss Peterson's booklet.

CANNING, PRESERVING AND JELLY MAKING

TO Preserve Foods by Canning we must do two things. First, we must provide sufficient heat to destroy all microscopic life that will cause spoilage in food; and, second, we must provide a perfect seal which will prevent the re-entrance of microorganisms. These problems of preventing spoilage have been practically solved by the improved methods of canning which are explained below.

Only the freshest of fruits and vegetables should be canned. Canning does not improve the product; it only preserves it for future use.

METHODS OF CANNING

OPEN KETTLE—This method involves cooking the product completely and pouring it into sterilized jars, using only sterilized equipment throughout. The jars are then sealed and stored. There is always the possibility of spoilage through contamination of product or jars, because there is no period of sterilization after the jars are sealed. Tomatoes may be safely canned by this method and so may preserves which are cooked in a thick sirup. For all other foods the following methods are safer.

COLD PACK—Foods that need to be arranged in the jars may be canned by this method. They are packed cold into jars and then are cooked and sterilized simultaneously by heating in the jars in boiling water or steam. The jars can be only partially sealed before processing because the food expands during heating and may cause the jars to crack if the seal is too tight.

HOT PACK is the preferred method. Foods are packed into the jars boiling hot and processed in boiling water or steam. The advantage of this method is that the jars may be completely sealed if the processing is to be done in water.

EQUIPMENT

GLASS JARS—Glass jars are sold with a variety of tops: glass, zinc with glass or porcelain lining and metal with a gasket which melts during the processing and automatically seals the jar. Rubber rings are used with all lids except those with automatic seal. New rings or new automatic seal lids must be used each year. Examine jars and lids for nicks. If there appear to be none, fit a new ring to the jar, partly fill with hot water, adjust lid and seal. Invert jar and watch for leakage or small bubbles rising through the water as it cools. An imperfect seal on jars having a wire bail can usually be corrected by removing the top bail, bending it down in the middle and in at the ends and replacing on jar. Test rings by bending double. If the rubber cracks the ring should not be used.

TIN CANS—Tin cans may be purchased plain or with enamel linings of 2 types. The R enamel cans are used for strongly acid foods and for those having a red color. They have a bright gold lining. The C type has a dull gold lining and is used for corn and other vegetables high in protein. To can meat, use plain tin cans, never the enamel lined ones. New lids for tin cans must be purchased each year but the cans may be reflanged and used as many as 3 times.

MECHANICAL SEALER—A mechanical sealer is necessary if tin cans are used and the adjustment of the sealer should be tested each time before using it. To test it, place 2 tablespoons of water in a can, adjust cover and seal. Submerge in boiling water and keep it below the surface until the steam formed in the can expands the ends. Air bubbles rising from the can indicate incorrect adjustment of the sealer. The sealer should be adjusted and the test made again.

WATER BATH CANNER—Fruits and acid vegetables may be processed in a water bath canner. This may be purchased or improvised from a wash boiler or large kettle. It must be deep enough to allow processing the jars in boiling water that is at least 1 inch over their tops and must have a rack in the bottom to prevent the jars from bumping when the water boils.

PRESSURE CANNER—All meats and nonacid vegetables should be processed only in a pressure cooker, in order to destroy the sporeforming bacteria. The pressure canner should be substantially constructed and should have a pressure indicator, a safety valve and a petcock.

PROCEDURE

Inspect and test all equipment before beginning to prepare the product to be canned. Wash jars and cans thoroughly in hot soapy water and rinse in clear hot water. If canning is to be done by the open kettle method, place jars, lids, rings, knife, spoon and funnel in a kettle of boiling water and boil 15 minutes. Leave in water until wanted. For cold or hot pack canning, leave jars in rinsing water or drain tin cans on a clean towel.

Choose vegetables that are young and that have made a quick growth.

Do not use very dirty vegetables as more microorganisms are present on these than on clean vegetables.

Do not attempt to handle too large a quantity of vegetables at once, especially in hot weather. The various steps in the canning process must be followed in rapid succession to prevent loss of flavor caused by what is known as flat sour, and large quantities can not be handled rapidly.

Can vegetables as soon as possible after they have been picked. This is particularly necessary with asparagus, peas, beans and corn.

Clean the vegetables thoroughly and prepare them as for cooking.

Select firm, well-grown, but not overripe fruit.

If possible, can fruit on the day that it is picked.

To can fruit without sugar, use boiling water or fruit juice instead of sirup to fill the jars. Proceed as directed.

If there is much variation in size, sort the fruit or vegetables so that the contents of each jar will be as nearly uniform as possible.

Precook all nonacid vegetables in order to heat them thoroughly. Use the water in which they are cooked to fill jars. Heat such foods as tomatoes or peaches only long enough to loosen the skins. Berries and fruits may be cooked in sirup a few minutes to insure a full pack.

Fill only as many jars at a time as the canner will hold. Work rapidly once the food has been heated and avoid letting it stand before processing, since objectionable bacteria develop most rapidly between 105° and 150° F.

Add 1 teaspoon salt to each quart of vegetables and ½ teaspoon to each pint. Fill jars to within ½ inch of top, using boiling water for vegetables and boiling sirup for fruits. Air bubbles will rise as the liquid is added. Assist them to rise and break by running a spatula down the side of the jar.

If the food in the jar is hot and if the processing is to be done in a water bath, seal completely. Otherwise seal only partially. If the contents of tin cans are not hot when ready to seal, exhaust the air from them by placing the filled cans in about an inch of water and boiling 5 minutes. Adjust lids and seal at once.

PROCESSING IN HOT WATER BATH

Place hot filled jars or cans on rack in canner and add boiling water to cover them to the depth of 1 inch. Heat quickly to boiling and count time as soon as bubbles break freely over the jars. Be sure the water covers the jars during the entire processing time. Add more boiling water if necessary. As soon as processing is completed remove canner from heat.

PROCESSING IN PRESSURE COOKER

Have enough boiling water in the cooker to come up to the bottom of the rack. Place filled jars or cans on rack, adjust cover of cooker and clamp down securely. Make sure that the petcock is open. Place over heat and watch for steam to escape from the petcock. Allow steam to escape for 7 minutes and then close petcock and allow pressure to reach the desired point. Count time from this point. Adjust heat to keep pressure steady. Fluctuations in pressure usually result in loss of liquid from the jars, particularly if the pressure goes high enough to release the safety valve and cause a sudden drop in pressure. Remove canner from heat as soon as processing time is completed. Allow to cool until pressure reaches zero. Then open petcock slowly. Do not open canner until pressure is entirely released. When number 2 cans are used, open petcock as soon as processing is complete, allowing pressure to go down rapidly. Open canner and remove cans, plunging them at once into cold water to prevent overcooking.

COOLING JARS AND CANS

Remove jars from the canner; complete the seal if jars are only partially sealed. Place jars on folded towels, away from drafts, inverting if they are not of the automatic seal type. Inspect the jars occasionally. Leakage or bubbles rising in the can mean that the contents must be used or recanned at once.

Submerge tin cans in water and watch for bubbles rising from seams or ends. When cans and jars are cold, wash, label and store in a cool dry place.

ALWAYS boil home-canned meats, beans, peas or corn for 10 minutes before using, even if they are to be served cold. These foods may be infected with Botulinus from the soil in which they were grown. Death has resulted from a single taste of food thus infected. Boiling destroys botulinus toxins. Never use food showing signs of spoilage.

SIRUPS FOR CANNING FRUITS

Boil sugar and water together for 5 minutes using the following proportions:

THIN SIRUP—4 cups water and 2 cups sugar.
MEDIUM SIRUP—4 cups water and 3 cups sugar.
THICK SIRUP—4 cups water and 4 cups sugar.

RECIPES FOR CANNING BY HOT WATER BATH

APPLES—Wash apples, pare and cut into slices, quarters or halves. Bake or stew, adding sugar to taste or heat to boiling in thin sirup and cook ½ minute. Pack hot into jars or plain tin cans, seal and process at once.

BERRIES—Wash and sort berries carefully. Can only perfect berries; use imperfect ones in making sirup. Pack berries into jars or R enamel tin cans and fill with boiling thin sirup or cook in sirup ½ minute before packing. Seal and process at once.

CHERRIES (Sweet)—Wash cherries; remove stems and pits. Cover with thin sirup, heat to boiling and cook ½ minute. Pack hot into jars or R enamel tin cans. Seal and process at once.

CHERRIES (Tart)—Proceed as above, using thick sirup instead of thin.

PEACHES—Immerse peaches in boiling water until skins will slip, plunge into cold water and drain. Peel, cut into halves and remove stones. Pack cut side down into jars or plain tin cans and cover with medium sirup or cook 5 minutes in sirup and pack hot into jars or cans. Seal and process at once.

PEARS—Wash and pare fruit. Cut into halves and core. Cover with thin sirup, heat to boiling and cook 4 to 8 minutes, depending upon hardness of fruit. Pack hot into jars or plain tin cans. Seal and process at once.

PLUMS—Wash fruit and prick several times with a needle to prevent bursting. Pack into jars or use R enamel tin cans for red plums and plain ones for yellow plums. Fill with boiling thin sirup. Partially seal glass jars and process. Exhaust tin cans before sealing and processing.

RHUBARB—Wash rhubarb and cut into ½-inch pieces. Pack into glass jars and cover with thick sirup. Partially seal and process at once. If preferred, measure cut rhubarb and add ¼ as much sugar. Bake in a covered baking dish until tender, pack hot into jars and seal. Process at once. Tin cans are not recommended for rhubarb.

TOMATOES—Select firm ripe tomatoes of uniform size for canning. Remove spots from any imperfect tomatoes, cut into pieces and cook until soft. Press through sieve and use as liquid for filling cans of whole tomatoes. Scald perfect tomatoes, plunge into cold water, drain and peel. Pack closely into jars or plain tin cans. Add salt and tomato juice. Partially seal jars; exhaust tin cans and seal. Process at once.

TOMATO JUICE—Prepare tomato juice as above. Heat to simmering and fill jars or plain tin cans. Add salt, seal and process.

RECIPES FOR CANNING IN PRESSURE COOKER

If not boiling hot, exhaust tin cans 5 minutes before sealing and processing in pressure cooker.

ASPARAGUS—Wash asparagus carefully and cut into lengths to fit container. Place in pan with boiling water over tough portions only. Cover closely and cook 3 to 4 minutes. Pack hot into jars or plain tin cans, stem end down, add salt and fill with cooking liquid. Partially seal jars; exhaust and seal tin cans. Process at once.

BEANS (String)—Wash beans, remove ends and cut into even lengths. Cover with boiling water and cook 3 to 4 minutes. Pack hot into jars or plain tin cans, add salt and boiling cooking water. Partially seal jars; exhaust and seal tin cans. Process at once.

BEANS (Lima)—Use only the small green beans for canning; the large white ones should be dried. Wash the beans thoroughly, shell; cook in water 5 minutes. Pour into jars or C enamel cans. Add salt; partially seal jars or seal tin cans. Process at once.

BEETS—Use only very small beets for canning. Wash thoroughly and cut off tops, leaving about 1 inch of stem. Cook in boiling water about 15 minutes, remove skins and pack into jars or R enamel cans. Add salt, fill with boiling water and partially seal jars or exhaust and seal tin cans. Process at once.

CARROTS—Wash carrots and either scrape skins off or cook in boiling water until skins will slip off. Pack into jars or plain tin cans. Add salt and fill with boiling water. Partially seal jars or exhaust and seal tin cans. Process at once.

CORN (Whole kernel)—Simmer ears of corn in water 4 to 5 minutes. Cut from cob but do not scrape cob. Weigh corn and add ½ the weight of water. Add 1 teaspoon salt and 2 teaspoons sugar for each quart. Mix well and heat to boiling. Pack at once into jars or C enamel tin cans. Seal tin cans at once; partially seal glass jars. Process immediately.

CORN (Cream style)—Remove corn, uncooked, from cob by cutting through grains and pressing out with the back of a knife. Add water, salt and sugar and proceed as above.

GREENS—Remove stems and any imperfect leaves. Wash thoroughly. Add water and simmer until leaves are wilted. Drain, saving liquid. Pack into jars or plain tin cans, loosen in center with a knife. Add salt and boiling cooking water. Seal tin cans at once; partially seal glass jars. Process at once.

PEAS—Use only very tender young peas for canning. Shell, discarding any imperfect peas. Wash and cook in boiling water 5 minutes. Pack into jars or C enamel tin cans. Add salt and boiling cooking water. Seal tin cans; partially seal jars. Process.

MINCEMEAT

3 pounds lean beef	2 pounds sugar
½ pound suet	2 cups cider vinegar
6 pounds sour apples	2 cups molasses
3 pounds seeded raisins	1 tablespoon cloves
2 pounds seedless raisins	1 teaspoon cinnamon
½ pound citron, minced	1 teaspoon mace
1 nutmeg, grated	1 tablespoon salt

Cut meat in cubes, cover with water and simmer until tender. Cool. Force meat, suet and pared and cored apples through a food chopper. Add remaining ingredients plus 2 cups stock and simmer 1 hour, stirring frequently. Fill into sterilized jars, seal and keep in a cool place. Makes about 9 quarts.

MOCK MINCEMEAT

6 green tomatoes	½ cup minced citron
6 tart apples	2 tablespoons orange rind
¼ pound seedless raisins	1 teaspoon salt
¼ pound seeded raisins	1 teaspoon cloves
1 tablespoon cinnamon	½ teaspoon allspice
¼ cup fruit juice	½ teaspoon ginger
¼ cup cider vinegar	¼ teaspoon nutmeg

Force tomatoes and cored apples through a food chopper. Add remaining ingredients and cook until thick. Fill into sterilized jars and seal. Makes about 1 quart.

TIME TABLE FOR HOT WATER BATH

	No. Minutes To Glass Jars		Process In Boiling Water Tin Cans	
PRODUCT	Quarts	Pints	No. 3	No. 2
Apples	15	15	10	10
Berries	15	15	15	15
Precooked	12	10	10	8
Cherries	25	20	20	15
Peaches	20	15	15	10
Pears	25	20	20	15
Plums	15	15	15	15
Rhubarb	10	8		
Tomatoes	45	40	40	35
Tomato Juice	5	5	5	5

TIME TABLE FOR PRESSURE COOKER

	No. Minutes To Process In Pressure Cooker				Pressure Pounds
	Glass Jars		Tin Cans		
PRODUCT	Quarts	Pints	No. 3	No. 2	
Asparagus	35	30	30	30	10
Beans (string)	35	30	30	25	10
Beans (Lima)	55	50	50	45	10
Beets	35	30	30	25	10
Carrots	35	30	30	25	10
Corn	80	75	75	70	15
Greens	65	60	60	55	15
Peas	55	45	45	40	10

Preserves

Preserves are fruits in which the tissues of the fruit have absorbed a heavy sugar sirup until they are filled with sirup instead of with water. A good preserved fruit is plump and tender in texture and filled with sweetness. It is bright in color, clear and sparkling.

Cook Hard Fruits Before Placing in Sirup—Stew hard fruits, such as hard pears, underripe peaches, pineapples, sweet apples, quinces, watermelon rind or citron, until tender before placing them in a heavy sirup. This makes the fruit soft, so that the sirup can enter the cells of the fruit. If these fruits are not treated in this way, the preserves will be hard and tough instead of plump and tender. Tender fruits such as berries, ripe peaches or cherries may be placed at once in a heavy sirup.

Cook Rapidly in Sirup—Cook the fruit rapidly in the sirup, and only long enough for the sirup to fill the fruit. Too long cooking gives a dark, stiff product.

When foods have been given a preliminary cooking to make them tender, drain them before adding them to the sirup. The water in which they were cooked should be used for making the sirup. Place the fruit in the sirup and bring it quickly to the boiling point; continue the cooking rapidly until the product has a bright, clear, shiny look, showing that the fruit is filled with the clear sirup.

Plumping—If an extra fine quality of preserve is desired, add the fruit to the sirup and heat it only until it bubbles; then set it away in a covered enamel preserving kettle for several hours, or overnight. Then continue the cooking. In this way, more sirup is absorbed by the fruit. If the amount of extra work entailed is not too exacting, the heating and cooling process may be repeated several times. Pears, peaches, green tomatoes, whole tomatoes, crab apples, citron and melon rind are especially adapted to plumping. Fruit to be candied should be plumped.

Sealing—The best method of keeping preserves is to seal them in hot clean jars. If trouble has been experienced with molds, it may be desirable to hold the jars of preserves in steam or boiling water for ten minutes as an extra precaution against molds. All jars, rubbers, spoons and utensils that are to be used in placing preserves in the jars should be sterilized in boiling water.

APRICOT PRESERVES

4 pounds apricots   6 cups sugar   2¼ cups water

Place apricots in wire basket or cheesecloth and immerse in boiling water. Plunge into cold water and drain. Peel apricots and remove stones or not as desired. Combine sugar and water and boil 5 minutes. Add apricots and cook until clear and tender. Pour into clean hot jars and seal. Makes 4 pints.

CHERRY PRESERVES

3 cups sugar   2 pounds tart cherries,
                                weighed after stoning

Add sugar to stoned cherries and heat quickly to boiling. Cook rapidly until fruit is clear, skimming as necessary. Pour into clean hot jars and seal at once. Makes 2 pints.

CRAB-APPLE PRESERVES

8 cups sugar   4 pounds crab apples
6 cups water   1 teaspoon whole cloves
2 tablespoons lemon juice   1 stick cinnamon

Combine sugar, water and lemon juice and heat to boiling. Wash apples, cut into quarters and remove stems and cores. Add to sirup with spices tied in a bag. Cook until clear and tender. Remove spices and pour apples into clean hot jars and seal. Makes 5 pints.

FIG PRESERVES

4 pounds fresh figs   4 cups sugar
1 lemon   1 cup water

Wash and peel figs; slice lemon. Combine sugar and water and cook 5 minutes. Add figs and lemon. Cook rapidly until clear. Seal in clean hot jars. Makes 3 pints.

GOOSEBERRY PRESERVES

1 pound green gooseberries   1¼ pounds sugar

Stem the berries, remove the blossom end, and wash the fruit in cold water. Half cover the gooseberries with water and scald the fruit until the skins are soft. Add the sugar to the hot mixture. Bring quickly to the boiling-point and cook until clear. Seal at once in clean hot jars.

GRAPE PRESERVES

4 pounds Concord grapes   1½ cups water
3 cups sugar

Wash grapes and remove skins and seeds. Boil sugar and water together 5 minutes, add grape pulp and cook until thick and clear. Pour into clean hot jars and seal at once. Makes 2 pints preserves.

GREENGAGE PRESERVES

4 pounds greengage plums   3 cups sugar

Place plums in a wire basket and immerse in boiling water until skins crack. Drain and peel. Place in layers with sugar in enamel kettle and let stand overnight. Then drain and heat juice to boiling. Cook 10 minutes, skimming as necessary. Add plums and cook rapidly until plums are clear and tender. Drain: boil sirup until it coats the spoon, adding juice as it drains from plums. Add plums and heat to boiling. Seal in clean hot jars. Makes 2 pints.

PRESERVED GINGER

1 pound fresh ginger roots   1½ cups water   1 pound sugar

Scrub roots of fresh green ginger thoroughly, using a brush. Pare with a very sharp knife, and place the roots at once in cold water. Rinse well and place in fresh cold water. Let stand overnight. Drain, weigh the ginger, place it in a preserving-kettle, and cover it with cold water. When the water is boiling, skim out the ginger and place it again in cold water. When quite cool, return to the kettle, add more cold water, and when the water is boiling, skim out the ginger and lay in cold water, as before. Do this three times, or until the ginger is tender.

Boil the sugar and water together for ten minutes. Drain the ginger and add it to the sirup. Bring quickly to the boiling-point; remove from the heat and let it stand overnight. Drain off the sirup, let it come to a boil and repeat the first process.

Drain off the sirup again, heat to boiling, add the ginger and simmer until clear. Pour into clean hot jars and seal. It will be ready to use in two weeks.

KUMQUAT PRESERVES

3 pounds kumquats   6 cups sugar

Make a deep slit in 1 end of each kumquat, cover with cold water and let stand overnight. Heat to boiling and cook until tender. Add sugar and cool until thick. Pour into clean hot jars and seal. Makes 4 pints.

PEACH PRESERVES

4 pounds prepared peaches   6 cups sugar
                3 cups water

Place peaches in wire basket or cheesecloth and immerse in boiling water until skins are loosened. Plunge into cold water and drain. Peel; remove stones if desired. Combine sugar and water and cook 10 minutes. Add peaches and cook until clear. Seal in clean hot jars. Makes 4 pints.

PINEAPPLE PRESERVES

3 pounds cubed pineapple   4½ cups sugar

Pare pineapple and cut out eyes. Cut from the core in cubes. Weigh and add water to half cover. Cook, closely covered, until tender. Drain; add sugar to liquid. Cook until it coats the spoon. Add pineapple and cook until clear. Pour into clean hot jars and seal. Makes 3 pints.

SUN-COOKED PRESERVES

3 pounds strawberries,   6 cups sugar
  raspberries or currants   3 cups water

Wash berries, pick over and weigh. Combine sugar and water and cook until it spins a thread (228° F.); remove from heat. Add berries and let stand overnight. Then skim berries from sirup and place in deep platters in a single layer. Cook sirup again to 228° F. and pour over berries. Cover with a piece of glass or cheesecloth and let stand in direct sunlight 3 to 4 days. When sirup has become thick, pour into clean hot jars and seal. Since dampness causes molds to form very quickly on this type of preserves, they must be brought indoors each night. If the sun does not shine, the cooking must be finished indoors. Makes 4 pints.

PLUM PRESERVES

3 pounds damson plums   4½ cups sugar   ½ cup water

Stem and wash plums and pierce each with a fork. Place in layers with sugar in an enamel kettle and add water. Let stand overnight. Drain and boil juice 5 minutes. Add plums and cook until clear. This takes only a few minutes; do not over-cook. Seal in clean hot jars. Makes 3 pints.

QUINCE PRESERVES

5 pounds quinces   4 cups water   6 cups sugar

Scrub quinces with a brush. Pare, quarter and core them, dropping the quarters into cold water to prevent discoloring. Cook parings and cores in water 15 minutes and strain liquid. Add quinces to liquid and cook until tender. Drain and add sugar to liquid; boil 10 minutes. Add quinces and cook until clear. Pour into clean hot jars and seal. Quince preserves are very rich. Sweet apples or pears may be used instead of half the quinces. Makes about 4 pints.

STRAWBERRY PRESERVES

3 pounds strawberries   6 cups sugar

Use firm deep red berries. Wash, hull and weigh. Place in layers with sugar in large kettle and heat to boiling, stirring carefully to avoid crushing. Boil rapidly until clear. Pour into clean hot jars and seal. Any berries except blackberries may be preserved by this method. Blackberries have too many seeds for preserves. Makes 4 pints.

TOMATO PRESERVES

2 pounds red or yellow tomatoes   3 cups sugar   1 lemon

Use the small yellow plum tomatoes. Cover with boiling water, cover closely and let stand 2 minutes. Drain and peel, taking care not to break them. Place in layers with sugar in bowl or enamel kettle and let stand overnight. Then drain and cook juice to 228° F. or until it spins a thread. Add lemon, thinly sliced, and tomatoes. Cook until clear and thick. Seal in clean hot jars. Makes 2 pints.

Jams

Jam is made from whole small fruits which are either mashed or cooked to a pulp with sugar. Good jam is soft, tender and jellylike in texture, bright and sparkling in color and of the same consistency throughout the mixture.

SOME UNDERRIPE FRUIT DESIRABLE—Portions of fruit left from canning, or broken fruit, may be used for jam, but at least a portion of the fruit should be underripe. Overripe fruit lacks pectin and some pectin, a jellying substance, is necessary for good jam.

COOK THE FRUIT BEFORE ADDING SUGAR—In order to develop the pectin substance, the fruit should be cooked for a few minutes before the sugar is added. If the fruit does not have sufficient juice, add just enough water to keep it from burning and cook it in a covered kettle.

NOT TOO MUCH SUGAR—The best jam is made by using not more than three-fourths pound of sugar to each pound of fruit.

COOK QUICKLY AND NOT TOO LONG—After the sugar is added to the fruit, continue the cooking quickly until the jam gives a jellylike appearance. It should hang in sheets from the spoon or set quickly if a portion is dropped on a cool plate. It should be tender and jellylike, not thick and tough. Jam thickens on cooling, and an allowance must be made for this or the jam will be overcooked. Overcooking also darkens the product. It is better to make a small amount of jam at a time. Use enamel or porcelain cooking utensils, if possible.

STIR TO PREVENT BURNING—Jam is a highly concentrated mass and will burn quickly unless it is stirred from the bottom. Use a wooden spoon and lift the mass from the bottom. It is better to cook jam briskly and watch it carefully for twenty or thirty minutes than to let it simmer for hours.

SEAL IN HOT, CLEAN JARS—Jams, like preserves, are safer from molds if they are sealed in hot, clean jars.

BLACKBERRY JAM

Mash berries and heat thoroughly. Press through sieve to remove seeds. Measure and add 1 cup sugar for each pint. Cook rapidly until thick, stirring frequently. Pour into clean hot jars and seal. One quart fruit makes 2½ cups jam.

BAR-LE-DUC

1 quart currants   2 cups sugar
1 cup water

Stem and wash currants. Combine sugar and water and heat to boiling, stirring until sugar is dissolved. Boil rapidly for 5 minutes. Add currants and boil rapidly for 15 minutes. Pour into clean hot jars and seal. Makes 3 (½-pint) jars.

BLUEBERRY JAM

3¾ cups crushed   ½ tablespoon grated lemon
  blueberries   rind
¼ cup lemon juice   8 cups sugar
1 cup liquid pectin

Pick over and wash berries. Crush well and add lemon juice and rind. Add sugar and heat to boiling, stirring constantly. Boil rapidly for 1 minute. Remove from heat and stir in pectin. Skim and pour into clean hot glasses. Seal with paraffin at once. Makes about 11 (8-ounce) glasses.

BLUEBERRY AND CURRANT JAM

1 quart blueberries   1 pint currants
2 cups sugar

Pick over and wash blueberries; stem and wash currants. Crush fruit and cook about 15 minutes. Add sugar and stir until dissolved. Cook rapidly until thick, pour into clean hot jars and seal. Makes 4 (8-ounce) jars.

DAMSON PLUM JAM

1 quart damson plums   1 cup water
About 2 cups sugar

Wash plums, add water and cook until skins are tender. Remove stones. Measure fruit and add ⅔ cup sugar for each cup plums. Cook quickly until thick. Color should be bright red. Pour into clean hot jars and seal. Makes 4 (8-ounce) jars.

VARIATIONS—Fruit may be cut from stones before cooking. Beach plums may be prepared in the same way.

FIG JAM

2 quarts ripe figs
2 slices lemon

1 cup water
4 cups sugar

Wash figs, peel and remove stems. Mash and add lemon and water. Cook until soft. Add sugar and cook until thick, stirring to prevent burning. Remove lemon, pour into clean hot jars and seal. Makes 6 (½-pint) jars.

GOOSEBERRY JAM

1 quart ripe gooseberries   3 cups sugar   1 cup water

Wash gooseberries and remove stem and blossom ends. Add water and cook until skins are tender. Add sugar and cook quickly until thick. Pour into clean hot jars and seal. Makes about 4 (8-ounce) jars.

GRAPE JAM

3 pounds Concord grapes   3 cups sugar, about

Remove grapes from stems, wash and press pulp from skins. Cook pulp until tender and press through sieve to remove seeds. Cook skins until tender in a small amount of water. Combine skins and pulp and weigh. Add 1 cup sugar for each pound and cook until thick. Pour into clean hot jars and seal. Makes 6 (½-pint) jars.

PEACH JAM

2 pounds sliced peaches
2 tablespoons lemon juice

1 cup water
3 cups sugar

Pour boiling water over peaches and let stand a few minutes. Drain. Peel and slice, discarding stones. Add lemon juice and water and cook until tender. Add sugar and cook until thick. Seal in clean hot jars. Makes 3 (8-ounce) jars.

RED RASPBERRY JAM

1 pound raspberries   1½ cups sugar

Wash berries and crush in preserving kettle. Add sugar and cook quickly until thick and clear. Seal in clean hot jars. Makes about 3 (8-ounce) jars.

STRAWBERRY JAM

1 quart hulled strawberries   3 cups sugar

Place berries in kettle over heat. Crush as they heat. When berries boil, add sugar and cook quickly until thick (not over 20 minutes), stirring frequently to prevent burning. Pour into clean hot jars and seal. Makes 4 (½-pint) jars.

GREEN TOMATO JAM

8 pounds green tomatoes   1 tablespoon preserved ginger
6 pounds sugar   6 lemons

Wash the tomatoes, remove any dark parts about the stems, and weigh them. Cover them with boiling water, let them stand five minutes, drain and slice them into a preserving-kettle, placing a layer of the tomatoes, then a layer of sliced lemon, then the sugar with the ginger sprinkled over it. Let the mixture stand over night. Drain and boil the sirup for ten minutes. Skim, add the tomatoes and cook rapidly until they are clear. Pour into clean, hot jars and seal.

Marmalades

Marmalades are usually made from fruits which have some jelly making properties, that is, in which both pectin and acid are present. Thin slices of fruit are used and the product shows a clear jelly or jellylike sirup in which the sliced or cut fruit is suspended. If a fruit is used which lacks these jellying properties, they are often supplied by adding sliced orange or lemon or by using some tart apple juice.

Marmalades are prepared in the same way as jams, except that the fruit remains in thin slices or cut portions and is not mashed. They should be clear and sparkling in color.

AMBER MARMALADE

1 grapefruit   3½ quarts water
1 orange, 1 lemon   10 cups sugar

Wash and dry fruit. Slice very thin, add water and let stand overnight. Cook until tender and let stand overnight. Add sugar, cook until jelly test is obtained. Pour into clean hot glasses and seal with paraffin. Makes 6 (6-ounce) glasses.

CARROT AND ORANGE MARMALADE

6 carrots   1 lemon
3 oranges   Sugar, about 4 cups

Scrape carrots, dice and cook until tender in as little water as possible. Slice oranges very thin and add juice and grated rind of lemon. Combine carrots and fruit, measure and add 2/3 as much sugar. Heat, stirring until sugar is dissolved. Cook rapidly until thick and clear. Pour into clean hot glasses and seal with paraffin. Makes 6 (6-ounce) glasses.

GRAPEFRUIT MARMALADE

2 pounds peeled grapefruit   2 quarts water
1/2 pound grapefruit peel   3 cups sugar

Wash grapefruit and remove peel in uniform sections. Select 1/2 pound peel free from blemish and cut into narrow slices. Cover with water, cook 10 minutes, drain and repeat process 4 times. Weigh and slice pulp. Add water and cook until tender. Drain through jelly bag, pressing out all juice possible. Filter juice through another jelly bag without pressing. Combine juice, cooked peel and sugar and cook rapidly until it gives the jelly test. Pour into clean hot glasses and seal with paraffin. Makes 6 (6-ounce) glasses.

ORANGE MARMALADE

8 oranges   Water
2 lemons   About 7 cups sugar

Wash and dry fruit. Remove peel and slice very thin. Cover peel with water, cook 5 minutes and drain. Repeat twice. Remove seeds and core from pulp and slice thin. Add drained peel. Measure and add 3 times as much water. Let stand overnight. Cook 40 minutes, weigh and add an equal weight of sugar. Cook rapidly until sirup gives jelly test. Pour into clean hot glasses and seal with paraffin. Makes 12 (6-ounce) glasses. For a pretty effect, remove most of white from peel and cut remaining orange part into fish-shaped pieces. Use glasses shaped like small goldfish bowls.

RHUBARB MARMALADE

1 pound rhubarb   1 lemon
2½ cups sugar

Wash rhubarb and cut into thin slices without peeling. Wash lemon and shave off the thin yellow rind. Add rind to rhubarb with sugar, mix and let stand overnight. Add juice of lemon and cook quickly until thick. Pour into clean hot glasses and seal with paraffin. Makes 3 (6-ounce) glasses.

CONSERVES

Conserves, like marmalades, may be made of large or small fruits. They differ from marmalades in that several fruits are often combined and nuts are usually added. In this way it is possible to develop pleasing combinations of flavors and to combine fruits that have good acid or pectin content with fruits that lack these qualities. When nuts are used, they are added after the cooking is finished because heat toughens the nut meats.

CANTALOUPE AND PEACH CONSERVE

2 cups diced peaches   2 lemons, shredded
2 cups diced cantaloupe   3 cups sugar
¾ cup broken nuts

Combine all ingredients except nuts. Heat slowly to boiling, stirring until sugar is dissolved, then cook rapidly until thick. Add nuts. Pour into clean hot glasses and seal with paraffin. Makes 5 (6-ounce) glasses.

VARIATION—Use 4 cups diced watermelon instead of peaches and cantaloupe.

CRANBERRY CONSERVE

6 oranges   1 pound dried currants
1 quart cranberries   Sugar
2½ cups shredded pineapple   1 cup boiling water
1 pound raisins   ½ pound almonds, blanched

Peel oranges and cut into pieces. Wash cranberries. Combine fruits and weigh. Add an equal weight of sugar. Add boiling water and cook rapidly until thick. Add almonds, pour into clean hot glasses and seal. Makes 8 (6-ounce) glasses.

STARTING POINT—
THE FINISHED PROD-
UCT WILL BE GOLDEN
ORANGE MARMALADE

SUCCULENT PEACH PRE-
SERVES WILL BRING A
BREATH OF SUMMER TO
YOUR WINTER MEALS

FRUITS AND BERRIES ARE ALWAYS IN SEASON IF YOU PRESERVE THEM

CURRANT CONSERVE

2 oranges	7 cups sugar
5 pints currants	1 cup broken walnuts

Combine grated rind and juice of oranges with currants and sugar and cook until thick. Add nuts, pour into clean hot glasses and seal with paraffin. Makes 10 (6-ounce) glasses.

GRAPE CONSERVE

2 pounds Concord grapes	1 cup raisins
1 cup water	2½ cups sugar
2 oranges	1 cup broken walnuts

Wash grapes and remove stems. Separate pulp and skins. Cook pulp until seeds are loosened; rub through sieve to remove seeds. Add water to skins and cook until tender. Squeeze oranges and grind the peels. Combine grape pulp and skins, orange juice, peel and raisins. Cook until thick. Add sugar and cook again until thick. Add nuts, pour into clean hot glasses and seal with paraffin. Makes 5 (6-ounce) glasses.

PINEAPPLE AND RHUBARB CONSERVE

4 cups shredded fresh pineapple	8 cups sliced rhubarb
1 cup water	2 oranges
	7 cups sugar

1 cup blanched almonds

Combine pineapple and water and cook, covered, until tender. Add rhubarb, juice and grated rind of oranges and sugar. Heat slowly, stirring until sugar is dissolved. Cook rapidly until thick and clear. Add almonds and cool slightly. Pour into clean hot glasses and seal with paraffin. Makes 10 (6-ounce) glasses.

GOOSEBERRY CONSERVE

3 pounds gooseberries	1 pound seeded raisins
3 pounds sugar	3 large oranges

2 cups broken nut meats

Remove stems and wash gooseberries. Mix with the sugar, raisins and grated rind and juice of the oranges. Cook until thick, add nuts and seal in clean hot jars. Makes 4 pints.

FRUIT BUTTERS

Fruit butters are among the most wholesome of fruit sweets, as they contain a large amount of fruit to a small amount of sugar. In making butters, the whole fruit is cooked until tender and then rubbed through a sieve. Sugar is added, and spice if desired, and the mixture is cooked until it is smooth and thick. Like jam, it must be carefully watched and should not be overcooked.

APPLE BUTTER

4 quarts sweet cider	2 cups sugar
2½ quarts quartered tart apples	Spices, if desired; cinnamon, cloves, ginger

Boil cider until it is reduced to 2 quarts. Add peeled, quartered apples and cook until very tender. Put through colander, add sugar and spices and cook until thick, stirring to prevent burning. Pour into clean hot jars and seal. Makes 3 pints.

APPLE AND PLUM BUTTER

3 pounds apples	1 cup water
1 pound plums	Sugar

Wash fruit. Quarter and core apples, cut plums into halves. Combine fruit and water and cook until tender. Rub through sieve. Measure pulp and add ⅓ as much sugar. Cook until thick, stirring almost constantly. Pour into clean hot jars and seal. Makes 3 pints.

CRAB APPLE BUTTER—Use 4 pounds crab apples instead of apples and plums and increase the water to 2 cups. Cook as above and use the same proportion of sugar. Makes 3 pints.

Crab apples may be used with plums in recipe above or the same quantity of blueberries or raspberries may be used.

GRAPE BUTTER

4 pounds ripe grapes	1 cup water	2 cups sugar

Wash and stem grapes. Add water and cook until tender. Rub through sieve. Add sugar and cook until thick and clear. Pour into clean hot jars and seal. Makes 3 (8-ounce) jars.

PEACH BUTTER

4 pounds peaches   2 cups water   Sugar

Peel peaches if very fuzzy. Slice, discarding stones, and cook with water until tender. Rub through sieve, measure pulp and add ½ the volume of sugar. Cook until thick, pour into clean hot jars and seal. Makes 3 pints.

DRIED PEACH AND APRICOT—Wash 1 pound dried peaches and 1 pound dried apricots. Cover with water and let stand 12 hours. Proceed as above using water remaining on fruit.

PLUM BUTTER

4 pounds plums   Sugar

Wash and stem plums. Crush a few plums to produce enough juice to prevent burning. Cover and cook until tender. Rub through sieve and measure pulp. Measure half as much sugar as pulp. Cook pulp until thick, add sugar and cook quickly until thick, stirring almost constantly. Pour into clean hot jars and seal. Makes 3 pints.

TOMATO BUTTER

5 pounds tomatoes   1 small stick cinnamon
1 cup vinegar   ¼ ounce ginger root
3 cups sugar   ½ tablespoon whole cloves

Peel and slice tomatoes. Add vinegar and sugar. Tie spices in a bag and add. Cook until thick, stirring almost constantly to prevent scorching. Remove spices. Pour into clean hot jars and seal. Makes 4 pints.

TOMATO AND APPLE BUTTER

2 cups tomato pulp   3 cups sugar
2 cups apple pulp   1 orange

Cook tomatoes and apples until tender and rub through sieve. Measure pulps and combine with sugar and juice and rind of orange. Cook until thick, stirring frequently. Pour into clean hot jars and seal. Makes 3 (8-ounce) jars.

JELLIES

Jelly is made by combining fruit juice and sugar in the correct proportions and cooking until the mixture will jelly when cool. A good jelly is clear and sparkling and free from sediment or crystals. It has the natural color and flavor of the fresh fruit. When turned from the glass it will hold its shape but will quiver. When cut, the edges are sharp and the jelly will not cling to the knife.

FRUITS SUITABLE FOR JELLY

To make a good jelly, fruit must be rich in both pectin and acid or it must be combined with another fruit which will supply whichever substance is lacking. Fruits which contain both acid and pectin in sufficient amounts are:

Apples, (tart)	Grapes
Blackberries	Loganberries
Crab apples	Plums
Currants	Quinces
Gooseberries	Raspberries

FRUITS LACKING SUFFICIENT PECTIN ARE:

Cherries	Pineapple
Peaches	Rhubarb
	Strawberries

FRUITS LACKING SUFFICIENT ACID ARE:

Apples (sweet)	Huckleberries
Blueberries	Pears

Slightly underripe fruit usually contains more acid and pectin than fully ripe fruit but the flavor is not as good. A proportion frequently used is $\frac{1}{4}$ underripe fruit and $\frac{3}{4}$ ripe fruit. Fruits lacking in either pectin or acid are often combined with tart apples since the apple juice affects color and flavor the least.

COMMERCIAL PECTIN

Juice from practically any fruit can be made into jelly by the addition of commercial pectin and a large amount of sugar. The advantages of this procedure are that much less time is required, any fruit may be used, the product has a fresher, more delicate flavor because of the short cooking time and, for the inexperienced at least, success is more certain.

The disadvantage is that the product lacks the rich full flavor which many people prefer and which is due to the concentration of the fruit juice by boiling. If a commercial pectin is used the directions which come with it must be followed exactly.

EXTRACTING FRUIT JUICE

Look over the fruit carefully, removing stems and any sign of decay. Cut up large fruits such as apples. Remove cores from quinces. Crush juicy fruits and add no water or only a small amount. To less juicy fruits add enough water to be seen through the pieces of fruit. If more water than necessary is added it must be evaporated from the juice which causes darker color and loss of flavor. Cover and cook until fruit is tender and juice runs freely but avoid overcooking. Apples require about 15 minutes, citrous fruits 1 hour and berries 1 to 3 minutes. Pour into a jelly bag and suspend over a bowl until the juice ceases to drip through. The jelly bag may be of flannel or a clean flour sack. For a clear jelly, do not squeeze the bag. More juice is obtained by squeezing, but the resulting jelly will be cloudy. A procedure frequently followed is to allow the juice to drip for the first extraction and then to squeeze the jelly bag when the second extraction is made. The two lots of juice are then made separately into jelly, the first to be used for special occasions and the second for general family use. To prepare the pulp for a second extraction, return it to the kettle, add water to nearly cover and simmer for 20 to 30 minutes. If preferred, only one extraction of juice for jelly may be made and the remaining pulp pressed through a sieve and made into jam or fruit butter.

TEST FOR PECTIN

To determine the proportion of pectin present in a fruit juice, combine 1 tablespoon extracted juice, 1 teaspoon sugar and 1½ teaspoons Epsom salts. Stir until salts are dissolved; let stand 20 minutes. If a solid mass or large flocculent particles are formed, the juice contains enough pectin to make a satisfactory jelly.

ADDING SUGAR

More jelly failures are caused by adding too much sugar than by any other factor. In general, ⅔ as much sugar as fruit juice is sufficient. Too little sugar will cause the jelly to be too firm; too much sugar will produce a weak sirupy jelly. The optimum amount of sugar varies with the amount of pectin, acid and water present and cannot be given exactly. In case of doubt it is always better to use less rather than more. Beet and cane sugar are equally suitable. Nothing is gained by heating the sugar.

COOKING THE JELLY

The best color, flavor and texture are obtained by cooking 2 quarts or less of juice at a time. Use an 8 to 10-quart kettle with a large diameter to allow rapid evaporation. Heat juice to boiling, then add sugar gradually, stirring slowly. Boil rapidly until the jellying stage is reached. This is determined by allowing a small amount of the juice to drop from the spoon. When the last 2 drops run together and sheet off from the spoon the jellying stage is reached and the jelly should be removed from the heat at once. Long cooking after the sheet test is obtained causes the pectin to break down so that the mixture will become a sirup and not a jelly. Skim the jelly and pour into clean hot glasses. Fill the glasses to within ⅜ inch of the top. There are 2 methods of sealing with paraffin. One is to pour the melted paraffin onto the jelly immediately. The other is to allow the jelly to cool and then cover it with very hot paraffin. When the paraffin has cooled, place the metal covers on the jelly glasses and store in a cool dry place.

Specific directions for making jelly from each kind of fruit are not necessary since the procedure is the same in most cases. A table follows showing the proportions in which various fruit juices may be combined and the proportion of sugar necessary for each. Recipes for a few unusual kinds of jellies are also given.

FESTIVE FLAVORS

Apple and crab apple jelly take on a note of gaiety if flavored with a spray of the leaves of rose geranium, lemon verbena or fresh mint. Drop the sprigs into the boiling jelly just before it is finished and allow to cool with the jelly while pouring. The

MINT JELLY

½ cup mint leaves   ¼ cup water
3 cups sugar   1 quart apple juice
              Green vegetable coloring

Wash mint and chop fine; add 2 tablespoons sugar and water and let stand for several hours, or overnight. Bring to boiling point, then strain. Combine remaining sugar (2⅞ cups) and tart apple juice. Cook and test for jelly, and when the jellying point is obtained, add green vegetable coloring and 2 tablespoons of prepared mint juice for each quart of apple juice. Pour into sterilized glasses and seal. Makes 7 (6-ounce) glasses.

If fresh mint leaves are not available, dried mint leaves may be used. Pour ⅓ cup boiling water over 3 tablespoons dried leaves, let stand 15 minutes, strain and use as above. Apple juice which is too red will give a brown jelly when green is added. Greening apple juice is preferable.

PARADISE JELLY

4 quarts red apples or   12 quinces
    crab apples   2 quarts cranberries
              Granulated sugar

Wash apples and quinces and remove the stems and blossom ends. Cut in quarters, cover with cold water and cook until tender. Wash cranberries and cook in 1 quart of water until tender. Pour apples, quinces and cranberries into a jelly bag and let drain overnight. Measure, add an equal amount, cup for cup, of sugar and boil until it gives the sheeting off test, about 10 minutes. Skim, pour into sterilized jelly glasses and seal. Makes about 20 (6-ounce) glasses.

QUINCE JELLY

Quinces require long cooking to become tender. They may be cooked in the fireless cooker or under steam pressure; in both cases they acquire a rich, dark red color.

Cut the quinces in small pieces, add sufficient water to float them and cook them until they are tender. Drain off the juice. Use two-thirds as much sugar as fruit-juice. Proceed according to the directions for making jelly. The pulp may be used for conserve or butter.

SAGE JELLY

½ cup boiling water
3 tablespoons sage
3¾ cups sugar

1½ cups sweet apple cider
Yellow food coloring
½ cup liquid pectin

Combine boiling water and sage, cover and let stand 15 minutes. Strain through fine cheesecloth and add water to make ½ cup. Add sugar and cider and heat to boiling. Add enough coloring to tint a light yellow. Add pectin, stirring constantly. Boil hard 1 minute. Remove from heat, skim and pour into clean hot glasses. Seal with paraffin. Serve with pork or poultry. Makes 5 (6-ounce) glasses.

SAVORY JELLY

2 tablespoons dried summer
   savory
½ cup boiling water

1 cup grapefruit juice
3¼ cups sugar
Green coloring
½ cup liquid pectin

Combine savory and water, cover and let stand 15 minutes. Strain through fine cheesecloth. Add water to make ½ cup. Combine with grapefruit juice and sugar. Heat to boiling and add just enough coloring to tint a light green. Mix thoroughly. Add pectin, stirring constantly. Heat to a full rolling boil and boil hard ½ minute. Remove from heat, skim and pour into clean hot glasses. Seal with paraffin. Serve with meat or poultry. Makes 4 (6-ounce) glasses.

THYME AND GRAPE JELLY

½ cup boiling water
1 tablespoon dried thyme

1½ cups grape juice
3 cups sugar
½ cup liquid pectin

Pour boiling water over thyme, cover and let stand 5 minutes. Strain through a fine cheesecloth. Add enough water to make ½ cup. Add grape juice and sugar and heat to boiling. Add pectin, stirring constantly. Boil hard for ½ minute. Remove from heat, skim and pour into glasses. Seal with paraffin. Serve with ham or beef. Makes 5 (6-ounce) glasses.

The same quantity of dried basil may be used instead of thyme if desired.

PICKLES AND RELISHES

WHEN foods are preserved with salt water or vinegar, the process is called pickling. Sweet pickles, sour pickles, and spiced pickles, either sweet or sour, are secured by varying the spices and seasoning.

Both fruits and vegetables may be pickled whole, or in halves, quarters, or slices. Cucumbers, tomatoes, onions, beets, carrots, cauliflower and cabbage, peaches, pears, crabapples and grapes are the vegetables and fruits most often preserved by pickling.

Preparing Food for Pickling

Clean vegetables carefully by scrubbing them in plenty of clear water. Then give them a preliminary soaking in a solution of salt and water—(one-eighth to one-fourth cup salt to one quart water)—for several hours or over night, or even for several days. Some vegetables must be parboiled in salt water before they are placed in the pickling solution. The salt draws the water from the tissues and makes them crisp and firm and better prepared to absorb the pickling solution.

Fruits need no preliminary treatment with salt and water. Prepare them as for canning and place them in the pickling solution.

Important Facts About Pickling

Use porcelain lined, graniteware or aluminum kettles for cooking pickles. Use a granite or wooden spoon for stirring or lifting the pickles.

Too much salt toughens and shrivels the vegetables to be pickled. Too strong vinegar may bleach the vegetables or cause it to soften after it is pickled.

The best results are obtained if pickles are sealed in glass or stone jars.

Varieties of Pickles

SWEET PICKLES—Fruits, ripe cucumbers and melon rinds are pickled in a sweet, spiced vinegar solution.

MIXED PICKLES—Various combinations of vegetables may be pickled together as mixed pickles.

CATCHUP AND SAUCES—Many fruits and vegetables, especially tomatoes, are chopped fine, cooked in the pickling solution and strained to form a thick fluid or sauce.

CHOWCHOW, CHILI SAUCE AND PICCALILLI are forms of relishes.

CHUTNEY—A sweet pickle highly seasoned, made from a variety of chopped vegetables or vegetables and fruits, is called a chutney. Chutneys are served with cold meats, sausages or stews.

RELISHES—Vegetables chopped fine and pickled are called relishes.

DILL PICKLES AND SAUERKRAUT—In these two forms of pickle the vegetable ferments in a salt solution. The acid present is the lactic acid formed by the action of the bacteria upon the sugar in the vegetable. In dill pickles, the dill is added for flavor. Plain salted cucumbers may be prepared in the same way without the dill. They are removed from the brine, soaked overnight in cold water, and prepared as needed.

TOMATOES, PEPPERS or other vegetables or fruit stuffed with various mixtures and pickled are favorites with many.

SPICED VINEGAR

4 cups vinegar
½ cup sugar
1 teaspoon salt
4 tablespoons horse-radish
1 tablespoon cinnamon
1 teaspoon allspice
1 tablespoon white mustard seed
1 teaspoon whole cloves
2 teaspoons celery seed

Combine vinegar, sugar, salt and horse-radish. The spices may be used either whole or ground, as preferred. If ground spices are used the pickles will be a darker color. Place ground spices in a cheesecloth bag and remove from the solution before the pickles are canned. If pickle is one that is to be heated in the vinegar, the vinegar and spices are not previously heated. If pickle is to be placed in the jars cold and the hot vinegar is poured over it, the solution is heated to boiling and poured over the pickle.

PICKLED BEETS

4 cups sliced cold cooked beets   ½ recipe Spiced Vinegar

Place beets in clean hot jars, cover with hot spiced vinegar, using horse-radish. Seal jars and let stand for 36 hours before using. Makes 2 pints. Add 1 sliced onion if desired.

RIPE CUCUMBER PICKLES

6 large yellow cucumbers   2 quarts vinegar
½ cup salt   4 cups sugar
4½ cups water   2 tablespoons mustard seed
          ⅓ cup mixed whole pickling spices

Pare cucumbers, quarter and remove seeds. Cut into strips, 1 x 2½ inches. Combine salt and water and stir until salt is dissolved. Add cucumber strips and allow to stand in brine 12 hours. Drain. Tie pickling spices in a cheesecloth bag. Combine vinegar, sugar, mustard seed and spices. Heat to boiling. Add only enough strips to vinegar at a time to cover the bottom of the pan, cook until just transparent, 3 to 5 minutes. Pack into sterilized hot jars. Fill with boiling vinegar mixture and seal at once. Makes 8 to 10 pints.

RICH CUCUMBER PICKLES—Prepare cucumbers and allow to remain in brine as above. Drain. Omit pickling spices and use 1 tablespoon whole cloves, 1 stick cinnamon and the mustard seed listed; tie in a cheesecloth bag. Reduce vinegar to 1 quart and increase sugar to 6 cups. Cook as above. For a dark pickle do not seal jars, just cover and each morning for the following 3 days drain off vinegar mixture, boil 5 minutes and pour over pickles. Seal on the third day.

CUCUMBER PICKLES

10 pounds small cucumbers   3 quarts vinegar
1 cup salt   1 quart water
1 gallon water   6 cups sugar
          1 ounce mixed whole pickling spices

Select cucumbers of uniform size, from 2 to 2½ inches long; wash thoroughly. Combine salt and 1 gallon water, add cucumbers and allow them to remain in the brine 24 hours. Drain. Tie spices in a cheesecloth bag. Combine vinegar, 1 quart water and sugar; add spices and cucumbers. Simmer (do not boil) 45 minutes. Let stand 2 to 3 days, then drain off pickle solution. Add 4 cups sugar to pickle solution and reheat. Pour over pickles and simmer 5 to 10 minutes. Let stand 2 to 3 days. Pack pickles in jars and fill with boiling pickle solution. Seal and store. Makes 4 quarts.

DILL PICKLES

50 cucumbers (4 to 5 inches long)
1½ cups salt
6 quarts water
½ small horse-radish root, diced
½ large bunch dill
¼ cup vinegar

Select thin cucumbers, wash and dry. Dissolve 1 cup salt in 4 quarts water, add cucumbers and let stand 12 hours. All cucumbers must be under the brine. It may be necessary to prepare more brine. Drain and wipe dry. Place in sterilized jars with layers of horse-radish and dill. Combine remaining 2 quarts water and ½ cup salt and vinegar; heat to boiling and pour over cucumbers. Partly seal. When fermentation stops, pour over enough fresh cooled brine containing vinegar to cover; seal. Makes about 6 quarts.

Instead of pouring hot brine containing vinegar over cucumbers, combine 5 quarts water, 1 pint vinegar and 1 cup salt; heat to boiling, cool and pour over cucumbers, horse-radish and dill in jars and seal.

MUSTARD PICKLES

1 pint cucumbers, about 2 inches long
1 pint large cucumbers, sliced
1 pint pickling onions
1 cup string beans, cut diagonally into 1-inch pieces
1 pint small green tomatoes
1 pint cauliflower, cut into small pieces
3 sweet red peppers, chopped
3 green peppers, chopped
1 cup sliced carrots
3 cups vinegar
3 cups water
1¼ cups sugar
½ cup flour
½ tablespoon turmeric
1 teaspoon celery salt
4 tablespoons dry mustard

Combine vegetables. Cover vegetables with a brine allowing 1 cup salt to 4 quarts water. Let stand overnight in the brine. Drain and soak vegetables in clear water 3 hours. Drain. Combine vinegar and water and pour over vegetables, let stand 1 hour, then heat to boiling. Combine sugar, flour, turmeric, celery salt and mustard. Drain vegetables and add vinegar gradually to flour mixture, stirring constantly to make a smooth paste. Cook the mixture over water until thickened. Pour mustard dressing over drained vegetables while they are hot and simmer 5 minutes. Pack into clean hot jars and seal. Makes about 3½ quarts.

PICKLED ONIONS

4 quarts small white onions	1/4 cup mixed pickling spices
3 pints boiling water	2 cups sugar
1 cup salt	2 quarts white vinegar
3 pints cold water	

Cover onions with the boiling water, let stand 5 minutes, drain, cover with cold water and peel. Dissolve salt in cold water listed, add onions and let stand 12 to 24 hours. Drain, cover with cold water and drain. Tie spices in cheesecloth bag, add to sugar and vinegar and heat to boiling. Remove spices, add onions, heat to boiling. Pack onions in sterilized jars, fill to overflowing with hot vinegar, then seal. Makes about 6 to 7 pints.

TART PICKLED ONIONS—Prepare onions as above. Instead of pickling vinegar used above use the following: Mix together 1 quart white vinegar, 1/4 cup sugar and 3 tablespoons each whole allspice, mustard seed and peppercorns; boil 1 minute and proceed as above.

PICKLED SWEET RED PEPPERS

6 or 7 large red peppers	1 1/2 cups vinegar
3/4 cup sugar	

Wash peppers, remove tops and seeds and cut peppers into strips. Cover strips with boiling water. Let stand 2 minutes. Drain. Pack peppers into hot sterilized jars. Boil sugar and vinegar together 5 minutes. Pour over peppers to fill jars. Seal. Makes about 3 (8-ounce) jars.

SPANISH TOMATOES

24 green tomatoes, sliced	1 tablespoon peppercorns
1 large onion, sliced	1 tablespoon mustard seed
2 green peppers, chopped	1 cup brown sugar
1/4 cup salt	2 quarts vinegar

Alternate layers of sliced tomatoes with layers of sliced onion and chopped green peppers, in a large crock and sprinkle each layer with salt. Let stand 24 hours, then drain. Combine vegetables, spices and sugar and cover with vinegar. Cook gently 45 minutes. Pack in sterilized, hot jars and seal. Makes about 4 pints.

For added color, cut 2 or 3 red sweet peppers into strips and add to tomatoes in crock.

BREAD AND BUTTER PICKLES

12 medium cucumbers
5 medium onions
1/4 cup salt
1 cup sugar
1 1/2 teaspoons mustard seed

1 1/2 teaspoons celery seed
1/2 teaspoon curry powder
1 cup vinegar
1/2 cup water

Wash cucumbers, peel onions and cut into 1/4-inch rings. Arrange in layers sprinkling salt on each layer. Let stand 2 to 3 hours. Drain. Combine remaining ingredients and heat to boiling. Add cucumbers and onions and simmer 10 minutes. Pack in hot sterilized jars and seal. Makes about 4 pints.

PICKLED SECKEL PEARS

7 pounds Seckel pears
1 tablespoon cinnamon
1 tablespoon allspice
1 tablespoon cloves

1 ounce ginger root
1 pint vinegar
1 pint water
3 1/2 pounds sugar

Pare pears leaving stems on. Tie spices in a bag and add to vinegar water and sugar, and boil mixture 5 minutes. Add pears a few at a time and cook until tender and clear. Place pears in a jar, pour in sirup and seal. Makes about 5 pints.

PEPPER MANGOES

1 quart chopped cabbage
1 onion, chopped
2 tablespoons salt
3 1/2 tablespoons mustard seed
3 1/2 tablespoons celery seed, crushed

1 1/2 cups sugar
11 cups vinegar
12 large sweet peppers
1/2 cup grated horse-radish
1 stick cinnamon

Combine cabbage, onion, 1 tablespoon salt, 2 tablespoons mustard seed, 2 tablespoons celery seed, 1/2 cup sugar and 3 cups vinegar and let stand 12 to 24 hours. Soak peppers in brine (1 cup salt to 1 gallon water) 24 hours. Rinse peppers in fresh water, cut a circle off top of each pepper and scoop out seeds and midribs. Then soak in cold water 1 to 2 hours. Combine remaining mustard seed, celery seed, sugar and vinegar, add horse-radish and cinnamon, heat to boiling and cool. Drain peppers, stuff with cabbage mixture, replace pepper tops and fasten with toothpicks. Pack in sterilized jars and fill with cold vinegar mixture.

SPICED CURRANTS

4 quarts currants	1 teaspoon whole allspice
2 pounds sugar	1 teaspoon whole cloves
1 pint vinegar	2 teaspoons cinnamon

Wash and stem fruit. Combine sugar, vinegar and spices and boil 5 minutes. Add fruit and cook until the mixture is thick and clear. Seal in sterilized, hot jars. Makes about 5 pints.

SPICED PLUMS

5 pounds plums	1 pint vinegar
3 pounds sugar	½ tablespoon whole cloves
1 tablespoon cinnamon	½ tablespoon whole allspice

Wash plums and prick with a fork or large needle. Boil remaining ingredients together 5 minutes. Pour boiling sirup over plums. Let stand 3 days, then lift out plums, boil down sirup until quite thick, add plums and heat to boiling. Pour into hot sterilized jars and seal. Makes about 5 pints.

PICKLED PEACHES

6 pounds peaches	3 pounds sugar
2 ounces stick cinnamon, broken	1 pint vinegar
1 ounce whole cloves	1 cup water

Dip peaches into hot water and peel. Tie spices in a bag. Combine sugar, vinegar, water and spices and boil together until clear, about 15 minutes. Add peaches, only enough at one time to fill 1 jar and cook until tender. Repeat until all are cooked. Lift out of kettle, pack into sterilized jars and cover to keep hot. Fill each jar to overflowing with hot sirup and seal. Makes about 5 pints.

Instead of breaking cinnamon add it whole to the sirup and stick several cloves into each peach before cooking.

Clingstone peaches are the most desirable for pickling.

PICKLED PEARS—Select pears of the hard variety. Pare pears, remove blossom end, but leave stem ends on pears. Cook in the same sirup and in the same manner as for peaches. If desired, add 1 ounce ginger to the spices listed above.

Stick cloves into pears instead of tying in a bag.

BRANDIED PEACHES

1 peck peaches, skinned
Sugar to half their weight

1 quart brandy

Alternate in stone jar, layers of peaches with sugar until filled. Add brandy. Cover closely, using cheesecloth or unbleached muslin under the jar cover. Keep peaches submerged in sirup at all times. May be used after 1 week. Keep in cool place.

PICKLED CRAB APPLES

4 quarts crab apples
2 cups vinegar
5 cups brown sugar

1 tablespoon whole cloves
2 sticks cinnamon
1 tablespoon whole allspice

Wash crab apples and remove blossom end. Do not pare. Combine remaining ingredients and simmer together 20 minutes. Add apples a few at a time and simmer until tender. Pack apples in hot sterilized jars adding sirup to cover apples. Seal. Makes 6 pints.

If a more spicy apple is desired, add 1 blade mace and 1 small piece of ginger root to sirup with other spices.

PICKLED WATERMELON RIND

2 pounds watermelon rind
2 cups vinegar
2 cups water
4 cups sugar

1 stick cinnamon
1 teaspoon whole cloves
1 teaspoon whole allspice
1 lemon, sliced thin

Pare watermelon rind and remove all pink portion. Cut rind into pieces 2 x 1 inches and $\frac{1}{2}$ inch thick or into $\frac{3}{4}$- to 1-inch cubes. Weigh. Soak rind overnight in brine made by dissolving $\frac{1}{4}$ cup salt in each quart water. Drain rind, wash in fresh water and drain. Cook rind in fresh water until tender. Combine remaining ingredients and boil together 5 minutes. Add rind a few pieces at a time and cook until rind is clear. Pack rind in hot sterilized jars, cover with boiling sirup and seal. Makes 2 pints.

Spices may be tied in a cheesecloth bag, if desired.

Cantaloupe rind, pumpkin or winter squash may be cut into pieces and pickled in the same way. Or slice green tomatoes and use salt instead of brine.

CORN RELISH

18 ears sweet corn
2 large green peppers
2 sweet red peppers
1 small cabbage
4 onions

1 cup chopped celery
1 quart vinegar
2 cups brown sugar
2 tablespoons salt
3 tablespoons mustard

Cut corn from cobs. Seed peppers and chop with cabbage and onions. Mix vegetables together, add remaining ingredients and cook until corn is tender, 20 to 30 minutes, stirring occasionally. Pack in hot sterilized jars and seal. Makes 5 pints.

DIXIE RELISH

1 pint chopped sweet green peppers
1 pint chopped sweet red peppers
1 quart chopped cabbage
1 pint white onions

2 tablespoons salt
4 tablespoons mustard seed
2 tablespoons celery seed
3 or 4 whole hot red peppers
¾ cup sugar
1 quart vinegar

Soak whole green and red peppers in brine for 24 hours, using 1 cup salt to 1 gallon water. Take from the brine and let stand in clear, cold water, from 1 to 2 hours. Drain well, cut open, remove seeds and white sections, and chop the peppers. Put cabbage and onions through the food chopper separately and measure before mixing. Add chopped cabbage and onions to chopped peppers. Add salt, spices, whole peppers, sugar and vinegar. Let the mixture stand overnight. Drain, and heat the liquid. When hot add the other ingredients and cook for 10 minutes. Seal in clean, hot jars. Makes about 5 pints. Hot peppers may be omitted.

PEPPER RELISH

12 red peppers
12 green peppers
12 onions, peeled

2 cups vinegar
1½ cups sugar
2 tablespoons salt

Split the peppers and remove the seeds. Chop peppers and onions coarsely, cover them with boiling water and let stand 5 minutes. Drain. Cover again with boiling water and let stand 10 minutes. Drain. Combine remaining ingredients and boil for 5 minutes, add vegetables and boil together 10 minutes. Pack in hot sterilized jars; seal. Makes 2 pints.

BEET RELISH

4 cups chopped cooked beets
4 cups chopped cabbage
½ cup grated horse-radish
2 teaspoons salt

¼ teaspoon pepper
2 cups vinegar
1 cup sugar

Combine the beets, cabbage and horse-radish and season with salt and pepper. Scald the vinegar, dissolve the sugar in it and add it to the first mixture. Cook until vegetables are tender. Seal in hot sterilized jars. Makes 5 pints.

QUICK BEET RELISH

2 cups chopped, pickled beets
5 tablespoons horse-radish
1 cup chopped red cabbage

Vinegar from pickled beets
Salt and pepper
Mustard

Mix beets, horse-radish and cabbage. Moisten with the vinegar left from the pickled beets and season with salt, pepper and a little dry mustard. Toss together and serve immediately or heat to boiling and seal in jars. Makes 1½ pints.

If desired, omit red cabbage and add 2 oranges, seeded and ground or chopped, including rind.

PICCALILLI

2 to 3 sweet green peppers
12 pounds green tomatoes
4 onions
1 cup salt
3 quarts vinegar

4 cups sugar
1 teaspoon ground ginger
1 teaspoon cinnamon
2 tablespoons mustard seed
1 cup grated horse-radish

Remove seeds from peppers. Chop vegetables very fine. Arrange vegetables in layers sprinkling each layer with salt and let stand overnight. Drain and add remaining ingredients. Cook until tender, stirring occasionally. Pour into hot sterilized jars and seal. Makes 12 pints.

Instead of using the above ingredients use the following: 2 sweet red and green peppers, 4 cups chopped green tomatoes, 1 cup chopped celery, 2 large onions, 1 small head cabbage, ½ cup salt, 3 cups vinegar, 1 pound brown sugar, 1 teaspoon dry mustard and 1 teaspoon turmeric. Prepare as above.

CHILI SAUCE

12 large ripe tomatoes
2 large onions
4 green peppers
2 tablespoons salt

½ cup sugar
1 teaspoon cinnamon
1 teaspoon ground cloves
2½ cups vinegar

Peel the tomatoes and onions, remove seeds from peppers and chop them fine. Stir all together and add salt, sugar, cinnamon, cloves and vinegar. Cook slowly for 45 to 60 minutes or until thick, stirring occasionally. Pour into hot sterilized jars and seal. Makes 4 pints.

If desired, add 2 hot red peppers, seeded and chopped.

CHOWCHOW

No. 1.

4 quarts green tomatoes
¼ cup salt
6 small onions
1 pint cucumbers
1 green pepper
1 bunch celery

1 quart vinegar
1 cup brown or white sugar
½ teaspoon cinnamon
½ teaspoon ground allspice
1 tablespoon dry mustard

Chop tomatoes and mix with salt. Let stand overnight. Next morning, drain tomatoes and add onions, cucumbers, pepper and celery, chopped fine, vinegar, sugar and spices. Cook mixture until vegetables are tender and clear, stirring well. Pack in clean sterilized jars and seal. Makes about 5 quarts chowchow.

No. 2.

18 green tomatoes
1 bunch celery
8 cucumbers
5 dozen small green onions
1 pound green string beans
1 cauliflower
3 red peppers

½ cup salt
2 quarts vinegar
1 cup brown sugar
2 tablespoons turmeric
4 tablespoons mustard seed
1 tablespoon cloves
1 tablespoon pepper

Dice tomatoes, celery and cucumbers, skin onions and remove tops, cut beans into small pieces, separate cauliflower into flowerets and chop peppers. Arrange vegetables in layers, sprinkling each layer with salt. Let stand 24 hours, then drain. Combine vinegar, sugar and spices and heat to boiling, stirring well. Pack in hot sterilized jars and seal. Makes 6 quarts.

CRANBERRY CATCHUP

1 pound onions	1 tablespoon ground cloves
4 pounds cranberries	1 tablespoon cinnamon
2 cups water	1 tablespoon allspice
4 cups sugar	1 tablespoon salt
2 cups vinegar	1 teaspoon pepper

Peel onions and chop very fine. Add cranberries and water and cook until tender. Rub through a sieve. Add remaining ingredients and boil until thick, stirring occasionally. Pour into hot sterilized jars and seal. Makes about 3 pints.

Serve as a relish with poultry or meat.

TOMATO CHUTNEY

4 pounds ripe tomatoes	2 cups brown sugar
1 pound apples, chopped	1 cup seeded raisins
3 onions, chopped fine	1 teaspoon cinnamon
1 pint vinegar	1 teaspoon dry mustard
2 tablespoons salt	½ teaspoon cayenne

Chop the tomatoes and add the apples and onions. Add the remaining ingredients and cook until the chutney is thick and clear, stirring occasionally. Seal it in hot sterilized jars. Makes 5 pints.

No. 2—If a hotter, more highly flavored chutney is desired, add to the above recipe:

½ teaspoon cayenne	2 teaspoons mustard
½ teaspoon allspice	2 cloves garlic, crushed
1 teaspoon cloves	

GRAPE CATCHUP

4 pounds grapes	2 teaspoons whole cloves
2 pounds sugar	2 teaspoons whole allspice
1 pint vinegar	2 tablespoons stick cinnamon
½ teaspoon salt	

Wash grapes and remove them from the stems. Place them in a pan and steam them without water, until they are soft. Rub fruit through a sieve, add remaining ingredients (spices tied in a bag) and simmer 20 minutes. Pour into hot sterilized jars and seal. Makes 2½ pints.

COLD TOMATO CATCHUP

1 peck ripe tomatoes
1 pint vinegar
2 tablespoons salt
2 teaspoons pepper

1 clove garlic, crushed
1 teaspoon ground allspice
1 teaspoon ground cloves

This is a recipe used in the kitchen of General Washington. Wash the tomatoes and force them through a wire sieve, then strain through a jelly bag. The liquid is not used in the catchup, but may be used as tomato juice. Thin the pulp with the vinegar. Season with salt, pepper, garlic, allspice and cloves. Pour into sterilized bottles and seal. This catchup retains the taste of the fresh tomatoes and is an excellent flavoring for soups and sauces. Makes about 4 quarts.

MUSHROOM CATCHUP

10 pounds mushrooms
½ cup salt
1 small onion, chopped
1 teaspoon ground allspice

1 teaspoon ground cloves
1 teaspoon horse-radish
Few grains cayenne
1 cup vinegar

Wipe mushrooms carefully with a damp cloth, chop them and mix them thoroughly with the salt. Let them stand overnight. Mash them, and to this pulp and juice add the chopped onion, spices and vinegar. Heat to boiling and cook slowly until thick, about 30 minutes, stirring occasionally. If desired, this catchup may be strained. If too thick, thin with vinegar. Seal in hot sterilized jars. Makes about 5 pints.

OLD VIRGINIA CATCHUP

1 peck green tomatoes
½ peck white onions
Salt
3 ounces mustard seed
1 ounce allspice
1 pound brown sugar

1 ounce cloves
1 tablespoon dry mustard
¼ cup water
1 tablespoon black pepper
1 ounce celery seed
1 quart vinegar

Chop tomatoes and onions, sprinkle with salt, and let stand 3 hours. Drain well and combine pulp with the other ingredients except vinegar. Cover with vinegar, and boil slowly 1 hour. Seal in clean hot jars. Makes 6 quarts.

TOMATO CATCHUP

1 peck ripe tomatoes	1 tablespoon whole allspice
5 onions, sliced	1 tablespoon celery seed
1 small clove garlic	1 teaspoon cayenne
2 red peppers, seeded	2 inches stick cinnamon
1½ bay leaves	½ cup sugar
1 tablespoon salt	2 cups vinegar

Boil first 6 ingredients until soft. Strain through sieve. Add spices (tied in a cloth bag) and sugar to tomato pulp and boil rapidly, stirring occasionally until thick or quantity is reduced one half. Remove spices, add vinegar and boil 10 minutes longer. Pour into hot sterilized bottles and seal. Makes about 6 quarts.

TOMATO PASTE

Spread thick tomato purée in flat oiled pans. As soon as a film forms over the top, loosen the paste with a spatula and turn it onto a screen covered with cheesecloth. Dry it in the sun or a very slow oven. When it is dry enough to handle without sticking, roll it in waxed paper and store it in a metal box or glass jar. The paste may be used for soup, sauces, scalloped dishes, etc. Soak it in cold water until it is soft, before adding it to any hot mixture. One teaspoon of the paste makes 1 cup soup.

TOMATO PURÉE

4 quarts tomatoes	1 bay leaf
1 small onion, sliced	2 teaspoons salt
1 stalk celery or celery leaves	¼ teaspoon paprika

Cook all ingredients until tomatoes are tender, then rub it through a strainer. Boil the pulp until it is reduced to one half the original volume. Seal in hot clean jars. Makes 3 pints.

PICKLED HORSE-RADISH

2 cups grated horse-radish	1 teaspoon salt
2 tablespoons sugar	2 cups cold vinegar

Mix all ingredients together thoroughly. Pour into cold sterilized jars, seal. Makes 4 half pints.

CASSEROLE AND OVEN COOKERY

THE expression "en casserole" is sometimes misunderstood because the word "casserole" is used in two quite different ways by writers on domestic subjects. Properly speaking, a casserole is the coarse clay saucepan, so common in France, in which meats and vegetables are not only cooked but served on the table. In its other usage the word is applied to a case or mold of potato, rice or fried bread, inside of which is placed some preparation of meat or vegetables. The word in this case really signifies a border or croustade. Directions for using this second form of casserole will be found in the chapter on entrées.

Varieties of Casseroles

Casseroles of different sizes, shapes and materials, are convenient additions to the cooking equipment, and should be chosen with consideration for the needs of the family. They come in many sizes from the individual ramekin up to one that will hold two chickens. They may be had in various shapes—oval and round, shallow and deep. They are made in a variety of materials—glass, vitrified china, earthenware, iron and aluminum—and in a color-range that allows one to choose according to personal preference—brown, yellow, green, blue and mixtures.

Care of Casseroles

Casseroles will last indefinitely if properly treated. It is wise to avoid a sudden and great change in temperature, such as occurs when a casserole is taken from a hot oven and placed in a wet sink. It is not advisable to set a glass or earthenware casserole over a high flame without an asbestos mat under it. A new casserole may be tempered and made more tough by pouring cold water into and about it, and bringing it gradually to the boiling-point.

Advantages of Cooking in a Casserole

THE CASSEROLE SAVES DISH-WASHING, because it makes it possible to bring food to the table in the dish in which it was cooked. Frequently, also, it contains a "one-dish meal" which eliminates all but the one cooking dish.

THE CASSEROLE MAKES IT POSSIBLE TO USE LEFT-OVERS in attractive, palatable combinations, to cook tough meats tender, and to prepare vegetables in an almost unlimited variety of ways. Any vegetable may be boiled, steamed, baked, scalloped or creamed, and cabbage, cucumbers, eggplant, onions, peppers, potatoes or tomatoes may be stuffed and cooked in the casserole.

FOOD COOKED IN THIS WAY NEEDS LITTLE WATCHING, it may be kept warm and still attractive if the meal is delayed, and there is no loss of vegetable or meat juices. These juices contain a valuable part of the food which is often thrown away, especially in the case of vegetables that are boiled.

A WHOLE MEAL MAY BE COOKING IN THE OVEN in the casserole while the oven is being used for some other purpose, such as baking cookies. The cover of the casserole should fit well into the dish, so that it is practically airtight, a fact that should be borne in mind when the casserole is purchased. If the oven must be kept very hot for something else, set the casserole in a pan of water so that the food within will simmer, not boil. As the water becomes hot, take out part of it and add cool water to keep it at the desired temperature.

CHICKEN EN CASSEROLE

1 chicken	12 potato balls
Butter, salad oil, or other fat	1 carrot, sliced
1 pint rich brown stock	6 small onions
12 button mushrooms	Salt, pepper, paprika

Wash the chicken and cut it up. Sauté the pieces in a little fat until well browned on all sides. Place in a greased casserole, add brown stock, cover and cook in a slow to moderate oven (350° F.) for an hour.

When the chicken has been cooking for an hour, sauté the carrot slices, the potato balls, the onions and the mushrooms in a little fat, stirring them lightly around until they are well browned. Put these with the chicken in the casserole, season with salt, pepper and paprika, add more salt if needed, cover and cook for three-fourths of an hour, then remove the cover and allow the chicken to brown before serving.

PIGEONS EN CASSEROLE

Pigeons or squabs
Bacon
3 tablespoons butter or other fat

1 Spanish onion
Veal broth or white stock
Vegetables, as desired
Flour

Clean and wash young pigeons and tie a strip of bacon around each one, or lard the breasts if preferred. Place the butter or other fat in a casserole, slice a mild Spanish onion over the fat, arrange the pigeons on the onion in the casserole, cover the casserole and set over a low heat with an asbestos mat under the casserole to protect it from direct heat and to insure slow cooking. Cook on top of the stove for fifteen minutes. Add enough veal broth or white stock to half cover the pigeons and set in the oven (350° F.) to cook until tender (2-2½ hrs.). When nearly done, vegetables may be added. At serving-time thicken the liquor in the casserole by stirring into it flour mixed smooth in a little water, allowing one tablespoon of flour for each cup of liquid.

STEAK EN CASSEROLE

3 tablespoons butter or other fat
3 tablespoons flour
2 cups stock
Salt
Parsley

Pepper
Turnip balls
Carrot balls
Potato balls
Small onions
2 pounds of 1½-inch steak

Make a brown sauce of the fat, flour, stock and seasoning. Add balls of turnip, carrot, potato and onions, which have been previously cooked in a little brown stock until tender. For each person, allow a half-dozen little balls of each of these vegetables and two small onions. Keep this sauce hot while you pan-broil the steak until about half done, then transfer steak to heated casserole, pour vegetables and sauce over steak, cover, and place in oven (350° F.) until steak is sufficiently cooked. When ready to serve, sprinkle the steak with finely chopped parsley.

CHOPPED BEEF EN CASSEROLE

2 pounds clod of beef
2/3 cup tomato catchup
1/3 teaspoon tabasco sauce

Boiled beets
Salt

Mix chopped beef with tomato catchup. Add tabasco sauce, using more if desired. Season well with salt. Place in casserole and bake (350° F.) slowly two to two and one-half hours, basting frequently with water and tabasco or Worcestershire sauce. A few strips of bacon across the top will add to the richness, and improve the flavor. Garnish with quartered beets.

TAMALE PIE EN CASSEROLE

1 cup yellow corn-meal
6 cups boiling water
1 teaspoon salt
1 medium-sized onion
2 tablespoons fat

2 cups chopped beef
2 cups tomatoes
2 pimientos
Cayenne

Cook corn-meal, water, and salt, as for mush, for about thirty minutes. Chop onion and fry in fat till brown. Add meat and fry until red color disappears. Add tomatoes, pimientos, and cayenne. Line oiled casserole with mush, put meat mixture in center, cover with mush, and bake in a moderate oven (350° F.; 2-2½ hrs.).

TURBANS OF FISH EN CASSEROLE

Prepare slices of halibut or other fish about the size of one's hand, with all bone and skin removed and sufficiently thin to roll easily. Trim all to uniform size, dip each in melted butter or other fat, squeeze over them lemon-juice and onion-juice, and sprinkle with salt. Beginning at the widest end, roll the slice of fish and secure with two toothpicks. Set the turban in a greased and heated casserole and pour in a little stock made by simmering the bones and trimmings of the fish in a little water, together with a few slices each of carrot and onion. Cook in a moderate oven (350° F.) basting occasionally. When done, drain off the liquid and thicken it with flour mixed with cold water. Return to the casserole, and reheat.

HUNGARIAN GOULASH EN CASSEROLE

4 onions	12 small onions
2 pounds **veal**	1 cup carrot slices
Bacon fat	1 cup turnip slices
1½ pints brown stock	Salt
Pepper	Paprika
1 pint potato balls	

Slice the onion and cut the raw veal in cubes. Cook together in a little bacon fat, until brown. Transfer to casserole, pour over it the brown stock and season with pepper and paprika. Place in moderate oven (350° F.). Add more fat to that in the frying-pan and brown in this the potato balls, small onions, and slices of carrot and turnip. Add the vegetables and salt to the casserole when the meat is partly cooked. Finish the cooking, adding more stock if necessary. This dish should cook two hours. If the broth is too thin when ready to serve, thicken slightly with browned flour rubbed smooth in water.

LAMB EN CASSEROLE

6 slices of lamb	1 pint vegetable balls
2 tablespoons melted butter or other fat	12 small onions
	Seasoning
2 cups brown stock	

Cut thick slices from a leg of lamb and sear, browning both sides. Brush with melted fat and place in casserole with one-half to one cup of brown stock. Cook over heat or in a moderate oven (350° F.) until tender, then add potato balls, carrot balls and onions, which have been previously cooked. Add more brown stock, salt, pepper and paprika.

PORK CHOPS EN CASSEROLE

6 pork chops	½ cup brown sugar
6 sweet potatoes	1 to 2 cups milk
Salt and pepper	

Place a layer of sweet potatoes, sliced crosswise, in a greased casserole, dust with salt, pepper, and a little brown sugar; continue the layers until the casserole is about two-thirds full. Heat the milk and pour it over the potatoes; it should just cover them. Place the pork chops on top of the potatoes, cover and bake (at 350° F.) for an hour, then remove the cover and season with salt and pepper. Leave the cover off and cook until the chops are tender and nicely browned on top.

Four tart apples, pared, cored and cut in eighths, used in place of the sweet potatoes, make an excellent casserole dish with pork chops.

CALF'S LIVER EN CASSEROLE

1 pound calf's liver
6 slices bacon
1 cup button mushrooms

3 cups potato balls
1 pint brown stock

Wash the calf's liver thoroughly and wipe dry. Fry some bacon in a pan, remove, place the liver in the bacon fat, and sear each side thoroughly. Transfer to a casserole, add slices of bacon, brown stock, and sautéd mushrooms. Cook for one hour and a half in the oven (350° F.) adding more stock if necessary. Just before serving add potato balls which have been fried in deep fat (395° F.) and drained.

CASSEROLE OF RICE AND LIVER

1 cup rice
1 quart water
2 tablespoons butter or other fat
1 pound lamb's or calf's liver
2 cups stock

1 teaspoon caramel
2 tablespoons browned flour
2 tablespoons fat
Crumbs
Salt and pepper

Boil the rice in the water and mash smooth with the fat. Season with salt and pepper to taste. Line a well-greased casserole with the mixture, pressing the paste firmly against bottom and sides, and leaving a large hollow in the center. Set in a cold place until firm. Meanwhile boil the liver, drain, chop fine and season with salt. Heat the soup stock, seasoned with caramel (See Index). Make a brown sauce with the fat, browned flour and soup stock, and add the minced liver. Fill the hollow in the center of the rice with the liver mixture, sprinkle with crumbs and brown in the oven.

RICE EN CASSEROLE

2 cups chopped cold meat
3 eggs
⅓ cup milk
2 cups boiled rice
Celery-salt

2 tablespoons butter or other fat
2 tablespoons tomato catchup
Salt

Season the meat and pile it in the center of an oiled casserole. Mix the eggs, milk, rice, fat and seasonings. Pour over the meat, cover, and bake (350° F.) for twenty minutes.

SPANISH RICE

¾ cup rice
2 tablespoons fat
5 cups water
2 onions
2 cups tomatoes

½ cup chopped green pepper or pimientos
Salt
Pepper
Paprika

Fry the rice in the fat until brown, then add water and boil until soft. Drain. Sauté the onions in a little fat; mix with tomatoes and chopped peppers or pimientos, and add to the rice. Add seasoning, and place in a greased casserole. Bake (350° F.) for thirty minutes.

RICE À LA CREOLE

1 cup chopped boiled ham
1 onion
1 cup boiled rice
1 can tomatoes

2 cups fine soft crumbs
2 tablespoons butter or other fat
Celery-salt
Pepper and salt

Mix ingredients in the order given. Bake in a greased casserole for one-half hour (350° F.). This dish makes a good one-dish meal.

SPAGHETTI, SPANISH MICHEL

2 cups spaghetti
1 quart tomatoes, fresh or canned
½ cup boiled ham

1 onion
1 green pepper
¼ teaspoon pepper
½ teaspoon salt

Break the spaghetti into inch pieces. Cook in one quart boiling water until tender, add the tomatoes, and cook fifteen minutes longer. Remove the fat from the ham and try it out. Dice onion and green pepper, and fry slowly in this fat until tender. Chop the ham and add it with the onion, green pepper and seasoning to the spaghetti and tomatoes. Put in casserole and bake fifteen minutes in a moderate oven (350°-400° F.).

SCALLOPED HAM AND POTATOES

6 potatoes
1 pound raw smoked ham
3 cups milk (or more)

1 green pepper (may be omitted)
Flour

Cover the bottom of an oiled baking-dish with sliced, raw potatoes. Sprinkle with flour add inch-square pieces of ham. Repeat until the dish is full. Pour in as much milk as the dish will hold. Bake (350°-400° F.) until the potatoes are tender (1-1½ hrs.). Chopped green pepper adds to the flavor.

SUMMER CASSEROLE

6 hard-cooked eggs
3 ripe tomatoes
3 tablespoons butter or other fat
3 tablespoons flour

2 teaspoons salt
1½ cups milk
½ cup grated cheese
Buttered crumbs

Cut hard-cooked eggs in half and arrange around the edge of a greased casserole or baking dish. Slice peeled ripe tomatoes in the center of the dish. Make a white sauce of the milk, fat, flour and salt. Add cheese, and stir over low heat until the cheese is well mixed and smooth. Pour over tomatoes and eggs. Cover with crumbs and bake twenty minutes in a moderate oven (350°-400° F.).

The centers of the tomatoes may be scooped out, and a whole egg placed in each, if desired.

BANANAS EN CASSEROLE

6 small bananas
1 glass currant or grape jelly

1 cup boiling water
1 lemon

Peel the bananas. Remove the coarse threads and divide in quarters, cutting first crosswise and then lengthwise. Place in a greased casserole and pour over them a sauce made by melting the currant or grape jelly in the boiling water, and mixing with it the juice of a lemon. Cover the casserole and bake in a hot oven (400°-450° F.) until the bananas are tender. The cover may be removed at the last moment and the bananas sprinkled with granulated sugar and allowed to brown slightly. Serve as an entrée with game, mutton, or beef.

AU GRATIN DISHES EN CASSEROLE

Au gratin dishes, many of which are given in this book, are particularly adapted to the casserole. The mixtures of chicken, sweetbreads, fish, macaroni and vegetables may be entirely prepared, then placed in the casserole, topped with buttered crumbs and cheese and placed in a hot oven (400°-450° F.) to brown.

EGGS YORKSHIRE—

½ cup fat	1 cup pastry flour
2 eggs, beaten	1 teaspoon baking powder
1 cup milk	½ teaspoon salt
4 hard or soft cooked eggs	

Place casserole with fat in oven to melt. Remove fat to use in batter, leaving enough to grease casserole thoroughly. Return casserole to oven to heat. Beat eggs and milk thoroughly; add baking powder, flour, salt and fat and beat mixture until smooth. Cover bottom of casserole with layer of eggs (whole, halved, quartered or sliced). Pour in batter until casserole is about ⅔ full and place in hot oven (450° F.) for 15 minutes until mixture begins to expand and brown slightly, then reduce to 350° F. for 25 minutes. The batter should puff nicely during baking, making an attractive uneven broken surface. Serve at once from baking dish.

SALMON CASSEROLE—

1 1-pound can salmon	2 cups prepared biscuit
⅓ cup milk	flour
½ pound American cheese	¾ cup milk

Flake salmon in casserole. Melt cheese in top of a double boiler; add ⅓ cup milk while stirring. Pour over salmon. Mix biscuit flour and ¾ cup milk and make biscuits. Cut each in half and place around edge of casserole. Bake in hot oven (425° F.) until lightly browned.

COOKING FOR TWO

~~~~~~~~~

THE problem here is really more one of planning and marketing than of actual cooking. No roast leg of lamb or baked ham of course, no standing rib roast of beef, not often a whole watermelon. But it is possible to buy cuts of meat and to plan the other marketing so that to all intents and purposes these favorites may form part of the menu even for the smallest family. Moreover, many dishes which are too expensive to be served to a large and hungry family are often possible for a family of two.

Cooking Equipment for Two

It is impossible to cook small quantities satisfactorily in large dishes; so the first thing to do is to buy dishes and utensils of the right size. The following list is given as a suggestion.

A small casserole or a large ramekin for soufflés and casserole dishes, to be used either for the meat course or for baked puddings.

Individual ramekins and custard cups.

A small frying-pan for cooking eggs, bacon, etc.

A small baking-pan for roasting meat.

Small saucepans and kettles for vegetables and other boiled foods. The saucepans that fit together, two or three on a single burner, are especially good for the small family.

A deep pot of small diameter for deep fat frying and a wire strainer that will fit down inside it to be used as a frying basket.

A double boiler holding one quart.

Muffin pans in sets of six.

Layer cake and pie pans five or six inches in diameter.

A small square or oblong shallow pan for baking sheets of cake, ginger-bread, etc.

A small loaf pan for breads, loaf cakes and meat loaves.

A set of skewers for serving "en brochette."

A cup sized egg beater.

Small bowls.

An ice cream freezer either of the crank or vacuum type, holding from one pint to one quart.

The small ovens for use on top of the stove are very convenient for baking two or three potatoes or apples or a small dish of rice pudding, custard and similar desserts.

How to Modify Recipes

Most of the recipes in the American Woman's Cook Book are planned for six persons. Many of them can be cut down to one-half or one-third and made exactly as though the entire quantity were used. It is often more advantageous to cut the recipe in half rather than thirds, since it is sometimes harder to work with small amounts and there is relatively greater waste from food adhering to pans and spoons.

IN COOKING OVER DIRECT FIRE or in the oven, the loss of moisture will be comparatively larger than in the larger quantity recipe, so a little more liquid may be used. This is true particularly in recipes that use cream sauces and in meat casseroles.

RECIPES INCLUDING EGGS are more easily made if they can be divided to the one or two egg quantity. If less than one egg has to be used, there are two ways of doing it: Either use a very small egg or beat the egg slightly and divide it, keeping the unused portion for some other dish. It might be well to say, however, that a little more egg than the recipe calls for will not generally do any harm. So if you are not considering economy you will be safe in using a whole egg even though the rest of the ingredients are cut down.

WITH YEAST DOUGH it is advisable to use a larger quantity of yeast, proportionately, than would be used in the full recipe. For instance, if the recipe calls for one yeast cake, and you are cutting it down to one-third or one-half, it will be wise to use the whole yeast cake, or the greater part of it, in order to hasten the process. Those recipes which demand no kneading are easier than the kneaded ones to handle in small quantities.

FOR SOUPS, allow from one-half cup to one cup for each person, the amount depending upon the kind of soup you are making and whether you are serving it in cups or plates.

FOR DESSERTS, allow from one-half cup to three-quarters cup for each serving.

OF CREAMED DISHES, vegetables, etc., about two-thirds cup is served, but an allowance for a second portion should be made.

To Use One Recipe in Different Ways

Often a full recipe can be made and used in different ways for several occasions.

THE RECIPE FOR CREAMED CHICKEN, for instance, will provide enough for an au gratin oven dish.

A RICH BAKING POWDER BISCUIT DOUGH will make short-cakes for one meal, toasted biscuits for another, and, if baked in a sheet and covered with cinnamon and sugar, coffee-cake for a third.

PIE DOUGH will make pies, tart shells for meat or dessert, cheese strips for soup or salad, and tiny jam turnovers for afternoon tea.

CAKE BATTER may be baked as loaves, layers, sheets or cup cakes, as cottage pudding, to be served hot with a sauce, or as a ring in which to serve fruit, jelly or a creamed dessert. A fruit cake mixture may be baked as fruit cake or steamed in small molds and served hot with sauce.

How to Use Left-Overs

The problem of cooking for two depends to a great extent for its solution upon the ability to use left-overs attractively at successive meals. In using this surplus food, it is important to supply whatever is lacking. If it is dry it needs to be moistened; if it is hard it needs to be softened; if it is not of any particular flavor it needs to be well seasoned or mixed with something that will give it a distinctive and appetizing taste.

SOMETIMES IT IS WELL TO KEEP YOUR LEFT-OVERS UN-COOKED. For instance, if you have a steak that is too large for one meal, because in order to have it appetizing you had to have it cut fairly thick, cut out the heart or tenderloin and broil it, keeping the rest for a fresh-meat casserole the next day.

ANY SMALL PIECES OF UNCOOKED MEAT may be made attractive by broiling on the skewer or preparing as a mixed grill or a mixed fried dish. For any of these there need be only a few small pieces of meat with accessories such as half a dozen mushrooms, a few slices of potato, an onion or two, small cubes of egg-plant or turnip or other vegetables, a few curls of bacon or a tiny sausage or two. To cook "en brochette" dip the small pieces of meat and vegetable in melted butter and impale them on the skewer. Bacon and sausage of course need no butter.

Put the skewer on the broiling rack and broil, turning occasionally. For a mixed grill, any meat or vegetable that can be put under the broiler may be used. Slices of tomato, eggplant and pineapple give interesting variety.

Meats for Two

The following types of meat dishes are as easily served to two as to six:

Hamburg balls or steak	Chop suey
Lamb, mutton, veal or pork chops	Sausages
	Scrapple
Liver	Dried beef
Kidneys	Sliced ham
Sweetbreads	Bacon
Ox tails	Salt pork

ROASTS—Instead of a large roast of beef, buy a thick steak, roll, tie and roast it in a very hot oven (450°-500° F.) for a short time. If even this is too large a roast, cut out the heart for roasting and keep the rest for a casserole dish.

FOR LAMB, MUTTON AND VEAL ROASTS, buy loin chops—as many as you require. Have the bones separated at the joints but do not have the meat cut through. Cook as a standing roast.

FOR BAKED HAM, buy a one-inch thick slice of raw ham. Brown it on both sides in the frying-pan, then cover it with mustard, flour and sugar and stuff the top with cloves. Add a little water and cook, covered, in a moderate oven (350° F.) for an hour.

IN PLACE OF STUFFED SHOULDER OF LAMB, mutton or veal, buy a slice of the meat and spread it with any desired stuffing. Roll, with the stuffing inside. This may be browned first and then baked, or may be put immediately into the oven.

FOR POT ROASTS a one pound or two pound piece will be quite as satisfactory as a larger one, though it may require a little more watching while it is cooking.

POULTRY—A whole turkey, of course, is out of the question, but poultry may be enjoyed in the shape of a broiling chicken or guinea chick, or squab and the smaller game birds, quail and grouse. These can be broiled, fried or baked. The pigeon is nice in a pie.

Fish

WHOLE FISH that will serve six or more persons are not a wise purchase for the small family. Either buy small fish, such as smelts, perch and butterfish, or a steak or fillet from one of the large fish—halibut, cod, haddock, salmon and the like.

SHELL FISH are particularly well suited to the needs of the small family. It is possible to buy just the right amount of clams, oysters, shrimps, hard and soft-shelled crabs, and sometimes a lobster just large enough for two is procurable. Shad roe and frogs' legs are luxuries that are more often possible for the small family than for the large family.

Vegetables

THE LARGE VEGETABLES will give left-overs that can be used in many ways. A small cabbage makes one nice salad, and, a few days later, one cooked dish. Winter squash can be used up in pies and custards. An egg-plant will give one-half for stuffing and baking and several slices for frying, with some, perhaps left to cook in Oriental style. Left-over cooked cauliflower may be served cold as a salad, or scalloped.

THE SMALLER VEGETABLES, fresh peas, beans, carrots, beets, potatoes, etc., can be bought and cooked in exactly the quantity required, though, as all of these are good for use in salads, it is generally wise to cook a little more than you need for one meal.

SPAGHETTI, MACARONI AND NOODLES are often served as a vegetable. These, of course, are easily managed if there are cooking utensils of the right size.

Soups

ANY CREAMED VEGETABLE SOUP can be made in a pint quantity.

A QUART OF MEAT STOCK can be made from the bones and trimmings of meat purchased for other cooking, and whatever is not needed for soup can be made into gravies and sauces for following days. A thickened meat stock containing small pieces of meat and plenty of diced vegetables makes a substantial dish.

Breads

ONE LOAF OF YEAST BREAD can be made at a time, and quickly, if the proportion of yeast is increased.

ANY BAKING POWDER MIXTURE can be mixed in the desired quantity, and almost any kind of loaf can be made with it—white, whole wheat, graham, oatmeal, bran, nut, raisin, etc. Baked in a small pan, these loaves will be used up before they are dry.

BISCUITS AND MUFFINS are the ideal home made bread for the small family.

PANCAKES AND WAFFLES are always possible, and may be served as breakfast or luncheon breads, as accompaniments to meat or chicken, or as a dessert, with fruit, honey, maple sirup or a sauce. With a table griddle or iron they can be cooked in the dining-room and served piping hot.

Cakes

A LAYER OR LOAF CAKE which can be consumed in one or two meals can be baked in small pans. Half of an average recipe will make two of these small layers as well as several cup cakes or a sheet which can be cut into squares and frosted or not as desired.

IF ROLLED COOKIES ARE TOO MUCH TROUBLE, use any recipe for drop cookies. These can be flattened out with a knife and made as thin as you wish.

Desserts

PUDDINGS—With individual custard cups or ramekins or with one large enough to serve two, practically any baked pudding is possible, and with these same molds, custards or any of the cold puddings are easily molded. The recipes need no change other than cutting them to the desired quantity. It is as easy to make one cup of custard or gelatin as it is to make a quart.

Most steamed puddings improve with keeping, so it is quite possible to make an entire recipe, steam it in small molds, and keep the extra ones for future need. They can be reheated in the top of a double boiler or in a pan, surrounded by water, in the oven. For strawberry shortcake of the old fashioned variety, cut the crust with a biscuit cutter and make individual shortcakes. For a sweet shortcake, bake the batter in muffin pans. Cottage pudding, soufflés, and similar desserts may be baked in custard cups or ramekins and either turned out or served in the dish with or without sauce.

PIES—A small sized pan will make as good a pie as a large one. If an extra shell is baked at the same time as a two-crust pie, it can be kept for several days, then reheated to freshen it and filled with a custard, cream or lemon filling. Individual tart shells made with the muffin tins, or turnovers just large enough to serve one person make a variation in form.

Fruits

These offer little difficulty, since most of them come in individual portions. If you feel impelled to buy the large fruits, such as watermelon, honeydew and casaba melons, and pineapple, serve them in different ways so that they do not become tiresome before they are eaten up. From the pineapple make a fruit cup, a salad, an open tart, frosting for cake or a delicious sherbet or ice-cream. After the first slices of melon have been used, cut balls and allow them to stand in fruit juice. Serve, chilled, as a fruit cup. Watermelon can be used for a cooling sherbet or frappé and the other melons make interesting fruit salads.

Nuts

These should not be forgotten in planning meals for two. Chestnuts, for example, make a delicious vegetable with meat when boiled and buttered or creamed. Chestnut purée with sweetened whipped cream is an unusual and delicious dessert. Blanched walnuts are particularly nice in making many dishes and can be roasted with a little oil or butter and served hot and crisp with meat.

Canned and Packaged Goods for Two

Although it is easy to feed a family of two with home cooked fresh foods, as shown by the preceding suggestions, an acquaintance with the possibilities of canned and packaged goods is important to the manager of a very small household. This is particularly so in the case of one who does work outside her home, or who makes her home in a kitchenette apartment where space-saving is a major consideration.

CANNED VEGETABLES eliminate the time-consuming operations of washing, scraping or paring, and simplify the problem of garbage disposal, which must always follow the preparation of fresh vegetables.

FRUITS, VEGETABLES, MEATS AND FISH of many kinds come in cans of various sizes, so that it is possible to buy the size that best suits your requirements.

READY-TO-MIX piecrust, pancake, cake and pastry flours shorten the time and reduce the number of utensils needed for mixing pies, biscuits, pancakes, muffins and cakes.

FRUITS AND NUTS IN CANS OR JARS of suitable size are always ready for salads, desserts, appetizers and garnishes.

CONDENSED, EVAPORATED AND POWDERED MILK may be kept in small space and, if not kept too long before they are opened, do not require a refrigerator temperature, as fresh milk does.

STEAMED PUDDINGS, pie-fillings, ready-to-mix pudding ingredients, canned Welsh rarebit, chicken à la king, baked beans, spaghetti in savory sauces, soups of all varieties and countless other aids are at your service to help you serve varied and appetizing meals however limited your time or culinary space.

Types of Recipes Especially Suitable for Two

Appetizers
Soups
Broiled meats and fish
Shell fish
Soufflés
Croquettes
Patties
Creamed, scalloped and au
    gratin dishes
Cheese recipes
Egg dishes
Mushrooms in all ways

Entrées
Salads
Substantial sandwiches
Vegetables of all kinds
Quick breads
Fruit desserts
Gelatin and cream desserts
Cookies, gingerbread and small
    cakes
Tarts and turnovers
Recipes suggested in the chapter Cooking at the Table

COOKING AT THE TABLE

THE small table cookers of various kinds—grills, chafing-dishes, waffle irons, muffin irons, pancake griddles, toasters and coffee percolators—make informal entertaining a pleasure to the hostess as well as to the guests.

Meals cooked at the table must of course be simple. It is usually wise to confine a supper to one hot dish, with such accessories as bread and butter, toast, crackers or cold sandwiches, a hot drink or a cold drink or both. If something more elaborate is desirable, the meal may begin with a fruit cocktail or a simple salad and end with a dessert that is easily served. Relishes, such as celery and olives, are easily provided.

Suggestions for Table Cookery

It will help you to entertain successfully in this manner, if you will keep in mind the following suggestions:

1. PREPARE AHEAD OF TIME everything that can be prepared. Have the table spread with all that is needed in the way of china, silver and glass. Arrange the sandwiches, relishes and other cold accessories attractively and conveniently.

2. HAVE ON HAND EVERYTHING THAT IS TO BE USED in the hot dish, and have it prepared as far as it is possible to prepare it. Meat or fish or vegetables should be nicely diced, cheese grated, oysters drained, and eggs broken into a bowl, unless they are to be cooked separately, as in poaching or frying. Lack of preparation often results in tiresome delays and unappetizing confusion, but with everything in readiness the one hot dish is easily put together before the guests become tired of watching the process.

3. BE SURE THAT YOUR EQUIPMENT IS SUFFICIENT to provide for the needs of your guests. If you are giving a waffle party, do not invite more guests than your waffle iron will easily serve, so that no one need wait hungrily while others are eating. The same thing holds true with table grills and chafing-dishes. There should be enough creamed chicken or Welsh rabbit to serve everyone generously at the same time.

4. IF YOUR COOKERS ARE ELECTRIC, be sure that your wires are heavy enough to bear the load without blowing out a fuse.

Unless you have special wiring and sturdy convenience outlets, it is safer not to attempt to use a grill or waffle iron plus a percolator on the same circuit. Plan to use first one and then the other, or you may melt a fuse when the meal is but half ready, leaving your guests hungry for that always indefinite period until it may be replaced.

Dishes That Are Especially Good for Table Cookery

BANANA SAUTÉ

1 tablespoon butter	Flour Sugar
3 bananas	3 to 6 slices sponge cake

Melt the butter in the blazer. Peel the bananas, cut in half lengthwise, roll lightly in flour and brown on both sides in the hot fat. Sprinkle with sugar and serve on oblongs of sponge cake.

CHICKEN HASH

1½ cups chopped chicken	1 tablespoon parsley
1 cup diced boiled potatoes	Salt Pepper
2 tablespoons fat	½ cup stock or water

Mix the chicken and the potatoes lightly together. Melt the fat in the blazer, add the potato and meat, parsley, seasoning and stock, and cook directly over the flame.

If desired, one-fourth cup of chopped green peppers may be added.

CRAB RAREBIT

1 tablespoon fat	Pepper Parsley
2 tablespoons flour	1 to 2 cups crab meat, fresh
2 cups cream	or canned
⅛ teaspoon soda	2 tablespoons Parmesan cheese
½ teaspoon salt	Toast

Make a white sauce of the fat, flour, cream, soda and seasonings. Add chopped cooked crab meat (see page 221). Arrange squares of buttered toast on a hot platter. Pour the crab mixture over them, sprinkle with grated cheese and serve piping hot.

ENGLISH MONKEY

1 cup bread-crumbs	1 egg
1 cup milk	½ teaspoon salt
1 tablespoon fat	¼ teaspoon pepper
½ cup mild American cheese	Toast

Soak the bread-crumbs in the milk until they are soft. Melt the fat in the blazer. Add the cheese cut in dice. When the cheese has melted, add the softened crumbs, the egg beaten, and salt and pepper. Cook three minutes longer and pour over squares of toast.

GRILLED SARDINES

12 large sardines   1 tablespoon lemon-juice   6 pieces toast

Drain sardines and heat thoroughly in chafing-dish. Turn frequently; add lemon-juice and serve on finger-length pieces of toast.

OYSTERS À L'INDIENNE

1 pint oysters	2 tablespoons Worcestershire
Bacon	sauce
Cloves	1 tablespoon minced parsley
2 tablespoons chutney	6 olives
sauce	½ teaspoon paprika

Drain large oysters, wipe them dry, wrap each in a slice of bacon, fasten with a toothpick, and stick two cloves in each oyster. Put the oysters in the blazer and cook until the bacon is crisp and the oysters plump. Mix the chutney sauce, Worcestershire sauce, minced parsley, olives cut fine, and paprika. Pour over the oysters, stirring it thoroughly into the gravy. This recipe will serve three or four.

LOBSTER À LA NEWBURG

2 tablespoons butter	1 pint milk
1 teaspoon flour	3 egg-yolks
1 boiled lobster or 1 can	Salt
of lobster	Cayenne

Place the butter in the blazer and stir it as it foams. Rub the flour into the butter, add the salt and pepper, then one-half of the milk, stirring all of the time and being careful that the flame is not too hot. Beat the yolks of the eggs until frothy, add the remainder of the milk and stir into the roux. When the mass is of the consistency of cream, add the lobster, cut up coarsely, and, when thoroughly heated, serve. If using the fresh fish, prepare as directed (see page 216). Just before adding the lobster, rub the coral and the fat together and stir in.

Food Suggestions for Table Service

Other dishes that lend themselves to this form of entertaining, as well as to the family breakfast or supper, will be found throughout the book under the following classifications. The index will supply page numbers for the recipes.

CREAMED DISHES—Creamed Chicken, Creamed Oysters, Chicken à la King, Tuna with Caper Sauce, Oysters with Mushrooms, Creamed Sweetbreads, Scotch Woodcock, Creamed Mushrooms, Curried Dishes.

HOT SANDWICHES—Grilled Cheese, Grilled Tongue and Egg, Club, Turkish, Savory, Sardine and Toast.

TOAST—Cream, Tomato Cream, Cinnamon, French.

QUICK BREADS—Griddlecakes, Pancakes, Waffles.

EGG DISHES—Omelet (with any desired variation), Scrambled Eggs, Poached Eggs, Cuban Eggs, Spanish Eggs, Egg Fricassee.

CHEESE DISHES—Welsh Rarebit, Cheese Fondue (on toast).

PANNED AND GRILLED DISHES—Panned Oysters, Pigs in Blankets, Peanut Butter Cutlets, Fried Tomatoes, Kedgeree, Hashed Brown Potatoes, Spanish Potatoes, Beef Hash à la Normandie.

CANDIES—Fudge (in any variation), Butterscotch, Maple Scotch, Peanut Brittle.

FOOD EQUIVALENTS

IN this list, the calculations are based on articles of medium size. These equivalents are not, of course, offered as exact, but merely as a guide for the housewife in estimating quantities.

Allspice (ground) — 1 oz. = 4 tablespoons.

Almonds (shelled) — 1 lb. = 2½ cups.

Apples (dried) — 1 lb. = 5 cups. Double in bulk when cooked.

Apricots (dried) — 1 lb. = about 3 cups. Double in bulk when cooked. (fresh) — 1 lb. = about 6 apricots.

Bacon (medium strip) — 1 lb. = about 30 full thin slices. (wide strip) — 1 lb. = about 15 full thin slices.

Baking powder — 1 oz. = 3 tablespoons.

Bananas — 1 lb. = about 3 bananas.

Beans (dried) — 1 lb. = about 2 cups. (fresh) — 1 qt. will serve 6 persons. Lima (dried) — 1 lb. = about 2⅓ cups. All dried bulk increases 2 to 3 times in cooking.

Beef (raw) — 1 lb. (lean) when cooked serves 3 to 4.

Bread — 1¼-lb. loaf = about 15 slices ½ inch thick. 2-lb. loaf = about 24 slices ½ inch thick. (sandwich) — 1 loaf = 36 to 40 slices ¼ inch thick.

Butter — 1 lb. = about 2 cups.

Celery Seed — 1 oz. = 4 tablespoons.

Cheese (cottage) — 1 lb. = 2 cups.

Cherries (candied) — 1 lb. = about 120 cherries. (Maraschino) — 1 qt. = 60 to 70 cherries.

Chocolate — 1 lb. = 16 squares. 1 square grated = 5 tablespoons.

Cinnamon — 1 oz. = 4 tablespoons.

Cloves (ground) — 1 oz. = 4 tablespoons.

Cocoa — 1 lb. = 4½ cups.

Coconut (shredded) — 1 lb. = 6 cups.

Coffee (ground) — 1 lb. = 5 cups.

Corn meal — 1 lb. = 3 cups.

Cornstarch — 1 lb. = 3 cups.

Crackers (graham) — 1 lb. = about 40 crackers. (oyster) — 1 lb. = 450 to 500 crackers. (saltine) — 1 lb. = about 125 crackers. (soda) — 1 lb. = 70 to 90 crackers.

Cranberries—1 lb. = about 4 cups. 1 bushel = 32 to 40 lbs.

Cream of Tartar—1 oz. = 3 tablespoons.

Currants (dried)—1 lb. = about 2⅔ cups.

Dates—1 lb. = 50 to 60 dates.

Egg whites—1 cup = 8 to 11 whites.

Egg yolks—1 cup = about 12 yolks.

Eggs (whole)—1 cup = 4 to 6 eggs. 1 lb. = 8 to 9 eggs.

Figs (pressed)—1 lb. = 25 to 30 figs.

Flour (graham)—1 lb. = about 4½ cups. (white)—1 lb. = about 4 cups.

Lard—1 lb. = 2 cups.

Lemons—1 lb. = 3 to 5 lemons. 1 cup lemon juice = 4 juicy lemons. 1 juicy lemon = 4 tablespoons of juice.

Mustard—1 oz. = 4 tablespoons.

Mustard Seed—1 oz. = 2½ tablespoons.

Nutmeg—1 nut, grated = 2¾ tablespoons.

Oats (rolled)—1 lb. = about 5½ cups.

Oatmeal—1 lb. = about 3 cups.

Oils—1 lb. = 2 cups.

Olives—1 qt. = 60 to 70 olives.

Peanut Butter—1 lb. = about 1¾ cups.

Peanuts (shelled)—1 lb. = about 2⅔ cups.

Peas (in pod)—1 lb. = 2 to 3 servings. 1 bushel = 60 lbs.

Pecans (shelled)—1 lb. = 3 to 4 cups.

Pepper (whole)—1 oz. = 4 tablespoons. (black)—1 oz. = 4½ tablespoons.

Prunes—1 lb. = 20 to 80 prunes, average 40 to 60.

Raisins (seedless)—1 lb. = about 2⅔ cups.

Rice—1 lb. = 2 cups.

Salt—1 oz. = 1¾ tablespoons.

Soda—1 oz. = 2½ tablespoons.

Spinach—1 lb. = about 2½ quarts (uncooked). 1 lb. makes 3 to 4 servings.

Sugar (brown)—1 lb. = 2½ to 2¾ cups, depending on moisture. (granulated)—1 lb. = about 2 cups. (loaf)—1 lb. = 50 to 70 lumps. (powdered)—1 lb. = 2½ to 2¾ cups.

Tapioca—1 lb. = 2½ cups.

Tea—1 lb. = 6½ cups.

Vanilla (liquid)—1 oz. = 2 tablespoons.

Walnuts (shelled)—1 lb. = about 4 cups.

THE FRIENDS
WHO HONOR US

For many families, the pleasant comings of friends and neighbors have no further purpose than warm interchange of plans and ideas over a cup of tea or coffee.

But some believe that life is lived with one's associates and that learning to know them simplifies business and professional as well as personal relationships. This does not mean that social life shall be stilted or rigid, even when formal—quite the contrary is usually the sought-after end. Clear thinking, honest motives and ease in management can develop a social life that is simple and charming.

The guest list must be carefully considered. When inviting persons for the purpose of introducing them to someone else, be sure that as far as can be discovered, there is no third person to inject a discordant note. One cannot take full responsibility for the emotional responses of all one's friends and acquaintances, but some caution can and should be exercised. When entertaining a group of professionals it is well to have several professions represented so that conversation will be general and pleasant, and not turn to moot professional questions that may start a sharp debate.

Many families, too, see in their social life an opportunity to train their children in the social graces and amenities. This, of course, can be overdone if not carefully thought out. Many guests are not interested in children and some are annoyed by them. But family parties are always the logical and pleasant opportunity to give the youngsters their chance. In any case, children should be prepared for what is ahead of them. Being more at ease in their own minds about what may happen and what is expected of them, they are much less likely to "show off" or behave like the "enfant terrible." Being reminded of the uses of knife, fork, and napkin beforehand, too, and not reprimanded in the presence of others, will make for better behavior.

ENTERTAINING WITHOUT A MAID

Many women can manage almost any form of entertainment without the help of a maid. For most, however, there are distinct limits to what should be attempted for pleasant and dignified results. The disappearance of the dining room and the substitution of a bay or alcove in the living room has increased the ease of servantless entertaining at the table. Many small pieces of furniture are especially designed to add to the efficiency of the hostess and the comfort of her guests, such as the drop-leaf, gate-leg and butterfly tables, double-decked tea carts, muffin stands and butler's trays. The menu should be planned to avoid last minute activities on the part of the hostess. She should be free to greet and attend her guests. All the extra china and glass necessary should be on one of the small tables within the hostess' reach and china removed can be placed out of sight on the lower shelf of the table or the low butler's tray. Extra bread, butter, wafers, sauces and water are also on the auxiliary table. If arrangements are well planned, the hostess need not leave her chair until it is time to clear, and serve the dessert. At that time, too, the coffee can be started. The coffee service has previously been placed at a convenient spot in the living room, and the screen to be used for enclosing the table when it has been left is at an easily accessible place. (See page 82.) As the guests leave the table for the living room, the hostess enters with the coffee while the host attends to placing the screen. By the time all have lighted a fresh cigarette, the coffee is being poured and the dining table has been forgotten.

BUFFET SERVICE

Until very recently the only buffet was an informal type of service in which everyone served himself and his partner from a refectory table set against one side of the living or dining room. The table is spread with the best cloth and laid with the best china and silver if the occasion is formal, or with an informal cloth and pottery, copper, chrome and wood for a man's buffet or a sports party. Decorations are in keeping with the occasion and the appointments. Silver is laid in groups, plates are stacked and napery is laid in a tilted pile. Only one or two hot dishes are served and all the food is brought to the table at the beginning, except for necessary replenishing.

The currently popular buffet dinner is another way to manage a maidless dinner. Guests are seated at card tables placed in the living room or other open space, wherever they can be comfortably seated and served. The extended dining table is set much as for the usual buffet, except that it is away from the wall so guests may walk around it. The small tables are set for the usual four with a complete service at each place. If there are flowers or other decorations they should be very small and low. Small fruits in low bowls are effective. The large table, however, may be very elaborately adorned with both flowers and candles. Friends or members of the family may be asked to assist and the host should be occupied in seeing that everyone is seated comfortably. Sometimes older people, unacquainted with this form of service, become confused and need help. Second helpings, fresh water and butter are brought to the small tables by host, hostess or those assisting.

For more hilarious parties, still on the grown-up side, there are those in which each couple brings one course, the hostess providing the hot one and coffee. There is also the dinner at which all hands help. This takes some organizing to keep the guests from colliding and from clogging the kitchen, but if well planned, can be a great source of fun and not much more formal than a studio party.

More formal and peculiarly adapted to servantless entertaining is after-dinner coffee and liqueurs. Invitations are usually issued for "9 p. m. to Midnight" and since these parties are particularly popular among bachelors and professional people —physicians, newspaper people and musicians—guests arrive at their own convenient time. There is usually music from 10 to 11, giving the earlier arrivals an opportunity to have their coffee and conversation first and the latecomers to have theirs afterwards.

THE "RUMPUS" ROOM

The retirement of solid fuels from domestic consumption has resulted, in recent years, in the rearrangement of basement space to provide for the Rumpus room. This room takes many forms and is as variously equipped as there are types of basements and of household ideas. It ranges from the simple, cleared space allotted to children's indoor play to the elaborate, professionally decorated English Taproom. In many of the simpler types there are provisions for some sort of cooking, an electric grill or a fireplace before which corn may be popped, or chestnuts, wieners and marshmallows roasted. Without cooking equipment, food prepared in the kitchen is served here. All Rumpus room parties are of the most informal type and the menus planned should reflect this spirit. Picnic menus serve best: hamburgs and wieners on rolls, small steaks, chops and bacon, sandwiches, whole pickles, radishes, tomatoes, olives, deviled eggs, whole fruit, doughnuts and cider, beer, lemonade or ginger ale. If there is a fireplace, use it for the camp cookery children enjoy on hikes— potatoes, sweet potatoes, whole eggs or onions done in the hot ashes. Clever boys and their fathers will be able to manage more complicated things. The room is, of course, the ideal spot for taffy pulls and popcorn-ball parties of the oldsters' childhood. Entertainment takes the form of games.

COCKTAIL PARTIES

Another form of entertaining that lends itself to the maidless home is the cocktail party. Men and women living alone, as well as householders, find this a simple method of bringing their friends together in both small and large numbers. The larger the party, the more formal it is apt to be but this need not necessarily hold. A refectory table against the wall is the usual setting but nothing is served that cannot be eaten with the fingers. No individual silver is necessary and only a tiny napkin is used. Drinks are the special province of the host. He will make up his own shopping list and often does his own buying. He will know the particular tastes and aversions of many of the guests (in a small party, of all of them) and guide himself accordingly. A woman alone will have a relative or friend act in this capacity. Likewise, a man entertaining alone may ask his sister or friend to attend to the menu. Served with the drinks are tiny and attractive open sandwiches, made of tart, smoked or spiced ingredients. Sweets are never used, except that in every group there are those who do not use spirituous liquors, for whatever reason. For them, there should be fruit juices, ginger ale, fruitades or whatever taste dictates. Then serve sweets. In addition there should be olives, small pickles, stuffed celery, carrot strips, potato chips in their various shapes or salted nuts. In cold weather hot hors d'oeuvres served with a toothpick are especially acceptable: small filled broiled mushrooms, broiled cocktail sausages with or without a bacon wrapping, broiled olives wrapped in bacon and many others. It is well to remember that all varnished furniture needs protection from the occasional careless guest. The foot of every stemmed glass should be provided with a jacket, and tall glasses equally well protected. Have plenty of coasters in addition.

OUTDOOR PARTIES

Interest in out-of-doors dining has long been evident in American families, somewhat colored by local facilities. When a lake and beach are available, then campfires, beach parties, fish fries and clambakes vie with picnics and steak fries. Many communities encourage these outdoor activities by providing picnic grounds and camp sites, often equipped with open-air fireplaces, tables, benches and other necessary facilities. Recently, however, many families have discovered that they may serve any meal out of doors on their own premises with very little effort and much pleasure. A screened-in porch, a level terrace, a planted back yard serves admirably or, if very fortunate, a garden planted and equipped as an outdoor living room. The handy man about the house or the local carpenter can build collapsible tables or hinged ones against the house wall, rush or picket screens and canvas-covered or wooden chairs, at little expense, using waterproof materials and finish. Since this is a warm-weather arrangement, there need be little concern for hot dishes, but it adds to convenience if an electric outlet can be available for making coffee and toast and keeping such dishes hot while serving. There need be little change in the menu when food is served at home. For transporting some distance, elaborate menus and complicated dishes should be avoided; steaks, chops, wieners, bacon, broilers and hamburgs to broil over an open fire if available; rolls of the proper shape; potato, cabbage, coleslaw or other small vegetable salad; whole tomatoes, radishes, olives, carrots; whole fruits, cookies, cupcakes or doughnuts. Beverages such as coffee, milk, or chocolate are carried in thermos bottles or in their own containers if beer or canned fruit juices. An ample supply of paper plates, cups, napkins, etc., should be at hand and used to build the fire that disposes of all refuse at the end of the meal. Be very sure the fire is completely extinguished before you leave it.

FORMAL PARTIES

The Formal Dinner or Luncheon served by the household staff will be found thoroughly discussed on pages 64 to 82.

A LIST OF HERBS, SPICES, EXTRACTS AND FLAVORS

HERBS

BAY LEAVES—Flavor particularly good in practically all meat cooking; also in vegetable and meat soups and sauces.

BORAGE—Young tender leaves excellent for salad or pot herbs.

CHERVIL—Flavor like parsley but milder. Young leaves may be used in meat and vegetable soups, salads, and as a garnish. More attractive than parsley as a garnish but not as lasting. Used in a powdered combination called *Fines Herbes*.

DILL—Both leaves and seeds of dill are used. Leaves may be used as a garnish or to cook with fish. Leaves or the whole plant may be used to flavor dill pickles.

FENNEL—Has a sweet hot flavor. Both seeds and leaves are used. Seeds may be used as a spice in very small quantity in pies and baked fruit. Leaves may be boiled with fish. Fresh leaves are valued by some people.

HOREHOUND—Used in candy making.

MARJORAM—May be used both green and dry for flavoring soups and ragouts; and in stuffing for all meats and fish.

MINT—May be used fresh in salads, fruit beverages, jellies, conserves, ices, iced tea, sauces for meats, and added minced to carrots and peas. Good with apple combinations.

PARSLEY—One of the most popular herbs, which may be used in many ways. A favorite garnish. May be used in fruit and vegetable salads, in sandwiches, in all soups and gravies, in meat sauces, minced and added just before serving to practically all vegetables, minced and added to white sauce.

PEPPER GRASS OR PEPPER CRESS—Excellent flavor. May be used in green salads and sandwiches.

SAFFRON—May be used to give pale yellow color to bread, cakes, and sauces, or to color confectionery. Has a pleasant flavor and good color.

SAGE—Used fresh and dried. May be used in poultry and meat stuffings; in sausage and practically all meat combinations; in cheese and vegetable combinations, as in vegetable loaf, or curry. The flowers are sometimes used in salads.

A List of Herbs, Spices, Extracts and Flavors (*Continued*)

SAVORY—Agreeable flavor, blends well with other flavors; may be used in stuffings in meat, in vegetable soups, in sausage, with meats and with horseradish.

SORREL—Green. May be used in salads or as a pot herb.

SWEET BASIL—Distinct flavor of cloves. May be used for flavoring salads, soups and meats.

TARRAGON—Leaves have a hot, pungent taste. Valuable to use in all salads and sauces. Excellent in Tartar sauce. Leaves are pickled with gherkins. Used to flavor vinegar.

THYME—Leaves, green or dried, valuable for use in stuffings, sauces, soups and meats.

SEEDS

ALLSPICE—Sold whole or ground. Better combined with other spices in fruit dishes, cakes, pies, pickles, etc.

ANISE—Leaves are used for garnishing and for flavor. Oil is extracted from the seed and used as anise extract.

CARAWAY—Seeds have a spicy smell and aromatic taste. Used in baked fruit, in cakes, breads, soups, cheese and sauerkraut.

CARDAMOM—Flavor especially good in honey combinations.

CLOVES—Should be dark brown in color. Usually used with other spices. The combination gives a better flavor than cloves used alone. Too much gives an undesirable color as well as a bitter flavor.

CORIANDER—Both leaves and seeds are used. Leaves are used in salads, soups and curry sauces. The seeds are used for flavoring pastries and confections in about the same way as caraway seeds.

CURRY POWDER—A number of spices combined in proper proportion to give a distinct flavor to such dishes as vegetables of all kinds, meat, poultry and fish.

MACE—The inner envelope of nutmegs. May be used both in "blade" and ground form in soups, sauces, pastry, pickles.

MUSTARD—Young tender leaves are used for greens and for salad. Seeds are used as a ground spice in salad dressings, pickles, sauces, in some vegetable cookery, and in some cheese dishes. Made into a paste and served with meats.

NUTMEG—Sold whole or ground. Gives good flavor used alone in small amount in various soups, meat dishes, pastry and in all dough mixtures. In combination with other spices for pickles.

PAPRIKA—A Hungarian red pepper. Bright red, in color. May be used in all meat and vegetable salads. In soups, both cream and stock. As a garnish for potatoes, cream cheese, salads or eggs.

PEPPERCORN—The whole berry of the pepper plant.

PEPPER, BLACK—Reduced to proper fineness by grinding and sieving. Used in all meat and vegetable dishes where the color does not affect the product.

PEPPER, CAYENNE—Usually obtained from small fruited varieties of capsicum. It should be of dull red color. May be used in very small amounts in vegetables and in some salad dressings and in cheese dishes. It must be used with care, however.

PEPPER, WHITE—Practically the same as black pepper except that the outer shell or pericarp of the berry is removed. Used where color of black pepper is undesirable.

PEPPER, WHITE CORIANDER—A product of especially attractive appearance screened to uniform size and bleached.

FLAVOR VEGETABLES

CELERY—Every part of the plant can be used to advantage. Stalks and heart may be used raw, plain or with various fillings. Outer stalks may be stewed, scalloped, or used in combination to give flavor to other vegetables such as potatoes. Trimmings may be used for flavoring soups or in any cooked meat or vegetable dishes. Dried seeds may be used in pickles, soups and salads.

CHIVES—Leaves are used in many ways. May be used in salad, in cream cheese, in sandwiches, omelet, soups, and in fish dishes. Mild flavor of onion.

GARLIC—Vegetable similar to a small onion but with the bulb divided into sections known as cloves. May be used in very small amounts in flavoring meats, soups, sauces, salads, pickles.

HORSERADISH—Valuable for its white, fleshy, pungent roots which are grated, mixed with vinegar and used as a condiment for meat, oysters, fish, sauces, and in some kinds of pickle. Young tender leaves may be used in salad or greens.

MUSHROOMS—Have a delicate characteristic flavor. May be used in meat or vegetable dishes, in sauces and soups.

ONION—Popular vegetable which combines in flavor with practically all vegetables, and some fruits—*e. g.*, apple, and orange; also with all meat and fish. Tender young tops may be minced and used as a garnish for soups and salads.

PEPPERS—All varieties of green peppers and some of the red peppers may be used to give flavor to most forms of vegetable cookery. The green peppers of mild flavor and thick-meated type are particularly good for stuffing and for salad.

SHALLOTS—A mild onion flavor used in the same way as onions.

A List of Herbs, Spices, Extracts and Flavors (Concluded)

FLAVORINGS AND EXTRACTS

ALMOND EXTRACT—Used in cakes and confectionery.

VANILLA EXTRACT—Particularly good with all chocolate, cocoa, coconut, date, raisin and coffee combinations. Good in most milk combinations; *e. g.*, ice-creams and custards.

LEMON EXTRACT—Used in cakes, puddings, pies, ice-cream and candy. Sometimes used in combination with vanilla. Excellent flavor. Lemon should be more sparingly used than vanilla.

ROSE EXTRACT—Used in angel and other white cake; also in fancy candies.

ORANGE, PINEAPPLE, STRAWBERRY, RASPBERRY, CHERRY (extracts)— Used in desserts, beverages and candies.

WINTERGREEN, PEPPERMINT, GINGER, CINNAMON, CLOVE (extracts) —Used largely in beverages and confections.

FRUIT VINEGARS—Blackberry, currant, elderberry, etc., made by steeping the fruit in the vinegar. Used in beverages, ices, and sauces.

LEMON—Used instead of vinegar in salads and sauces when a milder acid is desired or when vinegar is objectionable. Used in beverages, hot or cold. Also in salads, conserves, marmalades, etc. Citric acid found in lemons, oranges and limes.

TOMATO JUICE—Used in sauces to serve with bland foods, such as potato croquettes, or with foods having distinctive flavor, such as fish, also in beverages.

VEGETABLE FLAVORINGS—For use in sauces, gravies, etc.

VINEGAR—Low percentage natural acid, generally acetic acid. Used as a preservative for all pickling of vegetables and fruit. To give zest or tang flavor to salad dressing; for meat, fish and vegetable sauces. Different kinds are wine vinegar, malt or beer vinegar, white vinegar, cider vinegar, tarragon vinegar.

A LIST OF FOREIGN WORDS AND PHRASES

Often Used in Connection with Cooking

À LA, AU, AUX—Dressed in a certain style.

À L'ANCIENNE—In old style.

À LA BOURGEOISE—In family style.

À LA MODE—Literally, "in the fashion"; applied to ways of serving various dishes. For instance: "boeuf a la mode" is beef larded and pot roasted; "pie a la mode" is pie served with ice-cream.

ARTICHAUT—Artichoke.

ASPERGE—Asparagus.

AU GRATIN—Baked with a topping of crumbs, and often with grated cheese.

BISQUE—A rather thick soup, usually made from shell-fish; or an ice-cream containing finely chopped nuts.

BLANQUETTE—White meat in cream sauce that has been thickened with eggs.

BOMBE GLACÉE—A mold of ice-cream filled with a different kind of ice-cream or a water-ice.

BOUCHÉES—Small pastry shells or pepper cases filled with creamed meat or fish. The French word means "a mouthful."

CAFÉ AU LAIT—Coffee with milk.

CAFÉ NOIR—Black coffee.

CANARD—Duck.

CANAPÉ—A slice of bread, toasted or fried, spread with some highly flavored food and served as an appetizer.

CANNELON—Meat stuffed, rolled up and roasted or braised.

CAVIAR—The salted roe of the sturgeon.

CHAMPIGNONS—Mushrooms.

CHAUD-FROID—Literally hot-cold. In cooking, a jellied sauce.

CHOU—Cabbage.

CHOU-FLEUR—Cauliflower.

COMPOTE—A stew; often applied to fruits stewed in sirup.

CRÈME—Cream.

CROUSTADE—Case for creamed meat or fish, made of bread, rice, etc.

CROUTONS—Small cubes of fried or toasted bread served with soup.

DE, D'—Of.

DEMITASSE—Literally half a cup. Used to signify a small cup of black coffee generally taken at the close of a luncheon or dinner.

A List of Foreign Words and Phrases (Continued)

ÉCLAIR—A pastry or cake shell filled with whipped cream or custard.

EN BROCHETTE—Impaled on a skewer.

EN COQUILLES—In the shell.

ENTREES—Small made dishes served between the heavy courses at a formal dinner.

FARCI—Stuffed.

FILLETS—Long, thin pieces of boneless meat or fish.

FINES HERBES—Minced parsley, chives, chervil, etc.

FONDANT—Sugar, boiled and kneaded to a smooth creaminess. The basis of French candy.

FONDUE—Literally "melted"; usually applied to cheese, or a combination of cheese, eggs and crumbs.

FRAISES—Strawberries.

FRAPPÉ—Iced or semi-frozen.

FROMAGE—Cheese.

GÂTEAU—Cake.

GELÉE—Jelly.

GLACÉ—Frozen or glazed.

HARICOTS VERTS—Small green string beans.

HORS D'ŒUVRES—Side dishes or relishes. Usually served at the beginning of a meal.

HUÎTRES—Oysters.

JAMBON—Ham.

JARDINIÈRE—Mixed vegetables served in their own sauce.

JULIENNE—A clear vegetable soup, invented by Jean Julien in 1875, containing vegetables cut in matchlike strips.

LAITUE—Lettuce.

MACÉDOINE—A mixture; usually vegetables, with or without meat. Sometimes applied to fruit mixtures.

MARRONS—Chestnuts.

MERINGUE—Whites of eggs whipped to a standing froth with sugar.

MOUSSE—Having a mossy texture. Applied to whipped cream that has been frozen without stirring and to certain hot dishes of smooth texture.

NOIR—Black.

PAIN—Bread.

PÂTÉ—Paste, patty.

PÂTÉ DE FOIE GRAS—A paste of goose livers.

PÂTISSERIE—Pastry.

PÊCHE—Peach.

PETITS POIS—Small green peas.

PIÈCE DE RÉSISTANCE—The main dish in a meal; the roast.

POIS—Peas.

POMMES—Apples.

POMMES DE TERRE—Potatoes. Literally, "apples of the earth."

POTAGE—Soup.

POULET—Chicken.

PURÉE—Ingredients rubbed through a sieve to make a thick soup; any thick paste, such as mashed potatoes.

RAGOUT—A thick, highly seasoned stew.

RÉCHAUFFÉ—Reheated or warmed-over.

RIS DE VEAU—Sweetbreads.

RISSOLES—Minced fish or meat rolled in thin pastry and fried.

RÔTI—Roast.

SALADE—Salad.

SORBET—Frozen punch. This name is often given to water-ice when several kinds of fruit are used.

SOUFFLÉ—Literally "puffed up." A delicate baked custard which may contain fruit, cheese, flaked fish, minced poultry, meat or vegetables.

TARTE—Tart.

TARTELETTE—A little tart.

TIMBALE—An unsweetened custard, usually seasoned with fish, meat or vegetables, baked in a mold.

TIMBALE CASE—A small case of fried batter in which creamed mixtures and desserts are served.

TOURTE—A tart; a pie.

TRUFFLES—A species of fungi, similar to mushrooms, growing in clusters some inches below the surface of the ground. Used in seasoning and for a garnish.

TUTTI-FRUTTI—Mixed fruits.

VELOUTÉ—Velvety; smooth.

WINE SEASONS FINE FOOD

WINE seasons fine food and kindles delight in dining adventures. Until we have ample time in which to train our palates, the nice distinctions between the great vintages must remain an occult problem, but our education and our pleasure can be increased immediately by a somewhat cursory survey of the accepted laws for the serving of wine and for its use in cookery.

The fermented juice of grapes is the base of all wines. Except for the so-called fortified wines, there are two main headings for imported and domestics alike—red and white. The white types vary from a pale beige to a deep amber; the red ones show an even greater color variation. The latter should grow slightly light with age. If a red wine does not do so, it has been toned up in its youth. White wines, on the contrary, gain body and grow more golden with the lapse of years.

This passage of time affects wine as it does humans, for wine is a living thing. It becomes sick; it recovers; it is affected by the seasons, by heat and cold; it grows old; it dies—all this even after it has been bottled.

The term "good year" (we quote a chart on the opposite page for important French wines) merely means that the balance of sun and moisture of that particular year was propitious to superlative wine. In general, it is wiser to buy a fair wine of a good year than a famous brand of a poor year.

For daily use, still wines are suggested. If you are serving a single wine, serve a white wine when your main dish is a fish or a light type of meat; to accompany beef, lamb, and the like, a red wine is advised. Claret is the customary red wine for frequent service.

Claret at its best comes from the Bordeaux district of France. In that district the vineyards are large enough to permit the owners to carry out all the processes of growing, pressing, bottling and storing on their own land. Hence their brand names—usually the names of their châteaux—are guarantees of uniform quality. Red Bordeaux are lighter than most other red wines.

White Bordeaux come from the same district and are, generally spe king, sweet wines. Sauternes and Graves are two famed classific tions.

Burgundies come from a very small district extending southward from Dijon for some thirty-five miles. The upper portion produces the great red Burgundies; the southern portion supplies lighter kinds and the great white Burgundies. Bottling at the property is infrequent, for the holdings of a proprietor are small

VINTAGE CHART

YEAR	BORDEAUX RED (CLARET)	BORDEAUX WHITE	BURGUNDY RED AND WHITE	CÔTES DU RHÔNE	RHINE AND MOSELLE	CHAM-PAGNE
1933	Great	Great (c)	Great	Great	Great	(?)
1932	Poor	Poor	Poor	Poor	Fair	Poor
1931	Fair	Good	Poor	Poor	Very good	Fair
1930	Poor	Poor	Fair (c)	Fair	Good	Fair
1929	Great	Great	Great	Great	Great	Very good
1928	Great (a)	Great	Great (a)	Great (a)	Very good	Great
1927	Poor	Good	Poor	Poor	Fair (c)	Poor
1926	Great	Very good	Great (a)	Great (a)	Poor	Great
1925	Fair	Fair	Poor	Fair	Good	Poor
1924	Great	Very good	Good	Good	Poor	Good
1923	Very good	Good	Great	Great (b)	Good	Very good
1922	Fair	Good	Poor	Fair	Poor	Poor
1921	Good	Great	Very good (b)	Good	Greatest	Great
1920	Great	Fair	Fair	Good	Good (c)	Very good
1919	Great	Good	Great	Great	Fair	Very good
1918	Fair	Good	Fair	Fair	Poor	Fair
1917	Good	Very good	Poor	Poor	Good	Great
1916	Very good	Good	Fair	Poor	Poor	Poor
1915	Fair	Fair	Great	Great	Good	Great

Courtesy of Bellows & Co., Inc., Wine Merchants, New York.

(a) For laying down.
(b) For immediate consumption.
(c) With certain exceptions.

and scattered.   As a result Burgundies are commonly sold under the name of a township, and your greatest protection in their purchase is the reputation of the purveyor.

White Burgundies are dry, with one or two exceptions.

The term "dry" denotes a "less sweet" wine.   Rieslings and Chablis, for example, are dryer than Barsac or Sauterne.   However, there is no fixed standard of dryness for all Chablis or all Rieslings.   It is a relative matter that varies not only with the type and brand but with the particular years of growth.   Depend on your wine merchant for detailed advice.

In addition to Bordeaux and Burgundy, Anjou, Alsace, and the Rhone valley produce excellent French wines.   The best German wines are white and should be chilled.   Italian wines are heavier than either French or German, more heady.   Nearly every country in Europe grows grapes and makes wine.   Though France, Germany and Italy are the great wine exporting countries, the others ship their choicest varieties to the rest of the wine drinking world.   Our domestic wines cannot be charted reliably as yet.   We have some very fine vineyards and need only time to ripen our pressings and to establish uniform standards. Young wine is suitable for daily use, but fine wines must be ripened under expert supervision for eight or more years before they attain their full glory.

Fortified wines include sherry, madeira and port.   Brandy has been added to the natural wine.   This increase in alcoholic content prolongs their keeping qualities and permits storage in upright positions.

Champagne needs no introduction.   By complicated processes, the wine is aerated and the corking and recorking is a momentous and difficult technique.

WINE SEQUENCE (or Service Sequence)—Wines reverse the usual order of hospitality.   Your most august wine should be accorded the last place if you are serving more than one kind. The theorists hold that your wine tasting ability is not toned up to a proper appreciation of the unrivaled grandeur of a fine wine at the beginning of a dinner.

Englishmen customarily serve sherry with clear soups but Frenchmen consider that the sherry is too vivid a wine to precede the dry white wine that accompanies the entree or fish.

Never serve a sweet wine before a dry one, nor a rich, fruity Burgundy before a claret.

In serving two wines, select a rather dry white wine to accompany your fish or entree and a red wine for your meat course.

In serving three wines, the following make the best combinations:

A. White, red, Champagne
B. White, red, white
C. White, red, red.

In the case of "B," the second white wine should be sweet. In the case of "C," the greater of the red wines comes second.

Champagne is served with the dessert if several wines are provided.

Liqueurs are served with coffee in the drawing room or in the dining room at the close of dinner. Cognac is the most popular. However, Benedictine, Cointreau, Chartreuse and Crème de Menthe have many devoted admirers. Englishmen often drink port at the close of dinner.

Italians and Frenchmen habitually dilute their ordinary red wine with water for a daily beverage. Never add ice or very icy water to wine, for the sudden chilling ruins its flavor.

THE AMOUNT TO SERVE—Wine is best appreciated when it is drunk in moderation, as a food, as a pleasure and not as a thirst quencher or stimulant. Plan a total allowance of a half bottle to each guest. Thus a table of eight will require two bottles of each of the principal wines or four bottles if you are serving only one variety. However if you are ending dinner with a sweet wine, a Chateau d'Yqem, for example, one bottle should be ample.

Though it is sometimes convenient to serve one large and one half-size bottle, you will notice that the smaller bottles lack some of the fine qualities of the larger ones.

Try to gage the amount required for your dinner with rather nice exactitude, especially in the case of Champagne. Once iced, then warmed and re-iced at a later date, Champagne is nearly ruined, and other wines suffer to a lesser degree.

It may be pertinent to add that the larger the group of guests the more each one tends to consume.

TEMPERATURE—Broadly speaking, all red wines should be served at room temperature and all white wines chilled. The change in temperature from that of the storage space should be accomplished gradually, as sudden chilling or warming harms all wine.

Red wines should never be drunk cold. Fine red Bordeaux and Burgundies have scarcely any bouquet at a temperature that chills the hands. Red Bordeaux, or claret, is best at a temperature of 70°-75° F., approximately room temperature. If you keep your wines in a cool storage place—55° F. is ideal for storing—bring the claret to the dining room several hours before service time so that it may warm gradually. Never insert the bottle in hot water or put it near heat to hasten this process. Red Burgundy may be served slightly cooler than the other red wines. It loses its numbness speedily after it is poured into the glasses and by holding the bowl of the glass in the palm of the hand, to warm it further, the guest savors its expanding bouquet before tasting it.

Beaujolais, Arbois, Chinon and a few other red wines, with much bouquet and little body, are best drunk cool; they are exceptions to the general rule.

White wines should be drunk cool or chilled. The sweeter the wine, the longer it takes to chill it. Dry white wines cool quickly and a dry champagne quickest of all. On the other hand, a sweet sauterne takes a couple of hours in a mechanical refrigerator to reach its ideal temperature of 40° F. A half hour to an hour is ample refrigeration storage to cool white Burgundies, Rhone wines and the like.

All sweet white wines, all sparkling wines and some dry wines should be thoroughly chilled. They should approximate 40° F. This chilling is best accomplished by the use of an ice bucket, at least when the wine reaches the table. The first cooling may be done by laying the bottles, horizontally, of course, in the mechanical refrigerator. But wines, once iced, lose their grandeur if slightly warmed, and if they are allowed to stand outside a casing of ice for even ten minutes, the result may be disastrous. You can hasten even icing by turning your bottle in the ice bucket, which should be deep enough so that the entire bottle, except the very top, may be surrounded by ice.

Beer should be kept in a cool place so that it may be made icy cold quickly when needed. However, it should not be stored permanently in the refrigerator.

UNCORKING AND DECANTING—Careful uncorking is important. One least bit of cork dropped into the bottle will ruin great wines and can be detected in every case by the discerning palate.

A lever type corkscrew is ideal; its edges should be rounded so that it will not cut the cork. Insert it evenly, straight and to the full depth of the cork. Then withdraw it very slowly so that your wine will remain still. This prevents the mixing of any sediment in the bottom of the bottle with the clear liquid.

Note the condition of the cork. It should be long, moist and tightly inserted in the bottle. Short corks are an indication of slip-shod bottling, and dry corks, of poor after care (probably the bottle has been stored in an upright position). If the cork smells acid, the wine itself is turned and no longer in good drinking condition.

In recorking, it is usually advisable to cut off a little from the upper part of the cork (this obviates any taste of sealing materials) and insert this top end in your bottle. The moist end expands rapidly on exposure to air and can seldom be reinserted.

Decanting is the gentle transfer of wine from its bottle to a decanter. No two experts agree as to the advisability of doing this. However, there is no gainsaying the fact that old red wine with considerable sediment must be poured from the bottle by a very expert hand, or be decanted to prevent any sediment from reaching the wine glass. The simplest methods of decanting are to pour the wine slowly into a glass decanter and stop as soon as any sediment appears, or to pour the wine through a funnel topped with a thin layer of absorbent, not medicated, cotton. Decanting should be done just before the meal is served.

Fine white wines are seldom decanted. However, both white and red wines of the ordinary day-by-day sorts are often served from a handsome glass decanter. This fashion originated in Europe because wines of this grade are often bought in bulk. A decanter of white wine and another of red are frequently placed on the dinner table. It is a great convenience to own several sizes. Ordinary red wines will keep for a considerable period if the decanters are airtight. As you drink your wine, change it to a smaller decanter; the ideal is to have the wine and the stopper of the decanter meet each other. Liqueurs with high alcoholic content keep in partially filled decanters or bottles.

Sherry, Madeira, Port and Claret are served from the bottle or from a decanter with equal correctness.

CARE OF WINE—Wine should be kept at an even temperature and in a dark, dry place with some ventilation but no drafts. A closet equipped with metal bins is the best solution in city apartments. A cellar is, of course, ideal. Storing vegetables or other foods in such a cellar is unwise for they impart a disagreeable odor to wines even though they are bottled.

Fortified wines and brandy may stand upright. Keep all your other unopened wines in a horizontal position when stored. Upright bottles of natural wines spoil in a few days, because of the shrinkage of the corks. Do not disturb your wines by unnecessary movement, for if there are any dregs or sediment movement tends to cloud the entire bottle.

The ideal temperature for storing wines is about 55° F. Even temperature is important, for sudden changes ruin fine wines.

GLASSES—Sets of glassware make so charming a table decoration that most women will find it convenient to buy water goblets, glasses for red wines, and small ones for white wines and sherry in a single pattern. Champagne glasses should match the other glasses, for those who plan that luxury. Liqueur and cocktail glasses may differ, for they seldom appear at the same time as the other glassware. So select gay bits of contrast for these special services.

In choosing wine glasses, buy rather large ones and fill them partially; one-half to three-quarters is suggested. Since color is one of the great fascinations of fine wine, connoisseurs approve clear crystal glassware with sparse decoration. A ball or tulip shaped bowl atop a long stem conserves the aroma and permits swirling. By holding the stem between the thumb and forefinger, the guest may move his glass so that the wine picks up a slight motion and licks the sides of the glass. This swirling exhibits the fine texture of your wine and gathers its bouquet so that, when the glass is lifted to the mouth, the nose also gains full pleasure from the rich, fruity aroma. Dry wine spreads like water, and sweet wine hangs and makes runnels. A Bordeaux that does this is called "a fat one."

The glory of Champagne, its sparkling quality, is best conserved by serving it in a glass with a fluted top on a hollow stem. The effervescence has a longer road to travel before it is dissipated in the atmosphere.

A set of tall glasses suitable for beer, ale, juleps and lemonade may match your water goblets or differ in pattern. Steins for beer are preferred by some hosts.

WINE IN COOKERY—Wine is friendly to many foods but is equally antagonistic to other favorites. Egg is the outstanding example of the latter and cheese of the former. White and shell fish, poultry, game and meat, except pork, take on added luster by the addition of a small quantity of wine. Mushrooms, truffles and sweet potatoes complement wine flavors. Beware, beware, the combining of wine with acids in the form of gherkins, vinegar and similar condiments.

For fish or meat sauces, dry wines are the dicta of most experts. Riesling and Chablis are typical dry white wines, and claret is a typical dry red one. In the case of fish, the wine must be white, always, for red wine and fish do not mix. Meats may be cooked with either red or white wine. Occasionally a dash of a sweet cordial added at the last moment improves a meat. For instance, a tablespoon of Benedictine works magic in a pot roast.

Desserts and fruits combine to best advantage with sweet white wines, fortified wines, sweet liqueurs or a little brandy.

The amount of wine used in cookery is surprisingly small. To benefit by this trifling quantity, the flavor must permeate each morsel of food. Several methods aid the cook to this end. "To marinate" the food in the wine, for an hour or so, is suitable to some recipes. "To burn" is the easy means to benefit from a small amount of brandy; simply pour the brandy over the food, touch it with a lighted match and shake the food until the flame dies out. To cook the food with wine for a considerable period of time is the third and usual method.

Remember, however, that wine should never cook at a high temperature. A dozen bubbles spell disaster. This is especially true in the case of dishes that combine cream and wine. They should be cooked over hot water to prevent curdling. Another trick is to heat the fish or meat with the wine and add the cream or cream-egg mixture just before serving. If the amount of cream is large, heat it separately so that it will not chill the hot mixture. Do not heat eggs for sauces; merely add after the sauce is removed from the fire, for the heat of the cooked food will coagulate the egg.

When browning the top of a platter filled with a wine sauce and fish combination—sole or lobster, for example—place it as close to the flame as possible and leave only a second or two.

Never keep it in the broiler long enough to raise the temperature of the entire sauce. In olden days, a red hot poker seared the top—a nearly perfect method.

Never allow the aroma of your wine to escape and be squandered on the air. This bouquet should be part of the food. So cover your cooking utensils closely; cooking parchments may be used. Likewise, desserts should be closely covered while they chill in the refrigerator.

Taste your foods as you assemble and cook them. The requisite amount of salt and of wine will vary because of the differences in the wines themselves. Some sorts—sherry is one—run the gamut from quite sweet to very dry and from a rich, heavy, tawny quality to a light, flavorsome one.

Remember in your tasting adventures that, in the finest cooking, the wine flavor does not dominate; it merely accents and adds subtlety to the basic food flavor.

Remember, too, that all punches, with or without wine, should stand for thirty minutes or more after they are mixed. This is called the ripening process. Ice is added at the time of service.

COURT BOUILLON

1½ cups boiling water
½ cup white wine (dry)
¼ teaspoon salt
2 slices garlic
2 small onions

1 bay leaf
6 peppercorns
⅛ teaspoon thyme
6 slices carrot
3 sprigs parsley

Cook together for 30 minutes at simmering temperature. Strain and use as a substitute for water in poaching fish. If the recipe calls for a sauce, use this bouillon for its base. Any fish is improved by the added flavor-giving qualities of a court bouillon. Be sure to poach, not boil, your fish.

CHILLED TROUT

Try poaching brook trout in two tablespoons of butter and a half cup of court bouillon or of white wine. Turn once and cook a very short time. Lift out, chill and serve with tartar sauce. It may be covered with an aspic gelatin and garnished with shrimps and bits of truffle.

JELLIED CONSOMMÉ WITH SHERRY

3 cups seasoned consommé
2 tablespoons gelatin
½ teaspoon lemon juice

4 tablespoons sherry wine
½ cup cold water
Minced parsley

Soften the gelatin in the cold water. Dissolve in the hot consommé. Add the lemon juice and wine, and salt if required. Chill in the refrigerator. Chop lightly before putting in service cups. Top with minced parsley, a lemon crescent or a bit of tomato fringed with minced green pepper.

HALIBUT À LA NEWBURG

1 lb. halibut
1 tablespoon brandy
¼ cup sherry wine
2 tablespoons butter

1 cup evaporated milk (undiluted)
1 teaspoon lemon juice
3 egg yolks
Dash cayenne—salt to taste

Cut the halibut in small cubes. Steam over hot water or poach in court bouillon for five minutes. Beware of long or swift cooking as the halibut easily loses its shape. When poached, put the fish, butter, wine, brandy, salt and cayenne in a double boiler and heat smoking hot. Beat the yolks and combine with the evaporated milk (sour cream may be substituted for the milk and lemon juice) and cook with the hot fish for one minute. Remove from the fire and add the lemon juice. Serve on very hot plates. An excellent chafing dish innovation.

LOBSTER CURRY APPETIZER

½ cup fresh or canned lobster meat
2 tablespoons butter

¼ teaspoon curry powder
1 teaspoon sherry wine
⅛ teaspoon dry mustard

Sauté the lobster in the melted fat. Add the seasonings and the wine. When very hot serve on small bread croustades or packaged appetizer shells.

LOBSTER À LA NEWBURG

3 cups cooked lobster
3 tablespoons butter
1½ cups Madeira wine or
   sherry

1½ cups cream
3 egg yolks, beaten
¼ teaspoon salt
Dash cayenne

Cut lobster meat into large pieces and heat slowly in butter about 5 minutes. Add wine and simmer until wine is almost all reduced. Beat cream into egg yolks, add to lobster and season. Cook, stirring constantly until thickened. Do not boil. Serve at once. Serves 8.

SOLE THERMIDOR

1 lb. sole or fillet of flounder
2 cups court bouillon
1 tablespoon flour
3 tablespoons butter
1 teaspoon dry mustard

Salt and cayenne
½ cup sour cream
¼ cup brandy
4 tablespoons grated Swiss
   or Parmesan cheese

Neatly trim the fish fillets and poach in court bouillon. (See page 745.) Lift onto a hot baking platter. Combine the flour and melted butter and add the court bouillon in which the fish was poached. Add the seasonings, the cream, the brandy and 2 tablespoons of the cheese. Do not cook. Pour over the fish, sprinkle with the remaining cheese and put close under the flame to brown instantly. Serve as an entrée. Serves 3.

HAM PORTE MAILLOT

½ cup carrots
¼ cup onion
½ clove garlic
¼ cup celery
½ cup cauliflower

2 leaves lettuce
¼ cup fat
½ cup cooked Lima beans
½ to ¾ cup dry white wine
Baked ham

Originated by a restaurant just outside the Porte Maillot, one of the gates of Paris, this dish brings a new flavor to a baked ham. We have substituted dried Lima beans for the French white bean that is infrequently used in America. Cut the carrots, onion, garlic, celery, cauliflower and lettuce in long narrow shreds. Simmer them on the cooking fat but do not brown.

When cooked add the previously cooked Lima beans and the white wine. Cook together one minute and serve around a hot baked ham or as a sauce for left-over ham that has been re-heated over steam.

VEAL WITH OLIVES

1½ lbs. veal cutlets
⅓ cup Marsala wine
Salt and pepper to taste

¼ cup butter or cooking fat
10 green olives

The secret of the success of this delicious Italian meat is to have the veal pounded paper thin. Ask for veal scaloppini at markets in the East. Otherwise ask for veal cutlets and ask the butcher to pound the meat paper thin after cutting it ¼ inch thick. Wipe the veal, sprinkle with salt and pepper. Simmer very quickly in the melted butter, browning lightly on both sides, add the wine and the olives cut in narrow strips. Heat one minute and serve. The veal should cook in five minutes.

BURGUNDIAN BEEF

3 lbs. beef, rump or round
¼ lb. salt pork
3 cups minced onion
2 small shallots, minced
6 peppercorns
2 bay leaves
1 tablespoon tarragon vinegar
    or fresh minced tarragon
⅛ teaspoon thyme

2 tablespoons butter
3 tablespoons flour
½ carrot, in circles
1 clove garlic
2 tablespoons minced parsley
2 tablespoons minced chervil
1½ to 2 cups red wine
Salt to taste

Dice the salt pork and sauté in the butter. Cut the beef in two-inch cubes or leave in one piece as preferred. Sear thoroughly in the hot fat. Lift out. Add the onion, garlic, shallots and carrot. Simmer them in the fat till light yellow. Add all the other ingredients and the beef. Cook on a very slow fire three hours. Remove excess fat and serve. It may be re-heated with advantage.

LAMB CHOPS WITH MADEIRA

6 lamb chops
3 onions
2 tablespoons butter
1 teaspoon tomato paste
½ clove garlic

2 carrots
4 mushrooms
2 tablespoons Madeira
⅛ teaspoon pepper
½ teaspoon salt

Cut the vegetables in fine inch-length strips. Simmer them in the butter till tender. Cover during this cooking so that the zest will be preserved. Season. Add the tomato paste and Madeira. Serve on top of broiled lamb chops. Thick lamb chops boned and circled with bacon add elegance to this Madeira flavored dish.

CHICKEN BRAISED WITH WINE
(Coq au Vin)

1 frying chicken
8 small white onions
4 small shallots
1 tablespoon minced parsley
1 tablespoon minced chervil
2 tablespoons flour
1 tablespoon brandy
Salt and pepper to taste

3 tablespoons butter
¼ lb. salt pork diced
¼ lb. mushrooms
1 bay leaf
1 carrot
Pinch thyme
1 cup red or white wine
1 clove garlic

Lightly brown the salt pork in the melted butter, add the shallot, onions, garlic and the carrot cut in circles. Simmer till golden, but not browned. Lift out and brown the chicken. Sprinkle with the flour, seasoning and herbs. Return the sautéed vegetables and add the wine. Cook fifteen to twenty minutes on a rather hot fire. During the last five minutes add the mushrooms. Skim off excess fat and serve.

Red wine is usual in making this dish, but the white one gives a more delicate flavor.

Make your dinner perfect by serving with this chicken a salad of mixed greens with a simple French dressing made with lemon juice. The acid of vinegar devitalizes the subtle details in flavor of the wine-cooked chicken.

EGGS WITH SHERRY AND ORANGE

(Oeufs au Xérès et à l'Orange)

6 eggs
1 tablespoon sherry
3 tablespoons tomato sauce
Grated orange rind
½ teaspoon salt
Cayenne
Butter

Beat eggs until no longer stringy. Blend in sherry and tomato sauce. Add seasonings. Melt butter in a frying pan and pour in the mixture. Cook slowly, stirring until it begins to set. Then sprinkle with the grated orange rind and serve immediately.

PLANTATION SWEET POTATOES

6 sweet potatoes
¾ cup butter or other fat
Paprika
6 tablespoons sherry wine
1½ teaspoons salt
¼ teaspoon pepper

Bake washed sweet potatoes at 450° F. for 40 minutes. Cut off a slice from the top of each and hollow out. Mash the potato. Whip with the melted butter or other fat, the seasoning and the sherry. Re-stuff in the potato shells and sprinkle with paprika. Brown in the oven.

MUSHROOMS WITH MADEIRA

½ lb. mushrooms
3 tablespoons bouillon
¼ cup butter
2 tablespoons Madeira
Salt, cayenne
8 small white onions
3 teaspoons flour
1 tablespoon minced parsley
1 tablespoon minced chervil
½ bay leaf

Melt the butter and cook onions in it for five minutes. Do not brown. Add the mushrooms that have been washed but not peeled. Whole mushrooms make the most attractive service, so slice only the stems. When well coated with butter, add the minced herbs, the flour, the bouillon and the seasoning. Cook until the onions are tender—slowly of course. Add the Madeira and cook one minute. Serve garnished with croutons and minced herbs.

A delicious entrée or specialty for chafing dish parties.

WELSH RAREBIT

1 lb. grated American cheese	1 teaspoon butter
1 teaspoon paprika	½ pint ale or beer
Salt and prepared mustard to taste	

Melt the butter and stir so that it oils the bottom of your pan. (A chafing dish over hot water is ideal.) Add the cheese and gently stir into it one tablespoon of beer or ale. The cheese will at once thicken and another tablespoon of beer or ale should be added. Stir continuously. Add more liquid until the mixture is smooth and velvety. The exact amount of ale varies with different cheeses. Season to taste and serve on toast. Hot plates are essential. This will serve six single portions.

HOT WINE SAUCE FOR VENISON, GAME OR TONGUE

1 tablespoon butter	½ cup water
½ glass currant jelly	½ cup port wine
Juice of ½ lemon	3 cloves
Pinch cayenne	1 teaspoon salt

Simmer together for five minutes all ingredients except the wine. Strain and add the port wine. Add also a little of the meat gravy. Serve hot.

BRANDIED APPLE FRITTERS

4 medium apples	4 tablespoons brandy
1 egg	½ cup milk
1 tablespoon sugar	1 cup flour
1½ teaspoons baking powder	¼ teaspoon salt

Pare the apples, core and slice in circles or cut in segments. Pour over them the brandy, cover tightly with cooking parchment. Combine the well beaten egg yolk with the sugar and milk. Add the flour that has been sifted with the salt and baking powder. Fold in the egg white beaten stiff. Dip the brandied apples in this batter and fry in deep fat (360-370° F.) two to four minutes. Serve with sauce superb or powdered sugar.

SAUCE SUPERB

2 eggs	1 cup powdered sugar
1 cup whipping cream	4 teaspoons rum

Beat the eggs till thick and lemon colored. Add the sugar gradually and continue beating. Whip the cream very stiff, add the rum and combine the two mixtures. The secret of success in making this sauce is to beat it thoroughly. It will keep for hours in the refrigerator.

APRICOT RUM WHIP

1 #2½ can apricots	1 tablespoon rum
¾ cup whipping cream	3 egg whites

Drain the apricots and reserve the juice for beverages. Mash the fruit through a sieve and combine with the whipped egg whites and the whipped cream. Fold in the rum and serve cold.

BRANDIED CARAMEL BANANAS

6 bananas	3 tablespoons butter
1 tablespoon brandy	3 tablespoons brown sugar

Peel the bananas, divide in halves lengthwise. Melt the butter and sauté the bananas. Turn when brown on one side. Add the sugar and, when browned on the other side, add the brandy. Serve on very hot plates with the brandied sugar atop the bananas.

CRÊPES SUZETTE

¾ cup flour	6 lumps loaf sugar
2 teaspoons sugar	1 orange
1 teaspoon salt	6 tablespoons brandy
¾ cup milk	¼ cup Grand Marnier Liqueur
3 eggs	⅛ lb. sweet butter

This very famous but really very simple dessert is not difficult. A more awe-inspiring recipe for the crêpes is common at many great Parisian restaurants, but this is excellent and simple. The successful making of crêpes depends on the thinness of the batter.

Add sugar and salt to the eggs, beaten slightly, then alternately the flour and the milk and then beat thoroughly with a rotary beater. Lightly grease a small frying pan (7 inches) and pour in about two tablespoons of batter. Move the pan so that the batter spreads to the outer edge of the pan. Brown on both sides and roll. Keep in a warm place until ready to serve.

The Suzette sauce is made by rubbing the lump sugar with the white part of the orange peel, adding one teaspoon of very finely minced outer peel and dissolving the sugar in one tablespoon brandy. Combine with one-eighth of a pound of sweet butter. At service time, in the chafing dish, or Suzette pan preferably, melt prepared butter, add the cooked crêpes and turn. Then add the remaining brandy and the liqueur. Light with a match and when the flame goes out serve your crêpes.

BRANDIED APRICOT OMELET

Make a puffy omelet in the usual manner. Before folding it spread with apricot jam to which you have added a tablespoon of brandy. Around the omelet serve a foamy brandy sauce or a sauce superb.

GEORGIA CHRISTMAS PUDDING

½ cup chopped walnuts or pecans
½ cup sugar
6 egg whites
½ cup chopped raisins
½ cup sherry wine
¼ cup rum
1 teaspoon lemon juice

Soak the nuts and raisins in the wines and lemon juice for at least six hours—overnight if possible. Beat the egg whites stiff, add the sugar and beat till ropy. Fold in the wine-soaked fruits and nuts. Pour into a buttered baking dish. Set in a pan of hot water. Bake at 350° F. for one hour. Serve with the following sauce.

Make a custard of 6 egg yolks, ¼ cup sugar and 1½ cups of scalded milk. When smoothly thickened, flavor with sherry and serve on the Christmas Pudding. This is a famous old Georgia recipe.

FROZEN PUDDING WITH RUM

2 eggs
1 cup sugar
½ to ¾ cup rum
Pinch salt

1 cup assorted candied fruit
2½ cups milk
1 cup whipping cream

Cover the chopped candied fruits with rum and cover tightly. Stand two or three hours. Make a custard of the eggs, sugar, salt and hot milk. Cool. Fold in the whipping cream, beaten stiff, and the candied fruits. Pour into a tray of the mechanical refrigerator and freeze. Beat at the end of an hour and once or twice afterward to assure even textured cream. At the last beating, the cream may be placed in small molds or in little individual paper containers.

PINEAPPLE WITH KIRSCH

Cut a ripe pineapple in slices. Remove the rind and the eyes. Restack the slices in their original shape. Pass with the pineapple a bowl of powdered sugar and a bottle of kirsch.

Canned pineapple is also excellent with kirsch but, when using it, you gain in flavor by pouring the kirsch over the fruit and chilling in the refrigerator for an hour or more. Be sure to cover closely so that all the zest will be part of the fruit. Allow one tablespoon of kirsch to two slices of canned pineapple.

Many other fruits are delicious accompanied by this mild liqueur, strawberries, for example.

SYLLABUB

2 cups whipping cream
1 tablespoon rum

½ cup powdered sugar

A famous English recipe. Whip the cream stiff, fold in the sugar and rum. Ripen in the refrigerator for half an hour, covered, of course. Serve in sherbet glasses.

STRAWBERRIES CHANTILLY

Wash, stem and cut in half 1 quart ripe strawberries. Cover with powdered sugar and 2 tablespoons rum. Chill 30 minutes.

Whisk two egg whites stiff, beat in gradually 4 tablespoons powdered sugar. Fold in the chilled berries. Serve in sherbet glasses and top with sweetened whipped cream.

TIPSY PUDDING

One of the choice recipes of our Grandmother's era. It appeared in the place of honor on New Year's Day. The secret for a successful outcome is to use a very stale, very porous cake. A broken, not cut, sunshine cake at least four days old, should be soaked in sherry. Allow about one cup sherry to a quarter of a good sized cake. An hour later cover the cake with a soft custard flavored with rum. Serve very cold.

OLD FASHIONED WINE JELLY

2 tablespoons granulated gelatin	½ cup cold water
1 cup sherry or Madeira wine	1 cup boiling water
1 cup sugar	Grated rind 1 orange
⅔ cup orange juice	⅓ cup lemon juice

Soak the gelatin in the cold water until soft. Dissolve in the boiling water, add the sugar and other ingredients. Pour into molds that have been rinsed in cold water. Serve with whipped cream.

BRANDIED PEACHES

4 lbs. fruit	4 lbs. sugar
1 pint best white brandy	1 egg white
Cloves	3½ cups water

Pare the peaches with a silver knife. Insert 2 cloves in each whole peach. Make a syrup of the sugar and water. Add the egg white beaten to a froth. Skim. Put in fruit, one layer at a time, and boil five minutes or until it may be pierced with a straw. Remove the fruit to a platter to partially cool. Then pack in glass jars. Return any excess juice to the syrup and boil about ten minutes more, or till well thickened. Remove from the fire, add the brandy and pour over the fruit. Seal at once. White cling stone peaches are particularly good. Six pounds of fruit will yield about seven pint jars. Improves with age.

HASTY WINE GELATIN

2 packages lemon-flavored
gelatin
3½ cups hot water

½ cup Madeira wine or
¼ cup sherry wine

Dissolve the gelatin in the hot water. When perfectly clear add the wine. Pour in molds that have been rinsed in cold water. Serve with whipped cream. Garnish with grated orange peel on top the whipped cream. Orange flavored gelatin combines well with Madeira.

CLARET LEMONADE

12 cubes ice
1 bottle claret
Juice 3 lemons

Sugar syrup to taste
Orange slices

Half fill a glass pitcher with ice cubes or cracked ice. Add the lemon juice and a few slices of orange. Fill the pitcher nearly full with claret and add sugar syrup to taste. Stand twenty to thirty minutes to blend and ripen.

MULLED CLARET

1 qt. hot claret
1 piece stick cinnamon
Juice 1 lemon

½ cup sugar
8 cloves
½ lemon sliced

Heat the claret and add the other ingredients. Stir till dissolved and serve hot. Doughnuts were served with it in the nineties.

TUTTI FRUTTI

Into a stone jar put one cup of brandy, the best you own, one cup sugar and one cup ripe strawberries. Stir thoroughly. As each fruit comes to the height of its perfection, add it, with a cup of sugar for each cup of fruit. No more brandy is indicated. Be sure to stir at each addition. Large fruits like peaches should be cut in small pieces. Cherries and plums should be stoned. Atop vanilla ice cream this is an epicurean delight. Perhaps you will make enough to use it for preserves.

CHAMPAGNE CUP

½ cup Maraschino
½ cup Vermuth
½ cup Santa Cruz rum
Sugar to taste

2 qts. Champagne
Cucumber rind
Juice 4 oranges
Juice 3 lemons

Sweeten the fruit juices slightly. Combine all the ingredients. Let stand ten minutes after mixing with a large piece of ice in a punch bowl. It's well to use as large a piece of ice as possible, for it melts more slowly and adds less water to the punch.

EGGNOG, SOUTHERN

4 eggs
½ cup whipping cream
3 tablespoons powdered sugar

4 tablespoons brandy or whisky

Beat the yolks till thick and lemon colored. Slowly beat in the brandy and sugar. Fold in the stiffly beaten whites and the whipped cream. This must be eaten with a spoon. Excellent.

EGGNOG—OTHER TYPE

4 eggs
4 tablespoons powdered sugar

4 tablespoons brandy or rum
3 cups milk

Grating of nutmeg

Beat the egg white to a dry froth. Beat into the egg white the sugar and then the yolks of the eggs combined with the brandy. Add the milk and a slight grating of nutmeg. Serve at once. Famous at New Year's and Christmas.

ZABAGLIONE—

4 egg yolks
3 tablespoons honey

Cinnamon
2 tablespoons Marsala wine

Beat egg yolks with honey until thick and lemon colored in the top of a double boiler. Add wine gradually. While it heats continue to use rotary beater. Serve as drink or dessert sauce with dash of cinnamon.

CRACKERS 'N CHEESE
AND CHERRY PRESERVES
FOR WIT AND WISDOM
AFTER DINNER

Index

HOW TO FEED A FAMILY OF FIVE ON $20.00 PER WEEK

THE vital necessity for buying and preparing food with the highest possible nutritive value is imperative when the food budget is limited and there is no money to waste. This will be no new experience to the homemaker who has been feeding a family of two adults and three children on $20.00 per week. But for those who must learn to carry on when that figure is new to them, the following pages will help meet the challenge.

Whims and fancies break down well-laid plans for good nutrition. Everybody must eat all food prepared if there is to be a minimum of waste. This puts upon the homemaker the responsibility for careful selection and good cooking. The test of a good cook is the clean plate. And good cooking means conserving all the food values . . . minerals and vitamins.

Buy Carefully

Buy staples in quantities when permitted. Meats, fruits and vegetables need to be inspected carefully and bought in accordance with the market and the season. The woman who does her own marketing will have all the advantage over the woman who telephones or sends a child. Discriminating judgment at market is what saves money every day. Make a check list in your kitchen and then stick to it. Stay within your food budget every week. A dangerous pitfall is that of overbuying one week in the hope of making it up the next. If there is a little cash left, buy eggs or fruit. Raise a garden and poultry if you can. It will take pressure off the budget.

Buy Vitamins as a Bonus

Bake your own bread, cakes and cookies and be sure to buy enriched flour, thereby getting added B vitamins, thiamin and niacin, together with iron. When buying evaporated milk be sure it is irradiated, which adds vitamin D. Margarine when it is fortified adds vitamin A. Recipes for the menus are in the preceding or following pages.

BREAKFAST

Tomato Juice [1]
Waffles
Butterscotch Sauce [2]
Milk, Coffee

•

DINNER

Pork Shoulder Roast [3]
Sweetpotatoes [4]
Spinach [5]
Whole-wheat Rolls
California Slaw [6]
Cottage Pudding
Milk, Coffee

•

SUPPER

Oyster Stew [7]
Parsley Toast Triangles
Apple Betty [8]
Milk, Tea

•

Alternative Dishes

1—Or cantaloupe in season.
2—Or corn sirup flavored with orange.
3—Buy six-pound roast for economy and leftovers.
4—Or oven-browned potatoes.
5—Green beans, collards, mustard greens, kale, beet tops may be substituted.
6—Or cucumber salad. Same salad tomorrow night.
7—Or clam chowder, corn chowder, or soup made from scraps of vegetables may be used here.
8—Or blackberries, other fresh berries in season, or canned fruit.

BREAKFAST

Stewed Apricots [1]
Oatmeal [2]
Toast
Milk, Coffee

•

LUNCH

Scalloped Canned or
Fresh Mixed Vegetables
and Hard-cooked Eggs
Lettuce Salad
Muffins
Fruit Gelatin Mold
Milk, Tea

•

DINNER

Leftover Pork Slices in
Barbecue Sauce
Steamed Rice [3]
Buttered Carrots [4]
Celery Cabbage Salad
Enriched Bread
Steamed Molasses
Pudding [5]
Milk, Coffee

•

Alternative Dishes

1—If dried fruit is not available use sliced oranges, fresh peaches or berries in season.
2—Corn flakes, or other prepared cereal in warm weather.
3—Or potato chips. [Cook enough rice for tomorrow.]
4—Green vegetables would be a good choice.
5—Or use fresh cherry pie or pudding, or melon in season.

BREAKFAST

Applesauce [1]
Griddlecakes and
  Corn Sirup [2]
Slab Bacon
Milk, Coffee

•

LUNCH

Spanish Rice
Head Lettuce Salad
Whole-wheat Bread
Sliced Oranges,
Grapefruit with Honey [3]
Milk

•

DINNER

Broiled Lamb Patties
Parsley Buttered Potatoes
Canned Green Beans [4]
Pear and Grape Salad
Corn Sticks
Apricot Bavarian Cream [5]
Milk, Tea, or Coffee

•

Alternative Dishes

1—Or apple juice.

2—Or poached eggs on toast.

3—Fresh berries, peaches or pineapple
in season would be good here.

4—Fresh green beans, Lima beans,
peas, steamed summer squash are
other choices.

5—Use evaporated milk for whipping.

BREAKFAST

Grapefruit Juice
Omelet [1]
Toast, Dried Fruit Jam
Milk, Coffee

•

LUNCH

Boston Baked Beans
Carrot Sticks
Brown Bread
Canned Plums [2]
Milk

•

DINNER

Beef Chuck Roast [3]
Whipped Potatoes [4]
Gravy
Whole-wheat Bread
Buttered Beets [5]
Tossed Greens Salad
Chocolate Pudding
Milk, Tea, or Coffee

•

Alternative Dishes

1—Or soft-cooked eggs.

2—Or fresh ones.

3—Buy enough for Thursday. Boneless neck pot roast, or brisket may
be better buys.

4—Or brown potatoes with the pot
roast.

5—Alternate choices: celeriac, salsify,
parsnips, Brussels sprouts, cauliflower.

BREAKFAST
Stewed Prunes [1]
Corn-meal Mush
flavored with bits of
Cooked Bacon [2]
Toasted Buns
Milk, Coffee

•

LUNCH
Toasted Peanut-butter
or Cheese Sandwiches
Coleslaw
Sliced Bananas
Cocoa [3]

•

DINNER
English Meat Pie
(leftover beef) with
Carrots, Potatoes, Peas,
Potato Crust
Chicory and Lettuce
Salad [4]
Bread Pudding [5]
Lemon Sauce [6]
Milk, Tea, or Coffee

•

Alternative Dishes
1—Save juice for Saturday.
2—Make enough for tomorrow's lunch. Crisp rice cereal or other prepared breakfast food in warm weather.
3—Chocolate milk or milk shakes may be served.
4—Cucumber, lettuce salad, tomato salad, grapefruit salad are good choices.
5—Melon in season would be a good dessert.
6—Use another sauce if you serve tomato or grapefruit salad.

BREAKFAST
Orange Halves [1]
Scrambled Eggs
Toast
Milk, Coffee

•

LUNCH
Sautéed Corn-meal Mush
with Cheese Sauce [2]
Buttered Spinach [3]
Enriched Bread
Baked Apples [4]
Milk

•

DINNER
Baked Fresh Fish [5]
French Fried Potatoes [6]
Whole-kernel Corn [7]
Chicory Salad, [8]
Chili Dressing
Banana Ice Cream
Molasses Cookies [9]
Milk, Tea, or Coffee

•

Alternative Dishes
1—Or orange or grapefruit juice, fresh or canned.
2—Or cheese rarebit.
3—Or head lettuce salad.
4—Use fresh apples in season, or green applesauce.
5—Or make a fish casserole.
6—Or baked or mashed potatoes. Fish may be served creamed over baked potatoes.
7—Or corn on the cob, or beets.
8—Or tossed greens with tomato.
9—Make enough for several later meals.

BREAKFAST
Prune Juice (from
Thursday) with Lemon
Cooked Wheat Cereal
Toast, Jelly
Milk, Coffee

•

LUNCH
Baked Noodles with
Mushroom Sauce [1]
Buttered Peas
Carrot Sticks
Whole-wheat Muffins
Fresh or Canned Berries [2]
with Molasses Cookies
Milk

•

DINNER
Liver Loaf [3]
Boiled Cabbage [4]
Tomato Jelly Salad [5]
Enriched Bread
Mocha
Refrigerator Cake [6]
Milk, Tea, or Coffee

•

Alternative Dishes
1—Or scalloped potatoes.
2—Or fresh pineapple, peaches, pears,
applesauce in season.
3—Or braised pork or beef liver with
bacon. Add mashed potatoes to
menu.
4—Or cauliflower, broccoli, Brussels
sprouts, kohlrabi, leeks, artichokes.
5—Or fresh tomato salad.
6—Or brownies à la mode, or fruit
shortcake. Use remaining cake for
Sunday night supper.

BREAKFAST
Chilled Orange Juice [1]
French Toast
Maple-flavored Sirup
Crisp Bacon Strips
(Slab Bacon)
Milk, Coffee

•

DINNER
Fricassee of Chicken [2]
Mashed Potatoes [3]
and Gravy
Buttered Beets
Whole-wheat Rolls [4]
Head Lettuce Salad,
Thousand Island Dressing [5]
Raisin Pie [6]
Milk, Tea, or Coffee

•

SUPPER
Melba Toast or Thin Rye
Bread Sandwiches
Kidney Bean Salad [7]
Mocha Refrigerator Cake
Milk

•

Alternative Dishes
1—Or canned tomato or grapefruit
juice.
2—Or Swiss steak, braised beef, arm
pot roast, brisket or heel of round.
3—Mashed potatoes on the half shell
or Duchess potatoes.
4—Make enough for tomorrow.
5—Shredded leaf lettuce salad with
vinaigrette dressing, or salad of
mixed greens.
6—Fresh blueberry, peach, or strawberry pie. In warm weather a
jellied fruit pudding or whip.
7—Salad of whole tomatoes stuffed
with cottage cheese, or sliced tomato, cucumber and green pepper
ring salad with French dressing.

BREAKFAST

Grapefruit Halves [1]
Corn-meal Mush, Top Milk [2]
Cinnamon Toast
Milk, Coffee

•

LUNCH

Cream of Onion and Potato Soup
(Evaporated Milk)
Crackers
Pear Salad [3]
Milk, Tea

•

DINNER

Stuffed Cabbage Leaves [4]
Tomato Sauce
Buttered Peas
Carrot Sticks [5]
Whole-wheat Rolls
Baked Caramel Custards
Milk, Coffee

•

Alternative Dishes

1—Canned grapefruit juice, tomato
juice, pineapple or apricot juice.
2—Or cornflakes or other prepared
cereal with fresh strawberries or
raspberries in warm weather. Omit
grapefruit.
3—Salad of sliced peaches, bananas
and halved grapes, or jellied fruit
also good.
4—Ground beef patties or baked green
peppers stuffed with ground left-
over meat.
5—Cabbage and carrot salad with sour
cream or boiled dressing.

BREAKFAST

Stewed Prunes
Oatmeal with Top Milk
Toasted Whole-wheat
Rolls
Grape Jelly [1]
Milk, Coffee

•

LUNCH

Eggs Florentine [2]
Baking Powder Biscuits [3]
Honey Cookies [4]
Milk

•

DINNER

Baked Stuffed Spareribs [5]
Browned Potatoes [6]
Asparagus Salad
Enriched Bread
Fresh Fruit Cup, Three [7]
Milk, Coffee

•

Alternative Dishes

1—May be omitted, or another spread
may be used.
2—Egg salad sandwiches.
3—Omit baking powder biscuits.
Serve celery curls and radishes
with sandwiches.
4—Make enough for another meal
later this week (see 13).
5—Braised shoulder pork steaks,
baked cottage roll or fresh picnic
shoulder roast may be used here.
6—Potatoes au gratin, lyonnaise or
hashed brown potatoes.
7—Fresh sweetened raspberries, strawberries, or fresh berry tarts with
whipped cream topping. [Use
evaporated milk for whipping.]

BREAKFAST

Tomato Juice
Prepared Cereal
Poached Eggs on Toast
Milk, Coffee

•

LUNCH

Corn-meal Waffles [1]
Sorghum
Crisp Bacon
Orange Jelly with Fruit [2]
Milk

•

DINNER

Lamb Stew [3]
Raisin Bread
Jellied Fruit Salad
(left from lunch)
Gingerbread Squares
with Whipped Cream [4]
(use evaporated milk
for whipping)
Milk, Tea, or Coffee

•

Alternative Dishes

1—Or fried corn-meal mush if some
is left from Monday. Or plain
waffles.
2—Use fruit left from yesterday's fruit
cup.
3—Stuffed breast of lamb, stuffed
shoulder or spicy lamb shanks.
Substitute boiled potatoes and buttered carrots for vegetables in stew.
4—Or make banana cream pie, individual tarts or cottage pudding.

BREAKFAST

Sliced Oranges [1]
Cooked Wheat Cereal,
Top Milk
Raisin Bread Toast
Milk, Coffee

•

LUNCH

Welsh Rarebit
Celery Curls
Sliced Bananas with
Canned Cherries [2]
Milk, Tea

•

DINNER

Casserole of Sausages and
Lima Beans [3]
California Beets
Salad of Mixed Greens
(Lettuce, Chicory,
Watercress and Endive), [4]
French Dressing
Reheated Gingerbread [5]
Honey Rice
Milk, Coffee

•

Alternative Dishes

1—Use chilled cantaloupe slices or
honeydew melon slices in season.
2—Save part of cherries for tomorrow's dinner. Or serve sliced fresh
peaches or peach shortcake.
3—Or stuffed eggplant.
4—Use least expensive available
greens. Romaine, spinach, etc.,
might be investigated.
5—Use as bread in this meal.

823

BREAKFAST

Stewed Apricots [1]
Shredded Wheat Biscuits
with Hot Milk
Soft-cooked Eggs
Toast
Milk, Coffee

•

LUNCH

Creamed Carrots and
Peas in Buttered Noodle
Nests [2]
Rye Bread and Butter
Honey Cookies
Cocoa [3]

•

DINNER

Baked Whitefish [4]
Parsley Potatoes
Baked Broccoli [5]
Lettuce and Tomato Salad
Graham Muffins
Coconut Blanc Mange
Cherry Sauce
Milk, Tea, or Coffee

•

Alternative Dishes

1—Save some for dessert tomorrow
night.
2—Or use scraps of leftover vegetables—as many as you like.
3—Lemonade or iced chocolate may
be better in summer.
4—Investigate your local market for
the best buy.
5—Buttered mustard greens, spinach,
dandelion or other greens will be
good here.

BREAKFAST

Grapefruit Juice
Cooked Wheat Cereal
Toasted Rye Bread
Milk, Coffee

•

LUNCH

Cream of Corn Soup [1]
(made with evaporated
milk)
Peanut-butter and
Lettuce Sandwiches
on Whole-wheat Bread
Fresh Apples [2]
Milk, Tea

•

DINNER

Peanut Roast [3]
Enriched Bread [4]
Pennsylvania Cabbage Salad with
Sour Cream Dressing [5]
Apricot Whip (apricots
from Friday's breakfast) [6]
Milk, Coffee

•

Alternative Dishes

1—Or use another vegetable: celery,
onions, carrots, etc.
2—Fresh pears, peaches or berries in
season, applesauce, baked apples
would fit into the menu.
3—Or braise sliced liver and serve
with French fried onion rings and
parsley potato balls.
4—Crusty hard rolls.
5—Shredded cabbage and pineapple
salad, mixed greens would be as
good.
6—Or prune or fresh berry whip.